ZECHARIAH
A COMMENTARY ON HIS
VISIONS AND PROPHECIES

ZECHARIAH
A COMMENTARY ON HIS
VISIONS AND PROPHECIES

DAVID BARON

kregel
PUBLICATIONS

Grand Rapids, MI 49501

Zechariah: A Commentary on His Visions and Prophecies
by David Baron

Published by Kregel Publications, a Division of Kregel, Inc.,
PO Box 2607, Grand Rapids, Michigan 49501. All rights reserved. First published by Hebrew Christian Testimony to Israel, London, 1918.

For more information about Kregel Publications, visit our
Web page: http://www.kregel.com.

Library of Congress Catalog Card Number 70-180834

ISBN 0-8254-2090-3

Printed in the United States of America

6 7 8 9 10 11 / 11 10 09 08 07 06

Preface

MANY into whose hands this volume will come know its history in advance, and the character of its contents, but for the sake of others a few words of explanation are necessary.

Being earnestly asked by honoured friends and readers of *The Scattered Nation*, the Quarterly Record of the Hebrew Christian Testimony to Israel, to write connected expository "Notes on Zechariah," I undertook to do so, without sufficiently realising—as I must now confess—how formidable the task of a continuous exposition of this particular prophetic book would prove, especially to one whose life is subject to much strain and distraction on account of many other claims and responsibilities in connection with the work of God among scattered Israel.

But having once made a start, the conviction deepened within me that it was a task entrusted to me of God, and that such a handling of this great prophecy, which stands in close organic connection with the whole prophetic Scripture, and the last chapters of which deal so vividly with the solemn events of the end of this present age, might, with His blessing, prove of some use to earnest-minded believers and Bible students at this present time. I was also greatly encouraged in the process by the many spoken and written words of approbation and encouragement from esteemed brethren in Christ—Christian ministers, missionaries, and others—who read the expositions in the fragmentary form in which they first appeared. In the pages of the little Quarterly above named, these " Notes," under the heading of " The Prophet of Hope and of Glory," extended over a period of nearly eleven years. I have now gone through them again, and made a few slight alterations and corrections, but on the whole they are presented in this volume exactly as they originally appeared in *The Scattered Nation*—including the introductory remarks in the first chapter, which were written eleven years ago. This will partly account for the style. Did time and strength permit, I might have re-written parts with a view to their abbreviation, but certain circumstances made this impossible. Besides, my object was not to write a " Commentary " in the sense in which the word is usually understood, but to unfold and explain this great Scripture in such a manner as to make it at the same time spiritually profitable to the average intelligent Christian reader. That I am not unacquainted with the various works which already exist on Zechariah, the pages of this book will bear witness. To several scholars in particular—both English and Continental—I have either in the text, or in the footnotes, again and again expressed my indebtedness. I have indeed gleaned what I considered best and helpful for the elucidation of the text from many sources—and even from writers with whose general attitude to the Holy Scriptures and principles of interpretation I am altogether at variance. But almost all the existing works on this prophetic book are in one way or another defective, and some of them even misleading. The older commentaries, though commendable for their reverent spiritual tone and practical teaching, and some of them containing also a good deal of sound philological and historical matter, are more or less vitiated by the allegorising principle of interpretation by means of which all references to a concrete Kingdom of God on earth, a literal national restoration of Israel, and the visible appearing and reign of Messiah, are explained away; while most of the modern writers, biased at the outset by their committal to what is known as the Higher Criticism, with its attitude of suspicion of the authenticity and genuineness of the sacred text, spend themselves, so to say, on theories of reconstruction, and for the most part uncalled for alterations and emendations, with the result that there is much of criticism in their works, but very little which is worthy of the name of exposition.

As to my own effort now embodied in this volume, I am disposed to say little about it, for I am deeply conscious of the greatness and sublimity of the theme, and my inadequacy in handling it, but I may claim this much, that I have tried in constant dependence on the Spirit of God, who first moved holy men of old to utter the Divine oracles, to deal simply and conscientiously with this great Scripture, and that, while I have consulted many sources and " authorities," my chief guide and final authority has been the Hebrew text itself, viewed in the light of the whole of God's self-revelation in the Old and New Testaments.

The reader will find some parts both in the visions and in the prophecies more thoroughly handled than others, my object being first of all to elucidate as fully as possible the great Messianic prophecies in this book, and secondly to unfold and emphasise the great and solemn prophetic events which centre around the land and the people of Israel—events the rapid fulfilment of which men may now begin to see with their own eyes.

Let me add in conclusion that while the whole Scripture, which in each case stands at the head of the chapter in which it is treated, is now given for convenience' sake from

the American Standard Edition, which I consider the best
of all the English versions, in the exposition itself I have
had to do only with the original text, and have sought to
bring out shades of meaning which cannot be reproduced
in any one translation.

The Indexes at the close, prepared by other practised
hands, will, I trust, be found helpful for purposes of
reference.

DAVID BARON

Northfield
Chorley Wood, Herts

Contents

Part One

THE VISIONS

and the

Answer to the Deputation from Bethel

Chapter 1

INTRODUCTION AND THE PROPHET'S INTRODUCTORY ADDRESS
A CALL TO REPENTANCE
Zechariah 1:1-6

In the eighth month, in the second year of Darius, came the word of Jehovah unto Zechariah the son of Berechiah, the son of Iddo, the prophet, saying, Jehovah was sore displeased with your fathers. Therefore say thou unto them, Thus saith Jehovah of hosts : Return unto Me, saith Jehovah of hosts, and I will return unto you, saith Jehovah of hosts. Be ye not as your fathers, unto whom the former prophets cried, saying, Thus saith Jehovah of hosts, Return ye now from your evil ways, and from your evil doings: but they did not hear nor hearken unto Me, saith Jehovah. Your fathers, where are they? and the prophets, do they live for ever? But My words and My statutes, which I have commanded My servants the prophets, did they not overtake your fathers? and they turned and said, Like as Jehovah of hosts thought to do unto us, according to our ways, and according to our doings, so hath He dealt with us.

Chapter 1

INTRODUCTORY

I AM commencing a somewhat difficult task, in which I am much cast upon God for the help and guidance of His Spirit—the source of light and truth—for it is my desire and prayer that these " notes," though inadequate and unworthy of so great a theme, may yet prove in His hand not only helpful to a right understanding of this most precious part of Holy Scripture, but be made spiritually profitable, and a blessing, especially to " the poor of the flock " (xi. 11), who still believe that prophecy came not in olden times by the will of man, but that " holy men of God spake as they were moved by the Holy Ghost."

As I am writing here for Christians, and as these expositions are intended for average intelligent English readers, I shall avoid elaborate introductions, and as much as possible also minute critical points.[1]

There are some reasons why this portion of Old Testament Scripture should especially be precious to Christians. I will mention only two. First—because of the clear and striking manner in which it testifies of our Lord Jesus. Luther calls Zechariah *Ausbund der Propheten*—the quintessence of Old Testament prophecy—and this is especially true in reference to Messianic prophecy. Indeed it seems to be the special aim and mission of Zechariah to condense and concentrate in small compass, and in his own peculiar terse style, almost all that has been revealed to the " former

---

[1] An examination of critical points and the theories of "modern" critics against the authenticity of the last chapters will be found in the Introduction to Part II.

prophets" about the person and mission of Messiah—about His Divine and yet truly human character, and of His sufferings and of the glory that should follow.

His betrayal for thirty pieces of silver (chap. xi.); the Roman spear with which He was "pierced" by His own nation; the awakened sword of Jehovah's justice which, in love for a lost world, and for the sin of the guilty, smites the Good Shepherd, "the Man" who is God's own equal; and the outcome of His sufferings, when He alone shall bear the glory, and "shall sit and rule upon His throne," and when upon His blessed brow, once crowned with thorns, shall at last be put the crown of glory:—these, as well as other striking details, are brought before us in this prophecy very vividly and in small compass.

"The Messianic prophecies of Zechariah," says Hengstenburg, "are only second to those of Isaiah in distinctness. In this, the last prophet but one, the prophetic gift once more unfolded all its glory as a proof that it did not sink from exhaustion of age, but was withdrawn according to the deliberate counsel of the Lord."

Secondly, on account of the light it throws on the events of the last times preceding the great and terrible "Day of the Lord," which is fast approaching.

The presence in Palestine of a representative remnant of the Jewish people in a condition of unbelief; the fiery furnace of suffering into which they are there to be thrown; their great tribulation and anguish occasioned by the final siege of Jerusalem by the confederated Gentile armies under the headship of him in whom both Jewish and Gentile apostasy is to reach its climax; how in the very midst of their final sorrow the spirit of grace and supplication shall be poured upon them, and they shall look upon Him whom they have pierced and mourn; how this blessed One whom they so long rejected shall suddenly appear as their Deliverer, and His feet stand "in that day" on the Mount of Olives, which is before Jerusalem on the east; how God shall again say "Ammi" to the nation which during the long centuries of their unbelief were

"Lo-Ammi"—"not My people," and how Israel shall joyously respond, "Jehovah, my God"; how Israel's Messiah shall speak peace to the nations, and Israel himself enter at last on his priestly mission to the peoples for which he was originally destined, and Jerusalem become the centre of God's fear and worship for the whole earth—all these and other solemn events of the time of the end are spoken of in this book with a clearness and distinctness as if they were occurrences of history instead of prophecies of the future.

A very few words will suffice on the personality of the prophet.

Zechariah (*Zekharyah*, "he whom Jehovah remembers") is the central figure in the group of the three post-exilic prophets, and his voice was the last but one of that unique and wonderful succession of men who were, indeed, the oracles of God, and through whom "in divers portions and in different ways" He Himself "spake unto the fathers," revealing His eternal counsels to men.

Like Jeremiah and Ezekiel among the "former prophets," Zechariah was of honourable priestly descent; his grandfather, Iddo, being head of one of the twelve priestly families, or courses, who returned from Babylon with Zerubbabel, and with the high priest Joshua; and at a later period, when Jehoiakim, the son of Joshua, was high priest, Zechariah himself succeeded his grandfather Iddo as head of his priestly course (Neh. xii. 4–16), from which it is to be inferred that the prophet's own father, Berechiah, died young, and before he was able to succeed his father Iddo in the priesthood.[1] The above facts lead us to infer that when called to the prophetic office Zechariah was still very young. That he was scarcely a full-grown man may be inferred from the fact that in chap. ii. 4 he is addressed as נַעַר, *naar*—translated in the Authorised Version "young man." Now *naar* means "boy," "lad," or "youth." It is, for instance, the word

---

[1] This is probably the reason why, in Ezra v. 1 and vi. 14, Zechariah is called "Bar-Iddo," "the son of Iddo," and that his father is passed over.

used by Saul as a designation of David in 1 Sam. xvii. 33, when he said, "Thou art but a youth," and, therefore, not fit to go forth to fight with Goliath, who was "a man of war from his youth."[1]

By the same word, also, Jeremiah designates himself when, feeling the awful responsibilities of the prophetic office to which he was being called, especially in an age like his, he tried to excuse himself by exclaiming, "Ah, Lord God! behold, I cannot speak: for I am a child."

This fact should be an encouragement to those of any age who have a message from and for God. He can speak to and through men at any and every time of life. He presses into His service the hoary-headed, and sanctifies the experience of years; but He also reveals Himself "by the Word of the Lord" to the child Samuel, and speaks through him His message to the aged high priest: "I thank Thee, O Father, Lord of heaven and earth, because Thou hast hid these things from the wise and prudent, and hast revealed them unto babes. Even so, Father, for so it seemed good in Thy sight": yea, out of the mouths of babes and sucklings He can ordain strength, and perfect His praise, in order to silence His enemies and to confound the worldly-wise and experienced. Let us despise neither age nor youth in God's servants. The question to be asked in reference to those who profess to speak in the Name of God is not about age, experience, education, or worldly position; but are they really the Lord's messengers, and do they, like Haggai, speak "in the Lord's message"? Zechariah was contemporary and fellow-labourer with Haggai (Ezra v. 1) to this extent, that his first message was uttered in the eighth month of the second year of Darius; while Haggai's ministry—which, as far as it is known to us, spread over a period of scarcely four months altogether—closed on the 24th day of the ninth month of the same year; that is, scarcely two months after Zechariah

---

[1] Some, indeed, deny that the term נַעַר, *naar*, is used of the prophet; but we will enter into this question when we come to the exposition of that passage. See p. 60.

commenced.   The time and circumstances were, however, the same.

About eighteen years had elapsed since the first year of Cyrus, when a remnant of those who were carried into captivity—both of Judah and of Israel—returned under the leadership of Zerubbabel and Joshua the high priest.

The first zeal of the returned exiles was most beautiful. In the seventh month of the very year of their return they already rebuilt the altar of burnt-offering, and thus restored the sacrificial ritual which was suspended during the seventy years of captivity; and in the second month of the second year they solemnly set themselves to the task of rebuilding the Temple amid circumstances of great national joy—not unmixed with tears and sorrow on the part of those who remembered the Temple " in its first glory."

Soon, however, owing to causes into which I cannot enter here,[1] carelessness and indifference took possession of their hearts, and the holy task of building the House which served as the visible symbol of fellowship between Jehovah and His covenant people was neglected.   Then was raised up Haggai, the first of the great trio of post-exilic prophets, who, by scathing denunciations, blended with glorious promises of present help, and announcements of a special and " greater glory," which should be manifested in this " latter House," succeeded in rousing the nation zealously to resume the work of building the Temple.   It was then, right in the midst of the movement inaugurated by Haggai, that Zechariah was commissioned by God with further messages.   The difference between the two prophets seems to be this, that while Haggai's task was chiefly to rouse the people to the outward task of building the Temple, Zechariah took up the prophetic labours just where Haggai had left it, and sought to lead the people to a complete *spiritual* change, one of the fruits of which would of necessity be increased zeal in the building of God's House, the completion of which he witnessed four years later.

In structure Zechariah's prophecy has this in common

[1] See *Haggai's Prophecy—a Voice to the Present Time.*

with Haggai's, that they both consist of only four addresses of unequal length.

The four divisions in Zechariah are these:

I. The introductory address, which is a call to repentance (chap. i. 1–6).

II. A series of eight visions, followed by a striking symbolical transaction, all shown to the prophet in one night, mainly of a consolatory character, and though, having an historical foreground, lead up to the "last days," and to the *finale* of God's dealings with Israel and the nations (chap. i. 6 to end of chap. vi.).

III. An address in the fourth year of Darius—two years after his first message, in answer to a question on the observance of the national fasts put by a deputation from Bethel (chaps. vii. and viii.).

IV. A prophecy delivered at a later period, which, starting from the standpoint of a more immediate future, brings us up to the very climax of things when "the Lord my God shall come, and all the saints with Thee"; and when, as a result, "Jehovah shall be King over all the earth, and there shall be but one Lord, and His name One."

The Prophet's Introductory Address

The prophet's first words were startling enough to rivet their attention:

"*With great displeasure was Jehovah displeased against your fathers.*" [1]

That this was a fact, those to whom the prophet spoke could not deny. They had seen the proofs of it with their own eyes in the desolations of the land, and in the seventy years' captivity of the people.

But although Jehovah was angry against them on account of their long-continued apostasies and provocations,

---

[1] Literally, "Jehovah was indeed angry with your fathers," or, "wroth was Jehovah against your fathers with wrath": the verb קָצַף, *qatsaph*, has as its object the noun קֶצֶף, *qatseph*, to give it greater force. It expresses vehement displeasure, almost to the extent of abhorrence.

His anger was now turned away, and He was ready to
comfort them if they would but turn from the evils which
had brought those calamities on their fathers, and return
to God with all their hearts. To such a turning the
prophet, in the Name of God, now most solemnly invites
them :

" *Return unto Me, saith Jehovah of hosts, and I will* "
(or ' *that I may* ') *return unto you, saith Jehovah of hosts* "
—the repetition of the august Name of Jehovah being
meant to emphasise the Divine authority and sanction of
the call, and the certainty of the blessed result which would
follow from obedience to it ; since He who invites them to
come back is none other than " Jehovah of hosts," who,
while Lord of all things, at whose call all created forces
must marshal themselves as if for war, is at the same time
the Covenant God of the history of Redemption, whose
very Name is as " a strong tower " for the righteous, and
who is only " waiting to be gracious," and would therefore
most certainly return unto them.

The gracious invitation and assurance is followed by a
warning lest, following in the footsteps of their fathers'
disobedience, they would incur the like displeasure of God
and experience the like punishment:

" *Be not ye like to your fathers, to whom the former
prophets cried, saying, Turn, we beseech you, from your evil
ways, and from your evil doings : but they heard not, neither
did they hearken unto Me, saith Jehovah.* "

We have here incidentally given us a kind of inspired
résumé of one great part of the work " of the former
prophets " and its result. The mission of the prophets was
comprehensive and many-sided ; they spoke to all times,
making known to the children of men the counsels of the
Eternal. They spoke from the mouth of the Omniscient God,
foretelling things to come ; but to the current generations
in which they lived they were chiefly preachers of righteousness, and their constant cry was, " Repent."

They saw Israel—and in this respect Israel is but a
type of man—wandering ever further from God, and they

cried, "Turn ye, turn ye"; for why will ye wander from
the source of life and blessedness, and die, O House of
Israel? That repentance was the keynote in the preaching
of all "the former prophets" will be seen at a glance if I
quote here only a few of their chief utterances.

Taking the books as they are now arranged in the Old
Testament Canon, without strict regard to chronology and
beginning with Isaiah—his chief message to the generation
in which he lived, after denouncing their sins, may be
summed up in the proclamation found in the 55th
chapter:

*"Seek ye Jehovah while He may be found, call ye upon
Him while He is near. Let the wicked forsake his way, and
the unrighteous man his thoughts; and let him return unto
Jehovah, and He will have mercy upon him; and to our
God, for He will abundantly pardon."*

Jeremiah was again and again sent with the gracious
message:

*"Return, thou backsliding Israel, saith Jehovah; and I
will not cause My face to fall upon you in anger: for I am
the gracious One, saith Jehovah, and I will not retain anger
for ever. Only acknowledge thine iniquity, that thou hast
transgressed against Jehovah thy God"* (Jer. iii. 12, 13).

Ezekiel's touching appeal to the people in the Name of
God, who solemnly bids the prophet proclaim that He has
no pleasure in the death of the sinner, I have already
quoted. It was repeated again and again in the course of
his ministry. Hark, for instance, to his cry in the
18th chapter:

*"Repent, and be turned from your transgressions whereby
ye have transgressed, and iniquity shall not be your ruin.
Cast away from you all your transgressions; and make you
(or 'get you') a new heart and a new spirit: for why will ye
die, O house of Israel?"*

And these were but the continuance and repetition of
the still earlier voice of Hosea, Joel, Amos, and Zephaniah,
who cried:

"O Israel, return unto Jehovah thy God; for thou hast

fallen by thine iniquity " (Hos. xiv. 1). " *Turn ye, even to Me, with all your heart, and with fasting, and with weeping, and with mourning : and rend your heart, and not your garments, and turn unto Jehovah your God ; for He is gracious and merciful, slow to anger, and of great kindness, and repenteth Him of the evil* " (Joel ii. 12, 13). " *Seek ye Jehovah, and ye shall live* " (Amos v. 4–6). " *Before the decree bring forth, before the day pass as the chaff, before the fierce anger of Jehovah come upon you, before the day of the Lord's anger come upon you,* . . . *seek righteousness, seek meekness : it may be ye shall be hid in the day of the Lord's anger* " (Zeph. ii. 2, 3).

But, alas ! to all these cries Israel lent but a deaf ear. The result of all the ministry of the former prophets, as far as the nation was concerned, is summed up in the words : " *But they did not hear nor hearken unto Me, saith Jehovah.*"

On the last page of pre-exilic history are written the following solemn words : " Moreover, all the chiefs of the priests, and the people, transgressed very much after the abominations of the nations ; and polluted the house of the Lord which He had hallowed in Jerusalem. And the Lord God of their fathers sent to them by His messengers, rising up betimes and sending ; because He had compassion on His people, and on His dwelling place : but they mocked the messengers of God, and despised His words, and misused His prophets, until the wrath of the Lord arose against His people, till there was no remedy " (2 Chron. xxxvi. 14–16). They then went to Babylon, which inaugurated the period called in the New Testament " The times of the Gentiles," which are still running ; and when at the end of the seventy years a remnant was in the grace and faithfulness of God brought back, the tone and substance of the old message did not change. The cry was taken up by Haggai and Zechariah ; and with the proclamation, " *Return unto Me, and I will return unto you, saith Jehovah* " (Mal. iii. 7), the voice of Old Testament prophecy finally dies away.

For the sake of showing that the preaching of repentance is still the distinguishing mark of God's true messengers, let us note how this old cry is carried over, also, into the pages of New Testament history. After Malachi a pause of four long centuries intervened, during which there was no voice nor vision nor answer of God; but when the long silence was broken, the first words that fell on Israel's ear from the mouth of the Baptist were, " *Repent; for the kingdom of heaven is at hand*"; and when at last the Greatest and last of the prophets, who was Himself to inaugurate " the kingdom of heaven " on earth, stood in their midst, His first public utterance, too, was the same old familiar cry, " Repent! " (Matt. iv. 17). Oh, that Israel had known the day of his visitation, and hearkened at last to this gracious invitation—at least when uttered by the lips of the Son of God Himself! But they knew not, nor did they understand. The proud Pharisees and scribes, like so many of their fathers before, did not think they needed to repent. Did they not cry, " We are the Temple of the Lord "? Were there not the many voices of the *false* prophets who cried, " Peace, peace "? " Have we not Abraham to our father? " " We are God's favoured nation; no evil will befall us." And so again they showed themselves the successors of those who killed the prophets, and stoned them that were sent unto them and cried—as they did of all the prophets before Him—" Away with this disturber of our peace, He is no friend of our nation; it is expedient for us that one man should die for the people, and that the whole nation perish not."

Christ died and rose again, according to the Scriptures; but before His ascension He entrusted His disciples with a message for the world, and in that last commission (Luke xxiv. 46–49) " repentance " still finds a prominent place. And the keynote in the Apostolic preaching— whether in Jerusalem or in Athens, whether to Jew or to Greek—was, " God commandeth all men everywhere to repent." " Repent ye therefore, and be converted, that your sins may be blotted out, when the time of refreshing shall come from the presence of the Lord" (Acts iii. 19, xvii. 30).

And we may pause and ask, Is there less need for this kind of preaching now than there was in Jeremiah's or in Paul's time? Is man's attitude and tendency more God-ward and heavenward now than it was then? Is man all right, or is he radically wrong? Does man's natural course lead to life, or does the end of it lead to death? Upon the answer to these questions depends the answer as to who are the true prophets and genuine friends of man; whether those who cry, " Turn ye, turn ye; for why will ye die?" or those who speak of " the world's progress," and tell corrupt, sinful men that they are themselves potentially Christs, who need only develop " the good that is in them," and who still cry, " Peace, peace," although there is no peace. We may be forgiven for digressing somewhat beyond the limits of the passage before us; but we believe that this question of repentance touches the very heart of man's relationship to God. It shows us, as we have seen, man's condition as apostate from God, with his face turned away from the fountain of light and life. It tells us that man's great need is to forsake not only his outward ways, but also his *thoughts*, and to return to the Lord; and it reveals to us the grace and love of God, who has no pleasure in the death of the sinner, but yearns for his return, " because He delighteth in mercy," and has, at the cost of the sacrifice of His own Son, devised a means for reconciliation, " that His banished be not expelled from Him " (2 Sam. xiv. 14).

Let us return, therefore, unto the Lord, and He, accord-ing to His promise, will " return unto us "—we with our sins, He with His grace and forgiveness; we with our poverty and need, He with His exceeding " riches " and infinite fulness; we with our wretchedness and fears, He with His " everlasting consolation and good hope "—yea, with His peace, which passeth all understanding, and with His joy, which is unspeakable and full of glory. And if we find no power of ourselves to come to Him, let us pray, as Israel will by and by: " *Turn Thou us unto Thee, O Lord,*

*and we shall be turned." " Cause Thy face to shine, and we
shall be saved"* (Lam. v. 21 ; Ps. lxxx. 3).

We now come to the last two verses of Zechariah's
preparatory address, which may be summarised as a warning against disobedience, illustrated and enforced by the
sad experiences of their fathers. " *Your fathers, where are
they ?* " " They did not hear nor hearken"; they dis-
believed and disobeyed My word; but what was the consequence ? What good did they gain? what success did
they experience in resisting Me? " *Where are they ?* "
Did they not for that very reason spend their days in
wretchedness, and pine away in captivity? " *And the
prophets, do they live for ever ?* "

Probably we have here the record of a dialogue between
the prophet, speaking in the Name of God, and the people ;
at least so some of the leading Jewish commentators
understand it—namely, that when the prophet pointed them
to their fathers, saying, "Where are they?" the people
impudently answered, "*And the prophets, do they live for
ever ?* "—have they, too, not shared in the sorrows of the
nation and passed away like our fathers?[1]   And then the
prophet replies, "Yes; the prophets, though God's mouth-
piece, were but men, and are gone, '*but My words and My
statutes, which I commanded My servants the prophets, did
they not overtake your fathers, so that they had to return and
say, that as Jehovah of hosts hath thought* (or " *determined* ") to

---

[1] Kimchi, in his commentary on *Zechariah*, says, " Our Rabbis, of blessed
memory, have interpreted the words, 'The prophets, where are they?' as the
answer of the people.   They say that the congregation of Israel gave a controversial reply to the prophet.   He said to them : ' Return in true repentance, for
your fathers sinned ; and where are they?'   The people answered him : 'And
the prophets who did not sin, where are they?'   But they afterwards repented
and made confession to him."   The place in the Talmud to which he refers is
Bab. Sanhedrin, 105.

Among Christian interpreters, we are glad to see Keil adopting this view.   In
Lowe's *Hebrew Student's Commentary on Zechariah*, there is the following note :

" Another interpretation is that Zechariah's words are equivalent to this : The
light of prophecy is dying out ; while ye have the light, walk as children of the
light.   But to us it appears that to put the words, 'Do (or "did ") the prophets
live for ever?' into the mouth of Zechariah, is to destroy utterly his argument."

do unto us, according to our ways, and according to our doings,
even so hath He dealt with us?' "

Oh, that men would learn to distinguish between the
frailty and weakness of the best of God's messengers and
the eternal character and unfailing veracity of His message!
The prophets are no more, but the words which those holy
men of old spake as they were moved by the Holy Ghost
are still with us, verifying themselves, and in spite of man's
unbelief accomplishing, whether in judgment or in mercy,
that whereunto they were sent.

Oh, that men would take warning from the past history
of Israel, and note the faithfulness of God in carrying out
His threatenings as well as His promises!

Oh, that *you* would be wise and "give glory to Jehovah
your God before He cause darkness, and before your feet
stumble upon the dark mountains, and while ye look for
light He turn it into the shadow of death, and make it
gross darkness" (Jer. xiii. 15–17).

Chapter 2

THE FIRST VISION
THE ANGEL OF JEHOVAH
AMONG THE MYRTLE TREES

Zechariah 1:7-17

Upon the four and twentieth day of the eleventh month, which is the month Shebat, in the second year of Darius, came the word of Jehovah unto Zechariah, the son of Berechiah, the son of Iddo, the prophet, saying, I saw in the night, and behold a man riding upon a red horse, and he stood among the myrtle trees that were in the bottom ; and behind him there were horses, red, sorrel, and white. Then said I, O my lord, what are these? And the angel that talked with me said unto me, I will show thee what these are. And the man that stood among the myrtle trees answered and said, These are they whom Jehovah hath sent to walk to and fro through the earth. And they answered the angel of Jehovah that stood among the myrtle trees, and said, We have walked to and fro through the earth, and, behold, all the earth sitteth still, and is at rest. Then the angel of Jehovah answered and said, O Jehovah of hosts, how long wilt Thou not have mercy on Jerusalem and on the cities of Judah, against which Thou hast had indignation these threescore and ten years ? And Jehovah answered the angel that talked with me with good words, even comfortable words. So the angel that talked with me said unto me, Cry thou, saying, Thus saith Jehovah of hosts : I am jealous for Jerusalem and for Zion with a great jealousy. And I am very sore displeased with the nations that are at ease ; for I was but a little displeased, and they helped forward the affliction. Therefore thus saith Jehovah : I am returned to Jerusalem with mercies ; my house shall be built in it, saith Jehovah of hosts, and a line shall be stretched over Jerusalem. Cry yet again, saying, Thus saith Jehovah of hosts : My cities shall yet overflow with prosperity ; and Jehovah shall yet comfort Zion, and shall yet choose Jerusalem.

Chapter 2

ABOUT three months after the introductory address [1] which, as we have seen, was mainly a call to repentance, the series of eight visions, followed by the very significant symbolical transaction of the crowning of the high priest Joshua, the son of Josedech, was given to the prophet. In this case the exact day of the month is indicated, most probably because it was a day of special significance and of sacred association to the restored remnant. It was "*in the twenty and fourth day of the eleventh month, that is, in the month Shebat, in the second year of Darius.*" On that very day just five months before, the spirit of Zerubbabel and of Joshua, and "of all the rest of the people," being stirred up by God through the preaching of Haggai, commenced to work again in the rebuilding of the Temple (Hag. i. 14, 15).

On the same day also just three months later—that is, a month after Zechariah's introductory address—the same prophet delivered his last two stirring messages, the first ending with the promise, "From this day will I bless you," and the second containing the announcement that God would shake the heavens and the earth, and overthrow the thrones and kingdoms of the nations all with a view to the restoration and exaltation of the Davidic House, which was then represented by Zerubbabel (Hag. ii. 10–23); [2] so

---

[1] The exact day of the month is not given to the introductory address, but the omission is probably meant to imply that it was on the first day, or on the Feast of the New Moon, that it was delivered.

[2] It was also on the 24th of the month that Daniel, after having previously fasted and mourned for three full weeks, had received the vision of the things noted in the Scripture of truth (Dan. x. 4–21).

that there is probability in the suggestion that it is on account of its sacred connection with Haggai's ministry, and especially on account of it being the day on which they earnestly took in hand the work of rebuilding the Temple, that it was chosen as a day for further Divine revelations.

This 24th day of the eleventh month was, as already stated, exactly two months after the last promise issued through Haggai to the people that the Lord would henceforth bless His nation, and would glorify it in the future.

"To set forth in symbol and imagery this blessing and glorification, and to exhibit the leading features of the future conformation of the Kingdom of God, was the object of these revelations."[1]

These visions, which addressed themselves more to the prophet's mental and spiritual sight than to his ears, are called *debhar Yehovah*—"the word of Jehovah"—because the pictures seen in the spirit, together with their interpretation, had the significance of verbal revelations, and through them the will and purposes of Jehovah were communicated to him.

Divinely communicated visions were one of the "divers manners" in which God spake in times past in the prophets to the fathers, even as we read in Num. xii. 6 : "If there be a prophet among you, I, Jehovah, will make Myself known to him in a vision ; I will speak with him (literally, '*in* him') in a dream."

The whole series of visions which were granted to the prophet, probably in rapid succession one after the other with only short pauses between, in one night, though distinct and in a sense each one complete in itself—" form (as we shall see) a substantially connected picture of the future of Israel linked on to the then existing time, and closing with the prospect of the ultimate completion of the Kingdom of God."

The general plan in all these visions is first to present the symbol, and then, on a question being put, to supply the interpretation.

[1] Keil.

What the Prophet saw

In the dead of night—not in a dream, but in an ecstatic condition, in which his mental and spiritual faculties were altogether awake and attuned to God, so that he could fully respond to the operations and promptings of the Spirit, and pictures of divine objects could be reflected on his soul—he saw " a man " riding upon a red horse, standing among myrtles " in the bottom," or, more literally, " in " (or " by ") the " deep," and behind him, at his command, were horses (most probably with riders upon them), red, speckled (or " sorrel," or " bay "), and white.

Now, before passing from this verse we must consider :

(*a*) Who is "the man "? (*b*) What is represented by the myrtles ? and (*c*) the significance of the colour of the horses.

I. The "man," as we are told in ver. 11, was the *Malakh Yehovah*—the Angel of Jehovah, who is none other than the " Angel of His face," the Divine " Angel of the Covenant," the second person in the Blessed Trinity, whose early manifestations to the patriarch and prophets, as the " Angel " or Messenger of Jehovah in the form of man, were anticipations of His incarnation and of that incomprehensible humiliation to which He would afterwards condescend for our salvation. Some commentators (among them Keil and Dr. C. H. H. Wright[1]) do indeed distinguish between the two, but without sufficient reason. The chief ground of their objection to the identification of " the man " in the 8th verse with the Angel of Jehovah in the 11th, is that if the Angel of Jehovah was really identified with the rider on the red horse, that rider would have been represented as standing opposite to the other horseman (when giving in their report to him in ver. 11), and they would not have been spoken of as standing behind him.[2] To which surely it is sufficient to reply that it is

---

[1] " Zechariah and his Prophecies," being the Bampton Lectures for 1878.

[2] Dr. Wright further adds : " Moreover, though the rider on the red horse was the leader and chief of the band of angelic riders, he was also a member of one

not stated that they were behind him (or, as is more literal),
"after him," when giving in their report; and that there is
no necessity to suppose that their captain and leader could
not have turned his face toward them while they were
speaking.   Certainly, if the Angel of Jehovah is not
identical with "the man," and there were two prominent
commanding figures standing among the myrtles, apart
from the cohort of angelic riders, it would have been not
"the man" (who in that case would have been an inferior
being), but the Angel of Jehovah, who would have attracted
the attention of the prophet most, and who would have
been mentioned first.

II. It is pretty generally agreed that the myrtles
symbolise Israel, and it is not without significance that this
particular symbol is chosen.   Not the proud cedar, not the
lofty, far-spreading oak—the symbols of the great world-
powers—but the lowly, fragrant myrtle, growing for the
most part in the shady valley out of the world's gaze,[1] is
chosen to represent the covenant people.   Yes, it is with

of the subdivisions of which that band was composed, inasmuch as he was mounted
upon a steed of a red colour, and not of a colour distinct from the rest": but he
overlooks the fact that in answer to the prophet's question, "What are these,
my lord?" "The man," standing among the myrtles, answers, "These are
they," etc., not "*We* are they," showing that though he was the Captain of the
Lord's host, he was not to be confounded with them.   That he was mounted on
a steed of a red colour, and not a colour distinct from all the rest, is sufficiently
accounted for by the fact that this colour symbolised what was now the chief
characteristic of his attitude to the nations who were oppressing Israel, namely,
judgment and vengeance.

[1] Hadassah (Myrtle) became a favourite female name.   Esther bore it, perhaps
on account of the humility and modesty of her demeanour.   In Kimchi's
comment on this verse will be found the following curious passage : "We have
found in the words of our Rabbis, of blessed memory, the following exposition"
(it will be found in Talmud Bab. Sanhedrin, fol. 93, col. 1): "I saw in the
night that the Holy One—blessed be He !—sought to turn the whole world into
night; and, behold ! a man riding.   This man is no other than the Holy One—
blessed be He !—for it is said, 'The Lord is a man of war'" (a remarkable
testimony this from the Talmud, that He who appeared as the Angel of Jehovah
in the form of man was the God of Israel).   "'Upon a red horse.'   The Holy
One—blessed be He !—sought to turn the whole world into blood, but when He
looked upon Hananiah, Mishael, and Azariah, His anger was cooled, for it is
said, 'And he stood among the myrtle trees.'   The Hadassim can mean nothing
else but the righteous, for it is said, 'He brought up Hadassah,'" *i.e.*, Esther.

the lowly, with those of a contrite and humble spirit, that the High and Lofty One who inhabits eternity, ever dwells and identifies Himself (Isa. lvii. 15, lxvi. 2).

The myrtles among which the Angel of Jehovah is seen standing are represented as growing "in the bottom," as the Authorised Version has it; but the word is *metsulah*, from *tsul*—the verb *tsollal* being used of sinking in the water (Ex. xv. 10). The margin in the Revised Version suggests the rendering of "shady place," and various other translations as the basis of different interpretations have been given by Jewish and Christian commentators.

The Jewish Targum and the Talmud, followed by Kimchi and some Christian interpreters, translate "valley," and say that it represents Babylon, where the Jews had been banished on account of their sin; and some, like Hengstenberg, think that the *metsulah* was symbolical of the Kingdom of God in its then outwardly depressed condition, but still under the gracious protection of the Angel of Jehovah. But בַּמְּצֻלָה, *bammetsullah*, should, we think, be certainly rendered "in" or "by" "the deep." It is at least rightly so rendered in two passages in the Psalms. The first is Ps. lxxxviii. 6: "Thou hast laid me in the lowest pit, in the dark places in the deeps (*bimetsoloth*)," the next verse showing that it is in the deeps *of the sea*, since the writer goes on to say: "Thou hast afflicted me with all Thy waves." And the second passage in Ps. cvii. 23, 24, where we read that "they that go down to the sea in ships, that do business in great waters—these see the works of Jehovah and His wonders in the deep (*bimetsulah*)."

It might thus be a suitable figure of the unfortunate condition of Israel over whom the waves of troubles and oppression were rolling in their captivity among the Gentiles; but where dogmatic certainty is out of the question, we would venture to suggest what to us seems the most likely meaning of this symbol, namely, that "the deep" of "the great sea" represents the great Gentile world-power at that time, with whom commenced "the times of the Gentiles"—"the abyss-like power of the kingdom of the

world," as Baumgarten expresses it. By the side or in the
very midst of the great deep, or ocean of humanity, as if
threatened to be swallowed up by it, stands the group or
thicket of lowly myrtles; but the Angel of Jehovah—the
second Person in the Blessed Trinity, who, in His love and
in His pity redeemed and bore and carried them of old
(Isa. lxiii. 9)—is among them, in fulfilment of His word,
" When thou passest through the waters I will be with thee,
and the rivers they shall not overflow thee."

How rich in consolation to the prophet's own heart,
and to the people to whom he was to make known what he
saw, was this single item in the comforting vision! In the
very midst of that remnant of His oppressed and afflicted
people—though their eyes may be holden so that they cannot see Him—afflicted in all their afflictions, is ever Israel's
Redeemer, "the Angel of Jehovah," who "encampeth,"
with an invisible host, round about them that fear Him, to
deliver them.

Note, dear reader, governmental power and even
national independence had already been taken from Israel.
" The times of the Gentiles " had already commenced some
seventy years before, with Nebuchadnezzar; but that did
not mean Israel being, as a people, altogether cast off by
God. No; behold Him, not in the midst off the great
world-powers, into whose hands the sceptre of governmental
rule was parenthetically put, but identified with the comparative handful of people who, for their sins, were under
His severe chastisement, and given over for a time into the
hands of their enemies.

And the same is true of scattered, storm-tossed Israel
in the present day. Sometimes to the eye of man it would
almost appear true as Zion in her distress says of herself,
" Jehovah hath forsaken me; my Lord hath forgotten me."
And many Christian commentators even start with the
presupposition that, because the Jewish people is banished
and scattered, therefore it is also cast off; but hear the
faithful covenant-keeping God: " For I am with thee,
saith Jehovah, to save thee; for I will make a full end of

all the nations whither I have scattered thee, but I will not make a full end of thee; but I will correct thee with judgment, and will by no means hold thee guiltless." "And yet for all that, when they be in the land of their enemies, I will not cast them away, neither will I abhor them to destroy them utterly, and to break My covenant with them; for I am Jehovah their God" (Jer. xxx. 11; Lev. xxvi. 44).

III. Lastly, before passing on from the 8th verse, just a few words on the significance of the colours of the horses. That they symbolise the mission on which these angelic hosts are about to be sent forth, there can, I think, be no doubt, in spite of Dr. Wright's confident statement that "any attempt to assign any grounds for the employment of the special colours is futile."

The red is significant of judgment, blood, vengeance. It is to an angelic rider on a horse of this colour that a great sword is given, in Rev. vi. 4, to take peace from earth, so that men—the enemies of God and of His Christ—should slay one another; and in Isa. lxiii. it is in garments dyed red that the Messiah goes forth in the day of vengeance to tread the nations in His anger, and to trample them in His fury. In our vision it doubtless signifies the same thing— namely, the readiness of the Angel of Jehovah to go forth with His angelic cohorts to execute swift judgment on Israel's oppressors.

The exact colour to be understood by the word *seruqqim*, translated in the A.V. "speckled," or "bay," as in the margin, or "sorrel," as in the R.V., cannot be fixed with certainty.[1] I might fill several pages with the guesses and suggestions and disputations on this word by the learned, but it most probably is meant to describe a mixed colour—a combination of the first and last mentioned in the passage—and would signify that those mounted on these horses were to be sent forth on a mission of a *mixed* character—namely, of judgment and mercy; while the white is the symbol of victory, triumph, and glory

---

[1] The word does not occur elsewhere in the Hebrew as an adjective of colour.

(Rev. vi. 2), which shall be to God's people after their great champion rides forth "conquering and to conquer," and executing vengeance on their enemies.

And the vision of the legions of angels mounted and ready to obey the command of their great Captain was doubtless intended to convey to the prophet the message which he was to impress on the people, that "the chariots of God are twenty thousand, even myriads of angels"; that with Him was all the requisite power and resources for the deliverance of His people, and the destruction of their foes. It was not because His hand had become shortened and His ear heavy, or that there was a lack either of might or willingness to save on His part, that they had become subject to the power of the Gentiles; but because their sins had for a time separated them from their God, and their iniquities had caused His protecting and guiding power to be withdrawn from them.

But we proceed to the 9th verse.

"*Then said I, O my lord, what are these? And the angel that talked with me said unto me, I will show thee what these be.*"

Now, here we are introduced for the first time to this *malakh haddobher bi*—the angel that talked with me, or, literally, "*in* me"—and the question to decide is whether this angel who interprets is the same as the *Malakh Yehovah*—the Angel of Jehovah—whom the prophet saw standing among the myrtles, as some contend, or is he another being, simply angelic? The arguments advanced for the identity of the two are these :

(1) In the verse under our examination the prophet addresses this angel as "my lord" (*adoni*), and as no other person has been previously mentioned it would appear that it was the Angel of Jehovah he was speaking to. But this is by no means conclusive, for in the prophecies, and especially in the visions, on account of their dramatic character, persons are frequently introduced either as speaking, or as being addressed by others, without having been previously mentioned. Note the striking fact that the

prophet does not address this angel as *Adonai*, "my Lord"
—a Divine title addressed to the Angel of Jehovah, as, for
instance, in Gen. xviii. 3—but *adoni*, "my lord," which may
be addressed to man, or any created being.

(2) This angel promises to show or explain to the
prophet the meaning of the vision. Now, in the next
verse the explanation is given by the Angel of Jehovah,
therefore it is urged by some that they are the same. But
the word *arekha*, translated "I will show thee," literally
means, "I will make thee see," that is, "give thee an understanding heart and mind to understand the visions and
explanations which follow." Indeed, the very designation
of this Angel as the One "*that talked in me*" [1] seems meant,
as Pusey well points out, to convey the thought of an
inward speaking, "whereby the words should be borne
directly into the ¿ soul without the intervention of the
ordinary outward organs." An example as to how the
interpreting Angel prepared the heart and mind of the
prophet to behold and to understand the visions, we have
in chap. iv. 1, namely, by waking him out of his ordinary
condition into a spiritually ecstatic one, and preparing his
heart and mind subjectively for the objects presented to
him in the visions, and for the explanations which should
be given.

(3) In ver. 12 the *Malakh Yehovah* offers a supplication
to God on behalf of Jerusalem and the cities of Judah, and
in the next verse the answer is given to the interpreting
angel ; therefore, it is argued, they must be the same. But
to this it may be replied that the answer is addressed to
this angel because the Angel of Jehovah asked the question,
"How long?" not for himself, but that the consolation
contained in the answer may through the interpreting angel
be communicated to the prophet, and through the prophet
to the people.

[1] In the same manner the Lord says to Moses, in Num. xii. 6–9, "If there is
a prophet among you, I, Jehovah, will make Myself known to him in a vision ; I
will speak, not '*to* him,' as in the A.V., but *in* him, in a dream. My servant
Moses is not so. *In* him will I speak mouth to mouth" ; and Hab. ii. 1 speaks
of the same inward teaching : "I will watch to see what He will speak *in* me."

On the other hand, here are several reasons which seem to us unanswerable why the interpreting angel must not be confounded with the Angel of Jehovah.

(*a*) The title *Malakh haddobher bi* is quite different from the Angel of Jehovah. That it is a title there can be no doubt, for the prophet uses it eleven times (i. 9, 13, 14, 19, ii. 3, iv. 1, 4, 5, v. 5, 10, vi. 4) *without any variation*, and that not always after, or when conversation of any kind takes place, as, for instance, in this 9th verse of chap. i., and in chap. ii. 3. The variation in the Authorised Version, " The angel that communed with me," introduced in chap. i. 14, is unjustifiable.

(*b*) In chap. ii. 1–4 the prophet sees in vision " a man " engaged in measuring the site of Jerusalem. The interpreting angel who stood beside him leaves him to go forward, perhaps to ask the meaning of the vision, but before reaching his destination he is met by another angel, who comes forward with the command : " Run, speak to this young man " (the prophet). Now, assuming that the interpreter is the same as the Angel of Jehovah, directions would have been given him, and that too in word of command, by an inferior angel—a proceeding altogether irreconcilable with the Divine dignity ascribed by the prophet to the *Malakh Yehovah*.

Moreover, " the man " with the measuring line in his hand, in chap. ii., is, as we shall see, in all probability the same " man " whom the prophet saw in his first vision (comp. i. 8, 11), who, as we saw, was no other than the Angel of Jehovah himself; and as the interpreting angel was standing by the prophet and going forward toward " the man " with the measuring line, it proves that they are two, and not one.

(*c*) To " the angel that talked with (or ' in ') me " there is no Divine work ascribed, and no Divine name given at all.[1] Remarkable in this connection is the form of the

---

[1] This precludes the idea suggested by some that the interpreting ·angel was the Holy Spirit, though the work of this angel resembles one aspect of the mission of the blessed Paraclete.

prophet's address to him, which, as pointed out above, is not *Adonai*, my Lord, but *adoni*, my lord. Nothing higher is ascribed to this angel than the explanation of visions. Sometimes (as in i. 9, ii. 3, 4) not even that, but the preparation of the prophet's mind to *understand* the explanation which is given by the Lord Himself.

(*d*) To the same conclusion also we are led by the analogy of other apocalyptic places in the Old Testament Scriptures. In Dan. viii. 16 and x. 5–18, for instance, two heavenly beings are seen by the prophet, which stand in exactly the same relation as " the angel that talked with me " stands to " the Angel of Jehovah " in the visions of Zechariah ; and in the last apocalyptic book of the New Testament we have another parallelism in our Lord Jesus Christ : " The Angel of Jehovah " of Old Testament revelation, sending by the hand of an angel, to signify " unto His servant John," for him in his turn to make known to the Seven Churches the Revelation which the Father first gave to Him.

We see, then, that " the angel that talked with me " is not the same as the Divine Angel of Jehovah — the Messenger of the Covenant—but an *attendant angel* whose mission it was to be God's expositor to the prophet of the meaning of the visions.

The answer to the prophet's question, " What are these ? " in ver. 9, is given by " the man " that stood among the myrtles, in the 10th verse : " *These are they whom Jehovah hath sent to walk to and fro through the earth.*" How full of consolation for God's people is a statement like this ! Satan, when appearing as the accuser of Job in the presence of God, said that he came " from going to and fro in the earth, and from walking up and down in it." And what the aim and object of his restless activity in the earth is, we are told by the Apostle Peter in his earnest warning, " Be sober, be watchful, for your adversary the devil (full of hatred and fiendish cunning, as his names imply, and ever ready with fresh traps and snares for our destruction)—as

a roaring lion, walketh about seeking whom he may devour."
If left to ourselves and his devices for one day, where
should we be? But, blessed be God, "the Angel of
Jehovah encampeth (as with a great invisible host) round
about them that fear Him, and delivereth them"; and if
there are evil, malignant spirits (ever restlessly walking to
and fro in the whole earth on their mischievous intent of
hindering, if they cannot frustrate, the gracious purposes of
God and the manifestation of His Kingdom on the earth),
God also has *His* messengers who walk to and fro to
counteract and frustrate Satan's designs, and to succour and
shield, and in many more ways than we know, to be
ministering spirits to them who shall be heirs of salvation.

In our vision, however, the swift messengers were in the
first instance only sent out to reconnoitre the earth and the
state of the nations in their relation to the land and people
of Israel; for, as far as God's governmental dealings with
the nations are concerned, all things must be viewed in
their relation to that people in whom are bound up the
purposes of God for all mankind.

In "answer" probably to the unexpressed inquiry of
the Angel of Jehovah, these angelic messengers give in their
report: " *We have walked to and fro through the earth, and,
behold, all the earth sitteth still, and is at rest.*" [1]

This description of the Gentile world was intended by
contrast to bring more strikingly to light the mournful
condition of Israel. All the nations lived in undisturbed

---

[1] The words *yoshebheth veshoqateth* denote the peaceful and secure condition of a land and its inhabitants undisturbed by any foe. Pusey points out
that the last of the two words is used in the Book of Judges of the rest given to
the land under the judges, until its fresh departure from God (Judg. iii. 11, 30,
v. 31, viii. 28); of the undisturbed life of the people of Laish (Judg. xviii. 7,
27); in Josh. xi. 23, where we read "the land had rest from war"; and in a
number of other places, in later history, all describing a condition of profound
peace. Keil and Dr. Wright regard the report of the angelic messengers as
having reference to the prophecy of Haggai in chap. ii. 7, 8, 22, 23. "God had
then announced that He would shake heaven and earth, the whole world and
all nations, with a view to the overthrow of all kingdoms and powers hostile to
the welfare of Israel"; but instead of any such general commotion being apparent,
the report which the angelic riders bring is that the whole world is quiet and at
rest.

peace and prosperity. In short, all were at rest except the "tribes of the wandering foot and weary breast"; who, though a remnant of them had returned, were ground down under the yoke of the Gentiles, while Judea was still, for the most part, lying waste, and Jerusalem was still without walls—exposed in a most defenceless manner to all the insults of Israel's enemies.[1] The nations had scattered God's people and had taken possession of their land, and were now in undisturbed enjoyment of it. No one cared for the afflictions of Zion, or troubled himself for the sorrows of Israel.

" *Then the Angel of Jehovah answered* (i.e., ' *the implied longing' which was in his heart*) *and said, O Jehovah of hosts, how long wilt Thou not have mercy on Jerusalem and on the cities of Judah, against which Thou hast had indignation these threescore and ten years ?* "[2]

If the very fact of the presence amongst them of the Angel of Jehovah, who in ancient times led His people and brought them into the promised land, and smote all their enemies before them, was intended, as we saw when dealing with the 8th verse, to be in itself a message of comfort to the now oppressed and depressed Israel, how much more full of consolation must have been the fact of His appearing as the Advocate and Intercessor on their behalf ?

And He who here cries, " How long, Jehovah of hosts, wilt Thou not have compassion on Jerusalem and on the cities of Judah ? " has not changed in His attitude of longing and concern for His own nation. When in the fulness of time He permanently took upon Himself our human form, and became real man, we still read of Him as being moved with compassion on beholding Israel's weary

---

[1] This was the lament of even the restored remnant in the land : "Behold, we are servants this day, and as for the land that Thou gavest unto our fathers to eat the fruit thereof and the good thereof, behold, we are servants in it " (Neh. ix. 36).

[2] "The fact that the Angel of Jehovah addresses an intercessory prayer on behalf of Judah is no more a disproof of his essential unity with Jehovah, than the intercessory prayer of Christ in John xvii. is a disproof of His divinity."— Keil.

multitudes, who were as sheep having no shepherd, and as weeping over Jerusalem ; and we may be sure, also, that in those whole nights of prayer and intercession before the Father, the people which are " His own," and the city which was to be the seat of His throne, had a large and central place. Even on the cross He prayed, " Father, forgive them, for they know not what they do "; and when He rose and ascended to the right hand of God as the great High Priest of His people, Israel is still a subject of His intercessions. " For Zion's sake He doth not hold His peace; for Jerusalem's sake He doth not rest until her righteousness go forth as brightness, and her salvation as a lamp that burneth."

We will not enter into the chronological points which might be raised in connection with the words, " *against which Thou hast had indignation these seventy years*," and would merely point out in passing that there are different starting-points from which the period roughly spoken of as " the seventy years' captivity " in Babylon may be reckoned. But as these visions of Zechariah were granted to the prophet in the 2nd year of Darius Hystaspes, in B.C. 519, the " seventy years " foretold by Jeremiah had already expired, even if we calculate from the latest of the possible starting-points.[1] The Divine Advocate might well there-

---

[1] The definite prophecy of Jeremiah was that the inhabitants of Palestine and neighbouring lands "shall serve the king of Babylon seventy years." This began in the 3rd year of Jehoiakim, which was the 1st year of Nebuchadnezzar, *i.e.*, in B.C. 606, or before the 1st of Nisan (April) 605. Starting with this definite date the " seventy years " were brought to an end by the decree of Cyrus in the 1st year of his reign, in B.C. 536 (Dan. i. 1; Jer. xxiv. 1, 9–11; Ezra i. 1–3).

Another starting-point may be made with Jehoiachin's captivity in the 8th year of Nebuchadnezzar, *i.e.*, in B.C. 597 (598), when the city was taken and "all Jerusalem and all the princes and all the mighty men of valour, even 10,000 captives, and all the craftsmen and the smiths," together with the king and his mother and his wives, and the vessels of the Temple and the treasures of the palace were carried to Babylon (2 Kings xxiv. 10–17). From this date the "seventy years " came to an end in B.C. 528.

Then, finally, in the 17th year of Nebuchadnezzar and 9th of Zedekiah's reign, in B.C. 589 (588), commenced the final terrible siege of Jerusalem by the Chaldeans which lasted about a year and a half, and ended with the destruction

fore express "the reverent wonder" that the seventy years being accomplished, the *complete* restoration was not yet brought to pass, and that though a remnant had returned, "Jerusalem and the cities of Judah" were still practically desolate. This pitiable condition of things moves the Angel of Jehovah to intercession on their behalf.

The answer to the intercession of the Angel of Jehovah, given in the 14th verse, is addressed to the interpreting angel that he might make them sink in, so to say, into the prophet's heart and mind, so that he might be able to proclaim them to the people. What these "*debharim tobhim, debharim nichummim*" (literally, "words good ones, words comforting ones") were, we see in the last four verses: (1) Jehovah is jealous for Jerusalem and for Zion with a great jealousy—and He is *very sore displeased* (or, literally, "with great anger am I angered") against the nations that are at ease, "for I was but a little displeased," He says, "and they helped forward the affliction" (or, as it may also be rendered, "they helped for evil"). It is as if while a father was reluctantly punishing his froward but still beloved child with a stick, a stranger were to come and begin to smite him with an iron rod. No wonder that the father's jealousy is stirred, and that a quarrel ensues between him and the intermeddling stranger who dared to mix himself up in the controversy, and increase his child's sufferings. This is ever God's attitude to the oppressors of Israel.

That the nations from the very commencement of "the times of the Gentiles" have been guilty of helping forward the affliction, let the history of Israel, written for the most

of the city and Temple and the carrying away of the remnant of the people into captivity. With this date very probably begins more particularly the seventy years of "Indignation" referred to in this passage in Zechariah. Reckoning from this starting-point, the seventy years came to an end in the 2nd year of Darius Hystaspes, in B.C. 519—the year in which Zechariah saw these visions. A distinction is made by some between "the Captivity" and "the Desolations"; but the first has special reference to the condition of the people, and the other to the land during the same period. In post-Biblical Jewish literature the whole period of the subjection to Babylon is spoken of as the גלה, "captivity," and loosely, as "the seventy years,"

part in their blood, testify. God scattered Israel (Jer. xxxi. 10); but the nations among whom they have come trampled upon them, and put a yoke of iron upon their necks, and made them "to howl" all the day long (Isa. lii. 5), because of their oppressions. God gave them over to punishment, but, at the same time, warned the nations, saying, "Make not a full end" (Jer. v. 10); but they have tried, if possible, to destroy them, and to cut off their very remembrance from the earth. God gave over for a time "the dearly beloved of His soul into the hand of her enemies" (Jer. xii. 7): "I was wroth with My people," He says, addressing Babylon, the first, and also in many Scriptures the great, representative of all Gentile world-powers: "I polluted mine inheritance and gave them into thine hand, *and thou didst show them no mercy*" (Isa. xlvii. 6).

And this was not merely the attitude of the great nations of antiquity who have now for the most part perished from off the face of the earth—Israel's lot in the midst of Christendom has been even worse.

"Where shall we begin," writes an American brother, "in treating the awful truth which is put here in such simple language? Where shall we find words earnest enough to picture the terrible facts in connection with it, and sound a warning for our times? Some time ago a person said, 'The Jews are to-day more stiff-necked and blinder than ever before.' Who has made them thus? Surely judicial blindness and hardness of heart: ears which do not hear, are given by God; but, alas! the nations, or so-called Christendom, have helped forward their affliction; they have made matters worse a thousand times: and Satan, who hates Israel, has been the author of all things calculated to increase the affliction of this downtrodden nation. Surely the cause of the increased stiff-neckedness and the increased blindness of the Jewish people is one which is traceable to the nations. Every reader knows something of the history of the Jews, what it has been since they were driven from their land—a long, long tale of suffering, tears, and blood.

Most unjust outrages have been committed against them : torture upon torture, the stake, and worse than that—and all in the name of Jesus. It is a shameful history. Many a time Jews, after hearing the Word preached, have stood up and opened in answer this awful book of history with its blood-stained pages, asking the question, 'Can He be our Redeemer whose followers have treated us thus in His name?' And not a few can tell us of their own sufferings in being banished from foreign lands. Hardly a month passes without some new outrage upon this people. Cruelty, injustice, wickedness, and crime are practised against them, and thus their affliction has been increased."

And all this the Gentile nations have done to Israel out of cruel, selfish motives, and not out of regard for God at all. We are sometimes asked, " But have not the sufferings of Israel all been minutely foretold by Moses and the prophets in advance? " Yes, certainly they have all been foretold ; but have not the sufferings of Christ been even more minutely foretold and described also? And yet we read that it was " with wicked hands " that they took and crucified Him, and Israel was held responsible for their conduct and dealings in relation to Him. Prophecy, my dear reader, is given to us, not that it *may* be fulfilled, but because the omniscient God, who sees the end from the beginning, knows that it *will* be fulfilled, and man is left a free and responsible agent ; and the nations who know not that the great God is overruling all things, even their wicked actions, to the fulfilment of His predetermined counsel, are held accountable for their deeds.

And that the jealousy and hot displeasure of Jehovah against the nations because of their attitude to Israel are to be dreaded, history also testifies. Where are the great nations of antiquity who have lifted up their hands against the Jewish people? And in modern times the ancient word which He spoke to Abraham is still verifying itself in the experience of nations as of individuals : " I will bless them that bless thee, and him that curseth thee will I curse."

But not only is the prophet to proclaim the negative
comfort that Jehovah is very angry with the nations at
ease who help forward the affliction, but He has wonderful
purposes of grace concerning His people to announce:
" *Therefore, thus saith Jehovah, I am returned to Jerusalem
with mercies*"—which, on account of its certainty, is
expressed in the present or perfect tense.   This, which has
been already symbolically set forth to the prophet by the
standing of the Angel of Jehovah in the midst of the
myrtles, is the very heart and substance of " the good
words and comforting words " which are the message of this
vision.   It was the hiding of His face—the withdrawal of
Himself—that occasioned all these calamities in their
night of darkness.   So long as Jehovah was with them,
neither Assyria nor Babylon, nor all the forces of the
universe, could have prevailed against them ; but when His
glory was withdrawn, then they became a prey to the
Gentiles—" the boar out of the wood " came and wasted it ;
the " wild beast of the field " came and devoured it.   But
not *for ever* has Jehovah forsaken His people and the land
which He has chosen as the centre of the unfolding of His
purposes of mercy to all mankind.   " I will go," He says,
" and return to My place till they acknowledge their
offence " (or literally, " till *they declare themselves guilty* "),
" and seek My face ; in their affliction " (literally, " in their
tribulation ") " they shall seek Me early " (or earnestly),
and then He will return unto them with mercies ; and
" His going forth is sure as the morning, and He shall come
unto us as the rain, as the latter rain that watereth the
earth " (Hos. v. 15, vi. 1–3).
      In its fulness this promise will only be fulfilled when
" this same Jesus," whom at His first coming they handed
over to the Gentiles to be crucified, and who, after His
resurrection, ascended back into heaven into the glory
which He had with the Father before the world was, shall
" return " in the manner and under the circumstances
described by this same prophet in the last three chapters
of this prophecy.   Then, in the once marred face, and in

the wounded hands and feet of Him whom they once pierced, shall they fully learn the fulness and manifoldness of God's "mercies."

Two or three particular instances and outward signs of "that all-containing mercy" of His restored presence in their midst, are specially named : (*a*) "*My house shall be built in it, saith Jehovah of hosts*," as the visible sign and pledge of the restored fellowship between Him and His people; (*b*) And "*a line shall be stretched forth over Jerusalem*," to mark off the space it is to occupy in its restored condition, and the plan upon which it is to be arranged. (*c*) And not only shall His house be rebuilt and Jerusalem be restored on a grander scale than before, but *all the land* is to feel the blessed effect of the restored relations between Jehovah and His people. "*Cry yet again, saying, Thus saith Jehovah of hosts* : MY *cities*"—yes, they are peculiarly *His*, as is the case with no other land and no other cities, even as the people which shall inhabit it is peculiarly His, above all other nations of the earth—"*through prosperity shall yet be spread abroad*"—or "overflow," the word being used of the "gushing forth of a fountain" in Prov. v. 16, *i.e.*, they shall overflow, not only with spiritual prosperity, but with houses filled with citizens, and with abundance and plenty. (*d*) Finally, both as the ground and climax of all, come the last of the "good words." "*And Jehovah shall yet comfort Zion*," after her long night of sorrow, and however contrary to all appearance and human probability, "*shall yet choose Jerusalem*," or, by the above enumerated and many other acts of loving-kindness toward her, *demonstrate* in the sight of the whole world the fact and the immutability of His original choice of her—this last sentence being the first of a threefold inspired repetition by Zechariah[1] of the words of Isa. xiv. 1, where we read, "*For Jehovah will have compassion on Jacob, and yet choose Israel, and set them in their own land: and the stranger shall be joined with them, and they shall cleave to the house of Jacob.*"

---

[1] Here and in ii. 12 and iii. 2.

Now, there was no doubt a message in this vision and in the plain words of comfort with which it closes to the generation to which the prophet spoke, and in a very partial manner there was a fulfilment of these promises in the then immediate future. Thus God's "House," as applied to the Temple which they were then building, was completed about four years later, in the 6th year of Darius (Ezra vi. 15); and some time later Nehemiah succeeded also in rebuilding the city wall.

There is *some* truth also in the contention of those commentators who argue that there was a fulfilment of the good and comforting words about Jehovah's returning to Zion with mercies in the first advent of our Saviour. Thus, to quote one of them : "What is the highest good ? what the sweetest of solace in life? what the subject of joys? what the oblivion of past sorrow ? That which the Son of God brought upon earth when He illumined Jerusalem with the brightness of His light and heavenly discipline. For to that end was the city restored, that in it by the ordinance of Christ, for calamity, should abound bliss ; for desolation, fulness ; for sorrow, joy ; for want, affluence of heavenly goods "—all which is beautiful and true ; but to deny that in its fulness it will yet find an exhaustive fulfilment in the Jewish people, which for nearly two thousand years has been in much greater bondage than they were during the seventy years in Babylon, is to misapprehend and misinterpret the scope of this as of all the other visions. No ; these words which Zechariah is here commanded to "cry," or proclaim, *are a summary and divine reiteration of the permanent and irrevocable* " good words " of Jehovah through the former prophets in reference to Israel's future, and will assuredly be fulfilled, as already shown above, when, "after these things," our Lord Jesus shall return and will "build again the tabernacle of David which is fallen ; and will build again the ruins thereof, and will set it up, that the residue of men may seek after the Lord and all the Gentiles upon whom My name is called " (Acts xv. 14–18).

"For Jehovah shall comfort Zion; He will comfort all her waste places, and He will make her wilderness like Eden, and her desert like the garden of Jehovah; joy and gladness shall be found therein, thanksgiving and the voice of melody" (Isa. li. 3).

Chapter 3

THE SECOND VISION
THE HORNS AND THE
"CARPENTERS"
Zechariah 1:18-21

And I lifted up mine eyes, and saw, and behold four horns. And I said unto the angel that talked with me, What are these? And he answered me, These are the horns which have scattered Judah, Israel, and Jerusalem. And Jehovah showed me four smiths. Then said I, What come these to do? And he spake, saying, These are the horns which scattered Judah, so that no man did lift up his head: but these are come to terrify them, to cast down the horns of the nations, which lifted up their horn against the land of Judah to scatter it.

Chapter 3

THIS second short vision is in a sense a continuation of the comforting message contained in the first, for it shows how the Gentile nations against whom Jehovah is "very sore displeased," because they have each in turn "helped forward the affliction" by scattering Israel and treading down Jerusalem, shall themselves be broken and dissipated. The prophet had probably been absorbed in thought and meditation on what he saw and heard in the first vision ; but being directed, perhaps, by the interpreting angel to look up again, he beheld—not only with the outer eye, but with the eyes of his soul and whole inner being, which had been prepared for the reception of these Divine revelations—"*four horns*," and on his appealing to his angelic teacher, who stood by his side, for the meaning of these, the brief answer is given : "*These are the horns which have scattered Judah, Israel, and Jerusalem.*"

The "Horns"

Let us briefly ponder over the symbolism of these two verses before proceeding to the second part of the vision.

"Horns" are used in Scripture as emblematic of power and pride of conscious strength (Amos vi. 13 ; Ps. lxxv. 4, 5, xcii. 10), and are sometimes explained by the sacred writers themselves as representing *the ruling powers of the world* (Dan. viii. ; Rev. xvii. 3–12).

The number "four" may also, but in a secondary sense, stand, as some contend, for the four directions of heaven, or the four "corners" of the earth, and be designed to indicate the *universality* of the enmity which is directed against

Israel. In that case, to use the language of a learned commentator who thinks only of the past, the four horns would "represent the enemies of Israel on every side : Edom and Egypt in the south ; the Philistines in the west ; the Ammonites and Moabites in the east ; and from the north the Syrians, Assyrians, and especially the Chaldeans." Or, according to another commentator who views this prophecy in relation to the then present, " the number 'four' refers to the four cardinal points of the horizon, indicating that wherever God's people turned there were enemies to encounter."

But there can be no doubt, according to our judgment, especially if we remember the fact that it is the characteristic of Zechariah's visions and prophecies, that the Divine messages contained in them are generally based on revelations already granted to the former prophets, that in this vision of the four horns there is a direct reference to the four great world-powers, differently represented by the four metals in the great image, and four great beasts in chaps. ii. and vii. of Daniel's prophecies—the only four empires which were, or are, to rise till the kingdom of Messiah, the fifth of Daniel's visions, overthrows and absorbs all others in its universal dominion. This was the view of the most authoritative of Jewish commentators. Thus Kimchi says, " These are the four monarchies—and they are the Babylonian monarchy, the Persian monarchy, and the Grecian monarchy, and so the Targum of Jonathan has it (instead of four horns), the four monarchies."[1]

Some commentators have raised an objection to this

---

[1] He does not name the fourth. Abarbanel's explanation is to the same effect. The following passage is from Hengstenberg : "If we inquire more particularly what four empires are referred to, the first must be the Babylonian, which was not yet completely humbled, as the third vision shows, although it had received a fatal wound from the Persian smith (or 'carpenter'). The second is the Persian. That the Grecian must have been recognised by the prophet as the third, is evident from the expression in chap. ix. 13, 'I stir up thy sons, O Zion, against thy sons, O Javan.' The fourth is not named. The connection with Daniel is apparent here also, for in his prophecy the approaching dominion of Greece is expressly and amply referred to ; whilst the fourth monarchy, on the other hand, is left without a name."

view on the ground that the power which overthrew the
Israel of the northern kingdom was Assyria, and that other
powers besides, such as Egypt, etc., have had their share in
breaking up the two Israelitish states, and have argued
from the use of the perfect, or preterite *zeru* ("have
scattered"), that the dispersion was presented to the
prophet as an already accomplished fact by powers which
had already then been in existence; but to this objection
it is sufficient to answer that, though it is true that other
powers beside had had a share in afflicting and scattering
Israel, and that the northern kingdom had been overthrown
by Assyria, the prophetic Scriptures, and especially the
prophecies of Daniel, upon which this vision of Zechariah
is based, deal with a definite and particular period as pre-
eminently the one during which Israel is "scattered" and
Jerusalem "trodden down," and that these "times of the
Gentiles" begin, not with Shalmaneser, nor with Sennacherib, but with Nebuchadnezzar, king of Babylon, "the
head of gold" of the great image which he himself beheld
in a dream (Dan. ii. 1).

It is true that Israel, as far as the northern kingdom of
the ten tribes is concerned, had been overthrown and a
considerable number transported into Assyria; but it was
not till a hundred and thirty years later, when the sceptre
was finally plucked out of the hands of the last king of
the House of David who reigned in Jerusalem, by Nebuchadnezzar, that the united dispersion of Judah and Israel
commenced, and the special period of their national woes
and humiliations which were to extend during the whole
course of these four great Gentile world-empires, was
inaugurated.

As for the use of the perfect or preterite, and the fact
that the prophet sees the four horns together, we have to
remember that it is the tense of prophetic vision to which
everything appears present. In the same way the prophets,
for instance, described the sufferings and death of Messiah
—the perfect Servant of Jehovah who was to appear
centuries after their day—as already past, and speak of the

future glory of Israel as already come. And thus, also, these four powers, though successive in time, are exhibited to Zechariah together, and their antagonism and cruelty to God's people as already past and gone, "as each would be at the last, having put forth his passing might and perishing."

But the question may be asked, What *consolation* could the prophet derive or communicate to the people from a vision of four powers, two of whom at least had not yet arisen, who would in turn take up the work of scattering Israel? And the answer, dear reader, is, that though it may have been intended as an indication to the prophet, and a forecast that the *final* deliverance of Israel and the overthrow of Israel's foes, was, from the prophet's point of time, yet remote, the wonderful and consoling fact set forth in the vision remains; that in spite of all the great Gentile powers, who would each in turn take up the work of scattering and afflicting Israel, Israel would not be wholly swallowed up nor be overwhelmed, but would remain when all those powers should have disappeared, and would triumph in God's deliverance when the memory of their mighty enemies should be buried in shame and oblivion.

To us, looking back upon a period—the length of which was unforeseen even by prophets, embracing some two and a half millenniums—during which this comparative handful of people have been "scattered" and "tossed" about, by and among the nations, without being destroyed from off the earth, and without losing its national characteristics and identity, the marvel of Israel's continued preservation must appear much greater than to any one living in the time of Zechariah or Daniel, and can only be accounted for by the special providences and interpositions of Him who swore that so long as the sun and the ordinances of the moon and the stars continue, so long should Israel continue a nation before Him "for ever"; and who said in advance, even before the course of these four great Gentile world-powers, who would be permitted to scatter Israel, commenced: "For I am with thee, saith Jehovah, to save thee: for I will make a full end of all nations whither I have scattered thee ; but I will not make a full end of thee, but I will correct thee in measure (or ' with judgment '), and will in no wise leave thee unpunished " (Jer. xxx. 11). Well might the inspired writer of Ps. cxxix., looking back, not only on the particular period embraced in the prophetic " times of the Gentiles," but on the *whole course* of Gentile oppression, exclaim in the name of the remnant of Israel :

" *Many a time* (or, more literally, '*greatly* ') *have they afflicted me from my youth ; yet they have not prevailed against me.*"

" Israel's national youth, or childhood," to borrow words of our own from elsewhere, " was in Egypt, even as we find in Hos. xi. 1, which literally reads, ' When Israel was yet a child ' (the word being the same as '*youth*' in the 129th Psalm), I loved him, and from the time that he was in Egypt I called him my son "—that is, from the very beginning of their history, when God began to love Israel, the nations began to hate them ; and from the very time when God first called them " His son, His first-born " (Ex. iv. 22, 23), the nations began " to afflict them " (Ex. i. 12), and to lay plans for their extermination. Yes, from the very commencement of their history have the plowers mercilessly

" *Plowed upon his back ;*
" *They made long and deep their furrows* " (Ps. cxxix. 3).

And " yet," in spite of it all, " *they have not prevailed against him.*"

This is Israel's final shout of triumph, even as in a sense it has been their national song and their defiant answer to the nations all through the ages.

To commence with Israel's " youth "—deep and terrible was the pain and laceration when Egypt plowed upon his back ; but who came off worst in the end? Egypt was plagued ; Pharaoh and his host were drowned ; but of Israel we read, " The more they afflicted them, the more they multiplied and grew." Truly Egypt, with all its world-power, did " *not prevail against him.*"

Then—not to mention Canaanites, Philistines, Midianites, and other small powers—there came Syria, Assyria, Babylon, Persia, Greece, and Rome, each of whom in turn afflicted Israel much, and made deep and long their furrows; but where are all these powers? They have crumbled away and died, but Israel lives, and they have " *not prevailed over him.*"

Then came the centuries of dispersion, when it might be supposed that a comparative handful of men, scattered on the great ocean of humanity, would soon be swallowed up of the multitude. As a matter of fact, every force was brought to bear against them with terrible severity. Their enemies were united, and seemed confident of success. The Crusaders went from west to east with the cry " Hierosolyma est perdita ! "[1] and perpetrated wholesale massacres of the Jews as a commencement of their "holy" wars. Again and again apostate Christendom in the dark ages showed its zeal for the Jewish Messiah, who teaches His followers to love even their enemies, by burning whole communities of Jews, numbering sometimes thousands of souls, on one huge scaffold; but in spite of it all Israel lives —" *they have not prevailed over him* "; for there are more Jews in the world after all the centuries of banishments, massacres, and untold sufferings, than there have been at any previous point of the world's history; and the Jews at the present day, as is proved from official statistics, in some parts of the world increase in proportion to their Gentile neighbours at the ratio of three and four to one.

Alas! the sufferings of Israel are not ended, and even in this twentieth century we read almost daily of Jewish massacres and atrocities worse than any which disgrace the annals of the dark ages; but Czardom [2] and the corrupt bureaucracy of that unhappy empire will pass away, while Israel will still sing, " *Yet they have not prevailed against me.*"

---

[1] Or, "Hep! Hep!" which is an abbreviation formed from the three initial letters of this Latin phrase ; the English corruption of it is "Hip! Hip!"

[2] This was written in 1908.

And there is yet a future, or final, culminating "affliction," "trouble," or "tribulation," as the same Hebrew word is elsewhere rendered, awaiting Israel after a large remnant of them are returned to their land in a condition of unbelief, when all nations will be gathered in a final siege of Jerusalem (Zech. xiii., xiv.); but even then, when the nations cry, " Come, let us destroy them from being a nation, that the name of Israel be no more held in remembrance " (Ps. lxxxiii. 4)—one more blow, and the Jewish nation will be no more—the answer of the saved remnant, who are delivered by the sudden appearance of their Messiah, will be: "I shall not die, but live, and declare the works of Jehovah"—*Yet they have not prevailed against me.*

Israel is indestructible. The bush may burn, but it cannot be consumed, because God has said : " Though I make a full end of all nations whither I have scattered thee, yet will I not make a full end of thee."

But to come to the other points in this vision which need explanation. The peculiar structure of the sentence and the unusual designation of the chosen people as " Judah, Israel, and Jerusalem," in ver. 19, has given ground to many, and some of them very fanciful interpretations, but there can be no doubt that it is an all-inclusive term for the whole nation which for a time, as a punishment on the House of David, had been rent asunder and divided, so long as the northern kingdom continued, into " Judah " and " Israel," but which after " Jerusalem " (which was the metropolis and religious centre of those who feared Jehovah in both kingdoms, and is therefore mentioned separately) was overthrown, were together sharing the same destiny of being " scattered " by the horns of the Gentiles, even as they are included in the same common and united hope of restoration and blessing, no longer as two separate kingdoms, but as one, under the true Son of David.

The " Carpenters " or Smiths

Apart from the final and total overthrow of confederated
Gentile world-power at the time of the end, the prophet is
also made to see what we may describe as the gradual
process of the decay and overthrow of the four great
empires in turn.

" And Jehovah showed me four 'carpenters,' " literally,
" workmen," or " smiths," as the R.V. renders the word.
The Hebrew חָרָשׁ, ḥarash, designates a cunning workman
or artificer in either wood, stone, or metal. And as the
prophet evidently sees them coming on the stage of his
prophetic vision in readiness for work, with, perhaps, the
tools or implements of their trade in their hands, he asks :
" What come these to do ? " And the answer, evidently of
the Lord Himself, though it may have been through the
interpreting angel, is : " These (are) the horns which have
scattered Judah."

This first sentence in the reply is a repetition of the
statement in the preceding verse, but words are added
which are meant to emphasise the greatness of Israel's
sorrow and affliction during the period of their being tossed
about by these "horns"; for their sufferings have been
such (literally, "according to the measure," i.e., in such a
manner) " that no man did lift up his head," so heavily did
oppression weigh upon them, but these (the ḥarashim, or
" workmen ") are come to fray (literally, " to terrify ")
" them, and to cast down the horns of the nations which are
lifting up their horn against the land of Judah to scatter it "
(i.e., the inhabitants or population of it).

Who are these workmen, or smiths ? " Symbols of
Divine judgment " in a general way, says one learned commentator. " Symbols of the instruments of the Divine
Omnipotence by which the imperial power in its historical
forms is overthrown," says another. But while it is true
that this part of the vision is designed to show to the
people of God in a general way, " that every hostile power
of the world which has risen up against it, or shall rise up,

is to be judged and destroyed," the number *four* standing over against the four horns does not only suggest that " for *every* enemy of God's people God has provided a counter-acting power adequate to destroy it,"[1] but points to four powers *also successive, though in the vision, like the four horns, presented together.* And, if I am asked to state more definitely which four powers, I answer the first was the Medo-Persian, which by the hand of Cyrus broke down the horn of Babylon; the second was the Grecian, which by the hand of Alexander terrified and humbled the power of Persia; the third was Rome, which in its turn prostrated and trod down the power of Greece.[2]

This last, the most terrible of all, not only acted as one of the " workmen " or " smiths " to terrify and break down the great world-power which immediately preceded it, but, in relation to the Jewish people and the Church of God, still exists as the last of the four horns; and in its revived form, under the leadership of the Satan-possessed head of the final confederacy of apostate Gentile world-powers, will bring about the climax of all the sorrows and the sufferings of Israel in the last " great tribulation, such as hath not

[1] Lange.

[2] The following curious passage about the four carpenters or "smiths" is from Kimchi's Commentary:

" And the Lord showed me four workmen, . . . in order to cut off the horns —that is to say, each kingdom shall be a carpenter, to cut off the kingdom that preceded it, for the Babylonian monarchy fell by the hand of the Persians, and the Persian by the hand of the Greek, etc. Or, the carpenters may signify in a parable the angels—the supernatural princes who are appointed over the king-doms; and our Rabbis of blessed memory have interpreted the verse of the days of the Messiah, saying, ' Who are the four carpenters? R. Simon Chasida says they are Messiah the Son of David, the Messiah the Son of Joseph, and Elias, and the righteous priest.' This passage, quoted by Kimchi, is found in the Talmud, Succah, fol. 52, col. 2, where Rashi says, in his commentary on the authority of Bereshith Rabba, that ' the righteous priest' means Shem the son of Noah, who is there supposed to be identical with Melchizedek. The legend about the angels is thus given in the Pirke Eleazar: ' The Holy One, blessed be He, descended with the seventy angels who surrounded the throne of His glory,' and confounded their language into seventy nations and seventy languages, each nation with its own writing and language, and over each nation He appointed an angel, but Israel fell to His portion and lot, and therefore it is said, ' The Lord's portion is His people.' "

been from the beginning of the world until now, no, nor ever shall be." It is to that time that the 7th chapter of Daniel refers: "After this I saw in the night vision, and behold a fourth beast, dreadful and terrible and strong exceedingly, and it had great iron teeth; it devoured and brake in pieces, and stamped the residue with his feet, and it was diverse from all the beasts that were before it; and it had ten horns" (explained in ver. 24 of the same chapter as signifying "ten kings" or "kingdoms"). "I considered the horns, and behold there came up among them another, a little horn, before whom there were three of the first horns plucked up by the roots, and behold in this horn were eyes like the eyes of a man, and a mouth speaking great things" (Dan. vii. 6–8). But it is just then—when the strength and pride and ruthless cruelty and blasphemy of apostate world-power summed up in its head reaches its climax, that "the horn of the Gentiles" shall finally and for ever be broken and cast out; for then the last "workman" or "smith" who, though seen by the prophet with the other three, is altogether diverse from them, and is only included in the vision with the others in order to present a full and complete view of the overthrow of all the four horns, shall suddenly appear to accomplish *His* terrible work of judgment. "I saw in the night visions, and, behold, there came with the clouds of heaven one like unto a Son of Man, and He came even to the Ancient of Days, and they brought Him near before Him (to be invested formally with the Kingdom immediately before He comes in the clouds of heaven to take possession of it); and there was given Him dominion and glory and a kingdom, that all the peoples, nations, and languages should serve Him: His dominion is an everlasting dominion," and His kingdom "shall never be destroyed, nor shall the sovereignty thereof be left to another people, but it shall break in pieces and consume all these kingdoms, and it shall stand for ever" (Dan. vii. 13, 14, ii. 44, 45, R.V.).

Chapter 4

THE THIRD VISION
THE MAN WITH THE MEASURING LINE
Zechariah 2

And I lifted up mine eyes, and saw, and behold a man with a measuring line in his hand. Then said I, Whither goest thou? And he said unto me, To measure Jerusalem, to see what is the breadth thereof, and what is the length thereof. And, behold, the angel that talked with me went forth, and another angel went out to meet him, and said unto him, Run, speak to this young man, saying, Jerusalem shall be inhabited as villages without walls, by reason of the multitude of men and cattle therein. For I, saith Jehovah, will be unto her a wall of fire round about, and I will be the glory in the midst of her. Ho, ho, flee from the land of the north, saith Jehovah ; for I have spread you abroad as the four winds of the heavens, saith Jehovah. Ho Zion, escape, thou that dwellest with the daughter of Babylon. For thus saith Jehovah of hosts : After glory hath He sent Me unto the nations which plundered you ; for he that toucheth you toucheth the apple of His eye. For, behold, I will shake My hand over them, and they shall be a spoil to those that served them ; and ye shall know that Jehovah of hosts hath sent Me. Sing and rejoice, O daughter of Zion ; for, lo, I come, and I will dwell in the midst of thee, saith Jehovah. And many nations shall join themselves to Jehovah in that day, and shall be My people ; and I will dwell in the midst of thee, and thou shalt know that Jehovah of hosts hath sent Me unto thee. And Jehovah shall inherit Judah as His portion in the holy land, and shall yet choose Jerusalem. Be silent, all flesh, before Jehovah ; for He is waked up out of His holy habitation.

Chapter 4

THE second and third visions stand in closest possible connection with the first. " The good words and comfortable words" (i. 1 3), which were God's answer to the intercession of the Angel of Jehovah on behalf of " Jerusalem and the cities of Judah," contained a twofold message : First, that Jehovah is jealous for Jerusalem and for Zion with a great jealousy, and is sore displeased (or " very angry ") with the nations who are at ease, who helped forward the affliction of Israel (i. 14, 15). Secondly, that He would " return to Jerusalem with mercies," the outward proofs of which would be (a) that His house would again be built in it, as the visible sign and pledge of the restored communion between Him and His people. (b) And " a line shall be stretched forth over Jerusalem," i.e., as already explained in my notes on that vision, " to mark the space it is to occupy in its restored condition, and the plan on which it is to be arranged."

And not only should Jerusalem itself be rebuilt, but the whole land should feel the blessed effects of Jehovah's return to His people with mercies ; and its cities, which He calls " My cities," should " through prosperity yet be spread abroad," or " yet overflow with prosperity " (i. 16, 17).

Now, just as the second vision of the " horns," and " carpenters," or " workmen," is a continuation and sequel to the first part of the consoling message—for it shows how the Gentile nations, who " have helped forward the affliction" by scattering Israel and treading down Jerusalem, shall themselves be broken up and finally overthrown—so the third vision of the man with the measuring line is an amplification and realistic unfolding of the other " comfortable words " in the second part of the consoling message in reference to the future of the city, and the land, and the people, when Jehovah, in the Person of Messiah, shall " return to Jerusalem with mercies."

The Vision

Lifting up his eyes, the prophet sees a man with a measuring line in his hand, and on asking, " Whither goest thou ? " the answer is, " To measure Jerusalem, to see what (or ' how great ') is the breadth thereof and what (or how great) is the length thereof." While " the man " is thus actually engaged, the interpreting angel " goes out," or forward, from the prophet by whose side he had been standing, evidently in the direction of the measuring which was going on, to inquire the meaning of the symbolism, so as to communicate it to the prophet ; but is met on the way by " another angel," evidently sent forth by " the man " with the measuring line, who commands him to run and tell " this young man " from whose side he had just come, saying, " Jerusalem shall be inhabited as towns (or ' villages ') without walls, by reason of the multitude of men and cattle therein. For I, saith Jehovah, will be unto her a wall of fire, and will be the glory in the midst of her."

The Interpretation

In the above summary we have already indicated the character of the *dramatis personæ* in this prophetic vision, but it is necessary also to explain it in detail. First, who is " the man " with the measuring line ?

Some interpreters have confused him with the interpreting angel, though in the text itself this angel is clearly distinguished from " the man," since he does not " go out " till the latter had already gone to measure Jerusalem. Others, again, have regarded this " man " as " a mere figure in the vision"; while still others have confused him with the "young man" in ver. 4. Thus Dr. Wright says, rather dogmatically, "The man with the measuring line is not to be regarded as an angel ; he was sent forth on no mission from above. He appears as a mere figure in the vision, and one represented as acting unwisely. He may have been, as Neumann imagines, termed 'this young man' by the angel, in allusion to his simplicity."

But the suggestion of a "mere figure" in the vision is altogether out of keeping with the character of the whole series of these prophetic dramas in which every actor is of significance, and there is nothing whatever in the text of the vision to justify the above statement that this "man" was sent "on no mission from above," and is represented as acting "unwisely" or in "his simplicity."

In opposition to the above, it seems to me very clear that "the man" is none other than the One whom the prophet beheld in the first vision riding upon the red horse, and standing among the myrtles "in the bottom" or "by the deep" (chap. i. 8), who in the 11th verse of that same chapter is identified with the *Malakh Yehovah*—the Angel of Jehovah—who, as we have seen, is the same as "the Angel of His Face," the Divine "Messenger of the Covenant," the Second Person in the Blessed Trinity.

Nor are these the only places where the Angel of Jehovah is called "the man" in these series of visions, for in the symbolical transaction which follows the visions in chap. vi., which is an indisputably Messianic passage, we read: "Behold the Man, whose name is the Branch, and He shall grow up out of His place, and He shall build the temple of Jehovah." Now, He who in that scripture is represented as the builder of the true Temple of Jehovah, as the ultimate fulfilment of the "comfortable words" of promise in the first vision, "My house shall be built in it," is "the man" who in this third vision is represented as the Author of that future restoration and enlargement of the city expressed in the words which immediately follow in that first comprehensive message of consolation : " And a line shall be stretched over Jerusalem " (i. 16).[1]

Some (as Neumann, Lange, and others) identity the " other angel," in ver. 3, with the Angel of Jehovah ; but in that case it is difficult to see why he should not have been called simply by the title *Malakh Yehovah*, if he were that Divine Being, instead of by an indefinite designation which suggests in itself the idea that he was an angel of inferior dignity.   Besides, the expression, " went out," in ver. 3, which is the same as " went forth," as used of the interpreting angel, seems to me to indicate that just as the latter " went out " from the side of the prophet by whom he was standing, so this " other angel " was by the side and in attendance on the man with the measuring line, by whom he was sent to meet the interpreting angel with the message with which the latter, in his turn, was to run to the prophet.

The " young man," therefore, is neither " the man " with the measuring line, nor any other angelic being, as some have supposed ; for, apart from the fact that such an interpretation confuses the whole vision, the term *naar*, as Pusey well observes, " Common as our English term ' youth,' in regard to man, is inapplicable and unapplied to angels, who have not our human variations of age, but exist as they were created." [2]   The probable reason why

---

[1] The word translated a " line," in chap. i. 16, is not the same as the one rendered " a measuring line " in chap. ii., but there can be no doubt in our judgment that the idea expressed in that part of the consoling message of the first vision is taken up in this third vision, and the fulfilment realistically set forth by the symbolical act of the actual measuring.   It is, moreover, very probable that there is a reference in this second chapter of Zechariah to Ezekiel's vision in chaps. xl., xliii., where " the man whose appearance was like the appearance of brass," who was going forth " with a line of flax in his hand and a measuring reed " on the same errand, namely, to measure the site of the Jerusalem that is to be restored, is also the Angel of Jehovah.   In Rev. xxi. 15-27 the same symbolism is used in reference to the Jerusalem which is above—the city which hath foundations, " whose builder and maker," in a very special sense, is God in Christ.

[2] The term in Hebrew denotes a male from infancy, as Moses was in the ark of bulrushes, to the prime of life ; and is occasionally used for " minister " or " servant," without reference to age.

the prophet is thus styled, and the practical lessons which we may learn from this fact, I have already pointed out in my introductory remarks on the personality of Zechariah, at the commencement of these expositions.

The Message

The joyful tidings in explanation of the symbolical act of the measuring of the city, with which the interpreting angel is to " run," that he may quickly communicate them to the prophet, that he also in his turn may communicate them to the people, contain a twofold message.

I. Jerusalem shall not only be restored but greatly enlarged, extending much beyond the boundaries of its ancient walls, " *by reason of the multitude of men and cattle therein,*" it will " dwell " or " be inhabited " as *perazoth*, rendered in the A.V. " towns without walls," and in the R.V. " villages." But the word strictly describes " plains," or an open country in which there is nothing to circumscribe the inhabitants, or to prevent them from spreading themselves abroad : thus in Ezek. xxxviii. 11 it is used of the land where people dwell in peace and prosperity, " without walls, bolts, and gates," in contrast to those in walled cities ; and in Esth. ix. 19 the inhabitants of the *perazoth* (the unprotected towns and villages) are distinguished from those living in the fortified capital, Susa. It denotes also a condition of confidence and safety, since in danger men resort to strong cities and fortified towns.

This again is in accord with the words of the former prophets in reference to the marvellous increase of the people, and the extended boundaries of the city and the land after the restoration : thus, for instance, we read in Isa. xlix. 19, 20, " For as for thy waste places and thy desolate places, and thy land that hath been destroyed, surely now shalt thou be too strait for the inhabitants, and they that swallowed thee up shall be far away. The children of thy bereavement " (" the children that thou shalt have instead of those of which thou hast been bereaved "—it is addressed

to Jerusalem) "shall yet say in thine ears, The place is too
strait for me ; give place to me" ("make room") "that I
may dwell," so that the limits of the city and the land
shall be ever wider extended, and Jerusalem shall resemble
a succession of "villages" on the open plains.

II. But a promise much greater than mere outward
enlargement and material prosperity follows in the 5th
verse : " *For I, saith Jehovah, will be unto her a wall of fire
round about, and will be the glory* (or '*for glory*') *in the
midst of her.*" This is one of the most beautiful and comprehensive promises in the Old Testament. It contains
an assurance of *protection*—though inhabited as "villages"
in an open plain, without visible walls or fortifications, it
shall be "a strong city" and perfectly safe from all attacks
and danger ; for not only will Jehovah in that day "appoint
salvation for walls and bulwarks" (Isa. xxvi. 1), but He
Himself (the "I" in ver. 5 being very emphatic) will be a
wall of fire—"as an inner circle" of perfect defence to
those within, but for sure destruction to enemies who shall
dare to approach from without.

And as He shall be her protection from without, so
shall He be her glory from within, for "Jehovah shall be
unto thee an everlasting light, and thy God thy glory"
(Isa. lx. 19) ; and what is said of the heavenly Jerusalem
shall, in a degree, be true also in that day of the restored
earthly city, "The glory of the Lord shall lighten it, and
the Lamb shall be the lamp thereof" (Rev. xxi. 23).

But it might be as well, before proceeding further, to
pause and inquire if there is any truth in the assertion that
this promise has already been fulfilled, and to make quite
sure that *it is* of the literal Jerusalem that these beautiful
words are primarily spoken ; for there are some interpreters
who even deny this. Thus Pusey (whose otherwise devout
and scholarly work on the Minor Prophets is vitiated by
the so-called spiritualising method which seeks persistently
to explain away even the plainest prophecies about
Jerusalem, and applies every promise to "the Church,"
while it carefully leaves the curses to the Jews), after

explaining the words, "Jerusalem shall be inhabited as towns without walls," exclaims: "Clearly, then, it is no earthly city. To be inhabited as villages would be weakness, not strength; a peril, not a blessing. The earthly Jerusalem, as long as she remained unwalled, was in continual fear and weakness. God put it into the heart of His servant (Nehemiah) to desire to restore her; her wall was built, and she prospered. . . . This prophecy, then, looks on directly to the time of Christ. Wonderfully does it picture the gradual expansion of the Kingdom of Christ without bound or limit. . . . It should *dwell as villages*, peacefully and gently expanding itself to the right and to the left, through its own inherent power of multiplying itself, as a city to which no bounds were assigned, but which was to fill the earth." And another,[1] who, in an able and elaborate work, which, however, is chiefly a summary of the explanations and speculations of German commentators who, with very rare exceptions, have no place at all in their theological and exegetical schemes for any future for Israel—admitting that it is of the earthly Jerusalem that the words were spoken—tells us coolly that: "There is no need to suppose that the prophecy refers to a still future period, as Von Hoffmann imagines. The prophecy was fulfilled by the restoration of the city of Jerusalem under the protection of God even in troublous days.

"Though surrounded indeed by walls, Jerusalem grew so fast that a considerable number dwelt in villages outside the walls. Its population continually increased—the city was noted for its splendid appearance in the time of Ptolemy Philadelphus. . . . In the troublous times which intervened between the days of Zechariah and those of our Lord, notwithstanding the disasters which occasionally fell upon the holy city, abundant proof was given that the Lord was not forgetful of His promises, specially to shield and to protect it. The promises," he proceeds, "would

---

[1] Dr. C. H. H. Wright, "Zechariah and his Prophecies," Bampton Lectures for 1878.

have been fully accomplished if the people had kept the
covenant committed to them, and they were accomplished
in a great measure, notwithstanding their many sins."

A good deal is made of a letter of Aristeas, an
Egyptian Jew, to Philocrates, which is referred to by
Josephus in the 12th book of his *Jewish Antiquities*, in
which a description of Jerusalem after the restoration is
given ; also of a fragment of Hecatæus, who lived in the
time of Alexander the Great, and who describes the Jews
at the time as possessing " many fortresses and towns,
moreover one fortified city, by name Jerusalem, fifty stadia
in circumference and inhabited by 120,000 men " ; and of
Josephus' statement (see his *Jewish Wars*, v. 4. 2) that
at the time of Herod Agrippa, " as the city grew more
populous it gradually crept beyond its old limits, and those
parts of it that stood northwards of the temple and joined
that hill to the city made it considerably larger, and
occasioned that hill, which is in number the fourth, and is
called ' Bezetha,' to be inhabited also." All of which,
according to these interpreters, show that the glorious
prophecy in Zech. ii. has been fulfilled, and has no more
reference to a future period.

But first, in reference to those who explain away the
application to the literal Jerusalem altogether, we would say
that this method of interpretation does not " spiritualise "
but *phantomise* Scripture, for it does not really bring out
the meaning and true application of the Spirit, which alone
makes the Word of God " spiritual " and profitable to the
reader, but substitutes an unnatural and *shadowy* meaning
for what is plain and obvious, and thereby throws a vagueness and uncertainty over all the prophetic oracles. Surely
the fact that the Jerusalem whose greatly extended future
site is here measured is to overflow not only with men,
but with " cattle," who are to dwell therein, ought to be
sufficient proof that it is an earthly and not a heavenly
city that is spoken about. Was the " Jerusalem," against
which Jehovah had indignation " these threescore years and
ten " of the captivity, for which the Angel of Jehovah

intercedes in the first vision " the Kingdom of Christ " ?
And is not the third vision, as already shown, the expansion and sequel of the good and comfortable words
which are God's answer to that intercession ?

It is beside the mark to argue that it can be no
earthly city, because " to be inhabited as villages would be
weakness, not strength—a peril, not a blessing." So it
would in ordinary circumstances, but surely the words
which immediately follow make all the difference : " For I,
saith Jehovah, will be unto her a wall of fire round about " ;
and this is more than all visible walls and literal bulwarks.

It is true that at the time this prophecy was uttered,
and all along till now, " so long as Jerusalem remained
unwalled it was in continual fear and weakness," because
it was encompassed by enemies on every side, and its
inhabitants had not yet learned that it was Jehovah who
was in truth their refuge and strength, and that " Except
the Lord keep the city, the watchman watcheth but in
vain " ; but prophecy points to a time when, after " Jehovah
will have mercy on Jacob and choose Israel again, and set
them in their own land," their enemies shall no more be
permitted to afflict or molest them, and they shall have
rest from their sorrow and their fear, and from the hard
bondage wherein they were made to serve (Isa. xiv. 1–3).
Then also Jehovah, in the Person of their Messiah Jesus,
shall, from Jerusalem as the centre, " judge among the
nations, and rebuke many peoples : and they shall beat
their swords into plowshares, and their spears into pruning-
hooks : nation shall not lift up sword against nation,
neither shall they learn war any more " ; and it will be
quite safe for even the earthly Jerusalem, with " the King,"
" the Lord of hosts," in its midst, to be inhabited as
villages in an open plain, without visible walls or fortifications.

Then, secondly, in reference to those who tell us that
there is no need to suppose that there is any reference in
this prophecy to a future period, I would repeat my
remarks at the close of the exposition of the first chapter,

that though there was doubtless a message in this vision to the generation to which the prophet was first commissioned to relate it, and there was a very partial and shadowy fulfilment of the promise of the rebuilding of the house and the city in the work accomplished by Zerubbabel and Joshua the son of Jehozadak, and by Ezra and Nehemiah, yet to limit this glorious prophecy to any period of Jerusalem's history while it is still being "trodden down of the Gentiles," which has never ceased to be the case from the time of the Babylonian Captivity to this day, is to misapprehend and misinterpret the scope of this as well as of all prophecy.

But, in truth, these beautiful words, "For I, saith Jehovah, will be unto her a wall of fire round about, and the glory in the midst of her," are really an announcement of the return of the Glory of the Personal Presence of Jehovah to Jerusalem, and an amplification of the words in the first vision, "I am returned to Jerusalem with mercies." I have elsewhere tried to show the full significance of Ezekiel's vision of the departure of the Glory of Jehovah from Jerusalem, which synchronised with the removal of governmental power from Judah,[1] and the special characteristics of the present "Ichabod" period of Israel's history.

It was the withdrawal of Himself from their midst which has been the cause of all the helplessness and the sorrow and the darkness of the Jewish nation since the commencement of "the times of the Gentiles"; and that this period did not terminate with the first advent of our Lord is clear from Christ's own prophetic forecast of future events, in which He says: "And Jerusalem shall be trodden down of the Gentiles until the times of the Gentiles be fulfilled." It is true that if Israel's eyes had been opened to see the true character and divine majesty of that royal Babe born in Bethlehem and of the "mysterious man of Nazareth" (as a Jewish Rabbi has recently styled Him),

---

[1] See the chapter, "The Ichabod Period and the Return of the Glory of Jehovah," in *The Ancient Scriptures and the Modern Jew*.

they would have seen in Him a glory greater than that
which dwelt in the symbolic cloud which led our fathers in
the wilderness and which dwelt between the cherubim, and
the promises of the return of the Personal Presence of
Jehovah, no more to depart from their midst, might have
been fulfilled; but Israel's eyes were holden then, and only
a few Jewish disciples there were who saw the Glory of
God in the face of Jesus Christ and could joyfully exclaim:
"We beheld His Glory, the Glory of the Only-begotten of
the Father, full of grace and truth." The nation as a
whole saw "no form nor comeliness" to desire Him, so
they "despised and esteemed Him not." In the end, after
He had for three and a half years with outstretched arms
continued to call Israel to Himself, but without response—
that which was symbolised by the departure of the Glory
from the Mount of Olives, depicted by Ezekiel, received a
second personal and more striking fulfilment, when Jesus
also, slowly and reluctantly, after shedding tears of sorrow
for Jerusalem, and *from the same spot* whence the prophet
saw the Glory depart, finally (after His atoning death and
glorious resurrection) ascended out of sight.

But has the purpose of God been frustrated by Israel's
unbelief, and will the exceeding great and precious promises
in reference to the establishment of the Messianic Kingdom
on this earth, with Jerusalem as its centre, fail for evermore
because (as the writer quoted above asserts) the Jewish
people has not "kept the covenant committed to them"?
Oh no; man's unbelief and disobedience may, in accord
with the foreknowledge and infinite wisdom of God, cause
the delay and postponement of God's predetermined counsel,
which in this particular instance has been the occasion of
salvation and blessing to untold millions of Gentiles (Rom.
xi. 11–15), but it can never frustrate it.

Jesus Christ came as a minister of the circumcision for
the truth of God (not to annul or transfer), but *to confirm*
the promises made unto the fathers (Rom. xv. 8); and
since their ratification in His own precious blood, all the
promises of God in relation to the people and the land of

Israel, as well as in relation to the "mercy" which He purposed from the beginning to show unto the Gentiles, have been made doubly sure.

Both the New Testament as well as the Old teach us to expect and look for the revelation of the Glory of Jehovah, when "all flesh shall see it together"; and then, when the *Malakh Yehovah*, with whom the symbolic cloud of glory was associated from the very first mention of it in the Scriptures (comp. Ex. xiii. 21, 22 with xiv. 12, 20), shall appear in His glory, not only in the *form* of man, but as "the same Jesus," visibly to establish God's rule over this earth, and to sit upon the throne of His father David —these visions and prophecies of the return of the Glory of Jehovah shall be fulfilled: "*And Jehovah will create over the whole habitation of Mount Zion, and over her assemblies, a cloud of smoke by day, and the shining of a flaming fire by night: for over all the Glory shall be as a (marriage) canopy. And there shall be a pavilion for a shadow in the daytime from the heat, and for a refuge and for a covert from storm and from rain.*" [1]

But though not in the form of visibility, as shall be the case in restored Jerusalem by and by, the precious promise of outward protection and inward illumination, contained in the words, "For I, saith the Lord, will be a wall of fire round about, and the glory in the midst of her," is true to every one of you also, dear readers, who know experimentally the truth of the Apostle's words, "Whom, having not seen ye love, in whom though now ye see Him not, yet believing, ye rejoice with joy unspeakable and full of glory." The Angel of Jehovah even now "encampeth" (with an invisible host) round about them that fear Him and delivereth them (Ps. xxxiv. 7); and because He Himself is a wall of fire round about us, and our life is hid with Christ in God, therefore "when the wicked, even mine enemies and foes" (whether visible or invisible, whether evil men or "wicked spirits"), "come upon me" (full of determination and fury) "to eat up my flesh, it is *they*" (the "they" is very

[1] Isa, iv. 5, 6.

emphatic) " who stumble and fall," and we can confidently say :

> " *Though an host should encamp against me, my heart shall not fear ;*
> *Though war should rise against me, even then will I be confident.*"
>
> Ps.ˑ xxvii. 2, 3.

And as He is our protection from without, so He is our light and our salvation within ; for even now the word is true to those who walk with Him, " Jehovah shall be unto thee an everlasting light, and thy God thy glory."

But to return to the exposition. Because Jehovah hath spoken well concerning Zion, and hath such purposes of grace concerning Jerusalem, while the nations which were then " at ease," and in apparently undisturbed peace, were about to be visited with judgment, those still in the lands of the exile are exhorted to hasten back to their home.

> " *Ho, ho, flee from the land of the north, saith Jehovah ;*
> *for I have spread you abroad as the four winds of heaven,*
> *saith Jehovah. Ho Zion, escape, thou that dwellest with the*
> *daughter of Babylon.*"

The Hebrew הוֹי, *ho* or *hoi*, which has not always the same meaning, is here used simply as a particle of exhortation, and for calling attention.

" The land of the north " is the same as Babylon in the next verse, which, though really more an eastern, or south-eastern, power in relation to Palestine, is so called because, like Assyria before, it always invaded the Holy Land from the north, and the great caravan route entered the country from the same quarter. The whole passage seems to be made up of inspired echoes of similar utterances in the " former prophets " ; as, for instance, Isa. xlviii. 20 : " *Go ye forth of Babylon, flee ye from the Chaldeans ; with a voice of singing declare ye, tell ye this, utter it even to the end of the earth : say ye, Jehovah hath redeemed His servant Jacob.*" And again in chap. lii. 11 of the same prophet : " *Depart ye, depart ye, go ye out from thence, touch no unclean thing ; go ye out of the midst of her ; be ye clean, that bear the vessels of Jehovah.*" It is almost an exact reiteration also of the solemn words of Jeremiah : " *Flee out of the midst of*

Babylon, and save every man his life: be not cut off in her iniquity. . . . My people, go ye out of the midst of her, and save yourselves every man from the fierce anger of Jehovah" (Jer. li. 6, 45).

This also had a primary, though only a partial, reference to the time in which the prophet wrote his visions. Though a remnant had returned, by far the greater number were still in the land to which they had been exiled. Some of them had grown rich and prosperous in the strange land. Their love for Jerusalem and all that it stood for had cooled down, and they were content to become dwellers " with the daughter of Babylon." They were reluctant to leave their comfortable homes and vineyards (which they had indeed been encouraged to build and to plant, but only as temporary possessions during the seventy years of the Captivity, Jer. xxix.) for the rough journey and hard life in the desolated land.

And so they are exhorted to flee out of Babylon, not only because of the goodness of the Lord which is to be shown to His people in their own land, but because of the evil which was about to overtake the country of their sojourn, and the calamities which would come on its people, occasioned probably by the two great rebellions in Babylonia, and the two captures of the city of Babylon—one by Darius in person, and the other by one of his generals—which had just taken place when the prophet wrote his visions.[1]

At the same time, this call to come out of the Babylon

---

[1] An account of these events is given in the great inscription of Darius cut into the rock at Behistun, which was discovered by Sir H. Rawlinson, and supposed by him to have been made in the fifth year of the reign of Darius, *i.e.*, about three years before Zechariah's visions. The first of these rebellions was that of Nadinta-belus, or Nidantabel, as it is in the Median text. He pretended to be Nebuchadnezzar, raised a powerful army and fought a pitched battle, in which he was utterly routed and slain after the capture of Babylon. The second rebellion was that of Aracus (Arakua), who also became King of Babylon on the same pretence (of being Nebuchadnezzar) ; but who was afterwards defeated by Nitaphernes and crucified. Sir H. Rawlinson's translations of the Behistun inscription will be found in *Records of the Past*, vol. i. ; and the translation of the Median text by Dr. Oppert, in *Records of the Past*, vol. ii.

of that time, which met with only a very partial response, was also a foreshadowing of the future, when Jehovah shall lift up His hand again a second time to recover the remnant of His people which shall be left from Assyria and from Egypt, and from Pathros and from Cush, and from Elam and from Shinar, and from Hamath and from the islands of the sea : " And when they shall no more say, Jehovah liveth which brought up the children of Israel out of the land of Egypt, but Jehovah liveth which brought up and which led the seed of the House of Israel from the north country, and from all countries whither I had driven them ; and they shall dwell in their own land." This is evident from the fact that this passage in Zechariah is based on those prophecies in Isaiah and Jeremiah which are quoted above, and which link the last great judgment of Babylon with the final deliverance and salvation of Israel, as may be seen from a study of the context, and also from the expression : " For I have spread you abroad as the four winds of heaven "; which in the passage we are considering immediately follows a call to come out of Babylon, and which, therefore, as it seems to me, looks on to a return subsequent to the time when the scattering shall have been universal, which was not the case till the second stage in the dispersion was inaugurated with the destruction of the second temple.[1]

The verses which follow are among the most important

[1] Keil, Hitzig, Kliefoth, Lange, etc., and among English interpreters, Dr. Wright, W. H. Lowe, and others, in order to get over the apparent difficulty—why the exiles should be especially exhorted to return from the north if they had been " scattered to all the four winds of heaven " (as Hitzig expresses it), treat the word *perasti* as a *prophetic* perfect, and translate it in a good sense of the future, that is, " I shall spread you abroad," or "greatly multiply you as the four winds of heaven " ; but the verb is nowhere used of multiplying or diffusing, but generally " of spreading out what remained coherent—as hands, wings, a garment, tent, veil, cloud, letter, and light." In Ezek. xvii. 21 we have the same word and almost exactly the same phrase, and there it means certainly not to multiply or spread out, but to *scatter* towards every wind. It is probable that this expression in Ezekiel was in Zechariah's mind when he wrote this vision. Besides, this is not the only place where the north country in relation to Israel's scattering and gathering stands connected with the other lands of their dispersion —it is so in the passage quoted from Jeremiah.

in the Old Testament in reference to Messiah's character, and they sum up that part of His mission, in relation to Israel and the nations, which in the prophetic scriptures is always connected with His yet future glorious appearing.

"For thus saith Jehovah of hosts: After glory hath He sent Me unto the nations which spoiled you; for he that toucheth you toucheth the apple of His eye.

"For, behold, I will shake Mine hand over them, and they shall be a spoil to those that served them; and ye shall know that the Lord of hosts hath sent Me.

"Sing and rejoice, O daughter of Zion; for, lo, I come, and I will dwell in the midst of thee, saith the Lord.

"And many nations shall join themselves to the Lord in that day, and shall be My people, and I will dwell in the midst of thee, and thou shalt know that the Lord of hosts hath sent Me unto thee.

"And the Lord shall inherit Judah as His portion in the holy land, and shall yet choose Jerusalem."

First, about His character.

The One who speaks is a Divine being, for it is He who lifts up His hand in judgment over the nations and makes them a spoil to those who formerly served them; it is He who, as "Jehovah," comes to dwell in the midst of His people, in fulfilment of the many promises of the reign of God on Mount Zion, and before His ancients gloriously, and who shall receive the many nations in that day as "His people"; and yet He, who in the whole series of promises in this chapter affirms of Himself what belongs to Almighty God only, shall in that day be known as the One *whom Jehovah of hosts hath sent unto them.*

Mystery of mysteries—here is Jehovah, yet sent by Jehovah! but it is the mystery of light and not of darkness to those who have learned to know the blessed Triune God of Israel as He is self-revealed in the Scriptures, and whose eyes have been opened to see in Him Who, in that synagogue of Nazareth, applied to Himself the words from the ancient Hebrew scroll: "The Spirit of the Lord God is upon Me; because Jehovah hath anointed Me to preach good tidings unto the meek; *He hath sent Me* to bind up the broken-hearted," etc.—none other than "Jehovah Tzidkenu"—the "Wonderful Counsellor, the Mighty God, the Everlasting Father, the Prince of Peace," whose goings forth are from of old, even "from the days of eternity"— who as the *Malakh Yehovah*, the Divine Messenger of the Covenant, appeared of old to patriarchs and prophets, and in the fulness of time became incarnate, and was "sent" of God with the message of peace and salvation to man, and to be the Apostle and High Priest of our profession.

But it is no wonder that to modern Jews, who have lost the knowledge of the living, personal God of their fathers, and substituted for the scriptural faith of the unity of God the dogma of an abstract unicity, such a scripture is an enigma and insoluble mystery.

Secondly, the mission which He is to accomplish is described in the words, *Achar kabhod shelahani*, "*After glory hath He sent Me*"—a sentence which has been very variously interpreted by different writers, but which most probably means to *vindicate and to display* the glory of God, first in the judgments which He is to inflict on the nations who have oppressed Israel, and then in the exhibition of His grace in the deliverance and salvation of His own people, and also in the blessing which is to come to the Gentile nations after Israel is restored, and Mount Zion becomes not only the seat of Messiah's governmental rule over the nations, but the centre of the true worship of God on the earth. This is further explained by the words which follow: "*For, behold, I will shake Mine hand over them*"— even as in Isa. xi. 15 and xix. 16, where the same Hebrew word is used, God promised of old to do against Israel's enemies.[1] "*And they shall become a spoil to those that served them*," which is also an inspired echo of Isa. xiv., where we

---

[1] The figure also includes the *almighty power* of this Divine champion of His people's cause. He has only to shake (literally "wave") His hand, and the enemies of God and of His people, however formidable they may seem, become as women (Isa. xix. 16).

read that, after Jehovah shall have had compassion on Jacob, and have chosen Israel again, and set them in their own land, that "the stranger shall join himself with them, and they shall cleave to the house of Jacob; . . . and the house of Jacob shall *possess* them in the land of the Lord for servants and for handmaidens, and they shall take them captive whose captives they were; and they shall rule over their oppressors."

And the reason—"the subjective motive" of His lifting up His hand in judgment over the nations—is expressed in a phrase which gives us a glimpse of God's tender love for His people: "*For he that toucheth you toucheth the apple of His eye*"—the word literally is "the gate," the opening in which the eye is placed, but it is generally, and most probably correctly, understood to mean the *pupil* of the eye: "The aperture through which rays pass to the retina is the tenderest part of the eye—the member which we so carefully guard as the most precious of our members, the one which feels acutely the slightest injury, and the loss of which is irreparable." This is how God felt about Israel at the beginning; for already, in Deut. xxxii., Moses, in summing up their high privileges and God's great loving-kindness to them as a nation, says: "He found him in a desert land, and in the waste, howling wilderness. He compassed him about, He cared for him, *He kept him as the apple of His eye.*" Many and terrible have been Israel's sins and apostasies since, but He has never ceased to care and yearn for them.

Zion in her desolation may indeed sometimes say to herself, "Jehovah hath forsaken me, and the Lord hath forgotten me"; but God's answer comes: "Can a woman forget her sucking child, that she should not have compassion on the son of her womb? Yea, they may forget, yet will I not forget thee. Behold, I have graven thee upon the palms of My hands; thy walls are continually before Me." And even while "the dearly beloved of His soul" is in the hand of her enemies, He jealously watches the conduct of the nations toward her, and wishes it to be proclaimed that he that toucheth her toucheth the apple of His eye, and is accounted as His enemy.

And in this tender love and faithfulness of Jehovah to His unworthy Israel, you may see a picture of His unchangeable love and faithfulness to you also, dear reader ; for if you have learned to put your trust under the shadow of His wings, and in Christ have been brought into covenant relationship with Him, then you are loved of Him with the same love with which He loves His only-begotten Son, and are as dear and indispensable to Him as the dearest member of your body can be to you. You may therefore apply this figure also to yourself individually, and pray with David—

> "*Keep me as the apple of Thine eye ;*
> *Hide me under the shadow of Thy wings.*"

But the greatest promise in this vision and prophecy is that expressed in the words, "*Lo, I come, and I will dwell in the midst of thee, saith the Lord*" (ver. 10); which not only formed the ground and object of the expectations of the godly remnant of Israel in ancient times, but is still " the Blessed Hope" in the New Testament.

The speaker is still the *Malakh Yehovah*, the blessed, Divine Angel, in and through whom is fully manifested God's name (Ex. xxiii. 21), "the Angel of His Face," because he that seeth Him hath seen the Father. It is the same who speaks in the 40th Psalm : "Lo, I come ; in the scroll of the book it is written of Me," on which Luther well observes : "There is but one Person, and that is the Messiah ; and there is but one Book, and that is the Bible —in the whole of which it is written of Him."

And it is no wonder that in the glorious anticipation of His Advent, and the blessed consequences which are to follow, "the daughter of Zion " is called upon to "sing (or 'shout for joy') and rejoice"; which again (as is characteristic of the whole of Zechariah) is a terse summary of the joyful exclamations of the former prophets, whose hearts also glowed with joy and yearning whenever (though as yet from afar) they caught a glimpse of the King in His beauty, and their mouths were opened to announce His near approach. Thus Isaiah, at the close of the Book of Immanuel,[1] after describing the Glorious Person, and blessed reign of Him whose Name is " Wonderful," calls out, " *Cry aloud and shout, thou inhabitress of Zion, for great is the Holy One of Israel in the midst of thee* " (Isa. xii. 6); which again is repeated by Zephaniah, who exclaims: *Sing, O daughter of Zion ; shout, O Israel ; be glad and rejoice with all the heart, O daughter of Jerusalem ;* . . . *the King, even Jehovah, is in the midst of thee ; thou shalt not fear evil any more* " (Zeph. iii. 14, 15).

But there is a necessity, perhaps, once again to point out that the " Lo, I come," of these passages in Isaiah, Zechariah, and Zephaniah, are not the same as the " Lo, I come," of the 40th Psalm ; for though in Old Testament prophecy the principle of perspective is not observed, and events of the most distant future are sometimes linked on to those which are near, or nearer, the prophet's own time, yet the great *fact* of the two separate advents of the Messiah —once in humiliation to suffer and die ; and a second time in glory to dwell in the midst of Zion and to rule over the nations—stand out clear and distinct enough on the prophetic page, and to confound them is to throw the whole plan of God as revealed in the Scriptures into confusion.

The ancient Rabbis, puzzled by the two apparently contradictory series of prophecies in reference to Messiah's Person and mission—those which described Him as a Babe born in Bethlehem, and as a Man of Sorrows and acquainted with grief, who is stricken for the transgressions of His people, and in the end pours out His soul unto death ; and those which depict Him descending as a full-grown " Son of Man " in the clouds of heaven, in great power and glory, to build again the tabernacle of David, and to establish His kingdom—have formulated the belief in two Messiahs: a Messiah ben Joseph, who should suffer and die ; and a Messiah ben David, who should come to conquer and reign. But *we* know that there are not two persons, but only *two*

[1] Consisting of Isa. vii. to xii.

advents, and that it is " this same Jesus " who was born of a
Jewish virgin, and who minutely fulfilled the things written
in the scroll of the book, in reference to Messiah's sufferings
and atoning death, who shall " so and in like manner "
come again—that is, literally, visibly, bodily—to the Mount
of Olives, which is before Jerusalem on the east, and in the
clouds of heaven, even as the disciples saw Him go up into
heaven.

And this is the hope, not only of the Church, which is
His body, consisting of the whole blessed company of the
redeemed,—whether those who through the ages have fallen
asleep in Him, or those who shall be alive and remain till
the day of His appearing, who shall only be perfected
together " in that day,"—but of Israel and the nations ; for
then Israel's long night of weeping shall end—the true
" King," even Jehovah Jesus, shall be " in the midst of
them," and the many great and precious promises in reference to Messiah's reign, and the time of peace and blessedness for this earth, shall be fulfilled.

One great and blessed consequence of His judgments
which shall then be abroad in the earth, and of His coming
to dwell in the midst of Zion, is that the original purpose of
God in the call and election of Abraham and his seed—
namely, that in them all the families of the earth shall be
blessed—shall be fulfilled : " *And many nations shall join
themselves unto Jehovah in that day, and shall be My people ;
and I will dwell in the midst of thee ; and thou shalt know
that Jehovah of hosts hath sent Me unto thee.*" Yes, when
the Lord in His mercy shall rebuild Zion, and appear in
His glory, " then the nations shall fear the name of Jehovah,
and *all the kings of the earth His glory* " (Ps. cii. 13–22).
And not only shall they fear Him, but they shall willingly
" join themselves unto Him "—the word being the same as
that used of the " son of the stranger " who shall " join himself" to the Lord " to serve Him, and to love the name of
Jehovah " (Isa. lvi. 3–6) ; and of Israel themselves, who in
that day " shall join themselves to Jehovah in a perpetual
covenant which shall not be forgotten " (Jer. l. 4, 5).

During the present Dispensation, through Israel's temporary " fall," salvation has come to the Gentiles, and the " diminishing of them " has been overruled of God to " the riches of the Gentiles." But this " salvation " and " riches " extend only to individuals. God hath visited the " Gentiles " to " take out of them a people for His Name." It is only ignorance of God's plan, and self-delusion, which can boast of the gradual conversion of the world and of " Christian nations " in this present age. And even the partial blessing now experienced by the Gentiles has been brought to them, not only indirectly and passively (through Israel's unbelief), but directly and actively through those " who were of faith " in the chosen nation.

Through individual Jews whose hearts were set on fire with love and devotion to Jesus of Nazareth whom their nation despised and rejected, who went forth into the world, taking their lives in their hands, to preach Him among the Gentiles ; and through the inspired writings of Jewish apostles and evangelists — individuals from all nations—a multitude which no man can number have been, and are being, brought into the knowledge and fellowship of their Messiah. What *might have been* if the nation, as a nation, instead of rejecting, had accepted Christ, we can only guess and speculate about.

" Judging from the work accomplished by one Jew, Paul," says a Hebrew Christian brother in a recent ably-written work, " we can imagine what might have been achieved if the intellectual acumen and great learning of the scribes and Pharisees, together with the enthusiasm of the young patriotic zealots, had been enlisted in the cause of spreading Messiah's Kingdom in the world. If, instead of one Paul, there were thousands of Pauls. If the great learning, industry, and spiritual zeal which for centuries has been employed in rearing that great monument of wasted human industry, the immense literature of the Talmud, were used rather in the living work of propagating the gospel of Christ ! If Jerusalem, instead of Rome, had remained the capital of Christendom, and the Jew, instead of the Greek and Roman, the guiding spirit in the councils of the Church!"[1]

But our human "if" does not reach deep enough to fathom God's inscrutable purposes, nor is it high and broad enough to unravel all the thoughts and hidden counsels of the Infinite and Eternal One. This, however, we do know, that while Israel is held responsible for its rejection and present attitude to Christ and the gospel, that unto God all things were known from the beginning of the world, and that it was clearly forecast on the prophetic page that so it would be; it is only "*after these things*," when Messiah returns to build again the tabernacle of David which is fallen, and builds again the ruins thereof, and sets it up, *that the residue of men shall seek after the Lord, and all the Gentiles upon whom His name shall then be called*" (Acts xv. 13–18).

Then, when "*all Israel shall be saved*"; when the miracle of a whole nation being born in a day shall first be witnessed on the earth in the case of the Jews; when the full significance of the precious Name "Immanuel" shall be realised in Jesus "dwelling in the midst" of His own people, so that the name of Jerusalem from that day shall be "Jehovah Shammah" (Ezek. xlviii. 35); when there shall at last be not only "thousands of Pauls," but a whole nation who shall burn with the same love and zeal for the glorious Person of their Messiah, and for the extension of His Kingdom, which characterised the blessed apostle to the Gentiles, who in so many respects is the type of His nation,—then nations, as nations, "shall join themselves unto Jehovah," and the day of which prophets and psalmists sang, and for which they yearned, the day of universal peace and righteousness, when God's way shall be known in all the world, and His saving health among all nations, shall at last break on this earth.

But even when all nations of the earth shall walk in the light of Jehovah, the special position of Israel, as God's peculiar people on the earth, shall still be made manifest.

---

[1] *The Jewish Question and the Key to its Solution,* by Dr. Max Green.

"*And Jehovah shall inherit Judah His portion in the holy land, and shall choose Jerusalem again*": which reminds us of Isa. xix. 25, where we read that even after the blessing comes to the saved of the nations whom Jehovah of hosts shall bless, saying: "Blessed be Egypt, My people, and Assyria, the work of My hands," He will still say of Israel, "Mine inheritance," for the Lord's inalienable "portion" from among all the other nations of the earth "is His people, Jacob is the lot of His inheritance" (Deut. xxxii. 9); in which respect, again, Israel nationally is the type and counterpart of the Church, which, made up of saved individuals from among all men, is "the riches of the glory of His inheritance in the saints" (Eph. i. 18).

The expression '*al admath haqodesh*—" in the holy land "—is very beautiful, and reminds us of the fact that the land also which has been defiled and polluted, perhaps, above all others, shall then be cleansed of its defilement, and hallowed and sanctified by the presence of Immanuel, to correspond with the people who are to inhabit it ; who throughout their future existence on the earth shall be known and called by all other nations as "the holy people" (Isa. lxii. 12), on whose persons and homes and possessions, down to the very "bells of the horses," shall be written *qodesh layehovah*—" Holiness (or ' holy ') to the Lord."

The words, "and shall yet choose Jerusalem again," so to say, "round off" the glorious promises in this chapter, and are the second of a threefold reiteration by Zechariah of Isa. xiv. 1. The meaning, as already explained in my notes on the First Vision, is, that Jehovah shall then, by the various acts of lovingkindness to His people and to the land, which are enumerated in this prophecy, *demonstrate* in the sight of the whole world *the fact and the immutability* of His original choice of them.

The first cycle of these wonderful "visions" ends with the most solemn announcement of the great fact which forms the climax of all prophecy, namely, the visible appearing of Almighty God in the person of the Messiah as the Judge and Redeemer of men: "*Be silent, all flesh, before Jehovah; for He is waked up out of His holy habitation."*

The word חַס, *has*, is almost equivalent to the English " hush," only that there is more of solemnity and power expressed in the Hebrew. *"Kal basar"*—" all flesh "— is not only a universal term for all mankind, but is meant to express the weakness and impotence of man in presence of Almighty God. *Neor*, which is the Niphal of *ur*, is " to wake up," " to rise up," from rest or sleep, and is, so to say, a response to the many cries of His waiting, oppressed people. " Awake, why sleepest Thou, O Lord ? Arise, cast us not off for ever ! " (Ps. xliv. 23).

Mimme'on qadsho—" His holy habitation," or, literally, " the habitation of His holiness," an expression found also in Ps. lxviii. 6; Jer. xxv. 30; and Deut. xxvi. 15—is " heaven," the special and *permanent* dwelling-place of His glory. There are two somewhat parallel passages in the prophetic Scriptures—one in Hab. ii. 20, " But Jehovah is in His holy temple ; be silent before Him, all the earth "; and the other in Zeph. i. 7, " Hold thy peace " (*has*, the same word as " be silent " in the other passages) " at the presence of the Lord God."

The present Dispensation is the period of God's long-continued silence. How wonderful, how long, how deep, how mysterious, is this silence of God ever since the sound of the last words of Christ, " Surely I come quickly," and the inspired echo and response, " Even so, come, Lord Jesus," died away on the barren rock of Patmos nineteen centuries ago ! How often have the hearts of God's people grown impatient under the strain ! How often has not the Church cried, " How long, O Lord, how long ? " But there has been neither audible voice, nor sound, nor any *visible* interposition on the part of God. Moreover, while God has remained " silent," man has taken the opportunity of " speaking," and his words are becoming ever more foolish, arrogant, and blasphemous against the Most High ; but " our God cometh and *shall not keep silent*," and then it will not only be the turn of " all flesh " to keep silent, but to stand in solemn awe while "out of his own mouth" man shall be judged, and all his thoughts and words which spell out his own condemnation are set in order before him.[1]

But not only the ungodly and the sinners who have spoken "hard things" against God and His Anointed, but men in general, are called in a spirit of reverence and godly fear to await the solemn event announced ; for the coming and visible interposition of God on this earth, while it will mean judgment to some, will mean the consummation of grace and fulness of blessedness to others ; and when prophecy and vision is at last fulfilled, and "our God shall arise and His enemies are scattered, and they also that hate Him shall flee before His face"—then, also, "the righteous shaH be glad, they shall exult before the face of God, yea, they shall rejoice exceedingly."[2] The last practical word on this Scripture to you, dear Christian reader, is, "Abide in Him," that when He shall appear (when He shall be manifested) we may have confidence, and not be ashamed before Him at His coming.

[1] See the chapter, "The Silence of God : how it shall be Broken," in *The Ancient Scriptures and the Modern Jew.*

[2] See the Hebrew of Ps. xviii. 1–3.

Chapter 5

THE FOURTH VISION
JOSHUA BEFORE THE ANGEL OF JEHOVAH
Zechariah 3

And he showed me Joshua the high priest standing before the Angel of Jehovah, and Satan standing at his right hand to be his adversary. And Jehovah said unto Satan, Jehovah rebuke thee, O Satan ; yea, Jehovah that hath chosen Jerusalem rebuke thee : is not this a brand plucked out of the fire ? Now Joshua was clothed with filthy garments, and was standing before the Angel. And He answered and spake unto those that stood before Him, saying, Take the filthy garments from off him. And unto him He said, Behold, I have caused thine iniquity to pass from thee, and I will clothe thee with rich apparel. And I said, Let them set a clean mitre upon his head. So they set a clean mitre upon his head, and clothed him with garments ; and the Angel of Jehovah was standing by.

And the Angel of Jehovah protested unto Joshua, saying, Thus saith Jehovah of hosts : If thou wilt walk in My ways, and if thou wilt keep My charge, then thou also shalt judge My house, and shalt also keep My courts, and I will give thee a place of access among these that stand by. Hear now, O Joshua the high priest, thou and thy fellows that sit before thee ; for they are men that are a sign : for, behold, I will bring forth My servant the Branch. For, behold, the stone that I have set before Joshua ; upon one stone are seven eyes : behold, I will engrave the graving thereof, saith Jehovah of hosts, and I will remove the iniquity of that land in one day. In that day, saith Jehovah of hosts, shall ye invite every man his neighbour under the vine and under the fig-tree.

Chapter 5

THE fourth and fifth visions form a new chapter in this series of symbolic prophecies, which, though in a sense standing by themselves, are in the true psychological order, and in the closest possible relation with the wonderful things which had already been unfolded before the prophet's spiritual sight. "The good words, and comfortable words" (i. 13), which formed the message in the first three visions, contained the promises, not only of the overthrow of the Gentile world-powers "who lift up their horn to scatter Judah, Israel, and Jerusalem" (i. 18–21); not only of the restoration of the still-dispersed people to Palestine, and of the future enlargement and prosperity of the Promised Land, and of the Holy City, which shall then be inhabited as villages in an open plain "for the multitude of men and cattle therein" (ii. 4); *but of the restored spiritual relationship between God and His people,* and of the return of the glory of the personal Presence of Jehovah in the Person of Messiah, for evermore to dwell in their midst, the result of which would be that "many nations shall be joined to Jehovah in that day" and be His people, and the whole earth be made to know the immutable *fact* and gracious purpose in His election of Judah and Jerusalem as His peculiar "portion" (ii. 5, 10, 11).

But the question might well have suggested itself to the prophet's mind, How can these things be? Has not Israel by his grievous sins and moral defilement for ever forfeited his place and made himself unfit to be again Jehovah's sanctuary and appointed minister of blessing to the nations?

As if in answer to this probable inward questioning,

this fourth vision is shown to the prophet, from which he might learn for himself and communicate to the people (1*st*) the blessed fact that the fulfilment of the exceeding great and precious promises in reference to Israel's future, rests, not on their own merits or worthiness, but on the immutable purpose of Jehovah, who in His sovereign grace hath "chosen Jerusalem"; and (2*nd*) how the moral problem will be solved, and the sinful, defiled people be yet made, not only fit to be the sanctuary of the Holy One, but to be "the priests of Jehovah" and "the ministers of our God" in relation to the other nations, in accordance with His original purpose in their call and election: "Ye shall be unto Me a kingdom of priests and an holy nation" (Ex. xix. 6; Isa. lxi. 6). In brief, this vision depicts in a symbolic but very graphic manner *the inner salvation of Israel from sin and moral defilement, answering to their outward deliverance from captivity and oppression set forth in the preceding three visions.*

A somewhat similar thought is expressed in the 3rd chapter of Jeremiah, where, after a series of sublime promises of the restoration and conversion of "backsliding Israel," and how "at that time they shall call Jerusalem the throne of Jehovah, and all the nations shall be gathered unto it, to the name of Jehovah to Jerusalem," the question is asked: "But I said, How shall I put thee among the children (who art so unchildlike) and give thee a pleasant (or 'delightsome') land, the goodliest heritage of the nations?" (who hast forfeited all claims on God's favour). Then there follows the answer: "And I said, *Ye shall call Me 'my Father,'* and shall not turn away from following Me." "*I said . . . ye shall*": for what in His eternal counsels He has purposed, that His grace and power shall yet accomplish in His people, and Israel shall yet, not only be blessed, but be fitted to be the instrument in God's hand to spread abroad the blessings of their Messiah's gospel throughout the earth.

But now to come to the exposition of the fourth vision;

"*And he showed me Joshua the high priest standing before the Angel of Jehovah, and Satan standing at his right hand to be his adversary.*" It cannot be decided with certainty whether the subject of the verb "showed" was Jehovah, or the interpreting angel, but most probably it was the Lord Himself, as the office of the interpreter was not to introduce but to explain the visions. "Joshua" was, of course, the high priest who returned with Zerubbabel at the head of the first colony of 49,697 exiles from the Captivity some sixteen years before.

He was standing before the *Malakh Yehovah*, whose divine character shines out in this vision in a most striking manner, and whose identity with the "Angel of His Face," the Second Person in the blessed Trinity, who in a special sense is the *Sent* One of the Father, we have already seen.

The words '*omed liphnei*, "standing before," whether in relation to man or God, express *attendance upon*,[1] and when used of the priests, and especially of the high priest, is almost a technical term for their priestly ministry and service. Thus we read that the tribe of Levi was separated "*to stand before Jehovah*, to minister unto Him, and to bless in His Name."

But it is important at the outset to note that it is not in his individual or personal capacity that Zechariah beholds the high priest "standing" thus before the Angel of Jehovah—an erroneous supposition which has led some commentators into absurd and fanciful guesses as to the nature of the guilt of which Joshua stood accused [2]—but *as the type and representative of the nation*.

---

[1] Thus, for instance, it is used of Joseph before Pharaoh (Gen. xli. 46), of Joshua before Moses (Deut. i. 38), of David before Saul (1 Sam. xvi. 21), of Abishag the Shunammite before David (1 Kings i. 2-4), and many other instances.

Of standing to minister *before God*, the expression is used of the tribe of Levi in Deut. x. 8; of the high priest in Judg. xx. 28; of Elijah, 1 Kings xvii. 1; of Elisha, 2 Kings iii. 14-16; and other instances. It is used also of "standing" to *intercede* with God, Gen. xviii. 22; Jer. vii. 10. It is used also as an attitude of worship.

[2] Thus Ewald has invented a theory (which has for its support nothing but his own fancy, based on a misinterpretation of this sublime Scripture) that Joshua

This is brought out first by the emphasis on his official title, *ha-kohen ha-gadol,* the high priest; secondly, from the fact that the plea of the great Advocate, and His answer to Satan's accusations in the 2nd verse, is made, not on behalf of Joshua, but for "*Jerusalem,*" which, as in so many places, stands not only for the city but for the people; and thirdly, from a comparison of the 4th verse with the 9th, from which we see that the words addressed to Joshua, " I have caused thine iniquity to pass," are meant to set forth the blessed fact that God "*will remove the iniquity of that land in one day.*"

Standing thus as the high priest and mediator of the people, *it is the nation of Israel* which is on its trial. If he is rejected, they are rejected ; if he is justified, they are accepted.

The scene, then, to make free use of words of another writer, may be imagined as follows : " The high priest is in the sanctuary, the building of which had already commenced, and is engaged in some part of his priestly duty or prayer for mercy (on behalf of the people). The ' Angel of Jehovah ' comes down and condescends to appear in the Temple, as a proof of His favour, attended by a company of angels (ver. 7). Satan, the sworn enemy of the Church of God, looks on with jealous eyes, . . . and prepares to interrupt by his accusations." But, while this is in the main true, the fact that Satan was there to accuse invests the symbolic transaction, which is here presented to the prophet's spiritual sight, *with a judicial character,* and the

" was actually accused at the time, or was then dreading an accusation at the Persian Court," and that this accusation formed the superstructure on which the vision is based. " Zechariah, with peculiar sympathy, depicts the high priest as suffering under grievous accusations, and promises him a glorious acquittal. The garments of the high priest are represented as dirty because robes of that character were usually worn by accused persons as indications of mourning " (which, by the way, though a Roman custom, *was not at all the case among the Jews*). According to this father among German critics, " the ardent hopes of the prophet were soon to be justified by the event. On receipt of the Governor's report, which presented an impartial statement of facts, an inquiry was instituted by authority into the case, the accusation was repelled, and the decree of Cyrus, which had given permission for the rebuilding of the Temple, was duly confirmed and ordered to be carried into execution " ; for all which, as already observed, there is not even a shadow of historic ground,

high priest may be regarded also as "standing" on his trial before the Angel of Jehovah as Judge.[1]

Ha-Satan, which, with or without the definite article, is a proper name for the Evil One, is the same who in the New Testament is described as our "*adversary*" *the devil*, the Hebrew term having etymologically the sense of "enemy," or "adversary," and the Greek that of "accuser."

He is represented as standing at Joshua's "right hand," which is supposed by many to have been the usual position of the accuser in judicial procedure, the ground of the conjecture (for there is no positive proof of such a custom among the ancient Jews) being Ps. cix. 6, where we read, "Set a wicked man over him, and let an adversary ('Satan') stand at his right hand." Another suggestion is that Satan took the place *usually taken by the protector* (Ps. xvi. 8, cix. 31, cxxi. 5), "to show that Joshua, or those he represented, had none to save them, and that he himself was victorious." The passage itself, however, tells us clearly that he stood there "*l'sitno*"—to act as adversary, or "be Satan," to him—"that he," as an old writer observes, "who is called Satan, might thus fill up the measure of his name."

Here we are brought face to face with one of those mysteries of revelation which must be classed among the things which "we know not now," nor can as yet fully understand — namely, the position of Satan in God's economy in general, and his relation to the moral government of this world, and to man in particular.

How and why, we may not yet fully know, but the fact is clearly brought before us in Scripture that the great adversary of God and man is permitted to appear before God, not only in His earthly courts of the Temple, as in this vision, but in heaven, as "the accuser of the brethren."

And it is especially in his rôle as the accuser that the

---

[1] "To stand before" is used also in a judicial sense both of the plaintiff and the defendant in Num. xxvii. 2, xxxv. 12; Deut. xix. 17; Josh. xx. 6; 1 Kings iii. 16; so that Hengstenberg's statement, that this expression is never used of the appearance of a defendant before a judge, but always of a servant before his lord, is not quite accurate.

fiendish nature of the "old serpent" is brought out. It was he who brought sin into the world; it is he who deceives men and nations, and spurs them on to sin and rebellion against God; and yet, when the seduction is accomplished, he turns round and becomes their accuser—this truly is like himself.

But it is not merely his malice against Israel which brings him here as their accuser before God in the person of their high priest. Oh no; it is first and foremost his hatred of God, and his desire, if possible, to frustrate the accomplishment of God's purposes of mercy for this world, which, as he so well knows, are bound up with Israel. It was for this same reason that he sought all through the centuries to rouse the fury of the nations against them, with a view, if possible, to bring about their extermination.

The actual words of Satan's accusations are not given, but their nature may be inferred from the 3rd verse, where we read : "*Now Joshua was clothed with filthy garments, and stood before the Angel.*"

The word צוֹאִים, *tsoyim*, which is found only here as an adjective, is the strongest expression in the Hebrew language for *filth of the most loathsome character*, and the garments so defiled denote *the sins of the people* as viewed by the Holy One, in which the high priest as their representative stood, so to say, clad in His presence. Satan, therefore, might well have sought the rejection of Israel as the priestly nation, or to impugn the holiness of God's character in receiving the worship and services of those so morally defiled.

But, blessed be God, the adversary may accuse, but it is not in his power to condemn. He that sitteth as Judge, to justify or condemn, is the Lord. And note, it is the Divine Angel Himself, who in the 2nd verse is expressly called "Jehovah," who pleads the cause of His people. Well might the remnant of Israel say, therefore: "*He is near that justifieth; who will contend with me? Let us stand together; who is mine adversary? Let him come near to me. Behold, the Lord God will help me; who is he that shall condemn me? Behold, they all shall wax old as a garment; the moth shall eat them up*" (Isa. l. 8, 9)—a challenge which is thrown down still more triumphantly in the New Testament in the words, " *Who shall lay anything to the charge of God's elect? It is God that justifieth; who is he that condemneth? It is Christ that died, yea, rather, that is risen again, who is even at the right hand of God; who also maketh intercession for us*" (Rom. viii. 33, 34). Satan's malice and hatred against the Church and the individual believer in Christ is as great as it is against Israel. And he still appears as "the accuser of the brethren," before God and before our own conscience; but with such an "Advocate with the Father" as "Jesus Christ the Righteous," who has Himself become "the propitiation for our sins" (1 John ii. 1, 2), we need fear neither his fury nor his malicious accusations. Is Satan's hatred of us great? The love of Jesus is greater. Is Satan ever on the watch and restlessly walking about like a roaring lion seeking whom he may devour? Behold, He that keepeth Israel doth neither slumber nor sleep, and His eyes run to and fro throughout the earth to prove Himself strong on behalf of those whose hearts are perfect towards Him, and His myriads of blessed angels are sent forth specially to guard and to be ministering spirits to them who shall be heirs of salvation. Therefore we may continue the Apostle's song of triumph: " *Who shall separate us from the love of God? . . . for I am persuaded that neither death, nor life, nor angels, nor principalities, nor powers, nor things present, nor things to come, nor height, nor depth, nor any other creature shall be able to separate us from the love of God which is in Christ Jesus our Lord.*"

But to return to the context. The great Advocate bases His plea on Israel's behalf, first on the ground of Jehovah's immutable choice. " *Jehovah rebuke thee, O Satan.*"

The verb *yig'ar*, from *ga'ar* (" to rebuke," " to reprove "), " when applied to God, who accomplishes all things by His own power, includes the idea of actual suppression "; and in this case it " involved a withering rejection of the blasted spirit and his accusations, as when Jesus rebuked the unclean spirit and he departed out of his victim." [1]   The reason follows, " *Yea, Jehovah that hath chosen Jerusalem, rebuke thee,*" as much as to say, " Shall God cast away His people *which He hath foreknown?* " (Rom. xi. 1). And this is the best answer that can ever be given to the accusations of man or devil, directed either against Israel, or the Church, or the individual Christian. It is the answer which Paul gives in that section of his Epistle to the Romans which was indicted for the express purpose of instructing Gentile believers in God's mystery with Israel : " I say, then, hath God cast away His people ? " He shudders at the very thought, as inconsistent with the character of God, Who must abide true though all may prove liars, and whose gifts and calling of His people are without repentance (or " change of mind ") on His part— " By no means," or " God forbid," he exclaims.

Yes, if Israel's position as the Lord's peculiar people depended on their own faithfulness, then there would have been an end of them long ago; but Israel's hope and safety rest on the immutable character and faithfulness of the Everlasting, Unchangeable God, and that makes all the difference. Why did God choose Israel in the first instance ? Was it because of their righteousness or their lovableness above all other peoples ? Oh no! " Jehovah did not set His love upon you, nor choose you," He tells them through Moses, " because ye were more in number than any people ; for ye were the fewest of all people." " *Not for thy righteousness or the uprightness of thine heart*, but because Jehovah loved you, and because He would keep

---

[1] The following passages collected by Pusey show that "the rebuke of God must be with *power* " : "Thou hast rebuked the nations, Thou hast destroyed the ungodly " (Ps. ix. 5); "Thou hast rebuked the proud accursed " (Ps. cxix. 21); " They perish at the rebuke of Thy countenance " (Ps. lxxx. 16); "God shall rebuke him, and he fleeth far off, and shall be chased as the chaff of the mountains before the wind " (Isa. xvii. 13); " The foundations of the world were discovered at Thy rebuke, O Lord " (Ps. xviii. 15; Nah. i. 4; see also Ps. cvi. 9 and Mal. ii. 3, R.V,),

the oath which He hath sworn unto your fathers." A truly wonderful and God-like reason. "He chose you because He loved you; and He loved you because He loved you" = *the sole ground and motive being in His own heart of love*, and in the sovereign purpose of grace which He hath formed in and through them.

And having known and foreknown them—yea, with all their many and grievous sins and backslidings, and purposed in His heart to exhibit in and through them, not only His holy severity (as now in their unbelief), but even in a more wonderful way His infinite grace and goodness, and all the attributes of His character *for the blessing of all the nations of the earth*, He can never wholly cast them off.

Some of my readers may have visited the Wartburg and had pointed out to them the black spot on one of the walls of the room which Luther occupied during his benevolently intended imprisonment. The legend connected with it is this. One night during this mournful solitude, when suffering from great depression, because, as he himself expresses it in a letter to Melanchthon, dated May 24, 1521, "I do see myself insensible and hardened, a slave to sloth, rarely, alas! praying—unable even to utter a groan for the Church, while my untamed flesh burns with devouring flame" [1]—the great Reformer dreamt that Satan appeared to him with a long scroll, in which were carefully written the many sins and transgressions of which he was guilty from his birth, and which the evil one proceeded to read out, mocking the while that such a sinner as he should ever think of being called to do service for God, or even of escaping himself from hell. As the long list was being read, Luther's terrors grew, and his agonies of soul increased. At last, however, rousing himself, he jumped up and exclaimed: "It is all true, Satan, and many more sins which I have committed in my life which are known

---

[1] See *The Life of Luther*, by M. Michelet. Based almost entirely on his own letters and table talk, 2nd edition, translated by W. Hazlitt, pp. 101, 102.

to God only ; but write at the bottom of your list, ' *The blood of Jesus Christ, God's Son, cleanseth us from all sin,*' " and grasping the inkstand on his table he threw it at the devil, who soon fled, the memorial of it being left in the ink-splash on the wall.

We are always reminded of this story when reading anti-Semitic literature, or listening to accusations and disparagements of the Jewish people. No too-black a picture can ever be drawn of Israel's backslidings and apostasies ; no human lips can ever sufficiently describe the heinousness of Israel's sins and transgressions. All that can therefore be said against their past or their present is true. But when you have read through your long indictment against Israel, write at the bottom of your list words such as these : " *Thus saith Jehovah, If heaven above can be measured, and the foundation of the earth searched out beneath, I will also cast off all the seed of Israel, for all that they have done, saith Jehovah*" (Jer. xxxi. 37); or words taken from the very chapter which foretells in advance Israel's many sins and apostasies, and the terrible calamities which should come upon them in consequence: " *And yet, for all that, I will not cast them away, neither will I abhor them, to destroy them utterly, and to break My covenant with them, for I am Jehovah, their God*" (Lev. xxvi. 44). No, " Jehovah will not forsake His people, *for His great Name's sake*, because it hath pleased Jehovah to make you His people"—in which faithfulness of the God of Israel to the nation which He has chosen for His own inheritance, in spite of all its unworthiness, you may see a picture, dear reader, of His faithfulness to *you*, and a pledge of *your* eternal safety in Christ.

Secondly, the Angel of Jehovah bases his answer to Satan's accusations on the ground of the sufferings in punishment of their sins which Israel has already endured. " *Is not this a brand plucked out of the fire ?*" This same figure, with one slight variation, is found in Amos iv. 11, and is used (as Hengstenberg well explains) to " denote the occurrence of great misfortune, which, however, is prevented by the mercy of God from issuing in utter destruction."

It need scarcely be pointed out, after what has already been stated, that these words also must not be taken as applying to Joshua as an individual, but as the high priest, the type and representative of his people. The fire out of which Joshua had been rescued as a brand was neither the evil which had come upon him through neglecting the building of the Temple (as some German expositors explain), nor the guilt of allowing his sons to marry foreign wives (which the Jewish Targum, followed by Rashi and Kimchi, oblivious of the anachronism, assert); for, as Keil well observes, in the former case the accusation would have come too late, since the building of the Temple had been resumed five months before (Hag. i. 14 compared with Zech. i. 7); and in the latter case it would have been much too early, since these *mésalliances* did not take place till fifty years afterwards. No; the words are used by the Great Advocate *of the whole people*, against whom, as we have already seen, the adversary's accusations were really directed, and their general sense has been well given by one of the earliest Church Fathers—namely, " As if He should say, Israel confessedly has sinned, and is liable to these charges; yet it has suffered no slight punishment; it has endured sufferings, and has scarce been snatched out of them, as a half-burned *brand out of the fire.* For not yet had it shaken off the dust of the harms from the captivity; only just now, and scarcely, had it escaped the flame of that most intolerable calamity. Cease, then, imputing sin to them on whom God has had mercy." [1]

But though primarily the figure refers to " the fire " of the Babylonian Captivity from which the restored remnant at the time had been plucked as a " brand," the words are designed also to remind us of a deeper and more general truth in connection with Jewish history. Israel may be said to be *always* in the fire, yet God never permits them to be wholly consumed. Like the burning bush, the symbol of this indestructible people—it may burn, and must suffer by very reason of its being in a special sense

[1] Cyril.

the dwelling-place of the Holy One, until all its dross shall
have been consumed; *but it cannot be destroyed.*

When God first made His covenant with Abraham, the
symbols of His presence, which were meant to foreshadow
His whole future dealings with them, were "a smoking
furnace and burning lamp," or "flaming torch" (Gen.
xv. 17). Already in Egypt they found themselves in an
"iron furnace" (Deut. iv. 20), and from the human point
of view there was every reason to believe that they would
be wholly consumed; but along with and in the midst of
the furnace of the four hundred years' "affliction," there was
suspended the flaming torch of promise that God would
ultimately interpose on their behalf, and judge the nation
who was oppressing them, and bring them out "with
great substance" (Gen. xv. 13, 14).

Babylon was another such furnace, and though a
remnant had, according to God's promise, after the seventy
years, been plucked out "as a brand from the fire," we
have to remember that the Babylonian Captivity, in a very
important sense, *still lasts,* for it inaugurated the prophetic
period called "*the times of the Gentiles,*" which will only
be brought to a close when the kingdom is restored, and
governmental power over the earth is centred in Mount
Zion. But in this longer captivity also, in this more fiery
"furnace of affliction" (Isa. xlviii. 10), God has not left
His people without the burning lamp of promise that they
shall never be wholly consumed; that He will never forget
the Covenant which He made with their fathers; but that
He would be with them even when they walk through the
fires (Isa. xliii. 2); and in the end, when their sufferings
reach their climax in the great tribulation, when the filth of
the daughter of Zion shall finally have been purged away
"by the spirit of judgment and by the spirit of burning,"
He would save them as "a brand from the fire," and cause
them to multiply and to be a blessing to all the world.

If we may digress for a moment from the *interpretation*
of this familiar figure, and its primary significance in
relation to Israel, and make an *application* of it to the

individual believer in Christ, we would remind the reader, first, that we have a picture here of what, and where, we were in our natural condition. It is true, as Keil contends, that " fire is a symbol of punishment, not of sin," but in a very real and terrible sense sin is its own punishment; and apart from " the everlasting burnings " (Isa. xxxiii. 14) which await the impenitent in that place where " the fire is never quenched," wickedness (already in this life) burneth as a fire (Isa. ix. 18). And this, whether we have been conscious of it or not, has been the case with us all. We were in the fire which indwells our nature, and, but for the mercy of God, we should have ultimately been altogether consumed by it.

But, secondly, the figure also reminds us of the love and compassion of our Redeemer, Who, when there was no eye to pity, at the cost of infinite suffering to Himself, plucked us " as brands from the fire," and delivered us, not only from the punishment of sin in the future, but from the power and dominion of sin in the present.

But to proceed with the exposition. As already indicated, " the filthy garments " in which Joshua was clad symbolised the sin with which the nation as a whole was defiled, and which he, as high priest, represented in his official capacity. This was already clearly perceived by the Church Father whom I have already quoted, who observes : " The high priest having been thus taken to represent the whole people, the filthy garments would be no unclear symbol of the wickedness of the people ; for clad, as it were, with their sins, with the ill-effaceable spot of ungodliness, they abode in captivity subject to retribution, paying the penalty of their unholy deeds." [1]

The figure of the filthy garments as emblematic of moral pollution is also carried over into the visions of Zechariah from the former prophets. Thus in the confession of the remnant of Israel in Isa. lxiv. 6 we read : " *For we are all become as one that is unclean, and all our righteousnesses are as a polluted garment ; and we all do fade*

[1] Cyril.

as a leaf; and our iniquities, like the wind, take us away."
This is a true picture of Israel's moral condition before
God. But in contrast to the past and the present there
are other pictures painted for us by the prophets of Israel's
future, based on the fact of God's election of this nation to
be a peculiar people unto Himself, and on the exceeding
great and precious promises given to the fathers. The
Lord *shall wash away* " the filth of the daughter of Zion,"
and cleanse her from all her defilements, " *and it shall come
to pass that he that is left in Zion, and he that remaineth in
Jerusalem, shall be called holy, even every one that is written
among the living in Jerusalem* " (Isa. iv. 3, 4 ; Ezek. xxxvi.
16–32). Then, in contrast to the " polluted garment," [1] the
same prophet sings : " I will greatly rejoice in Jehovah, my
soul shall be joyful in my God ; for *He hath clothed me
with the garments of salvation*, He hath covered me with
the robe of righteousness, as a bridegroom decked himself
with ornaments (or, ' with his priestly head-dress ' or
' turban '), and as a bride adorneth herself with her jewels "
(Isa. lxi. 10).

Now this same glorious truth, so clearly announced in
verbal prophecy, is here realistically set forth to Zechariah
in symbol. The symbol, however, is immediately interpreted by the Angel of Jehovah Himself, who, after commanding the attendant angels " who stood by," saying,
" Take away the filthy garments from him," addresses the
comforting words to Joshua himself : " *Behold I have caused
thine iniquity to pass from thee* " (which, as already pointed
out, answers to the glorious promise in ver. 9 : " *I will
remove the iniquity of the land in one day* "), " *and I will
clothe thee with rich apparel* " ; which, in brief, answers to
the garments of salvation and pure robe of Messiah's
own perfect righteousness, in which Israel shall then be
attired.

But the word מַחֲלָצוֹת, *machalatsoth*, which is in the
plural, translated in the Authorised Version " change of
raiment," and in the Revised " rich apparel "—and which is

---

[1] Not " filthy rags," as rendered in the A.V. of Isa. lxiv. 6.

found elsewhere only in Isa. iii. 22, where it is used of the "changeable suits of apparel" which the haughty daughters of Zion of that time reserved to be worn on great occasions—probably stands here for the specifically priestly or high priest's outfit ; and these being put upon Joshua as the representative of Israel would indicate, not only pardon and justification before the Lord, on the ground of the righteousness which He Himself provides for His people, but their *reinstatement and reconsecration to their priestly calling as a nation.* And this, it seems to me, is brought out still more clearly in the 5th verse.

The prophet has hitherto been a silent but eager spectator of the wonderful scene which he was made to witness, but as he beholds the transformation which had taken place in the high priest's outfit, after the filthy garments were taken from him, and as the symbolical character of the transaction becomes clear to him in its very process (since he does not in this vision ask for any explanation of its meaning, nor is there one given to him by the interpreting angel), he bursts out in the prayer that the gracious work may be completed : " *And I said, Let them set a fair* (or '*clean*') *mitre upon his head* "—which prayer, being in accordance with the good pleasure of Jehovah, and that for which it asked having apparently been omitted only in order to leave *something*, and that the completion of all, to be done at the intercession of the prophet, it is also immediately answered, " *So they set a fair mitre* (literally, ' *the mitre, the clean or fair one*') *upon his head.*"

Now the word *tsaniph* (rendered "mitre") is not "a turban such as might be worn by anybody" (as Koehler and other commentators assert), but is, as Keil rightly explains, "the head-dress of princely persons and kings," and is here used as a synonym for *mitsnepheth*, which is the technical word for the tiara prescribed for the high priest in the law.

And this mitre, or turban, was the glory and comple-ment of the high priest's sacred and symbolical attire—the portion of his dress " in which he carried his office, so to speak, upon his forehead " ;[1] for to it was attached the plate of pure gold with the words קֹדֶשׁ לַיהֹוָה—*qodesh layehovah* ! " Holy to Jehovah," engraven on it. " It shall be always upon his forehead," we read, " that he may bear the iniquity of the holy things which the children of Israel shall hallow, . . . *that they may be accepted before the Lord* " (Ex. xxviii. 36–38). The answer, therefore, of the prophet's prayer, and the putting of the fair mitre upon Joshua's head, signified in his own case his full equipment and fitness for his high-priestly functions ; and in relation to the people, the removal of their guilt, and an assurance of their acceptance before the Lord.

But we have also to remember that the Aaronic priesthood, summed up as it was in the person of the high priest, while appointed to meet Israel's felt need of a Mediator between them and God, was at the same time designed not only to foreshadow some of the aspects of the everlasting priesthood of Him Who ever liveth to make intercession for us, *but to be also a continual reminder of God's purpose with the nation as a whole,* and, symbolically at least, ever to keep before them the significance of priesthood, which is to be " chosen " ; to be " His," in a peculiar sense ; to be " holy," and to " draw near " unto Him in priestly service and intercession (Num. xvi. 5).

To the ultimate realisation of God's original purpose in the election and call of His people, that they should be unto Him " a kingdom of priests and an holy nation " (Ex. xix. 5, 6), the prophetic Scriptures bear unanimous testimony ; and the wonderful transformation which Zechariah is permitted to witness in this vision, in the case of Joshua, symbolically sets forth the same great truth, and describes the change which will come over Israel as a nation, and their equipment in that day when they shall be named throughout the earth " the priests of Jehovah," and when men everywhere shall call them " the ministers of our God " (Isa. lxi. 6).

[1] Keil.

And the process which the prophet witnesses in the case of Joshua as the representative of the Jewish nation, answers also to the experience of each individual believer.

By nature, dear reader, " we are all "—whether we be Jew or Gentile—" as one that is unclean " in God's sight, and " all our righteousness "—the very best moral outfit which we can manufacture for ourselves—is, " as a polluted garment " (Isa. lxiv. 6), not only of no avail, but, together with our sins, must be " taken away."

Man, in his own name, and on the ground of his own merits, has no approach and no standing in the presence of God—he must find his moral fitness outside of himself if he desires to " ascend into the hill of the Lord, and to stand in His holy place."

There must first be a stripping of self. Like the great and blessed Apostle, we must each one be brought to say : " What things were gain to me, those I counted loss for Christ. Yea verily, and I count all things but loss, for the excellency of the knowledge of Christ Jesus my Lord : for Whom I have suffered the loss of all things, and do count them but dung, that I may win Christ, and be found in Him, not having my own righteousness, which is of the law, but that which is through faith in Christ, the righteousness which is of God through faith " (Phil. iii. 7–9).

From the very beginning of the history of redemption we have the same truth set forth under the same figure. Already in the garden of Eden, as soon as sin entered into the world, and man, losing the consciousness of God, became self-conscious, we read of the man and the woman that " they sewed fig-leaves together, and made themselves aprons." These " aprons " or " girdles " which men continue to sew or " weave " for themselves (Isa. lix. 6) are of no avail to hide their shame or to cover their misery. But already then, God in His infinite compassion began to preach the gospel to man by direct promise, and to set it forth also by type. He not only announced the coming of " the Seed of the woman," who should bruise the serpent's head and destroy the devil and his works (Gen. iii. 15), but Jehovah God, we read, also " made for Adam and his wife coats of skins (from animals which He probably first commanded the man to slay) and clothed them " (Gen. iii. 21).

And these two " garments "—the one symbolic of the meetness for fellowship with God, which man tries to work out for himself, and the other of the beautiful robe of Messiah's own righteousness which is provided for all who, conscious of their own utter unworthiness to appear in His presence on the ground of anything in themselves, look for the mercy of our Lord Jesus Christ unto eternal life (Jude 21)—are contrasted throughout Scripture until the day when the " wedding feast " which the Great King made for His Son, to which men are now invited, merges into the " marriage of the Lamb " and " the great supper of God." Then there shall be a final scrutiny and separation between those arrayed in " fine linen, bright and pure " and clothed in " festal attire," and those who refused to put on the wedding robe provided by the King, because they deceived themselves, or made belief to think that their own " polluted garment " was good enough : these shall then be bound hand and foot and cast into outer darkness, where there shall be weeping and gnashing of teeth (Matt. xxii. 1–14 ; Rev. xix. 6–18).

And this " robe of righteousness," which is ours first of all by faith, and which is the only ground of our standing before God, becomes also a blessed subjective experimental reality to the Christian.

In this world men walk in a vain show, and there is often no inward correspondence between their actual character and the robe of office which they wear. There are kings who are not kingly, princes who are by no means princely, and priests who are far from being priestly ; but it can never be so in the kingdom of God—in it there are no deceiving appearances. As many as are justified in Messiah's righteousness are also being regenerated and sanctified by His blessed Spirit, and there is not one arrayed in the beautiful robe of His perfection who does not also make it the aim of his life to perfect holiness in the fear of God now, and who shall not in the end be conformed to His image, and be actually and fully like Him in character.

And what Israel shall be nationally in the day when, stripped of their own filthy garments, they are clothed in *machalatsoth* (the new priestly outfit), and, with the fair mitre with *qodesh layehovah* on their foreheads, go forth as "the priests of Jehovah" and as "the ministers of our God" among the nations—that also all believers in Christ are already now as individuals. We, too, are "a chosen generation, *a royal priesthood*, a holy nation, a people for God's own possession," and are sent forth into the world, not only with our lips, but also in our lives and conduct, "to show forth the praises (the excellences) of Him Who hath called us out of darkness into His marvellous light."

But let us now proceed to the second half of this chapter.

The symbolical transaction of the removal of the filthy garments from Israel's high priest, and his being fitted out in *machalatsoth*, or "rich apparel," with the "clean mitre" on his head, is followed by a solemn charge and most glorious promises.

"*And the Angel of Jehovah protested unto Joshua, saying, Thus saith Jehovah of hosts : If thou wilt walk in My ways, and if thou wilt keep My charge, then thou also shalt judge My house, and shalt also keep My courts, and I will give thee places to walk among these that stand by.*"

The word *va-ya-'ad* ("protested") means *solemnly* to protest, or "testify." Etymologically it signifies "to call God to witness." It occurs, for instance, in the words of Solomon to Shimei, "Did I not make thee swear by Jehovah, *and protested* unto thee," etc. (1 Kings ii. 21)— and is intended to express the solemnity and importance of the charge about to be made.

The expressions "Walk in My ways" and "Keep My charge" (*mishmarti thishmor*) are frequently used in the Pentateuch for "holding on in the way of life, well-pleasing

to God, and for keeping the charge given by God."[1]   It
was the injunction of the dying David to Solomon : " Keep
the charge of the Lord thy God to walk in His ways, to
keep His statutes." The first part of the charge, " If
thou wilt walk in My ways," refers particularly to Joshua's
personal attitude towards the Lord—to fidelity in his
personal relations to God ; and the second, " If thou wilt
keep My charge," to the faithful performance of his *official*
duties as high priest.

And the reward of his thus (in his personal and official
capacity) studying to present himself approved unto God,
will be (*a*) " Then thou also shalt judge My house." " My
house " may be used metaphorically of the people, as in
Num. xii. 7 : " My servant Moses, . . . who is faithful in
all My house," and the judging of the house would in that
case refer to the high priest's function as the representative
of God in all matters of controversy, to give the sentence of
judgment (Deut. xvii. 8–10) ; or Hengstenberg, Keil, and
Pusey may be right in limiting it to the high priest's
administration of the literal House or Temple—to the
decisions, namely, which devolved upon him in all matters
of the sanctuary.   Probability is added to this more
limited meaning of the expression by the next parallel
clause, which certainly is to be understood in a literal sense
as referring to the Temple, namely, (*b*) " And shalt also keep
My courts "—as a faithful watchman or porter, not only " to
keep away everything of an idolatrous nature from the
House of God," but to see to it that nothing that is unclean
or which defileth shall enter into it (2 Chron. xxiii. 19).
(*c*) But the climax of promise in this verse is reached in the
last clause, " And I will give thee places to walk among
these that stand by."   The Hebrew word מַהְלְכִים, *mah'lekhim*,
translated " places to walk," and which the Revised Version
renders " a place of access," has been variously translated
and interpreted by different commentators.   Thus Gesenius,
Hengstenberg, Hoffmann, etc., have rendered the sentence,
" I will give thee leaders among those that stand by."   But

[1] Pusey.

the rendering in the Authorised Version, which is supported by almost all modern scholars, is doubtless the true one. " These that stand by "—as we see by comparing the expression with ver. 4—are, the angels, who were in attendance on the Angel of Jehovah, and who " stood before Him " ready to carry out His behests. The promise is usually limited by Christian commentators to signify that God would yet give to Joshua, and to the priesthood generally, fuller and nearer access to Him than they possessed hitherto, or than was possible in the old dispensation ; but the Jewish Targum is, I believe, nearer the truth when it paraphrases the words, " In the resurrection of the dead I will revive thee, and give thee feet walking among these seraphim." Thus applied to the future, the sense of the whole verse would be this : " If thou wilt walk in My ways and keep My charge, thou shalt not only have the honour of judging My house and keeping My courts, but when thy work on earth is done thou shalt be transplanted to higher service in heaven, and ' have places to walk ' among these pure angelic beings who stand by Me, hearkening unto the voice of My word " (Ps. ciii. 20, 21). Note the " if's " in this verse, my dear reader, and lay to heart the fact that, while pardon and justification are the free gifts of God to all that are of faith, having their source wholly in His infinite and sovereign grace, and quite apart from work or merit on the part of man, the honour and privilege of acceptable service and future reward are conditional on our obedience and faithfulness : therefore seek by His grace and in the power of His Spirit to " walk in His ways and to keep His charge," and in *all things*, even if thine be the lot of a " porter " or " doorkeeper " in the House of God, to present thyself approved unto Him, in remembrance of the day when " we must all be manifested before the judgment-seat of Christ, that each one may receive the things done in the body, according to what he hath done, whether it be good or bad " (2 Cor. v. 10).

But there are still greater and more wonderful promises following, in vers. 8 to 10 ; and to rouse Joshua, and us also through him, to a sense of their significance and importance, his attention is again attracted by the words, "*Hear now, O Joshua*"—not only with the outer ear, but with the ears of the heart, namely, *hearken and consider.*

The words *ha kohen ha-gadol—the high priest*—which are added, are intended once more to remind us that it is not in his private personal capacity, but as the head of his order and *official representative* of the people, that he is thus addressed. This is made clear by the words which immediately follow: "*Thou and thy fellows which sit before thee, for they are men which are a sign.*"

"Thy fellows" (or "companions") which sit before, are the ordinary priests who, in meetings of the order for the purpose of discussing or deciding matters connected with their office, "sat before" the high priest, who was the president of the assembly [1]—not that they were there and then sitting before Joshua. The words *anshei mopheth*, rendered in the Authorised Version " men wondered at," and in the Revised Version " men that are a sign," are men who attract attention to themselves by something striking, *and are types of what is to come.* Thus Isaiah's sons, with their prophetic names, Shear Jashub ("a remnant shall return "), Maher-shalal-hash-baz (" Haste spoil speed prey "), were, with his own name "Isaiah," which signifies "the salvation of Jehovah," for signs and *moph'thim*—portents and types to the people of what was going to take place in the nation (Isa. viii. 18 ; see also Isa. xx. 3 ; Ezek. xii. 6–11). And if we ask wherein were Joshua and the whole order of Aaronic priesthood portents or types of things which were then yet to come, the answer is that in their persons they were imperfect images of the true Priest after the order of Melchizedek, " who is made, not after the law of a carnal commandment, but after the power of an endless

---

[1] We find the expression in 2 Kings iv. 38 and in vi. 1, used of the sons of the prophets as " sitting before " their master Elisha ; and in Ezekiel it is used again and again of the elders of Judah who came and " sat before " the prophet, professing the desire to be taught by him the Word of God (Ezek. viii. 1, xiv. 1, and xx. 1). Thus also in later times the Rabbinical students "sat before " and "at the feet of " their Rabbis, in the *yeshibahs* or Talmudic seats of learning.

life," and whose priesthood is therefore "unchangeable"; and in their ministry, the essential part of which was "to make atonement"—but which in the old economy could never be perfectly accomplished, since "it was impossible that the blood of bulls and goats should take away sins"— they typified the great redeeming work of Him who, through the Eternal Spirit offered Himself without spot unto God, and thus once and for ever "put away sin by the sacrifice of Himself."

But Kliefoth, Keil, Dr. C. H. H. Wright, and Pusey may be right in considering that the words that Joshua and the other priests are *anshei mopheth*—men who are a portent or type—have a reference also to the previous incidents of the vision. "The vision had pictured to the eye of the priest-prophet the manner in which the priest-hood of Israel, represented by Joshua, though defiled with iniquity, had been cleansed by Divine grace, and rendered acceptable to God. By that grace priest and people had been snatched like half-burnt brands from the fire of a well-deserved punishment. That deliverance was, however, typical of a greater salvation, which the angel was now about to reveal. Hence Joshua and his fellows were typical men." [1] "For this miracle of grace which has been wrought for them points beyond itself to an incomparable, greater, and better act of the sin-absolving grace of God which is still in the future." [2]

The key and explanation of the enigmatic words addressed to Joshua, and to his fellow priests "that sat before him," are contained in the last sentence of the 8th verse:

"*For, behold, I will bring forth My servant the Branch.*"

This and the words which immediately follow in the 9th verse form one of the richest and most beautiful Messianic passages in the Old Testament; and again, on careful examination, we find it to be (as is the manner of Zechariah) a terse summary of glorious announcements concerning the coming Redeemer in the "former prophets." Thus, "My Servant" is the title of Messiah in the second

---

[1] Wright.   [2] Keil.

half of the Book of Isaiah, and our minds are taken back to such passages as, " *Behold My servant, whom I uphold; Mine Elect, in whom My soul delighteth. I have put My Spirit upon Him; He shall bring forth judgment unto the Gentiles. . . . It is a light thing that thou shouldest be My servant to raise up the tribes of Jacob, and to restore the preserved of Israel: I will also give thee for a light of the Gentiles, that thou mayest be My salvation unto the end of the earth.*" [1]   But it is perhaps particularly to Isa. liii.— " the crown of all Old Testament prophecy," as it has been well called—that our thoughts are directed by the introduction of this title of Messiah in our prophecy—to the innocent and absolutely holy One who is wounded for our transgressions, bruised for our iniquities, who pours out His soul unto death as an atonement for sin—to the "Righteous Servant" through the knowledge of whom the many are justified, or " made righteous," and in whose redeeming work Zechariah, like Isaiah himself and all the other prophets, saw the solution of the great moral problem, how those morally defiled, as Joshua was represented to be in his filthy garments, can be acquitted and justified by a holy God, and how " the iniquity of the land shall be removed " in one day.

But the designation, " My Servant " stands here in combination with another well-known Messianic title, which in the visions of Zechariah is turned into a proper name of the promised Deliverer—" My Servant *the Branch*." [2]

[1] Isa. xlii. 1-6, xlix. 6.

[2] Kimchi's comment on the words " My Servant the Branch " is : " This is Zerubbabel " ; but the interpretation thus proposed is (as shown in a note by Dr. Alexander McCaul in his translation of Kimchi's Commentary) untenable. " Kimchi here follows Rashi in interpreting ' My servant the Branch' of Zerubbabel.   Their reason for this probably was that if they acknowledged the person thus designated in this chapter to be the Messiah, they must have made the same admission in the parallel passage, chap. vi. 12 ; and by so doing they would have admitted that Messiah was to be a priest as well as a king.

" Perhaps they also saw some polemical danger in this chapter, in connecting the promise of the Messiah with the promise occurring in the next verse, ' To remove the iniquity of that land in one day,' which would seem to favour the Christian doctrine that the Messiah ' by one offering perfected for ever them that are sanctified' (Heb. x. 14).   But, however that be, the interpretation which

In the former prophets we find *Tsemach* first used as a title of Messiah by Isaiah in chap. iv., where, too, it stands in connection with the prophecy of the washing away of " the filth of the daughter of Zion " and the purging of the blood of Jerusalem from the midst of her," so that all that shall be left in Zion, and he that remaineth in Jerusalem, shall be called holy, " even every one that is written among the living in Jerusalem." Then Jeremiah, in chaps. xxiii. and xxxiii. 15, uses the term *Tsemakh Tsaddik,* " the Branch of Righteousness," or " Righteous Branch," as a designation of the Divine King who should spring out of David's line, in whose days Judah shall be saved, and Israel dwell safely, and whose name shall be called *Jehovah Tsidkenu.*

Including, therefore, the prophecies of Zechariah, we find the Messiah brought before us in the Old Testament Scriptures by this title of *Tsemach* in four different aspects of His character :

(1) As the ideal *King* who shall reign in righteousness —the Branch of David in whom shall be fulfilled all the promises made to the Davidic house (Jer. xxiii. 5, 6, xxxiii. 15, 16).

(2) As " My *Servant* the Branch " (Zech. iii. 8).

(3) As " The *Man* whose name is the Branch " (Zech. vi. 12).

they propose is not tenable : 1*st*, Because it departs from the old received interpretation of the Jewish Church. Both Kimchi and Rashi admit that there was an interpretation referring this passage to the Messiah ; and Jonathan, in his Targum interprets both these passages of the Messiah ; 2*nd*, Because it contradicts the analogy of the prophetic language. Messiah is elsewhere called ' The Branch,' as in Isa. iv. 2 and Jer. xxiii. 5, in both of which passages Kimchi himself freely admits that ' Branch ' means the Messiah. 3*rd*, Because the words do not agree with the circumstances of Zerubbabel. God says, ' I will bring My Servant the Branch.' But, as Abarbanel remarks, Zerubbabel had come long before, and was already a prince among them. Kimchi felt this difficulty, and therefore tries to twist the words to mean ' that his dignity should increase still more, and his greatness should grow as a branch,' etc. But Abarbanel remarks again that God does not say that He will make him great, but that He will bring him ; and adds, that ' after this prophecy Zerubbabel attained to neither royalty, dominion, or other dignity more than be already possessed ' " (see Abarbanel, *Comment. in loc.*).

(4) As " *The Branch of Jehovah* " who in that day shall be " for beauty and for glory, . . . for excellency and comeliness to them that should be of the escaped in Israel " (Isa. iv. 2). The promised King—the Servant—the Man —the Branch, or Son of God.

And this fourfold prophetic picture of Messiah on the pages of the Old Testament, as I have elsewhere shown many years ago,[1] answers to the fourfold portraiture which the Holy Spirit has given us in the four different Gospels of the Christ of history. One probable reason why the Divine artist has seen fit to sketch the person and character of Messiah for us in four Gospels instead of one, has been well expressed by the late Professor Godet, who says : " Just as a gifted painter, who wished to immortalize for a family the complete likeness of the father who had been its glory, would avoid any attempt at combining in a single portrait the insignia of all the various offices he had filled ; at representing him in the same picture as general and as magistrate ; as man of science and as father of a family ; but would prefer to paint four distinct portraits, each of which should represent him in one of these characters. So has the Holy Spirit, in order to preserve for mankind the perfect likeness of Him who was its chosen Representative, God in man, used means to impress upon the minds of the writers, whom He has made His organs, four different images."

And these " four different images " in the historic narrative correspond in a striking manner, as already stated, with the fourfold outline of Messiah's character as delineated on the page of prophecy. Although the same blessed features of our Redeemer are easily recognisable in all the Gospels, there is a special aspect of His character brought out in each. (1) In Matthew, which is primarily " the Jewish Gospel," and was very probably in the first instance written in Hebrew or Aramaic (though afterwards rewritten by the same evangelist in Greek), we have the promised

[1] In *Rays of Messiah's Glory*, 2nd edition, published in 1886, now out of print.

Malkha Meshicha — the theocratic "King Messiah" —
presented to us, and the fulfilment of the prophecy, "Behold,
I will raise unto David a Righteous Branch, and a King
shall reign and prosper, and shall execute judgment and
justice in the earth," gradually unfolded before us. In
keeping with its primary design is its very style. The
keynote throughout is "that it might be fulfilled." For
this reason also is Christ presented to us in this Gospel,
more than in any of the others, as the Prophet like unto
Moses, the great lawgiver of the Old Covenant, and yet
above Moses and the whole prophetic order, not only in the
new unfolding and application of the law in the so-called
"Sermon on the Mount," but in His four other great discourses, to which the narrative portion supplied by Matthew
forms the framework. For the same reason also the
genealogy in this Gospel traces back Christ's earthly descent
only as far as Abraham, for the aim of the Evangelist is to
unfold the thesis laid down in the 1st verse, which is in
itself a summary and fulfilment of all the Messianic hope
of the Old Testament: "The book of the generation of
Jesus Christ, *the son of David, the son of Abraham.*

(2) But if "Behold thy King" (Zech. ix. 9) is the keynote of the Gospel of Matthew, the inscription written by
the Spirit of God on the Gospel of Mark is, "Behold My
Servant." This, the shortest of the four Gospels, which,
though written by the pen of John Mark, has most probably
"come to us from the lips of Peter"—and was apparently
designed in the providence of God primarily for the practical,
busy Roman world—is a graphic and living sketch of that
Blessed One Who spoke of Himself in the Spirit long before
His advent—"Lo I am come: in the scroll of the book it
is written of Me, I delight to do Thy will, O My God, yea,
Thy law is within My heart." It is a record, not so much
of the words of Jesus as of His *acts.* It is composed of
two sections only—the ministry in Galilee and the death
on Calvary.

"His ministry moves in widening circles—first in the
synagogue, then in the open field, to the interested groups

who gathered round Him, afterwards to the teeming multitudes." [1]

Characteristic of this Gospel is the rapidity of its movements, and the promptness of the obedience to the Father's will and to the impulses of the Spirit, expressed in the word rendered "straightway," "immediately" (i. 10–12).

Mark gives no genealogy, because a servant needs not such recommendation, he being judged by his work alone.

(3) But, if Matthew is the Gospel of the King and the Kingdom, and Mark that of the perfect Servant, the prominent feature of our Lord in the Gospel of Luke, which probably was primarily intended for the cultured Greek world, is that of "*the Son of Man.*" In it Christ is portrayed as the Man *par excellence*—the *true* Man, who is both the ideal and the representative of the race; the second Adam, who, in contrast to the first, who brought sin and ruin to the race, is the *Saviour* of men. The chief characteristic of this Gospel is its *universality*. The Christ depicted on its orderly pages is indeed the Messiah of Israel, "who is sent in fulfilment of the promises made to our fathers," and of the oath which God sware "to our father Abraham" (i. 67–80); and Who, even after His rejection by Israel, commands that, in the proclamation of His gospel among all nations, His disciples should " begin at Jerusalem " (xxiv. 47)—but He is shown as caring also for all who are sitting in darkness and in the shadow of death. " Already in the narrative of the infancy there are hints of the Light which is to enlighten all nations; in the parable of the Good Samaritan and the recital of the mission of the seventy, there is the promise of the advancing outreach of the Divine mercy to men of every nation and tongue; and in the call of Zacchæus, the parable of the Pharisee and the publican, and the salvation of the penitent robber, we have tokens of a grace which reaches out to the uttermost. The author does not aim at being a theologian ;

[1] See the chapter, " The Fourfold Portrait," in *The Spirit in the Word*, by D. M. McIntyre. The subject is also fully and beautifully unfolded in Bernard's *Progress of Doctrine in the New Testament*, Lecture ii.

he is an evangelist, and his message is, " The Son of Man came to seek and save that which was lost." [1]

It is for this reason also that this evangelist took upon himself the laborious task of tracing the genealogy of Jesus right back to Adam, in order to show His relation as the promised " Seed of the woman," not only with Israel, as does Matthew, but with men of all nations and kindreds, and peoples and tongues, who are thus traced back to one common stock.

(4) And the picture of our Lord in the Gospel of John is undoubtedly that of " *the Branch of Jehovah* " ; for though it is true that " no other evangelist so sounds the depths of our Lord's humiliation, nor rises with such adequacy to the exaltation of His glorified manhood, as John, the son of Zebedee, the eagle of the Church," and it would not be true to say that in the Fourth Gospel the emphasis rests entirely on the deity of Christ and ignores His perfect humanity ; yet the light that shines most transcendently through this most sublime narrative is His *Divine Sonship*—that glory which He had with the Father from all eternity. Hence we have no genealogy in this Gospel tracing back His relations to Abraham, for He of Whom it speaks was " before Abraham " (viii. 58) ; nor yet, as in Luke, to Adam, for by Him were all things made (i. 3), and Adam himself was created in His image. No, John traces not His human, but His divine pedigree, and shows us that, although the Word " became flesh and dwelt among us," He that tabernacled with the children of men was none other than the Only-begotten of the Father, full of grace and truth, Who in the very " beginning " was with God, and Himself was God.

But just as in each of the Gospels, though one feature of our Lord's character is brought more prominently to the fore, His twofold nature is always steadily kept in view ; so it is also in each of the four different prophecies to which we have referred. Jeremiah speaks of Him as the " Branch of David," thus dwelling more particularly on His human nature, but he proceeds to add : " And this is the name

[1] *The Spirit in the Word*, by D. M. McIntyre.

whereby He shall be called, *Jehovah our Righteousness,*" by which he proclaims Him to be Divine. Isaiah introduces Him as the *Tsemach Yehovah* (*Branch of Jehovah*), but he also designates Him *Ph'ri ha-arets* (" Fruit of the earth "), which, as the construction demands, must be regarded as another title of the *Tsemach,* and which brings before us more particularly His *human* nature, and His relation to our earth.

He is " the Servant " in Zechariah, and is pointed to as the One who will bring in a perfect righteousness, on the ground of which Israel shall be justified and the iniquity of the land be removed " in one day "; but it is the Servant, " *the Branch,*" and by Zechariah's time the title *Tsemach* had already become a proper name for the Messiah, and carries with it all that the former prophets had spoken of His divinity, as well as of His humanity.

Lastly, in Zech. vi., we are told to " behold *the Man* "; but this chapter proceeds to tell us that this Man shall not only rule and be Counsellor of Peace, but that He shall be a " Priest upon His throne "—the true Melchizedek, the King of Peace, and King of Righteousness, Who unites in His one person different functions which were formerly vested, not only in different persons, but in different tribes.

The climax of the Messianic references in this great prophecy is reached in the 9th verse: " *For behold, the stone that I have laid before Joshua ; upon one stone are seven eyes : behold, I will engrave the graving thereof, and I will remove the iniquity of the land in one day.*"

Many fanciful explanations have been given of this beautiful scripture, overlooking the fact that here again (as I have so frequently pointed out to be the case in these visions of Zechariah) we have a terse summary of well-known predictions in the former prophets, in the light of which we must interpret the passage.[1] " Behold the stone

[1] Baumgarten thinks the stone laid before Joshua represented the jewels belonging to the high priest's breastplate (the Urim and Thummim, which, by the way, never existed in the Second Temple), or even some single precious stone which supplied the place of the jewels that were lost.

which I have laid" carries our minds back to Isa. xxviii.
16: "Behold, I lay in Zion for a foundation a stone, a
tried stone, a precious corner-stone, a sure foundation; he
that believeth shall not make haste"; and to Ps. cxviii. 22:
"The stone which the builders refused (or 'despised') is
become the head-stone of the corner."

There may have been some allusion to the foundation-
stone of the Second Temple—the *eben shetiyah*, as it was
afterwards called—"the very foundation as well as the
centre of the world," about which there are many traditions,
true and false, absurd and beautiful, in the Talmud and in
later Jewish Midrashim; but if so, it is because the literal
foundation was a type of Him who is the "precious corner-
stone" and unshakable foundation of the spiritual temple,
into which believers also are built as living stones, and
which through eternity shall be for the habitation of God
through the Spirit.

Upon this one stone "are seven eyes."

If, according to Jewish commentators, we are to understand the words that the eyes are *directed toward* this
stone, then they are "the seven eyes of Jehovah" (chap.
vi. 10), which have rested from before the foundation of
the world upon this precious corner-stone; and the figure
would in that case express, not only the assurance of His
watchful care and protection over it, but the Father's complacency and delight in His only-begotten Son. Or the
sacred and covenant number "seven" may be taken in a

Keil says: "The stone is the symbol of the Kingdom of God." Hengstenberg explains it as "the Kingdom or people of God, outwardly insignificant
when compared with the great mountain (chap. iv. 7) which symbolises the
power of the world"; and Köhler regards the stone as signifying Israel, "which
nation was entrusted to the care of the high priest Joshua, that, by the due
discharge of his high priestly office, the purity and freedom from iniquity required
by God should be attained by the people."

Many interpret it simply of the foundation of the Temple, while Von
Hoffmann and others say that "the stone here represents the entire collection of
materials required for the erection of the (second) Temple." All of which
interpretations are more or less fanciful and beside the mark, since (as shown
above) "the Stone" which Joshua was to behold, like "the Servant, the
Branch," in the previous verse, are well-known titles of Messiah carried over in
these visions of Zechariah from "the former prophets."

more general sense as meaning " *all* eyes," that is, the eyes
of God, and of the holy angels, and of men, all directed
toward Him thus symbolised by the Foundation Stone, as
the object of love and of admiration, of yearning desire and
hope.

But it seems to me that the view adopted by most of
the modern scholars, namely, that there were actually seven
eyes carved, or engraven, on this stone of vision, is most
probably the correct one, in which case the thing signified
by the symbol would be the *manifold intelligence* or
omniscience of this " Living Stone "—the seven reminding
us of the sevenfold plenitude of the One Spirit of Jehovah,
" the spirit of wisdom and understanding, the spirit of
counsel and might, the spirit of knowledge and of the fear
of the Jehovah," which should rest upon Him, and which
was so wonderfully fulfilled in Him whom the New Testament seer beheld as the Lamb which had been slain
" having seven horns (all power) and seven eyes (omniscience), which are the seven spirits of God sent forth into
all the earth " (Rev. v. 6).

" For this stone to have seven eyes," says one of the
Fathers, " is to retain in operation the whole virtue of the
Spirit of sevenfold grace. For, according to the distribution
of the Holy Spirit, one receives prophecy, another knowledge, another miracles, another kinds of tongues, another
interpretation of words ; but no one attaineth to have all
the gifts of that same Spirit. But our Creator taketh on
Him our infirmities, because through the power of His
Divinity He showed that He had at once in Him all the
virtues of the Holy Spirit, uniting beyond doubt the bright
gleams of the sevenfold constellation." [1]

The next sentence in this verse, *hineni mephateach
pituchah*—" Behold I will grave the graving thereof "—is
probably not unconnected with the words which we have
just considered, and denotes, as it seems to me, that what
the prophet had seen on the stone of vision, God Himself
would accomplish in the day of fulfilment.

[1] St. Gregory, quoted by Pusey.

What the graving will be is not stated, but those are far from the mark who conjecture some kind of an inscription. Rather is it that which makes this Living Stone the *precious* corner-stone (or, " *the corner-stone of preciousness*," as it is literally), namely, the perfect equipment of the Messiah by the Father for His Messianic office and mediatorial work of redemption—the spiritual glory and beauty which God would bestow upon Him when He shall have anointed Him with all the fulness of the Spirit; which indeed had already in symbol been set forth by the " seven eyes " which the prophet saw traced on the stone.

According to the Talmud, the *Eben Shetiyah*—the foundation-stone of the Second Temple, which was some inches higher than the level of the Holy of Holies—had the sacred Tetragrammaton (the four Hebrew letters making up the ineffable name " Jehovah ") graven upon it; and although in later times all sorts of absurd legends gathered around this tradition, there is no reason to doubt the fact itself, and the words used in reference to the Everlasting Foundation of the spiritual temple, " Behold, *I will engrave the graving thereof*," may be an allusion to it.

On Messiah, too, the ineffable name was graven. Of the Divine Angel of Jehovah we read already in the Old Testament, " My Name " (which stands for all the attributes of God's character, for all the perfections of His glorious Being) " is in Him." And, when in the fulness of time, He who of old so often appeared as the Angel of the Covenant in the *form* of man, became *real* man, and " tabernacled among us," then this sacred mystical " graving " became more and more clear and legible. Then " the Name " became fully *manifested*, and men saw " the glory of God in the face of Jesus Christ."

But the most glorious display of all the attributes belonging to that " holy Name " was when on the cross of shame He laid down His life a ransom for us; hence those early Fathers, and some also of the modern interpreters, are not far wrong when they say that the " graving " of the stone took place when, " through the providence and will of God He caused Him to be wounded by the nails of the cross and the soldier's lance." " For what even in the body of the Lord can be lovelier or more lightful," says a Catholic writer, " than those five wounds, which He willed to retain in His immortal Being, lest the blessed work should be deprived of that splendour surpassing far the light of sun and stars "; to which I would add the words of yet another, namely : " Beautiful were the gifts and graces which Christ received as man ; but beautiful beyond all beauty must be those glorious scars with which He allowed His whole body to be riven, that throughout the whole frame His love might be engraven."

The last sentence of this 9th verse, " *And I will remove the iniquity of this land in one day*," may in a sense be regarded as the key to the whole vision, for it demonstrates (1) the fact we have so frequently emphasised in the course of the exposition, namely, that it is to Israel as a nation that the vision primarily refers, and that what the prophet beheld as happening to Joshua was meant *typically* to set forth the experience of the whole people, which, in his official capacity as high priest, he represented ; and (2) that the removal of Israel's iniquity, and their acceptance and reinstatement as Jehovah's priestly nation, are yet to take place in the future.

For which is this *yom echad*—" one day "—of which the prophet speaks ? The Jewish answer is expressed in the words of their most popular commentator,[1] who says, " One day ; I know not what that day is." Christian commentators all substantially agree in saying, " It is the day of Golgotha," which is true, but yet does not express the whole truth.

What is here predicted will assuredly be fulfilled only on the ground and as a blessed consequence of " the day of Golgotha," when Christ through the Eternal Spirit offered Himself without spot unto God, and thus once and for all put away sin by the sacrifice of Himself ; but the " one day " on which the iniquity of this land and people

---

[1] Rashi.

shall be removed is none other than the "that day" of the last chapters of this same Book of Zechariah—the "day," namely, of Israel's national repentance and great Day of Atonement, when the spirit of grace and supplication shall be poured out upon them, and they shall look upon Him whom they have pierced.

"In that day," we read, "*there shall be a great mourning in Jerusalem :* . . . *every family apart and their wives apart. In that day there shall be a fountain opened to the House of David and to the inhabitants of Jerusalem, for sin and for uncleanness*" (Zech. xii. 10–14 and xiii. 1).

"But, again we may be asked, how can this be reconciled with the statement that the true Day of Atonement is the Day of Calvary ; and was not the 'fountain for sin and uncleanness' opened when our Saviour was nailed to the cross, and when the soldier with the spear pierced His side, and forthwith there came out blood and water?" Yes, but to the sinner actually and experimentally the Day of Calvary is the day when his eyes are opened to the true meaning *to himself* of the great redeeming work there accomplished, and when the Spirit of God *applies* Jesus' blood and righteousness and high-priestly intercessions to his own need. Thus, "in that day" it will be with Israel nationally.[1]

A simple illustration from the experience of Hagar in the wilderness of Beer-sheba may help us to understand this. When the water in her bottle was spent, and she put down the lad, as she thought to die, she herself went to a distance, and in the anguish of her spirit lifted up her voice and wept. But God heard not only her voice, but the voice of the lad, and had pity on them. "*And God opened her eyes, and she saw a well of water.*" The well was most probably there all the time, but her eyes, dimmed by her very sorrow and tears, could not see it ; and it was to her, as she was filling her skin bottle, as if the well had just

---

[1] This section about the future prophetic significance of the Day of Atonement is quoted from the chapter, "The Sacred Calendar of the History of Redemption," in *Types, Psalms, and Prophecies*, to which I would refer the reader,

sprung up. So it will be with Israel. The fountain for sin and for uncleanness has been opened in the wounds of their Messiah nineteen centuries ago, but "in that day," when the Spirit of grace and of supplications is poured out upon them as a nation, "*the eyes of the blind shall be opened*" (Isa. xxxv.), and the Spirit of God will apply to their hearts and consciences as a people the great redeeming work accomplished on Calvary, and the words used in connection with the Day of Atonement shall receive a fulfilment as never before : "*For on this day He shall atone for you to cleanse you from all your sins ; before Jehovah ye shall be clean*" (Lev. xvi. 30, Heb.).

On that day the high priest, as I have fully described in another place,[1] entered twice within the veil—first, with the blood of the sin-offering for himself and his house, and then a second time with the blood of the goat of the people's sin-offering on which the lot fell "*la-yehovah*"; and it was not till he came forth a second time, and the remaining part of the ceremonial was gone through, that the people could rejoice in the knowledge that atonement was fully accomplished, the whole of which, in this sense also, may be regarded as a figure of the work of Christ in relation to the Church and to Israel. For Himself, the Holy One needed not as the Aaronic priests to offer sacrifice, but for those who in this interval, and in a special sense, constitute His redeemed family, atonement is fully accomplished, not only as an objective fact, but as a blessed subjective reality ; and in proof that it is not only "finished," but accepted, the Great High Priest, after His Resurrection, showed Himself again, "but not to all the people" (Acts x. 41), but only to His own family of faith.

But in relation to Israel the High Priest may still be regarded as inside the veil, or in the Holy Place, and the people as "waiting without," marvelling that he tarries so long (Luke i. 10, 21). But soon He will come forth again, in the hour of their deepest sorrow and humiliation, to cleanse them before Jehovah, so that they shall be known

[1] See the exposition of Ps. xxxii., in *Types, Psalms, and Prophecies.*

(and called in all the earth) as " the holy people, the Redeemed of the Lord," that He may be glorified (Isa. lxii. 12).

Finally, " when the high priest came forth from the sanctuary and appeared again unto the people, he first dispatched the scapegoat bearing all their iniquities into the wilderness, and then united with them in offering the burnt-offering unto the Lord. And such shall be the result of the Second Advent of our Saviour. Then shall sin be completely put away, and every trace of it removed for ever. In one sense sin is already put away—it is no more imputed unto them who believe in Jesus ; but sin itself remaineth, yea, and will remain, until He comes again. But then it shall be for ever banished, and all its consequences shall be removed for ever. Then *there shall be no more sin*, nothing of it shall remain but the blessed consciousness that we are redeemed from its power and its curse. And then, too, *shall Jesus and His people unite to offer the burnt-offering unto God.* Then, in the midst of His redeemed, He shall head up all their pure and holy service ; and blessed and consecrated by the presence of incarnate Godhead, the untiring energies of the redeemed people shall be for ever consuming, yet unconsumed, upon the altar of eternal love."

It was on the evening also of the Day of Atonement, after the complete cycle of seven sevens of years were fulfilled, that the " Jubilee " was proclaimed (Lev. xxv. 9, 10), which was the signal of liberty, not only to the people but for the land itself, which that year was neither to be ploughed, sown, nor reaped, the typical significance of which was already discerned by the prophets in the Old Testament, who rejoiced in spirit, and by faith greeted from afar the time when, after Israel's iniquity shall have been purged, Messiah will not only " proclaim liberty to the captives," [1] but when the earth itself shall at last enjoy her rest, and the whole creation, which has been groaning

---

[1] The very words used in Isa. lxi. 1 are taken from the command in reference to the Jubilee in Lev. xxv. 9, 10.

and travailing in pain together until now, shall at last be delivered from the bondage of corruption into the glorious liberty of the children of God.

And when once Israel's sin and guilt shall be removed, their sorrows and suffering, too, shall end. The vision closes, therefore, with the beautiful picture of tranquillity and happy contentment depicted in the last verse, "*In that day, saith Jehovah of hosts, ye shall call every man his neighbour under the vine and under the fig-tree.*"

I close with the following quotation : " We are told in the Talmud (Yoma, vii. 4) that, when, on the great Day of Atonement, the high priest had performed the various duties of that solemn day, he was escorted home in a festive manner, and was accustomed to give a festal entertainment to his friends. The maidens and youths of the people went forth to their gardens and vineyards with songs and dances ; social entertainments took place on all sides, and universal gladness closed the festival of that solemn day."

And thus, in the last verse of this chapter, a picture is given of a day of similar gladness and joy of heart, when, on account of sin pardoned, free access to God's throne granted, and the Deliverer having come anointed with the plentitude of the Spirit and sealed by God the Father, each true Israelite would invite his friends as joyful guests to partake of festal cheer under his own vine and fig-tree. The days of peace once more are seen. The glorious era of the earthly Solomon has indeed returned in greater splendour under the reign of the Prince of Peace. " Paradise lost " has become " Paradise regained."

"THE BODY OF MOSES"

NOTE TO CHAPTER III

It has been a point much disputed whether the reference in the Epistle of Jude to Michael's contention with the devil about " the body of Moses," where the same formula (" the Lord rebuke thee ") is used by the Archangel in silencing Satan as by the Angel of

Jehovah in this chapter, does, or does not, refer back to this vision. Origen, and some of the other Church Fathers, state that the quotation in Jude is from an apocryphal book, the title of which is " The Ascension," or " Assumption of Moses "; but, in the fragments of that legendary apocalyptic writing which have come down to us—either in Latin, Hebrew, or Arabic (in which elements belonging to various dates as far apart as the first or second and the thirteenth and fourteenth centuries after Christ are discernible)— no such tradition as a strife between Michael and the Evil One over the body of Moses is to be found, nor is there anything to prove that it ever existed in those parts of this apocryphal book which are missing—the confused allusions in the Fathers being probably to legends in the Talmud and Midrashim to a contest between Samael, the Angel of Death, and Michael, which had reference, not to the body of Moses after his death, but to his soul while he was still living. There are also different legendary accounts of contests between Moses himself and the Angel of Death, whom he put to flight when he came to take his soul by striking him with his rod, on which the ineffable name Jehovah was inscribed. In the end (so one legend proceeds) God Himself, accompanied by Gabriel, Michael, and Zagziel (the former teacher of Moses), descended to take Moses' soul. " Gabriel arranged the couch, Michael spread a silken cover over it, and Zagziel put a silken pillow under Moses' head. At God's command Moses crossed his hands over his breast and closed his eyes, and God took his soul away with a kiss."

On the other hand, there is just a possibility that the expression " the body of Moses," in Jude, is used in an allegorical sense of the Jewish people; in which case the reference would certainly be to this vision.

" It is true that no instance can be cited in which ' the body of Moses,' or any similar expression, is used of the people of Israel; but it is possible that the phrase *might* have been employed by Jude in that signification in imitation of the expression ' the body of Christ,' which is used in reference to the Church of Christ in the Epistles of St. Paul, and in view of the fact that the Jewish Church in the writer's day had become bitterly opposed to the Church of Christ, while it looked back to Moses as its teacher—a claim which might well be admitted as true in the most real sense of the Jewish Church in the days of Zechariah " (C. H. H. Wright).

I must refer those who are desirous to enter more fully into this question to Baumgarten's *Die Nachtgeschichte Sacharias*; Dr. C. H. H. Wright's *Zechariah and his Prophecies*; and to Dean Alford's note on the passage in Jude, where they will find the subject fully discussed. For my own part, while not committing myself to the allegorical interpretation of the passage in Jude, which may have reference to a very early tradition about a dispute about the literal body of Moses not recorded in any writing now extant, there can be no doubt that the incidents and the words of the vision we are considering were in the Apostle's mind when he wrote his short epistle. This is proved not only by his use of the formula, "The Lord rebuke thee," but by two other undoubted allusions to this vision in ver. 23—namely, the "pulling out of the fire," which is an echo of "the brand plucked from the fire" (Zech. iii. 2), and "the garment spotted by the flesh," which is an allusion to the "filthy garments" in which Joshua was at first seen standing before the Lord.

Chapter 6

THE FIFTH VISION
THE CANDLESTICK
Zechariah 4

And the angel that talked with me came again, and waked me, as a man that is wakened out of his sleep. And he said unto me, What seest thou? And I said, I have seen, and behold, a candlestick all of gold, with its bowl upon the top of it, and its seven lamps thereon ; there are seven pipes to each of the lamps, which are upon the top thereon ; and two olive trees by it, one on the right side of the bowl, and the other upon the left side thereof ; and I answered and spake to the angel that talked with me, saying, What are these, my lord ? Then the angel that talked with me answered and said unto me, Knowest thou not what these are ? And I said, No, my lord. Then he answered and spake unto me, saying, This is the word of Jehovah unto Zerubbabel, saying, Not by might, nor by power, but by My Spirit, saith Jehovah of hosts. Who art thou, O great mountain ? before Zerubbabel thou shalt become a plain : and he shall bring forth the top-stone with shoutings of Grace, grace unto it. Moreover the word of Jehovah came unto me, saying, The hands of Zerubbabel have laid the foundation of this house ; his hands shall also finish it ; and thou shalt know that Jehovah of hosts hath sent me unto you. For who hath despised the day of small things ? for these seven shall rejoice, and shall see the plummet in the hands of Zerubbabel ; these are the eyes of Jehovah, which run to and fro through the whole earth. Then answered I, and said unto him, What are these two olive trees upon the right side of the candlestick and upon the left side thereof ? And I answered the second time, and said unto him, What are these two olive branches, which are beside the two golden spouts, that empty the golden oil out of themselves ? And he answered me and said, Knowest thou not what these are ? And I said, No, my lord. Then said he, These are the two anointed ones, that stand by the Lord of the whole earth.

Chapter 6

INTRODUCTORY [1]

A S stated in the introduction to the 3rd chapter, the
fourth and fifth visions form a new chapter in
this series of symbolic prophecies, which, " though
in a sense standing by themselves, are in true psychological
order, and in the closest possible relation with the wonderful
things which had already been unfolded before the prophet's spiritual sight." We there saw that the fourth vision
depicts in a symbolic but very graphic manner *the inner
salvation of Israel from sin and defilement, answering to
their outward deliverance from captivity and oppression* set
forth in the preceding three visions.

We feel it, however, necessary, even at the risk of being
guilty of repetition, to cast once more a brief retrospective
glance at the progressive unfolding of God's counsel in
relation to Israel, and the establishment of Messiah's
Kingdom, in the series of visions which we have already
considered.

The first three visions were meant to convey to the
prophet, and through the prophet to the people, the " good
and comfortable " assurance that God had neither cast off
nor forsaken the people which He hath foreknown ; that,
though they found themselves under the oppressive yoke of
Gentile world-power (which was true of the remnant which
had returned as well as of the bulk of the nation which was

---

1 The exposition of this chapter was originally written out and read as "a
paper" at a meeting of the " Prophecy Investigation Society," by whom it was
also privately circulated among the members. This will account for its being
slightly different in form and style from the rest of the exposition.

127

still in the far land of the Captivity), the Angel of the Covenant was in their midst, identified with them, and pleading their cause (i. 8–12). Jehovah Himself, far from being indifferent to their sorrows and sufferings, is very angry with the nations who are helping forward the affliction (i. 14, 15), and wishes it to be proclaimed that he that toucheth them "toucheth the apple of His eye" (ii. 8). These Gentile world-powers "who lift up their horn" to scatter and oppress "Judah, Israel, and Jerusalem," would be broken and cast out (i. 18–21); the beloved city should be rebuilt on a much grander scale, and according to plans and measurements devised by God Himself, Who would henceforth be her Light and her Defence—"a wall of fire round about, and the glory in the midst of her" (ii. 1–5).

And not only Jerusalem, but the whole land, shall experience the blessed effects of Jehovah's "return to His people with mercies," and its cities shall spread abroad and overflow with material prosperity and with the multitude of men and cattle which shall be found therein (ii. 4). "The name of the city from that day shall be Jehovah Shammah; and thus the first cycle in this series of visions ends with the joyous proclamation: "Sing and rejoice, O daughter of Zion: for, lo, I come, and I will dwell in the midst of thee, saith the Lord" (ii. 10).

And the blessed consequence of Israel's return to the land, and of the return to the glory of Jehovah, for evermore to dwell in the midst of His people, will be that the original purpose of God in the call and election of Abraham and his seed—namely, that in and through them all the families of the earth should be blessed—shall be fulfilled. "And many nations shall join themselves to the Lord in that day, and shall be My people, and I will dwell in the midst of thee, and thou shalt know that Jehovah of hosts hath sent Me unto thee" (ii. 11).

But (as shown in the exposition on chap. iii.) the question might have suggested itself to the prophet: How can these things be? Has not Israel, by his grievous sins and moral defilement, for ever forfeited his place, and made himself unfit to be again Jehovah's sanctuary and appointed minister of blessing to the nations?

As if in answer to this question, the vision in the 3rd chapter is shown to the prophet, from which he is to learn (1) that the fulfilment of "the good words and comfortable words" of promise, rests, not on Israel's merits or worthiness, *but on the immutable purpose of Jehovah*, Who, in His free sovereign grace, hath "chosen Jerusalem," and Whose gifts and calling are without repentance.

(2) The solution of the moral problem, how the Holy One can dwell in the midst, and accept and use the ministry of those who are defiled by sin, is realistically presented to the prophet in the transformation which he witnesses as taking place in the case of Joshua, who stands before the Angel of Jehovah, not in his private capacity, but as the high priest and representative of the people.

Like the filthy garments in which their representative had been clothed, so shall the Lord remove the moral filth of the daughter of Zion, and cause her iniquity to pass away in that "one day" when her eyes shall be opened to behold the glorious Person and atoning work of her Messiah, who, in allusion to the prophecies in the second half of Isaiah (especially chap. liii.), is called "My Servant," and also by the well-known Messianic title, "The Branch" (iii. 8).

Thus, clothed in the righteousness of Him, Who "by His knowledge makes the many righteous," and arrayed in the "rich apparel," or festal attire of priestly garments, with the high-priestly mitre, to which was fastened the plate of gold with *Qodesh la-Yehovah* on his head, Israel shall be fitted, not only for fellowship with Jehovah, but to go forth on the mission for which he was originally chosen and destined, namely, *to disseminate the truth and the blessings of Jehovah among the nations.* Now, in beautiful order of sequence we have the vision in chap. iv., which presents to us Israel as the Light of the world.

The Fifth Vision

We shall now give an explanation, first, of the symbolism of this vision ; and, secondly, of the message.

I. *The Symbolism* (vers. 1–5)

A brief pause had intervened, during which the prophet was lying probably in a state of ecstatic slumber still contemplating the wonderful things he saw and heard in the last vision ; or Hengstenberg may be right in regarding the prophet's "sleep" as a return to his ordinary conditions of life in comparison to the *spiritually wakeful* state in which he was when receiving the visions. If so, then we have here, as he suggests, "the deepest insight into the state in which the prophets were, during their prophecies, as compared with their ordinary condition. The two bear the same relation to each other as sleeping and waking. A man's ordinary state, in which he is under the control of the senses, and unable to raise his spiritual eye to the contemplation of Divine objects, is one of spiritual sleep; but an ecstatic condition, in which the senses with the whole lower life are quiescent, and only pictures of Divine objects are reflected in the soul, as in a pure and untarnished mirror, is one of spiritual waking."

Being thus wakened by the interpreting angel, and his powers of spiritual vision stimulated by the question, "What seest thou?" he looks, and beholds a candlestick, all (of it) of gold, with a bowl, or oil vessel, "at the top of it" (indicating that it is designated as a fountain of supply for the candlestick), with seven מוצקות (*mutsaqoth*) "pipes," or little canals (literally "pourers"), connecting this vessel with each of the seven lamps on the candlestick.[1]

On either side (*i.e.*, one on the right and one on the left of the bowl) were two olive trees, each with a specially fruitful bough, or branch, which, as Kimchi puts it, "were

---

[1] For it is in the *distributive* sense that the expression *Shibh'ah v' Shibh'ah* must doubtless be understood.

full of olives, as ears are full of grain," and are therefore called *Shibalei hazēthim*—" ears of olives "—which poured golden oil from themselves, by means of two " spouts " or channels, into the vessel, for the supply of the candlestick.

On the prophet's asking, " What are these, my lord ? " the Interpreter answers, " Knowest thou not what these be ? " as much as to imply that the symbolism of this vision was such that the prophet might himself have been able to interpret had he understood the symbolism of the Tabernacle and Temple.

As a matter of fact, neither the Interpreter nor the Angel of Jehovah explain the symbolism of this vision, but only indicate the *message* which it conveyed to Zerubbabel at that time, and to the people of God generally in all time.

The candlestick itself—the central object in this vision—is doubtless a figurative representation of the seven-branched candlestick in the Temple. There it stood in the Holy Place (the figure of heavenly places not made with hands), not only as the emblem and representation of what the whole redeemed family shall finally be " when in union with their risen, glorified Lord they shall for ever shine in the sanctuary of God," but also *as typifying Israel's high calling in relation to the other nations.*

In his midst a great light had shone—the light of the self-revelation of the glory of Jehovah—not only for his own illumination, but that he might be the candlestick, the light-bearer, and light-diffuser all around.

It is for this reason that " when the Most High gave to the nations their inheritance, when He separated the children of men, He set the bounds of the peoples according to the number of the children of Israel " (Deut. xxxii. 8).

We know how terribly and sadly Israel failed to respond to God's purpose concerning Him. " *Thus saith the Lord God*"—through His prophet Ezekiel, in chap. v. of his prophecy—" *This is Jerusalem : I have set her in the midst of the nations, and countries are round about her,*"—that she may shine as a light in their midst, so that these nations and countries may see of her good works and glorify God,

—BUT *she hath changed My judgments into wickedness more than the nations, and My statutes more than the countries that are round about her : for they have rejected My judgments, and as for My statutes, they have not walked in them."*

Often did God in effect threaten Israel through the prophets to remove his candlestick ; but in His long-suffering for a long time, even after the sceptre, *the emblem of governmental power,* had been removed, the candlestick— *which is the emblem of Israel's religious or ecclesiastical position as witness for God in His corporate capacity*—was not taken away till the cup of his national iniquity was filled up in the rejection of Him who is the " Light of light," for the diffusion of which this very candlestick was formed, and in their final resistance of the Holy Spirit. Then the Kingdom of God was taken from them and "given to a nation bringing forth the fruits thereof."

On the disappearance of the candlestick from Israel, the *seven* golden candlesticks come into view as representing the new people of God, the Church of this dispensation planted on the earth, that during the period of Israel's blindness and darkness it might fulfil Israel's mission of shining before the Lord in His sanctuary, and letting its light stream out into the night of the world's darkness : the seven as representing the Church, instead of the one as representing Israel, is not without significance.

The seven Christian *ecclesiai* selected by the Lord out of the many Christian assemblies which already then existed even in that one pro-consular province of Asia, to be symbolised by the seven golden " *luchniai* " (lampstands), *are meant to represent the one Church of Christ through all time, and in all places, during the present dispensation.* It has not, like Israel, one earthly centre, and cannot be presented as an absolute unity. The seven are all mutually independent as to external order and government, yet were they meant to be one in the unity of the Spirit, under the one headship of Christ. But not only in relation to the Lord and to one another, but also in relation to the world outside, did the

Church of Christ, as originally *constituted*, possess both a *local* and a *catholic* unity. " The first," to quote a great master now with the Lord, " was symbolised by each of the candlesticks regarded individually; the second by all the seven collectively. At Ephesus, for example, all the saints who dwelt in that city were gathered into visible communion with each other. All light was with them; everything else in Ephesus was darkness; and therefore one candlestick fitly represented their condition. There was one point of concentrated light. But what each Church was in its own locality, that all the Churches unitedly were to the world around them. They were together separated; had a common calling and service; were alike one to the other; were ordered and nourished by the same hand. This was *catholic* unity, symbolised by the seven candlesticks standing together with the Lord in their midst. The proper unity of the Church is gone if either of these be wanting."[1] How glorious was the Apostolic Church in its original purity and lustre! How brightly did it shine! And how rapidly did it disseminate its light! Thus the Apostle Paul, for instance, writing to the Thessalonians only such a very brief while after the Church in that city was founded by him, could say : " *From you hath sounded forth the word of the Lord, not only in Macedonia and Achaia, but in every place your faith to Godward is gone forth, so that we need not to speak anything* " (1 Thess. i. 8).

But how long did this beautiful condition of things continue ? Already in the lifetime of the Apostles, germs of corruption began to manifest themselves, and they have continued ever since to develop; and though the long-suffering of God manifested in His dealings with Christendom has been as great, and even greater, than in His dealings with Israel, He has had, nevertheless, to remove from His sanctuary, one by one, the candlesticks of Gentile Christianity, and to disown them in their corporate capacity from being witnesses for the truth and representatives of Christ on the earth.

[1] *Thoughts on the Apocalypse*, B. W. Newton.

The history of corporate Gentile Christianity is not as the shining light that "shineth more and more unto the perfect day," as some who boast in the supposed progress and speak of the conversion of the world before the glorious appearing of Christ ignorantly suppose, but rather that of a bright dawn, developing into an increasingly dark and cloudy day, and ending in blackness of darkness. And there is no hope for Christendom which continued not in the goodness of God when once it is "cut off"; nor is there any promise of the restoration and relighting of *its* candlestick when once its light has been quenched in anti-Christian apostasy. But it is different with Israel. There is always hope in his end.

Not only shall the sceptre of governmental rule and the kingdom come back to the daughter of Jerusalem, after the long centuries of subjugation and oppression, but her candlestick, too, shall be restored after the long period of Israel's spiritual darkness and blindness, to shine in more resplendent glory than even in the past. This is the meaning of Zechariah's fifth vision, and it sets forth in symbol the great truth proclaimed by the former prophets in relation to Israel's future glory as the centre of light and blessing to all the nations of the earth, as, for instance, in Isa. lx. 1–3 : "*Arise, shine ; for thy light is come, and the glory of Jehovah is risen upon thee. For behold, darkness shall cover the earth, and gross darkness the peoples : but Jehovah shall arise upon thee, and His glory shall be seen upon thee. And nations shall come to thy light, and kings to the brightness of thy rising*"; and Isa. lxii. 1, 2 : "*For Zion's sake will I not hold my peace, and for Jerusalem's sake I will not rest, until her righteousness go forth as brightness, and her salvation as a lamp that burneth. And the nations shall see thy righteousness, and all kings thy glory : and thou shalt be called by a new name, which the mouth of Jehovah shall name.*"

That the light of Israel's restored candlestick will shine on throughout the millennial period in undiminished purity, and in greater—yea, in sevenfold brilliancy as compared with the past—is, I think, indicated by the additions to the candlestick in this vision as compared with the original in Exodus.

In the Tabernacle, in keeping with the Mosaic dispensation, the continuity of its light depended on the offerings of the people, who were commanded to bring "pure olive oil, beaten for the light; to cause a lamp to burn (lit., to ascend) continually"; and on the ministry of Aaron and his sons, who had to fill, and trim, and order, and light them every morning and evening (Ex. xxvii. 20, 21, xxx. 7, 8); but in our vision no attendant priests are necessary, nor offerings of oil from the people. The lamps are fed spontaneously from the *gullah*, or oil vessel, above the candlestick, the plentifulness of the flow of oil (emblematic of the abundant outpouring of the Holy Spirit) being set forth by the seven pipes (or "pourers"), which carried the supply to each.

There is yet one item in the symbolism of the candlestick which requires our attention—namely, the two olive trees (ver. 3), or "sons of oil" (ver. 14), which, by means of the two *tsanteroth*, or spouts, empty golden oil out of themselves into the *gullah*, or bowl.

Many fanciful interpretations have been given of this part of the vision, which, for lack of time and space, we will not stop to examine, but it is most in harmony with the scope of these visions (one of the great objects of which was to encourage the two heads, or leaders, of the restored remnant of the nation in their task of rebuilding the Temple) to regard the olive trees as representing Joshua the high priest, and Zerubbabel the prince. These were the two persons by whom the whole covenant people was then represented, and through whom it, in a very important sense, received the grace and the promises of God.

The words, "*These are the two that stand before the Lord of the whole earth*," must also lead us to the same conclusion. In the previous vision (iii. 1), which is so closely connected with that we are considering, Joshua is thus represented as " standing " before the Angel of Jehovah ; and in chap. iv. it is Zerubbabel who is specially mentioned by name.   It is fitting, therefore, that in the end the two who are so often mentioned together by Haggai and Zechariah should again be represented together in their united ministry. Though differently occupied, the one in more particularly " religious," and the other in civil duties, they both stand (intent on their ministry) before the Lord of the whole earth.

But, while in relation to the remnant of Israel at that time, and to the Temple then in building, we are to understand by these two " sons of oil " the actual persons of Joshua and Zerubbabel, it is certain that these two, considered *merely as individuals*, do not exhaust the symbol, for the simple reason that the supply of oil for the candlestick in a vision designed to describe the *abiding*, and especially the *future* position and mission of the congregation of Israel, could not be represented as dependent on the lives of two mortal men.   They must therefore be viewed standing here as the types or representatives of the kingly and priestly offices to which they respectively belonged —the only two orders (with the one other exception of the prophetic) which could properly be designated by the term " sons of oil," because of their being originally consecrated for their office by the ceremony of *anointing* (with oil), by which act they were, so to say, appointed as the *media* through whom " the spiritual and gracious gifts of God " were to be conveyed to His Church.

And both these divinely-appointed offices and functions in Israel, we must remember, were from the beginning designed to shadow forth what should ultimately be united in Him who, as set forth by Zechariah himself (vi. 13), would be " a Priest upon His throne "—the true and everlasting great High Priest, of whom Joshua and the whole order of the Aaronic priesthood were " men that were a sign " (iii. 8) ; and the just and ideal King (ix. 9), of whom the kingly function in Israel was also a type and prophecy. It is in *His* light, and by means of the golden oil of His

Spirit, which shall then be shed upon them abundantly, that Israel's candlestick shall yet shine with a sevenfold brilliancy for the illumination of all the nations of the earth.

II. *The Message* (vers. 6–10)

The contemplation of God's determinate counsel and the glimpse of Israel's future glory are to serve as a stimulus and encouragement to the leaders and people in the then present.

The prophet having with humility confessed his ignorance of the true import of the symbolism, the interpreting angel answered and said: " *This (vision in as far as it embodies a prophecy) is the word of Jehovah unto Zerubbabel, saying, Not by might, nor by power, but by My Spirit, saith Jehovah of hosts.*" The word חַיִל, *ḥayil* (" might "), which also means an " army," or " host," probably stands for the strength of many; while כֹּחַ, *ko'ach*, stands for that of one man. The two might be taken to express human strength and power of every description—physical, mental, and moral— individual, or the combined strength of the multitude. All of themselves can neither advance nor retard the accomplishment of His purpose. The real motive power by which Israel's mission, as set forth by the candlestick, shall eventually be fulfilled, namely, " My Spirit, saith Jehovah," must be the only resource also of Zerubbabel in the prosecution of the task of rebuilding the Temple which shall be the visible proof and symbol of the restored fellowship between Jehovah and His people, and hence an indispensable preparation for the accomplishment of Israel's mission as the light of the nations.

Now this Almighty Spirit of Jehovah " of Ts'bhaoth " was now present, dwelling in the midst of the returned remnant of the people; for, in effect this message through Zechariah is but an amplified reiteration of the word of Jehovah to Zerubbabel and his companion by the mouth of Haggai about four months before: " *Be strong ; for I am with you, saith Jehovah of hosts, according to the word that I covenanted with you when ye came out of Egypt, so My*

Spirit remaineth among you : fear ye not" (Hag. ii. 4, 5), which again (as is characteristic of all the notable utterances of the post-exilic prophets) is based on a great word of Jehovah through one of the former prophets, namely, Isa. lix. 21 : *" As for Me, this is My covenant with them, saith Jehovah : My Spirit that is upon thee, and My words which I have put in thy mouth, shall not depart out of thy mouth, nor out of the mouth of thy seed, nor out of the mouth of thy seed's seed, saith Jehovah, from henceforth and for ever."*

Relying only on God's Spirit, " the great mountain "— whether we understand it as a figurative expression for " the colossal difficulties, which rose up mountain high," and of the hindrances which were then in the way before the building could be completed ; or, with the Jewish Targum and Kimchi, and some eminent Christian interpreters, as the symbol of Gentile world-power, which is the real obstacle to the restoration of the theocratic kingdom, before Zerubbabel, as the instrument of God's Almighty Spirit—shall be turned into " a plain "; and he, who some fifteen years before was permitted amid great demonstrations of joy, not unmixed with sobs and tears, to lay the foundation (Ezra iii. 8, 13), shall yet bring forth the " headstone," accompanied by shoutings of joy and admiration, " Grace, grace (is) unto it ! "

In vers. 8–10 we have, so to say, a corroborative message from the mouth of the *Malakh Yehovah*, of the explanation given to the prophet by the angelic interpreter :

" *Moreover the word of Jehovah came unto me, saying, The hands of Zerubbabel have laid the foundation of this house ; his hands shall also finish it"* ; which, so far as the Temple which they were then building was concerned, was, as we know, fulfilled about four years after the prophesying of Haggai and Zechariah, namely, " on the third day of the month Adar, which was in the sixth year of the reign of Darius the king " (Ezra vi. 14, 15); but the words, " And thou shalt know that Jehovah of Ts'bhaoth hath sent me unto you " (which, as appears clear from a comparison with chap. ii. 9, must be ascribed, not to the *angelus interpres,* but to the *Malakh Yehovah*), show that the promise was not exhausted then, but that the work on which Zerubbabel was engaged is regarded as a type and pledge of the sure fulfilment of that which was set forth by the symbolism. The last words of the message sound a special note of encouragement to the dispirited remnant.

Toward so great a consummation the work they were then engaged upon might seem insignificant. Indeed this feeling had been one of the chief causes of the slow progress made in the work of building the House, and disposed them only too readily to yield to the opposition of their enemies, and for a time to desist from their task altogether, till Haggai and Zechariah were raised up " to prophesy to them in the Name of the God of Israel " (Ezra v. 1, 2).

When its foundation was laid, in the midst of the great joy which accompanied it, " many of the priests, and Levites, and chief of the fathers, which were ancient men," when they saw the modest dimensions, and remembered the very limited resources at their command, " wept with a loud voice, . . . so that the people could not discern the noise of the shout of joy from the noise of the weeping of the people " (Ezra iii. 10–13).

Even in comparison with the glory of the first House which had been destroyed, the one that was then building " was as nothing in their eyes " (Hag. ii. 3); but particularly in relation to the greater glory of their restoration and of the future House predicted by the former prophets, which should become the centre from which the light of Jehovah should stream forth to all the nations, the actual circumstances in which they then found themselves must have seemed indeed " a day of small things." Yet from God's point of view the task of the rebuilding on which they were then engaged was—because of its being a necessary step toward the fulfilment of His purpose as set forth in the symbolism of the candlestick—*the greatest and most important thing in the world, and formed the centre and motive of His providential dealings on the earth at that time.* Not on the great world-movements, but on the little " stone of lead " or "plummet" in the hand of Zerubbabel, who is thus indicated as superintending the work of building, do the seven eyes of God's special providence rest with complacency and joy; and as those eyes run to and fro through the whole earth, and nothing is hid from His omniscience, He will see to it that *nothing from without* shall now prevent the work being brought to a happy completion.

This is "the word of Jehovah unto Zerubbabel"; but as we look more closely at the message we seem to see the lineaments of Zerubbabel melt away into the features of the true Prince of the House of David, and the task on which he was then engaged merge into the building of the true "Temple of Jehovah" by "the Man whose name is The Branch," as set forth by the prophet in chap. vi. Messiah, the true Son of David, shall not only be the real builder of the future literal Temple, which through the millennial period shall be the centre of the true worship of Jehovah on this earth, and the House of Prayer for all nations; but also of the much more glorious mystical Building, which through eternity shall be for the habitation of God through the Spirit. Of this spiritual Temple He is Himself the "sure Foundation," the precious Corner-stone and Head-stone of the Corner, as well as the Master Builder.

Nineteen centuries ago, in His life of suffering, death of atonement, and glorious resurrection, the foundation of that Temple was laid. Since then living stones, both Jewish and Gentile, from all parts of the earth are being gathered by His Spirit, and "the building fitly framed together" is growing toward completion; but the exceeding magnificence and the spiritual glory of this mystical Temple will not be manifested until, at the glorious appearing of our Lord Jesus, the Head-stone is, so to say, brought forth, and Christ is for ever joined with His Church.

Then, when covered with the beauty of her Lord, and made perfect in the comeliness which He shall put upon her, there shall be shouting of joy and admiration, not only by men, but by the hosts of heaven, חֵן חֵן לָהּ, " Grace, beauty, loveliness (is) unto it!" *Ḥen, Ḥen, lah!*

Chapter 7

THE SIXTH VISION
THE FLYING ROLL
Zechariah 5:1-4

Then again I lifted up mine eyes, and saw, and behold, a flying roll. And he said unto me, What seest thou? And I answered, I see a flying roll; the length thereof is twenty cubits, and the breadth ten cubits. Then said he unto me, This is the curse that goeth forth over the face of the whole land : for every one that stealeth shall be cut off on the one side according to it ; and every one that sweareth shall be cut off on the other side according to it. I will cause it to go forth, saith Jehovah of hosts, and it shall enter into the house of the thief, and into the house of him that sweareth falsely by My name : and it shall abide in the midst of his house, and shall consume it with the timber thereof and the stones thereof.

Chapter 7

THE first five visions are indeed prophecies " of Hope and of Glory." They abound, as we have seen, in most glorious promises of restoration and enlargement, of temporal and spiritual prosperity and blessing—promises which, in their full and exhaustive sense, are yet to be fulfilled, when " Jehovah shall arise and have mercy upon Zion," and yet again " choose Israel."

But before that longed-for day of blessing can at last come ; before the beautiful symbolism of the fifth vision shall at last be realised, and Israel's restored candlestick shall once again, and in greater splendour and purity than ever before, shed abroad the light of Jehovah throughout the millennial earth—both the land and people must be cleansed from everything that defileth, or worketh abomination, or maketh a lie. This is the import of the dark episode unfolded in the two visions in the 5th chapter, which we are now to consider.

The God of Israel has two methods in dealing with sin and removing iniquity, both of which are in perfect accord with the absolute holiness of His character. One of these methods—the one He delights in—is the method of *grace*. This is beautifully unfolded in the 3rd chapter, where we are shown how that, on the ground of His sovereign immutable " choice " (ver. 2), and because of the full atonement and perfect righteousness accomplished by His Righteous Servant, " The Branch," the iniquity of that land shall be removed " in one day," and repentant Israel (upon whom the Spirit of grace and supplication shall in that day

143

be poured) shall be cleansed from all defilement (as signified by the removal of the "filthy garments") and clothed in "rich apparel," and with the "fair," or "clean," mitre on his head, on which the words *Qodesh la-Yehovah* —"Holy to Jehovah"—are graven, shall be fitted to go forth among the nations as the priests of Jehovah and the ministers of our God.

But what about those who persist in their wickedness, and, in spite of the marvellous display of God's grace, "will not learn righteousness," but continue even "in the land of uprightness" (as Immanuel's land shall then be called) "to deal unjustly, and will not behold the majesty of Jehovah" (Isa. xxxvi. 10)? With them God's method is that of *judgment*. Sin must be purged away, iniquity must be stamped out in the city of God; and when the sinner is so wedded to his sin that he is no longer separable from it, he becomes the object of God's curse, and must be "cleansed away" from the earth. In short, then, the two visions in chap. v. give us the reverse side of the truth unfolded in the first four chapters.

They show us that if there is grace and forgiveness with God, it is not in order to encourage men to think lightly of sin, but that "He might be feared" (Ps. cxxx. 4). They also take us, so to say, a step backward, and show us that, before the glorious things symbolically set forth in the first five visions will finally be fulfilled, a period of moral darkness and corruption, and of almost universal apostasy, was yet to intervene.

The Flying Roll

But now for a brief exposition of the sixth vision.

The prophet having for a season been absorbed in meditation on the wonderful things which had been presented to him in the last vision, "turns" himself, his attention being very probably called anew by the interpreting angel—and, lifting up his eyes, sees a roll twenty cubits in length and ten cubits in breadth flying in the air.

On addressing a silent look of inquiry to his angelic instructor as to the meaning of this strange sight he is told, " This is the curse that goeth forth over the whole land," etc.

The מְגִלָּה, *megillah*, " roll " or " scroll," as the emblem of a message or pronouncement of solemn import from God to man, is used in other scriptures. Thus, in Ezek. ii. 9, 10 we find a strikingly parallel passage : "*And I looked, and behold an hand was put forth unto me ; and, lo, a roll of a book (megillath sepher) was therein ; and he spread it before me, and it was written within and without : and there was written therein lamentations, and mourning, and woe.*"

The *megillah* which Zechariah beheld was also " spread " out, or open, else its dimensions could not have been seen ; and it also was written " within and without," as may be gathered from the words " *on this side and on the other side, according to it,*" which I take to be the most satisfactory rendering of the Hebrew *mizzeh kamoah*, which is twice repeated in ver. 3.

The same was true of the tables of the law, of which the same words are used to describe the fact that " they were written on both sides : *on the one side and on the other* (מִזֶּה וּמִזֶּה, *mizzeh-u-mizzeh*) were they written " (Ex. xxxii. 15).

What was written on this roll may be gathered from the words, " This is the curse" *ha-alah* (answering to the " lamentations and mourning and woe " of Ezekiel's *megillah*)—which might refer to the awful catalogue of curses which Moses foretold would come upon Israel in case of their disobedience, recorded in Deut. xxviii. 15–68, and which in chap. xxx. 1 of the same book are spoken of in the singular as " *the curse.*"

But it seems to me more satisfactory to regard the word as describing in a more general way the curse which *the law as a whole* contains within itself—the sequel, so to say, to the breaking its commands expressed in a solemn sentence : " *Cursed be he that confirmeth not the words of this law to do them.*"

It is true that only two transgressions are here specified
for which their perpetrators are to be pursued and overtaken by the curse—namely, perjury and theft; but these
two are most probably mentioned as samples and summaries of the whole. For the expression "everyone that
sweareth" must be understood as explained in the 4th verse,
as "*swearing falsely by the Name of Jehovah*," and is thus a
violation of the Third Command, which is found in the first
table of the law which summarises man's duty to God; and
"everyone that stealeth" breaks the Eighth Commandment,
which is found on the second table, which summarises
man's duty to his neighbour.[1] So that Baumgarten and
Hengstenberg are not far wrong when they write that one
side of the roll contained the judgments of God against the
transgressors of the Command, "Thou shalt love the Lord
thy God with all thine heart, and with all thy soul, and
with all thy might"; and on the other the judgments
against the transgressors of the Command, "Thou shalt
love thy neighbour as thyself."

Against all such the *megillah*, with its awful contents,
"*goeth forth*," being set in motion (as we see from the 4th
verse) by "Jehovah of hosts"; and is therefore seen "flying"—that is, travelling rapidly over the whole land,[2] and

---

[1] Baumgarten points out that the prophet selects the middle Command from
each of the tables.

[2] אֶרֶץ, *eretz*, means *earth* as well as *land*, and several commentators have
defended the rendering in the A.V., "over the face of the whole earth." But
the translation adopted in the R.V. is doubtless the correct one—first, because,
as Pusey points out, those upon whom the curse was to fall were those who
swore falsely by the Name of Jehovah, which was true of *Judah* only; secondly,
as Keil observes, in the vision of the Ephah, which is closely connected with that
of the Flying Roll, "the land" is contrasted with "the land of Shinar." The
reference to the two tables of the law also confines the vision primarily to those
who were under the law. Yet it is true also that "since the moral law abides
under the gospel there is an ultimate application in these two visions in the
5th chapter also to Christendom, which was to spread over *the whole earth*."
Remember, dear reader, whatever the primary application of this vision, that
God's curse will finally overtake *all* workers of iniquity, and that He will
"render to every man according to his works: to them that by patience in well-
doing seek for glory and honour and incorruption, eternal life; but to them that
are factious, and obey not the truth, but obey unrighteousness, wrath and
indignation, tribulation and anguish, upon every soul of man that worketh evil--

signifying the *swiftness* with which the judgments of God shall finally overtake the wicked.

The special dimensions of the roll, which the prophet so carefully notes, are also not without significance. It was twenty cubits long and ten cubits broad, which corresponds both with the porch of Solomon's Temple (1 Kings vi. 3) and with the Holy Place of the Tabernacle. This is certainly not accidental. Hengstenberg, who, together with Kimchi and other Jewish commentators, considers the reference to be to the Temple, says: " The porch, the uttermost portion of the actual Temple, was the spot from which God was supposed to hold intercourse with His people " (1 Kings vii. 7). Hence the altar of burnt-offering stood before the porch in the forecourt of the priests, and when any great calamity fell upon the land the priests approached still nearer to the porch to offer their prayers, that they might, as it were, embrace the feet of their angry Father (Joel ii. 17).

By giving to the flying roll (the symbol of the Divine judgments upon the covenant nation) the same dimensions as those of the porch, the prophet appears to intimate that these judgments were a direct result of the theocracy, and originate in the very fact of Israel's relationship to God, in accordance with His Word through the prophet Amos: " You only have I known of all the families of the earth, therefore will I visit on you all your iniquities " (iii. 2), for which reason also judgment begins first at the house of God.

But there is a greater probability in the suggestion of Keil, Kliefoth, and others, that the dimensions are taken, not from the porch of the Temple, but from the Holy Place of the Tabernacle, just as the symbolic candlestick in the preceding vision is also the Mosaic candlestick of the Tabernacle, and not of the Temple. And the true reason *why* the dimensions of the roll containing God's curse against the breakers of His law are taken from the

of the Jew first, and also of the Greek ; but glory and honour and peace to every man that worketh good, to the Jew first, and also to the Greek : for there is no respect of persons with God " (Rom. ii. 6-11).

sanctuary is probably that suggested by Kliefoth, who says :
" The fact that the writing which brings the curse upon
sinners has the same dimensions as the Tabernacle signifies
that *the measure will be meted out according to the Holy
Place* "; or, in the words of an English theologian : " Men
are not to be judged as to sin by their own measures, or
weighed in their own false balances—*the measure of the
sanctuary* is that by which man's actions are to be weighed "
(1 Sam. ii. 3).[1] And the judgment which is to fall on the
unrepentant, unpardoned transgressor will not only be
" according to the measure of the sanctuary," but in strict
correspondence with the majesty and holiness of the law
which has been broken : " For every one that stealeth shall
be purged out " (literally, *cleansed away*, " as something
defiled and defiling which has to be cleared away as
offensive ") " on (or ' from ') this side according to it "
(namely, as already explained, *according to the writing* on
the one side of it); " and every one that sweareth shall be
cleansed away according to " (the writing) " on the other
side of it." [2]

---

[1] Dr. C. H. H. Wright.

[2] The verb נִקָּה (*niqqah*) is here the *Niphal*. The *Piel* is alike in form. The
probable meaning of the root is to *carve out*, to *hollow*, then to *be empty*, to *be
pure, free from fault*. Hence the *Niphal* is used in the sense of to *be pure, free
from fault*, followed by מִן (*min*, " from," " out of "). Luther has taken it here
in this meaning, translating " for all thieves shall according to this letter be
pronounced pious" (*denn alle Diebe werden nach diesem Briefe fromm
gesprochen*). That is, it is a curse upon the land that theft and perjury are
regarded no more as crying evils, nor as deserving of punishment. Similarly the
Syriac. But this is evidently not the meaning. Modern scholars rightly render
it *shall be cleared*, or *cleansed away*. " The verb is used of a city being emptied
of inhabitants, *i.e.*, laid waste and ruined (Isa. iii. 26). Here the verb may be
employed in the sense of being rendered solitary, emptied of society, driven out
of communion (Fürst), or as signifying extirpated (Gesenius). It has probably
the signification of cleaning away, as the Greek καθαρίζω in Mark vii. 19, as
Pusey suggests, or as ἐκκαθαίρω in I Cor. v. 7, as Pressel has given."

The late Rev. D. Edwards, for many years an honoured missionary to the
Jews in connection with the Free Church of Scotland, wrote some thirty-five
years ago a striking pamphlet, which is not now in my possession, on the two
visions of this 6th chapter of Zechariah, in which he gave expression to the view
that the Flying Roll symbolised the false, counterfeit law, namely, the Talmud,
and doctrines of modern Judaism, which (in contrast to the holy law of God)
justified, or " declared innocent," all manner of transgressors.

The 4th verse is one of the most solemn in the whole Bible, as showing what an awful thing it is to come under God's curse against sin. *"And I will cause it to go forth"* —that is, the curse, with its doom of judgment, which God keeps, so to say, in His storehouse, against the day of vengeance—*"and it shall enter into the house of the thief, and into the house of him that sweareth falsely by My Name."*

(*a*) " I *will bring it forth,* and *it shall enter."*

Here we see the certainty with which God's judgments shall finally overtake the wicked. Man may avoid detection of his sins and punishment at the hands of his fellowman, but he cannot escape God. " Be sure your sin will find you out " ; and so will its inevitable punishment.

" It shall enter into *the house* "—the place where the transgressor may think that he can hide himself, where he may think himself most secure ; but he shall find that God's avenging justice cannot be kept out, even by strong walls or iron gates.

(*b*) " And *it shall abide* in the midst of his house." [1] Here we see the continuance, or *permanency* of God's judgment against the wicked. The word for " abide," or " remain," as in the A.V., is לָנֶה, *laneh,* from לֻן, *lun,* " to lodge," " to spend the night in " ; the idea being that the curse will not only pay him a passing visit, but shall " lodge " there—that is, abide by night as well as by day, until it accomplish that for which it was sent, its utter destruction.[2]

Among Jewish commentators Rashi interprets נקה (*niqqah*) in the sense of being freed, or justified—the same as adopted by Luther and Mr. Edwards ; but Kimchi says the meaning of נקה is " *shall be cut off.*" And this, or rather " *shall be cleansed away,*" *i.e.,* extirpated, is here doubtless the true meaning of the verb, as shown above.

[1] The same verb is found in Ps. xci. 1, but there it is used to describe the blessed privilege of the righteous, who, " dwelling in the secret place of the Most High " (by day), shall also " abide," literally " lodge " (*i.e.,* at night), under the shadow of the Almighty.

[2] Pusey.—Dr. Wright, in a note, quotes by way of illustration the classical instance recorded by Herodotus (Book vi. 86), which shows that the moral law of God was not only revealed to Israel and graven on the tables of stone, but was originally also written by His finger on the conscience of man, who still retains a shadowy tracing of it, so to say, in his consciousness. It is the story

And the punishment which these transgressions often bring down upon man, even in this life, must be regarded as "mere premonitory droppings of the tempest of wrath which will one day overwhelm the ungodly."

(*c*) But there is yet a climax in the train of calamities which the curse will bring to the house of the wicked. It shall not only "dwell" there, but it "*shall consume it with the timber thereof, and the stones thereof*." Here we see the *terribleness* of the punishment which sin brings down upon itself. It shall be utterly "cleansed away," or "consumed" from the midst of God's congregation, together with those sinners who are no longer separable from it.

The terms in the last sentence are almost identical with those used of the house stricken with leprosy in Lev. xiv. 45, which, too, had to be destroyed, "both the stones thereof and the timber thereof"; and this undoubted allusion supplies another hint of the fact that already in the Old Testament leprosy was regarded as a type of sin, and that what that terrible and loathsome disease did for men's bodies and their earthly habitations, sin does for men's souls, not only in relation to the life that now is, but also in relation to that which is to come. There is only one way by which we can escape the curse of a broken law, and that is, instead of being "cleansed away" *with* our sins by God's wrath into perdition, to be cleansed *from* our sins in that fountain which God has opened in the pierced side of Messiah for sin and uncleanness, and which makes the

about Glaucus. The name of this man was held in high repute for integrity, and hence a Milesian came to him to deposit a sum of money on trust. The deposit was accepted by Glaucus. But when the money was required by the sons of the depositor, who presented the tallies in support of their claim, Glaucus hesitated to restore it. He consulted the oracle of Delphi whether he might perjure him-self and appropriate the money. The priestess told him that it was best for the present to do as he desired, because death was the common lot of the honest and the dishonest. "Yet oath has a son, nameless, handless, footless, but swift ; he pursues until he seize and destroy the whole race and house." On hearing this, Glaucus begged to be pardoned for his question ; but the priestess replied that it was as bad to have tempted the god as to have done the deed. Glaucus ulti-mately restored the money to its owners. Yet it was noted that his whole family became extinct, which was considered as a punishment for consulting the oracle whether he might perjure himself.

vilest "whiter than snow." Yes, blessed be God! for as many as can say with the Apostle, "Christ hath redeemed us from the curse of the law, having become a curse for us; for it is written, Cursed is he that hangeth on a tree" (Gal. iii. 13).

Yet one word more in conclusion in reference to the yet unfulfilled prophetic element in this vision.

The more immediate application may have been to the remnant which returned from Babylon, to whom Zechariah spoke; and there may be some truth in the suggestion of Dr. Fausset that the "theft" and "false swearing" specially referred to in this vision has a reference to the *sacrilege* of which the Jews then were guilty in withholding the portions due from them for the Levites (Neh. xiii. 10), and in holding back the due tithes and offerings from the Lord (Mal. iii. 8).

Thus "they *robbed* God by neglecting to give Him His due in building His house, whilst they built their own houses foreswearing their obligations to Him."

There is also, as we have seen, a general application of the solemn truth contained in this vision to all who make any profession of the name of God at all times; yet the full and manifest fulfilment of this symbolic prophecy will not take place till the time of the end, when, in the final stage of both Jewish and anti-Christian apostasy, iniquity shall reach its climax, and the majority of those who profess to be the Lord's people shall join in "*transgressing and lying against Jehovah, and in departing away from their God, speaking oppression and revolt, conceiving and uttering from the heart words of falsehood*" (Isa. lix. 13). Then the final separation shall take place, and the wicked be "cut off" from the congregation of the Lord, and all sin and iniquity be finally cleansed away from the "holy land" (Zech. ii. 12), and from "off the face of the whole earth."

Chapter 8

THE SEVENTH VISION
THE EPHAH
Zechariah 5:5-11

Then the angel that talked with me went forth, and said unto me, Lift up now thine eyes, and see what is this that goeth forth. And I said, What is it? And he said, This is the ephah that goeth forth. He said moreover, This is their appearance in all the land (and behold, there was lifted up a talent of lead); and this is the woman sitting in the midst of the ephah. And he said unto me, This is wickedness; and he cast her down into the midst of the ephah: and he cast the weight of lead upon the mouth thereof. Then lifted I up mine eyes and saw, and, behold, there came forth two women, and the wind was in their wings; now they had wings like the wings of a stork; and they lifted up the ephah between earth and heaven. Then said I to the angel that talked with me, Whither do these bear the ephah? And he said unto me, To build her a house in the land of Shinar: and when it is prepared, she shall be set there in her own place.

Chapter 8

WE now come to the second of the two visions contained in the 5th chapter, which, together, set forth the full and final removal, not only of the *guilt* of sin, but of sin itself (especially in its final and yet future form of "*wickedness*" or *lawlessness*)—and that by means of judgment—from off the "holy land," and from the very presence of His redeemed and purified people.

What the Prophet saw

After instructing the prophet as to the meaning of the preceding vision, the Interpreting Angel had again withdrawn for awhile, and the prophet was left to himself to meditate on the solemn significance of the Flying Roll. Then the angel "went forth" (probably from the choirs of angels among whom he had retired in the interval, as Pusey suggests), and telling the prophet once more to lift up his eyes, he beholds another object, which the Angel tells him is "*the ephah which goeth forth*," and adds the enigmatical words: "*This is their resemblance* (lit., '*their eye*') *in all the land.*"

As the prophet looks, the cover, consisting of a circular mass, or "talent," of lead, was lifted up, and he beheld a woman (lit., "one woman") sitting in the midst of the ephah, of whom the angel said, pointing to her: "*This is the Wickedness.*" As there is evidently an attempt on the part of the woman to get out, or escape, the angel casts her down into the midst of the ephah: "*And he cast the weight* (lit., '*stone*') *of lead upon the mouth thereof.*"

Then the prophet saw two women with wings like the

155

wings of a stork "coming forth" from the invisible, and
the wind was in their wings, and they lifted up the ephah
between the earth and the heaven.   On his inquiring of the
angel : " *Whither do these bear the ephah ?* " the answer was :
" *To build her an house in the land of Shinar : and when*
(or ' *if* ') *it be prepared* (or ' *established* ') *it shall be set
there upon her own base.*"

The Significance of the Symbolism

Let me now try very simply to explain the various
items in this vision in the order in which they occur in the
text.

(*a*) The *ephah*, the same as *bath*, was the largest
measure for dry goods in use among the Jews,[1] though
there is still some difference of opinion as to its exact size
and capacity.   The most general interpretation of this
symbol—the one which I myself have previously held—is
that it signified the (full) measure of Israel's sins, beyond
which there is to be no more forgiveness, but a carrying
away, or banishing from the land, or (as some interpreters
will have it) from " the earth."   Thus, already one of the
Church Fathers, quoting the solemn words of our Lord,
" *Fill ye up the measure of your fathers,*" says : " The
measure, then, which the prophet saw pointed to the
filling-up of the measure of the transgression against
Himself " ;[2] and another says : " The angel bids him
behold the sins of the people Israel heaped together in a
perfect measure, and the transgression of all fulfilled, that
the sins which escaped notice one by one, might, when
collected together, be laid open to the eyes of all, and
Israel might go forth from its place, and it might be shown
to all what she was in her own land." [3]

A somewhat similar interpretation is given by Kliefoth
(who is followed by Keil and others), who says : " Just as

---

[1] The '*omer*, which contained ten ephahs, appears, as Keil points out, to
have had only an ideal existence, namely, for the purpose of calculation.

[2] Cyril.   [3] Jerome.

in a bushel the separate grains are all collected together, so will the individual sinners over the whole earth be brought into a heap when the curse of the end (contained in the Flying Roll) goes forth over the whole earth." [1]

But, though it is a solemn truth that God allows evil fully to develop itself, and iniquity to fill up its full measure of guilt before He finally interposes in judgment, the usual interpretations quoted above overlook the fact that the ephah instead of being represented as the measure into which the people pile up their iniquities, is spoken of as itself "*going forth*" (הַיּוֹצֵאת, the same expression as is used of the Flying Roll in ver. 3) to pervade the people with its influence, and to stamp upon it, so to say, its own characteristic features, so that "this shall be their appearance ('their aspect,' or 'resemblance') in all the land." [2]

If we ask ourselves what was this new power, or principle, which exercised such a mighty formative influence over the Jewish people ever since the Babylonian Captivity, and which is gradually also bringing all the other nations of the earth under its sway, the answer is *trade* or *commerce, of which the ephah is the natural emblem.*

With their banishment to Babylon and subsequent dispersion and peculiar position among the nations, there not only began an altogether new period of Jewish history, but there commenced also the processes by which the bulk of the nation became gradually transformed from an agricultural and pastoral people into a nation of merchant-men,[3] and the new occupations into which they were forced

---

[1] So also Bredenkamp, in his *Prophet Sacharja*, in almost exactly the same words : "Wie in einem Scheffel die einzelnen Körner gesammelt werden, so werden alle Gottlose in diesem epha gesammelt, so dass sie ein Weib ausmachen."

[2] The LXX have either had another MS reading, namely, עֲוֺנָם (*avonam*), "their iniquity," instead of the present Hebrew text of עֵינָם (*'ēnam*), "eye," or appearance, or have simply blundered in their translation, for they render the sentence, "this is their iniquity in all the earth," a reading which has been adopted by several of the German commentators. But there is no reason to doubt the correctness of the Masoretic text.

[3] This is the explanation given in the Targum and by Rashi. Kimchi, who quite unjustifiably applies this vision to the Ten Tribes, gives the following far-fetched interpretation : "He showed him an ephah, which is a measure, to

by the altered circumstances tended in a peculiar sense to develop the two transgressions (namely, *theft* and *perjury*) which are specified in the preceding vision of the Flying Roll, with which this vision of the Ephah stands very closely related. Idolatry, into which they were so liable to fall, was for ever left behind in Babylon; but a godless commercialism, with its temptations "to make the ephah small and the shekel great, and to deal falsely with balances of deceit" (Amos viii. 5), eventually becomes not less hateful to God—not only because it has too often been supported by *theft* and *perjury*, which, as we have seen, are transgressions of the central commands of both tables of the Law, but because it was destined to develop a new *system* in which all iniquity would finally be summed up.

(*b*) In conjunction with the ephah we have the כִּכָּר, *kikar*, which the English Version renders "talent." The Hebrew word literally means "a circle," and thus *kikar*

signify that God had measured out to them measure for measure ; for, according as they had done by continuing many days in their wickedness, from the day that the kingdom was divided until the day that they were led away captive ; and as they had not had one out of all their kings who turned them to good, but, on the contrary, they all walked in an evil way : according, I say, as they had continued long in evil, so they shall be many days in captivity—this is measure for measure ; therefore the prophet saw an ephah which is a measure."

Among German commentators, Pressel, in his *Commentar zu Haggai, Sacharja, und Maleachi*, is the only one who, as far as I know, has caught what, on mature consideration, seems to me the true significance of the ephah, and he is followed by Dr. C. H. H. Wright.

Lange, in his *Bibelwerk*, refers somewhat contemptuously to Pressel's view, his great objection being expressed in the words : "Wie wenn etwa von einem heutigen judenviertel die Rede wäre, und nicht von der Geheiligten Colonie zu Jerusalem" ("as if the subject dealt with was a modern Jewish quarter instead of the sanctified colony in Jerusalem"). But the answer to this objection is that the present state of the Jewish people as seen "*im heutigen judenviertel*" cannot be dissociated from Israel's past or future. That the beginning of the new power of commercialism as associated with the Jewish people can be traced back to the dispersion, and began already to assert itself in Zechariah's time, is a matter of history. Beside this, these two visions in chap. v. do not set forth the "sanctified colony in Jerusalem," but rather show how transgressors shall be "cut off" (or "cleansed away"), and how the evil which is the very embodiment of "wickedness," or "lawlessness," shall finally be banished from the "holy land," so that *those who remain* after the purifying judgment shall "be called holy, even every one that is written among the living in Jerusalem" (Isa. iv. 3).

leḥem, "a circle of bread," is used to denote a round loaf.[1]

The word, as Dr. Wright points out, is not elsewhere found in the signification of a *cover,* though that is a possible sense. " It is constantly used of a fixed weight, by which gold, silver, and other things are weighed and measured, and is naturally spoken of in such a meaning here in connection with the Ephah, as the latter was the usual measure of capacity. The talent was the largest measure of quantity, and the weight was made of lead as the most common heavy metal, and was used in all commercial transactions for weighing out money."

That a " talent," the other chief emblem and instrument of trade, should have been seen by the prophet as forming the *cover* of the ephah, is of solemn significance, as will be shown further on.

(*c*) The " talent," or circular mass of lead, being lifted,[2] the prophet beheld a *woman*[3] sitting in the midst of the ephah.

" And he said " (*i.e.*, the Angel, as if to call anew the prophet's special attention), " this is the Wickedness "—the very embodiment of iniquity, rendered in the Septuagint ἀνομία, *lawlessness.*

---

[1] Ex. xxix. 23 ; 1 Sam. ii. 36.

[2] According to Pressel and Dr. Wright the woman was sitting (as it were, enthroned) in the ephah carrying the *kikar,* or talent of lead (the emblem of the means by which her traffic is carried on), in her lap. They render the 7th verse thus : " And behold a talent of lead was being lifted up (*i.e.* carried), and I saw, and this was one woman sitting (or ' as she sat ') in the middle of the ephah." But, though this is a possible though somewhat forced rendering of the verb נשׂאת (which is the Niphal participle fem. of נשׂא), it seems to me clear from the 8th verse that the " talent " formed the *cover.* The impression left on the mind by reading the narrative of the vision in the original is certainly that there is an attempted escape on the part of the woman from the ephah, and that the Angel casts the talent on the mouth of the ephah with a view to secure her, that she may be safely carried to the land of Shinar. It is for this reason, I suppose, that it may serve as a cover, or circular lid—apart from its emblematic significance as the instrument of trade—that a talent of *lead,* consisting of a large, circular, undefined mass, is seen in the vision, instead of one of gold, or of silver, which in size would be very much smaller.

[3] *Isshah achath*—literally, " one woman " The words, " and this is one woman," are those of the Interpreting Angel, who proceeds in the next verse to describe her character.

The woman is usually taken by commentators to symbolise the Jewish people, which, when the measure of sin shall have become full, would be carried away into captivity. But the seventy years' captivity in Babylon was now at an end, and the idea of a retrospective significance of the symbolism of this vision, which Jerome and Rosenmüller adopt, seems to me untenable. All the other visions of Zechariah relate to the future—as Hengstenberg well observes, why should this be the sole exception? In the judgment of the Flying Roll a coming judgment is foretold. Why should this one of the Ephah be referred to the past?

Neither can it be properly referred to the subsequent captivity, as Hengstenberg and others attempt to do. There was, indeed, another dispersion of the Jewish people after the restoration from Babylon, but that could not well be represented in any special sense as a carrying away " into the land of Shinar." Besides, as I have tried to show in the introductory remarks to the exposition of the preceding vision of the Flying Roll, the scope and purport of the two visions in chap. v. are not the *punishment of the nation*, but the *cleansing* of the restored people and land, and the stamping out and banishment *from their midst* not only of the *guilt* of sin, but of iniquity or " wickedness " itself.

We regard, therefore, the woman in this vision, not as a personification of the Jewish people, nor as a collective representation of individual sinners who are finally gathered into one heap in the ephah, *but as delineating the (then as yet hidden) moral system of which the ephah is the emblem.*

And it is not inappropriate that the system engendered by the ephah, which in its essence is the worship of Mammon, should be represented by a woman, " because of the power it displays as a temptress, whereby it exercises such an enticing and dangerous influence over the souls of men." Or, as Grotius observed: This form of wickedness is here described as a woman " because she is the mother of thefts and perjuries, and of all crimes." But though this vision, like all the rest, has primary reference to *the* land and *the* people—and the purport of its message is that the system which is characterised as the Wickedness (and is altogether alien and opposed to the principles of the redeemed and sanctified community in the land in which the King of Righteousness shall have His seat) shall be banished to the place, or sphere, to which it originally belongs—it is a solemn truth that this same evil power of the ephah, with its all-pervading controlling influence, is " going forth " also in the whole world; so that of all the civilised nations in particular it must be said : " This is their aspect, or resemblance, in all the earth." [1]

It is a striking and noteworthy fact, which no intelligent man can fail to observe, that commerce is more and more bringing the nations under its sway.

It now sets up the governments and dictates the policies of the nations. It is for it that the mighty armaments are being built and that wars are being made.

In all the earth and among all nations that which is symbolised by the ephah is becoming the great controlling centre of society. " The producing power of manufacture, the distributing skill of the merchant, the controlling power of those who trade in money and command the circulating medium of commerce—these and similar interests, when combined, are able to speak with a voice which no government can refuse to hear. Their will is potent. Legislation and government accommodate themselves to their demands."

That, for instance, " which is *most* distinctive in the present condition of England is her commercial system. Commerce, or the wealth and influence thence arising, has become the mainspring of England's energies—the chief bulwark of her social institutions, the pillar of her government. When ecclesiastical power fell, and the feudal aristocracy became gradually enfeebled, and when the steady advance of the people seemed to make democracy (perhaps revolutionary democracy) the sure end of the

---

[1] אֶרֶץ, *eretz*—as already explained—means both " land " and " earth," though its primary use in this vision is of the " land."

social movement, there was gradually being formed in this country a new aristocracy, more potent than any, whether ecclesiastical or hereditary, that had preceded—the aristocracy of wealth. The expressions 'commercial interest,' 'manufacturing interest,' 'moneyed interest,' 'Indian interest,' and the like, suggest sufficiently intelligible ideas to English minds. The ramifications of these interests are so various and so extended that the mass of society is effectually reached and controlled by their influence; and thus a power has been consolidated the like to which has never before existed. In England this power is learning to work in harmony with the State. Indeed, the State has virtually become its organ. Plutocracy is a comprehensive, not an exclusive system. Its elasticity is great. It can adapt itself to the changing circumstances of the hour, and receiving within its circle both the aristocrat and the democrat, it provides a place of honour and influence for both.

" In its relations to ancient systems, it seeks, not to annihilate, but rather to modify, adapt, harmonise, and employ. It possesses, therefore, not only its own intrinsic weight, but is acquiring also all the weight which governmental authority can give. No other interest, whether royal or ecclesiastic, aristocratic or popular, is allowed to throw any effectual impediment in its course. Virtually, its will is paramount. The appropriate device of England would not be either the crown or the mitre, the coronet or the sword, but some emblem of commerce. An 'ephah' should be emblazoned on her banners. Our Government is a commercial Government, not because England happens to be a mercantile country, but because manufacturing and trading interests supremely sway her councils, and all other interests are being made subordinate. Such are the features which characteristically mark the period during which the powers of civilisation have been renovated in this Western corner of the Roman world.

" The abasement of ecclesiastical *supremacy*, the establishment of constitutional monarchy, and the rise of commerce into sovereign influence, may be regarded as accomplished facts. They distinctively characterise England; and finally they will equally characterise every other kingdom that falls within the Roman world. The success of England naturally causes her to be imitated. Her influence, which is great, is exerted, as might be expected, for the propagation of her principles, and the circumstances of the hour favour these principles. We cannot marvel at this, for the Scriptures plainly declare that such shall be the principles of the closing period of our dispensation. Whatever opinion may be formed as to the particular city indicated in the 18th of the Revelation, this at least is evident, that that chapter describes a closing scene in the world's present history, and speaks of ' merchants being the great men of the earth,' and of a commercial city being ' queen of the nations.'

" But it may be asked, Why should this be regretted ? Is an ephah the symbol of evil ? In other words, Is commerce *necessarily* sinful ? We reply, No ; commerce is not *necessarily* sinful. Commerce may be the mere exchange on just and righteous principles of the productions of various regions, or of various labourers. The effecting such exchange may involve no course of conduct that militates against the principles of God, or sacrifices His truth. But it may be otherwise. If commerce comes into such supremacy as to make her merchants the great men of the earth, the influences that governmentally order the nations would in that case fall into her hand. The world —educationally, politically, religiously, socially—would be virtually under her control. How blessed if her principles were the principles of God ! But if the arrangements which are to characterise the nations as the latter day draws nigh are as evil as the Scriptures declare them to be, then they who by means of their commercial greatness control or sustain these arrangements must be the very pillars of the last great system of evil, and the commercial period of the world's history becomes the period of its systematised transgression." [1]

[1] *Babylon and Egypt*, by B. W. Newton.

It is most probably, then, because of the part this system is to play in connection with the final apostasy, that it is characterised by the Angel with such emphasis as הָרִשְׁעָה—" *the* wickedness," or " the lawlessness."

But to return to the Scriptures immediately before us.

The Angel's action in throwing the woman back into the ephah, and casting the circular mass of lead "upon the mouth thereof," is meant, I believe, to set forth, not only the fact that the instruments of sin become the instruments of her punishment, but the still more solemn truth that men and nations who sell themselves to sin are, after a time, kept down and tied to that particular sin; or, to use the language of Prov. v. 22 : "*His own iniquities shall take the wicked, and he shall be holden with the cords of his sin.*"

Not only in relation to the future *eternal* destiny of the individual (of which the words are primarily used), but already also in the earthly history of men and nations, there comes a time when the solemn judicial sentence goes forth from the mouth of God : "*He that is unrighteous, let him do unrighteousness still: and he that is filthy, let him be made filthy still*" (Rev. xxii. 11, R.V.).

Thus, when the woman attempts to escape, she is thrown back into the ephah, which becomes, so to say, the chariot in which she is carried away as something which is defiled and defiling, from the land in which God shall dwell; and the talent with which she carries on her unrighteous trade becomes the heavy weight by which she is held down till she is landed safely "in her own place," where, after a season of lawless liberty in which she will allure men to their own destruction by her seductive attractiveness and luxury, she will be judged and destroyed, together with him who is pre-eminently styled "The Wicked One," by the brightness of the Lord's *parousia* (2 Thess. ii. 8).

(*d*) We come now to the last act in the drama of this vision, which, as already said, is primarily intended to set forth the removal of "wickedness" from the holy land without occupying itself with its final destiny in the land to which, by the aid of evil powers, it was for a time to be transplanted.

That every item in the description of the actors in the 9th verse is of symbolical significance (as is the case with all the details in the other visions), and not merely picturesque figures of speech with a view " to give distinctness to the picture " (as Keil, Hengstenberg, Bredenkamp, and others assert), there can be no doubt ; but it is impossible to speak with absolute positiveness as to *what* each particular is intended to signify.[1]

In a general way I agree on this point with those writers who regard these women as typifying instruments or systems of evil, who for a time deliver the woman in the ephah from the vengeance which was about to destroy her. " By reason of the curse described (in the previous vision) as overtaking all who followed in her wicked ways," observes Dr. Wright, " no place is left for her any longer in the land of righteousness, among a people whose trangressions are forgiven and who are sanctified to bring forth fruit unto holiness. The winged women, therefore, bear off the evil one to the land of Shinar, there to build for her a home and a house." [2]

---

[1] Keil, whose remarks are repeated almost verbally by Bredenkamp and others, easily passes over this verse with the following remarks : " Women carry it because there is a woman inside ; and two women because two persons are required to carry so large and heavy a burden, that they may lay hold of it on both sides. These women have wings because it passes through the air ; and a stork's wings because these birds have broad pinions," etc.

[2] It may be remarked that the final cleansing of the land and people of Israel does not, in point of time, take place until after the full development of " Wickedness," and the manifestation of the " Wicked One," who shall be destroyed by the " brightness " (or " shining forth ") of Christ at His coming (2 Thess. ii. 8). Not until the King of Righteousness reigns over Mount Zion, will Palestine be " the land of righteousness," and the nation of Israel " a people whose transgressions are forgiven, and who are sanctified to bring forth fruits unto holiness."

But we are not to expect in these visions, or indeed in Old Testament prophecy generally, a clear setting forth of eschatological events *in their true chronological order*.

The *fact* is clearly, though symbolically, set forth, that among a people, and in a land whence " iniquity has been removed " (chap. iii. 9), and which should thenceforth be known as the " holy land " (chap. ii. 12), and the holy people, the system of " wickedness " outwardly symbolised by the ephah, can have no place.

Incidentally, it also sets forth the fact that for a time this system *will* find a place in the land and sphere to which it, so to say, belongs.

And if we are asked what two evil systems, helped and impelled by evil spirits (as may be gathered from the fact that they had the wings of a stork, which is an unclean bird, and that "the wind," or "spirit," certainly not of God, "was in their wings"), would thus eventually unite in finding a home for the ephah and the woman, which for a season would be permitted to dominate the nations through its power, we can only suggest that it may be apostate Christianity united in the last days to apostate Judaism, and both given over to the worship of Mammon, on which the power of the ephah is based ; or, as in these series of visions, the *civil* and *ecclesiastical* powers, as represented by Zerubbabel and Joshua, are frequently brought before us ; and in the fifth vision (chap. iv. 14) are probably "the two" who are represented "as standing before the Lord." The two women here may, perhaps, be meant to signify *civil government* broken loose, even outwardly, from every acknowledgment of God (and, therefore, an instrument in the hand of lawlessness), and a corrupt anti-Christian and anti-theistic *priesthood*—both Jewish and Gentile—ready to unite as sponsors and protectors to a system which, though as yet not so regarded, even by the elect, is characterised by God as "the Wickedness."

(*e*) There is yet one more point that we must briefly touch on before taking our leave of this vision—namely, what are we to understand by "the land of Shinar," which, according to the words of the Interpreting Angel, is to be the destination to which the two women bear the ephah, there for a time to establish it on its own base ? According to the commentators, the name "Shinar" is not to be taken geographically here, as an epithet applied to Mesopotamia, but "is a national, or real, definition, which affirms that the ungodliness carried away out of the sphere of the people of God will have its permanent settlement in the sphere of the imperial power that is hostile to God."[1] Or, as another explains it : "The name Shinar, though strictly Babylonia, carries us back to an older power than the world-empire of

---

[1] Keil.

Babylon, which now was destroyed. In the land of Shinar was the first attempt made, ere mankind was yet dispersed, to array a world-empire against God. And so it is the apter symbol of the anti-theistic or anti-Christian world, which, by violence, and falsehood, and sophistry, wars against the truth." [1]

But while there is truth in the words of yet another writer that Shinar was the land of unholiness, and stands here contrasted with Palestine, which shall be "the holy land" (chap. ii. 12), and that the chief point in the vision is the renewal of the special form of "wickedness" which is symbolised by the ephah from the land of Israel to find its resting-place "in the land of world-power which is antagonistic to God," we cannot altogether agree that "the picture is an ideal one," and that "the land of Shinar is an ideal land contrasted with the land of Israel." [2]

Without any spirit of dogmatism, and without entering at this place into the question of the identity and significance of the Babylon in the Revelation—whether mystical or actual—we would express our conviction that there are Scriptures which cannot, according to our judgment, be satisfactorily explained except on the supposition of a revival and yet future judgment of literal Babylon, which for a time will be the centre and embodiment of all the elements of our godless Western "civilisation," and which especially will become the chief *entrepôt* of commerce in the world, in which will be gathered "*merchandise of gold, and silver, and precious stone, and pearls, and fine linen, and purple, and silk, and scarlet ; and all thyine wood, and every vessel of*

---

[1] Pusey.

[2] Dr. C. H. H. Wright. According to Hengstenberg, who, as I believe erroneously, regards the woman in the ephah as symbolising the Jewish people, who, when the measure of their sin became full, was to be banished again from the land and carried away into captivity, Shinar stands for the lands of their present dispersion : that is, "the future dwelling-place of the Jews, who were to be banished from their country, is called by the name of the land in which they were captives before." And he finds in it a "striking example of the custom which the prophets adopted of representing future events by images drawn from the past, and at the same time transferring to the former the names which belong to the latter."

ivory, and every vessel made of most precious wood, and of brass, and iron, and marble; and cinnamon, and spice, and incense, and ointment, and frankincense, and wine, and oil, and fine flour, and wheat, and cattle, and sheep; and merchandise of horses and chariots and bodies; and souls of men," [1] until it shall finally and for ever be overturned by one terrible act of judgment from God.

To this conviction we are led chiefly by the fact that there are prophecies in the Old Testament concerning the literal Babylon which have never in the past been exhaustively fulfilled, and that Scripture usually connects the final overthrow of Babylon with the yet future restoration and blessing of Israel.

And it is very striking to the close observer of the signs of the times how things at the present day are rapidly developing on the very lines which are forecast in the prophetic Scriptures. "The fears and hopes of the world—political, commercial, and religious," writes one in a monthly journal which lies before me, "are at the present day being increasingly centred upon the home of the human race—Mesopotamia. . . . As the country from which the father of the Jewish nation emigrated to the land of promise, it is also occupying the thoughts and aspirations of the Jews."

Whatever may be the outcome of the negotiations which have been carried on recently with the Turkish Government by the Jewish Territorialists "for the establishment of a Jewish autonomous State" in this very region, in which many Zionists and other Jews were ready to join, there is so much truth in the words of another writer that when once a considerable number of such a commercial people as the Jews are re-established in Palestine, "the Euphrates would be to them as necessary as the Thames to London or the Rhine to Germany. It would be Israel's great channel of communication with the Indian seas, not to speak of the commerce which would flow towards the Tigris and Euphrates from the central and northern districts of Asia! It would be strange, therefore, if no city should

[1] Rev. xviii. 12, 13.

arise on its banks of which it might be said that her merchants were the great men of the earth."

" Noteworthy in this connection," observes another writer, " is the watchful eye of the German Imperial Government upon the railway in course of construction from Konia (the biblical Iconium) to Bagdad. Some six hundred miles of the Anatolian, or Euphratean, line have already been opened to traffic." In short, there is a general impression that this region, the highway between Asia and Europe, and contiguous to Africa, is about to become a great " commercial centre of gravity." The new Turkish Government (in contrast to the old régime) is very keen on the development of the resources [1] of that ancient and naturally fertile region, and alive to the very important aid which Jewish capital and energy could render in that direction. Very recently, therefore, they engaged the services of a distinguished English hydraulic engineer, Sir William Willcocks, K.C.M.G., to survey the district and report on the establishment and development of irrigation works. He returned full of enthusiasm, declaring that his " future hopes, ambitions, and work are bound up with the re-creation of Chaldea."

A very interesting paper which he read at a meeting of the Royal Geographical Society last November is published in *The Geographical Journal* for January 1910. The following are his concluding remarks : " In her long history of many thousands of years, Babylonia has again and again been submerged, but she has always risen with an energy and thoroughness rivalling the very completeness and suddenness of her fall. She has never failed to respond to those who have striven to raise her. Again, it seems that the time has come for this land, long wasted with misery, to rise from the very dust and take her place by the side of her ancient rival, the land of Egypt.

" The works we are proposing are drawn on sure and truthful lines, and the day they are carried out the two great rivers will hasten to respond, and Babylon will yet

[1] All this was written in 1910.

once again see her waste places becoming inhabited, and the desert blossoming as the rose." [1]

All this may be regarded by some as a long digression from the subject before us; but it is not altogether so, for it shows from actual facts and events which are before us the very strong probability that " the land of Shinar "—which in the past was so " prominent in connection with the manifestation of evil on the part of man, and of judgment on the part of God, that it stands peculiarly as a memorial of proud ungodliness met by the visitation of righteous vengeance from above "—will yet, as Scripture forecasts, play a very important part in the consummation of human " wickedness " in the final anti-Christian apostasy, in which a godless Judaism and a corrupt, unbelieving Christianity will be united for the sake of the false peace, and pomp, and luxury, and a humanitarianism dissociated from God and the truth, which the system, outwardly symbolised by the ephah, will for a time minister to them, but which, as Scripture also warns us, will end in the most terrible judgment which has yet befallen man upon the earth.

---

[1] The following paragraph forms the concluding remarks of an article in the London *Standard* for August 30, 1910, in which the beginnings of the great irrigation works proposed by Sir William Willcocks are described :

" These gigantic schemes cannot be carried out in their entirety without the co-operation of great capitalists ; but an experiment might well be made with a limited area, when the feasibility of the whole would be apparent. Nowhere in the world do the natural conditions and the possibilities of hydraulic science offer a greater field to the agricultural capitalist. One hears from time to time of one or other scheme of Jewish colonisation on a vast scale. If Baron Hirsch's committee, who have, apparently, ransacked the world for a suitable locality, would give the scheme the attention it deserves, it might mean great things for the Jewish race. Here, in the very cradle of their race, in the land so intimately and so sadly associated with their subsequent history, a new Psalmist may arise, converting the sadness of the ' Super flumina ' into joy ; the old-time captivity may yet be turned, ' as the rivers in the South.' Here is the land, and here is the water ; it only needs money, intelligently applied, to convert a wilderness into another Garden of Eden.

" One cannot take leave of this subject without reference to the certain advent of the railway, possibly of more railways than one. It will, indeed, be a wonderful revival. Ur of the Chaldees as the centre of an important trade and railway system, must appeal to the dullest imagination ; yet such it assuredly will be in the not very distant future. Such great possibilities as here exist cannot, at this stage of the world's history, be allowed to lie dormant for ever."

Chapter 9

THE EIGHTH VISION
THE FOUR CHARIOTS
Zechariah 6:1-8

And again I lifted up mine eyes, and saw, and behold, there came four chariots out from between two mountains; and the mountains were mountains of brass. In the first chariot were red horses; and in the second chariot black horses; and in the third chariot white horses; and in the fourth chariot grisled strong horses. Then I answered and said unto the angel that talked with me, What are these, my lord? And the angel answered and said unto me, These are the four winds of heaven, which go forth from standing before the Lord of all the earth. The chariot wherein are the black horses goeth forth toward the north country; and the white went forth after them; and the grisled went forth toward the south country. And the strong went forth, and sought to go that they might walk to and fro through the earth: and He said, Get you hence, walk to and fro through the earth. So they walked to and fro through the earth. Then cried He to me, and spake unto me, saying, Behold, they that go toward the north country have quieted My spirit in the north country.

Chapter 9

WE come to the eighth, or last vision, in which the prophet's eyes are opened to see the invisible chariots of God which are being sent forth for the overthrow of Gentile world-power, and to prepare the way for the Kingdom of Messiah, which "shall never be destroyed."

What the Prophet saw

Probably directed again by the interpreting angel to do so, the prophet lifts up his eyes and beholds four chariots coming forth from between two mountains of brass.[1] These chariots were drawn by horses of various colours. In the first were red horses, in the second black, in the third white, and in the fourth grisled, or speckled, horses, to which also are applied the epithet אֲמֻצִּים (*amutsim*, "strong").[1]

The Significance of the Symbolism

I. The two mountains, which in the Hebrew have the definite article, indicating that they are well known, and which, as we may gather from the 5th verse, are associated with the "presence," or special dwelling-place, of "the Lord of the whole earth," are very probably Mount Zion and Mount Olivet, "viewed as ideal mountains, and as the place whence God's judgments go forth over the world."

---

[1] The Rabbis understood a chariot as signifying a team of four horses. Their reason is a curious one. In 1 Kings x. 29 it is said: "And a chariot came up and went out of Egypt for six hundred shekels, and a horse for a hundred and fifty." The price of a chariot is here four times that of a horse. Thus, therefore, Kimchi says, "A chariot is a team of four horses."

This is the more likely true explanation, since the Valley of Jehoshaphat (the meaning of which is " Jehovah shall judge "), which lies between these two " mountains," or " hills," is associated in the prophetic Scriptures with God's judgments upon the nations (Joel iii. 2).[1]

At any rate, this much is clear (as Dr. Wright points out), that the chariots are represented as going forth from a place situate between " north " and " south "—*i.e.*, from Palestine, and from that place in the Holy Land where Jehovah was wont to display His gracious presence. From this spot, which God has chosen as His earthly dwelling-place, and as the centre of His governmental dealings with the nations, blessing goes forth in all the world, and from it also judgments proceed.

They are spoken of as mountains of " brass," or, more literally, " copper," to indicate the strength and *inaccessibleness* of God's dwelling-place. He can, and does, send forth His chariots to build up, or to pull down and destroy, but no one can penetrate into *His* presence. Or, as Pusey observes, " the mountains of brass may signify the height of the Divine wisdom (in all His plans and purposes concerning the nations), and the sublimity of the power which putteth them in operation. As the Psalmist says : ' Thy righteousness is like the mountains of God.' "

---

[1] All sorts of fanciful explanations have been given by interpreters of these two mountains. Hengstenberg regards them as merely emblematic of the power of God, which shields and protects His people. Baumgarten says that they represent the east and west as the two central points of the world-power. But these in Zechariah's visions, as Dr. Wright properly points out, are rather the north and south. Hitzig would, it seems, locate them in heaven, and regards the chariots as having been seen coming forth from the dwelling-place of the Most High.

Von Hoffmann, Pressel, and others have explained them to be the mountains of Zion and Moriah, " for from these two mountains in Messianic days the Kingdom of God should be spread abroad " (Pressel) ; " and they will be the mountains whence God should send forth His last judgments upon the world." The opinion of Jasper Svedberg, the father of the renowned Swedenborg, may be mentioned as a curiosity of exposition. According to him, the prophet, when speaking of mountains of brass or copper, evidently alluded to the country of Dalarne, in Sweden, which, he thought, was destined to be of great importance in the latter days !

II. The Chariots. If, with the prophet, we ask, What are these? the answer of the Interpreting Angel in ver. 3 is: " *These are the four winds of heaven, which go forth from standing before the Lord of the whole earth.*" We must therefore regard them either as ideal appearances, personifying the forces and providential acts which God often uses in carrying out His judgments on the earth, or, what seems to me the simplest and most natural explanation, *angelic beings, or heavenly powers* — those invisible " messengers " of His " who excel in strength, and who ever stand in His presence, hearkening unto the voice of His word," and then go forth in willing obedience, as swift as the " winds," to carry out His behests (Ps. ciii. 20, 21, civ. 4).

These, no doubt, are also meant by " the chariots of God, which are twenty thousand, even thousands upon thousands," of which we read in Ps. lxviii. 17, though the word " angels " (used in the Authorised Version) is not found in the original of that verse. Indeed, there is a striking connection between the first and the last visions. In the first vision (chap. i. 7–17), at the beginning of this, to the prophet, memorable night, he saw the angelic riders with the Angel of the Lord, Himself mounted on a red horse at their head, appearing in the presence of the Lord, to bring in, as it were, their report after " walking to and fro through the earth " as to the condition of the Gentile nations and their attitude to *the* people and *the* land. And now, toward morning, as the visions were about to be brought to an end, he sees the same angelic hosts, now turned into God's war chariots, actually being sent forth (no longer to *report*) but to carry out the judgments of God upon those nations with whom He is " very sore displeased," because " they helped forward the affliction " of His own people, whom, even in the time of their banishment and scattering, He has never cast off.

III. We now come to the difficult point of the number of the chariots and the significance of the colours of the horses.

The number, four, clearly brings to our mind again the four great Gentile world-powers, whose successive course makes up "the times of the Gentiles," and whose final overthrow must precede the restoration and blessing of Israel, and the visible establishment of the Messianic kingdom.

In this connection it is again interesting to observe that these four "chariots" are explained to be the "four winds." Now, in Dan. vii. 1–3 we read of the four winds of heaven "striving," or "breaking," upon "the great sea," which caused the four great Beasts, "diverse one from the other" (symbolical of the four great Gentile world-powers), to *arise*; and here we see the "four winds" sent forth to *break up* these same empires; from which we may surely learn that it is by the will and power of God, and by His direct interposition, either by visible, natural, or by angelic agency, that empires rise and fall.

There is a certain parallelism to be observed also between this vision and the second act of the historical prophetic drama unfolded in the vision of the four horns and four carpenters (chap. i. 18–21)—only here we have the great fact still more clearly brought out, that behind visible phenomena and all human motives and actions there is the eternal purpose and power of God, and the invisible active agency of His angelic hosts.

But there is a difficulty in connection with the number of the chariots, and in the description of the colours of the horses, which we must face before proceeding further. The difficulty, briefly stated, is this: In the vision itself (vers. 2, 3) the prophet beholds four chariots, in the first of which were red horses, in the second black, in the third white, and in the fourth grisled horses, to which last is also added the epithet אֲמֻצִּים (*amutsim*, "strong"); but in the interpretation by the interpreting angel (vers. 5–7) the first with the red horses is passed over. The black and the white are explained as going forth into the north country, the grisled into the south, and then we read of the *amutsim* ("strong"), which in ver. 3 are the same as the "grisled," wanting to go forth on a separate, or yet another mission.

The explanations of this difficulty which have been given by interpreters both Jewish and Christian, ancient and modern, are many, but for the most part are far-fetched and unsatisfactory. Some get over the difficulty lightly by the very simple method of correcting the text and substituting אֲדֻמִּים (*adummim*, "the red") in the 7th verse for אֲמֻצִּים (*amutsim*, "the strong"), which they regard as a scribal error. This, I might mention, had been done already by the translators of the ancient Syriac version. But this solution of the difficulty, apart from other objections, does not explain why the description "the strong" should be used as an additional epithet of the "grisled" in the 3rd verse, nor why the red, which in the vision was seen *first*, should in the Angel's interpretation be spoken of as going forth *last*.

Another explanation already adopted in the Septuagint version, the Targum, Kimchi, etc., and by some Christian interpreters, including Calvin and Koehler, is that *amutsim* does not here mean "strong," but denotes a colour. They regard אָמֹץ (*amots*) as a softened form of חָמוּץ (*hamuts*), a word found in Isa. lxiii. 1, and there signifying "red."[1] But apart from the fact that it is impossible (as Keil observes) to see why so unusual a word should have been chosen by the prophet in the 7th verse to describe the colour "red," instead of the intelligible word *adummim*, which he had already used in the 3rd verse, there is no satisfactory ground for identifying *amots* with *hamuts*.

Moreover, as Dr. Wright points out, there is a serious difficulty in the way of this explanation, that the same word would then be used in ver. 3 and in ver. 7 in two totally different significations—in the first place as an additional description of the "grisled," or "speckled," and in the latter to denote the "red."

Hengstenberg attempts to solve the difficulty in the following manner: According to him there can be no doubt as to the meaning of the word *amutsim*; it can only

---

[1] This conjecture is the basis of the rendering "bay" in the Authorised and Revised Versions.

signify "powerful," or "strong," but he argues that this predicate, although only formally connected with the horses in the fourth chariot, at the end of the 3rd verse, "cannot apply to them in contrast with those of the other three chariots, but must, in fact, belong equally to all the four." The "strong" horses therefore, seen to go forth last, in the 7th verse, are in reality the "red" of the first chariot. He lays emphasis on the article, "*the* strong ones," in ver. 7, and says, "*the* strong ones, that is, those in comparison with which the others were to be regarded as weak, although in themselves they were really strong ; . . . in other words, the strongest among them. They are mentioned last because in the consciousness of their strength they were not content like the rest with one particular portion of the globe, but asked permission of the Lord to go through the whole earth."   But, excepting on the supposition that a word in the 3rd verse has dropped out, Hengstenberg's exposition is, as is now pretty generally agreed, on grammatical reasons "impossible." [1]

.   .   .   .   .   .

Let us now give what appears to be the most likely and satisfactory solution of the difficulty.   We have already observed that though these four chariots, which with their horses are interpreted by the angel to be "the four winds," or "spirits," of the heavens, *cannot be identified* with the four Gentile world-powers of Dan. ii. and vii., on which Zechariah's second vision, that of the horns and carpenters, is, as we have seen, based—they are *closely connected,* and

---

[1] If אֲמֻצִּים (*amutsim,* "strong"), in the 3rd verse, were intended to be referred to the horses in all the chariots, the phrase would have been expressed by אֲמֻצִּים כֻּלָּם, *amutsim kulam*—"all of them strong." As to Hengstenberg's argument that the article before *amutsim* (the strong), ver. 7, is to be regarded as emphatic, it must not be forgotten that all the adjectives used in reference to the horses when first mentioned naturally occur without the article ; but when spoken of by the interpreting angel are all used most naturally with the article. "The use of the article with the adjective in ver. 7 can no more be regarded as emphatic *than when used with the black, the white, and speckled* (or '*grisled*') *horses. Amutsim* is similarly used at first without the article ; but when mentioned the second time it takes the article just as the other adjectives."

primarily refer to those empires whose united successive course make up the "times of the Gentiles."

These four are the Babylonian, the Medo-Persian, the Grecian (or Græco-Macedonian), and the Roman. "These are the horns (or Gentile powers) which have scattered Judah, Israel, and Jerusalem" (chap. i. 19), and it is the *overthrow* and *judgment of these*, by means of invisible heavenly powers appointed of God as a necessary precursor to the establishment of Messiah's kingdom, and the blessing of Israel, which is symbolically set forth to the prophet in this last vision.

But these powers, though in vision and prophecy seen together, are, as a matter of fact, *successive in time.*

Now, when these visions were shown to Zechariah, Babylon had already been overthrown, and its world-empire taken away, visibly and apparently, by the Medo-Persians, behind whom, however (as the prophet beholds), there was the invisible chariot of God, with its red horses of blood and vengeance.

This act of judgment on the first great Gentile world-power which had oppressed Israel and laid waste his land being already an accomplished fact (though in the 3rd verse, for completeness' sake, all the four are shown to the prophet together, as is the case in the vision of the four horns, one of which had also been already overthrown), this first chariot is passed over by the Angel in the interpretation, and is not seen among those who "go forth" in ver. 6—its mission, as far as the Babylonian Empire is concerned, having already been fulfilled.

The black horses, significant probably of sorrow and mourning in consequence of sore judgments to be inflicted, go forth toward the north country, and "after them," going forth in the same direction, are the white, symbolical of victory, triumph, and glory over Gentile world-power—for both the Medo-Persian and Græco-Macedonian Empires, being each in turn successors of the great Babylonian Empire, were the great hostile *northern* powers in relation to Palestine.

In contrast to these who went forth to the north country, the *beruddim* ("grisled," or "speckled" horses) —the exact colour of which it is difficult to give with certainty, but which probably answers to the *seruqqim* ("speckled") in chap. i. 8—go forth to the south country.

Now, the south country is Egypt, the other direction from which hostile world-power came into contact with Israel and Palestine; and "the king of the south," as, for instance, in Dan. xi., is the king of Egypt. But *there* it was that the fourth great world-empire came into collision with the declining Macedonian power, and *that it was first brought into direct contact with the Jewish nation.* It is most probable, therefore, that the fourth chariot, appointed for the overthrow and destruction of the fourth great world-empire, is seen to go forth, first to the south, as if to encounter this fresh hostile power at the point at which it first came into contact with Israel.

But the Spirit of God, foreseeing that the fourth empire, unlike its predecessors, would spread itself, not only to the north, and south, and east, but westward also, and practically embrace the whole known world; and that it would, in the different stages of its existence, endure for a considerably longer period than its predecessors—the horses of this same chariot are represented as desiring also, after having accomplished their mission in the south, to go forth to walk to and fro through the earth. "And He" (that is, the Lord of the whole earth, before whom they were all seen "standing" in the first instance) "said, Get you hence, walk to and fro through the earth," in order to meet this power in every place where it shall establish itself, to hold it in check, and to counteract its evil plans, until the signal shall be given for its final overthrow.

If we are asked why the horses in this last chariot are seen first going forth as the "grisled" or "speckled," and then, in the 7th verse, as the "strong" (which, be it noted, was the additional epithet applied to them already in the 3rd verse), the true answer is probably that suggested by Bredenkamp, who says that "speckled strong horses" are such as, regarded from the point of view of their colour, are " speckled " (*gefleckte*), but from the point of view of their special characteristic, are " strong."

Viewed as going forth like the other chariots into a particular direction, and as encountering a particular power, they are described, like the previous ones, by their colour, which is in itself symbolical ; but when the fact is brought into view that this particular power which these horses are to encounter is unlike its predecessors, but will assert its dominion over the whole earth, then their special characteristic as " the strong ones " is emphasised.

To this we may add the striking fact that *strength* was to be an outstanding feature of the fourth great world-empire, even as we read in Dan. vii. 7 : " After this I saw in the night visions, and behold a fourth beast, terrible and powerful, and *strong exceedingly* ; and it had great iron teeth ; it devoured and brake in pieces, and stamped the residue with his feet : and it was diverse from all the beasts which were before it ; and it had ten horns."

Now, over against the might of man, and of all the powers of darkness which assert themselves in this last great world-power, there is the might of God ; and we are reminded in this vision that His invisible hosts are a match for the mightiest, and that God is ever stronger than His foes.

We now come to the 8th verse :

" *And He cried unto me, and spake unto me, saying, Behold, those which go toward the north country have quieted* ('*caused to rest*') *My spirit in the north country.*"

The idiom, " to cause to rest upon " a person, or, as in this case, upon a land, involves, as Pusey rightly observes, that that person (or land) is the object *on whom it abides*, not that the spirit is quieted in him whose it is, as some interpreters have explained it. The word רוּחַ (*ruach*, " spirit ") must, I believe, be understood here as *anger*, in which sense it is found also in other scriptures.[1] The meaning of the 8th verse, then, is that that company of

[1] Judg. viii. 3 ; Eccles. x. 4.

the invisible host whose mission was toward the north country caused God's anger to rest on it —*i.e.*, "have carried it thither, and deposited it there (made it to rest upon that people or kingdom) as its abode"; as John says of the unbelieving, "*The wrath of God abideth on him.*"[1] The reason why "the north country" is specially singled out for the region on which God's anger was already resting, is to be found, perhaps, first of all in the fact that there the first great world-power—namely, the Babylonian —was already overthrown by God's judgments.   Secondly, because it was probably intended as a message of comfort more directly to the restored remnant, to whom the prophet was primarily commissioned to relate the visions— to indicate, namely, that the second great northern world-power, the successor of Babylon, under whose yoke they were then groaning,[2] was already the object of God's anger, and would soon be trodden down under the feet of the horses of God's war chariot which was being sent forth in that direction.

And, thirdly, as Bredenkamp suggests, God's wrath is specially spoken of in this last vision as being caused to rest on "the north country," because not only was it there that the attempt was first made to array a world-empire against God, and where apostasy sought, so to say, to organise and fortify itself; not only did Babylon also, at a later time, become the final antagonist and subduer of God's people and the destroyer of His Temple, but probably because there, "in the land of Shinar," the metropolis of world-power, Babylon, the great rival of the city of God—wickedness, as we have seen in the consideration of the last vision, will once again establish itself, and all the forces of evil again for a time be concentrated.

Then God's judgments shall be fully poured out, and anti-Christian world-power be finally overthrown to make room for the Kingdom of Christ, whom the Father has invested with all power and dominion and glory, "that all nations and languages should serve Him."   His dominion

---

[1] Pusey.   [2] Neh. ix. 36, 37.

is an everlasting dominion, "and His Kingdom shall never be destroyed."

And this, dear reader—the establishment of Messiah's throne of righteousness on Mount Zion, that from it, and Israel as a centre, His beneficent rule may extend over the whole earth and bless all peoples—is the appointed goal of history toward which all things are moving. It is the motive, also, of all God's providential dealings with the nations. "Political changes," as one has expressed it, "are the moving of the shadow on the earth's dial-plate that marks the mighty motions going forward in the heavens"; and however conflicting and confusing to our poor human judgments, they mark but the various stages of a plan and counsel which God formed from eternity.

In reference to the four great world-powers, whose successive course was to make up "the times of the Gentiles," we have to note that three of them have already long ago disappeared, in accordance with the clear predictions of Scripture, and the fourth, which (as also foreseen and foretold) was to drag on longest, is now, as is generally agreed by all students of the sure Word of Prophecy, fast approaching its very last phase of existence. We may, therefore, say with confidence that we are on the eve of the most solemn events in the world's history, and are very fast approaching "the day," not only of our own final and complete "redemption" as believers at the manifestation of Christ, but the "set time," when God shall again arise and have mercy upon Zion, and when, through the restoration and blessing of Israel, "the nations shall fear the Name of Jehovah, and all kings of the earth His glory."

Chapter 10

THE CLIMAX OF THE VISIONS
THE CROWNING OF JOSHUA
Zechariah 6-9:15

The word of Jehovah came unto me, saying, Take of them of the captivity, even of Heldai, of Tobijah, and of Jedaiah ; and come thou the same day, and go into the house of Josiah the son of Zephaniah, whither they are come from Babylon ; yea, take of them silver and gold, and make crowns, and set them upon the head of Joshua the son of Jehozadak, the high priest ; and speak unto him, saying, Thus speaketh Jehovah of hosts, saying, Behold, the Man whose name is the Branch : and He shall grow up out of His place ; and He shall build the Temple of Jehovah ; even He shall build the Temple of Jehovah ; and He shall bear the glory, and shall sit and rule upon His throne ; and He shall be a priest upon His throne ; and the counsel of peace shall be between them both. And the crowns shall be to Helem, and to Tobijah, and to Jedaiah, and to Hen the son of Zephaniah, for a memorial in the Temple of Jehovah. And they that are far off shall come and build in the Temple of Jehovah ; and ye shall know that Jehovah of hosts hath sent Me unto you. And this shall come to pass, if ye will diligently obey the voice of Jehovah your God.

Chapter 10

THE series of eight visions is followed by a very significant symbolical transaction, which must be regarded as the crowning act—the headstone of the rich symbolico-prophetical teaching which was unfolded to the prophet on that memorable night.

It shows us what will follow the banishment of evil from the land, and the overthrow of world-power in the earth, as set forth particularly in the last three visions—namely, *the crowning of the true King*, the Mediator of Salvation, who shall be "a Priest upon His throne," and build the true temple of Jehovah, into which not only Israel, but "they that are far off"—the Gentiles—shall have access.

To indicate that the visions are now ended, the prophet adopts the usual formula by which the prophets always authenticated that they spake, not of themselves, but as they were moved by the Holy Spirit: "*And the word of Jehovah came unto me, saying.*" The whole section divides itself into two parts—the first (vers. 9–11) gives the account of the symbolical transaction ; and the second (vers. 13–15) records the verbal prophecy.

The symbolical act was occasioned by the following circumstance : There arrived in Jerusalem, probably on the very morning after the vision, three prominent men as a deputation from the *Haggolah*, "the Captivity"—that is, from those who were still settled in Babylon, whither they were originally carried "captive"—bringing with them an offering of silver and gold for the Temple, which was then still in building. The sight of these men from "far-off" Babylon, bearing their offering for the Lord's House, was the occasion of the opening of the prophet's eyes by the Spirit of God to behold the future glorious Temple, which in Messiah's time shall be established in Jerusalem as an House of Prayer for all nations, and to which even the Gentile peoples which are " far off " shall flock, bringing their worship and their offerings. The incident recorded in John xii. 20–33 may in a sense be regarded as parallel to this. There the coming of Andrew and Philip to our Lord with the touching request made in the first instance to the latter of these two disciples by the Greeks who came up to Jerusalem among those who came up to worship at the feast : " Sir, we would see Jesus," took our Saviour's mind to the time when " all men," without distinction of race or nationality, shall be " drawn " unto Him, and to the only possible way by which this could be brought about. In the temple of His pre-resurrection body, as the Son of David, there was no room for these poor Gentiles. The Son of Man must be lifted up : except the corn of wheat fall into the ground and die, it abideth alone ; but *if it die*, it bringeth forth much fruit. So here the appearance in Jerusalem of these strangers takes the prophet's mind from the Temple they were then building, over the second outer court of which when completed there was the inscription put up in Greek and Latin : " *No stranger may enter here on pain of death*," [1] to the

---

[1] The interesting discovery in 1871 by Clermont-Ganneau, the learned Oriental archæologist (the same who discovered and translated the inscription of the Moabite Stone), of the block of stone with the Greek version of this inscription, which was actually built into the wall or enclosure of the Second Temple, separating the "Court of the Gentiles" from the "Court of the Women," is now well known. I have myself more than once seen and examined the block with the inscription on it, which, with many other precious archæological treasures, is now in the Constantinople Museum. The actual words of the Greek inscription upon which our Lord Jesus and Paul most probably looked more than once, read, translated, thus : "No stranger born may enter within the circuit of the barrier ($\tau\rho\nu\phi\acute{a}\kappa\tau o\nu$) and enclosure ($\pi\epsilon\rho\iota\beta o\lambda o\hat{\nu}$) that is around the sacred court ($\tau\grave{o}\ \iota\epsilon\rho\acute{o}\nu$). And whoever shall be caught there, upon himself be the blame of the death which will consequently follow." Josephus (*Antiq.* xv. 11. 5), speaking of the enclosures, or Courts of the Temple, which he describes as very spacious and surrounded by cloisters of much grandeur, says : "Thus was the first enclosure. In the midst of which, and not far from it, was the second, to be gone up by a

future Temple, which Messiah, the true Prince and Priest, of whom Zerubbabel and Joshua the son of Josedech, were types, would build ; which, as already said, shall be an House of Prayer for all nations, and in which those that are " far off "—by which we must understand not only the Jews who were still in the far lands of their " captivity," but the Gentiles, " from the rising of the sun even unto the going down of the same," as the last post-exilic prophet Malachi predicts—" shall come and build."

The symbolical act itself which the prophet is commanded to perform was as follows :

He was to go to the house of Josiah the son of Zephaniah, " whither they (*i.e.*, these distinguished strangers) are come from Babylon," as the original words in the 18th verse are properly rendered in the Revised Version—the 14th verse indicating, as we shall see, that this Josiah, like a true son of Abraham, was a man " given to hospitality," and lodged these strangers in his house as an act of " kindness." Having gone that " same day " to that hospitable house, he was to take some of the silver and gold which they had brought as an offering from those still in Babylon, and make '*ataroth*. The word is in the plural, and is rendered in the Authorised Version and in the text of the Revised Version " crowns," [1] some commentators supposing that there were at least two crowns—one made of silver and the other of gold : the first for the high priest, or at any rate as an emblem of the priestly dignity ; and the other of royalty. But what follows does not at all agree with this supposition, for the prophet is commanded to put the '*ataroth* upon the head of Joshua ; and, as Keil and Lange well observe, " You do not put two or more crowns upon the head of one man." Ewald, Hitzig, and others, to

few steps ; this was encompassed by a stone wall for a partition, *with an inscription which forbade any foreigner to go in under pain of death.*"

How significant, in the light of this fact, are the words of the apostle : " But now in Christ Jesus ye who sometimes were far off are made nigh by the blood of Christ. For He is our peace who hath made both (*i.e.*, Jew and Gentile) one, and hath broken down the middle wall of partition " (Eph. ii. 13, 14).

[1] In the margin of the R.V. it is rendered in the singular, "a crown."

meet the supposed difficulty, would interpolate the words " and upon the head of Zerubabbel " in the 11th verse, as if one crown was to be put upon the head of Zerubbabel and the other upon Joshua; but there is no justification whatever for such a free-and-easy method of handling the sacred text, and the interpretation based upon their " reconstruction " only obscures the rich significance and spiritual beauty of the truth set forth in this symbolical transaction.

There is no mention whatever of Zerubbabel in this passage, neither was a silver crown, or indeed any crown, ever worn by the high priest—the priestly mitre being never so designated.[1]   In fact, the whole significance of the incident lies in the fact that these crowns, or crown, was placed *upon the head of Joshua.*   The plural " *'ataroth* " is used in Job xxi. 36 for one crown, and what most probably is meant is a single " splendid royal crown," consisting of a number of gold and silver twists or circlets woven together.

The Verbal Prophecy

Having placed this crown upon the head of Joshua, the prophet was, by the Lord's command, to deliver to him the following message : " *Thus speaketh Jehovah of hosts, saying, Behold the Man whose name is the Branch, and He shall grow up out of His place, and He shall build the Temple of the Lord : even He shall build the Temple of the Lord : and He shall bear the glory, and shall sit and rule upon His throne ; and He shall be a priest upon His throne ; and the counsel of peace shall be between them both.*"

This is one of the most remarkable and precious Messianic prophecies, and there is no plainer prophetic utterance in the whole Old Testament as to the Person of the promised Redeemer, the offices He was to fill, and the

---

[1] " The silver might have formed a circlet in the crown of gold, as in modern times the iron crown of Lombardy was called iron because it had a plate of iron in its summit, being else of gold and most precious."—Pusey.

In Rev. xix. our Lord Jesus is spoken of as wearing many crowns (διαδήματα πολλά) ; but what is probably meant is a diadem composed of, or encircled with, many crowns.

mission He was to accomplish. Let us examine the
sentence in detail.

הִנֵּה אִישׁ—ἴδε ὁ ἄνθρωπος—Ecce Homo!—"Behold the
Man!"—an expression which has become famous and of
profound significance, since some five centuries later, in the
overruling providence of God, it was used by Pilate on the
day when He Who came to bring life into the world was
Himself led forth to a death of shame.

Here, however, it is not to the Son of Man in His
humiliation, to the "Man of Sorrows and acquainted with
grief," that our attention is directed by God Himself, but
to the only true Man after God's own heart—the Man *par
excellence*—the Ideal and Representative of the race, Who,
after having for our salvation worn the crown of thorns,
shall, as the reward of His sufferings, be "crowned with
glory and honour," and have all things put in subjection
under His feet.

"Behold the Man!" "Behold My Servant!" (Isa. xlii. 1,
lii. 13), "Behold thy King!" (Zech. ix. 9), "Behold your
God!" (Isa. xl. 9): thus variously, as calling attention to
the different aspects of the character of the same blessed
Person, is this word "Behold" used by God Himself.

"Behold the Man!"—the words are indeed addressed to
Joshua, but by no possibility can they be made to apply
to him as the subject, as modern Jews and some rationalistic Christian interpreters seek to do.[1]

[1] Rashi, Aben Ezra, and Kimchi assert that "the Man, the Branch," is Zerubbabel; but, for obvious controversial reasons, they have departed from the older
received interpretation, as is seen from Targum of Jonathan, where the passage
(ver. 12) is paraphrased thus: "Behold the Man; *Messiah is His Name*. He
will be revealed, and He will become great and build the Temple of God."

The Messianic interpretation is also defended with great force by Abarbanel,
who thus decisively refutes the interpretation adopted by the great trio of
Jewish commentators, Rashi, Aben Ezra, and Kimchi. He says, "Rashi has
written that the words, 'Behold the Man Whose Name is the Branch,' have by
some been interpreted of the Messiah." He here means Jonathan, whose interpretation he did not receive, for he adds that the building here spoken of refers
altogether to the Second Temple; but I wish that I could ask them, if this prophecy refers to the Second Temple and Zerubabbel, why it said, "The Man
Whose Name is the Branch," "and He shall grow up from beneath Him."
Surely we know that every man grows up to manhood, and even to old age and

Joshua himself knew of a certainty that that which was set forth by the symbolical act of his being crowned, and the great prophecy contained in the words which followed, could not refer to himself.

Perhaps if it had been Zerubbabel—who was a prince of the House of David—who had been so crowned, and to whom the words had been addressed, there might have been some shadow of ground for such a mistake; but Joshua, as priest, never could wear a crown, nor sit and rule upon a throne, since as long as the old Dispensation lasted the priesthood and royalty were, by God's appointment, apportioned to different tribes, and no true prophet would ever think or speak of any one but a son of David as having a right to sit and rule on a throne in Jerusalem. This, in all probability, was the reason why the crown was placed on the head, not of Zerubbabel, but of Joshua. But Zechariah, who was a priest-prophet, and Joshua, to whom the words are addressed, knew well that there were pre-

---

hoary hairs. Rashi, perceiving this objection, has interpreted this to mean that He shall be of the royal seed; but this is not correct, for the word מִתַּחְתָּיו ("from beneath Him") teaches nothing about the royal family. . . . But, at all events, I should like to ask them, if these words be spoken of Zerubbabel, why does the prophet add that "He shall build the Temple of the Lord: even He shall build the Temple of the Lord." Why this repetition to express one single event? The commentators have got no answer but this, "It is to confirm the matter." But, if this be the case, it would be better to repeat the words three or four times, for then the confirmation would have been greater still. I should further ask them how they can interpret of Zerubbabel those words, "He shall bear the glory, and shall sit and rule upon His throne"; "*for he (Zerubbabel) never ruled in Jerusalem, and never sat upon the throne of the kingdom, but only occupied himself in building the Temple, and afterwards returned to Babylon*" (Abarbanel, *Comment. in loc.*).

Dr. Alexander McCaul says on this passage, "The prophecy promises these particulars: first, 'He shall be a priest upon His throne'; secondly, 'He shall build the Temple of the Lord'; thirdly, 'He shall bear the glory (הוֹד, the "majesty"), and shall sit and rule upon His throne, and they that are far off shall come and build the Temple of the Lord.'" It is not necessary to point out the well-known passages which prove that these four particulars are all features of Messiah's character, and in that of no one else. It is also easy to identify these features in the character of Jesus of Nazareth. He is represented in the New Testament as a High Priest, as a King; and it is certain that the Gentiles, who were then afar off, have acknowledged His dignity; and, as for building a Temple, He did this also. (See John ii. 29; Eph. ii. 22.)

dictions in the former prophets that in a time to come the Redeemer, whom God promised to raise up in Israel out of the House of David, would combine in His own Person the two great mediatorial offices of Priest and King, and be at the same time the last and greatest Prophet, through Whom God would reveal Himself more fully and perfectly to man. Thus, for instance, in the 110th Psalm it is predicted of the theocratic King, Who "shall strike through kings in the day of His wrath," and "judge among nations"—

   " *The Lord hath sworn, and will not repent.   Thou art a priest for ever, after the order of Melchizedek.*"

   Now, of this royal Priest, whose priesthood was to be " for ever," Joshua was already told in the 3rd chapter that both he and his " fellows of the Aaronic family were *anshei mopheth*—literally, " men that are a sign," *i.e.*, *types*— so that there could be no shadow of a possibility of his understanding this new and fuller message about the Priest-King in the 6th chapter as referring to himself, beyond the fact that in his official capacity as high priest he (like all the other priests of the House of Aaron) fore-shadowed the Person and office of the One who should be the true and only Mediator between God and man.

   To return for a moment to the symbolical action which preceded the delivery of the verbal message, there is truth in Pusey's observation, that the act of placing the crown on the head of Joshua, the high priest, pictured not only the union of the offices of Priest and King in the person of the Messiah, but that He should be King, being first our High Priest. " Joshua was already high priest; being such, the kingly crown was added to him. It says in act what the Apostle says in plain words, that Christ Jesus, being found in fashion as a man, humbled Himself, and became obedient unto death, even the death of the Cross. Wherefore God also hath highly exalted Him."

   But to remove any possibility of mistake or doubt, " the Man " to whom the attention of Joshua is directed away from himself is introduced by the well-known

Messianic title, which in the Book of Zechariah is used as a proper name of the promised Deliverer.

"*Behold the man Tsemach—The Branch—is His Name.*"

We have fully entered into this point in the exposition of the 8th verse of chap. iii., and have there shown also how, under this title, the Messiah is brought before us in the Old Testament prophecy in the four different aspects of His character to which reference has already been made above—namely, as the King (Jer. xxiii. 5, 6), the Servant (Zech. iii. 8), the Man (Zech. vi. 1 2), and as "the Branch of Jehovah " (Isa. iv. 2) : which answer so beautifully to the fourfold portraiture of the Christ of history which the Spirit of God has, through the Evangelists, given us in the four different Gospels. We therefore pass on to the next clause.

"*And He shall grow up out of His place*"—*umitachtav itsmach* [1]—literally, " He shall branch up from under Him " —from His own root or stock.

First, as to the race or nation, He shall be of the seed of Abraham, of the tribe of Judah, and of the family of David ; and, secondly, as to the soil or country, it shall be " Immanuel's Land," and out of Bethlehem Ephratha, that this glorious Branch shall spring up, as foretold by the former prophets.

At the same time it is true, as Hengstenberg observes, that the expression presupposes the lowliness from which He will first rise by degrees to glory. " Thus," to quote another writer, " in this one significant sentence the lowly origin of the Messiah on the one hand, and His royal dignity on the other, are both not obscurely referred to." [2]

From His glorious Person and family, or place of His origin, as " the Man," or " Son of David," our thoughts are next directed to the great *work* He is to accomplish :

"*And He shall build the Temple of Jehovah ; even He* (or, literally, *He Himself*) *shall build the Temple of Jehovah.*"

---

[1] The only other place where "*umitachtav*" is found in the Old Testament is Ex. x. 23, where it means " out of his own place."

[2] Dr. Wright.

The repetition and the strong emphasis laid upon the pronoun " He " being intended as an affirmation both of the *certainty of the fact, and the greatness of the task* to be accomplished by Him. Joshua the priest and Zerubbabel the prince were then engaged in the building of a Temple, and one primary object in the visions and prophecies of Zechariah—even as it was of Haggai—was to encourage them in the task which was now nearing completion. But, perhaps as a reward for his faithfulness, or as an encouragement to those who sorrowed because of the apparent insignificance of the House they were then able to build,[1] the prophet is commissioned of God to reveal to Joshua that another, greater than he and his companion, but whom they in their respective offices had the honour to *foreshadow* —He who would combine in His own Person the dignities of priesthood and royalty—would build *the* Temple of Jehovah, of which also that they were now engaged in building was a type and pledge.

But, we may ask, what Temple is it which the Messiah, according to this and other predictions, was to build ?

In answer to this question we would say first of all that we cannot exclude from this prophecy the reference to a literal Temple in Jerusalem, which shall, after Israel's national conversion, be built under the superintendence of their Messiah-King, and which will, during the millennial period, be " the House of Jehovah " on earth, to which " the nations will flow " and many peoples go, in order that they may be taught His ways, and learn to walk in His paths, and which will be literally " An House of Prayer " and worship " for all nations."[2]

But there is something greater and deeper in this prophecy than the reference to a future material Temple on earth, however glorious that may be. The Temple in Jerusalem was the outward visible symbol of communion between God and His people, which in the past has never been perfectly realised. And let us remember, mysterious

---

[1] Ezra iii. 10-13 ; Hag. ii. 3 ; Zech. iv. 10.
[2] Isa. ii. 2-4, lvi. 6, 7 ; Mic. iv. 1-7 ; Ezek. xl. to xliii.

and wonderful as it may appear to us, that not only is the blessedness of man created in the image of God conditional on communion with his Maker, but the infinite and ever-blessed God, the Father of spirits, *seeks* communion with man. Indeed, it might be said that this was the chief object which God had in creating man—that he might be a temple to contain His perfection and fulness; that the mind with which He had endowed him might comprehend and admire His infinite wisdom, and his heart respond to His love. In the Garden of Eden we get a beautiful glimpse of what was intended as the beginning of a fellow-ship between God and man, which was to go on and unfold through limitless ages.

But soon *sin*—that hateful and accursed thing in God's universe—entered, and communion between God and man was interrupted. The outward token of this was the banishment of the man from the garden, and the placing of the cherubim with the "flaming sword which turned every way" to bar the way against his re-entering that blessed abode.

But the heart of God yearned for man, and in His infinite wisdom and grace He devised a means by which His banished be not for ever an outcast from Him.

He chose Israel, whom He suffered to approach to Him through the sprinkling of blood, which in His mind pointed to the blood of the everlasting covenant which the Messiah, who was to be "led as a lamb to the slaughter," was to shed as an atonement for sin ; and to them His proclamation went forth, "*Make Me a tabernacle, that I may dwell among you.*" The tabernacle was built, and then the Temple on Mount Moriah; but soon, alas! this Temple, too, was defiled, and sin in its progress made such rapid strides that it penetrated even into the Holy of Holies, and God was obliged entirely to withdraw His manifest presence even from His chosen dwelling-place.

After the destruction of the first Temple by the Chaldeans under Nebuchadnezzar (2 Kings xxv.) the Jews built another one after their restoration from Babylon ; but the manifest presence of Jehovah no more returned to it; for Rabbi Samuel Bar Juni, in the Talmud (Yoma, f. 21, c. 2), and Rabbis Solomon and Kimchi, in their comment on Hag i. 8, all agree that five things that were in the first Temple were wanting in the second—*i.e.*, the *ark*, wherein were the tables of the Covenant, and the cherubim that covered it; *the fire* that used to come down from heaven to devour the sacrifices; the *Shekinah Glory*; the *gift of prophecy*, or the Holy Ghost; and the miraculous *Urim and Thummim*.

But before that Temple was destroyed by the Romans, another Temple, not built by the hands of man, arose, and in it dwelt the fulness of the Godhead bodily (Col. ii. 9). One came, and in sight of the magnificent structure which had then become more a "den of thieves" than a "house of prayer," proclaimed, "Destroy this Temple, and in three days I will raise it up again; and this He spake of the Temple of His body." Who was this who thus spoke but the promised Messiah, with whose advent the presence of Jehovah should again return to His people, as is implied in His very name Immanuel, which being interpreted means "God with us." Behold, "the tabernacle of God is with men" once more, "and He doth dwell with them." For "the Word was made flesh, and dwelt among us; and we beheld His glory, the glory as of the only-begotten of the Father, full of grace and truth" (John i. 14).

Behold, therefore, O Christian, in the Person of the Redeemer Himself, the fulfilment of these words, "*He shall build the Temple of Jehovah*," for in Him we have the fullest manifestation of the Divine glory, and "in Christ Jesus" is the true meeting-place where communion between God and man is consummated.

But there is another Temple of which the Messiah Himself is actually the builder, and in which we may see a fulfilment of this and other prophecies.

"Thou art Peter," were the words of Jesus on a certain solemn occasion, "and upon this rock (*i.e.*, the confession

Peter had just uttered, " Thou art the Christ, the Son of the
living God ") I will build My Church, and the gates of
Hades shall not prevail against it." And what is the
Church but the Temple of the living God, of which the
Tabernacle and material Temple in Jerusalem were but
types, and in which His fulness and glory shall be *eternally*
manifested ?   Thus the Apostle Peter, addressing primarily
Jewish believers, says : " Ye also as living stones are built
up *a spiritual House*" ; and in a yet fuller manner, Paul,
addressing Gentile believers, writes : " Ye are no more
strangers and sojourners, but ye are fellow-citizens with the
saints and of the household of God, being built upon the
foundation of the apostles and prophets, Christ Jesus
Himself being the Chief Corner-stone ; in whom each
several building, fitly framed together, groweth into a *holy
temple in the Lord*; in whom ye also are builded together
for an *habitation of God* in the Spirit " (Eph. ii. 19–22,
R.V.).   And how glorious is this Temple which " the Man
Whose Name is the Branch " is now, by His Spirit through
His servants, building !   It is He Who, as the Eternal
Word, built the material Temple of the Universe, which is
filling the minds of men in successive generations more and
more with wonder and astonishment.   What a spectacle,
for instance, do the starry heavens present to us !   The
more we contemplate them, the more we are lost in wonder
at their immeasurable immensity, and the more do our
hearts go up in reverent adoration of the God Whose
eternity, glory, power, and wisdom they ceaselessly proclaim
in language intelligible to every human heart.   But the
spiritual Temple which He is now engaged in building,
when completed, will astonish even the admiring angels,
and will throughout eternity show forth *to principalities and
powers* in heavenly places " the *manifold wisdom*" as well
as the infinite grace of God (Eph. iii. 10).

But to proceed to the next sentence :

" *And He shall bear the glory, or regal majesty.*" [1]

[1] The word הוד—*hōd*—is used in different significations, but it is *especially*

The pronoun is again emphatic: *He Himself*, and none other, shall build the Temple of Jehovah, and *He Himself* shall bear the glory, or regal majesty, as none other has borne it. He is *peerless* in His work and in His reward. His is the glory of *the only-begotten of the Father*, full of grace and truth.

Already, as the result of His sufferings, having by the grace of God tasted death for every man, He is " exalted and extolled, and lifted very high," " crowned with honour and glory "; but this prophecy speaks especially of the royal majesty which He shall bear when He shall come forth again from the presence of the Father—and, all His enemies having been made a footstool for His feet, He shall sit down upon *His own throne* as the theocratic King of Israel.

Then, indeed, upon His head there shall be " many crowns "; for, not only will God the Father invest Him with glory and majesty, but men too, especially His own nation, will glorify Him; " and He," as the true Son of David, the One Whose right it is to reign, " shall be for a throne of glory to His Father's house: *and they shall hang upon Him all the glory of His Father's house*, the offspring and the issue, every small vessel, from the vessels of cups to the vessels of flagons " (Isa. xxii. 23, 24). We come to the next sentence of the prophecy:

" *And He shall sit and rule upon His throne*,"

i.e., He shall not only possess the honour and dignity of a king; He shall not be " a constitutional " monarch, who reigns but does not rule; but He shall Himself *exercise* all royal power and authority. Yes, the rule of King-Messiah will be absolute and *autocratic*, but autocracy will be safe

employed to describe *royal* majesty (Jer. xxii. 18; 1 Chron. xxix. 25; Dan. xi. 21). Pusey observes: " This word is almost always used of the special glory of God, and then, although seldom, of the majesty of those on whom God confers majesty, as Moses or Joshua (Num. xxvii. 20), or the *glory of the kingdom given to Solomon*" (1 Chron. xxix. 25). It is used of the glory or majesty to be laid on the ideal King in Ps. xxi. 5—which the Jews themselves interpreted of the Messiah.

and beneficent in the hands of the Holy One, Who is
infinite in wisdom, power, and love.   The result of His
blessed rule will be that—

> "In His days shall the righteous flourish ;
> And abundance of peace till the moon be no more.
> He shall have dominion also from sea to sea,
> And from the River unto the ends of the earth.
> Yea, all kings shall fall down before Him';
> All nations shall serve Him.
> He shall judge the poor of the people,
> He shall save the children of the needy,
> And shall break in pieces the oppressor ;
> For He shall deliver the needy when he crieth,
> And the poor that hath no helper.
> He shall redeem their soul from oppression and violence :
> And precious shall their blood be in His sight. . . .
> And men shall be blessed in Him :
> All nations shall call Him blessed."
>
>   (Ps. lxxii.)

The *character* of His blessed rule is further explained
in the next sentence :

" *And He shall be a priest upon His throne.*"

How full of significance is this one sentence of Holy
Writ !   As is the manner of Zechariah, we have in these
four Hebrew words a terse summary of nearly all that the
former prophets have spoken of Messiah and His work.

Here is the true Melchizedek, Who is at the same time
King of Righteousness, King of Salem, which is King of
Peace, and the great High Priest, whose priesthood, unlike
the Aaronic, abideth " for ever."   " He shall be a Priest
upon His throne."

Now He royally exercises His high priestly office as
the Advocate with the Father, and only Mediator between
God and man, at the right hand of God in heaven.   From
thence He shall come forth again to take possession of His
throne, and to commence His long-promised reign on the
earth.   But, even when as King he exercises His sovereign
rule, He will still be " a *Priest* upon His throne," who will
have compassion upon the ignorant and erring (Heb. v. 2),

and cause His righteous severity to go forth only against the wilfully froward and rebellious.   For our Lord Jesus is " the same yesterday, to-day, and for ever "; and that which will eternally constitute His *chief* glory will be, not His power, but *His grace*, manifested once in His laying down His life—a ransom for many—and since in His priestly *mediatorial* rule, whether in heaven or on earth.

" *And the counsel of peace shall be between them both.*"

The expression *atsath shalom*, " counsel of peace," means not merely " peace," for if that alone were meant, the simple idiom וְהָיָה שָׁלוֹם, *vehayah shalom*, " there shall be peace between them both," would be used.   The word used here signifies a *counsel planning or procuring* peace for some other than those who counsel.

But who are " the twain " who thus devise peace for man between them ?

Some commentators consider that the offices of Priest and King are alluded to, but the phraseology naturally constrains us to think of persons, not of things or abstract offices.   The explanation advocated by Hengstenberg, and adopted by Koehler, is a probable and reasonable one— namely, that " the reference is to the two offices of Priest and King combined in the Person of Messiah, and that the prophecy speaks of a plan *devised by Messiah in His double character*, whereby peace and salvation should be secured for the people of God," and on the earth during His reign. " This fact," observes Dr. Wright, " agrees with the New Testament statements in which the angelic choirs are re- presented announcing ' Peace on earth ' as one of the results of Christ's birth ; and with our Lord's own words, ' Peace I leave with you—My peace I give unto you,' the full realisa- tion of which is exhibited in the final vision of the Book of Revelation."   But I am personally inclined to think that another view, which is held by many scholars, is the right one—namely, that " the two " are Jehovah and the Messiah, or " Jesus and the Father." [1]   " It is clear, no doubt, that the

[1] Pusey.

pronoun '*His*' in the expression ' His throne ' is used twice
in ver. 13 in reference to the Messiah, and cannot well be
regarded as relating to Jehovah. The royal dignity of the
Messiah is specially referred to, inasmuch as the Messiah,
as King, would have power to perform the work which He
had to do. But the fact that the pronoun in the phrase
' His throne ' cannot refer to Jehovah, does not prove that
Jehovah cannot be one of the two persons referred to at
the close of the verse. Two, and only two, persons are
referred to in the verse—namely, the Lord and the Lord's
Christ ; and many eminent scholars—as Vitringa, Reuss,
Pusey, and Jerome—have considered that these are the two
Persons to whom reference is made in the clause, ' the
counsel of peace shall be between them both.'

" The prophecy indeed is closely connected with Ps. cx.,
where a ' counsel ' between the Lord and His Christ is
plainly referred to, and where Messiah is predicted as King
and Priest. This is the natural meaning, and the way in
which the words were no doubt interpreted by the hearers
of the prophet Zechariah." [1]

" In Christ," to quote another writer, " all is perfect
harmony. There is a counsel of peace between Him and
the Father whose Temple He builds. The will of the
Father and the Son is one. Both have one will of love
toward us, the salvation of the world, bringing forth peace
through our redemption. God the Father *so loved the world
that He gave His only-begotten Son, that whosoever believeth
in Him should not perish but have everlasting life* ; and God
the Son *is our peace, who hath made both one, that He might
reconcile both unto God in one body by the cross, and came and
preached peace to them which were afar off, and to them that
were nigh* " (Eph. ii. 14, 16, 17).

In all fulness, however, the blessed fruit of this
" counsel of peace," and the " thoughts of salvation " between
the Father and the Son, will only be realised by Israel
and the nations of the earth during the period of Messiah's
reign, and by the one Church of the living God through

[1] Dr. Wright.

the eternity that is to follow. *Then*—in the limitless ages
to come—" He will show the exceeding riches of His grace
in kindness toward us in Christ Jesus, according to His
good pleasure which He purposed in Him unto a dispensation of the fulness of the times, to sum up all things in
Christ, the things in the heavens, and the things upon the
earth . . . according to the purpose of Him who worketh all
things after the counsel of His will " (Eph. i. 9–11, ii. 7, R.V.).

We now come to the 14th verse. First let me give a
word of explanation in reference to the difference of the
names here as compared with the 10th verse. As to חֵלֶם,
Helem, it is the same as חֶלְדַּי, *Heldai*, the difference being
probably occasioned by a very slight scribal error of
running two separate Hebrew letters into one. " *Hen* " is
not a proper name at all, but an appellative, meaning "the
favour," or " grace," and is rightly rendered in the margin
of the R.V. and by all scholars, "and for *the kindness*
of the son of Zephaniah."

This is very beautiful. The crowns were to be
deposited in the Temple of God as a memorial, not only
of these three distinguished strangers who had brought
their own and their brethren's offerings for the House of
God, but as a memorial also of " the kindness " of this true
son of Abraham, who, as stated at the beginning of this
exposition, was evidently a man given to hospitality, and
received these three strangers into his house. It was
apparently a small service rendered to the cause of God,
but it was very *precious* to Him because it was doubtless
done for His Name's sake. And so many a little and
apparently insignificant deed done out of love for our Lord
Jesus—yea, even the cup of cold water given in the name
of a disciple—is treasured up in His memory, and shall in
no wise lose its reward—" For God is not unrighteous to
forget your work, and labour of love, which ye have showed
toward His Name, in that ye have ministered to the saints,
and do minister " (Heb. vi. 10). " As we have therefore
opportunity, let us do good unto all men, especially unto
them who are of the household of faith " (Gal. vi. 10).

But while the crowns were to be thus deposited in the Temple as a memorial of these four men, they were also to serve as a pledge and earnest of the fulfilment of the prophecy, and of the realisation of the symbolical action on which it was based : " *And they that are far off shall come and build in the Temple of the Lord.*"

These words not only refer to those Jews who were still in the far lands of the dispersion, who in Messiah's time would be gathered, and take their share in the building of the future Temple, as some have explained, but are a glorious promise, as I have already stated at the beginning, of the conversion of the Gentiles, and of the time when all nations would walk in the light of Jehovah. " It is probable," as another writer suggests, " that the great Apostle of the Gentiles may have had this prophecy in his view when he reminded his converts in Ephesus that now in Christ Jesus ye who sometimes were *far off* have become nigh through the blood of Christ (Eph. ii. 13)." On the other hand, Peter probably understood the similar expressions to which he gave utterance as referring (primarily) to the dispersed of Israel. " The promise is to you and to your children, *and to all that are afar off,* even as many as the Lord our God shall call " (Acts ii. 39).

But again, I repeat, that whatever fulfilment of the words we may already see, the full realisation of them will not be until Messiah sits and reigns a " Priest upon His throne " over Israel. Then, when the law shall go forth out of Zion, and the word of the Lord from Jerusalem, and converted Israel goes forth declaring among the peoples the wonderful works of God, shall the nations which are still " afar off " learn His ways and walk in His paths, and come with their tribute of worship and service to His Temple.

" *And ye shall know that Jehovah of hosts has sent Me unto you.*" The fulfilment, or realisation, of what had here been predicted in symbol and verbal prophecy would be, so to say, the Divine authentication of the Message and Messenger, and " Israel will perceive that the speaker had been sent to them by Jehovah of hosts." Keil, however, from whom I quote the last sentence, contends that it is not the prophet who thus speaks, but the Angel of Jehovah. " For although in what precedes, only the prophet, and not the Angel of Jehovah, has appeared as acting and speaking, we must not change the 'sending' into 'speaking' here, or understand the formula, or expression, used in any other sense here than in chap. ii. 8–11 and iv. 9. We must therefore assume that just as the words of the prophet pass imperceptibly into words of Jehovah, so here they pass into words of the Angel of Jehovah, who says, concerning Himself, that Jehovah hath sent Him."

The final sentence of the prophecy reads : " *And this shall come to pass (vehayah : ' this shall be ') if (or when) ye diligently obey* (lit., ' *if hearkening ye shall hearken* '—i.e., ' *give heed with a view to obey* ') *the voice of Jehovah your God.*"

Not that the fulfilment of the prophecy will be conditional on their obedience—that is, conditional on the *will and unchangeable purpose of God alone*—but *their participation in it* depends on their faith and obedience. " Because He had said, ' And ye shall know that Jehovah of hosts hath sent Me unto you,'" observes an old writer. " He warns them that the fruit of that coming will reach to those only who should hear God, and with ardent mind join themselves to His Name. For as many as believed in Him were made sons of God, but the rest were cast into outer darkness."

The whole Hebrew phrase, I may point out, is taken bodily from Deut. xxviii. 1, where it is rendered : " And it shall come to pass, if thou shalt hearken diligently unto the voice of the Lord thy God "—then all the blessings promised to them under the old covenant would be enjoyed by them. Under the law, however, though they were very ready to promise, they had no power " diligently to hearken " or to obey the voice of Jehovah their God, and instead of enjoying the blessings they came under the *curse* of the law. But what was impossible under the law shall be realised under grace. Then, as one great blessing of the New Covenant under which they shall be brought, the law of God shall be put *in their inward parts* and written in their hearts, or, as we read in Jer. xxxii. 38–41, " *They shall be My people, and I will be their God ; and I will give them one heart, and one way, that they may fear Me for ever, for the good of them, and their children after them : and I will make an everlasting covenant with them that I will not turn away from them, to do them good ; and I will put My fear in their hearts, that they shall not depart from Me. Yea, I will rejoice over them to do them good, and I will plant them in this land assuredly with My whole heart and with My whole soul.*"

And then, also—after Israel shall yield ready and joyful obedience to the voice of Jehovah their God—" shall come to pass " what is stated in the first part of the last verse of the prophecy which we have been considering, and the Gentile nations " that are afar off shall come and build in the Temple of Jehovah." " *And Jehovah shall be King over all the earth : in that day shall Jehovah be One, and His Name One.*"

Chapter 11

ADDRESS TO THE DEPUTATION FROM BETHEL ON THE QUESTION OF THE CONTINUED OBSERVANCE OF THE FASTS
THE NEGATIVE ANSWER

Zechariah 7

And it came to pass in the fourth year of King Darius, that the word of Jehovah came unto Zechariah in the fourth day of the ninth month, even in Chislev. Now they of Bethel had sent Sharezer and Regem-melech, and their men, to entreat the favour of Jehovah, and to speak unto the priests of the house of Jehovah of hosts, and to the prophets, saying, Should I weep in the fifth month, separating myself, as I have done these so many years? Then came the word of Jehovah of hosts unto me, saying, Speak unto all the people of the land, and to the priests, saying, When ye fasted and mourned in the fifth and in the seventh month, even these seventy years, did ye at all fast unto Me, even to Me? And when ye eat, and when ye drink, do not ye eat for yourselves, and drink for yourselves? Should ye not hear the words which Jehovah cried by the former prophets, when Jerusalem was inhabited and in prosperity, and the cities thereof round about her, and the South and the lowland were inhabited? And the word of Jehovah came unto Zechariah, saying, Thus hath Jehovah of hosts spoken, saying, Execute true judgment, and show kindness and compassion every man to his brother; and oppress not the widow, nor the fatherless, the sojourner, nor the poor; and let none of you devise evil against his brother in your heart. But they refused to hearken, and pulled away the shoulder, and stopped their ears, that they might not hear. Yea, they made their hearts as an adamant stone, lest they should hear the law, and the words which Jehovah of hosts had sent by His Spirit by the former prophets: therefore there came great wrath from Jehovah of hosts. And it came to pass that, as He cried, and they would not hear, so they shall cry, and I will not hear, saith Jehovah of hosts; but I will scatter them with a whirlwind among all nations which they have not known. Thus the land was desolate after them, so that no man passed through nor returned: for they laid the pleasant land desolate.

Chapter 11

NEARLY two years had elapsed since that memorable night on which the series of eight visions were shown to the prophet—in which are unfolded, as in a wonderful panorama, the thoughts and purposes of God concerning Israel and the nations from the beginning to the very end of this age—when the word of Jehovah came again to Zechariah. The day, the month, and the year of this divine oracle are clearly given—it was "*in the fourth day of the ninth month, even in Chislev*" (answering to December), "*in the fourth year of King Darius.*"[1]

The occasion when the prophet was inspired to utter this great and comforting prophecy, which stands separate and complete in itself, though going over in plain, verbal prophecy the same line of thought as unfolded by the visions, is clearly stated in the first three verses of chap. vii.

To understand the circumstances which brought about the very significant incident recorded in these verses, we have to remember that the fourth year of Darius was a time when things seemed to go well, and looked promising to the remnant who had returned to the land. Every hindrance to the completion of the building of the Temple had been removed by the royal decree of Darius, as recorded in Ezra vi. Even the city of Jerusalem, in spite of the desolations which still prevailed in some of its quarters, and the ruinous condition of its walls, was beginning to improve and revive, and contained already some fine private residences, as we may judge from Hag. i. 4.

The question, therefore, naturally agitated the minds of

[1] Compare chap. i. 7. From Ezra vi. 15 we learn that it was just about two years before the final completion of the Temple, which they were then building.

the people whether, with these signs of apparent prosperity the restored remnant should continue to observe the days of national sorrow and fasting which had been instituted in commemoration of the destruction of the Temple, and the desolation of the land at the commencement of the seventy years' captivity.

The initiative in bringing this point to an issue was taken by the inhabitants of Bethel, who sent a deputation of two of their prominent citizens, "with his men"[1] (*i.e.*, attendants or retainers of Regem-melech—he being probably a man of importance), "*to entreat the favour of Jehovah, and to speak unto the priests of the house of Jehovah of hosts, and to the prophets, saying, Should I* (or, '*Shall I continue to*') *weep in the fifth month, separating myself as I have done these so many years?*"

One or two further explanatory notes are necessary on these first verses before we can proceed.

(1) It will be noticed that, together with the Revised Version, and almost all modern scholars, we discard the rendering given of the first line of the 2nd verse in the Authorised Version, namely, "*When they sent unto the House of God.*" Now, Bethel does mean literally "House of God"; but it is never used of the Temple, but only and always of the well-known town of Ephraim, one of the great centres of the Israelitish idolatrous worship set up by Jeroboam the son of Nebat.[2] Some commentators, with the Septuagint and some of the Jewish interpreters, have taken Bethel in the accusative, and have rendered the words, "When they (the Jews) sent to Bethel"; but no reason can be assigned for such a deputation being sent to Bethel, since the "priests of the House of Jehovah of Hosts," which all agree must mean the Temple, "and the prophets," whom the deputation was to consult, most

---

[1] The rendering "their men" in the Authorised and Revised Versions is not accurate according to the Massoretic text.

[2] בית יהוה ("Beth Jehovah") is used altogether about two hundred and fifty-nine times, and בית אלהים ("Beth Elohim"), or בית האלהים ("Beth ha-Elohim"), about fifty times in the Hebrew Scriptures of the Temple; but בית אל ("Bethel") not once.

certainly lived in and about Jerusalem. Besides, considering its previous history as a centre of Israelitish idolatry,
the Jews were not in the least likely to have gone, or sent
there, " to entreat the face of Jehovah." On the other
hand, it is not only in accord with Bible history, but there
is a special significance in a deputation coming from Bethel
to Jerusalem. According to the original division of the
land by Joshua, Bethel fell to Benjamin (Josh. xviii. 13);
but at the great schism from the House of David under
Jeroboam it went with that part of Benjamin which fell
away with the northern tribes, and became the chief centre,
as already stated, of the idolatrous worship set up by the
son of Nebat, who built there a " sanctuary," or temple, in
imitation of, and as a rival to, the Temple in Jerusalem, as
well as a royal palace for his own residence (Amos vii. 13).

It was overthrown and became desolate in the overthrow, first of the northern kingdom of Israel by Assyria,
and again in the subsequent overthrow of Judah, and the
desolation of the whole land by the Babylonians; but it
was rebuilt after the partial restoration at the conclusion of
the seventy years' captivity, and a considerable number of
the former inhabitants, mixed probably with some from the
other tribes, once again settled in it (Ezra ii. 28; Neh. vii.
32, xi. 31).

Now, the special significance in this deputation from
Bethel to the " House of Jehovah " in Jerusalem lies in the
fact that it is, as J. P. Lange and Dr. Wright well point
out, an evidence " that the lessons taught by the Assyrian
and Babylonian captivities were not lost upon the men of
Bethel." The men who had formerly belonged to the
northern ten-tribed kingdom no longer cherished hopes of
a separate destiny, nor looked to a different centre than
their brethren of Judah. "Notwithstanding the many
sacred memories connected with their city, and the fact
that it had been the seat of a Temple in the days of the
Israelitish kingdom, to which the tribes of Israel had
resorted in numbers, no attempt was now made on their
part to dispute the legitimate right to Jerusalem being

regarded as the only place where the sacrifices and services
enjoined by the precepts of the Mosaic Law could be
offered."

(2) Owing to the omission of the particle אֵת (*eth*)
after Bethel, which in such cases usually indicates the
accusative, Ewald, Koehler, Dr. Wright, and others have
taken the clause, " Sharezer Regem-melech and his men,"
as in apposition with Bethel, and have translated the
2nd verse thus: " And Bethel, that is Sharezer Regem-
melech and his men, sent to entreat Jehovah," etc.; but we
agree with Keil that there is something so harsh and
inflexible in the assumption of such an apposition as this,
that, in spite of the omission of the particle, it is preferable
to regard the names as in the accusative, even as the
Revised Version has done.

(3) As to the names of these men, it is a rather
striking fact that, while those who came as a deputation
from Babylon with the offering to the House of the Lord,
in chap. vi. 9–15, bore names all expressive of some
relationship to Jehovah, those who came from Bethel have
foreign names which originally were associated with the
false worship of their oppressors. שַׂרְאֶצֶר (*Sharetser*) was
the name of one of the parricide sons of Sennacherib (Isa.
xxxvii. 38), and also of one of the princes of Babylon who
desolated Jerusalem and destroyed the Temple (Jer. xxxix.
3–13). The full Assyrian name was Nergal-Sarusur, or
Nergal-Shar-Ezer, which, according to Schrader, means
" May Nergal protect the king." Here Nergal, the name
of the Assyrian false god, is dropped, but the prayer,
originally idolatrous, is retained.

רֶגֶם (*Regem*) is found as a proper name in 1 Chron.
ii. 47. Gesenius explains Regem-melech as signifying
" friend of the king." It may originally also have been
an Assyrian name, though Regem has not been found in
that language, but has been explained from the Arabic.
But it is probable that, as in the case of Daniel, Hananiah,
and Mishael, so these men also, apart from the names
bestowed upon them by their Gentile conqueror, in whose

service they stood, had also their proper Jewish names; and the reason why their Babylonian or Assyrian names are given here is probably to mark them out as men of importance, who very likely held positions of office in the Court of Assyria or Babylon.

(4) The deputation, after entreating the favour of the Lord by presenting gifts and offerings,[1] was instructed to address the inquiry "to the priests of the House of Jehovah of hosts," because according to the Mosaic institution they in all such matters were to teach Jacob God's judgments, and Israel His law (Deut. xxxiii. 8–10); or, as we have it in the beautiful picture in Mal. ii. 5–7, "the priest's lips should keep knowledge, and they should seek the law at his mouth." That they should also consult "the prophets"—that is, Haggai and Zechariah—was very natural, since by their ministry, and its immediate powerful effect in rousing the people to the long-neglected task of rebuilding the Temple, they had indeed proved and authenticated themselves in the sight of the whole people to be "Jehovah's messengers in Jehovah's message" (Hag. i. 13).

(5) The question itself was, "*Shall I* (i.e., *the city of Bethel*) *weep in the fifth month, separating myself* (הַנָּזֵר— *hinnazer*—like the Nazarite who 'separated himself,' or abstained from strong drink and other bodily indulgences);[2] *as I have done these many years?*"

The fast of the fifth month, which is the month of Ab, answering to August, is still observed by the Jews on the ninth day, in celebration of the destruction of Jerusalem by Nebuchadnezzar; but, according to the Talmud and Jewish historians, the following list of calamities all happened on

---

[1] The phrase חִלָּה פְּנֵי (*ḥilah penei*) primarily signifies to "*stroke the face*," hence to entreat favour, or to appease, or propitiate. It is used of entreating the favour of the rich with gifts (Job xi. 19; Prov. xix. 6; Ps. xlv. 12), and is often used in reference to God. No intelligent reader is, of course, in any danger of misunderstanding these anthropomorphic expressions in the Bible when applied to God.

[2] Fasting and mourning were generally accompanied with weeping (comp. Judg. xx. 26; 1 Sam. i. 7; 2 Sam. i. 12; Ezra x. 1; Neh. i. 4, etc.).

the same day, namely: (1) On that day the decree went forth
from God in the wilderness that the people should not
enter the land because of their unbelief; (2) on the very
same day of the destruction of the First Temple by the
Chaldeans, the Second Temple also was destroyed by the
Romans; (3) on that day, after the rising under Bar
Cochba, the city of Bethar was taken, "in which were
thousands and myriads of Israel, and they had a great
king whom all Israel and the greatest of the wise men
thought was King Messiah"; but (4) he fell into the
hands of the Gentiles, and they were all put to death, and
the affliction was great, like as it was in the desolation of
the Sanctuary; (5) and lastly, on that day "the wicked
Turnus Rufus, who is devoted to punishment, ploughed up
the (hill of the) Sanctuary, and the parts round about it,
to fulfil that which was said by Micah, 'Zion shall be
ploughed as a field.' "[1]

Here, however, the inquiry doubtless had reference only
to the fast in celebration of the destruction of the First
Temple by the Chaldeans, the continued observance of
which, now that the new Temple was almost finished,
might seem to them almost incongruous, especially as the
prophets proclaimed that the restoration of the Temple
would be a sign that Jehovah had once more restored His
favour to His people. The question, as Keil observes, also
involved the prayer "that the Lord would continue permanently to bestow upon His people the favour which He
had restored to them, and not only to bring to completion
the restoration of the Holy Place, but accomplish generally
the glorification of Israel which had been predicted by
the earlier prophets"; or, to quote another writer, "the
question was in some respects similar to that asked by the
Apostles of the Lord after His resurrection, 'Lord, wilt
Thou at this time restore again the Kingdom to Israel?'"[2]

The Lord's answer to this question through the mouth
of His prophet divides itself into two parts—the first,

---

[1] See Maimonides yad ha-chazaqah, Hilchoth Taanith, c. 5.
[2] Dr. C. H. H. Wright.

which may be described as the negative part of the answer, being contained in chap. vii. 4–14 ; and the second, or positive part, in chap. viii. Each of these two larger divisions is, however, again subdivided into two sections. The whole answer, thus falling into four parts, each of which begins with the words, " *And the word of Jehovah of hosts came to me, saying* " (vii. 4, 8, viii. 1, 18)—the usual formula, as has already been poined out, by which the prophets authenticated their messages as being not of, or from, themselves, but from the mouth of the Lord.

We said at the beginning that, though these two chapters are a prophecy separate and complete in itself, it will be found on close examination to go over the same line of thought as unfolded in the series of visions in the first six chapters. The outstanding feature of this prophecy, even as it was of the visions, is that they are *debharim tobhim*, *debharim nichummim* (" good words, even comforting words," chap. i. 13). In both there are the consolatory anounce- ments that " Jehovah is jealous for Zion with great jealousy," and will " return to Jerusalem with mercies " ; and that not only would the people be restored and the land be rebuilt, but that He Himself would dwell in the midst of Jerusalem, which should be known henceforth as the " city of truth " and " the holy mountain "—the centre to which the Gentile nations shall come to seek Jehovah to be taught in His way.[1]

But as the consolatory messages in the visions are introduced by a call to repentance, and the reminder that all their sorrows and troubles were occasioned by their disobedience to the words which Jehovah had spoken to them through the former prophets (chap. i. 1–6), so also the wonderful prophecy of the future blessing of Israel and the future glory of Jerusalem in chap. viii. is preceded by what is practically also a call to repentance in chap. vii. 4–14, and the exhortation to give heed at last to the words of the same " former prophets."

[1] Comp. chap. i. 14 with viii. 2 ; chap. i. 16 with viii. 3 ; chap. ii. 4 with viii. 4, 5 ; chap. ii. 10, 11 with viii. 3, 20–23.

But let us now examine in detail the different parts of the answer.

The first "word of Jehovah" which the prophet was commissioned to speak not only to the deputation from Bethel, but to "*all the people of the land*" whose thought the men of Bethel expressed, "*and to the priests*," who, instead of answering to the ideal "messengers of Jehovah of hosts" (Mal. iii. 5), and being able to give answer in such an emergency, had, in Haggai's and Zechariah's time, sunk to the same level as the people—was designed to show the worthlessness before God of mere outword acts, or forms of repentance and piety, if the inner spirit of them be wanting.

"*When ye fasted and mourned in the fifth month and in the seventh, even these seventy years, did ye at all fast unto Me, even Me?*"

In these words the Lord overthrows the false notion which they may have entertained, which certainly the Jews now do entertain, that fasting in itself is a meritorious act. He admits that they had fasted *long*, "seventy years," and often, not only in the fifth but also "in the seventh month," which was the fast appointed for the murder of Gedaliah, which completed the calamities of Jerusalem, and led to the migration of the little remnant to Egypt for fear of the vengeance of the Chaldeans.

Moreover, they were very thorough and earnest about their fasts; they not only abstained from food (as in Jewish fasts still, which are one unbroken abstinence from food and drink from sunset to sunset), but they accompanied their fasting with mourning and lamentations—the word used in the 5th verse being used for mourning *for the dead* or for special great public calamities—and yet their observance of these fasts was a matter of utter indifference to God. Why? Because even in their fasting and mourning they were centred on themselves; **they fasted** not *unto God*. It was not the outward sign and **accom**paniment of true sorrow and repentance for sin, **but of** sorrow for their calamities. They were self-imposed, to begin with ; and they regarded them, not only as intrinsically meritorious, but as an end in themselves rather than as the means of turning away from self and all idea of self-merit to the grace of God. And not only in their fasts but also in their feasts there was the same concentration on self and regardlessness of God. "*And when ye eat and when ye drink, do not ye eat for yourselves and drink for yourselves ?*" which is the very opposite of the apostolic exhortation, which really sums up the intention and spirit of the many precepts and commandments of the law— "*Whether, therefore, ye eat or drink, or whatsoever ye do, do all to the glory of God.*"

But apart from the special message which they conveyed to those to whom they were originally addressed, and their application to the Jewish people at the time, there is a solemn lesson in these words which men at the present time, both Jews and Christians, should lay to heart. Are there not thousands now who are very zealous and regular in religious observances, and who think that they are acquiring great merit before God, to whom Christ in that day will say, " Depart from Me ; I never knew you ? " *Did ye at all do it unto Me, even Me ?* Was it not for the most part will-worship and mere religiousness, without any knowledge of, or real regard for, the will of God ?

The 7th verse begins in the Hebrew with the words, *Halo eth haddebharim asher qara Yehovah*—to which most translators and commentators have supplied a verb, on the supposition that the sentence is elliptical, and have rendered it, " Should ye not hear the words which Jehovah hath cried," as the Authorised and Revised Versions do ; or, " Should ye not *do* the words," etc., as Maurer and others translate ; or, " Do ye not know the words," according to Ewald, Koehler, Pusey, and others. But the sentence is also capable of another rendering, which we are inclined to think is the correct one, namely : "*Are not these the very things which Jehovah cried* (that, is ' *did He not have the same complaints to make, and the same remonstrances to*

*address'), through the former prophets, when Jerusalem was
inhabited and in prosperity* (or '*in safety*'), *and her cities
round about her, and the South and the lowland were
inhabited?* " the three districts named being those into which
the land of Judah was divided, namely, the *Negebh*, which
is " the southern district," extending as far as Beersheba
(Josh. xv. 21); the *Shephelah*, or "lowland" district,
toward the west; and the "hill country of Judah," which
is here included under "Jerusalem and the cities round
about."

There are many Scriptures in the former prophets
which bear witness to the truth of what Zechariah here
affirms, namely, God's repudiation of mere outward acts of
religious observances, and particularly of *fasting*, as being
in any way pleasing to Him. "Wherefore have we fasted,"
we read, for instance, in Isa. lviii., "and thou seest not?
Wherefore have we afflicted our soul, and Thou takest no
knowledge?" Then the answer, which is very much the
same as in Zechariah, "Did ye at all fast unto Me, even
Me?"—"*Behold in the day of your fast, you find your own
pleasure. . . . Ye shall not fast as ye do this day to make
your voice to be heard on high. Is it such a fast that I have
chosen? A day for a man to afflict his soul? Is it to bow
down his head like a bulrush, and to spread sackcloth and
ashes under him? Wilt thou call this a fast, and an acceptable day to the Lord?*" (Isa. lviii. 3–5).

But it is quite true, as another writer observes, that
reference is here made, not so much to the passages in the
former prophets, in which fasting is specially referred to (as,
e.g., the one from Isaiah just quoted) as to those numerous
Scriptures in which the general principle was taught which
was enunciated by Samuel in his question, "Hath the
Lord as great delight in burnt-offering and sacrifices as in
obeying the voice of the Lord?" (1 Sam. xv. 22, 23); or,
as set forth in the words of the great lawgiver, "And now,
Israel, what doth the Lord thy God require of thee, but to
fear the Lord thy God, to walk in His ways, and to love
Him, and to serve the Lord thy God with all thy heart and

with all thy soul, to keep the commandments of the Lord,
and His statutes, which I command thee this day for thy
good " (Deut. x. 12, 13).

This—that " to obey " is in God's sight " better than
sacrifice," and " to hearken " " than the fat of rams," and
that obedience to the great moral precepts of the law is
infinitely more important than meaningless ceremonies and
abstinence from meat and drinks, is brought out still more
clearly in the second section of the first part of the answer
(vers. 8–10).

" *And the word of the Lord came unto Zechariah, saying,
Thus hath the Lord of hosts spoken, saying, Execute true
judgment, and show mercy and compassion every man to his
brother : and oppress not the widow, nor the fatherless, the
stranger, nor the poor ; and let none of you imagine evil
against his brother in your heart.*"

Here we are reminded of Isa. lviii. 6–12, and many
other scriptures in the earlier prophets, where the Lord
tells us the kind of fast in which He does takes pleasure—
" *Is not this the fast that I have chosen ? to loose the bonds
of wickedness, to undo the bands of the yoke, and to let the
oppressed go free, and that ye break every yoke ? Is it not to
deal thy bread to the hungry, and that thou bring the; poor
that are cast out to thy house ? when thou seest the naked,
that thou cover him ; and that thou hide not thyself from
thine own flesh ?* (Isa. lviii. 6–8, R.V.).

But Zechariah, in the passage we are now considering
(vers. 8–10), instead of quoting the exact words of the
former prophets, gives the substance of their preaching on
this subject in words renewed to himself by the direct
inspiration of the Spirit of God.

We note also that it is particularly man's duties to his
neighbours which are here summarised ; but man's duty to
God is presupposed, for even the precepts which inculcate
love and mercy to our fellow-men, are enforced by the
words, " I am Jehovah *thy God,*" which remind us of our
relation and obligations to Him, even as in the New Testament it is our debt of love and gratitude to Christ which is

the impelling motive of love to the brotherhood. And let
me remind you, dear reader, that Christians do have need
to lay these moral precepts to heart, for though we are not
under the law, the law of God is written on our hearts, and
it is His purpose that the righteousness of the law should
be fulfilled in us who walk not after the flesh but after the
Spirit. Beside, whatever be our relation to the law of
Moses, we are "under law to Christ," and it is in the New
Testament that we are commanded to live and act justly
and righteously, and to "have compassion one upon the
other," and "to think no evil," which is the equivalent of
the beautiful word we have in this passage in Zechariah,
"Let none of you imagine evil against his brother in your
heart."

But to return to our context. This was the summary
of the teaching of the former prophets ; the result is stated
in vers. 11 and 12 : "*But they refused to hearken, and pulled
away the shoulder, and stopped their ears that they should not
hear. Yea, they made their hearts as an adamant stone, lest
they should hear the law, and the words which the Lord of
hosts had sent by His Spirit by the hand of the former prophets : therefore came there great wrath from the Lord of
hosts.*"

We have already pointed out the parallelism between the
line of thought in the consolatory message contained in
chaps. vii. and viii. and that which is unfolded in the series
of visions. The same is true also of the introductory
addresses, or calls to repentance, which in each case precede the prophecies of hope and of future glory. The
parallel to chap. vii. 8–14 is chap. i. 4–6. There also we
read, "Be not as your fathers, to whom the former prophets
cried, saying, Thus saith Jehovah of hosts, Return ye now
from your evil ways and your evil doings ; *but they did not
hear* nor hearken unto Me, saith Jehovah." Here, however,
the process of Israel's self-hardening and disobedience,
which brought about the desolation of the land and the
scattering of the people, is enlarged upon. (*a*) "*They
refused to hearken*" or to give heed to the word of God

through the prophets. (*b*) "*They pulled away the shoulder,*" *vayyitt'nu khatheph sorareth,* a Hebrew phrase which is found elsewhere only in that great confession in Neh. ix. 29, and means literally they offered a recusant, or unwilling, *rebellious shoulder,*[1] instead of serving Jehovah "with joyfulness and gladness of heart" (Deut. xxviii. 47), and finding His yoke easy and His burden light. (*c*) "*And stopped their ears,*" הִכְבִּידוּ (*hikhbidu*), literally, "*made it heavy,*" the word being the same as in that solemn passage, Isa. vi. 10, " Make the heart of the people fat, and *make their ears heavy,* and shut their eyes; lest they see with their eyes, and hear with their ears, and understand with their heart, and turn again, and be healed."

It is one of the terrible moral consequences of men turning away from *doing* the will of God, that the more they hear, the duller their perceptions become, so that in the end, though having eyes, they see not. (*d*) The final stage of this process of rebellious self-hardening is expressed in the first line of the 12th verse: " *And they made their hearts as an adamant stone.*" It is not quite certain what stone is meant by שָׁמִיר (*shamir*), but it was harder than flint (Ezek. iii. 9). In Jer. xvii. 1 it is rendered "diamond." " It was hard enough to cut ineffaceable characters; it would cut rocks, but could not be graven itself or receive the characters of God."[2]

Truly a fit figure to set forth the hardness and obduracy of the natural unregenerate heart. It is altogether hopeless, and nothing can be done to improve or soften it; the only hope for men in such condition being in this stony heart being altogether taken away by the power and grace of God, and in the creation within them of " an heart of flesh," responsive and impressionable to the Spirit and Word of God.

The enormity of the guilt of Israel is magnified by the

---

[1] That is, they shook off the yoke which was sought to be laid upon them, "as if they had been a refractory heifer struggling with all its might against the yoke laid upon it."—Wright; comp. Hos. iv. 16.

[2] Pusey.

fact that that which they refused to hear and to receive into
their hearts in order to obey was the תּוֹרָה (*torah*) "law,"
which we must take in the usual sense as describing the
law of Moses, and the דְּבָרִים (*debharim*), "words" of "the
former prophets," neither of which originated with man,
both being " *sent by Jehovah of hosts through the Spirit* ";
which is a very remarkable incidental statement of the Bible's
own claim to inspiration.[1]

The human channel of communication used of God
may be Moses, or Isaiah, or Jeremiah, or any of the other
"prophets," but the wonderful things they spoke came
not by the will of man, but these holy men of God
"spake as they were moved by the Holy Ghost" (2 Pet. i.
20, 21).

And the process of apostasy here described by Zechariah
did not end with the rejection of the law and the words
which God spoke through the prophets. It continued even
after the partial restoration, as far as the great majority of
the people was concerned. The climax was reached when,
after the continued process of disobedience and self-hardening, and because their hearts were already alienated from
God, Israel turned their backs upon Him Who was not only
the greatest of the prophets, but was Himself "the Word
of God"—"the brightness of His glory, and the express
image of His person."

Nor, alas! can Christendom boast or glory over the
Jews, for its history, too, is one of continued rebellion, not
only against the law and the prophets, but against the
greater light of New Testament revelation, and culminates
in the greatest apostasy in the history of the human race,
when Satan shall be worshipped instead of God, and Antichrist preferred to Christ.

The consequence of this continued provocation of God
and the hardening of their hearts against His word was
that *there came great wrath from Jehovah of hosts*," for God
is not mocked, and, however great and wonderful His

[1] The same we have in Neh. ix. 30; "And testifiest against them *by Thy Spirit through* the prophets."

patience and long-suffering, His anger is in the end poured out upon all who are obdurately impenitent.

On the last page of the Hebrew Bible—which, as the books are there arranged, closes with 2 Chronicles—we read these very sad and pathetic words: "*Moreover all the chiefs of the priests, and the people, trespassed very greatly after all the abominations of the heathen; and they polluted the house of the Lord which He had hallowed in Jerusalem. And the Lord, the God of their fathers, sent to them by His messengers, rising up early and sending; because He had compassion on His people and on His dwelling-place: but they mocked the messengers of God, and despised His words, and scoffed at His prophets, until the wrath of the Lord arose against His people, till there was no remedy*" (2 Chron. xxxvi. 14–16)—"till *there was no remedy*" and "*there came great wrath from Jehovah.*"

How His wrath showed itself is next described: "*And it came to pass as He cried* (that is, '*called, remonstrated, and reasoned with them through the prophets*') *and they would not hear, so they shall cry*" (*in their distress and anguish*) "*and I will not hear*"—solemn and awful words, which have not only verified themselves in the terrible history of the Jewish people these past two thousand years, but are a warning to the individual sinner, whether Jew or Gentile, of whom similar language is used,[1] when he hears God's voice, not to harden his heart and refuse to obey His word as Israel did, "in the provocation and the day of temptation in the wilderness," and who entered not into God's rest because of unbelief.

The last verse of the 7th chapter shows the awful consequences of the "great wrath" which came from Jehovah:

(*a*) In relation to the people. "*But I will scatter them*" וַאֲסָרֵם (*ve'esa-areim*—"*as with a whirlwind,*" or, "*I will toss them*") "*among all the nations whom they have not known*"; who will therefore have no pity or compassion upon them —a process which only *began* with the destruction of the

---

[1] Prov. i. 24–33.

First Temple and the seventy years' captivity in Babylon, but has continued all through the centuries since, during which the Jewish nation continues to be " sifted," or " tossed about among all nations as corn is tossed about in a sieve " (Amos ix.) [1]—until the times of the Gentiles shall be fulfilled, and " He that scattered Israel shall gather him and keep him as a shepherd doth his flock."

(b) In relation to the land. "And the land was desolate (or most probably, 'shall be desolate,' the perfect tense standing here for the future, or 'prophetic perfect') after them, so that there shall be no one passing through or returning" (meobher umishabh)—an idiom expressing the fact that the land shall be destitute of a population, so that there shall be none to pass to and fro, or " up and down " in it; a prophecy also which has not only verified itself during the seventy years' captivity, but in the course of the many centuries since the destruction of the Second Temple by the Romans, during which the land has in the providence of God been practically without a people, while the people has been without a land.

Hitherto in vers. 13 and 14 God in the first person has been the speaker, but the last sentence with which the chapter closes seems to be a reflection or ejaculation of the prophet's, in which he gives God the glory by ascribing the desolation which has come upon the land as due entirely to their sins: "And they made the pleasant land" (eretz ḥemdah, a beautiful and true description of the promised land which is carried over from Jer. iii. 19) "a desolation"; for, just as all nature was involved in Adam's sin, and ever since the Fall "the whole creation groaneth and travaileth in pain together until now" (Rom. viii.); so Palestine, which is indeed naturally "a delightsome" and fertile land, has in a special manner become involved in the sin of Israel, and lies desolate until the people's covenant relationship to

---

[1] See also Deut. xxviii. 49, 50, 64, 65; Jer. xvi. 13; and other places. Pusey rightly observes that the expressions "nations whom they know not," "whose tongue thou shalt not understand," are meant to set forth the intensification of their sufferings in captivity because the common bond between man and man, mutual speech, shall be wanting.

God is restored, when the land shall once again, and more than ever before, flow with milk and honey, and "the wilderness and the solitary place shall be glad, and the desert shall rejoice and blossom as the rose."

Now, in conclusion, to sum up the negative part of the answer to the question put by the deputation from Bethel. Its purport was as follows : There is no occasion as yet to abrogate the observances of the fasts in which you call to mind the calamities which you and your fathers have brought upon the land, by your evil ways and doings, for the underlying cause of the evil which came upon you— namely, sin and rebellion against the word which God spake to you through the former prophets—you have not yet truly repented of. Your fasting and mourning, however, are in themselves nothing to God so long as they are not the accompaniment of a real sorrow for sin, and a heart-desire to do His will as expressed in His moral law. Take warning, therefore, from the experience of your fathers— who kept on hardening their hearts, until there was no more remedy, and great wrath from God came upon them —lest the same, and something worse yet, happen to you.

The positive part of the answer, which tells when and how the fasts *shall* be abrogated, yea, turned into *feasts*, follows in chap. viii.

Chapter 12

ADDRESS TO THE DEPUTATION FROM BETHEL ON THE QUESTION OF THE OBSERVANCE OF FASTS

THE POSITIVE ANSWER

Zechariah 8

And the word of the Lord of hosts came to me, saying, Thus saith Jehovah of hosts : I am jealous for Zion with great jealousy, and I am jealous for her with great wrath. Thus saith Jehovah : I am returned unto Zion, and will dwell in the midst of Jerusalem : and Jerusalem shall be called The city of truth ; and the mountain of Jehovah of hosts, The holy mountain. Thus saith Jehovah of hosts : There shall yet old men and old women dwell in the streets of Jerusalem, every man with his staff in his hand for very age. And the streets of the city shall be full of boys and girls playing in the streets thereof. Thus saith Jehovah of hosts : If it be marvellous in the eyes of the remnant of this people in those days, should it also be marvellous in Mine eyes? saith Jehovah of hosts. Thus saith Jehovah of hosts : Behold, I will save My people from the east country, and from the west country ; and I will bring them, and they shall dwell in the midst of Jerusalem ; and I will be their God, in truth and in righteousness. Thus saith Jehovah of hosts : Let your hands be strong, ye that hear in these days these words from the mouth of the prophets, that were in the day that the foundation of the house of Jehovah of hosts was laid, even the Temple, that it might be built. For before those days there was no hire for man, nor any hire for beast ; neither was there any peace to him that went out or came in because of the adversary : for I set all men every one against his neigh- bour. But now I will not be unto the remnant of this people as in the former days, saith Jehovah of hosts. For there shall be the seed of peace ; the vine shall give its fruit, and the ground shall give its increase, and the heavens shall give their dew ; and I will cause the remnant of this people to inherit all these things. And it shall come to pass that, as ye were a curse among the nations, O house of Judah and house of Israel, so will I save you, and ye shall be a blessing. Fear not, but let your hands be strong. For thus saith Jehovah of hosts : As I thought to do evil unto you, when your fathers provoked Me to wrath, saith Jehovah of hosts, and I repented not ; so again have I thought in these days to do good unto Jerusalem and to the house of Judah : fear ye not. These are the things that ye shall do ; Speak ye every man the truth with his neighbour ; execute the judgment of truth and peace in your gates : and let none of you devise evil in your hearts against his neighbour ; and love no false oath : for all these are things that I hate, saith Jehovah. And the word of Jehovah of hosts came unto me, saying, Thus saith Jehovah of hosts : The fast of the fourth month, and the fast of the fifth, and the fast of the seventh, and the fast of the tenth, shall be to the house of Judah joy and gladness, and cheerful feasts ; therefore love truth and peace. Thus saith Jehovah of hosts : It shall yet come to pass, that there shall come peoples, and the inhabitants of many cities : and the inhabitants of one city shall go to another, saying, Let us go speedily to entreat the favour of Jehovah, and to seek Jehovah of hosts : I will go also. Yea, many peoples and strong nations shall come to seek Jehovah of hosts in Jerusalem, and to entreat the favour of Jehovah. Thus saith Jehovah of hosts : In those days it shall come to pass, that ten men shall take hold, out of all the languages of the nations, they shall take hold of the skirt of him that is a Jew, saying, We will go with you, for we have heard that God is with you.

Chapter 12

A S shown in the exposition of the 7th chapter, of which the scripture we are now to consider is a continuation, the message which the prophet was inspired to deliver, not only to the deputation from Bethel, but "to all the people of the land," in answer to the question whether they should continue to observe the fasts which had been appointed in celebration of certain sad anniversaries connected with the destruction of the Temple and the desolations of the land by the Chaldeans, divides itself into two parts.

The first, which I have described as the *negative* part of the answer, is contained in chap. vii.; and the second, or *positive* part, in chap. viii. "Each of these two larger divisions," to repeat some sentences from the previous exposition, "is, however, again subdivided into two sections —the whole answer thus falling into four parts, each of which begins with the words, '*And the word of Jehovah of hosts came to me, saying*' (vii. 4, 8, viii. 1, 18)—the usual formula, as has already been pointed out, by which the prophets authenticated their messages as being not of, or from, themselves, but from the mouth of the Lord."

The negative part of the answer in the 7th chapter may, moreover, be regarded in a very important sense as preparatory to the *debharim tobhim debharim nichummim* ("good words, even comforting words," i. 13), which the prophet proceeds to unfold in the glorious prophecy in chap. viii., inasmuch as chap. vii. is practically *a call to repentance*, and a solemn reminder that their sorrows were the direct consequence of their sins, and that before Israel's fasts shall at last turn to feasts, and they shall enjoy the

"good thing" which Jehovah has promised them, they
must give heed to the voice of the prophets, and be no
more like their fathers, who brought all these calamities
upon themselves by obdurate disobedience and progressive
apostasy from God.

The first section of the consolatory message in chap.
viii. consists of vers. 1 to 17.

The first thing which strikes us in reading the series of
great and precious promises in this scripture is the frequent
reiteration of the sentence—"saith Jehovah of hosts."
Apart from the authenticating formula, "The word of
Jehovah of hosts came unto me," by which each of the
four sections is introduced, it is repeated eleven times in the
first seventeen verses of the 8th chapter; and the object and
reason for it is to strengthen our faith, and to assure us at
the very outset that, however incredible from a natural or
human point of view the fulfilment of these things may be,
they will most *certainly* come to pass, because the Name of
the infinite, eternal, and faithful Jehovah, with Whom
nothing is too hard or impossible, stands pledged to their
accomplishment.[1]

Let us bear this in mind as we proceed, and not stagger
at the promises of God through unbelief, saying, as many,
alas, do say, "How is it possible?" The series of
promises commences with the words, " *Thus saith Jehovah
of hosts, I am jealous for Zion with great jealousy, and I
am jealous for her with great wrath* (or '*fury*')."

This is a repetition, with one slight variation in the
original, but "in the same rhythm," of the declaration of
His tender love for Zion in the first of the series of visions

[1] "At each word and sentence in which good things, for their greatness
almost incredible, are promised, the prophet declares, ' *Thus saith Jehovah of
hosts,*' as if he would say, Think not that what I pledge you are my own, and
refuse me not credence as man. What I unfold are the promises of God."—
Jerome.

So also Lange: "Es handelt sich darum eine ganze Reihe scheinbaren un-
möglichkeiten durch die Gewähr des Namens Jehovah Zebaoth in Gewissheiten
zu verwandeln." By making the name of Jehovah of hosts surety for their
accomplishment, a whole series of apparent impossibilities are thus turned into
certainties.

(chap. i. 14).[1] And because His love for Zion is so great, He is jealous on her account, and His anger is stirred to the heat of "*fury*" against the nations, for the reason already stated in the first vision, namely, because when He was but "a little displeased" and gave over "the dearly beloved of His soul" for a time into the hands of her enemies (Jer. xii. 7), the nations among whom they were scattered "showed them no mercy," but rather "helped forward the affliction."

We have dwelt fully on these solemn and fervent words of Jehovah and their application, not only to the great world-powers of antiquity, but to the nations of Christendom, in my exposition of the first vision, so we need not tarry on this point here. But I may take the opportunity of again emphasising one fact in connection with the warning to the nations contained in these words, and this is the testimony which history supplies, that God's jealous anger and hot displeasure against the nations, because of their oppression and cruelty to Israel, is to be greatly dreaded. "Where," to repeat a few sentences, "are the great nations of antiquity who have lifted up their hands against the Jewish people?"

And in modern times the ancient word which God spake to Abraham is still verifying itself in the experience of nations as of individuals: "I will bless them that bless thee, and him that curseth thee will I curse."

And the fervent inalienable love of Jehovah for His people will manifest itself, not only in His wrath and indignation against the nations who have oppressed and persecuted them, but in the full restoration of the long-interrupted communion.

"*Thus saith Jehovah, I am returned to Zion, and will dwell in the midst of Jerusalem*"—the glad announcement of which, contained in the two verbs *shabhti* and *shakhanti*

---

[1] Only חֵמָה גְדוֹלָה, *ḥemah gedolah,* "great heat of anger," or "fury," is here substituted for קֶצֶף גָּדוֹל, *qetseph gadol* (chap. i. 14), there rendered, "very sore displeased" in the English versions, but literally "great anger," though not quite so strong an expression as here.

("I am returned" and "I will dwell," which are in the prophetic perfect tense), being again an inspired repetition of the "good and comfortable words" which were set forth in the first vision.

Thus the word *shabhti* ("I am returned") takes us back to chap. i. 16 ("*I am returned—shabhtti—to Jerusalem with mercies*"), and *shakhanti* ("I will dwell") to chap. ii. 10, where we read, "*Sing and rejoice, O daughter of Zion : for, lo, I come, and I will dwell in the midst of thee, saith Jehovah.*"

According to some commentators these glad announcements of the return and dwelling of Jehovah in the midst of His people, in chap. viii., "signify nothing more nor less than the restitution of His favour and goodwill toward Israel,"[1] as shown in their partial restoration from Babylon, and in the relief which the remnant then experienced. But this is a very poor and inadequate view to take of this prophecy, as its very connection with the glorious predictions in chaps. i. and ii. itself shows. No, as I have shown in my notes on the first vision, the announcement, "I am returned to Zion with mercies," is itself the very heart and substance of the consoling part of the message which the prophet was commissioned to deliver ; and the fulfilment of the promise, "I will dwell in the midst of thee," is the goal to which all the former prophets looked forward, and will in its fulness be realised only in the visible and manifest reign—in and from Mount Zion, in the midst of restored and converted Israel, of Him Whose Name is "Immanuel" —which, being interpreted, is "God with us."

We take this promise, then, not only in a more literal, but, if we may use the expression, also in a more *personal* sense. At the commencement of "the times of the Gentiles," which began with the Babylonian Captivity, when God was about to give Israel over into the hands of their enemies, the prophet Ezekiel saw the slow and reluctant departure of the glory of Jehovah from the Temple and City of Jerusalem. And with this withdrawal

[1] C. H. H. Wright.

of the presence of Jehovah from the midst of His people, commenced Israel's *Ichabod* period, and the long night of darkness which has rested on the people and on the land. But not for ever has Jehovah forsaken His land and cast off His people. " I will go," He said through the prophet Hosea, " and return to My place *till* they acknowledge their offence " (or, lit., " till they declare themselves guilty "), " and seek My face: in their affliction (lit., ' in their tribulation') they shall seek Me early." Then He will return unto them with mercies, and "*His going forth is sure as the morning ; and He shall come unto us as the rain, as the latter rain that watereth the earth*" (Hos. v. 15, vi. 1–3).

In its fulness, to repeat again some sentences from the notes on the first vision, this promise will only be fulfilled when this same Jesus, Whom at His first coming they handed over to the Gentiles to be crucified, and Who, after His resurrection, ascended back into heaven to the glory which He had with the Father before the world was, shall return in the manner, and under the circumstances, described by the same prophet in the last three chapters of his prophecy.

Then Jehovah, in the person of the Messiah, " *will dwell in the midst of Jerusalem,*" which shall become the centre of His governmental dealings with the world, and the place whence light and truth shall go forth unto all the nations. " *And Jerusalem shall be called 'Ir ha-emeth, the City of Truth*"; first, because it shall be the seat of the *El-emeth*, " The God of Truth " ; and, secondly, because " the remnant of Israel," which shall then dwell in it, " shall not any longer do iniquity, nor speak lies " (Zeph. iii. 13), but be known throughout the earth for their truth and fidelity toward God and man. " *And the mountain of Jehovah of hosts,*" i.e., Mount Zion, shall be called " *The Holy Mountain,*" because there the Holy One of Israel shall once more take up His abode, and by His presence in their midst sanctify His people, so that they, too, shall be holy ; and, *Qodesh la-Yehovah*—" Holiness (or ' holy ') unto Jehovah," shall be written, not only upon their hearts and foreheads, but upon all their possessions, down to the very "bells of their horses," and the "pots" which they shall use to prepare their food.[1]

Now follows a beautiful picture of restored and flourishing Jerusalem. No longer shall the holy city, and the land of which it is the metropolis, be depopulated by wars and other grievous calamities, and lie desolate; no longer shall such terrible sights be witnessed in her streets as are described by inspired writers who witnessed the siege and capture of the city by the Babylonians, which, however, were surpassed in the still more awful and horrible conditions which prevailed during the siege and destruction of Jerusalem by the Romans, and in subsequent sieges since then—when old and young were cut off without mercy, and those children and sucklings who were not destroyed by the sword "fainted for hunger in the top of every street."[2] But the promises contained already in the law, of prolongation of life and numerous offspring, which in the past have been only at certain intervals partially fulfilled, because of Israel's sin and disobedience, shall, under the new and unconditional covenant, into which the people shall then be brought, be fully realised. There and then "*there shall be no more an infant of days, nor an old man that hath not filled his days.*" Then "they shall not build and another inhabit; they shall not plant and another eat; for *as the days of a tree shall be the days of My people*, and My chosen shall long enjoy the work of their hands" (Isa. lxv. 20–22). And thus it shall come to pass, *saith Jehovah of hosts*, that "*there shall yet old men and old women dwell in the streets of Jerusalem, every man with his staff in his hand, for multitude of days. And the streets of the city shall be full of boys and girls playing in the streets thereof.*" "The two opposite pictures," to adopt words of

---

[1] Chap. xiv. 20, 21. See also Isa. i. 26: "Thou shalt be called The City of Righteousness, The Faithful City"; lx. 14: "They shall call thee The City of Jehovah, the Zion of the Holy One of Israel"; lxii. 12: "They shall call them The Holy People, the Redeemed of the Lord."

[2] Lam. ii. 11–19; Ps. lxxviii. 63, 64.

another writer, " the old man so aged that he has to lean
on his staff for support because of the multitude of his
days," and the young in the glad buoyancy of recent life,
fresh from their Creator's hands (shall in that day) " attest
alike " (as in measure they do now in all communities of
men) " the goodness of the Creator Who protecteth both,
the children in their yet undeveloped strength, and the
very old, whom He hath brought through all the changes
and chances of this mortal life, in their yet sustained weakness ; for the tottering limbs of the very old, and the
elastic, perpetual motion (and playfulness) of childhood,
are like far distant chords of the diapason of the Creator's
love." [1]

Then, as if doubly to confirm the immutability of His
counsel, and to strengthen our hearts in the certain fulfilment of the things just announced, as well as of those
which follow—however " marvellous " or " impossible " they
may appear to human sight—there follows a brief parenthetical statement (ver. 6) which is closed in, so to say, by
a twofold use of the divine attesting formula, " saith Jehovah
of hosts."

Even the saved remnant, contemplating the actual
fulfilment of these great and precious promises, will exclaim,
" This is Jehovah's doing " (or, lit., " *This is of Jehovah* ";
for by no human or natural means could this have been
brought about)—" it is marvellous in our eyes " (Ps. cxviii.
23). But " *thus saith Jehovah of hosts, If it is marvellous
in the eyes of the remnant of this people in those days,*[2] *should
it also be marvellous in Mine eyes? saith Jehovah of hosts.*"

The word נִפְלָא, *yipalei*, used in this verse, from פָּלָא,
polla, rendered variously " wonderful," " marvellous," " hard,"
" difficult," " hidden," in the Authorised Version, reminds us
of its use in at least two other places in the Old Testament
in which God wants to teach us the great and prominent
lesson which He has designed the whole of mankind to

---

[1] Pusey.
[2] *Bayyamim hahem.* The Authorised Version has " these days "; but this is
incorrect.

learn from the history of Israel. One is in Gen. xviii.
There we read that "Sarah laughed within herself" when
she heard the Angel of Jehovah give the definite promise
to Abraham of the birth of Isaac, for to nature and human
reasoning it was no longer possible for Sarah to bear a child.
But "Jehovah said to Abraham, Wherefore did Sarah laugh,
saying, Shall I of a surety bear a child, which am old?
Is anything *too hard* (or '*wonderful*') *for Jehovah?*"

Indeed, one great reason of the long delay of the
fulfilment of the promise of the birth of the child, in whom
the great promise of blessing for all nations was to be
handed down, was because God wanted to lay a supernatural basis for the history of Israel; and that both Israel
and the nations of the future might learn that the things
which are *naturally* impossible are not *supernaturally*
impossible, and that nothing which Jehovah has ever spoken
is "too hard" for Him to accomplish.

The other place where the word is used is in Jer. xxxii.,
a prophecy which is in some respects parallel to Zech. vii.
and viii. Jeremiah was shut up in the court of the prison
adjoining the palace, when the word of the Lord came to
him that his uncle's son, Hanameel, would come to him
with the request that he should buy a piece of ground
which belonged to him in Anathoth; and the prophet, in
obedience to God's command, went through all the legal
formalities connected with the purchase of land in Palestine.
Now, from the human and natural point of view, the whole
transaction seemed a mere farce and absurdity. The
Chaldeans had already laid waste the whole land, and were
even then besieging Jerusalem. How unlikely, so far as
human probabilities went, that houses, or fields, or vineyards, would ever again be possessed by Jews in Palestine.

Jeremiah's own faith in the promises of God in reference to the future of the people and the land, was strongly
put to the test by this symbolical transaction which he was
commanded to carry through, but he stood the test; he
staggered not at the promise of God through unbelief.
He looked away from human improbabilities and natural

impossibilities to the Almighty and covenant-keeping God, and exclaims (ver. 17), "*Ah, Lord God, behold Thou hast made the heaven and the earth by Thy great power and stretched-out arm, and there is nothing too hard*" (or '*wonderful*') *for Thee*"—to which God Himself adds, so to say, His "Amen," by repeating in ver. 23 the prophet's own words—"*Behold, I am Jehovah, the God of all flesh; is there anything too hard*" (or '*marvellous*') *for Me?*" and proceeds to tell him that, though the city and land would now be given over to desolation, and the people carried into captivity because of their great sin and manifold provocations of the Holy One, yet the time would assuredly come when "*men shall buy fields for money, and subscribe the deeds and seal them, and call witnesses in every part of the promised land; for I will cause their captivity to return, saith Jehovah.*"

Before passing on to the following verses, let me ask you, dear reader, Have you learned this great lesson? Have you experienced personally the supernatural power of the living God, the Creator of the ends of the earth, Who brought again from the dead our Lord Jesus, and with Whom nothing is impossible, or "marvellous," in your own heart and life? For only then can you believe in the great and marvellous things which God promised to do for Israel in the future, and through them for the whole world.

But let us proceed to the next brief paragraph (vers. 7, 8). "*Thus saith Jehovah of hosts, Behold I will save My people from the east country, and from the west country: and I will bring them, and they shall dwell in the midst of Jerusalem; and they shall be My people, and I will be their God, in truth and righteousness.*"

This is one of the greatest and most comprehensive promises in reference to Israel's restoration and conversion to be found in the prophetic Scriptures, but on which I may not tarry long for want of space, and because I have fully dwelt on this subject in some of my other writings.[1]

---

[1] *The Jewish Problem—Its Solution*; also, *The Shepherd of Israel and His Scattered Flock.*

But let me very briefly point out in passing—first, that it is a promise which has manifestly not yet been fulfilled. The expression מֵאֶרֶץ מִזְרָח וּמֵאֶרֶץ מְבוֹא הַשָּׁמֶשׁ, literally, "*from the land of the rising of the sun, and from the land of the going down of the sun*," properly rendered, " from the east country, and from the west country," in the English versions, really includes *all parts of the earth*, as may be seen from Ps. l. 1, cxiii. 3 ; Mal. i. 11, etc., where the same Hebrew idiom is used. Now, never in the past has such a restoration taken place. A representative section, but a mere handful out of the whole people, was indeed brought back to the land after the seventy years' captivity in Babylon, of which Zechariah himself was a witness, but that could not possibly be the restoration here promised ; first, because, as is to be inferred from the whole prophecy, this was to be something which should take place at a time *future* in the point of view, or outlook, of this post-exilic prophet, to whom, what we may call the chief act in the restoration from Babylon was already an accomplished fact ; and, secondly, because that partial restoration was only from one direction, namely, from the east, or " north " (as Babylon and Persia were called, because their invasions of Palestine were from the north). From the " west " they could not then have been brought back, since very few of the Jewish nation had as yet wandered westward.

It was only at the second stage of Israel's dispersion, which was brought about by the destruction of Jerusalem and the Temple by the Romans, that Israel became in the fullest sense a *Diaspora*—scattered over all the face of the earth—the majority always found in lands more or less to the *west* of Palestine. No ; the promise here is a divine summary and repetition of the many promises of the yet future restoration which were uttered by the former prophets, as, for instance, Isa. xliii. 5, 6, where we read, " *Fear not : for I am with thee : I will bring thy seed from the east, and gather thee from the west; I will say to the north, Give up ; and to the south, Keep not back : bring my sons from far, and my daughters from the ends of the earth* " ; and will be fulfilled when "*Jehovah shall set His hand again the second time to recover the remnant of His people ; . . . and He shall set up an ensign for the nations, and shall assemble the outcasts of Israel, and gather together the dispersed of Judah from the four corners of the earth*" (Isa. xi. 11, 12).

That the restoration spoken of here is yet future, is proved also by the fact that it is to be followed by Israel's national conversion, which has certainly never yet taken place. "*And they shall be My people, and I will be their God, in truth and in righteousness.*"

The restoration of Israel to their own land after the many centuries of dispersion and wanderings, will, as I have stated elsewhere, "be a great mercy and a wonderful event in the world's history"; but a still greater mercy, and a still more wonderful thing, will be the restoration of the long - interrupted covenant relationship and communion between them and their God. This is what is promised in the last words of the 8th verse: "*They shall be My people*" — the "*Lo-ammi*" period, during which Israel, separated from God, is given over into the hands of his enemies, shall at last be ended, and God shall again receive them graciously and acknowledge them as "*Ammi*," and He, Jehovah, shall be their God, *be'emeth u-bhits'dakah*, "in truth and in righteousness"—even as we read in Hos. ii. 19, 20: "*And I will betroth thee unto Me for ever ; yea, I will betroth thee unto Me in righteousness, and in judgment, and in loving-kindness, and in mercies. I will even betroth thee unto Me in faithfulness ; and thou shalt know the Lord.*" But the expression *be'emeth u-bhits'dakah*—"in truth and in righteousness"—belongs to both clauses of the brief statement which announces the restoration of the covenant relationship between Israel and God, for not only will God act toward them (as, indeed, on His part He has ever done) in truth and in righteousness, but this also shall henceforth be the condition of the people. No longer shall it be said of them that "they swear by the name of Jehovah, and make mention of the God of Israel, *but not in truth nor in righteousness*" (Isa. xlviii. 1), but like the man after God's

own heart, of whom the expression is first used (1 Kings
iii. 6), and their other fathers, who "walked with God"; so
also restored and converted Israel shall walk before Him
"*in truth and in righteousness, and in uprightness of heart*"
throughout the rest of their national history—even as we
read in Jer. xxxii. 38–41, which, as already stated, is in
some respects parallel to Zech. viii.: "*And they shall be My
people, and I will be their God; and I will give them one
heart, and one way, that they may fear Me for ever, for the
good of them, and of their children after them: and I will
make an everlasting covenant with them, that I will not turn
away from them, to do them good; and I will put My fear
in their hearts, that they shall not depart from Me. Yea, I
will rejoice over them to do them good, and I will plant them
in this land assuredly with My whole heart and with My
whole soul.*"

A word more, perhaps, needs to be said on the expression in the 8th verse, "And they shall dwell *in the
midst of Jerusalem*," upon which the allegorising commentators have fixed as a proof that it is not a literal
restoration of literal Israel which is spoken of.

Thus Pusey, Dr. Wright, Keil, and others are quite
dogmatic that it is not the literal Jerusalem, because this,
to quote the words of the first of the above-named authors,
" could not contain the Jews from all quarters of the world,
whom, as they multiplied, the whole land could not contain ;
but the promised Jerusalem, the Jerusalem which should be
inhabited as towns without walls, to which the Lord should
be a wall of fire round about," which, as is to be seen from
his comments on the 7th verse, he interprets of the Church.

To this I would reply that the enlarged Jerusalem,
which " should be inhabited as towns without walls," and of
which Jehovah Himself shall be the defence and "the glory
in the midst thereof," is also the *literal* Jerusalem, as I have.
I think, clearly shown in my exposition of the 2nd chapter.
As to the expression, " in the midst of Jerusalem," even Dr,
Wright, who denies any future fulfilment of this prophecy
to literal Israel, says : " The allusion is evidently to Jeru-

salem, not so much as the actual residence of all the people, but as the place where Israel should worship Jehovah." Jerusalem stands here for the land of which it is the centre and metropolis, to which restored and converted Israel (in whatever part of the country they may be located) will turn, as the place where the glory of their Divine Messiah will then be especially manifested—even as in times past the tribes from all parts of the land went up during the three great festivals, there to appear before God, being thus taught to regard the place where His honour dwelt, and His glory was specially manifested, as their true home.

The great and glorious promises contained in the first eight verses of this chapter, like all prophecy about the future, are to be turned to practical account. Not only is the restored remnant to derive comfort and stimulus from " these words," but they are to act as incentives in the path of obedience and to the more perfect accomplishment of the will of God in the present: " *Thus saith Jehovah of hosts: Let your hands be strong, ye that hear in these days these words from the mouth of the prophets which were in the day that the foundation of the house of Jehovah of hosts was laid, even the Temple, that it might be built.*"

" Let your hands be strong," which is an idiom for the expression "Be of good courage" (Judg. vii. 11; 2 Sam. ii. 7; Ezek. xxii. 14, etc.), reminds us of the words of Zechariah's contemporary and colleague, whose voice was now silenced by death: " *Be strong, O Zerubbabel, saith Jehovah; and be strong, O Joshua, son of Jehozadak, the high priest; and be strong, all ye people of the land, and work*" (Hag. ii. 4)—though here, in the 8th chapter of Zechariah, the phrase is used as an exhortation not merely or especially to the continuation of the building of the Temple, as is the case in Haggai, but with reference to their doing, individually and collectively, the will of God *in all things.*

" *These words*" refer particularly to the words of promise which had just been uttered by Zechariah in the preceding verses of this chapter, and by Haggai in the prophecy from which I have just quoted, who are together

spoken of as "*the prophets*," who were God's mouthpieces to
the people since a beginning was made by them in rebuilding the Temple, and are thus contrasted with the "*former
prophets*," to whom Zechariah so often refers.

The word לְהִבָּנוֹת, *l'hibanoth* ("that it might be built"),
is added as a more precise definition of the time to which
the prophet refers in the expression, "in the day that the
foundation of the house of Jehovah of hosts was laid";
for there had, in fact, been two beginnings, or foundation-
layings, of the Temple. Already, in the seventh month of
the very year of the return of the first colony of exiles,
under the leadership of Zerubbabel and Joshua the high
priest, the altar of Jehovah was rebuilt, and the sacrificial
service restored in Jerusalem; and in the second month of
the second year the foundation was laid amid solemn and
joyous scenes described in the 3rd chapter of Ezra. But
very soon difficulties and hindrances came in the way.
There were the Samaritans and their intrigues and accusations at the Persian Court; and there were the still more
insidious and dangerous enemies in their own midst, and
in their own hearts—namely, the selfish love of ease and
comfort, and their unwillingness to devote their time and
means to the building of the house of God, because they
wanted to build "ceiled houses" for themselves (Hag.
i. 3–5). And so they neglected the work, excusing themselves that "the time is not come, the time that Jehovah's
house should be built"; with the result that for about
thirteen years the work which they began was suspended
and "lay waste." But in the second year of Darius the
king the word of Jehovah came to Haggai and Zechariah,
whose rebukes, exhortations, and appeals, "in the Name of
the God of Israel" (Ezra v. 1, 2), roused the people to
make a new beginning, and then it was that they took up
the task "*with set purpose of heart*," *l'hibanoth*—"that it
might be built" (Hag. i. 12–15).

And with "the day" in which they set their hearts to
obey the voice of Jehovah their God in this matter, there
began a new epoch in the history of the remnant of the

people, and their leaders, for "from this day will I bless you," saith Jehovah (Hag. ii. 19).

Then there follows a contrast between the time before they obeyed the voice of Jehovah their God and took up the work of building the Temple, and the condition of things *since* they hearkened to the voice of the Word of God through Haggai and Zechariah. Before, when they cared only for their own affairs, nothing prospered with them, and there was nothing but disaster and disappointment: " For *before those days there was no hire* (or ' *wages* ') *for man, nor any hire for beast,"* so little was the produce that it did not pay the labour of man and beast; which answers to the description of those same days by Haggai : " *Ye have sown much, and bring in little ; ye eat, but ye have not enough ; ye drink, but ye are not filled with drink ; and he that earneth wages earneth wages to put into a bag with holes* " (Hag. i. 6). And not only so, but (to return to our passage in Zechariah) "*for him that went out and for him that came in (literally) there was no peace, because of the adversary,"* which is most probably a true and graphic description of the conditions which then prevailed ; for, to quote words from another writer, " in such an empire as the Persian there was large scope for actual hostility among the petty nations subject to it; so that they did not threaten revolt against itself, or interfere with the payment of tribute, as in the Turkish Empire now." [1]

On the rebuilding of the walls (a little later) we actually read that " the adversaries "—*i.e.,* the Samaritans, Arabians, Ammonites, and Ashdodites—conspired to fight against Jerusalem, and to slay the Jews, but were frustrated because the Lord's protection was now over the little remnant of the people.

And not only was there no peace " in those days " to him that went out and to him that came in, because of the

---

[1] According to Ilitzig the expedition of Cambyses to Egypt occurred at this time ; and though it was not referred to in the Book of Ezra, the march of the Persian army through the land southward must have caused no little affliction to the colonists under their then distressing circumstances.

adversary without, but the misery was increased because there was strife and contention which prevailed among themselves, for "*the Lord hath set (vaashallach) all men every one against his neighbour.*" But now, having entered on the path of obedience, and made God's service their delight, God was going to "make their wants His care": "*But now I will not be unto this people as in the former days, saith Jehovah of hosts.* For there shall be the seed of peace*" (or, the seed of peace even) ; "*the vine*[1] *shall give her fruit, and the ground shall give her increase, and the heavens shall give their dew,*" which reminds us somewhat of the promise in Hos. ii. 21, 22 : "*And it shall come to pass in that day, I will answer, saith Jehovah, I will answer the heavens, and they shall answer the earth ; and the earth shall answer the corn, and the wine, and the oil,*" etc.

And not only shall the blessing of the Lord resting on their toil produce plentiful harvests and abundant vintage, but no one shall despoil them of these gifts of God's bountifulness.

"*And I will cause the remnant of this people to inherit all these things.*"

And the improvement in the condition of the restored remnant since they set themselves earnestly to the task of building God's house, was only a pledge of the greater things which God has promised them, and which yet await their fulfilment in the day of Israel's national restoration and conversion, as announced by the prophet in the first part of this chapter. The whole may be said to be summed up in the words in the 13th verse : "*And it shall come to pass that, as ye were a curse among the nations, O house of Judah and house of Israel, so will I save you, and ye shall be a blessing : fear not, let your hands be strong.*"

---

[1] The expression זֶ֫רַע הַשָּׁלוֹם הַגֶּ֫פֶן (*zera-hashalom haggephen*) is peculiar, but I think that the rendering adopted by Keil, Koehler, Wright, and others is the correct one, and that *zera-hashalom*, "seed of peace," is a noun which stands in apposition to *haggephen*, "the vine." Keil thinks that the vine may especially be called "the seed of peace," inasmuch as it can only prosper in days of peace, its cultivation requiring much care and attention, which it is impossible to bestow in times of war or adversity.

Here we note first of all how both "Judah" and "Israel"—*i.e.*, the entire nation, which had previous to the Exile been for a time divided into two kingdoms—are now after the partial restoration from Babylon, included in undivided unity in one common destiny, both of wretchedness and blessedness. *Together* they are, during the Lo-ammi period—the time during which God's face is averted from them—"a curse," for the solemn and terrible words which He spoke through Jeremiah have been literally fulfilled in the whole nation: "I will give them up to be tossed to and fro among all the kingdoms of the earth for evil; *to be a reproach and a proverb, a taunt and a curse, in all places wherein I shall drive them*" (Jer. xxiv. 9, xlii. 18).

But, as they have been together in their entirety "a curse," or the object of curse, *i.e.*, so smitten of God as to serve the object of curses, and "the nations when imprecating curses on their foes were wont to wish them the fate of Israel"[1]—and not only so, but as the unbelieving majority of the nation had also *actually and actively* in the period of their separation from God and bitter hostility to their Messiah and His gospel been a curse to the nations—so says Jehovah, "*will I save you*" (not only from your captivity, but *from your sin*; not only from your outward enemies and oppressors, but from the evil of your own hearts—*from yourselves*), "and *ye shall be a blessing.*" This glorious promise is to be understood, not only as "equivalent to being so blessed as to be used as a benedictory formula,"[2] but is a revival and an application of the original promise to Abraham, "*thou shalt be a blessing*," as Pusey well observes, and reiterates the oft-expressed purpose of God to make *saved* and *blessed* Israel the *source* and *instrument* of blessing to all the nations of the earth, even as we read in Isa. xix. 24, "*In that day shall Israel be . . . a blessing in the midst of the land*"; and Ezek. xxxiv. 26, "*I will make them and the places round about My hill a blessing.*"

---

[1] C. H. H. Wright.   [2] Keil.

In measure this has already been the case, for all the great blessings which have come to the world have come to it through the seed of Abraham ; " for of them," to quote another, "*according to the flesh Christ came, Who is over all God blessed for ever*: of them were the apostles and evangelists, of them every writer of God's Word ; of them those who carried the gospel throughout the whole world." [1]   But, so far, the blessing which has come through Israel to the world has been only partial, and has extended only to individuals ; but when Israel as a nation is " saved in Jehovah with an everlasting salvation," and their hearts are set aflame with love to the long-rejected Messiah and zeal for His cause, then " the receiving of them " shall indeed be " as life from the dead " to the whole world, and the great Messianic blessings shall universally be spread by them throughout the whole earth.   In Abraham and his seed—which includes Christ and *Israel*—shall *all the families of the earth be blessed.*

And it is God's faithfulness and the steadfastness of His purpose which form the grounds for our hope of His certain fulfilment of His promises.   This is brought out in vers. 14 and 15 : "*For thus saith the Lord of hosts : As I thought to do evil unto you, when your fathers provoked Me to wrath, saith the Lord of hosts, and I repented not ; so again have I thought in these days to do good unto Jerusalem and to the house of Judah : fear ye not.*"

The remnant of Israel to whom Zechariah spoke knew from their own experience that Jehovah is faithful—yes, faithful in carrying out His *threatenings* as well as in fulfilling His promises ; for when, after repeated warnings, their fathers continued in their impenitent provocations of Him through their many sins, the " evil " which He foreannounced that He would do unto them came.   They may, therefore, be assured that when He announces to them through the prophet that His thoughts toward them now are " thoughts of peace and not of evil," and that His purpose " in these days " is " to do good unto Jerusalem

[1] Pusey.

and to the house of Judah," He will not repent or prove false to His word. This passage again reminds us of Jer. xxxii.—a scripture which, as we observed before, is in some respects parallel to Zech. vii. and viii., where we read (ver. 42): " *Thus saith Jehovah : Like as I have brought all this great evil upon this people, so will I bring upon them all the good that I have promised them.*"

But these great promises of God, to be experimentally realised, must be responded to by the faith and obedience of God's people, and, as has been well said, " God's covenanted grace leads those truly blessed by it to holiness, not to licentiousness." Hence the exhortation to practical godliness which follows in vers. 16 and 17 :

" *These are the things (debharim,* literally, ' *words* ') *which ye shall do : Speak ye every man the truth with his neighbour ; truth and judgment of peace judge ye in your gates : and let none of you imagine evil in your hearts against his neighbour, and love no false oath : for all these are the things that I hate, saith Jehovah*"; which is an inspired repetition and application of the preaching of the former prophets, which Zechariah had already summarised in chap. vii. 9, 10, an exposition of which will be found in my notes on those verses. I would only here add that the *mishpat shalom,* "judgment of peace," which they are exhorted to judge " in their gates " (the place where justice and judgment were wont to be administered, Deut. xvi. 18, xxi. 19, etc.), means "judgment which issues in peace," or " such an administration of justice as tends to promote peace and establish concord between those that are at strife." [1]

The sins enumerated in the 17th verse which are con-

---

[1] Keil. The remarks of the Jewish commentator, Kimchi, on this expression are as follows : "If ye judge righteousness there will be peace between the parties in the lawsuit ; according as our Rabbis have said in a proverb, 'He that has his coat taken from him by the tribunal, let him sing and go his way'—in proof of which they have adduced the verse, ' And all this people shall also go to their place in peace' (Ex. xviii. 23) : 'ALL the people,' even he that is condemned in judgment. And our Rabbis, of blessed memory, have interpreted *mishpat shalom* (judgment of peace) of reconciliation between the litigants, for it is said (in Sanhedrin, fol. 6b), 'What sort of judgment is that in which there is peace ? It is that of arbitration.' "

trary to " truth and peace " are emphatically described as
the very things which God hates, אֵת כָּל אֵלֶּה אֲשֶׁר שָׂנֵאתִי, *eth
kol-elleh asher sanethi*—as if He meant to say, " This is
the sum of what I hate " ; for they sum up in brief the
breaches of both tables of the law—that which sets forth
man's duty to God, and that which sets forth his duty to
his fellow-man.

And because God hates these sins we, too, must hate
them, for " religion consists in conformity to God's nature,
that we should love what God loves and hate what God
hates."

We now come to the last of the four sections into which
the whole of chaps. vii. and viii. are divided. Here we
have the direct positive part of the reply to the original
question by the deputation from Bethel (chap. vii. 1–3)
to ask whether there was still occasion to observe the fasts
which had been appointed to celebrate the anniversaries of
the destruction of the Temple and the desolation of the
land by the Chaldeans : " *And the word of Jehovah of hosts
came unto me, saying, Thus saith Jehovah of hosts : The fast*
(or '*fasting*') *of the fourth, and the fast of the fifth, and the
fast of the seventh, and the fast of the tenth (months) shall
be* (or ' *become* ') *to the house of Judah joy and gladness, and
cheerful feasts*—מוֹעֲדִים טוֹבִים, *moadim tobhim* ('*good seasons*,'
or ' *holidays* ') ; *therefore love truth and peace*." The fast of
the ninth day of the fourth month was instituted to celebrate the taking of the city by Nebuchadnezzar in the
eleventh year of Zedekiah's reign ;[1] the fast of the fifth
month (the blackest day of all in the Jewish calendar)
commemorates the destruction of both the city and the
Temple,[2] and many other calamities which, according to
Jewish tradition, happened on this same day (some of which
are enumerated in my notes on chap. vii. 3) ; the fast of
the seventh month, as already stated in the exposition of
chap. vii., was appointed for the murder of Gedaliah ;[3]
and the fast of the tenth commemorated the commence-

[1] Jer. lii. 6, 7.   [2] Jer. lii. 12, 13.
[3] 2 Kings xxv. 25, 26 ; Jer. xli. 1–3.

ment of the siege of Jerusalem on the tenth day of that month in the ninth year of Zedekiah.[1]

All these days are still observed as fasts by the Jewish nation in all parts of the earth, for it is still the night of weeping for Israel, and Zion still sits desolate and mourns. But the long night of weeping is to be followed by a morning of joy, when Jehovah shall accomplish the "good" which He has purposed and promised to Israel and Jerusalem (vers. 14, 15), and then the former troubles and calamities shall be "forgotten" (Isa. lxv. 16), and the very days which commemorate them shall be turned into "joy and gladness" and *moadim tobhim*—cheerful feasts or *sacred festivals.* "Therefore," the prophet turns again to the remnant whom he was addressing, "love *ha-emeth ve ha-shalom—truth and peace*"—for the promises of future blessedness and glory, whether national in relation to Israel, or spiritual in relation to the individual believer in Christ, are intended in every case to act as incentives to holiness of life and consecration to God's service in the present ; and though God's covenants and promises to the nation are unconditional, and "without repentance," or any change of mind as far as He is concerned, and are not made to depend on Israel's goodness or righteousness, yet righteousness, truth, and love must be blessed fruit of these promises.

What the consequence of Jehovah's dwelling in the midst of Israel will be to the other nations, and how Israel's blessing will react upon the whole earth, we see in the last four verses of our chapter.

" *Thus saith Jehovah of hosts : It shall yet come to pass* " (or, "it shall yet be ")—however unlikely it may have appeared in the eyes of the remnant of the people to whom Zechariah prophesied, and however "wonderful " or impossible it may appear in our eyes—" *that there shall come peoples* " (a collective and representative name for *all* peoples), " *and the inhabitants of many* (or ' *great* ') *cities : and the inhabitants of one city shall go to another, saying, Let us go speedily* (literally, ' going, let us go '—נֵלְכָה הָלוֹךְ—or 'let us go on and on,' *i.e.*, 'perseveringly until we attain' the blessed goal)[1] *to entreat the favour* (literally, to 'entreat the face') *of Jehovah,[2] and to seek Jehovah*"—to which the ready and glad response of those invited will be, "*I will go also—and many peoples and strong nations shall come to seek Jehovah of hosts in Jerusalem, and to entreat the face of Jehovah*"—all which is but an iteration by the central figure in the group of post-exilic prophets of the glorious announcements concerning "the latter days" made by the former prophets. Thus, for instance, we read both in Isaiah and in Micah, "*And it shall come to pass in the latter days, that the mountain of the Lord's house shall be established in the top of the mountains, and shall be exalted above the hills ; and all nations shall flow unto it. And many peoples shall go and say, Come ye, and let us go up to the mountain of the Lord, to the house of the God of Jacob ; and He will teach us of His ways, and we will walk in His paths : for out of Zion shall go forth the law, and the word of the Lord from Jerusalem*" (Isa. ii. 2, 3, R.V.).

The allegorising commentators, according to whom "the literal fulfilment of such passages is a sheer impossibility"[3]—as if it had not been foretold in this very scripture that the fulfilment of the great and glorious things which are here prophesied would appear too "wonderful" and impossible in the eyes of men—would have us believe that what is predicted by Isaiah, and Micah, and Zechariah (indeed, by *all* the prophets) in

---

[1] Pusey wrongly applies this, as all the other great promises in this chapter, to the present ; yet there is some truth in his observation that "the words seem to speak of that which is a special gift of the gospel, namely, continued progress, 'forgetting those things which are behind and reaching forth unto those things which are before, to press forward toward the mark of the prize of the high calling of God in Christ Jesus.' *Let us go on and on*; whence it is a Christian proverb, *Non progredi est regredi*—Not to go on is to go back. Augustine observed, 'The whole life of a good Christian is a holy longing to make progress'; and again, 'The one perfection of man is to have found that he is not perfect.' 'If thou sayest it sufficeth, thou art lost.' *Nolle proficere deficere est*— To be unwilling to increase is to decrease."—St. Bernard, quoted by Pusey.

[2] See footnote on this phrase in the exposition of chap. vii. p. 213.

[3] C. H. H. Wright.

reference to the universal spread of the knowledge of Jehovah through the instrumentality of Israel, has already been fulfilled, or is now exhaustively fulfilling itself in this gospel dispensation.

Thus one of them, commenting on these verses, writes: " Zechariah describes vividly the eagerness and mutual impulse with which not only many, but mighty nations should throng to the gospel, and every fresh conversion should win others also, till the great tide should sweep through the world."

" *The inhabitants of one city shall go to another.* It is one unresting extension of the faith, the restlessness of faith and love. ' They shall not be satisfied with their own salvation, careless about the salvation of others; they shall employ all labour and industry, with wondrous love, to provide for the salvation of others as if it were their own.' It is a marvellous stirring of minds. Missionary efforts, so familiar with us as to be a household word, were unknown then. The time was not yet come. *Before the faith* in Christ *came*, the Jewish people were not to be the converters of mankind. They were to await Him, the Redeemer of the world, through Whom and to Whom they were to be first converted, and then the world through those who were of them. This mutual conversion was absolutely unknown. The prophet predicts certainly that it would be, and in God's time it was. ' From you,' St. Paul writes to a small colony in Greece, ' sounded out the Word of the Lord, not only in Macedonia and Achaia, but also in every place your faith to Godward is spread abroad. *Your faith*,' he writes to the heathen capital of the world, ' *is spoken of throughout the whole world*.' Within eighty years after our Lord's ascension the Roman governor of Bithynia reported, on occasion of the then persecution, that it spread as a contagion. ' The contagion of that superstition traversed not cities only, but villages and scattered houses too.' Before the persecution the temples had been desolated, the solemn rites long intermitted, the sacrificed animals had very rarely found a purchaser. An impostor of the same date

says : ' Pontus is full of atheists and Christians.' ' There is no
one race of men,' it was said before the middle of the second
century, ' whether barbarians, or Greeks, or by whatsoever
name called, whether of those wandering, homeless tribes
who live in waggons, or those pastoral people who dwell in
tents, in which there are not prayers and eucharists to the
Father and Creator of all things, through the name of the
crucified Jesus.' ' The word of our teacher,' said another,
' abode not in Judæa alone, as philosophy in Greece ; but was
poured out throughout the whole world, persuading Greeks
and barbarians in their several nations and villages and
every city—whole houses and each hearer individually—
and having brought over to the truth no few even of the
very philosophers ; and if any ordinary magistrate forbid
the Greek philosophy, forthwith it vanishes, but our teaching
forthwith, at its first announcement, kings and emperors and
subordinate rulers and governors, with all their mercenaries
and countless multitudes, forbid, and war against us and
try to extirpate, but it rather flourishes.' " [1]

That there is a *measure* of truth in all this no one will
gainsay, nor can any one deny the fact of the marvellous,
rapid spread of the gospel in the first two or three
Christian centuries, through those Jewish apostles and
messengers whose hearts were all aflame with love and zeal
for their all-glorious Redeemer, and through their first converts from among the Gentiles.   But what about the subsequent history of the professing Church ?   Has it continued in
its first love ?   Has it " gone on and on " in faith and purity,
and in zeal for Christ's cause and the salvation of men ?
Alas ! instead of converting the world, the Gentile Church
became more and more merged *into the world*, and their
candlesticks of corporate testimony were one by one
removed from the earth.   Not as if the Word of God has
failed in that whereto it was sent : a people for His Name
from among the Gentiles—a multitude which no man can
number, out of all nations, and kindreds, and tongues—

---

[1] Pusey.   The quotations are from Justin Martyr, Trypho, Clement of
Alexandria, and Tertullian.

have been, and are being, gathered into the fold of the One Great Shepherd. But this dispensation, according to the predictions of Christ and His apostles, instead of ending in the universal knowledge of God, and in peace and righteousness among the nations, is to end in almost universal apostasy and failure, and in the greatest conflict among the nations that the world has yet known.

Beside this, what is here predicted is something which, as we have seen, is to take place subsequent to the restoration and national conversion of Israel. Has that yet taken place? No; as we observed in 'the notes on chap. ii., it is only ignorance of God's plan and self-delusion which can boast of the gradual conversion of the world, and speak of " Christian *nations* " in this present dispensation. But when Jehovah will have mercy upon Jacob, and will yet choose Israel again and set them in their own land—when, after the long centuries of darkness and unbelief the eyes of the blind shall be opened and Israel nationally is converted, and the heart of each of them is fired with that love and zeal which burned in the heart of Paul after the Lord revealed Himself to him, saying: " *I am Jesus whom thou persecutest*"—then this prediction of Zechariah shall be fulfilled, and " *many peoples and strong nations shall come and seek Jehovah of hosts in Jerusalem, and to entreat the face of Jehovah* "; and the still more ancient promise shall be realised : " *As truly as I live, saith Jehovah, all the earth shall be filled with the glory of Jehovah,*" " for the earth shall be full of the knowledge of Jehovah, as the waters cover the sea." [1]

All this is confirmed and brought to a climax in the last verse: " *Thus saith Jehovah of hosts : In those days it shall come to pass that ten men out of all the languages of the nations shall take hold of the skirt of him that is a Jew, saying, We will go with you, for we have heard that Jehovah is with you.*"

Ten is used in Scripture for an indefinite number; [2]

---

[1] Num. xiv. 21 ; Isa. xi. 9.
[2] Gen. xxxi. 7 ; Lev. xxvi. 26 ; Num. xiv. 22 ; 1 Sam. i. 8.

here it stands for " a great and complete multitude." The unusual Hebrew phrase, *mikol leshonoth haggoyim*—" of all the languages of the nations "—is an echo of Isa. lxvi. 18, where we read that " all nations and tongues " (or " languages "—*haggoyim vehalleshonoth*) shall be gathered to see God's glory in Jerusalem. They shall lay hold on the *khenaph*, which is the corner of the long flowing garment worn in the East. Among the Jews, to each of the four *kenaphayim* of the outer garment of white, the צִיצִת (*tsitsith*, " fringes," or tassels (of blue) were attached ; and some writers have supposed that this is what is referred to, since it was the distinctly visible sign of " a man, a Jew." It is spoken of as being laid (or caught) hold of, first with a view to detain the Jew, so as to beg his permission to accompany him. But it has the sense of keeping *firm* hold, expressive of the earnest *determination* of the Gentile seekers of Jehovah to accompany the Jew, who is himself represented as travelling towards Zion, with his face turned thitherward. Like Ruth, the Moabitess, to her Jewish mother-in-law, so the Gentile converts to the God of Israel shall say : " Entreat us not to leave Thee, or to return from following after Thee: for whither Thou goest *we will go:* . . . *Thy people shalt be our people, and Thy God our God.*" " We will go with you, *for we have heard that Jehovah is with you.*"

It is because the Jew shall then not only " believe in one God " (which is their boast now), but shall be so *one with God* that for a Gentile convert to call himself by the name of Jacob will be equivalent to saying, " I am the Lord's " ; and to surname himself " by the name of Israel," equal to " subscribing with his hand unto Jehovah " (Isa. xliv. 1–5). It is because the glorious hope and promise contained in the Name " Immanuel " shall then be fulfilled in a literal and personal sense to Israel nationally, and Jehovah Himself, the Holy One of Israel, in the Person of their Messiah Jesus, shall dwell in the midst of them ; and because, finally, *Qodesh l' Yehovah*—" Holiness (or ' holy ') unto Jehovah "—shall then be written upon their foreheads, yea, upon all that they possess, that the

Gentiles shall honour and reverence them "as the priests of Jehovah, the ministers of our God" (Isa. lxi. 10), and cleave unto them as the appointed messengers of salvation and instruments of blessing, saying, "We will go with you, for we have heard that Jehovah is with you."

A pledge and prophecy of it we have in the history of the gospel in this dispensation, for it is a remarkable and wonderful fact that "the religion introduced by a Jew, the religion which consists of faith in the person of One who was indeed a Jew—namely, our blessed Lord—is that which has been embraced" by multitudes from among the Gentiles. Those are, therefore, not far wrong who have interpreted the words "a man, a Jew," of Christ; for although, as the whole context shows, it is not primarily and directly of the Messiah, but of the Jews in the days of their future blessing, that this prophecy is spoken; yet, as we have seen, it is only when Israel shall be the Messianic people and the representatives of Christ among the nations, Who will then be the King of the Jews, that this prophecy will be fulfilled. In this connection it is interesting to observe that even the Jews saw a reference in this scripture to the Messiah. Thus in an ancient Midrash we read: "All nations shall come, falling on their faces before the Messiah, and the Israelites saying, Grant that we may be Thy servants, and of Israel. For, as relates to the doctrine and the knowledge of the law, the Gentiles shall be their servants, according as it is written: 'In those days it shall come to pass that ten men shall take hold out of all the languages of the nations, shall even take hold of the skirts of him that is a Jew, saying, We will go with you, for we have heard that God is with you.'"[1]

---

[1] Pesikta Rabbathai, in Yaklut Shimoni.

Part Two

THE PROPHECIES

Chapter 13

INTRODUCTION TO THE SECOND
PART OF ZECHARIAH
AN EXAMINATION OF THE
MODERN CRITICISM IN REFERENCE
TO THE LAST SIX CHAPTERS

Chapter 13

THE aim which we set before us in these "Notes" on Zechariah was by God's help to make this precious portion of Old Testament revelation intelligible, and spiritually profitable, to the ordinary intelligent English reader, and in doing so to avoid as much as possible minute critical points, and lengthy discussions of the questions of dates and authorship.

We might, therefore, have accepted the contention of the more "moderate" of the modern critical writers, that the contents and "religious" or spiritual value of these sacred oracles are independent of the question as to whether they were, or were not, actually composed by the person, or persons, and at the time "traditionally" attached to them —and have proceeded at once to the exposition of chap. ix. But this contention is only partially true. The ethical and spiritual character of a writing is not altogether independent of its authorship and the circumstances in which it originated; and then, too, as far as these chapters are concerned, it is not a question merely as to what "religious" value we can find in them for ourselves, or for the professed people of God at the present day. The true believer and disciple is anxious above all to understand the *meaning* of the divine oracles, which holy men of old spake as they were moved by the Holy Ghost; and we are concerned here not only with the application, but with the interpretation of these chapters. Both Jews and Christians have always believed that they contain fore-announcements of great and solemn events, and that we have in them divine forecasts of things which were to transpire at a time, or times, which from the prophets' then point of view, at any rate, are contemplated as future.

Now in order rightly to understand or explain the prophetic element in these chapters, and to know whether these forecasts have already been fulfilled or not, much will depend on the question of the date of their origin. It makes all the difference, for instance, whether chaps. xii.–xiv. were composed by an unknown contemporary of Jeremiah, whose prophecies of a siege of Jerusalem, and "anticipations" of God's manifest interposition on behalf of His people in the hour of their greatest extremity (which, however, were falsified by the events), refer to the siege of Jerusalem and the destruction of the Temple by the Chaldeans, or whether the writer is the inspired post-exilic prophet under whose name these chapters stand, who not only lived after the destruction of the Temple, but witnessed the rebuilding of the Temple after the partial restoration from Babylon, and who therefore must speak of another Temple and a yet future siege.

Now, while Zechariah's authorship of the first eight chapters (with which I have already dealt so far) is universally acknowledged, strong objections have been raised in modern times against the assumed authorship and date of the last six chapters.

The Spirit of the Early English Criticism

On examining the great amount of criticism on this subject, we find that it divides itself into two separate streams, which are impelled by two different motives.

The earliest critics of the traditional authorship of these chapters were learned English divines, men who believed in the plenary inspiration of Holy Scripture, whose actuating motive was to justify the inerrancy of the citation in Matt. xxvii. 9, 10, which ascribes to Jeremiah a prophecy found in Zech. xi. Thus Joseph Mede [1] (the very first who sought to establish a pre-exilic authorship of these chapters) says, in his note on the above passage in Matthew: " It

---

[1] Joseph Mede, born in 1586 at Berden, Essex, author of the *Clavis Apocaliptica*; died in 1638.

would seem the Evangelist would inform us that those latter chapters ascribed to Zachary . . . are indeed the prophecies of Jeremy, and that the Jews had not rightly attributed them : . . . there is no scripture saith they are Zachary's, but there is a scripture saith they are Jeremy's, as this of the Evangelist." And proceeding from this point of view, he discovered, as he thought, internal proof that these chapters belonged not to Zechariah's, but to Jeremiah's time. He was followed by Hammond, Kidder, Newcome, etc.[1]

We shall see when we come (D.V.) to the exposition of chap. xi. as to whether there is any other possible explanation of the occurrence of Jeremiah's name in that passage in Matthew ; meanwhile, without entering more fully into this point here, we would adopt the words of another English Biblical scholar,[2] and say :

" Is it not possible, nay, is it not much more probable, that the word Ιερεμιου (Jeremiah) may be written by mistake by some transcribers of Matthew's Gospel, than that those of the Jewish Church, who settled the canon of scripture, should have been so grossly ignorant of the right author of these chapters as to place them under a wrong name ? It is not, I think, pretended that these chapters have been found in any copy of the Old Testament otherwise placed than as they now stand. But in the New Testament there are not wanting authorities for omitting the word Ιερεμιου (Jeremiah). Nor is it impossible to account plausibly for the wrong insertion of Jeremiah (Matt. xxvii. 9) by observing that exactly the same words occur in Matt. ii. 17, where we read Τοτε επληρωθη το ρηθεν υπο (in some copies δια—see Wetstein) Ιερεμιου του

---

[1] Archbishop William Newcome on the *Twelve Minor Prophets*. The spirit of these early English critics may be judged from the following words. After stating his reasons for accepting Mede's view that chaps. ix.–xi. were written by Jeremiah, Newcome says : " But whoever wrote them, their divine authority is established by the two quotations from them in the New Testament." How different this from modern criticism, which takes no account of the New Testament in this respect, nor even of the direct testimony of Christ !

[2] Dr. Benjamin Blayney, author of *Dissertation on the Seventy Weeks of Daniel*, etc. ; died in 1801.

προφητου, λεγοντος (Then was fulfilled what was spoken by Jeremiah the prophet, saying). Now supposing a transcriber to have had in his copy either δια του προφητου (through the prophet) only, or δια Ζαχαριου του προφητου (through Zechariah the prophet), yet carrying in his mind what he had written a little before, he might inadvertently and without intention have written the same over again, as will easily be granted by those who are at all used to transcribe."

The Rationalistic Criticism which reduces Prophecy to Human Divination

The other stream of criticism directed against the date and authorship of these chapters rises from a different source, and is impelled by the same motive which, alas, underlies the whole of the so-called " modern criticism." There are, no doubt, exceptions ; but reading the many, and for the most part conflicting opinions of modern writers on this question, one is struck with the truth of Keil's remarks, that the objections which modern critics offer to the unity of the book (and the same may be said also of much of their criticism of other books of the Bible) do not arise from the nature of these scriptures, but " partly from the dogmatic assumption of the rationalistic and naturalistic critics that the Biblical prophecies are nothing more than the productions of natural divination ; and partly from the inability of critics, in consequence of this assumption, to penetrate into the depths of the divine revelation, and to grasp either the substance or form of their historical development so as to appreciate it fully." [1]

In illustration of these remarks of Keil, it may not be out of place to quote a striking instance of the elimination of any reference to a distant future, and, indeed, of any supernatural element from the prophetic scriptures on the part of modern critics. Before me lies the last edition of what is regarded by many as a standard work on the

[1] Keil, in the Introduction to his *Commentary on Zechariah*.

Literature of the Old Testament. The author (Canon Driver) is esteemed as one of the more " moderate " of this school. Like many others, he divides chaps. xii.–xiv. from chaps. ix.–xi., but he follows those of the German rationalistic school, who ascribe a post-exilic origin to the second half of Zechariah, though he denies Zechariah's authorship. These are his words on the last three chapters :

" As regards the *occasion* of the prophecy it is impossible to do more than speculate. It is conceivable that in the post-exilic period where our history is a blank (B.C. 518–458 ; 432–300) the family of David assumed importance in Jerusalem, and supplied some of the leading judges and administrators, and that they had been implicated with the people of the capital in some deed of blood (xii. 10–14), on the ground of which the prophet depicts Jehovah's appearance in judgment. In the heathen invaders of xii.–xiv. he perhaps has not in view any actual expected foe, but pictures an imaginary assault of nations, like Ezekiel (*c.* 38–39), from which he represents Jerusalem, though not without severe losses, as delivered. In other features the prophecy appears to be one of those (cf. Isa. xxiv.–xxvii.) in which not merely the *figurative*, but the *imaginative*, element is larger than is generally the case, especially in the pre-exilic prophets. But even when allowance has been made for this, many details in the prophecy remain perplexing, and probably no entirely satisfactory explanation of it is now attainable." The italics are Canon Driver's.

We refrain from characterising the remarks which ascribe the origin of some of the sublimest prophecies in the Old Testament in reference to the last things to the exercise of the "*imaginative*" faculty of the writers, but let us, for lack of space, look at one point only. The first reference, which is so easily disposed of with a stroke of the pen, is chap. xii. 10–14. Now this passage begins with the words :

" *And I will pour upon the house of David, and upon the inhabitants of Jerusalem, the spirit of grace and supplication ; and they shall look unto Me Whom they have pierced : and they shall mourn for him as one mourneth for his only son, and they shall be in bitterness for him, as one that is in bitterness for his first-born*"—and proceeds to describe an intense universal mourning throughout "the whole land," when every tribe shall mourn apart, and "their wives apart."

Even Jews believed that this is a prophecy of solemn events in the future—though, on grounds which we cannot stop here to indicate, they wrongly applied ver. 10 to a "Messiah ben Joseph," who, according to them, was to precede the Messiah ben David.

Certainly the remarkable correspondence in this case, between the prediction and that part of it which has already been fulfilled in the Gospel narrative, is one of the most striking proofs of the divine inspiration of the prophecy, as well as of the Messiahship of our Lord Jesus of Nazareth. But for Canon Driver and the school which he represents, New Testament history is evidently non-existent, or, if it exists, it has no relation whatever to Old Testament prophecy; and rather than admit the possibility of a divine fore-announcement in reference to a distant future, this sublime scripture is made to refer to "some deed of blood" in which the leaders and the people were implicated some time *before these chapters were written,* which, according to him, was some time between 518 and 300 B.C.—of which "deed of blood" which could occasion such deep and universal mourning, *history knows nothing !*

Now, to quote another author:

"The human authorship of any books of Holy Scripture —and so of these chapters of Zechariah—is, in itself, a matter which does not concern the soul. It is an untrue imputation that the date of books of the Bible is converted into matter of faith. In this case Jesus has not set His seal upon it; God the Holy Ghost has not declared it. But, as in other cases, what lay as the foundation of the theory was the unbelief that God, in the way above nature, when it seemed good to Him, revealed a certain future to His creature man. It is the postulate (or axiom, as appears to these critics), that there is no superhuman prophecy, which gives rise to their eagerness to place these and other prophetic books, and portions of books, where they can say to themselves that they do not involve such prophecy. To believers it has, obviously, no religious interest at what time it pleased Almighty God to send any of His servants the prophets. Not the dates assigned by any of these self-devouring theories, but the grounds alleged in support of those dates, as implying unbelief of God's revelation of Himself, make the question one of religious interest, namely, to show that these theories are as unsubstantial as their assumed base is baseless." [1]

That it is not unjust to say that to most of these critics either prophecy in the Christian sense of the term does not exist; or, to quote one of them, that "all definite prophecy relates to an immediate future" and has reference to events which, as men imbued with the ethical principles which determine God's dealings with men and nations, and as careful observers of the signs of the times, the propnets could well conjecture, or "anticipate," as likely to come to pass—the following quotation from one of the chief fathers of the modern criticism shows :

"That which is most peculiar in this prophet" (writes Ewald, of the supposed unknown author of the last six chapters of Zechariah) "is the uncommon high and pious hope of the deliverance of Jerusalem and Judah, notwith-standing all visible greatest dangers and threatenings. At a time when Jeremiah, in the walls of the capital, already despairs of any possibility of a successful resistance to the Chaldees and exhorts to tranquillity, this prophet still looks all these dangers straight in the face with swelling spirit and divine confidence; holds, with unbowed spirit, firm to the like promises of older prophets, as Isa. xxix.; and antici-pates that, from that very moment when the blind fury of the destroyers would discharge itself on the sanctuary, a wondrous might would crush them in pieces, and that this must be the beginning of the Messianic weal within and without." [2]

[1] Pusey.
[2] Professor H. Ewald, *Die Propheten des Alten Bundes.*

Chap. xiv. is, according to Ewald, a modification of the earlier " anticipations " of this prophet.

"This piece," he says, "cannot have been written till somewhat later, when facts made it more and more improbable that Jerusalem would not anyhow be conquered, and treated as a conquered city, by coarse foes. Yet then, too, this prophet could not part with the anticipations of older prophets, and those which he had himself at an earlier time expressed so boldly, amid the most visible danger, he holds firm to the old anticipation (in remembrance of) the great deliverance of Jerusalem in Sennacherib's time (Isa. xxxvii.), which appeared to justify the most fanatic hopes for the future (comp. Ps. lix.). And so now the prospect moulds itself to him thus, as if Jerusalem must indeed actually endure the horrors of the conquest, but that then, when the work of the conquerors was half-completed, the great deliverance already suggested in that former piece would come, and so the sanctuary would notwithstanding be wonderfully preserved, the better Messianic time would notwithstanding still so come."

Principal George Adam Smith, to whose work, *The Book of the Twelve Prophets*, we shall have occasion to return presently, and who, like Canon Driver, follows those German critics who ascribe a post-exilic origin to these chapters, though denying Zechariah's authorship, after mentioning some grounds for a later date, says:

" But though many critics judged these grounds to be sufficient to prove the post-exilic origin of Zech. ix.–xiv., they differed as to the author and exact date of these chapters. Conservatives, like Hengstenberg, Delitzsch, Keil, Köhler, and Pusey, used the evidence to prove the authorship of Zechariah himself after 516, and interpreted the references to the Greek period as pure prediction. . . . But on the same grounds Eichhorn saw in the chapters not a prediction, but a reflection, of the Greek period. He assigned chaps. ix. and x. to an author of the time of Alexander the Great; xi.–xiii. 6 he placed a little later, and brought down xiii. 7–xiv. to the Maccabæan period."

But it is a sad fact that the grounds, when closely examined, on which Eichhorn and the others, who, admitting a post-exilic origin of these chapters, yet deny that they were written by Zechariah, are neither "the geographical references" nor the historical or philological indications in the scripture in question, but the underlying presupposition on the part of these critics that "pure prediction" is an impossibility, and the attempt to eliminate or explain away the supernatural element in the prophetic scriptures. And since, as an instance, there is too marked and striking a resemblance between the historic events connected with the march and conquest of Alexander the Great through Syria, Phœnicia, and Palestine, with the description in chaps. ix. and x., they cannot be prophetic of these events (for that would be admitting the possibility of "pure prediction"), but must be "a reflection," or, in other words, a *description* of the events after they had taken place.

But to come back to Ewald and those who ascribe a pre-exilic origin to the second part of Zechariah, it must be pointed out that the prophecy, had it *preceded* the destruction of Jerusalem by the Chaldeans, could not have been earlier than the reign of Jehoiakim, since the mourning for the death of Josiah is spoken of as a proverbial sorrow of the past. But in that case the prophecy which "anticipates" a miraculous interposition of God for the deliverance of Jerusalem would have been in direct contradiction to Jeremiah, "who for thirty-nine years in one unbroken dirge predicted the evil" which should come upon the city; and the inventive prophet would have been "one of the false prophets who contradicted Jeremiah, who encouraged Zedekiah in his perjury, the punishment whereof Ezekiel solemnly denounced, prophesying his captivity in Babylon as its penalty; he would have been a political fanatic, one of those who by encouraging rebellion against Nebuchadnezzar brought on the destruction of the city, and in the name of God told lies against God.

" It is such an intense paradox that the writing of one

convicted by the event of uttering falsehood in the name of God, incorrigible even in the thickening tokens of God's displeasure, should have been inserted among the Hebrew prophets, in times not far removed from those whose events convicted him, that one wonders that any one should have invented it.   Great   indeed   is   the   credulity   of   the incredulous!"[1]

The Uncertainties and conflicting "Results" of Rationalistic Criticism

But though the preponderating weight of modern critical opinion since the beginning of the nineteenth century is that these chapters belong to a period before the Captivity (chaps. ix.–xi., somewhere in the reigns of Uzziah, Jotham, Ahaz, or Hezekiah, and chaps. xii.–xiv., because of the mention of the mourning for that king as an event of the past in chap. xii., after the death of Josiah[2]), yet over against them stands another group of critics of equal repute, who transfer these chapters to late post-exilic, post-Zecharian days.

We have already referred to Eichhorn, who, "after long vacillation," assigned these chapters (which, according to him, are made up of different fragments) to different epochs of the Greek-Maccabæan period (332 B.C. to 161 B.C.). And to him must be added H. E. G. Paulus, Böttcher, Vatke, Bernard Stade, and others.

Principal George Adam Smith is so sure of the correctness of Stade's theory, who assigns "between 300 and 280 B.C." as the date of these chapters, that he has carried it out even in his arrangement of the order of the books. In his *Book of the Twelve Prophets* he places Malachi after the first part of Zechariah (chaps. i.–viii.); then Joel,

---

[1] Pusey.

[2] Some have not been satisfied with merely two unknown writers for these six chapters.   One B. G. Flügge, in a work published in Göttingen in 1818, entitled, *Die Weissagungen welche die Schriften des Propheten Zacharias beigebogen sind*, not only referred these chapters to pre-exilic days, but split them up into nine fragments, of different dates.

for whose assignment to so late a date there is no justification in fact, and is only part of the newest destructive critical theories of the Pentateuch, to the baselessness of which (if the generally accepted older date be admitted) Joel's prophecy testifies. Then, after Malachi and Joel, as a section by itself, he places Zech. ix.–xiv.[1] But there is truth in the remark that "Criticism which reels to and fro in a period of nearly 500 years, from the earliest of the prophets to a period a century after Malachi, and this on historical and philological grounds, certainly has come to no definite basis, either as to history or philology. Rather, it has enslaved both to preconceived opinions ; and at last, as late a result as any has been, after this weary round, to go back to where it started from, and to suppose these chapters to have been written by the prophet whose name they bear."[2]

[1] In the large edition of *Die Heilige Schrift des Alten Testaments* (the New Critical German Translation of the Old Testament), by Kautzsch and others, in the notes and appendices to which are embodied all the "results" of German scholarship and criticism of the nineteenth century, I read the following note to Zech. ix.–xiv. :

"In Betreff dieser sechs Kapitel die wegen ihre Stellung hinter den Weissagungen Sacharyas schon frühzeitig diesem Propheten zugeschrieben worden sind, ist noch immer streitig, ob wenigstens ein vorexilischer Kern (und zwar für kap. ix.–xi. aus dem 8 Jahrhundert, für xii.–xiv. aus dem Ende des 7 Jahrhundert). Auzunehmen, oder ob das Ganze erst aus der spätern nach exilischen Zeit (dem 4 oder gar 3 Jahrhundert) herzuleiten sei—namely, ' In reference to these six chapters, which, on account of their position after the prophecies of Zechariah, were already in early times ascribed to this prophet, it is still a matter of dispute if we are to regard them as containing at least a pre-exilic kernel (or foundation—namely, for chapters ix.–xi. from the eighth century, and for chapters xii.–xiv. from the end of the seventh century, B.C.), or if the whole is to be referred to the later post-exilic time (namely, the fourth or even the third century B.C.).' "

[2] Pusey. In the last sentences he has, no doubt, the case of De Wette in his mind, who, after advocating a pre-exilic origin of these chapters in the first three editions of his *Einleitung ins Alte Testament*, changed his mind in the 4th edition.

Stähelin, in his *Einleitung in die Kanonische Bücher des Alten Testaments*, says : "De Wette often assured me orally, that since he felt himself compelled to admit that this portion evinces acquaintance with the latest prophets, he could not deny it to be Zechariah's." De Wette's characterisation of these chapters was that they are "prophecies of fanatic contents, which deny all historical explanation."

It is obvious that there must be some mistake either in the tests applied or in their application, which admits of a variation of at least 450 years from somewhere in the reign of Uzziah (say 770 B.C.) to later than 330 B.C.

The Arguments against the Unity of Zechariah examined

But now let us very briefly examine the arguments against the unity of the Book of Zechariah. They are summarised by Professor von Orelli of Basel, one of the " moderate " of the modern school,[1] whose own conclusion in the end is that "chaps. ix.–xi. is a prophecy of a later contemporary of Hosea," and chaps. xii.–xiv. are " by an unnamed prophet at Jerusalem in the time of Jeremiah.' The critical grounds are these :

(*a*) " The great diversity of literary form and manner existing generally between Parts I. and II. In Part II are wanting those careful headings with indications of author and date which are found in Zechariah I. and Haggai. The style in Parts I. and II. is very different, both as relates to the phraseology in particular and the tenour of discourse generally. . . . The peculiar expressions of Part I. are not found in Part II., and conversely. The different tenour of the whole is of still greater importance. To put it in brief, the first part on the whole offers a somewhat awkward prosaic style ; whereas in the second, where there are no visions, exhibits in the discourses a spirit and a fire of enthusiasm such as one meets with elsewhere only in the early prophetic writings, but there all the oftener."

Now, in reference to the arguments based on supposed differences of literary form and style, which play such an important part in modern criticism, which is directed not only against these chapters, but against almost all the books of the Bible, it is sufficient to repeat a truism which

[1] In his Introduction to Zechariah in his *Commentary on the Twelve Minor Prophets.*

has been often stated, *that diversity of subject is sufficient to account for differences of form and style where such exist.* Headings and indications of authorship and date were necessary as introducing the series of visions at the beginning of the prophet's ministry, and to the address which formed the reply to the deputation from Bethel (chaps. vii., viii.); but no argument can be based on their absence from the oracles in the second part.

Some of the other prophets, too, use headings and attach dates to *some* of their utterances, and omit them in others.[1] Introductory formulas are, for instance, " made use of by Hosea in the first five chapters of his book, which are completely wanting in the last nine chapters, and yet no doubt is entertained of the integrity of that book. The style, moreover, of that prophet is very different in chaps. i.–iii. from what it is in chaps. iv.–xiv.; and the style of Ezek. iv., v., is totally different from that of chaps. vi., vii., or of xxvii., xxviii."[2]

But even those critics who agree in denying the unity of Zechariah do not agree among themselves on the points of style. Thus, Rosenmüller speaks of the first eight chapters as being " prosaic, feeble, poor," and of the last six chapters as " poetic, weighty, concise, glowing "; while Böttcher, on the other hand, speaks of the " *lifeless language* " of the last chapters, and compares them with the " amazingly fresh " style of the Psalms attributed to the time of the Maccabees.

The argument from style, however, to quote from W. H. Lowe's *Hebrew Student's Commentary*, must always remain a doubtful one. Pusey has given an instance of the precarious nature of such arguments in the following: " An acute German critic imagined to have proved from their style that the *Laws of Plato* were not the work of Plato ; and yet Jowett (trans., *Plato*, Dialog. iv. p. 1) has shown their genuineness by twenty citations in Aristotle (who must have been intimate with Plato for some

---

[1] Isa. i. 1, vi. 1 ; Ezek. i. 1–3, viii. 1, 2, xl. 1, 2.
[2] C. H. H. Wright.

seventeen years), by allusions of Isocrates (writing a year after Plato's death), by references of the comic poet Alexis (a younger contemporary), besides the unanimous voice of later antiquity.

" But it would not at all be surprising, as Keil, Stähelin, and others have observed, to find that the style of Zechariah varies in chaps. i.–viii. from that in chaps. ix.–xiv., as the subject-matter treated of in the two portions is radically different. ' In the former portion the prophet had to narrate a series of visions seen by him in one night, and to record divers exhortations of a practical kind suggested by the inquiry of the deputation from Bethel ; in the second portion he speaks of the distant future. In the former he might be expected to write in simple prose ; in the latter he might at times rise to lofty heights of poetry.

" ' Moreover, and this must not be forgotten, it is exceedingly probable that the second portion was composed many years after the first—long after the Temple had been completed—and matters had assumed a kind of normal condition as regards the Jewish colony, and also at a time when the realization of the bright hope of attaining their national independence seemed to be as far off as ever.' " [1]

" *That Gentle Lover of Peace.*"

Principal George Adam Smith finds a great argument against Zechariah's authorship of the last six chapters in the fact that " the peace, and the love of peace, in which Zechariah wrote, has disappeared. Nearly everything in the last part breathes of war, actual or imminent. The heathen are spoken of with a ferocity which finds few parallels in the Old Testament. There is revelling in their blood, of which the student of the authentic prophecies of Zechariah will at once perceive that gentle lover of peace could not have been capable."

We confess that we fail to " perceive " the truth of this statement, or to find any " ferocity," or " a revelling in the

[1] C. H. H. Wright.

blood of the heathen," on the part of the writer of these chapters.

What is true is that the prophet, who already in the First Part was commissioned to announce God's "great fury" against the nations who oppressed Israel, and already there foretells the overthrow of Gentile world-power, does in the last chapters, when he comes to prophesy more particularly of the last days, and of the solemn events which are to usher in the day when Jehovah shall at last be "*King over all the earth*," set forth in realistic language the final great conflict, and the terrible judgments which are to come, not only on "the heathen," *but on Israel also.*

It might be true that, according to his natural disposition, Zechariah, "that gentle lover of peace," might not find it a congenial task to prophesy of war and judgment, or to describe the destruction of the enemies of God and of His people; but other "gentle lovers of peace" among Israel's inspired prophets also had to utter some terribly heavy things against the ungodly in Israel and the nations who forget God, when compelled so to do by the hand and the Spirit of God.   There was no gentler man nor greater lover of peace than Jeremiah, and when he had to announce impending calamities and judgments he shrank from his task and did it with a broken heart; but Jehovah's word came to him saying, "*Behold, I have put My words in thy mouth: see, I have set thee over the nations and over the kingdoms, to pluck up and to break down, and to destroy and to overthrow ; to build and to plant.*"   He who was the embodiment of gentleness and love, and loved to reveal the Father's heart, had yet to warn men of the place of doom—"where the worm dieth not, and where the fire is not quenched."

But let us turn briefly to the other arguments against the unity of Zechariah, as summarised by Von Orelli.   We pass over the statement under the heading (*b*), namely, that "*the circle of thought is quite different in the two parts of the book*," for, as he himself observes, "this cannot be conclusive against the unity of the author, as, *e.g.*, we cannot demand that Zechariah, in his later discourses, should use again the entire angelology of the visionary part: the figure of Satan, the seven eyes of God," etc.

(c) "*A much more important point is that the outward, historical, and political situation presupposed in chaps. ix.–xiv. is not that of the age of Zerubbabel.*" But is that so really? Let me put over against this statement, one by another German commentator, who was certainly not less scholarly nor less painstaking than those against whom he contends. "*The current opinion of these critics, that the chapters in question date from the time before the Captivity*," writes Professor Keil, "*is completely overthrown by the circumstance that even in these oracles the condition of the covenant nation* AFTER THE CAPTIVITY *forms the historical ground and starting-point for the proclamation of the picture of the future development of the Kingdom of God*," which statement he proceeds to prove (to my mind satisfactorily) by a number of references in these chapters. And that the historic foreground and starting-point of these chapters are not only post-exilic, but might *very well* fit in with the time of Zerubbabel, is also shown by Hengstenberg, Stähelin, Hävernick, Koehler, Kliefoth, Lange, Bredenkamp, and other prominent Bible scholars and commentators.

To show that the critics themselves are far from sure of " the historic and political situation presupposed in chaps. ix.–xiv.," we might point again to the group which includes Eichhorn, H. E. G. Paulus, Vatke, B. Stade, etc., and their English exponents—Driver, George Adam Smith, etc., who, though denying Zechariah's authorship, *yet ascribe a post-exilic origin for these chapters, some of them as late, or even later, than 300 B.C.,* which guesses are also based chiefly on the supposed " historical and political situation " which they discover in these chapters.

Misconceptions and Misinterpretations

It can be shown, however, that many of the supposed " results " and conclusions of modern critics are based, not only on misconceptions as to the " outward, historical, and political situation presupposed " in the scriptures with which they deal, but on misunderstandings and misinterpretations of the text.

This will appear more clearly when we come to the exposition of these chapters ; but an illustration of this fact is found in the summarised arguments against the unity of Zechariah given by Von Orelli under the last two headings of (*d*) and (*e*). We will quote them one by one, and very briefly examine them. The italics in all cases are, of course, ours.

(i.) "*As relates to the circumstances of Israel in chaps. ix.–xi., chap. ix. is of the nation as found in foreign lands* (ix. 11); *but a more general exile is still to come* (x. 2–9)."

We confess we cannot see how, supposing this is admitted, it would go to prove a pre-exilic origin of these two chapters, but we may quote words written by an English divine already before the end of the eighteenth century. "*It is urged,*" says Benjamin Blayney, "that many things are mentioned in these chapters which by no means correspond with Zechariah's time, as when events are foretold which had actually taken place. But it may be questioned whether those subjects of prophecy have been rightly understood, and whether that which has been construed as having a reference to past transactions may not in reality terminate in others of a later period, and some perhaps which are yet to come."

Taking it for granted, as we do, that it *is* possible for an inspired prophet, speaking by the Spirit of God, to utter things not only in reference to an immediate, but also of a distant future, the references quoted from chaps. ix. and x. "as relates to the circumstances of Israel," answer exactly to the facts as contemplated from the starting-point of Zechariah's time ; for the actual conditions were these : A remnant had returned after the seventy years' Captivity, but many of Zion's children—indeed by far the majority—were "prisoners of hope" (ix. 12) in the hands of the Gentiles. In the end, all the dispersed, wherever they may be found —whether in the lands "of the rising of the sun," or in those

" of the going down of the sun " (viii. 7, 8)—will be gathered ; but that Zechariah foresaw a second stage in the dispersion, a more universal scattering before the final and universal gathering, we have already seen in the exposition of vers. 10 and 11 of chap. ii., and of vers. 7 and 8 of chap. viii.

(ii.) " *The Temple in Jerusalem was still standing* (xi. 13)." Why not? Did not Zechariah early in his ministry see the completion of the building of a temple in Jerusalem after the partial restoration? And here again, supposing the difficult prophecy in chap. xi. refers (as, in the light of its striking and manifest fulfilment in Christ, it assuredly does) to a more *distant* future from the point of view of the prophet, when a temple would exist in Jerusalem?

(iii.) " *Nay, even Ephraim has not gone into exile,* . . . *but is presupposed as a still existing power* (ix. 10–13, x. 6, xi. 7–14)."

Now, this would be a very serious argument against the post-exilic date of these chapters if the statement were true ; but here also the conclusion is not justified by a proper understanding of the references given. It is based on the mention of " Ephraim " or " the house of Joseph," which are used as designations of " Israel " (xi. 14) in the narrower sense—namely, for those who during the long schism belonged to the northern kingdom in contrast to " Judah," or " the house of Judah," or " Jerusalem," which stand, when thus contrasted, for the southern kingdom. But if the mention of Ephraim, or " Israel," together with " Judah " and " Jerusalem," is to be taken as a proof that " Ephraim had not gone into exile " when these chapters were written, then on the same ground we might conclude that the northern kingdom still existed when chaps. vii. and viii. were written ; and not only chaps. vii. and viii., but even the vision of the Horns and Carpenters in chap. i., for there also we read of the " house of Judah and the *house of Israel*" (viii. 13), and of " Judah, Israel, and Jerusalem " (i. 19, ii. 2) ; and yet it is universally admitted, even by the critics, that chaps. vii. and viii., as well as the visions, *were* written by Zechariah long after the overthrow—not only of Ephraim or the northern kingdom, but even of "Judah."

But in truth these full designations, "house of Judah and house of Joseph," or "Judah and Ephraim," or "Judah, Israel, and Jerusalem," are used by the prophet as *all-inclusive terms*, for the whole people, after both kingdoms had been overthrown, and the schism which had existed so long had ceased with the Captivity. "The entire nation," as I wrote in my note on chap. viii. 13, "which had previous to the Exile been divided for a time into two kingdoms, are now, after the partial restoration from Babylon, included in both parts of the book, in undivided unity in one common destiny." Together they are, during the Lo-ammi period, "scattered" and "a curse among the nations," and together (the prophet foretells) Jehovah shall "redeem" and gather them, "so that they shall be a blessing."

(iv.) The last of the internal grounds against the unity of Zechariah advanced by the critics, as summarised by Von Orelli, is that "*the chief moral and religious faults presupposed in Part II. are pre-exilic. This part still contends chiefly against idolatry* (x. 2), *and regards the extirpation of false prophets as still future ; their number must still have been great at the time when Zechariah xiii. 2–6 was written.*"

In reference to idolatry, let me quote the words of another writer :

"Idolatry certainly was not the prevailing national sin after God had taught the people through the Captivity. It is commonly taken for granted that there was *none*. But where is the proof ? Malachi would hardly have laid the stress on *marrying the daughters of a strange god*, had there been no danger that the marriage would lead to idolatry. Nehemiah speaks of the sin into which Solomon was seduced by 'outlandish women,' as likely to occur through the heathen marriages ; but idolatry was that sin. Half of the children could only speak the language of their mothers. It were strange if they had not imbibed their mothers' idolatry too. In a battle in the Maccabee war it is related,

' Under the coats of every one that was slain they found things consecrated to the idols of the Jamnites, which is forbidden the Jews by their law ' (2 Macc. xii. 40).

" The Teraphim were, moreover, an unlawful and forbidden means of attempting to know the future—not any coarse form of idolatry; much as the people now, who, more or less, earnestly have their fortunes told, would be surprised at being called idolaters." [1]

But it is very probable that Zechariah is speaking in chaps. x. 2, xiii. 2, etc., of *the sin which brought on the Captivity*, and not of it as existing in his own day. The prediction repeated from one of the former prophets, that God will *cut off* the very names and memory of idols from restored and converted Israel of the future, does not necessarily imply that they existed when the prophet wrote. And as to false prophets, they continued to exist after the Captivity—such, for instance, were Shemaiah, who *"prophesied" against Nehemiah*, and the prophetess Noadiah, and " the rest of the prophets " of whom we read in Neh. vi. 12–14.   But here again it is overlooked that it is *the distant future of Israel's final deliverance* and cleansing which is before the prophet's range of vision, though it is linked to promises which have for their starting-point the more immediate future.   There were false prophets at the time of the Lord's first advent, and He Himself warns His disciples against " false prophets " who would appear in the professing Church " in sheep's clothing, but inwardly are ravening wolves," and predicts that before the time of the end " many false prophets would arise and deceive many " (Matt. vii. 15, xxiv. 11–24, etc.).

Internal Marks of the Unity of Zechariah

We must draw this already lengthy disquisition to a close. We think we have shown that the objections raised by modern critics against the unity of Zechariah have no sufficient basis in fact.

[1] Pusey.

On the other hand, there are strong reasons, even apart from "tradition" (which in this case includes the testimony of the compilers of the Old Testament Prophetic Canon centuries before Christ, and of the Talmud)—which has always ascribed this scripture to Zechariah—to believe that it was the same human pen which committed to writing the series of visions in chaps. i.–vi. and the address to the deputation from Bethel in chaps. vii., viii., that the Spirit of God used also to write the last six chapters. The internal proofs of the integrity of the whole book have been thus summarised by another writer, of which, for the sake of conciseness, I gladly avail myself:

"(1) Both portions exhibit an extensive acquaintance with the writings of the *later* prophets.

"(2) They both exhibit also an extensive acquaintance with the *earlier* books, thus: In chap. i. 4–6, chap. vii. 12, reference is made to 'the former prophets' generally.[1]

"(3) In both divisions there are similar if not identical expressions to represent the whole people, such as 'the house of Israel and the house of Judah' (viii. 13), 'the house of Judah and the house of Joseph' (x. 6).

"(4) Chap. xi. 11 is very similar to ii. 9–11, and the promise x. 1 to that of viii. 12. In both portions Jerusalem is bid rejoice (ii. 10, ix. 9), and in both the only King of Israel mentioned is the Messiah.

"(5) In both portions there are promises of the bring-

---

[1] Chap. ii. 12 (E.V. 8) recalls the thought, though not the phraseology, of Ps. xvii. 8; chap. iii. 8, vi. 12, alludes to Isa. iv. 2, as well as to Jer. xxiii. 5 and xxxiii. 15; chap. iii. 10 is from Mic. iv. 4; chap. vi. 13 evidently refers to Ps. cx. 4; chap. viii. 8 recalls Hos. ii. 21 (E.V. 19); chap. viii. 20–22 in substance may be compared with Mic. iv. 1, 2, Isa. ii. 2, 3. And in the Second Part, chap. ix. 1–8 bears some resemblance to Amos i. 3, ii. 6; chap. ix. 10 (first half) is borrowed from Mic. v. 10, and (second half) from Ps. lxxii. 8; chap. xiii. 2 is a quotation from Hos. ii. 17 or Mic. v. 12, 13 (comp. Isa. ii. 18, 20); and ver. 9 from Hos. ii. 20 (E.V. 23); compare also chap. ix. 16 with Isa. xi. 12; chap. x. 12 with Mic. iv. 5; chap. x. 10–12 with Isa. xi. 15, xiv. 25, x. 24–27, xxx. 31, etc.; chap. xii. 8 with Joel iv. 10; chap. xii. 10 with Joel iii. 1, 2; chap. xiv. 3 with Isa. xxxiv. 1–4; chap. xiv. 6, 7 with Amos v. 18–20; Joel iv. (E.V. iii.) 15; Isa. xxx. 26; chap. xiv. 8 with Isa. xi. 9, ii. 3, Mic. iv. 2; chap. xiv. 11 with Amos ix. 13–15; chap. xiv. 20 with Isa. xxiii. 18; chap. xiv. 21 with Isa. iv. 3, xxxv. 8, Joel iv. (E.V. iii.) 17, etc.

ing back of the exiles (comp. ii. 6–13, viii. 6–8, with ix. 11, 12 and x. 10–12).

"(6) In both there is the habit of dwelling on the same thought or word (e.g., ii. 10, 11, vi. 10, vi. 12, 13, viii. 4, 5, viii. 23, xi. 7, xiv. 10, xiv. 4, xiv. 5). In both the whole and its part are mentioned together for emphasis, as v. 4, x. 4 ; and in xii. 12 we have 'every family apart,' and then in ver. 13, the specification. In both parts we have the unusual number of *five* sections to a verse, *e.g.*, vi. 13, ix. 5–7.

"(7) Both divisions are written in Hebrew free from Aramaisms. In both the expressions *mě'ōbhêr umishábh* occurs (vii. 14, ix. 8), an expression which occurs elsewhere only in Ezek. xxxv. 7.

"(8) The highly poetic language and deep prophetic insight of chaps. ix.–xiv. we consider as an additional argument in favour of the unity of authorship of the whole book. For the man to whom in his youth such mystic visions as those of chaps. i.–vi. were vouchsafed, is just such an one to whom we should not be surprised to find that in his later years such profound revelations as those contained in chaps. ix.–xiv. were revealed, and who from his poetic and imaginative temperament would be likely to find suitable poetic language and metaphors wherewith to clothe them when revealed to him.

"The *internal* evidence being favourable to the hypothesis of the post-exilian origin of chaps. ix.–xiv., as well as of chaps. i.–viii., and to that of unity of authorship, rather than adverse to it, and there being no positive external evidence to the contrary, we conclude that it is probable that the whole of the so-called Book of Zechariah is the work of Zechariah, grandson of Iddo." [1]

[1] W. H. Lowe, M.A., "*Hebrew Student's Commentary.*"

Chapter 14

THE GENTILE WORLD-CONQUEROR
AND ISRAEL'S PRINCE OF PEACE

Zechariah 9

The burden of the word of Jehovah upon the land of Hadrach, and Damascus shall be its resting-place (for the eye of man and of all the tribes of Israel is toward Jehovah); and Hamath, also, which bordereth thereon; Tyre and Sidon, because they are very wise. And Tyre did build herself a stronghold, and heaped up silver as the dust, and fine gold as the mire of the streets. Behold, the Lord will dispossess her, and He will smite her power in the sea; and she shall be devoured with fire. Ashkelon shall see it, and fear; Gaza also, and shall be sore pained; and Ekron, for her expectation shall be put to shame: and the king shall perish from Gaza, and Ashkelon shall not be inhabited. And a bastard shall dwell in Ashdod, and I will cut off the pride of the Philistines. And I will take away his blood out of his mouth, and his abominations from between his teeth, and he also shall be a remnant for our God: and he shall be as a chieftain in Judah, and Ekron as a Jebusite. And I will encamp about My house against the army, that none pass through or return; and no oppressor shall pass through them any more: for now have I seen with Mine eyes. Rejoice greatly, O daughter of Zion; shout, O daughter of Jerusalem: behold, thy king cometh unto thee: He is just, having salvation; lowly, and riding upon an ass, even upon a colt the foal of an ass. And I will cut off the chariot from Ephraim, and the horse from Jerusalem; and the battle-bow shall be cut off; and He shall speak peace unto the nations, and His dominion shall be from sea to sea, and from the river to the ends of the earth. As for thee also, because of the blood of thy covenant I have set free thy prisoners from the pit wherein is no water. Turn you to the stronghold, ye prisoners of hope; even to-day do I declare that I will render double unto thee. For I have bent Judah for Me, I have filled the bow with Ephraim; and I will stir up thy sons, O Zion, against thy sons, O Greece, and will make thee as the sword of a mighty man. And Jehovah shall be seen over them, and His arrow shall go forth as the lightning, and the Lord Jehovah will blow the trumpet, and will go with whirlwinds of the south. And Jehovah of hosts will defend them, and they shall devour, and shall tread down the sling-stones; and they shall drink, and make a noise as through wine; and they shall be filled like bowls, like the corners of the altar. And Jehovah their God will save them in that day as the flock of His people: for they shall be as the stones of a crown, lifted on high over His land. For how great is His goodness, and how great is His beauty! grain shall make the young men flourish, and new wine the virgins.

Chapter 14

THE overthrow of world-power, and the establishment of Messiah's Kingdom, may be given as the epitome of the last chapters of Zechariah, to which we have now come. The two oracles which make up the whole of the second half of the book (chaps. ix.–xi. and xii.–xiv.) show by their headings, as well as by their contents, and even by their formal arrangement, that they are corresponding portions of a greater whole. Both sections treat of war between the heathen world and Israel, though in different ways.

In the first (chaps. ix.–xi.), the judgment *through which Gentile world-power over Israel is finally destroyed*, and Israel is endowed with strength to *overcome all their enemies*, forms the fundamental thought and centre of gravity of the prophetic description. In the second (chaps. xii.–xiv.), the judgment *through which Israel itself is sifted and purged* in the final great conflict with the nations, and transformed into the holy nation of Jehovah, forms the leading topic.

" The formal or structural resemblance between the two long oracles into which the last six chapters divide themselves appears also in the fact that in the centre of each the announcement suddenly takes a different tone without any external preparation (chaps. xi. 1 and xiii. 7), so that it appears as if it were the commencement of a new prophecy ; and it is only by a closer study that the connection of the whole is brought out and the relation between the two is clearly seen—namely, that the second section contains a more minute description of the manner in which the events announced in the first section are to be realised. In the threatening word concerning the land of Hadrach, chaps. ix. and x. form the first section, chap. xi. the second. In that concerning Israel the first section extends from chap. xii. 1 to xiii. 6, and the second from chap. xiii. 7 to the end of the book."[1]

Chaps. ix. and x., as has just been observed, go together and form a continuous proohecy. The foreground, or more immediate future, to which it refers, is the course of the victories of Alexander the Great, "which circled round the Holy Land without hurting it," and ended in the overthrow of the Persian Empire—though the foreground merges, as we shall see, into solemn events both of judgment and of mercy of a more distant future.

The prophecy begins with the word מַשָּׂא (*massa*), which the Authorised Version, together with all the ancient versions (with the exception of the Septuagint), have rendered "burden"; but the majority of modern scholars translate simply "oracle," or "utterance," or "sentence."

It is not necessary to enter here into a long critical examination of the actual force of this word when used as a superscription to prophetic utterances; but it is certainly true that מַשָּׂא (*massa*), which is from the verb נָשָׂא (*nasa*), "to lift," or "take up," as a man takes up a burden, "is never placed in the title," as is observed already by Jerome, "save when the vision is heavy, and full of burden and toil."

It is used by Isaiah entirely as the heading to the prophecies which contain threatenings and announce judgments against the nations who have acted as oppressors of Israel,[2] and in Nahum it forms the introductory formula to the prophetic description of the destruction of Nineveh. In short, in ordinary Hebrew "*massa* is unquestionably used in the sense of a *burden*, and the prophecies to which it is affixed are mainly prophecies of woe and disaster." Here, moreover (in Zech. ix. 1 and in chap. xii. 1), *massa*

[1] Keil. I have taken the liberty of recasting and slightly condensing his valuable remarks.

[2] Isa. xiii. 1, xiv. 28, xv. 1, xvii. 1, xix. 1, xxi. 1, 11, 13, xxii. 1, xxiii. 1. A full and able criticism, five pages long, on the use of the word will be found in Hengstenberg (*Christology*) on Zech. ix.

does not stand alone as the introductory formula, as is the case in Isaiah and Nahum, but is followed by דְּבַר יְהֹוָה (*debhar Yehovah*), "the word of Jehovah"; as is the case also in Mal. i. 1, which begins, "*The burden of the word of Jehovah to Israel.*"

Very many pages have been devoted by commentators to the discussion as to the meaning of *Hadrach*. Because the name occurs nowhere else in the Bible, and because of the difficulty in identifying it with any known place or district in Syria, it has been generally understood by Jewish and Christian commentators as having a *symbolical* or mystical significance. Thus Kimchi says, " We find in the words of our Rabbis of blessed memory that Rabbi Benaiah says Hadrach is the name of the Messiah, who is sharp— חַד (*had*)—to the Gentiles, and tender—רַךְ (*rakh*)—to Israel." And this interpretation of Rabbi Benaiah is echoed also by other Jewish expositors. The explanations given by most Christian commentators have been quite as fanciful. Thus Hengstenberg (who devotes eight learned pages to it in his *Christology*), Kliefoth, Keil, and others explain Hadrach to be " a symbolic epithet, descriptive of the Medo-Persian Empire, which is called 'sharp-soft,' or 'strong-weak,' on account of its inwardly divided character." [1]

Gesenius, Bleek, and others have taken *Hadrach* as the name of some Syrian king who is supposed to have reigned in Damascus between Benhahad III. and Rezin, which utterly baseless supposition (since there is no trace whatever in history of the existence of such a king) has been taken by them as a support for the theory of a pre-exilic origin of these chapters.

Others have wrongly understood the word as standing for " an Assyrian fire-god," or as the name of " a deity of Eastern Aramea," of which also there is no trace in history ; while Olshausen, Von Ortenberg, Bredenkamp, and others regard Hadrach as a scribal error for *Hauran*, which is a district south of Damascus, and is mentioned also in connection with Hamath and Damascus in Ezek. xlvii. 18.

[1] Keil.

But it is now pretty certain that there was a city called Hadrach in the neighbourhood of Damascus, for comparatively recent monumental historical discoveries have in this, as in so many instances beside, confirmed and thrown light on the Hebrew text. In the list of Assyrian eponyms—that is, the list of the various officers after whom the Assyrian years were named in a certain definite order, the kings themselves acting in due course as eponyms—we read, in B.C. 772, in the eponymy of Assur-bel-ezer, governor of Calah, of an " expedition to Hadrach " (Ha-ta-ri-ka). This statement immediately follows the name of the governor of Sallat (or *Salmat*, as Rawlinson and Schrader give the name), who was the eponym in the previous year, when an expedition was made to the city of Damascus. Hadrach (or Hatarika) figures also in the expeditions in the eponyms of later Assyrian kings and generals.

Sir Henry Rawlinson says that in the catalogue of Syrian cities tributary to Nineveh (of which we have several copies in a more or less perfect state, and varying from each other both in arrangement and extent) there are three names which are uniformly grouped together, and which read Manatsuah, Magida (Megiddo), and Du'ar (Dor). " As these names are associated with those of Samaria, Damascus, Arpad, Hamath, Carchemish, *Hadrach* (or Hatarika) and Zobah, there can be no doubt about the position of the cities." [1]

We proceed to the next line—"*And Damascus shall be its resting-place*"; [2] that is, the judgment which is the " burden " of this prophecy shall first of all have Damascus

---

[1] Those interested in this subject will find full notes and long quotations from Rawlinson, Schrader, etc., in Dr. Wright's *Zechariah and his Prophecies*, and in Pusey in his *Minor Prophets*.

[2] מְנוּחָה (*menuchah*) is indeed commonly used of " quiet, peaceful resting," and some (as already the Targum) have understood it as indicating the conversion of the people of Damascus. But this idea is contrary to the context. Rather is it to be understood of the lighting down of God's wrath, which shall there *rest* until it has accomplished His purpose of judgment. Dr. Wright suggests as a parallel Jer. xlix. 38, when, in allusion to His judgment impending over Elam, God says, " I will set My throne in Elam."

as its goal, and from that centre it shall spread itself over the whole district which the passage goes on to describe.

The easiest and most natural translation of the second half of the first verse—*Ki la-Yehovah 'ein adam ve khol shibhte Israel*—is that given in the Authorised Version and in the text of the " Revised "—i.e., "*for the eye of man and of all the tribes of Israel is toward the Lord*"; but the margin of the Revised Version has another rendering, which is supported by the LXX, the Syriac, and the Targum, and is adopted also, with slight variations, by some modern scholars—namely, "*for Jehovah has an eye* (or '*to Jehovah is an eye*') *upon* (or '*over*') *man and the tribes of Israel*"— which is regarded as a parallelism to Jer. xxxii. 19: "*Great in counsel and mighty in work, for Thine eyes are open upon all the ways of the sons of men, to give every one according to his ways, and according to the fruit of his doings.*" But the rendering given in the Authorised Version is doubtless the true one.

It primarily describes the consternation into which men would be thrown at the approach of the conqueror, who would be the executor of God's judgment, or, as another has expressed it, when the fulfilment of this prophecy takes place " upon Hadrach and Damascus, and the wrath of God descends upon those cities and districts, the eyes of the nations, as well as those of the people of Israel, will look toward Jehovah, and marvel at the wonders of judgment which will then be performed in their sight, in accordance with the solemn warnings of the prophet."

The eye of all the tribes of Israel is particularly specified as directed then toward Jehovah, probably because the Jews had special reason to fear the wrath of Alexander, their high priest having from a sense of loyalty to the Persians refused at first to pay tribute or allegiance to the Macedonian conqueror. But what is here foretold as primarily taking place as the result of the terror inspired among the nations which then constituted parts of the

Medo-Persian Empire by the rapid march and conquests of Alexander the Great, also foreshadows what will take place in a yet future time, when, driven by fear and consternation of God's judgments which shall then be in the earth, the eyes of all men, and "of all the tribes of Israel" in particular, shall be directed toward Him who was once pierced, but now marches forth conquering and to conquer (Rev. i. 7).

In Isa. xvii. we have a somewhat parallel prediction of men's eyes, and specially of the eyes of Israel, being turned to God as the result of judgment, and there also it is primarily coupled with the burden, or oracle, against Damascus: "*In that day*," we read, "*shall a man look unto his Maker, and his eyes shall have respect to the Holy One of Israel ; and he shall not look to the altars, the work of his hands, neither shall he have respect to that which his fingers have made*"—a passage which reminds us also of the language of the godly remnant in the 26th chapter: "*Yea, in the way of Thy judgments, O Lord, have we waited for Thee : to Thy Name and to Thy Memorial is the desire of our soul. With my soul have I desired Thee in the night ; yea, with my spirit within me will I seek Thee early : for when Thy judgments are in the earth the inhabitants of the world learn righteousness.*" [1]

But to proceed to the 2nd verse: "*And Hamath, also, which bordereth thereon*"—*i.e.*, on Damascus—shall be involved in the like fate, and share in the burden of wrath of which Damascus is the "resting-place."

There was a district or small kingdom in Syria, as well as a city of that name (which was its capital), the present Hamath, and within its bounds "in the land of Hamath" Riblah was situated, associated in Jewish memory with terrible sufferings and humiliations at the hands of their conquering foes (2 Kings xxiii. 33, xxv. 6, 7, 20, 21).

Then, having spoken of the two capital cities which represent Syria, the prophet proceeds to speak of the two

[1] Isa. xvii. 1-8, xxvi. 8, 9.

capitals of Phœnicia: " *Tyre and* (or ' *with* ') *Sidon,*[1] *because*
(or ' *although* ') *she is very wise.*"

How Tyre especially showed her worldly wisdom, and
the great material prosperity which she attained thereby,
we see in the 3rd verse: " *And Tyre built herself a stronghold, and heaped up silver as the dust, and fine gold as the
mire of the street.*" The words in the Hebrew are *vatibhen
Tsor matsor.* There is a kind of play on the word Tyre
(*Tsor*). The similarity of the sound and meaning may be
somewhat imitated, as Dr. Wright suggests, by the English
rendering, " *Tyre* built herself a *tower,*" though the Hebrew
word " *matsor* " has a much wider significance than the
English " tower." " Tyre " (*Tsor*) was perhaps, in the first
instance, so called because of her natural *strength*, or strong
fortifications, the word suggesting *a rocky stronghold.* But
she was not satisfied with that—she built herself in addition
a *matsor*—a strong rocky fortress. This refers, no doubt,
to the *new* Tyre, which was on an island thirty stadia
(about seven hundred paces) from the mainland. This new
Tyre is called in Isa. xxiii. 4, מָעוֹז הַיָּם, *maoz hayyam*, " the
stronghold of the sea," because, although very small in
extent, it was surrounded by a wall a hundred and fifty
feet high, and was so strong a fortification that Shalmaneser besieged it for five years without success, and
Nebuchadnezzar for thirteen years, and apparently was
unable to conquer it. This is confirmed by the heathen
historian Diodorus Siculus, who says, " Tyre had the
greatest confidence owing to her insular position and
fortifications, and the abundant stores she had prepared." Thus, thinking herself doubly strong and im-
pregnable, she gave herself up, as the capital of Phœnicia,
to commercial enterprise, and " heaped up silver as the

---

[1] Sidon is regarded as an annexe of Tyre, which, as Keil points out, answers
to the historical relation in which the two cities stood to one another. Tyre was,
indeed, originally a colony of Sidon, but it very soon overshadowed the mother
city, and rose to be the capital of all Phœnicia, so that even in Isaiah and
Ezekiel the prophecies concerning Sidon are attached to those concerning Tyre,
and its fate appears interwoven with that of Tyre. Hence, after the mere
mention of Sidon, Tyre only is spoken of in vers. 3 and 4 of this prophecy.

dust, and fine or shining gold (*ḥarutz*) as the mire of the
street." [1]

But worldly wisdom, natural strength, and material
resources are of no avail if it is *the Lord* who rises in
judgment against us ; and that is true of nations as of
individuals.

"*Behold, the Lord will dispossess her, and He shall smite
her power* (or '*her wealth*') *in the sea ; and she shall be
devoured with fire.*" " Behold " (*hinneh*), by which word
our special attention is directed to something very
important. " Behold," though Tyre is so wise, so doubly
strong, so rich—yea, even though her strength were a
hundred times as great, and she enclosed herself in a
hundred strong walls of one hundred and fifty feet high,
" *the Lord* will dispossess her "; for cities or peoples cannot
barricade themselves against God, and " it is altogether
useless to build strongholds to keep *Him* out." It was *the
Lord* who did it through Alexander, whom He used as His
scourge against Phœnicia and the Persian power at that
time.

" If the reference of a prophecy can be judged of by the
event," says another writer, " there can be no doubt whatever to what period this prophecy must refer. The judgments denounced against Damascus, Hadrach, and Hamath
are expressed in such general terms that several events
which occurred at very different periods might be adduced
as fulfilments of the prophecy. But the prophecies referring
to Tyre were not accomplished until the capture and
destruction of that city by Alexander the Great. Tyre
was unsuccessfully attacked, during the supremacy of the
Assyrian power, by Shalmaneser. It was again besieged
for many years by Nebuchadnezzar, and it is still a matter
of doubt whether it was actually taken by that monarch.
It is, indeed, highly probable that Nebuchadnezzar, though
he failed in his attack on the island fortress, was so far

---

[1] Compare especially Ezek. xxviii. No wonder the Prince of Tyre became
the foreshadowing of Antichrist, and the King of Tyre (Ezek. xxviii. 12) the
earthly foreground and type of the chief of the fallen angels.

successful as to gain possession of the city on the mainland, which was possibly denuded of all that was valuable, and that the Tyrians after the loss of the city on the mainland made peace with the Chaldean monarch on favourable terms. But it is certain that if Tyre was captured at all by Nebuchadnezzar, it was not then burned with fire——her sea-girt fortress was not destroyed nor her naval power ruined. Though she may have lost her independence, she did not lose the important position she occupied as the greatest commercial and naval city in the world, and the naval power of the Phœnicians proved in the Persian period of the greatest possible importance to that empire.

" The case was very different when Alexander the Great, having completely shattered the might of Persia in the decisive battle of Issus, marched with his victorious army into Syria. Alexander directed the main division of his army against Phœnicia, while he dispatched Parmenio with a strong detachment to operate against Damascus. Damascus, where Darius had deposited his riches, opened its gates to that general, who overran all the land of Hadrach, and must also necessarily have occupied Hamath, which probably submitted without a struggle. Sidon surrendered without making any resistance; but Tyre, after a vain attempt at negotiation, ventured to resist.

" Proudly confident in the strength of their island fortress, the Tyrians mocked the attempts of Alexander to reduce their city. Every engine of war suited for defence had been stored up in their bulwarks, and every device which their skilful engineers could suggest was had recourse to, and for a time with marked success. ' Ye despise this land army through confidence in the place that ye dwell in is an island, but I will show you that ye dwell on a continent,' was the language of Alexander. The shallow channel between the mainland and the island was at last bridged over by a huge dam of earth erected after repeated failures, and the city which had stood a five years' siege from the Assyrians, a thirteen years' siege from the Chaldeans, was taken after a short siege of seven months by Alexander.

Ten thousand of its brave defenders were either massacred or crucified, the rest were sold into slavery, and none escaped save those who were concealed by the Sidonians in the ships.   O. Curtius adds distinctly that ' Alexander having slain all save those who fled to the temples, ordered the houses to be set on fire.' [1]

"The city of Tyre was afterwards repeopled by fresh settlers, and recovered some of its prosperity.   During the reigns of the Seleucidian monarchs it rose again to considerable importance.   But the prophecy of Zechariah had been fulfilled to the letter.   The city lost its insular position ; for the mole of Alexander was never removed, and covered over and strengthened by the deposits of sand and other matter, it .remains even to this day a monument of the execution of the Divine wrath upon the proud, luxurious, and idolatrous city." [2]

But the burden of judgment travels south.   The overthrow of the Phœnician stronghold and the approach of the powerful enemy greatly terrifies Philistia : " *Ashkelon shall see it* (or '*let Ashkelon see it*') *and fear ; Gaza also shall be sore pained* (or '*greatly tremble*') *; and Ekron, for her expectation* (or '*her hope*') *shall be ashamed ; and a king shall perish from Gaza, and Ashkelon shall not be inhabited* (or '*shall not abide*').   *And a bastard shall dwell in Ashdod, and I will cut off the pride of the Philistines.*"

Only four of the five capital cities of the Philistines are mentioned, Gath being usually omitted in the later prophets, perhaps because it belonged, for a time at any rate, to the kingdom of Judah, and was, according to some, ultimately incorporated with it.

The order in which these Philistine cities are named is the same as in Jer. xxv., which prophecy was certainly not unknown to Zechariah.

[1] There is a full and graphic account of the siege and capture of Tyre by Alexander in Professor George Rawlinson's *Phœnicia* ("The Story of the Nations" Series), pp. 216-236.

[2] At present Tyre, now called Sur, is an unimportant place with 6000 inhabitants, about half of whom are Moslems and the rest Latin Christians and " United Catholics."

Though no special mention is made of Ashkelon, Ekron, or Ashdod in the histories of Alexander's march, they were no doubt occupied by the Macedonian troops. The fate of Gaza, however, at that time is fully recorded. " Strongly fortified, and occupying an important position, its very name, ' the strong,' testified to its natural strength. Despite, therefore, of the terror caused by the overthrow of Tyre, Gaza ventured to resist Alexander, and was not reduced to submission for five months. Its king perished, and the city lost the semi-independence which it seems to have had under the Persian Empire. For the Persians, like their predecessors, the Assyrians and the Babylonians, were wont to permit many of the cities and districts which formed a portion of their empire to retain a state of semi-independence. Hence frequent mention is made of kings subject to the Persian ' King of kings.' "

The one who actually bore the name of King of Gaza at the time of the siege of the city by Alexander was Betis, or Batis, who, though a Persian satrap and commander of the city, had assumed a relatively independent position. His end was tragic. After the fall of Gaza, when ten thousand of the inhabitants were slain and the rest sold into slavery, Batis was bound to a chariot with thongs thrust through the soles of his feet, and dragged through the city.

We cannot with certainty define what is meant by " a bastard shall dwell in Ashdod." The word מַמְזֵר, *mamzer*, is only found in one other place in the Hebrew Scriptures (Deut. xxiii. 3), and its etymology is somewhat obscure. Among the Jews the term is used of one born out of lawful wedlock, but some think that it properly describes only one who is *mixed*, or of ignoble birth, and not necessarily one illegitimately born. The ancient versions (the LXX, Syriac, Targum, Vulgate) render the word in our passage by " a foreigner." In any case, as Keil observes, it describes one whose birth has some blemish connected with it, so that he is " not an equal by birth with the citizens of a city or the inhabitants of a land." Hengstenberg has rendered it freely by " *Gesindel* " (a rabble).

The second line in the 6th verse may be taken as explanatory of the first.   By the dwelling of the *mamzer* in Ashdod " the pride of *the Philistines shall be cut off.*"

" It would appear that the Philistines were wont to pride themselves upon their nationality, their prowess, and their independence.   Their pride would be humbled by Gaza's being deprived of any ruler bearing the name of king, by the city of Ashkelon being removed from its ancient place (*i.e.,* ceasing to exist), and by Ashdod being inhabited by a mixed and bastard population." ¹

In the 7th verse there is a ray of promised mercy shining out of the thick cloud of judgment which was to alight upon Philistia, for the end of the judgment is the deliverance of the people from their idolatrous abominations, and the incorporation of the remnant which shall remain, among God's people.

"*And I will take away his blood and his abominations from between his teeth, and he also shall be a remnant* (or ' *shall remain* ') *for our God: and he shall be as a chieftain* (or, ' *as a small tribe, or family* ') *in Judah, and Ekron shall be as a Jebusite.*"   It is the Philistine nation or people personified as one man who are here spoken of in the singular.   The blood (or, literally, " bloods," for the word is in the plural) which God will " take," or " cause to pass away " from his mouth, is the blood of his idolatrous sacrifices, which in the next sentence are called *shiqqutsim*—" abominations "—and thus deprived of, or delivered from, their polluting idolatry, the remnant that remains shall belong to " our God "—the living God of Israel—who stands out so glorious in His holiness when contrasted with the " abominations " of the heathen, " and He shall be as a chieftain in Judah." ²

---

¹ Wright.

² The word אַלֻּף (*alluph*) is used in the earlier books of the Bible of the "dukes," or tribal chiefs or princes of Edom and of the Horites (Gen. xxxvi.; Ex. xv. 15) ; but is applied by Zechariah in chap. xii. of the princes or chieftains of Judah.   It is connected with אֶלֶף (*elleph*), " a thousand," and stands perhaps literally for chief, or " head of a thousand.''   Some critics would substitute *eleph* for *alluph* in our passage, and render it " he shall be as a thousand," *i.e.,* a small

"*And Ekron shall be as the Jebusite,*" which latter, to quote the word of another commentator, "stands here for the former inhabitants of the citadel of Zion," who adopted the religion of Israel after the conquest of this citadel of David, and were incorporated into the nation of the Lord. "This is evident from the example of the Jebusite Araunah, who lived in the midst of the covenant nation (2 Sam. xxiv. and 1 Chron. xxi.) as a distinguished man of property, and not only sold his threshing-floor to King David as a site for the future Temple, but also offered to present the oxen with which he had been ploughing, as well as the plough itself, for a burnt-offering."

Here we are reminded once again that though the more immediate reference of the prophecy in this chapter was to Alexander's march and conquests, it looked on and merges into a more distant future. Koehler rightly points out that this 7th verse was not fulfilled by the deeds of Alexander, "since neither the remnant of the Phœnicians nor the other heathen dwelling in the midst of Israel were converted to Jehovah through the calamities connected with his expedition." On this ground this German scholar regards the conquests of Alexander as the *commencement* of the fulfilment, which was then continued through the calamities caused by the wars of succession—the conflicts between the Egyptians, Syrians, and Romans—until it was completed by the fact that the heathen tribes within the boundaries of Israel gradually disappeared as separate tribes, and their remnants were received into the community of those who confessed Israel's God. But, as Keil observes, "we must

tribe or "clan" in Judah. Calvin, however, gives quite a different interpretation to this somewhat difficult passage. He paraphrases the 7th verse thus : "I will rescue the Jew from the teeth of the Philistine" (the figure, according to him, being taken from wild beasts rending their prey with the teeth), "who would have devoured him as he would devour blood or flesh of his abominable sacrifices to idols ; and *even he*, the seemingly ignoble remnant of the Jews, shall be sacred to our God ; and though so long in a servile position, and bereft of dignity, I will make them all to be as governors, or princes, ruling others ; and Ekron shall be as a tributary bondservant, as the Jebusite." Then the antithesis would be between the Jew that remaineth and the Ekronite. But the interpretation I have given above is doubtless the correct one.

go a step further, and say that the fulfilment *has not yet* reached its end, and will not, until the kingdom of Christ shall attain that complete victory over the heathen world " which is foretold in the following verses of this chapter. Then, as has already been stated, when God's judgments are in the earth, the inhabitants of the world shall learn righteousness, and after Israel as a nation is converted, all the tribes and families of the earth shall be blessed with and through them.

But while Israel's enemies in the north and south have occasion to tremble at the approach of the hostile army, God Himself would be the shield and protector of His people and His special dwelling-place in their midst. "*And I will camp about My house*, וְחָנִיתִי לְבֵיתִי—*vechanithi lebhethi* (or ' for '—i.e., *on account, or for the protection of My house*) *because of the army*" (which is most probably the correct reading, though some, by a slight alteration of the first vowel, would read מַצָּבָה (*matsabhah*), instead of מִצָּבָה (*mitsabhah*), and translate : " I will encamp about, or for, My house, as a garrison, or guard "), "*because* (or ' *on account*') *of him who passeth through or returneth* ; [1] *and no oppressor shall pass through them any more, for now have I seen with Mine eyes.*"

" My house " stands not for the congregation of Israel, as some suppose, but for the Temple ; but the protection of the house carries with it also the protection of the people, which it is supposed will henceforth be under God's favour, so that in the next, or parallel line, the plural is used in the expression, " no oppressor shall *pass through them* any more."

The word נוֹגֵשׂ (*noges*), translated " oppressor," primarily means " *taskmaster* "—one who compels slaves to perform their appointed tasks (Ex. iii. 7, v. 6–10). It is used

---

[1] The phrase מֵעוֹבֵר וּמִשָּׁב (*me'obher umishabh*), "because of him that passeth by and because of him that returneth " ; or, " because of him that passeth to and fro," occurs altogether only four times in the Hebrew Scriptures, and as it is found in Zech. vii. 14 and here in chap. ix. 8, it has rightly been taken (as the expression is so unusual) as an indication of the common authorship of the first and second halves of this book, as is pointed out in the Introduction to the second part of this book.

also of *cattle-drivers* and tax-gatherers.   Once only, and in
this very prophecy (chap. x. 4), it is used in a good sense,
as describing one who has absolute rule ; but here it
stands for the foreign tyrants, the heads of the great
Gentile kingdoms who oppressed Israel.

In the last sentence in the 8th verse, " For now have
I seen with Mine eyes," we have an echo and reminiscence
of Ex. iii. 7 : "*I have surely seen* (or '*seeing I have
seen*') *the affliction of My people which are in Egypt, and have
heard their cry by reason of their taskmasters ; for I know
their sorrows*"; where also the word "for I have seen "
stands in connection with Israel's affliction at the hands of
their "taskmasters," which is the same word in plural form
as rendered "oppressor" in Zech. ix. 8.   Yes, the God who
delivered Israel from under the oppression of Egypt, and
with Whom only to "see" the afflictions of His people is
to be moved with compassion for their sorrows, will yet
again look "with His own eyes," and interpose, and deliver
them from the power of their oppressors ; which promise,
whatever the more immediate reference, will not be
exhaustively fulfilled until the final national deliverance of
Israel, of which the deliverance from Egypt is regarded in
the prophetic Scriptures as a type, and until the final overthrow of the enemies of God and of His people, of which
the overthrow of Pharaoh and his host in the Red Sea was
a foreshadowing.

With regard to the special fulfilment of the prediction
in the 8th verse in the more immediate future from the
prophet's point of view, let me remind my readers of the
account given by Josephus of the remarkable episode in
Alexander's march through Palestine, which agrees also
with traditions preserved in the Talmud and Midrashic literature.   At the commencement of his campaign against
Phœnicia, Alexander the Great sent messengers to the
Jewish high priest in Jerusalem demanding aid from the
Jews and the payment of the tribute which they used
to pay to the King of Persia.   The high priest, however, refused to break the oath of fidelity which he had

sworn to Darius, and Alexander in consequence threatened
to inflict a severe chastisement on Jerusalem as soon
as he had captured Tyre, and reduced the Philistine
strongholds.

" Now Alexander, when he had taken Gaza, made
haste to go up to Jerusalem ; and Jaddua the high priest,
when he heard that, was in an agony, and under terror,
as not knowing how he should meet the Macedonians, since
the king was displeased at his foregoing disobedience.

" He therefore ordained that the people should make
supplications, and should join with him in making sacrifices to God, whom he besought to protect that nation, and
to deliver them from the perils that were coming upon
them ; whereupon God warned him in a dream, which came
upon him after he had offered sacrifice, that he should take
courage, and adorn the city, and open the gates ; that the
rest should appear in white garments, but that he and the
priests should meet the king in the habits proper to their
order, without the dread of any ill consequences, which the
providence of God would prevent.   Upon which, when he
rose from his sleep, he greatly rejoiced ; and declared to
all the warning he had received from God.   According to
which dream he acted entirely, and so waited for the coming
of the king.

" And when he understood that he was not far from
the city, he went out in procession with the priests and the
multitude of the citizens.   The procession was venerable,
and the manner of it different from that of other nations.
It reached to a place called Sapha, which name, translated
into Greek, signifies a prospect; for you have thence a
prospect both of Jerusalem and of the Temple.   And when
the Phœnicians and the Chaldeans that followed him
thought they should have liberty to plunder the city and
torment the high priest to death—which the king's displeasure fairly promised them—the very reverse of it
happened ; for Alexander, when he saw the multitude at a
distance in white garments, while the priests stood clothed
in fine linen, and the high priest in purple and scarlet

clothing—with his mitre on his head—having the golden plate whereon the name of God was engraved, he approached by himself, and adored that name, and first saluted the high priest. The Jews also did altogether, with one voice, salute Alexander and encompass him about; whereupon the kings of Syria and the rest were surprised at what Alexander had done, and supposed him disordered in his mind. However, Parmenio alone went up to him and asked him how it came to pass that, when all others adored *him*, he should adore the high priest of the Jews? To whom he replied, 'I did not adore him, but that God who hath honoured him with his high priesthood; for I saw this very person in a dream, in this very habit, when I was at Dios in Macedonia, who, when I was considering with myself how I might obtain the dominion of Asia, exhorted me to make no delay, but boldly to pass over the sea thither, for that he would conduct my army, and would give me the dominion over the Persians; whence it is, that having seen no other in that habit, and now seeing this person in it, and remembering that vision, and the exhortation which I had in my dream, I believe that I bring this army under Divine conduct, and shall therewith conquer Darius and destroy the power of the Persians, and that all things will succeed according to what is in my own mind.

"And when he had said this to Parmenio, and had given the high priest his right hand, the priests ran along by him and he came into the city; and when he went up to the Temple, he offered sacrifice to God according to the high priest's direction, and magnificently treated both the high priest and the priests. And when the Book of Daniel was showed him wherein Daniel declared that one of the Greeks should destroy the empire of the Persians, he supposed that himself was the person intended; and as he was then glad, he dismissed the multitude for the present, but the next day he called them to him and bade them ask what favours they pleased of him; whereupon the high priest desired that they might enjoy the laws

of their forefathers, and might pay no tribute on the
seventh year." [1]

Israel's Prince of Peace and His Mission in the World

From the victorious progress of the great Gentile world-
conqueror, with his great army, which God uses as His rod
to chastise the peoples and cities enumerated in the first
verses of this chapter; and from the deliverance of the
people and land of Israel by Jehovah, who would camp
round about His house with an invisible host, " because of
him who passeth by, and because of him that returneth "
(the primary reference of which, as we have seen, was to a
more immediate future)—the prophet passes to the true
King of Israel, whose strength rests not in chariots and
horses, or in the multitude of an host; and to the *great*
deliverance and salvation which He shall bring, not only to
Israel, but to " the nations."

And it is quite in keeping with the character of Old
Testament prophecy that there is no perspective observed,
nor clear indications given of the pauses and intervals
between the different stages and acts by which Messiah's
work would be accomplished, and His Kingdom finally
established.   Like the traveller who from a great distance
beholds a whole mountain range as one mountain, without
discerning the different peaks, with the long valleys
between, so do the Old Testament seers often behold

---

[1] Josephus' *Antiquities of the Jews*, xi. 8. 3.   " Rationalism, while it remains
such," observes Pusey, "cannot admit of Daniel's prophecies which the high
priest showed him, declaring that a Greek should destroy the Persian empire,
which Alexander rightly interpreted of himself.   But the facts remain that the
conqueror, who above most gave way to his anger, bestowed privileges almost
incredible on a nation, which under the Medes and Persians had been ' the
most despised part of the enslaved' (Tacitus), made them equal in privileges .o
his own Macedonians, who could hardly brook the absorption of the Persians,
although in inferior condition, among themselves.   The most despised of the
enslaved became the most trusted of the trusted.   They became a large portion
of the second and third then known cities in the world—they became Alex-
andrians, Antiochenes, Ephesians, without ceasing to be Jews.   The law commanded faithfulness to oaths, and they who despised their religion respected its
fruits."

Messiah's Person and Mission without clearly discerning from their distant point of view the interval between the sufferings and the glory that should follow. And not only are their eyes always fixed on the distant and ultimate future, and the final great national and spiritual deliverance of Israel at the time of the end, but the distant future was always connected by them with the more immediate or proximate future. Every promised deliverance they regarded as a pledge of the final *great* deliverance, and in every redemption which God wrought for His people they saw already the last great redemption which was to be brought to the world by the advent of the Messiah. This we must bear in mind as we proceed to examine the prophecy which is now before us.

We shall not stop to argue with those who would give a non-Messianic, non-Christian interpretation to this great prophecy. Fortunately, such are in the minority, even among the critics.

The attempts of one and another rationalistic writer to apply this passage to Zerubbabel, or Nehemiah, or Judas Maccabeus, or to the entrance of Uzziah into Jerusalem after his victories over the Philistines, or to the entry of Hezekiah into Jerusalem on the day of his coronation (of which there is no historic record, and which, as well as its application to Uzziah, is bound up with the theory of a pre-exilic origin of the second part of Zechariah), have been sufficiently refuted by scholars of the same school.

"When we brush aside all the trafficking and bargaining over words that constitutes so much of modern criticism, which in its care over the letter so often loses the spirit, there can, at least, be no question that this prophecy was intended to introduce, in contrast to earthly warfare and kingly triumph, another Kingdom, of which the just King would be the Prince of Peace, who was meek and lowly in His Advent, who would speak peace to the heathen, and whose sway would yet extend to earth's utmost bounds. Thus much may be said, that if there ever was a true picture of the Messiah-King and His

Kingdom, it is this; and that, if ever Israel was to have a Messiah, or the world a Saviour, He must be such as is described in this prophecy—not merely in the letter, but in the spirit of it. And, as so often indicated, it was not the letter but the spirit of prophecy—and of all prophecy—which the ancient synagogue, and that rightly, saw fulfilled in the Messiah and His Kingdom. Accordingly, with singular unanimity, the Talmud and the ancient Rabbinic authorities have applied this prophecy to the Christ."[1]

But let us approach the Scripture itself. In view of the magnitude and the joyful character of the announcement about to be made, the prophet exclaims, " *Rejoice greatly, O daughter of Zion; shout, O daughter of Jerusalem,*" which reminds us of the similar summons in the first part of this book: " *Sing and rejoice, O daughter of Zion : for, lo, I come, and I will dwell in the midst of thee, saith Jehovah,*"[2] which again is an inspired post-exilic echo of the joyous proclamation with which the Book of

---

[1] Edersheim.   Many pages could be filled with quotations from the Talmud, the Midrashim, and Jewish commentators, in which this passage is applied to the Messiah.   In the Talmud Bab., fol. 98, we read Rabbi Joshua ben Levi asks : " It is written in one place, 'Behold, one like the Son of Man came with the clouds of heaven,' but in another place it is written, 'lowly, and riding upon an ass.'   How is this to be understood ?   The answer is, If they be righteous (or deserving) He shall come with the clouds of heaven ; if they be not righteous, then He shall come lowly, and riding upon an ass."

With the exception of Rabbi Moshe ha-Kohen (quoted by Aben-Ezra, who applied the prophecy to Nehemiah) and Aben-Ezra (who applies it to "Judas, the son of the Hasmonean") all the Jewish commentators apply it to the Messiah.   Rashi says, " This cannot be explained except of King-Messiah, for it is said of Him, 'And His dominion shall be from sea to sea' ; but we do not find that such a one ruled over Israel in the time of the Second Temple."

Saadiah Gaon, commenting on the words in Dan. vii., " Behold, one like the Son of Man came with the clouds of heaven," says, " This is the Messiah our righteousness.   But is it not written of the Messiah, ' Lowly, and riding upon an ass ' ?   Yes, but this shows that He will come in humility, and not in pride upon horses."

Non-Jewish readers interested in Rabbinic interpretations must be referred to Schöttgen, vol. ii. p. 20 ff. ; Pusey, *The Minor Prophets* (who has a fairly full collection of passages with references) ; Wünsche, *Die Leiden des Messias*, pp. 66, 103, etc. ; Hengstenberg, in his *Christology* ; Alexander McCaul, in his *Observations on the 9th chapter of his* (Kimchi's) *Commentary*, etc.

[2] Chap. ii. 10.

Immanuel [1] closes: "*Cry aloud and shout, thou inhabitress of Zion : for great is the Holy One of Israel in the midst of thee.*" But when the infinite Jehovah, the Holy One of Israel, whom no man hath seen, or can see, manifests Himself, and comes visibly to dwell in the midst of His people, it is always in the person of the Messiah, and the " Lo, I come, and will dwell in the midst of thee," is explained therefore by the equivalent announcement, " Behold, thy King (Messiah) cometh unto thee."

The coming of the King, which is announced in our passage in Zech. ix. is, however, a different one from the coming foretold in the passages quoted from Isa. xii. and Zech. ii. For although, as already stated, there is no perspective observed in Old Testament prophecy, and the two advents of the Messiah are often seen and spoken of by the prophets as one, we know now, in the fuller light of the partial fulfilment, that there is a coming of the Redeemer first in humiliation to suffer and die, before He shall come again a second time in divine majesty to reign over this earth, and to fulfil in a literal sense the hope and promise contained in the name " Immanuel," by Himself, the God-Man, visibly dwelling " in the midst of them," so that Israel will at that time be able to say to the nations, " God is with us," [2] not only in the spiritual sense, in which His presence is a reality to us now, but in the literal sense of having their Divine Messiah-King dwelling and reigning among them.

It is to the first advent of Messiah, then, that attention is especially called by the word " Behold," in the 9th verse of the chapter we are now considering, although, as we shall see, this very prophecy looks on also to the second advent, and beyond the sufferings of Messiah, to the glory that should follow.

I have already, in the exposition of chap. vi. 12, pointed out how the Messiah is introduced to us four different times in the Old Testament, and under four

---

[1] Isa. vii.-xii. has been appropriately so styled.

[2] Hebrew, "Immanu-El," Isa. viii. 10, the same as Isa. vii. 14.

different aspects, by this word " Behold," which correspond
also to the fourfold portraiture of Christ in the four Gospels.
Here it is especially as Zion's King that we are called
upon to contemplate Him : " Behold, *thy King cometh unto
thee.*" He does not say " a King," but " *thy* King ; thine
own, the long-promised, the long-expected ; He who, when
they had kings of their own given them by God, had been
promised as *the* King ;[1] *the Righteous Ruler among men,*
of the seed of David ; He who, above all other kings, was
their King and Saviour, whose Kingdom was to absorb in
itself all kingdoms of the earth, the King of kings and
Lord of lords."[2]

" *Cometh unto thee* "—that is, to Zion, or Israel. He
was in a manner, then, " of her," and *not* of her, as another
writer observes. " *Of* her, since He was to be *her King*;
not of her, since He was to *come* to her. As man He was
born of her ; as God, the Word made flesh, He *came* to
her."

But the word, לָךְ, *lakh*, rendered " unto thee," means also
"*for thy good*," as Keil points out, as is implied also from
the whole context, " *He cometh unto thee,*" that is, as thy
Deliverer, or, as an ancient cabalistic Jewish writing paraphrases it, " He shall come to thee to upraise thee ; He
shall come to thee to raise thee up to His temple, and to
espouse thee with an everlasting espousal."[3]

Zion's coming Saviour-King is described first as צַדִּיק
(*tsaddik*), " righteous " (rendered in the English version
" just "), which means, not " one who has a right cause," as
one or two commentators have explained, nor merely " one
righteous in character, answering in all respects to the
will of Jehovah," as Koehler expresses it, but one *animated*
with righteousness, and maintaining and displaying in
His righteous rule this fundamental attribute of the ideal
king.

Secondly, He is נוֹשָׁע (*nosha'*), which the English Bible
renders " having salvation," in which it is supported by the

---

[1] *e.g.*, Ps. ii., lxxii. ; Isa. xxxii. 1 ; Jer. xxiii. 5, 6 ; 2 Sam. xxiii. 3.
[2] Pusey.   [3] Zohar.

authority of the ancient versions (*e.g.*, the LXX, the Targum, the Syriac, and Vulgate), who all render the word " Saviour."

A Jewish controversialist, who has written, perhaps, the best-known polemical work against Christianity, accuses the Christians of corrupting the text here, saying :

" The Nazarenes have altered the word נוֹשָׁע, *nosha'* (*saved*), and written instead of it מוֹשִׁיעַ, *moshia'* (Saviour), in order to add some auxiliary confirmation to their faith." [1] But in the first place the accusation as it stands is false. The Christians have never altered this word. In every Christian edition of the Hebrew Bible it stands just as it does in those edited by Jews. But, in " the next place, allowing him to mean what he does not say, that some Christians, as the Vulgate, have translated the word ' Saviour,' and not ' saved,' as he would have it, they did not do this with a fraudulent intention to confirm their faith, but were led by *Jews* to think that this was the right ּsense of the word. The Jews, who translated Zechariah into Greek before the rise of Christianity, translated נוֹשָׁע (*nosha'*) by σωζων, ' saving,' or ' Saviour,' and Christians simply followed them. The mistake, therefore, is not to be attributed to the Christians, but to the Jews themselves. But if Jews say that the Greek text has been altered, then we refer them to the Targum of Jonathan, who translates the word by פְּרִיק (*Phariq*), ' Redeemer,' or ' Saviour '; and surely Jonathan had no fraudulent desire to favour Christianity. His translation shows that the meaning of the word originated, and was common, amongst the Jews themselves; they, therefore, and not the Christians, are answerable for it." [2]

But it is pretty generally agreed now that נוֹשָׁע (*nosha'*) is the Niphal participle of the verb יָשַׁע (*yasha'*), and is used in the *passive* sense, so that the word must be rendered not "saving," but "*saved*"; though it may be used here, as

---

[1] Rabbi Isaak ben Abraham, of Troki (born 1533, died 1594), in his *Chizzuk Emunah*.

[2] Alexander McCaul.

Hengstenberg suggests, in a more general sense (as in Deut. xxxiii. 29 and Ps. xxxiii. 16, where *nosha'*—" saved " —is found) as describing one " who is *endowed* with salvation," or "furnished with the assistance of God " requisite for the fulfilment of His mission.

We shall see presently the application of the prophecy contained in this word to our Lord, Jesus of Nazareth, but to the prophet's contemporaries the expression would probably recall, as Dr. Wright suggests, the language of the 2nd Psalm, " where the Messiah is represented as saved and delivered, in spite of all the combinations made against Him, and destined to be one day seated on His royal throne."

But taken in its passive sense as meaning "saved," there is none the less promise in the word for the people as well as for the Messiah ; for, as has been well observed, if the King of Israel is "saved," His people (whose Head and Representative He is) must be saved likewise.   " His deliverance, or salvation, is a sure sign of the deliverance of His people, which is to be accomplished by His means."

The ideal King of Israel is further characterised as עָנִי ('*ani*), which is rendered in the English versions " lowly," but which primarily means "*poor*," " *afflicted*."   This word, as is properly observed by Hengstenberg, Keil, and others, gathers up "the whole of the lowly, miserable, suffering condition" of the righteous Servant of Jehovah, as it is elaborately depicted in Isa. liii. ; [1] and those who feel themselves constrained to recognise in that great prophecy in Isaiah a vivid description of the suffering and death of the Messiah, cannot regard it as strange that Zechariah, who

---

[1] Keil.   The apparent paradox that the King who is endowed with salvation and comes to deliver should be "afflicted," or "poor," led the translators of the LXX, the Targumists, the majority of Jewish commentators, and many critics in modern days, to adopt the translation "lowly," or "meek," which is also the rendering given by the evangelists in the Gospels, who, however, simply quote the word from the Greek LXX. עָנִי ('*ani*), and עָנָו ('*anav*), both come from עָנָה ('*anah*), to be "bowed down," to be "humbled "; but עָנִי ('*ani*) seems, as Von Orelli points out, to refer more to the physical state (in the sense of being "*poor*," "*wretched*," "*afflicted*"), and עָנָו ('*anav*) to qualities of the spirit (in the sense of being "harmless," "humble," "meek," etc.).

was doubtless acquainted with the writings of Isaiah, and who in all his Messianic passages—both in the first and second parts of his book—tersely summarises the great predictions of "the former prophets," should be led to describe Israel's Redeemer-King as "afflicted" and suffering. And in keeping with His character shall be the manner in which He shall present Himself to His people. Not in outward pomp or with display of worldly power, shall He appear, but "*riding upon an ass, even upon a colt, the foal*[1] *of an ass.*"

The second sentence in this line more precisely defines the kind of ass which the Messiah shall ride upon. It shall be a young animal not yet ridden on, but still accustomed to run behind the she-asses, as the last qualifying words of the description imply.

The question is discussed by commentators whether the riding upon an ass is to be regarded as an emblem of Messiah's "lowliness," in keeping with the description of Him as "*'ani*," "poor," "afflicted," or as an outward sign of the *peacefulness* of His mission. But it seems to me that both ideas are merged in the prophecy of this symbolic action. It is true that in the East the ass is generally of a nobler breed, and is not so despised as in the West, and in the earliest times of Jewish history we read of judges and rulers riding on asses; but that was only, as Hengstenberg has shown by a full discussion of all the references, until horses were introduced, when it was no longer in accordance with the dignity of kings and rulers of Israel to ride on asses.[2] "In fact, *from the time of Solomon downwards, we do not meet with a single example of a king, or of any distinguished personage, riding upon an ass.*"

In Jeremiah's time, for instance, it was certainly regarded as becoming royal dignity for kings and princes to be "sitting in chariots and riding on horses,"[3] so that when the Messiah is here represented as "riding on an ass,"

[1] Lit., "the son of she-asses."   [2] Hengstenberg.
[3] Jer. xvii. 25.

it does suggest the idea of lowliness, in keeping with what had just been said of Him as being "poor" or "afflicted." At the same time, as there is a contrast suggested in the context between the great Gentile world-conqueror, who with his chariots and horses comes to subdue and tread down, and Israel's Redeemer-King, who comes to "speak peace," and as in the 10th verse, the horse is certainly one of the emblems of war, His riding upon an ass does also symbolise the *peaceable character of His mission.*

Before passing on to the 10th verse, let me very briefly point out the fulfilment of this prophetic picture of the Messiah in the Christ of history :

(*a*) The Messiah was to be, in a peculiar manner, *Zion's King*, and our Lord Jesus Christ was born "King of the Jews," and the very inscription on His cross, *Jesus Nazarenus, Rex Judæorum*, still proclaims this everlasting, indissoluble relationship between Christ and Israel. It is true that the Jews as a nation still say, "We will not have this Man to reign over us," and that the "many days during which the children of Israel abide without a king and without a prince" still continue. But Jesus of Nazareth *is Israel's King*; and, as sure and certain as there was once a cross raised for Him on Golgotha, so certain is it that "the Lord God" will yet "give unto Him the throne of His Father David," and that He will "reign on Mount Zion and before His ancients gloriously."

(*b*) "Behold, thy King *cometh unto thee*," which reminds us of the pathetic lament of the evangelist, "*He came unto His own*," *i.e.*, His own estate, His own possession (the word being in the neuter), the land and people where above all other places in the world He had a right to expect a welcome, and to be greeted with the enthusiastic joy depicted by the prophet; but, alas! as the sequel proved, "His own"—they that were His by reason of peculiar and manifold relationship, and who ought to have been prepared for Him as a bride for the bridegroom—"*received Him not.*"

(*c*) And Christ is the only Person in all history whose character and experience answer to the description of the ideal King in this prophecy. He alone, among the sons of men, can be described as the true *Tsaddik*—the Righteous One, who did no violence, nor was deceit found in His mouth ; the One who always loved righteousness and hated iniquity, whose purity and beauty of character is borne witness to even by those who have not learned to bow their knees in allegiance before Him as the Son of God.

(*d*) The Lord Jesus Christ, for us men and our salvation also became " poor " and " afflicted "—so poor that He Himself could say : " The foxes have holes, and the birds of the air have nests, but the Son of Man hath not where to lay His head."

(*e*) And of Him alone also is it true that He is endowed with, and is the bringer of, salvation, because He was Himself " saved " or " delivered," or " made victorious " (as some would render) in the great conflict which He came to wage on our behalf with the powers of darkness. " He trusted in Jehovah that He would deliver Him," [1] and the chief priests and scribes taunted Him with it on the cross, saying : " *Let Him deliver Him now if He desireth Him : if He is the King of Israel, let Him now come down from the cross, and we will believe on Him : He saved others, Himself He cannot save.*" [2] Thus in their blindness and ignorance uttering unconsciously an eternal truth, for it was *because* He came to save others, and His life, as He Himself had predicted, had to be laid down " a ransom for many," that He could not save Himself.

But though He willingly drank the cup of shame and sorrow which the Father had given Him to drink, and was not delivered from the death on the cross, " He was delivered in very deed from the hand of the great destroyer, for God raised Him from the dead, having loosed the pains of death, because it was not possible that He should be holden of it." [3] Thus He was saved by the almighty power of the Father, " and declared to be the Son of God with power, by the resurrection from the dead. And because He

[1] Ps. xxii. 8.   [2] Matt. xxvii. 39–43.   [3] Acts ii. 23, 24.

became obedient unto death—even the death of the cross —He was made perfect as Redeemer and Mediator, and is now the Author of eternal salvation unto all them that obey Him." [1]

We cannot enter here into the significance of Christ's triumphal entry into Jerusalem, which believers in the New Testament can never dissociate from this prophecy in Zechariah.

But I agree with the view of Vitringa, Hengstenberg, and Koehler, that though this scripture then received a literal accomplishment, " that triumphal procession was not, in the main, the fact which the prophecy was designed to depict. The prophecy would have been as truly and really fulfilled if the triumphal procession had never taken place. That single incident in the life of our Lord is not the point which the prophet had in view. It was rather the whole of the Saviour's life, the entire series of events connected with Christ's first advent, which was presented in one striking picture. The actual entrance of Christ into Jerusalem in the manner described in the Old Testament prophecy was an express declaration that this passage was indeed Messianic in the fullest sense, and was fulfilled in His Person and work." [2]

It is in this sense that Matthew and John [3] quote this passage in connection with that entry ; not, however, in the stiffness and deadness of the letter. " On the contrary (as so often in Jewish writings), two prophecies—Isa. lxii. 11 and Zech. ix. 9—are made to shed their blended light upon this entry of Christ, as exhibiting the reality, of which the prophetic vision had been the reflex. Nor yet are the words of the prophets given literally—as modern criticism would have them weighed out in the critical balances— either from the Hebrew text, or from the LXX rendering ; but their meaning is given, and they are " Targumed " by the sacred writers according to their wont. Yet who that sets the prophetic picture by the side of the reality—the

[1] Rom. i. 3 ; Phil. ii. 8 ; Heb. v. 9.   [2] C. H. H. Wright.
[3] Matt. xxi. 4, 5 ; John xii. 14, 15.

description by the side of Christ's entry into Jerusalem—can fail to recognise in the one the fulfilment of the other?"[1]

From the Messiah's humiliation, the depths of which are reached in the words "poor," or "afflicted," and "riding upon an ass" (ver. 9), the prophet's vision is directed to the glory that should follow, and to the blessed *results* of the advent of this Redeemer-King, not only in relation to Zion and Israel, but to the whole earth :

"*And I will cut off the chariot from Ephraim,*[2] *and the horse from Jerusalem, and the battle-bow shall be cut off ; and He shall speak peace unto the nations : and His dominion shall be from sea to sea, and from the river to the ends of the earth.*"

As the deliverance which Israel's Prince of Peace shall bring will not be by means of chariots and horses, or by the multitude of a host, so also shall His Kingdom not be founded on worldly might ; nor shall those subject to His rule have need to rely on any of these things. This is in keeping with what the Lord had already spoken through one of the earlier prophets : "*I will have mercy upon the house of Judah, and I will save them by* (or ' *in* ') *Jehovah their God, and will not save them by bow, nor by sword, nor by battle, by horses, nor by horsemen.*"[3] In other words, Jehovah alone, in the Person of the Messiah, shall then be the hope and confidence of His people, for " He is their Help and their Shield " ;[4] or, as He had already said of restored Jerusalem, through Zechariah, in the third vision : "*I, saith Jehovah, will be unto her a wall of fire round about, and I will be the glory in the midst of her*"[5]—that is, her all-sufficient outward protection and inward illumination.

[1] Edersheim.

[2] The mention of Ephraim alongside of Jerusalem in this place is considered by some commentators as proof of the pre-exilic origin of the second half of Zechariah—" when the kingdoms of Israel, on the one hand, and of Judah on the other, were independent nations." Von Orelli even sees in this passage a proof that Ephraim " at the time, apparently, rejoiced in considerable military strength." But, as I have shown in the "Introduction to the Second Part of Zechariah," the argument rests on a misconception, and has no real basis in fact.

[3] Hos. i. 7.   [4] Ps. cxv. 9.   [5] Chap. ii. 5.

He will, therefore, "cut off" the instruments of war and emblems of worldly power, first of all from His own people because they shall have no need of them, and lest they should still be tempted to be like the Gentile world-powers, some of whom "trust in chariots and some in horses." [1]

But the mission of the Jewish Messiah—the Prince of Peace—extends not only to Israel and Palestine: "*He shall speak peace to the nations*"—an expression which does not mean exactly that Messiah would *command* peace to the nations, as Koehler and others interpret; or that He "would bring about peace by compassing the disputes and quarrels of the contending nations," as some other writers understand it. The phrase דְּבֶּר שָׁלוֹם, *daber shalom* ("to speak peace"), is used in some instances in the sense of *speaking that which avowedly has peace for its object*, whether the profession be sincere or not; [2] or simply speaking in the sense of *announcing peace and the removal of hostility*. Thus God is said to "speak peace to His people and to His saints." [3]

It is in this latter sense, I believe, that the words are to be understood here. Israel's Redeemer-King comes to *publish* peace to the nations—not only peace from outward strife and conflict with one another, but that deeper inner peace, and the removal of hostility *between man and God*, which has been the cause of all outward restlessness and strife—though it is implied also that there is both *power* and authority in the word which He shall speak to *bring about* the blessed end which He has in view.

"*And His dominion shall be from sea to sea, and from the river to the ends of the earth*"—which is a verbal quotation by our prophet from the 72nd Psalm, where the effects of the blessed reign of the true Son of David, Israel's ideal "King," is so beautifully depicted, and where we read that "*He shall have dominion also from sea to sea, and from the river unto the ends of the earth. They that dwell in the wilderness shall bow before Him; and His enemies shall lick the dust. . . . Yea, all kings shall fall down before Him; all nations shall serve Him.*"

[1] Ps. xx. 7.   [2] Ps. xxviii. 3, xxxv. 20.   [3] Ps. lxxxv. 8.

The phrase מִיָּם עַד יָם, *miyyam ad yam*—from sea to sea—is idiomatic, and equivalent to "from the sea to the other end of the world where the sea begins again." The *nahar* ("river") is the Euphrates, and is mentioned as the remotest eastern boundary of the promised land, according to Gen. xv. 18; Ex. xxiii. 31.

In short, from the Holy Land, which will then be extended to the limits originally promised to the fathers, and which will be the *centre* of Messiah's blessed rule, His dominion will extend even "unto the ends of the earth."

Before finally taking leave of the 10th verse, we must note once more that, in keeping with the special style and characteristic of our prophet (which we had occasion to observe again and again in our study of the first half of the book), Zechariah not only bases his prophecy of Messiah's Person and Mission on the utterances about Israel's coming Redeemer of the "former prophets," but gives, so to say, a terse summary of God's previous revelations on this great theme. This indeed is one reason why this short prophetic book of only fourteen chapters is so marvellously rich in its contents; for, in addition to new Divine communications granted to this priest-prophet, we have in it, as it were, an inspired condensation, or summary, of the great prophecies and promises contained in the earlier prophets.

We have already noted the verbal quotation from the 72nd Psalm, but there are also earlier prophetic utterances which are interwoven in this inspired picture of Messiah's Person and Mission as presented by Zechariah. The chief of these is Mic. v.: "*But thou, Bethlehem-Ephratah, which art little* (or '*least*') *to be among the cities of Judah, out of thee shall One come forth unto Me that is to be Ruler in Israel; whose goings forth are from of old, from everlasting. . . . And He shall stand and feed in the strength of Jehovah, in the majesty of the name of Jehovah His God: and they shall abide, for now shall He be great unto the ends of the earth. And this One shall be our peace. . . . And it shall come to pass in that day, saith Jehovah, that I will cut off thy horses out of the midst of thee, and I will destroy thy chariots, and I will cut the (walled) cities of thy land, and I will throw down all thy strong holds.*" [1]

Here we have a Child born in time, in a small obscure place in Palestine, and of a race despised by the other nations, whose " goings forth " are from eternity, and who would be great unto the ends of the earth, and not only be the bringer of peace, but *Himself " be our peace.*"

And the same picture of the true Son of David and ideal King of Israel, with the same enigmatical and apparently paradoxical combination of characteristics of humiliation and helplessness on the one hand, and of power and dominion on the other, which is to spread over the whole earth, not by force of arms but by means of His simple Word, is given also by Micah's contemporary Isaiah the son of Amos,[2] and was also doubtless in the mind of Zechariah as he spoke of the King who should appear in lowliness but would yet speak peace to the nations, and exercise a sway which would extend to the ends of the earth.

Secondly, I must once again repeat what has been stated at the beginning of my remarks on the 9th verse, that there is no perspective observed in the Old Testament prophecy, and that the prophets behold from their distant point of view the two advents of Messiah as one, not observing the different stages and long pauses in the process of the fulfilment of His mission on earth.

A pause of nearly two thousand years has already ensued between the 9th and 10th verses of this great prophecy—between the time when Jesus, " that it might be fulfilled which was spoken by the prophet " Zechariah, presented Himself to the daughter of Zion as her true King, " meek, and riding upon an ass, and upon a colt, the foal of an ass,[3] and the time when He shall " speak peace to the nations," and shall visibly " stand and feed (or ' *rule* ') in the strength of Jehovah, in the majesty of the name of Jehovah His God."

[1] Mic. v. 2, 4, 10, 11.   [2] Isa. ix. 1-7 (R.V.).   [3] Matt. xxi. 4, 5.

Indeed, we know by comparing scripture with scripture that before the instruments of war shall finally be "cut off," and the Messiah is manifested as the Judge and "Reprover" of strong nations, so that they "shall beat their swords into ploughshares and their spears into pruning-hooks," and neither learn nor practise war any more, the greatest war which this afflicted earth has ever seen is to take place, during which time the nations will "beat their plough-shares into swords, and pruning-hooks into spears."

But this is sure and certain, that however long the pause may last, God never loses the thread of the purpose which He has formed for this earth; and as surely as the prophecies of the sufferings of Christ have been literally fulfilled, so surely will those also be which relate to His glory and reign; and although Israel and the nations have had to wait long for it, the angels' song at the birth of our Saviour, "Peace on earth and goodwill toward men," will yet be realised, and Christ will not only be owned by His own people as "the King of the Jews," but His rule will extend "from sea to sea, and from the river even unto the ends of the earth."

Meanwhile, while He is still rejected on earth, He is exalted at the right hand of God in heaven; and to those who already recognise Him as King, and render to Him the glad allegiance of their hearts, He already "speaks peace," yea, a peace which passeth all understanding even in the midst of outward strife and travail—such as the world can never give nor take away.

The last seven verses of the 9th chapter (to which the whole of the 10th chapter is linked) set forth in fuller detail the results of the advent and mission of the Redeemer-King, more particularly in relation to Israel nationally. The prophet had spoken of Messiah in the 10th verse, as the One who would also "speak peace to the (Gentile) nations," whose dominion would extend even "to the ends of the earth"; now he turns again to Zion and Israel. "*As for thee* (or, literally, '*thou also*'), *by* (or 'because of') *the blood of thy covenant I have sent forth*" (or release, or send free) "*thy prisoners*" (or captives: literally, "thy bound ones ") "*out of the pit wherein is no water.*"

It is the whole nation which is thus addressed, as we see from the context, where the inclusive terms " Ephraim and Judah " and " Judah and Ephraim "[1] are used. This is clear also from the words which follow, for the covenant which God made, whether with Abraham or with the people at the foot of Mount Sinai, included the whole people, and there was no provision or promise in it which applied to one part, or to some of the tribes and not to the others.

The primary reference of the phrase בְּדַם בְּרִיתֵךְ, *bedam berithekh*—" the blood of thy covenant "—is most probably to Ex. xxiv., when, at the ratification of the Sinaitic covenant, we read that Moses took the blood of the slain animals in basins, and, after sprinkling half on the altar, which represented God, and half on the people, he exclaimed, " *Behold, the blood of the covenant, which the Lord hath made with you concerning all these words.*"[2]

To that covenant Israel proved itself unfaithful; and as they still persist as a nation in taking their place before God on the ground of a broken law, and strive, though vainly, to establish a righteousness of their own, they have been permitted to have a long and bitter taste of the curses which the law proclaims against disobedience to its precepts. But though Israel proved themselves unfaithful, and this particular covenant itself was " broken,"[3] " *the blood of the covenant,*" on which emphasis is laid in this prophecy, was a sign and pledge of the faithfulness of God (though all men prove liars), and typically set forth the provision which God has made by which eventually His disobedient and rebellious people would be brought back within the sphere of blessing.

But the covenant of Sinai was not the only one which God made with and for Israel; there was a much earlier one—the one He made with Abraham, which was in the nature, not of a contract between two parties, but of a promise to the fulfilment of which God alone was pledged.

---

[1] Vers. 10–13.   [2] Ex. xxiv. 8.   [3] Jer. xxxi. 31.

And in connection with that covenant, too, there was the shedding of the blood of the animals and birds which Abram was commanded to slay [1]—which, as well as the blood-shedding on Sinai, and indeed of all the blood of the sacrifices which were " on Jewish altars slain," pointed to the great sacrifice " of nobler name," and to the much more precious blood which alone secures to sinful man God's covenanted blessings.

The antitypical ratification of the covenant, therefore (whatever the primary reference of these words in Zechariah), took place when Israel's Messiah, Jesus, appeared as the " minister of the circumcision to confirm the promises made unto the fathers." [2]

" This is My blood of the new covenant," He said, when about to lay down His life a ransom for many; and since the great sacrifice on the cross, all the promises of God, " how many soever," or whatever they may be, whether made to Israel nationally, or intended for all men generally —ratified as they now are in His own precious blood, have become, so to say, *doubly sure and certain*, for " in Him is the Yea, and in Him the Amen, to the glory of God by us." [3]

But to return to our prophecy. Because of the ever-lasting covenant-relationship which exists between Him and His people, sealed and ratified with blood, " *I have sent forth,*" God says, " *thy prisoners out of the pit wherein is no water.*"

The perfect tense of the verb שִׁלַּחְתִּי (*shillachti*)—" I have sent forth," or " released "—is prophetic of what God intends to do, there being many instances in the prophetic Scriptures where the perfect is used for the future. With the eternal, unchangeable God, His promises, however distant be the set time of their fulfilment, are already as good as accomplished.

The description " prisoners " in a " pit," or " dungeon," " wherein is no water," primarily describes, figuratively, Israel's condition in captivity, out of which God, in virtue of His covenant promise, will deliver them.

It reminds us of the description of Jacob, when given

over for a time "for a spoil," and "Israel to the robbers,"
which we find in Isaiah: "*But this is a people robbed and
spoiled; they are all of them snared in holes, and they are
hid in prison houses: they are for a prey, and none delivereth;
for a spoil, and none saith, Restore.*"[1] But though in
"prison," and "robbed," and "spoiled," they are not given
over to death, this being already hinted at in the expression *bor ein mayim bo*—"the pit (or 'dungeon') *without
water in it,*" which is an echo of Gen. xxxvii. 24 (where
exactly the same phrase is found), with an evident allusion
to the story of Joseph.   It was with a view to save him
from a violent death that Reuben proposed that Joseph
should be thrown into the pit, which was doubtless a dis-
used cistern, such being on occasion also used as dungeons.
But it made all the difference to Joseph that there was no
water in that pit or cistern; for had there been water in it,
he would have been drowned.

So it is with Israel.   They are likened to one bound
and in a "pit," or "dungeon," which, alas! has also been
literally the case with multitudes of Israel's sons and
daughters during the period of their "captivity"; but God
sees to it that there should be no water in the pit, and that
His people, which is still bound to Him by covenant blood,
should not utterly perish.   And eventually, at the word of
God, Israel, like Joseph, shall be freed from the pit and
lifted from the position of humiliation and suffering to
become a nation of princes on the earth.

And Israel's deliverance from national bondage will
synchronise, and be, so to say, the outward sign of their
still greater spiritual deliverance, for the words "prisoners"
(*asirim*, literally, "bound ones") and "pit" (*bor*) are used
in other scriptures to describe the condition of men,
who are not only in outward bodily captivity, but who are
in the bondage of sin and captives to Satan.

Thus the Messiah is anointed and sent to open the
prison-gates "to them that are bound";[2] and in the day

[1] Isa. xlii. 22.
[2] *Asurim*, Isa. lxi. 1; the same as "prisoners" in Zech. ix. 11.

when Israel, by a look at their crucified Messiah, is "redeemed from all his iniquities" and experiences God's "plenteous redemption,"[1] it will be this greater spiritual deliverance that they will celebrate in words which are already familiar and precious to us who know the Messiah of Israel as our personal Redeemer.

"*He brought me up also out of an horrible pit, out of the miry clay; and He set my feet upon a rock, and established my goings*" (Ps. xl. 2, 3).

And the same double promise of national and spiritual deliverance and blessing is contained also in the 12th verse: "*Turn ye to the stronghold, ye prisoners of hope.*"

The בִּצָּרוֹן, *bhitsaron*—"stronghold," or "fortress"—to which the captives are invited to return, is perhaps primarily their own land, which is as a rocky and fortified "fastness" as compared with the low-lying "pit" of their captivity. But even the Jewish commentator Kimchi sees in it a reference also to God, who is the strength and sure refuge of His people, and paraphrases the first words of this verse, "Turn ye to God, for He is a stronghold and tower of strength." And this agrees also with earlier prophetic utterances in which God Himself is spoken of as the safe hiding-place and defence of His people, as, for instance, Joel iii. (which seems to me to be one of the scriptures from the earlier prophets which was in the mind of Zechariah when writing the last verses of the 9th chapter), where we read that in the day when the Lord shall gather the nations for judgment, and the whole order of nature shall be shaken, "*Jehovah will be the refuge of His people, and a stronghold to the children of Israel.*"[2]

The expression אֲסִירֵי הַתִּקְוָה, *asirei hatiqvah* — "prisoners of hope," or of "*the* hope"—truly describes the Jewish people in their banishment and scattering, and marks the difference between the nation which stands in an indissoluble relationship to God by reason of the "blood of the covenant," and all other nations as nations. The

---

[1] Ps. cxxx. 7, 8.
[2] Joel iii 1–6. Here the word for stronghold is מָעוֹז (*maoz*).

Jewish nation may for its sins be sent into captivity as
"prisoners"; Jacob may be "given over for a spoil, and
Israel to the robbers," "but there is hope (*tiqvah*) for thy
latter end, saith Jehovah,"[1] or, to quote from an earlier
chapter of the same prophet: "*For I know the thoughts
that I think towards you, saith Jehovah, thoughts of peace,
and not of evil, to give you* אַחֲרִית וְתִקְוָה (*acharith vethiqvah*)"—
literally, "a latter end and hope"[2]—that is, a "latter end"
according to the hope based on God's own promise.
Therefore the Psalmist, in response to the agonising cry of
the remnant of Israel "from the depths" of their national
tribulation and anguish in Ps. cxxx.—which at the same
time breathes such a spirit of confident reliance on God's
word of promise as is expressed in the words: "*I wait on
Jehovah; my soul doth wait, and in His word do I hope*"—
is inspired to address to them the encouraging exhortation:
"*O Israel, hope in Jehovah* (for it is a hope which will not be
put to shame); *for with Jehovah there is mercy, and with Him
there is plenteous redemption, and He shall redeem Israel from
all his iniquities.*"[3]   And since his iniquities have been the
underlying cause of all his sufferings and sorrows, when
God forgives Israel his sins, and removes his transgressions,
He shall "redeem" him also "out of all his troubles."[4]

And there is a certain analogy in this respect between
Israel and the Church, or rather between Israel in their
present condition as "prisoners of hope," and those who, in
and through Christ, have already set their hope upon God.
We are not in outward or bodily dispersion and banishment, as Israel is; nor, praise be to God, are we in
bondage to sin or Satan.   In Christ we have even now
"redemption by His blood, the forgiveness of sins according
to the riches of His grace"; already we have been delivered
out of the power of darkness and are translated into the
kingdom of the Son of His love, and are made heirs and
joint-heirs with Christ of an inheritance which is incor-
ruptible and undefiled, and that fadeth not away.   Yet,

---

[1] Jer. xxxi. 17.   [2] Jer. xxix. 11.
[3] Ps. cxxx. 7, 8.   [4] Ps. xxv. 22.

inasmuch as we are still environed by an unrenewed creation, which, on account of man's sin, was subjected to vanity; so long as we still carry about "the body of this death" and know the motions of sin and death within us; so long as we are still in this present evil age, and not actually in our glorious promised land, and our Father's own house—we are "prisoners of hope," for not only do we still form part of that creation which groaneth and travaileth in pain together until now, *but ourselves also, which have the first-fruits of the Spirit, even we ourselves groan within ourselves, waiting for our adoption, to wit, the redemption of our body. For by hope are we saved; but hope that is seen is not hope: for who hopeth for that which he seeth? But if we hope for that which we see not, then do we with patience wait for it.*"[1]

We are therefore longing and looking for the realisation of "the Blessed Hope," namely, "the appearing of the glory of our great God and Saviour Jesus Christ," who also shall bring rest and deliverance to a groaning creation and fashion anew the body of our humiliation that it may be conformed to the body of His glory, according to the working whereby He is able even to subject all things unto Himself.[2]

---

[1] Rom. viii. 22–25.

[2] Zech. ix. 12 is the only place in the Hebrew Bible where the word for hope has the article. It is therefore, as has been observed, not any hope, or general hope, that the prophet speaks about, but THE SPECIAL hope of Israel, "the hope which sustained him through all the years of patient expectation." The centre and essence of it is the Messiah, and the great promised national and spiritual redemption which He was to accomplish, and which will not be fully realised till He shall appear a second time apart from sin unto salvation, and to establish His righteous rule on the earth.

The hope is carried over therefore from the Old Testament into the New. Paul speaks of it as "the hope of Israel," for which the Jews of Rome saw him bound as a prisoner in a chain (Acts xxviii. 20), or, as he said in his defence before Agrippa: "I stand here to be judged for the hope of the promise made of God unto our fathers, unto which promise our twelve tribes earnestly serving God night and day hope to attain. And concerning this hope I am accused by the Jews, O King" (Acts xxvi. 6, 7).

It was doubtless in his mind when he spoke of "the blessed hope and the appearing of our great God and Saviour Jesus Christ" (Tit. ii. 13), for then the hope as regards the Church, and Israel, and the world, will be fully realised.

But, to proceed to the second half of the 12th verse, "*even to-day*," in thy present adversity and in spite of all appearances, "*do I declare*" (or "tell" you as good news, from which you may already draw consolation and hope) "*that I will render*" (or "cause to return") "double unto thee."

There are several scriptures in which the word "double" occurs as expressing a principle of God's dealing with His own people. The key and explanation of it is found in His own appointment in reference to the first-born. According to the law, the first-born son inherited a double portion of his father's property as compared with the other members of the family. This, except it were forfeited by personal unfitness, or transgression, was his inalienable right. If, contrary to God's original appointment, any man of Israel had two wives, "the one beloved and the other hated, and they had borne him children, both the beloved and the hated, and if the first-born son be hers that was hated, then it shall be in the day that he causeth his sons to inherit that which he hath, that he may not make the son of the beloved the first-born before the son of the hated, . . . but he shall acknowledge the first-born, the son of the hated, by giving him a double portion (*shenayim*) of all that he hath ; . . . the right of the first-born is his."[1] An illustration of this principle we have in the case of Joseph. Reuben having, by an act of personal moral defilement, disqualified himself to inherit the birthright, it was transferred to Joseph,[2] and as a consequence his descendants were counted as two tribes—Ephraim and Manasseh—who had two portions of the land instead of one ; and Joseph himself became by this act entitled to a double portion of Jacob's personal possessions. Now Israel is God's "son," God's "first-born" in relation to the other nations,[3] and He deals with them on the principles of His own law. In his own land, and under the protection of the Covenant-keeping God of his fathers, Israel enjoys a "double portion" of favour and

[1] Deut. xxi. 15-17.   [2] 1 Chron. v. 1, 2.   [3] Ex. iv. 22.

blessing. But commensurate with privilege is responsibility, and of him to whom much is given much is required. Therefore when Israel sinned he was visited with " double " punishment. This is the explanation of such passages as " She hath received of the Lord's hand double " (*kiphlayim* —" twofold ") " for all her sins " ;[1] or, " I will recompense their iniquity and their sin double " (*mishneh*—" a *repetition* "; once and again) " because they have defiled My land . . . and have filled Mine inheritance with their abominations."[2] This is the key and explanation of the woeful history of the Jewish people during the centuries of their banishment and dispersion. This is why under the whole heaven it hath not been done as has been done upon Jerusalem ;[3] and that, as Josephus complains, Israel's sorrows and sufferings surpass that of all the rest of mankind.

But Israel's disobedience and consequent sufferings are not to last for ever. Even in their dispersion they are, as we have seen, " prisoners of the hope," and when restored to their land and brought back into favour as God's " firstborn " among the nations, then "*for their shame they shall have double*"—*mishneh*—"*and for the*" (or, instead of) "*confusion they shall rejoice in their portion ; therefore in their land they shall possess the double. Everlasting joy shall be unto them.*"[4]

And it is particularly this grand prophecy in Isa. lxi., to which, as it seems to me, there is this inspired reference in our passage in Zechariah when he announces to them in their then still national day of gloom that God will cause the double to return to them.

From the final results to Israel and the nations of the advent and mission of the Messiah we are in the next three verses taken back to *the process*.

Before Judah shall finally be saved, and Israel possess again in their land the " double " portion of blessing and privilege, Gentile world-power must be broken, and the

---

[1] Isa. xl. 2.   [2] Jer. xvi. 18.
[3] Dan. ix. 12.   [4] Isa. lxi. 7.

enemies of God's kingdom be finally overthrown. The
figures in vers. 13 to 15 are very bold and graphic: " *For
I will bend* (or ' *stretch* ') *Judah for Me as a bow, and I will
fill it with Ephraim ;* [1] *and I will stir up thy sons, O Zion,
against thy sons, O Greece, and I will make thee as the
sword of a mighty man. And Jehovah shall appear above
them, and His arrow shall go forth as the lightning : and
the Lord Jehovah shall blow the trumpet, and shall go forth*
(or ' *march* ') *with whirlwinds* (or ' *in the tempests* ') *of the
south.*" Judah is the drawn bow, Ephraim the arrow, and
Zion the sword in the hand of Jehovah, by means of which
the foe is thoroughly subjugated.

The יָוָן בְּנֵי, *Benei-Yavan*, sons of Javan, who come
within the range of the prophet's vision in this passage,
are "the Greeks as the world-power," or the Græco-
Macedonian kingdom ; but, as we shall see, the more
immediate merges here also into the more distant future.
The "weak beginnings" of the fulfilment of this prophecy,
to borrow an expression from Keil, is to be seen "in the
wars between the Maccabees and the Seleucidæ, or Greek
rulers of Syria," to which also some ancient Jews applied
this prophecy :

" The wars of the Jews against Greece, under the heroic
leadership of the Maccabees, were occasioned by the attempt
to overturn the Jewish religion and substitute in its place
Grecian customs (comp. 1 Macc. viii. 9–18 ; 2 Macc. iv.
13–15). Those wars were essentially religious in their
character. The Maccabean heroes went forth to the contest with the full conviction that the cause in which they
were engaged was the cause of God, and that the Lord
was with them in all their various difficulties and trials.
In the glowing language of the prophet (ver. 14), Jehovah
was seen over them, and His arrow went forth as the
lightning ; yea, the Lord Jehovah blew with the trumpet,
for He was the real Captain of His host, and the war
waged by the Jews was in defence of His truth. The

---

[1] אֶפְרַיִם מִלֵּאתִי. Von Orelli regards Ephraim as the quiver—the object filled
with arrows for God's use.

Lord is further described as going forth in the storms of
the south; because the storms from that quarter, coming
from the desert, were generally the most violent (Isa.
xxi. 1). The language used is highly figurative, but it
need not surprise us that the exploits of the Maccabees
should be so described when we call to mind the vivid
language in which David depicts his own deliverance in the
remarkable song in the day when God delivered him from
his foes.[1] Small as were the armies which Judas and his
brethren commanded, those armies were the armies of
Israel, and they went forth to battle in the name of the
Lord of hosts, the God of the armies of Israel, who was
then defied by the Grecian foe, even as in former days He
had been defied by the Philistine (1 Sam. xvii. 45). Thus
doing battle against the enemies of their God, 'out of
weakness they were made strong, they waxed valiant in
fight, and turned to flight the armies of the aliens' (Heb.
xi. 34)."

But that the prophecy cannot be altogether restricted
to the Maccabean struggle with the Syrian Greeks is manifest, for the whole passage points to the complete subjugation of imperial world-power.

No; Zion and Greece, as has been well observed by
another writer, are in this prophecy of Zechariah opposed
to one another as the city of God and the city of the world
(the "*civitas Dei*, and the *civitas mundi*," as Augustine has
it), and the defeat of Antiochus Epiphanes and his successors at the hands of comparative handfuls of despised
Jews, to which this passage may primarily refer, foreshadows
the final conflict with world-power, and the judgments to
be inflicted on the confederated armies who shall be
gathered against Jerusalem, not only directly by the hand
of God, but also by the hand of Israel, who shall then be
made strong in Jehovah, so that "the feeble among them
shall in that day be as David, and the house of David shall
be as God, as the Angel of Jehovah before them."

[1] Ps. xviii. 6–9 ; comp. also Ps. cxliv. 6, 7 ; Ps. lxxvii. 16–19 ; and especially
Hab. iii. 12–14.

Then, in a literal sense, Jehovah in the person of their Messiah "*shall be seen over them*, and His arrow shall go forth as the lightning," and He Himself as the Captain of the Host "shall blow the trumpet,"[1] and "shall go forth and fight against those nations as when He fought in the day of battle."[2]

The 15th verse illustrates the word of the Psalmist, "Through God we shall do valiantly, for He it is that shall tread down our adversaries."[3]   "*Jehovah of hosts,*" we read, "*shall defend them ;*[4] *and they shall devour, and they shall tread down the sling stones ; and they shall drink, and make a noise as through wine : and they shall be filled like bowls, like the corners of the altar.*" The devouring (or "eating ") and "drinking " must, of course, be understood in a figurative sense—for it is only to a perverted imagination, worthy of those who from time to time seek to revive the diabolical lie which is known by the name of the "Blood Accusation," that the thought could ever occur that the Jews did literally eat the flesh and drink the blood of their conquered adversaries.[5]

The figure which is here before the prophet's mind is

---

[1] See the somewhat parallel passage Isa. xxx. 30-33, where the enemy primarily referred to is the Assyrian.

[2] Chap. xiv. 3.

[3] Ps. lx. 12, cviii. 13.

[4] עֲלֵיהֶם יָגֵן, *yagen 'aleihem*—literally, "shall be a shield over them." Pusey points out that the word is used before only by Isaiah (xxxvii. 33, xxxviii. 6). This image of *complete protection* stands first in God's word to Abraham, "I am thy shield" (Gen. xv. 1).   But it is laid hold of by David when he appeals to God : "*Thou, O Lord, art a shield around me*" (Ps. iii. 3).

[5] A German scholar named Ghillany, in a treatise on *Die Menschenopfer der Alten Hebräer*, published in Nüremberg in 1842, does actually descend to this absurdity. He adduces this verse in Zechariah in proof that the prophet "in his dreams of victory let us have an insight into the barbarism of the victorious Hebrews," who, according to him, "did actually in ancient times eat their fallen foes as food, and drank their blood in the rage of victory, as well as partook of portions of their bodies"!

But whatever cannibal "barbarisms " may have existed among some of the *Gentile* nations, both in the East and in the West, Israel had never sunk quite so low even in the most "ancient " times, and the very idea of actually drinking blood is repugnant to the Jewish religion, as Dr. Wright well observes, and is condemned in both the Law and the Prophets.

that which was used by Balaam ages before: "Behold the people (Israel) shall rise up as a great lion, and lift up himself as a young lion.   He shall not lie down till he eat the prey and drink the blood of the slain " (Num. xxiii. 24). It is also found in Mic. v. 8 : " And the remnant of Jacob shall be among the nations, in the midst of many people as a lion among the beasts of the forest, as a young lion among the flocks of sheep : who, if he go through, treadeth down and teareth in pieces, and there is none to deliver."

" The idea of actually drinking blood was repugnant to the Jewish religion, and condemned in both the Law and the Prophets ; but when nations are compared to wild animals, language must be used characteristic of the habits and usages of such animals."[1]   " The one thought seems to be that their enemies should cease to be, so as not to molest them any more. . . . They should disappear as completely as fuel before the fire, or food before the hungry."[2]

The Authorised Version renders וְכָבְשׁוּ אַבְנֵי קֶלַע (vekha-bhshu abhnei qela'), " and they shall subdue with sling stones " ; but the sling stones cannot, as Keil points out, for grammatical reasons, if the whole sentence be considered, be taken in an instrumental sense—that is, that Israel would overcome their enemies with mere sling stones, as David did Goliath.

The true meaning is rather that given in the Revised Version, "they shall tread down sling stones " ; and since in the next verse Israel is likened to the precious stones set in a crown, it is probably correct to suppose, with Hengstenberg, Keil, Hitzig, Pusey, etc., that " the sling stones " are, in comparison, to be taken " as a figure *denoting the enemy*, who is trampled under the feet like stones."

The idea is further carried out in figurative language when the victorious Israelites are described in the second half of the 15th verse as making a noise like men drunk with wine—the drink with which they are made drunk being the blood of the enemies of the Lord.   " With this

---

[1] Wright.   [2] Pusey.

blood the prophet describes the victorious Jews as being *filled*, like the sacrificial bowls in which the priests were wont to catch the blood of the victims which were slain ; and they would be sprinkled with it like the corners of the altar, which expression includes the *horns* of the altar, which were wont to be sprinkled with the sacrificial blood." [1]

The climax is reached in the last two verses. The final overthrow and subjugation of world-power is followed by the exaltation and the glorification of the people of God. "*And Jehovah their God shall save them in that day as the flock of His people : for they shall be as the stones of a crown lifted on high.*"

The picture in the 16th verse changes from war and bloodshed to that of the Shepherd and His flock, which plays so prominent a part in the last chapters of this prophetic book.

Jehovah in that day shall "*save them.*" This does not mean here merely that He will help and deliver them. This, as another writer points out, would affirm much too little after what has gone before. "When Israel has trodden down his foes, he no longer needs deliverance." The meaning is rather that God will in that day endow them with salvation, not only in the negative sense of deliverance, but in the *positive* sense ; and, if we want to know what is implied in it, we have it in the figure of the next clause. He will do for them and be to them *all that a shepherd does and is to his flock*, which implies that He will not only *seek*, and *deliver*, and gather them, but He Himself, in the person of the Messiah, as all the prophets bear witness, will *tend*, and *feed*, and lead, and rule over them— all which is implied in the Hebrew word "Shepherd." That most beautiful "nightingale song," Ps. xxiii., which is so precious to us now, will then express the experience of saved Israel. "*Jehovah is my Shepherd, I shall not want*" —because in His Shepherd-care the fullest provision is made for every need, both spiritual and temporal, for His own flock.

[1] C. H. H. Wright.

Another aspect of this positive " Salvation " which
Jehovah shall then bestow upon His people, is brought
before us in the second half of this verse. In contrast to
their enemies, who are likened to " sling stones," which shall
then be contemptuously trodden under foot, saved Israel
shall be אַבְנֵי נֵזֶר, *abhnei-nezer* " stones of a crown " (*or jewels
set in a consecrated crown*),[1] lifted on high over His land—
which reminds us of Isa. lxii., where we read that after
" Zion's righteousness shall go forth as brightness, and her
salvation as a lamp that burneth," so that " the nations shall
see thy righteousness, and all kings thy glory "—then
" *Thou shalt also be a crown of beauty in the hand of Jehovah,
and a royal diadem in the hand of thy God.*" We note the
expression in this verse, " over *His* land," which reminds us
of the unique relationship in which Jehovah stands to the
land, as well as to the people of Israel. " The land is
Mine," [2] He said of Palestine in a very special sense, though
the whole earth belongs to Him ; and this, as Pusey observes,
" was laid down as the title-deed to its whole tenure." He
appointed it in His sovereign right, and with a gracious
purpose in view, as the inheritance of the seed of Abraham ;
but the ownership remains vested in *Him*. It is called also
" *Immanuel's Land*," [3] because the theocratic King-Messiah
is the true heir to it, not only by reason of His being the
true Son of Abraham, and Son of David, to whom the land
was promised, but because He is the Son of God, to Whom
it, in a special sense, belongs.

For a long time Israel has been banished from their
possession on account of sin, and Jerusalem and Palestine
are being trodden down of the Gentiles ; but the counsel of
Jehovah, both as regards the land and the people, standeth
for ever, the gifts and the calling of God are without
repentance ; and when the covenant relations between God

[1] The primary meaning of the masculine noun נֵזֶר, *nezer*, is separation, or consecration. Then it is used also of the *sign of consecration*—as, for instance, the
long hair of the " Nazarite," and the crown of the king, or *priest*. The word is
first found in Ex. xxix. 6, where it is used of the " *holy crown* " which the high
priest was to wear over the " mitre."

[2] Lev. xxv. 23.　　　　[3] Isa. viii. 8

and "His own" people Israel are restored, "*Jehovah shall inherit Judah, His portion in the Holy Land, and shall choose Jerusalem again.*"[1]

The prophet ends this section of the prophecy with the exclamation : "For how great is His goodness, and how great is His beauty!——כִּי מַה טּוּבוֹ וּמַה יָפְיוֹ, *Ki mah tubho umah yaphyo—corn shall make the young men to flourish and new wine the maids.*"

There is difference of opinion among commentators to whom the first half of this verse is to be applied. On strict grammatical grounds it must be applied to God, to whom the suffixes " His land," " His people," refer in the verse immediately preceding ; but it is argued by Koehler and others that since beauty is never attributed to Jehovah Himself in the Old Testament, it is better to understand the words as applying to the people. And this is the view taken by most modern scholars. With this contention, however, I cannot concur ; for, first, though it be true that the term יְפִי, *yaphi* (*beauty*), was not used before of God, it is used of the Messiah in such scriptures as, " Thou art fairer " (or more beautiful) "than the sons of men," and " Thine eyes shall see the King in His beauty." And it is in the face of their Messiah-King that Israel shall behold, even as we do already, the glory and beauty of the invisible God.

" Goodness " is very frequently attributed to God in the Old Testament, as, for instance, in Ps. xxxi. 19 : "*Oh how great is Thy goodness, which Thou hast laid up for them that fear Thee. Which Thou hast wrought for them that put their trust in Thee, before the sons of men*" ; and Ps. cxlv. 7 : "*They shall utter the memory of Thy great goodness.*"

I take the words then, with Hengstenberg and others, as referring to God, " whose great doings had been the prophet's theme throughout."

Let me, in closing the exposition of this chapter, echo this exclamation of the prophet, "*How great is His goodness!*" "Goodness is that attribute of God whereby

---

[1] Chap. ii. 12.

He loveth to communicate to all who can or will receive it, all good—yea, Himself, who is the fulness and universality of good, Creator of all good, not in one way, not in one kind of goodness only, but absolutely, without beginning, without limit, without measure, save that whereby without measurement He possesseth and embraceth all excellence, all perfection, all blessedness, all good."

" This good His goodness bestoweth on all and each, according to the capacity of each to receive it; nor is there any limit to His giving, save His creatures' capacity of receiving, which also is a good gift from Him. From Him all things sweet derive their sweetness, all things fair their beauty, all things bright their splendour, all things that live their life, all things sentient—their sense, all that move their vigour, all intelligences their knowledge, all things perfect their perfection, all things in any wise good their goodness." [1]

" *And how great is His beauty !* " This we cannot fully know until we are fully transformed into His image and can gaze upon His unveiled glory. But even now we may pray with David : " One thing have I asked of the Lord, that will I seek after, that I may dwell in the house of the Lord all the days of my life, *to behold the beauty of the Lord*, and to inquire in His temple " (Ps. xxvii. 4). And the more we behold it even now by faith and with the veil of flesh between, and inquire about it, the more shall we be changed into the same image from glory to glory, even as by the Lord the Spirit.

But, to come back to the context, this goodness and beauty of Jehovah shall in that future day also be reflected by restored and converted Israel, when " they shall be as precious stones of a crown lifted up high over His land."

And of the abundance of spiritual blessing and " glory " which shall then dwell in the land,[2] material prosperity and temporal abundance will, as is not the case in the present dispensation, be the outward sign and accompaniment. " *Corn*," exclaims the prophet, " *shall make the young men*

---

[1] Quoted by Pusey. [2] Ps. lxxxv. 9.

cheerful" (*yenobhabh*, literally, *to* " *grow*," or *to* " *increase* "), " *and new wine the maids* (or ' *virgins* ')."

But the mention of young men and maidens is, as has been observed, merely intended to " heighten the picture of prosperity given by the prophet," and is in some respects a parallel to the prophetic description of the prosperity of the land and people in the earlier portion of the book, where the streets of Jerusalem are spoken of as being again " full of boys and girls playing in the streets thereof " [1]

[1] Chap. viii. 5.

Chapter 15

WHAT ISRAEL'S SHEPHERD-KING WILL
BE AND DO FOR HIS PEOPLE

Zechariah 10

Ask ye of Jehovah rain in the time of the latter rain, even of Jehovah that maketh lightnings ; and He will give them showers of rain, to every one grass in the field. For the teraphim have spoken vanity, and the diviners have seen a lie ; and they have told false dreams, they comfort in vain : therefore they go their way like sheep, they are afflicted, because there is no shepherd. Mine anger is kindled against the shepherds, and I will punish the he-goats : for Jehovah of hosts hath visited His flock, the house of Judah, and will make them as His goodly horse in the battle. From him shall come forth the corner-stone, from him the nail, from him the battle bow, from him every ruler together. And they shall be as mighty men, treading down their enemies in the mire of the streets in the battle ; and they shall fight, because Jehovah is with them ; and the riders on horses shall be confounded. And I will strengthen the house of Judah, and I will save the house of Joseph, and I will bring them back, for I have mercy upon them ; and they shall be as though I had not cast them off ; for I am Jehovah their God, and I will hear them. And they of Ephraim shall be like a mighty man, and their heart shall rejoice as through wine ; yea, their children shall see it, and rejoice ; their heart shall be glad in Jehovah. And I will hiss for them, and gather them ; for I have redeemed them : and they shall increase as they have increased. And I will sow them among the peoples, and they shall remember Me in far countries ; and they shall live with their children ; and shall return. I will bring them again also out of the land of Egypt, and gather them out of Assyria ; and I will bring them into the land of Gilead and Lebanon ; and place shall not be found for them. And he will pass through the sea of affliction, and will smite the waves in the sea, and all the depths of the Nile shall dry up : and the pride of Assyria shall be brought down, and the sceptre of Egypt shall depart. And I will strengthen them in Jehovah ; and they shall walk up and down in His name, saith Jehovah.

Chapter 15

THE blessed and prosperous condition of restored and converted Israel under the care and leadership of their true Shepherd-King may be given as the summary of the chapter to which we have now come. The first verses are linked on, and are a continuation of the promises contained in the last section (vers. 7–11) of the 9th chapter.

Of the abundance of spiritual blessings and glory which shall then dwell in the land, to repeat a few sentences from my notes on chap. ix. 19—"Material prosperity and temporal abundance will, as is not the case in the present dispensation, be the outward sign and accompaniment." "Corn," exclaims the prophet at the conclusion of that chapter, "shall make the young men cheerful (or, literally, 'grow' or 'increase'), and new wine the maids (or 'virgins')."

But for Palestine to become once again, yea, even more than before, a land "flowing with milk and honey," after its many centuries of barrenness and desolation, the fertilising showers are essential; and though this is promised to them, they are yet exhorted to "ask" for it, even as in Ezek. xxxvi., where, after promising, among many other great things, that "this land which was desolate shall become like the garden of Eden, and the waste and desolate and ruined cities shall become fenced and inhabited," we read: "*Thus saith the Lord God, yet for this will I be inquired of by the house of Israel to do it for them*"[1]— for the promises of God, whether in relation to temporal or spiritual blessings, are only turned into experience by the faith and prayers of His people.

[1] Ezek. xxxvi. 37.

But it is perhaps necessary to repeat and emphasise that it is literal rain which is meant here, in the first instance, in which connection it is important to observe that Israel was taught to regard the giving or withholding of this great temporal blessing, upon which the prosperity of the land and the life of man and beast are dependent, as entirely in the hand of God. *"Are there any among the vanities of the heathen that can cause rain?"* exclaimed the prophet Jeremiah, *"or can the heavens (of themselves) give showers? art not Thou He, O Jehovah our God? therefore we will wait upon Thee: for Thou hast made all these things."* [1]

In these modern times men have grown wiser, and no longer recognise or acknowledge God in what to them is entirely due to "natural causes"; but such wisdom is based on a science only falsely so called, and is foolishness in the eyes of those who *know* that there is a living, personal God, the Creator and Upholder of all things, who, though He in His infinite power and wisdom appointed certain "laws" to govern His creation, is Himself all the time behind and above these laws, to guide and control; and does, either by using "natural means" which are known to us, or apart from them, interfere in the affairs of men and nations with a view to deliver, or instruct, or correct. To Israel, rain in due season, so that the land should yield her increase, was promised as the direct reward of national obedience.

"And it shall come to pass, if ye shall hearken diligently unto My commandments which I command you this day, to love the Lord your God, and to serve Him with all your heart and with all your soul, that I will give the rain of your land in its season, the former rain and the latter rain, that thou mayest gather in thy corn, and thy wine, and thine oil." [2]

And it is a notorious fact that the withholding of the showers and the scarcity of the rainfall—whatever the secondary causes by which it may be accounted for—was one of the chief factors in the predicted desolation of

---

[1] Jer. xiv. 22.   [2] Deut. xi. 13-15; Lev. xxvi. 3, 4; Deut. xxviii. 1-12.

Palestine, during the many centuries that the people has been banished from it on account of apostasy.

But to return to our passage. It is especially "the latter rain" which in Palestine is so important as strengthening and maturing the crops, that they are here exhorted to ask of the Lord, so that He may graciously complete "what He had begun by the former rain, filling the ears before the harvest." [1]

But though the primary reference is to literal showers, "on which the successful cultivation of the fruits of the ground depends," I agree with the German Bible scholar who says that the exhortation to ask for rain "only serves to individualise the prayer for the bestowal of the blessings of God, in order to sustain both temporal and spiritual life."

Indeed, there is a blending of temporal and spiritual blessings in the promise in the 9th and 10th chapters, the outward and visible being the types and symbols of the spiritual and eternal. When, on coming out of Egypt,

---

[1] There are four words in the Hebrew Bible for rain, three of which occur in this 1st verse of our chapter.

(1) יוֹרֶה, *yoreh* (also מוֹרֶה, *moreh*), which stands for the "first" or "former," or very early rain.

(2) מָטָר, *matar*, the ordinary word for "rain" during the rainy season.

(3) גֶּשֶׁם, *geshem*, which stands for heavy, or torrential rain.

(4) מַלְקוֹשׁ, *mal'qosh*, "the latter rain."

The variations of sunshine and rain, which in England extend throughout the year, are in Palestine confined chiefly to the latter part of autumn and winter. The autumnal, or "early" rain, commences in October (in the Lebanon about a month earlier) and continues to November, with long spells of beautiful weather—the whole fall being very small. It prepares the soil for ploughing and sowing. November to February inclusive is the rainy season, the storms and showers often being extremely heavy; but during these months also there may be many days at a time of fine weather.

In March and April is the time of the latter rain. The period of sowing varies according to situation from the end of October right into December (barley is not, as a rule, sown till January or February). Harvest-time also differs according to situation from early in May, or even April (in the low-lying parts), to June and even July, as we have ourselves witnessed on the higher slopes of the Lebanon. From May to the end of September is the very dry and hot season. The almost uninterruptedly cloudless and burning sun dries up all moisture, and, as the heat increases the grass withers, the flower fades, the bushes and shrubs take on a hard grey look, the soil becomes dust, and many parts of the country assume the aspect of parched and barren deserts.

Israel was brought into covenant relationship with God, we read, " *Thou, O God, didst send a plentiful rain; Thou didst confirm Thine inheritance when it was weary.*" [1]

And when Jehovah shall have mercy upon Zion again, and bring back His people after the long centuries of their "weary" wanderings, the light of His blessed countenance shall be as "life" to them, "and His favour *as a cloud of the latter rain*" [2]—yea, in response to the spirit of grace and of supplication which shall then be created in them, God says, " *I will pour water upon him that is thirsty, and streams* (or '*floods*') *upon the dry ground; I will pour My Spirit upon thy seed, and My blessing upon thine offspring.*" [3]

Viewed as a symbol of spiritual gifts and blessings, there is a message also for you and me in this ancient exhortation, dear reader. Indeed, I look upon this passage as one of the most beautiful scriptures in the Old Testament in reference to prayer, and God's manner of answering.

I. " Ask ye of Jehovah, . . . *and Jehovah shall give,*" which reminds us of the word of our Lord Jesus: "Ask, and ye shall receive," for the God of Israel is a God who *does* answer prayer. Sometimes the answer may be brought about by apparently natural causes, but all the same it is " Jehovah that maketh lightnings," [4] and commandeth the clouds to discharge their fertilising showers.

II. " Ask ye of Jehovah RAIN, . . . and He shall give them *showers of rain,* מְטַר גֶּשֶׁם, *m'tar geshem*"—literally, " *rain of plenty,* or *pouring rain*"; for our God is able to do *exceeding abundantly* above all that we *ask* or think, and this both in relation to temporal and spiritual things.

III. " *And He will give to every one grass in the field,*" for He individualises His gifts and blessings, and not one is left out of His gracious and bountiful provision and care.

But one great condition of effectual prayer is that our hearts and expectations be set wholly upon God. " *Hear,*

---

[1] Ps. lxix. 9.   [2] Prov. xvi. 15.
[3] Isa. xliv. 3.
[4] The lightnings are spoken of as the harbingers of rain ; see also Jer. x. 13, " He maketh lightnings for the rain," which is a verbal repetition of Ps. cxxxv. 7.

O My people, and I will testify unto thee: O Israel, if thou
wouldest hearken unto Me; there shall no strange god be
in thee; neither shalt thou worship any strange god. I am
the Lord thy God, which brought thee up out of the land of
Egypt: open thy mouth wide, and I will fill it." [1]

It was Israel's divided heart, the turning away from the
true and living God to follow after the vanities of the
Gentiles, which was the cause of Israel's calamities and
ruin in the past.   This is what the prophet reminds them
of in the 2nd verse: "*For the idols* ('*teraphim*') *have*
spoken vanity, and the diviners have seen a lie; they have
told false dreams (or, '*and dreams speak vanity*'), *they*
comfort in vain: therefore they went their way (or
'*wandered*') *like sheep, they are oppressed* (or '*afflicted*'),
because there was no shepherd."

It is the *teraphim*, or "*speaking*" oracles of the heathen,
and their consulters, or diviners, that the prophet specially
speaks of in this verse.

"Apart from our passage there are only seven other
scriptures in the Hebrew Bible where the teraphim are
introduced; but these suffice to show that they were not
only *idols*, the use of which is classed by God with 'witch-
craft, stubbornness, and iniquity,'[2] but that they were a
peculiar kind of idols, namely, those used for oracular
responses.   The first mention of the teraphim is in connection with Jacob's flight from Laban, in Gen. xxx.; and in
the light of the other passages there seems probability in
the explanation of Aben Ezra that Rachel stole them in
order that her father might not discover the direction of
their flight by means of these oracles.[3]

"The second place where we find them is in that
strange narrative about the Ephraimite Micah, and the
Danite expedition to Laish, in Judg. xvii. and xviii., where
we get a sad and characteristic glimpse of the condition of
some among the tribes in those days, 'when there was no

---

[1] Ps. lxxxi. 8–10.   [2] 1 Sam. xv. 23.

[3] See Aben Ezra *in loc.* Gesenius traces "teraphim" to the unused root
"*taraph*," which in the Syriac has the significance, "to inquire."

king in Israel, and every man did that which was right in his own eyes.' This narrative supplies an illustration of the fact that not only is man incapable of himself to find God, but that, left to himself, he is incapable of retaining the knowledge of God in its original purity even when once divinely communicated ; and that even the things revealed, apart from the continued teaching of God's Spirit, are liable to become corrupted and distorted in his mind. Here we have a sad instance of a certain knowledge of Jehovah mixed up with the worship of 'a graven image and a molten image,' which were an abomination in His sight, and the illegitimate use of the divinely instituted ephod, which was only to be borne by the high priest, joined together with the pagan teraphim. But the point to be noted is that here also these teraphim were used for oracular consultations, for it was of them that the apostate Levite of Bethlehem asked for counsel for the idolatrous Danites.[1] In Ezek. xxi. 21 we find the exact antithesis to David's consulting the ephod, in the pagan king of Babylon 'consulting with images' (literally, 'teraphim'), in reference to his projected invasion of Palestine.[2]

" Now it is clear that in olden times, whenever by apostasy and disobedience fellowship with Jehovah was interrupted, and when in consequence there was no revelation from Him, 'neither by dreams, nor by Urim, nor by prophets,' Israel turned to the pagan teraphim, or, like poor Saul, they 'sought unto such as had familiar spirits and wizards that peep and mutter.'

" A parallelism, in its spiritual significance, is to be found in Christendon. What the ephod or the prophet was in olden times, Holy Scripture is now. It is even a 'more sure word' than voices from heaven, or answers by

---

[1] Judg. xviii. 5, 6.

[2] The only other instances where teraphim are mentioned are 1 Sam. xix. 13-16, from which we gather, first, the sad fact that idolatry was practised by Michal, the daughter of Saul ; and, secondly, that the teraphim must have had some resemblance to the human form, since the idol could be mistaken for the body of David. There were no doubt larger ones in the temples, and smaller ones of all sizes, and for idolatrous purposes, in the houses.

Urim and Thummim. The Scriptures, first spoken by holy men of God as they were moved by the Holy Spirit, are now '*the oracles of God*,' themselves *speaking* with voices which carry their own conviction to hearts honestly seeking for truth, and ever confirming themselves in the world's history and in the Christian's experience ; but men in the present day, even in Christendom, stumbling at the supernatural, as if there could be a revelation of the Infinite and Everlasting One without such an element in them, turn away from these oracles often on the flimsiest grounds, and instead are giving heed on the one hand to the speculations of a ' science falsely so called,' and on the other hand ' to seducing spirits and doctrines of devils,' and are thus in a measure supplying an illustration of the solemn words of the apostle, that if men receive not the love of the truth that they might be saved, ' God shall for this cause send them strong delusion that they should believe a lie.' [1]

" For of the modern Christian teraphim it is as true as of the ancient pagan ones, that ' *they speak vanity*,' or ' wickedness '; and as for their ' diviners,' or false prophets representing them, ' they *see a lie*, and tell false dreams, they comfort in vain ' ; for it is a comfort not well founded, and will not stand the test of death, or of a judgment to come." [2]

But to return to our passage : " *Therefore* "—the prophet continues, because they followed lying oracles, and they who should have strengthened them in God, and in His truth, told them their own false dreams, and comforted them with vain expectations—" *they went their way* (or ' *wandered* ') [3] *like sheep, they are afflicted* (or ' *oppressed* '), *because there is no shepherd*."

The primary reference is very probably to their wandering and oppression in the Babylonian Captivity, but the picture is true also of the much longer exile and greater

[1] 2 Thess. ii. 11, 12.

[2] Quoted from *The Ancient Scriptures and the Modern Jew.*

[3] נָסַע, *nas'u*. The metaphor of the verb is taken from the pulling up the stakes of a tent or sheep-fold, a breaking up which involves an idea of wandering, and in this connection of wandering into captivity.

affliction which commenced with the destruction of the second Temple.

This is how our Lord Jesus beheld Israel's multitudes, and " was moved with compassion on them,[1] because they were distressed (or ' plagued,' or ' harassed ') and scattered," *i.e.*, they were troubled, neglected, uncared for. Their outward condition, as they followed Him about from place to place, a disorganised mass, hungry and weary, was pitiable enough, but this was but a faint picture of their spiritual condition, of the wretchedness of their souls, in consequence of the misguidance and tyranny of their false leaders.

And there in Matt. ix., even as in this passage in Zechariah, which may have been in our Lord's mind at the time, the saddest touch in the gloomy picture of Israel's distressed and helpless condition is contained in the words, *" because there is no shepherd,"* or, *" as sheep having no shepherd,"* *i.e.*, no one to guide, or control, or care for them. There were indeed in the time before the Captivity, as later in our Lord's time, many who called themselves " shepherds," but they were false, *deceiving* shepherds, who devoured the flock, and sought only to feed themselves.

But to proceed to the 3rd verse.

Because their appointed shepherds have proved false, Jehovah Himself, in the Person of the Messiah (as we shall see from the 4th verse), is going to act the part of the Good Shepherd to them. And first He will show His care for His people by delivering them from their false shepherds. *" Mine anger is kindled against the shepherds, and I will punish the he-goats."* It is not necessary to suppose, with Hengstenberg, Keil, Koehler, etc., that by these false shepherds and he-goats, the " heathen governors and tyrants " who ruled over them in captivity, are meant. It is much more likely that the prophet has such scriptures from the " former prophets," as Jer. xxiii. and Ezek. xxxiv., in his mind, where the false shepherds are their own faithless princes, priests, and prophets—in short, those in their

[1] Matt. ix. 36, R.V.

own nation who should have led them, but only misled them ; and of whom, alas ! there has been no lack at any time or period in Jewish history.

עַתּוּדִים, *atudim*—" he-goats," though it does sometimes (as in Isa. xiv. 9) signify rulers or princes, must not here be confounded with " the shepherds," but must be viewed in the light of Ezek. xxxiv., where, after judgments are announced against the false shepherds (or rulers), we read, " *And as for you, O My flock, thus saith the Lord God, Behold, I judge between cattle and cattle, as well (as between) the rams and the he-goats (atudim)* "[1]—where the latter stand for the rich and strong ones among the people themselves who oppressed the humble and the poor.

And not only will He deliver them from the false shepherds, the best part of the promise is contained in the second half of the verse, " *For Jehovah of hosts hath visited* (or ' *visits* ') *His flock, the house of Judah, and makes them as His goodly horse in the war* (or ' *battle* ')." The perfect tense of *paqad*, " to visit," is used here also prophetically of what God has resolved to do and will assuredly carry out. And when He visits His flock for good, and assumes His shepherd-care of them, they will be no more like distressed and scattered sheep, a prey to any wild beast, but they shall be strong in Jehovah and in the power of His might. He shall make them (or " set them ") " as His goodly horse," or, as the phrase may be rendered, " the horse of His Majesty "—that is, the horse fit and equipped for the God of Majesty to ride forth upon " in battle," to execute His judgments upon the nations.

We now come to the 4th verse of the 10th chapter, which I regard as one of the richest Messianic prophecies in the Old Testament. In keeping with Zechariah's style, which I have so often had occasion to point out in my notes on the earlier chapters, we have in this short verse not only allusions, but *a terse summary of a number of utterances by the "former prophets"* in reference to the character and mission of Israel's promised Redeemer.

[1] Ezek. xxxiv. 17.

" From him the corner (or *' corner-stone '*), *from him the nail* (*or 'peg'*), *from him the battle bow, yea, from him shall proceed every ruler together* (or, *' he that will exercise all rule '*)." [1]

[1] Many different interpretations of this verse have been given by commentators, who for the most part ignore any reference to the Messiah. Dr. Wright admits that "the corner" means the corner-stone, and that in Isa. xxviii. 16 this title, with others, is used in reference to the Messiah (p. 272) : and so evidently the term "nail," which is taken from Isa. xxii. ; but a few pages further on he blames Dr. Pusey, Bishop Wordsworth, and others for explaining these terms of the Messiah (which the Jewish Targum also does), and says that "such explanation cannot be defended on any rational principles of exegesis." But if in those passages in Isaiah (which there is every reason to believe were known to Zechariah, and to which he very probably alludes) these titles refer to the Messiah, what "rational" grounds are there for saying that they do not refer to the Messiah in this passage in Zechariah?

Hengstenberg, who translates, "Out of him the corner-stone, out of him the peg, out of him the war-bow, out of him will every ruler come forth together," explains in a general way as follows : "Having attained perfect freedom by the help of the Lord, who gives success to their arms, they will now receive rulers and officers from among themselves, and a military force of their own ; and whereas they formerly were a prey to strange conquerors, they will now terrify even foreign nations."

Keil, who translates the same as Hengstenberg, explains *phinnah*, the "corner," as "a suitable figure for the firm stately foundation which Judah is to receive." *Yathed*, "nail" or "plug," is a suitable figure for the supports or upholders of the whole political constitution. The war-bow stands for weapons of war and the military power ; and *noges* (which I have rendered ruler in the absolute sense), according to him (as well as Hengstenberg), "has the subordinate idea of *oppressor* or *despotic ruler* in this passage also ; but the idea of harshness (which is implied in the title) refers not to the covenant nation, but to its enemies." Kliefoth, explaining each word on the principle of a part of the whole, interprets "the corner-stone" to indicate the walls or fortifications ; the "tent peg," to denote the camp ; "the battle bow," warlike weapons of offence in general. All these are, according to him, included in the last phrase, *Khol noges yachdav*, which he translates, "All which rules."

Lange maintains that the four terms are expressions denoting the leaders of the people—two of them indicating the leaders required for war, and the other two the leaders in the days of peace. According to him, the "corner-stone" denotes the fixed and established government ; the "tent peg," those who took charge of travel ; while the "battle bow" is supposed to indicate the regular leaders on the battlefield ; and the *noges*, which he renders "assaulter" or "oppressor," the man who breaks through the hostile line of battle. But the explanation is fanciful, as are others which may be quoted.

On the rendering of the last clause see the note on p. 355.

I must add that in my notes on this verse I have embodied some paragraphs from the chapter, "Four Precious Titles of the Messiah," in my book, *Rays of Messiah's Glory*, which is out of print.

"From him," must be understood of Judah — the sense being equivalent to "*out of himself*," with a probable allusion to Deut. xviii. 15–19, where the promised great prophet like unto Moses, but who should yet be greater than Moses, is spoken of as coming forth "*from the midst of thee, of thy brethren*"; and Jer. xxx. 25, where we read: "*And their Prince* (literally, their 'glorious one') *shall be of themselves, and their ruler shall proceed from the midst of them.*" It is partly in explanation how, and through whom, the promise in the 3rd verse shall be fulfilled, namely, that when Jehovah visits "the house of Judah" they shall suddenly be transformed from a flock of scattered, troubled sheep, into His stately irresistible war-horse.

It is also in harmony with the whole testimony of prophetic scripture that the family of David, of the tribe of Judah, should be the human stock, and Bethlehem Ephratha in the portion of Judah, the place on earth where He should come forth "*that is, to be Ruler in Israel*," though we are at the same time reminded that, according to His Divine nature, "His goings forth are from of old from the days of eternity," as the passage in Mic. v. 2 reads literally.

I. *The Corner-stone*

Out of Judah then shall come forth "the corner" (פִּנָּה, *phinnah*, the *corner-stone*). The allusion is doubtless to Isa. xxviii. 16, where, contrasting the sure refuge which He Himself provides for His people with the refuges of lies which men make for themselves, which shall be swept away by the hailstorms of His judgments, the Lord says, "*Behold, I lay in Zion for a foundation, a stone, a tried stone, a precious corner-stone, a sure foundation* ('*a foundation well founded*') ; *he that believeth shall not make haste*"—a scripture which has always been regarded as Messianic by both Jews and Christians. The Christian cannot also forget the fact that in the New Testament the figure of the foundation stone, and head-stone of the corner, is applied to our Lord Jesus both by Himself and by the apostles.[1] But the question is, What is implied in it? Writing as I do here, primarily for Christians, and in the full light which the New Testament revelation casts upon the ancient prophecies in the Old Testament, I would say that the first and most obvious truth which the Spirit of God would have us learn from this figure is that the Messiah is the sure foundation of "the House of God, which is the Church of the living God."

For the safety and stability of a building almost everything depends on the foundation. The plan and material may be ever so perfect ; the ornamentation ever so elaborate and beautiful—but all is of no avail if the foundation be sand, for it cannot abide the storm or flood. On the other hand, the materials of a building may be of more humble quality, the ornamentation may be less elaborate or plain ; but if the foundation be sound, the rain may descend, the floods come, and the winds blow and beat upon that house, it will not fall, for it is built upon a rock. Now the great God, the Divine Architect of the universe, has purposed within Himself from all eternity to raise out of frail, imperfect, human materials a glorious Temple for His own eternal habitation through the Spirit, which, when completed, shall show forth, even more than the material temple of the universe, to principalities and powers the infinite power and manifold wisdom of God ; and in order to ensure its eternal safety He has bestowed great care on the foundation. He Himself has laid it : "Behold, *I lay* in Zion for a foundation," for it is a task which could not be entrusted to, or accomplished by, men or angels.

And the "tried" and "precious" corner-stone which He laid as the basis of this mystical structure is His own Son, who is "perfected for evermore," against whom even the gates of hell shall not prevail.

This accounts for the continuance and immovableness of the Church of Christ, in spite of the many storms it has had to brave, and the insidious attacks from enemies and false friends. Let the storm rage ; let infidelity assail ; let

[1] Matt. xxi. 42 ; Acts iv. 11 ; 1 Pet. ii. 4–8.

men and devils do their utmost. Has it not been foretold in advance that the same precious foundation stone upon which millions would build unto their eternal safety, would also become a stone of stumbling and rock of offence against which many would stumble, and fall, and be broken to pieces ?[1]

But "the foundation of God remains sure," and those whose feet are firmly planted on it have no occasion to fear. Therefore the prophet adds : "*He that believeth shall not make haste*"—that is, to flee in alarm at the threatened judgments, in the day when God ariseth to shake terribly this earth, but shall abide safe on the unshakeable Rock of Ages and Eternal Refuge.

But, secondly, the corner-stone served not only as a foundation, but, to quote a dictionary definition, it is "that stone which unites the two walls at the corner." It is a point of much interest that the original foundation stone of Solomon's Temple was actually discovered as one of the early results of the exploration carried on by the Palestine Exploration Fund. I take the following from a small work by one of its agents, which gives the account of this discovery :

" Among the ancient Jews the foundation corner-stone of their sanctuary on Moriah was regarded as the emblem of moral and spiritual truths. *It had two functions to perform : first, like the other foundation stones, it was a support for the masonry above ; but it had also to face both ways, and was thus a bond of union between two walls. . . .*

" The engineers, in order to ascertain the dimensions of this foundation stone, worked round it, and report that it is three feet eight inches high and fourteen feet in length. At the angle it is let down into the rock to a depth of fourteen inches ; but, as the rock rises towards the north, the depth of four feet north of the angle is increased by thirty-two inches, while the northern end seems entirely embedded in the rock. The block is further described as squared and polished, with a finely dressed face.

[1] Isa. viii. 14, 15 ; Matt. xxi. 42–44.

" It does not appear to have any marginal draft at the
bottom, and indeed this was not necessary, as the lower
part, being sunk in the rock, would always be hidden from
view ; but the absence of the lower draft indicates that the
block was dressed in the quarry in a somewhat peculiar
style, with a view to its being the foundation corner-stone.
The draft on the upper margin of the stone is four inches
wide. Fixed in its abiding position 3000 years ago, it
still stands sure and steadfast, a fitting emblem of the
' Rock of Ages,' that cannot be removed, but abideth fast
for ever." [1]

And in this respect also the corner-stone is a fit
emblem of our Lord Jesus Christ. "*For He is our peace,
who hath made both one, and hath broken down the middle
wall of partition between us ; having abolished in His flesh the
enmity, even the law of commandments contained in ordinances ; for to make in Himself of twain one new man, so
making peace.*" [2] In spite of mutual prejudice and the
otherwise impassable legal and ceremonial gulf that separated
the Jew from the Gentile, Christ is the angle at which they
both meet to be united as one building, or, even more
closely, as the members of one body. This indeed is the
connection in which Paul speaks of Christ under this figure
in that great scripture from which I have already quoted.

After reminding the Ephesian believers how that
formerly they were " Gentiles in the flesh, called uncircum-
cision by that which is called circumcision in the flesh
made by hands, . . . without Christ, aliens from the
commonwealth of Israel, and strangers from the covenants
of promise, having no hope and without God in the world,"
he proceeds to say :

" *But now, in Christ Jesus, ye who sometimes were far
off are made nigh by the blood of Christ. . . . Now therefore
ye are no more strangers and foreigners, but fellow-citizens
with the saints, and of the household of God ; and are built
upon the foundation of the apostles and prophets, Jesus Christ*

---

[1] *Recent Discoveries in the Temple Hill of Jerusalem*, by J. King, M.A.
[2] Eph. ii. 14, 15.

Himself being the chief corner-stone ; in whom all the building, fitly framed together, groweth unto an holy temple in the Lord, in whom ye also are builded together for an habitation of God through the Spirit." [1]

I must not tarry here to point out the difference between the " corner-stone " and the " head-stone of the corner," to which there are also many allusions in the Hebrew Scriptures, and of the important truths which are set forth under the figures in reference to Israel's past and future attitude to their Messiah, having elsewhere fully entered into these subjects." [2]

I proceed therefore to the second designation of the Messiah in this passage.

II. *The Nail in the Sure Place*

The word יָתֵד, *yathed,* translated here " nail " (rendered in the Septuagint πάσσαλος), is used first of a tent-pin, or stake, which is driven into the ground and to which the tent is fastened ; [3] and, secondly, of the strong peg inside the Oriental tent, or which is built into the wall of the Eastern building, on which is hung most of its valuable furniture.[4]

The primary allusion is to Isa. xxii., where we read : *" And the key of the house of David will I lay upon his shoulder, and he shall open and none shall shut ; and he shall shut and none shall open. And I will fasten him as a nail in a sure place ; and he shall be for a throne of glory to his father's house.* And they shall hang upon him all the glory of his father's house, the offspring and the issue, every small vessel, from the vessel of cups even to all the vessels of flagons." [5]

Now this prophecy in Isaiah, though uttered primarily of *a* son of David—namely, Eliakim—merges into *the* Son

---

[1] Eph. ii. 19-22.
[2] See " The Conclusion of the Hallel, a Prophetic Drama of the End of the Age," in *The Ancient Scriptures and the Modern Jew.*
[3] Ex. xxvii. 19, xxxv. 18 ; Isa. xxii. 22, 23.
[4] Ezek. xv. 3.
[5] Isa. xxii. 22-24 (R.V.).

of David, the Messiah, in whom all the promises given to
the Davidic house finally centre and are being fulfilled.   It
is He who is "the glorious throne to His Father's house,"
the true heir and perpetuator of the throne of His father
David, and of His Kingdom, "to establish it, and to uphold it
with judgment and with righteousness from henceforth, even
for ever,"[1] and who, as we have seen in the exposition of
chap. vi., "shall bear the glory, and shall sit and rule upon
His throne."   Anyhow, to us it is not without significance
that the risen Christ in His message through His servant
John to the Church in Philadelphia, in allusion to the
words addressed to Eliakim, claims to be the one who is in
possession of the key of the house of David—"*These things,
saith He that is holy, He that is true, He that hath the key of
David, He that openeth and none shall shut, and that shutteth
and none openeth.*"[2]

The reference in Isa. xxii., and in our passage in
Zechariah which is based upon it, is not to the "nail," or
pin, or stake, to which the ropes of the tent are fastened,
but to the strong peg inside the tent, or built into the wall
of the house.

(*a*) The "nail," or peg, when thus fastened in a sure
place, was used *to hang burdens upon*.   This we see from
Isa. xxii. 25, where, speaking of the overthrow of the
unfaithful Shebna, the treasurer of the king's house, who
thought himself quite safe in his position, as a nail in a sure
place, the Lord says, "And the burden upon it" (הַמַּשָּׂא,
hammassa—"the heavy weight," used here figuratively of
the weight of office and responsibility as governor of the
king's house) "shall be cut off."

In the light of this fact we easily perceive the applica-
bility and preciousness of this figure as applied to the
Messiah.   He is not only the Foundation of the mystical
temple, and the uniting "Corner-stone" in whom all
believers, either Jew or Gentile, are made one, but *to those
inside the spiritual house* He is the Nail in a sure place, upon
whom they may hang their "burdens."   Ah, how many

[1] Isa. ix. 7.   [2] Rev. iii. 7.

there be among God's people who know Christ as the Foundation of their hopes for eternity, but little as their Burden-bearer, "who bears their grief and carries their sorrows"! Cast thy burden upon the Lord, O Christian, whatever it may be, "and He will sustain thee."

(*b*) But, secondly, the chief purpose of the nail, or peg fastened in a sure place, is, that *upon it may hang all the glory of the house*, "all vessels of small quantity, from the vessels of cups (or 'goblets') even to all the vessels of flagons." A great portion of the wealth of the ancient Orientals (and the same is still true in measure) consisted in gold and silver vessels and in changes of raiment. These, as well as shields, swords, and suits of armour taken in battle, they were wont, with Eastern ostentation, to hang on the "pegs" in their tents or houses for the admiration of all who entered.

And this, to pass from the figure to the great truth it is meant to represent, is what God expects us to do with Christ. When it is said, "They shall hang upon Him all the glory of His Father's house," it means that Israel shall yet render to Him that honour and glory, that joyful allegiance and willing consecration of themselves and their possessions, to which He is entitled as the true heir of the Davidic "house," and Lord of the theocratic kingdom. And it is our privilege also even now, during the period of His rejection, to "hang upon Him," that is, consecrate to Him and His service all that which we may regard as "our glory." Nor is there any one, even the least and the weakest of His redeemed people, who can say that he has nothing which he can dedicate to Him, for that which is most precious in His sight is a loving, confiding heart and an adoring spirit. But next to, and together with, the offering of *ourselves*, we are to "hang upon Him" whatever possessions or gifts or talents which He may have entrusted to us. And it is precious and beautiful to note that there is a place on the peg for "the cup or goblet" as well as for the "flagon": and "the vessel of small quantity," when fully consecrated to the Master's use, is of greater use, and brings more " glory " to Him, than the " vessel of large quantity " when not so fully surrendered. And as with our persons, so with our gifts. The " small offerings " from those who have but little, and to whom the giving implies real sacrifice for His blessed Name's sake, are at least equally if not more precious in His sight than the " large offerings " from those who have much. Above all, it is the *motive* which Jehovah, " by whom actions are *weighed* " (not counted or measured), takes into account.

III. *The Battle Bow*

It is generally agreed that every one of the four terms used in this verse (*phinnah*, " corner "; *yathed*, " nail "; *qesheth milchamah*, " battle bow "; and *noges*, " ruler " or " exactor ") are all used *metaphorically*, and denote persons, or, as I verily believe, one Person, who Himself fulfils these different functions. The last two terms bring before us an aspect of the Messiah's character which will be manifest at His Second Coming. Then He will be the " Battle bow " —the mighty and skilful Archer, who shall send forth His " sharp arrows " in the heart of the king's enemies, " whereby the people shall be made to fall under Him." [1]

This is an aspect of Christ's character on which men do not like to dwell; but let it not be forgotten that the same prophet, Isaiah, who pictures Him in the 53rd chapter as the suffering Lamb of God, who " as a sheep before her shearers is dumb, openeth not His mouth," describes Him in the 63rd chapter as clothed in majesty, marching forth in the greatness of His strength to take vengeance on the nations : " *Wherefore art thou red in thine apparel, and thy garments like him that treadeth in the winefat? I have trodden the winepress alone, and of the peoples there was no man with Me : yea, I trod them in Mine anger, and trampled them in My fury ; and their lifeblood is sprinkled upon My garments, and I have stained all My raiment* " [2]—an Old Testament vision which will be fulfilled at " the revelation

[1] Ps. xlv. 5.　　　　　　　　　[2] Isa. lxiii. 2-4 (R.V.).

of the Lord Jesus from heaven with the angels of His
power, in flaming fire, rendering vengeance on them that
know not God, and that obey not the gospel of our Lord
Jesus, . . . when He shall come to be glorified in His
saints, and to be marvelled at in all them that believe." [1]

"*And I saw the heaven opened ; and behold, a white
horse, and He that sat thereon, called Faithful and True ;
and in righteousness He doth judge and make war. And
His eyes are a flame of fire, and upon His head are many
diadems ; and He hath a name written, which no one knoweth
but He Himself. And He is arrayed in a garment sprinkled
with blood : and His name is called The Word of God. And
the armies which are in heaven followed Him upon white
horses, clothed in fine linen, white and pure. And out of His
mouth proceedeth a sharp sword, that with it He should smite
the nations : and He shall rule them with a rod of iron :
and He treadeth the winepress of the fierceness of the wrath
of Almighty God. And He hath on His garment and on
His thigh a name written,* KING OF KINGS AND LORD OF
LORDS." [2]

IV. *The Autocratic Ruler, or "Exactor"*

It is not possible to speak with absolute certainty of
the exact meaning of the last clause in the verse which we
are considering, as the construction of the sentence in the
original is unusual and peculiar, and has led to conflicting
translations and interpretations. In rendering the words
כָּל נֹגֵשׂ יַחְדָּו, *khol noges yachdav*—"every ruler together," or,
"he that will exercise all rule,"—I am guided more by the
context and obvious sense than by strict principles of
Hebrew grammar.[3]   It seems to me that, as the first terms

---

[1] 2 Thess. i. 7-10 (R.V.).   [2] Rev. xix. 11-16 (R.V.).

[3] It is capable also of the following renderings, for which some have contended : "Out of him (Judah) shall come (or 'go') forth every exactor (in the
sense of absolute ruler) together." But, even if this be the most correct reading,
it would still apply to the Messiah, inasmuch as He embraces in Himself a
variety of different functions. Thus, for instance, He is represented by the
prophets as being "a Priest upon His throne" (Zech. vi.), and not only as

in this verse undoubtedly refer to the Messiah in allusion to utterances about His person and mission by the " former prophets," so must this last clause also. Certain it is that the Messiah at His Second Coming shall gather up in Himself all authority and rule. He shall be then not only the *Nasi*—the chosen Prince from among the people; not only the *Moshel*, God's Viceroy or Deputy Ruler on the earth; not only a constitutional *King*, who reigns but does not rule—but He shall be the *Noges*, the absolute Ruler, or " Exactor "—the most absolute and autocratic King the world has yet seen.

In Messiah's reign on the earth God's sovereignty will be fully manifested, but it is blessed to remember that it will be sovereignty exercised by One who is not only " glorious in holiness," infinite in wisdom and power, but by Him who is also infinite in compassion, and whose very nature is love. His absolute autocratic rule, therefore, though a terror to the ungodly, is a thought full of comfort to the righteous, for it will mean righteousness, peace and joy to this long-afflicted earth, and the very consummation of blessedness to His own people. But there is truth in Israel's King, but as the Prince (Ezek. xxxvii. **24, 25**). The Messiah was to be like unto Moses (Deut. xviii. **15**), who, in himself, united the different offices of prophet, priest, and king ; so that the phrase is quite applicable to Him on that account. Just as His atoning death can be spoken of in the plural (see Hebrew of Isa. liii. 9), on account of the various sacrifices receiving their fulfilment in His own body, which He offered once and for all—so, in a sense, He is many also in His reign, because all authority will meet in Him as the Centre. Aaron Pick, formerly Hebrew Professor at the University of Prague, in his *Literal Translation of the Twelve Minor Prophets*, renders our text thus : " From Him the Corner, from Him the Nail, from Him the Battle Bow, yea, from Him shall come forth He that conquereth all together."

The last sentence may also be understood as gathering up the ideas in the first three terms, *Phinnah*, *Yathed*, and *Qesheth milchamah*. From him (Judah) the Corner, from him the Nail, from him the Battle Bow ; yea, from him shall proceed He who shall unite in Himself, not only all that is implied in these three terms, but *every* power and authority "together." Yet another rendering, but in the sense just suggested, is given by George Adam Smith in his *Book of the Twelve Prophets*, namely, " From him the Corner-stone, from him the Stay (or 'Tent-pin'), from him the War-bow, from him the Oppressor—shall go forth together." That נוגש, *noges*, is here used in a *good* sense, is pretty generally admitted by lexicographers and commentators. Hitzig renders it " *Feldherr* " (commander). The cognate word in Ethiopic, Negus, signifies king.

the suggestion that the title *noges* (absolute ruler or
" exactor ") is applied here to Israel's ideal king or absolute
ruler in His relation, *not to His own people, but to their and
His enemies*, from whom He will " exact submission and
allegiance with a rod of iron," and who will make downtrodden Israel to rule over those who have long oppressed
and ruled over them.

> " *Now therefore be wise, O ye kings :*
> *Be instructed, ye judges of the earth.*
> *Serve Jehovah with fear,*
> *And rejoice with trembling.*
> *Kiss the Son, lest He be angry, and ye perish in the*
> *   way,*
> *When His wrath is kindled but a little.*
> *Blessed are all they that put their trust in Him.*"

In the 5th verse the line of thought unfolded in the
first three verses of this chapter is resumed, and the change
which will come over the people after Jehovah of hosts, in
the person of the Messiah, shall " visit His flock, the house
of Judah " (ver. 3), is now fully described.

Instead of being like a troubled and helpless flock of
sheep (ver. 2), they shall suddenly be transformed into His
" goodly horse " (or " the horse of His Majesty ") in battle,
and instead of being " afflicted " and at the mercy of their
adversaries, they shall be as " mighty men " treading upon
their enemies. The " mire of the streets " is used here as
a figure of their enemies, and is parallel to chap. ix. 15,
where it is said, " they shall trample on the sling stones "
(which is the figure of contempt used there to describe
their adversaries), while they themselves are likened to the
abhnci nezer, " stones of a crown " (or jewels set in a consecrated crown), lifted on high over the land. The figure
is found elsewhere in the prophetic Scriptures. Thus
Micah says, " Mine eyes shall behold her (' mine enemy ');
now shall she be trodden down (or, a ' treading down.'), as
the mire of the street " ;[1] but Zechariah, by a yet bolder

[1] Mic. vii. 10.

image, " pictures those trampled upon as what they had
become—the mire of the streets—as worthless, as foul." [1]
But not in their own strength shall they prevail, they shall
be and " fight " as heroes, " *because Jehovah is with them*,"
the source and secret of their strength—therefore, " *the
riders upon horses* "—the enemies' cavalry, the most formidable arm of the hostile forces—shall be put to shame, or
confounded.

Yes, Israel in that day shall experience the truth of
the words of their sweet Psalmist :

> " *Some trust in chariots and some in horses ;
> But we will make mention of the Name of Jehovah our
>   God ;
> They are bowed down and fallen ;
> But we are risen up and stand upright.*"

And the great deliverance which Jehovah shall then
accomplish for Israel will embrace the entire nation, which
in Zechariah's prophecies are regarded as no longer divided
into two separate kingdoms, but as one people, with a
common and inseparable destiny.   " *And I will strengthen
the house of Judah ; and I will save the house of Joseph ; and
I will bring them again, and make them dwell* (or ' *settle
them* ') : *for I have mercy upon them, and they shall be as
though I had not cast them off ; for I am Jehovah their God,
and I will hear them.*"

In keeping with Zechariah's very terse style, and the
summaries which we find sometimes in single words and
expressions, both in the first and second parts of his book,
of utterances by the " former prophets," we have here
embodied in the one word וַהֲשֵׁבוֹתִים (which the Authorised
Version has translated, " I will bring them again to place
them "), the promise uttered fully by Jeremiah, namely : " *I
will bring them again into this place, and I will cause them to
dwell safely*," [2] for the most satisfactory grammatical
explanation of the Hebrew word is that it is a blending of
two verbs which have the respective meanings of " I will

---

[1] Pusey.   [2] Jer. xxxii. 37.

make them dwell," and " I will bring them back "—both
ideas, as already the Jewish commentator Kimchi points
out, being expressed in the one word, namely, " He will
cause them to return to their own land, and will cause
them to dwell there in peace and security."

And He will do all this—strengthen, save, restore, and
establish them, because " *He shall have mercy upon them,*"
for, " The goodness and loving-kindness of God, and not
any merit of theirs, is the first and principal cause " of
Israel's whole salvation and grace, and the words of the
inspired Psalmist : " *They got not the land in possession by
their own sword, neither did their own arm save them* " ;
but—

> " *Thy right hand, and Thine arm, and the light of Thy
> countenance,*
> *Because Thou hadst a favour unto them* "—

will be true of the future restoration, as it was true of their
original possession of the land !

And His mercy and loving-kindness will blot out all
the past of sin and sorrow. " *And they shall be,*" He says,
" *as though I had not cast them off* " (or, literally, " as though
I had not loathed them," the word being expressive of
God's strong abhorrence of sin, and of sinners when they
become wedded to it)—which reminds us of the greater
promise of the new covenant : " *I will forgive their iniquity,
and their sin will I remember no more* " ;[1] and of the promise
in Ezekiel : " *And I will settle you as in your old estates, and
I will do better unto you than at your beginnings.*"[2]

The 5th verse ends with a beautiful glimpse of the
restored relationship between Jehovah and His long-
wandering people :

" *For I am Jehovah* "—that is, the everlasting, unchangeable, covenant-keeping God—which is the reason
why the sinful sons of Jacob have not been consumed.
And He is now " *their God,*" for the Lo-ruhamah and Lo-
ammi period of Israel's history shall then be ended, and no

[1] Jer. xxxi. 34.   [2] Ezek. xxxvi. 11.

longer shall He say: " Ye are not My people, and I will
not be your God."[1]   No; then He "*will hear them*"—or,
as we read more fully in the 13th chapter, " *They shall call
on My name, and I will hear them ; and I will say it is My
people* ; and they shall say Jehovah is my God,"[2] which
reminds us of many similar, if more general, promises in
the prophetic Scriptures, as, for instance: " *Then shalt thou
call, and Jehovah shall answer ; thou shalt cry, and He shall
say, Here I am* "; and again: " *I, Jehovah, will hear them,
I the God of Israel will not forsake them.*"[3]

And the joy and blessing and victory here promised is
henceforth to be shared alike by the whole nation, which
the prophet, in keeping with the peculiarity of his style,
designates by the separate names, " House of Judah," and
" House of Joseph," or " Ephraim," which together include
the whole people which had, indeed, previous to the Exile,
been for a long time divided into two frequently hostile
kingdoms, but are from the time of the partial restoration
from Babylon regarded as one nation, with one common
hope and destiny.

" *And they of Ephraim shall be like a mighty man, and
their hearts shall rejoice as through wine ; yea, their children
shall see it and rejoice ; their hearts shall rejoice* (or ' *be glad*')
in the Lord "—which is in effect a repetition more particularly in reference to " Ephraim " of what is stated in
chaps. ix. 15 and x. 5 of Judah. And the reason why
" Ephraim," or those previously belonging to the northern
kingdom, are specially mentioned as included in the word
of promise, is probably to be found (as suggested by Calvin
and Hengstenberg) " in the circumstances of the times," or
in the historic foreground of this prophecy. If the predictions of the earlier prophets in reference to Judah were now
(that is, in Zechariah's time) only *beginning* to be fulfilled,
and therefore needed to be renewed lest the nation should
think itself deceived, much more was this the case with
regard to Ephraim.

The great body of the people belonging to the northern

[1] Hos. i. 8.		[2] Zech. xiii. 9.		[3] Isa. xli. 17, lviii. 9.

kingdom was still in exile, though a small fraction of them had joined the children of Judah on their return, and there was outwardly but little in existing circumstances to support the hope of that grand restoration, which, according to the declaration of the former prophets, was one day to occur.

They of the "house of Joseph," as being in an apparently even more hopeless condition, are therefore especially assured that under the true son of David, the Redeemer-King, whose advent to "Zion" and "Jerusalem" the prophet had jubilantly announced in the 9th chapter, and who, in the 4th verse of the 10th chapter is spoken of as coming forth *out of Judah*, would fully share in all the blessings promised to the "house of Judah." They too would be brought back and made strong in the Lord and in the power of His might for the final conflict with their adversaries, so that they "*shall be like a mighty man*," or hero (that is, in "treading down their enemies in the mire of the streets," ver. 5), "*and their hearts shall rejoice as through wine*"—which exhilarates and "maketh glad the heart of man" with a gladness which is not natural, and is a fit emblem, therefore, of the strength and exhilaration which are imparted by the Spirit of God.[1]

And it will not be an evanescent joy which will soon fade away. No; "*their children (also) shall see it*," that is, the great things which God shall then do unto them—and be glad. "*Their heart shall rejoice in Jehovah*"—as the highest and only lasting source of joy "to whom," as an old writer puts it, "is to be referred all gladness which is derived from created things—that whoso glorieth may glory in the Lord, in whom alone the rational creature ought to take delight."

Most commentators suppose that ver. 8 to the end of the chapter still speak of Ephraim; but the supposition is, I think, without sufficient warrant. Having spoken of the "house of Judah" and the "house of Joseph" separately, the prophet now proceeds to set forth the purpose of God

---

[1] Eph. v. 18.

in reference to both parts of the nation who constitute one people with one common destiny :

"*I will hiss for them, and gather them ; for I have redeemed them.*"

This verb שָׁרַק, *sharaq*, to "hiss," or "whistle," or "pipe," is used several times in the earlier scriptures to describe God's signal in calling together nations and peoples to accomplish His purposes. Thus, in Isaiah He uses this word when He threatens to gather the Gentile nations to chastise His people : "*It shall come to pass in that day, that Jehovah shall hiss* (or '*whistle*') *for the fly that is in the uttermost part of the rivers of Egypt, and for the bee that is in the land of Assyria. And they shall come and rest all of them in the desolate valleys, and in the holes of the rocks, and upon all thorns, and upon all bushes.*" And again : "*He will lift up an ensign to the nations from far, and will hiss* (or '*whistle*') *unto them from the end of the earth. And behold they shall come with speed swiftly ; none shall be weary or stumble among them.*" [1] That is, He would gather the hostile nations against them "like the countless numbers of the insect creation, which, if united, would irresistibly desolate life. He would summon them as the bee-owner by his shrill call summons and unites his own swarm." But now the time to favour Zion having come, this same word is used in our passage in Zech. x. for the signal which He will use for the gathering together of His own dispersed people from the four corners of the earth.

The word *sharaq*, however, describes not only the shrill noise used to call together a swarm of insects—it means also, as already suggested above, to "pipe," [2] and *is used of the shepherd signal for the gathering of his scattered flock.*

This, indeed, is the picture presented to our minds in this chapter. At present, because they have given heed to false dreamers, "they go on their way (or wander about)

[1] Isa. v. 26, 27, vii. 18, 19.
[2] In the Song of Deborah, Judg. v. 16, translated in the A.V. : "Why abodest thou among the sheepfolds to hear the bleatings of the flocks?" is properly rendered in the R.V. : "Why satest thou among the sheepfolds to hear the pipings for the flocks ? שְׁרִקוֹת עֲדָרִים (*sheriqoth 'adarim*)."

like sheep; they are troubled (or 'afflicted') because there is no shepherd" (ver. 2); but when Jehovah of hosts, in the person of the Messiah, again "visits His flock," namely, "the house of Judah" (ver. 3) and "the house of Joseph" (ver. 6), He "will pipe for them and gather them."

If I may digress for a moment, and mention incidents of personal experience, I would say that on more than one occasion I have had the figure referred to in this passage illustrated before my eyes. On one occasion (it was in 1891) while camping for a few days with missionary friends in a wild part high up on the Lebanon, a picturesque-looking young Bedouin shepherd was leading a small flock of sheep to some distant part in search of pasturage. Passing our encampment he stopped for a while to converse with us, and in the meantime his flock got scattered among the rocks; but by and by, when he was ready to start, he pulled out from under his burnoose a reed pipe, and began to play on it a not very melodious tune; and it was interesting and beautiful to notice how, as he was playing, his scattered sheep, some of which had wandered off to some distance, collected closer and closer around him, and formed into a flock; and when they were all there he started off again at their head. Involuntarily this passage from Zechariah came to my mind: "*I will pipe for them and gather them.*" On another occasion, when travelling in 1889 one whole night in a diligence in inland Algeria, we stopped about dawn at an inn in a small Arab village to change horses. While this was being done, an Arab who stood near began to play, or whistle, on one of the same kind of rough reed or bamboo pipe. At first I thought he was playing for our benefit in order to get *baksheesh*, but I soon observed that as he continued "piping," sheep and cows and goats came toward him from all directions. It was the village shepherd gathering his flock to lead them forth to pasture.

Thus also the Shepherd of Israel is going to gather His flock and lead them into their own pastures. "*If any of thine outcasts be in the uttermost parts of heaven,*" He says, "*thence will Jehovah thy God gather thee, and from thence*

*will He fetch thee ; and Jehovah thy God will bring thee into
the land which thy fathers possessed, and thou shalt possess
it ; and He will do thee good, and multiply thee above thy
fathers."* [1]

And He will do this, He says, because " *I have redeemed
them* "—with a full and complete redemption, not only from
outward captivity, but "*from all their iniquities,*" [2] so that
they shall be known and called in that day " *The holy
people, the redeemed of Jehovah* "—henceforth to serve and
glorify Him, " Who hath ransomed them from the hand of
him that was stronger than he." [3]

And when thus redeemed and gathered in their own
land again, " *they shall increase as they have increased* "—
which latter phrase, as already Kimchi in his commentary
explains, is meant to remind us of God's wonderful and
gracious dealings with them during the last days of their
sojourn in Egypt, where " *the children of Israel were fruitful* " because of the blessings of Jehovah upon them, " *and
increased abundantly, and multiplied, and waxed exceeding
mighty ; and the land was filled with them.*" [4]   And thus,
again after the future greater redemption, the spared
remnant, who shall have been brought through the fiery
purging ordeal described in the last chapters of this very
prophecy, shall increase mightily, even " as they have
increased " (that is, in Egypt), and become a mighty
nation on the earth.

And this increase will characterise the seed of Israel
in a striking degree, even while still scattered among the
nations.   This I believe to be the meaning of the words
which follow in the 9th verse : " *And I will sow them
among the peoples ; and they shall remember Me in far
countries : and they shall live with their children, and shall
return.*"   The controversy among commentators as to
whether the expression, " *I will sow them among the
peoples,*" is to be understood as a prediction of a scattering
of the people among the nations subsequent to the partial

---

[1] Deut. xxx. 4, 5.   [2] Ps. cxxx. 8.
[3] Isa. lxii. 12 ; Jer. xxxi. 11.   [4] Ex. i. 7.

restoration from Babylon, is, according to my judgment, settled by the fact that the verb זָרַע (*zara'*), which is employed, is never used of scattering, or dispersing, in a bad sense, but always " to sow "; and the prediction in this verse cannot therefore refer to a dispersion of the Jewish people to be inflicted as a punishment. It is most probable that this passage in Zechariah is based on two utterances of the former "prophets." The first is Hos. ii. 23, where we read : "*And I will sow her unto Me in the earth ; and I will have mercy upon her that had not obtained mercy ; and I will say to them which were not My people, Thou art My people ; and they shall say, Thou art my God.*" And the second is Jer. xxxi. 27 : "*Behold, the days come, saith Jehovah, that I will sow the house of Israel and the house of Judah with the seed of man, and with the seed of beasts.*"

It is not necessary then to understand the words in Zechariah as referring to a future act of dispersion (though, as a matter of history, a dispersion subsequent to the partial restoration from Babylon—or rather, a new and more terrible and universal phase of the dispersion which was inaugurated by the Babylonian Captivity, did take place after Israel's national apostasy from God was completed in the rejection and crucifixion of their Messiah), but rather as a prediction first of all that in the dispersion which had already begun with the destruction of the city and Temple by the Babylonians, and which would last till the full and final restoration of the whole nation (Judah and Israel) to their own land, which is still in the future— God would cause them to multiply. This increase (to judge from the analogy of their experience in Egypt, to which allusion is made more than once in this chapter) would take place toward the end of the time of their sojourning among the nations, and would be a precursor of their national restoration.[1]

[1] The marvellous increase of the Jewish people since their so-called "emancipation" in the nineteenth century, is, indeed, a striking sign of the times. The statement of a recent writer in the *Jewish Chronicle*, that at the commencement of the sixteenth century there could scarcely have been more than a million Jews left in the entire world after the untold sufferings, dispersions,

And not only would they be preserved even in dispersion, and increase and multiply even as they did during the last days of their sojourn in Egypt, but in those "far countries" where they shall be found "*they shall remember Me*," saith Jehovah—which is perhaps an inspired echo by Zechariah of the words of Ezekiel: "*And they that escape of you shall remember Me among the nations whither they shall be carried captive, and they shall loathe themselves for the evil which they have committed in all their abominations. And they shall know that I am the Lord.*" [1]

The next sentence in the 9th verse, "*They shall live with their children, and turn again,*" must be connected with the words which immediately precede. Because they shall remember Jehovah "in the far countries" *they shall live.* Here we probably have an allusion (as Hengstenberg suggests) in one word (in the Hebrew) "to the figure which Ezekiel has so beautifully carried out in chap. xxxvii." They who, while dispersed among the nations, are seen by the prophet as dry bones scattered over the valley of vision, are to live again, for: "*Behold, I will open your graves, and cause you to come up out of your graves, O*

and massacres which they had to endure in the dark and middle ages—is probably true. The historian Basnage, in his *History of the Jews from Jesus Christ to the Present Time*, calculated that in his time (end of the seventeenth and beginning of the eighteenth century) there were three million Jews in the world. Since then, however, the growth of Jewry has been phenomenal. At the commencement of the nineteenth century there were said to be five millions. Half a century later the numbers reached six or seven millions; and at the end of another half a century — in 1896 — the greatest living authority on Jewish statistics gave their number as eleven millions. And now after this short interval it is officially established that there are over thirteen million Jews in the world. And the surprising feature of this latest calculation is the officially-authenticated fact that, in the country where they are most persecuted, and which during the past three decades has driven forth millions to seek an asylum in other countries, there are more Jews to-day than ever before; and this in spite of pogroms, and baptisms, and overcrowding, and starvation, and the pursuance of a merciless policy of repression which led Pobiedonostsef to prognosticate that, in the end, a third of Russia's Jews would emigrate, a third would die, and a third would join the dominant faith. The old story of Israel in Egypt renews itself to-day in Russia : "The more they afflicted them, the more they multiplied."

[1] Ezek. vi. 9.

*My people ; . . . and I will put My Spirit in you, and ye
shall live, . . . and ye shall know that I am Jehovah.*" [1]
Neither shall this new national and spiritual life be
transient in its character. No; not only shall they live,
but "their children" also, the thought expressed in these
words being the same as "their children also shall see it,"
in the 9th verse. "*And shall return*" (or "turn again ")—
not only to their land but to their God, the word being the
same which the prophets constantly used when calling to
Israel to repent—as, for instance: "*Turn ye, turn ye from
your evil ways : for why will ye die, O house of Israel ?*" [2]

In the 10th verse the gathering and leading back by
the Shepherd of Israel of His scattered flock are more
minutely described :

"*I will bring them back out of the land of Egypt, and
from Assyria will I gather them*"; which two Powers, to
quote another writer, may perhaps be regarded as "standing
here as of old, for the two conflicting empires (Egypt to
the south and Assyria to the north) between which Israel
lay, at whose hand she had suffered, and who represent the
countries which lay beyond." But there is no need to
allegorise the names of Egypt and Assyria, as almost all
the commentators do, as used only typically of the lands of
Israel's oppression. I believe it to be a prophecy which
merges into the most distant future (from the prophet's
then point of view), and will be literally fulfilled at the
final restoration, "when *Jehovah shall lift up His hand*

---

[1] Ezek. xxxvii. 11–14.

[2] This is one of those scriptures which seem to speak of a turning of Israel to
God while still in the "far countries" of their dispersion, and may appear to be
in conflict with the many prophecies which predict a restoration of Israel in
unbelief, and their conversion in the land at the visible appearing of Christ.
But there is no real conflict or contradiction between these various scriptures,
the solution of the apparent difficulty being in the fact that while a large representative section of the nation will be in Palestine in a condition of unbelief
when the Lord appears, and will be converted there, the remaining part of
the nation will still be in the dispersion, and upon them the spirit of grace
and supplication will come in the "far countries" where they shall be found.
The subject is fully dealt with in *Types, Psalms, and Prophecies*, pp. 364–
377.

*again the second time to recover the remnant of His people,
. . . and shall assemble the outcasts of Israel, and gather
together the dispersed of Judah from Assyria and from
Egypt, . . . and from the four corners of the earth."* [1]
It is a fact that there are now many Jews scattered in the
regions which formed the " Assyrian " or Babylon empire [2]
as well as in Egypt, and with the revival and progress of the
East their numbers in those countries will greatly increase.

And when Jehovah thus gathers them and leads
them back, He will bring them *" into the land of
Gilead and Lebanon,"* which probably represent the whole
promised land east and west of the Jordan.   But even
there *"place will not be found for them,"* which reminds us
of Isa. xlix. 20, 21, where we read : *" The children of thy
bereavement shall yet say in thine ears, The place is too strait
for me : give place to me that I may dwell.   Then shalt
thou say in thine heart, Who hath begotten me these, seeing I
have been bereaved of my children, and am solitary, an exile,
and wandering to and fro ? Who hath brought up these ?
Behold, I was left alone ; these, where were they ? "*—which
again reminds us of the jubilant exclamation in Isa. liv. :

> *" Sing [exult], O barren, thou that didst not bear ;
> Break forth into singing, and cry, thou that didst not
>   travail :
> For more are the children of the desolate
> Than of the married wife, saith Jehovah."*

[1] Isa. xi. 11, 12.

[2] Ewald, Hitzig, and other writers who deny the post-exilic origin of the
second half of Zechariah, have argued from the mention of " Assyria (and not
Babylon) that these chapters must have been written before the Babylonian
Captivity and soon after the overthrow of the northern kingdom of Israel " ; but
it must be borne in mind that in post-exilic times the King of Babylon was
sometimes styled " the King of Assyria " (Ezra vi. 22 ; 2 Kings xxiii. 29 ; Judith
i. 7, ii. 1 ; comp. Herod. i. 178, 188), inasmuch as his authority extended over
Assyria.   In later books the expressions, " King of the Persians " and " King of
Assyria " are interchanged.   Compare Ezra (1 Esdr. ii. 30) with vii. 15.   The
King of Persia is also styled King of Babylon (Ezra v. 13 ; Neh. xiii. 6), and
references are sometimes made to Assyria when Babylon is really signified, or
when, as in this passage, allusion is made to the enemies of the covenant people
north and south of their land (comp. Lam. v. 6 ; Jer. ii. 18).

The words are addressed to Jerusalem, the counterpart of Sarah, in her barrenness at first and her fruitfulness afterwards. She is barren now—not, indeed, because she had never borne children, but because in her captivity and exile she had been robbed of her children, and as a holy city had all this time given birth to none. But she is to awake and sing, because the children that shall gather around her after her long period of desolateness would be more than when in the time before her calamity came upon her she had as a married wife—yea, so great will be the increase of Zion's future population, that, instead of bewailing her lonely and desolate condition, she shall even hear her children say " in her own ears " that the place is too strait, and the call to the surrounding nations : " Give place (literally, ' give way,' or ' fall back '), that I may be able to settle down."

I have elsewhere pointed out [1] that the land which God by oath and covenant promised to the fathers is about fifty times as large as the part which hitherto the Jews actually possessed, and that it is only pitiable ignorance which made the superficial Voltaire utter the blasphemy that the God of the Jews must have been a little God, because He gave His people a land no larger than Wales, and called it " a good land and a large " (Ex. iii. 8). Surely a land which includes within its boundaries an area at least one-third more than the whole of France may with right be called " a large land " ; but it is possible that even the larger land, with its desert parts transformed into fruitful fields, will not suffice to hold the whole of blessed Israel in the millennial period, so great and rapid will be the increase of the saved remnant.

In the 11th verse God's wonderful works on behalf of His people in the past are again alluded to as the basis and illustration of what He will do for them in the yet greater deliverance of the future. When He brought them out of Egypt, He went before them in the pillar of cloud ; and when pursued by Pharaoh and his host, and there

[1] See *The Jewish Problem.*

seemed no way of escape, He made a way in the sea, and a path in the deep waters for His redeemed to pass over.[1] Now, "as in the days of thy coming forth out of the land of Egypt," He says, "will I show him marvellous things."[2] Once again He Himself will march at their head, and no obstacle shall be allowed to hinder the progress of His redeemed people on their way back to Zion. Should any hindrance present itself, even if it be as formidable as the Red Sea at the exodus from Egypt, "*He shall pass through the sea of affliction* (or straitness), *and shall smite the waves in the sea, and all the depths of the river* (or Nile) *shall dry up* (even as the Jordan did before the Ark of the Covenant): *and the pride of Assyria* (Israel's former oppressor from the north) *shall be brought down, and the sceptre of Egypt* (Israel's enemy from the south) *shall depart.*"

But these two empires may also represent Gentile world-power in general, which will then give way to the Kingdom of the Messiah which the God of heaven shall set up, Whose blessed rule shall extend from Mount Zion even unto the ends of the earth.

And not only will the Shepherd of Israel gather them and lead them back to their own habitation, removing by His Almighty power and grace every obstacle out of the way, but there in their own land, when the Spirit shall have been poured upon them from on high, they shall be "strong in the Lord and in the power of His might," and ready to do exploits in His name. "*I will strengthen them in Jehovah,*" we read in the last verse of our chapter, "*and in His Name shall they walk up and down*"—which last expression may denote first their life, or walk and conversation, which shall all be rooted in God, and be in full accord with "*His Name,*" which stands for His revealed character, which shall then be fully and gloriously manifested in their midst in the person of their Messiah, the image of the invisible God. But the phrase וּבִשְׁמוֹ יִתְהַלָּכוּ, *u-bhish'mo yithallakhu,* probably means also that they shall *walk up and down* in His Name, as His messengers and representatives, dispensing

[1] Isa. li. 10.   [2] Mic. vii. 15.

the blessings of Messiah's gospel among the nations by whom they shall be known as the " priests of Jehovah," and be welcomed as " the ministers of our God," [1] נְאָם יְהֹוָה, *neum Yehovah*—" the saying, or ' utterance,' of Jehovah."

These are the last words of the chapter, and form, so to say, the *signature* which stands pledged to the fulfilment of the contents of the prophecy.

And yet even evangelical writers and commentators deny that there ever will be a literal fulfilment of these plain and solemn predictions, and see in them at the most only forecasts of the gradual spread of Christianity and of the absorption of a certain number of Jews into the Church. Thus, one German scholar, after summarising the contents of the whole prophecy from chap. ix. 11 to the end of chap. x., says : " The principle of fulfilment is of a spiritual kind, and was effected through the gathering of the Jews into the Kingdom of Christ, which commenced in the times of the Apostles, and will continue till the remnant of Israel is converted to Christ its Saviour." [2]

And another, to whose elaborate and, in some respects, useful work reference has often been made in these " notes," says : " In the remarkable position occupied by Israel in the early Christian Church—for our Lord and His apostles were Jews, and the majority of the early evangelists were men of this nation—in the wonderful fact that the Jews, though politically crushed beneath the Gentile yoke, conquered the nations of the earth by means of that religion which sprang from their midst—in such facts this prophecy, and other similar prophecies, found a most glorious and real fulfilment. The nations have been enlightened by the Jews, and books written by Jewish pens have become the laws and oracles of the world." [3]

But, as I have had occasion to remark more than once, such method of interpretation turns the great prophetic utterances in the Bible into mere hyperbole, and substitutes an unnatural and shadowy meaning for what is plain and obvious, thereby throwing a vagueness and uncertainty over

[1] Isa. lvi. 6.   [2] Keil.   [3] Wright.

all Scripture.   No, no ; just as the scattering of Israel was
literal, so the gathering also will be *literal* ; and it is not in
the absorption of a remnant of the Jewish people into the
Church, and in the gradual spread of " Christianity " that
" these prophecies find a most glorious and real fulfilment,"
but in a yet future nationally restored and converted Israel,
which shall yet be the centre of the Kingdom of God and
of His Christ, and the channel of blessing to all the nations
of the earth.

Chapter 16

A DARK EPISODE
THE REJECTION OF THE TRUE SHEPHERD AND THE RULE OF THE FALSE
Zechariah 11

Open thy doors, O Lebanon, that the fire may devour thy cedars. Wail, O fir-trees, for the cedar is fallen, because the goodly ones are destroyed : wail, O ye oaks of Bashan, for the strong forest is come down. A voice of the wailing of the shepherds ! for their glory is destroyed : a voice of the roaring of young lions ! for the pride of the Jordan is laid waste. Thus said Jehovah my God : Feed the flock of slaughter; whose possessors slay them, and hold themselves not guilty ; and they that sell them say, Blessed be Jehovah, for I am rich : and their own shepherds pity them not. For I will no more pity the inhabitants of the land, saith Jehovah : but, lo, I will deliver the men every one into his neighbour's hand, and into the hand of his king : and they shall smite the land, and out of their hand I will not deliver them. So I fed the flock of slaughter, verily the poor of the flock. And I took unto me two staves : the one I called Beauty, and the other I called Bands, and I fed the flock. And I cut off the three shepherds in one month ; for my soul was weary of them, and their soul also loathed me. Then said I, I will not feed you ; that which dieth, let it die ; and that which is to be cut off, let it be cut off; and let them that are left eat every one the flesh of another. And I took my staff Beauty, and cut it asunder, that I might break my covenant which I had made with all the peoples. And it was broken in that day ; and thus the poor of the flock that gave heed unto me knew that it was the word of Jehovah. And I said unto them, If ye think good, give me my hire ; and if not, forbear. So they weighed for my hire thirty pieces of silver. And Jehovah said unto me, Cast it unto the potter, the goodly price that I was prised at by them. And I took the thirty pieces of silver, and cast them unto the potter, in the house of Jehovah. Then I cut asunder mine other staff, even Bands, that I might break the brotherhood between Judah and Israel. And Jehovah said unto me, Take unto thee· yet again the instruments of a foolish shepherd. For, lo, I will raise up a shepherd in the land, who will not visit those that are cut off, neither will seek those that are scattered, nor heal that which is broken, nor feed that which is sound ; but he will eat the flesh of the fat sheep, and will tear their hoofs in pieces. Woe to the worthless shepherd that leaveth the flock ! the sword shall be upon his arm, and upon his right eye : his arm shall be clean dried up, and his right eye shall be utterly darkened.

Chapter 16

THE 11th chapter stands in the same relation to the verbal prophecies which make up the second part of Zechariah, as the 5th does in relation to the first part of the visions.

"*All the ways of the Lord are mercy and truth*." . . . And again, "*I will sing of mercy and of judgment: unto Thee, O Lord, will I sing*."[1]

These words of the inspired Psalmist may, as an old writer well observes, be written over the whole Book of Zechariah.

In the first part we have first a series of five visions which in various symbols set forth "the good and comfortable words"[2] of promise concerning restoration, enlargement, and temporal and spiritual blessing which God has yet in store for the land and the people of Israel. But to complete the prophetic forecast of the future, and also (to borrow an expression from another writer) "to prevent an abuse of the proclamation of salvation," the obverse side of the picture, which sets forth a yet future apostasy and judgment, had to be presented. This is done in the visions of the Flying Roll and the Ephah, in the first of which we hear God's great curse pronounced against sin; and in the second we see its banishment from His own land and presence "to the land of Shinar"—the original place of rebellion and apostasy against God—where it shall meet with its final doom.

In the 6th chapter, however, we emerge again from the dark valley of sin and apostasy, and we are shown in the symbolical transaction there set forth how, in spite of it all,

[1] Ps. xxv. 10, ci. 1.　　　　　　　　　[2] Chap. i. 13.

Israel's Messiah will yet be crowned, and sit and rule upon His throne, and be a Priest upon His throne; and how, not only Israel, but "they that are far off," shall find a place in the glorious Temple which He shall build.

And thus it is also with the second part. First, we have a series of verbal prophecies, which are full of promise of future restoration and blessedness; and then, in order to prevent a carnal misuse of the promises of salvation on the part of the godless majority in the nation, and also as a hint that the full realisation of the promises was, from the prophet's point of view, in the yet distant future—we are suddenly in the 11th chapter brought to the precipice of a tremendous gulf of national apostasy and consequent judgment.

But even from this deep abyss we shall emerge again in the last three chapters, where Israel's national repentance and mourning over Him whom they have sold for thirty pieces of silver, and "pierced," are depicted for us in inspired language, which reads almost like history instead of prophecy. And the end and blessed issue of Israel's national conversion and reunion with their Messiah will be, that "Jehovah will be King over all the earth: in that day shall Jehovah be One, and His Name One." [1]

The first brief section into which our chapter is divided, consisting of vers. 1–3, may be regarded as the prelude of what follows. In dramatic style the prophet announces the desolating judgment which will sweep over the whole land:

"*Open thy doors, O Lebanon, that the fire may devour thy cedars.*

"*Howl, O fir-tree, for the cedar is fallen, because the goodly ones are spoiled: howl, O ye oaks of Bashan, for the strong forest is come down.*

"*A voice of the howling of the shepherds! for their glory is spoiled: a voice of the roaring of young lions! for the pride of Jordan is spoiled.*"

There is a blending of the literal with the figurative in these verses. The primary reference is very probably to

[1] Chap. xiv. 9.

the physical desolation which is to befall the land in consequence of its being invaded by an enemy. The progress of the devastating scourge which is here depicted has been graphically described by another:

"Lebanon is bidden to open its doors; that is, its steep mountain paths, in order that the fire of the enemy might consume its cedars. The firs, or cypresses, are called upon to howl or lament because the cedars are fallen; for if the more excellent and valuable trees were felled without mercy, the poor firs and cypresses must needs expect a similar fate.

"From the heights of Lebanon the destructive storm sweeps down on the land of Bashan, and the oaks—the pride of the land (with their kindly shade from the burning heat)—are likewise felled by the enemy to meet the wants of the invading army, and to construct his means of offence and defence. Thus, the wood hitherto practically inaccessible is brought low. The desolating storm sweeps from the high lands to the low lands. The very shepherds are forced to howl, because their splendour is laid waste; namely, the pasture lands in which they were wont to feed and tend their flocks in the day of peace and quiet. The conflagration extends even to the south of the land. Judah is wrapped in flames. The close thickets which fringed the Jordan river, as it ran along through the territory of the southern kingdom, are consumed by the fire. The thickets which shut in that stream so closely that its waters could not be seen till the traveller was close on its banks, which were wont to be the abode of lions and other beasts of prey in those days, are likewise described as destroyed. 'The pride of Jordan' is rendered desolate, and hence the voice of roaring of lions is heard wailing over the general ruin."

But while the physical desolation of the land is that which is primarily set forth in this brief opening section of the chapter, there is also contained in it, if not directly, at least indirectly, an announcement of a destructive judgment of the people, "inasmuch as the desolation of the land also involves the destruction of the people living in it."

Most interpreters, indeed, both Jewish and Christian, regard the language as figurative. Thus, the "cedars" are taken to mean the highest and noblest in the land, while the "cypresses," or "firs," represent the common people, who are commanded to "howl," because since the "cedars" have fallen there is no hope of their being spared. Certainly in Ezek. xvii. 3 the family of David is represented by a lofty cedar, and in Isa. xiv. 8 and Jer. xxii. 6–7 the cedars of Lebanon stand as "the emblem of the glory of the Jewish State." But even though "the scientific expositor" may regard the allegorical interpretation of this particular passage as "fanciful," [1] and we ourselves would by no means wholly commit ourselves to it, it is none the less of interest that a very ancient Jewish interpretation identifies Lebanon here with the Temple "which was built with cedars from Lebanon, towering aloft upon a strong summit —the spiritual glory and eminence of Jerusalem, as the Lebanon was of the whole country." Thus Kimchi, after explaining these verses as a prophecy of the destruction of the kings of the Gentile nations, in accordance with the interpretation of the Targum of Jonathan, who paraphrases, "A voice of the howling of the shepherds because their glory is spoiled" (ver. 3), as : "The voice of the crying of the kings because their provinces are desolated," he says : "This interpretation is according to the Targum, but our Rabbis of blessed memory have interpreted the chapter of the desolation of the Second Temple, and Lebanon is the Holy Temple." [2]

---

[1] Dr. Wright.

[2] The remarkable tradition which Kimchi here quotes, is found in the *Talm. Bab.*, *Treatise Yoma* (fol. 39, col. 2), and is as follows : "Our rabbis have handed down the tradition, that forty years before the destruction of the Temple, the lot (for the goat that was to be sacrificed on the Day of Atonement) did not come out on the right side, neither did the scarlet tongue (that used to be fastened between the horns of the scapegoat) turn white (as, according to tradition, it used to do, to signify that the sins of the people were forgiven), neither did the western lamp burn ; the doors of the sanctuary also opened of their own accord, until R. Johanan, the son of Zacchai, reproved them. He said : 'O sanctuary, sanctuary ! why dost thou trouble thyself?' R. Isaac, the son of Tavlai, says : 'Why is the Temple called Lebanon (white mountain)?' Answer :

But whether literal or figurative, the passage announces a judgment which would embrace, as already stated, the land and the people, and not stop short of the holy city, or sanctuary.

In the next and longest section of the chapter (vers. 4–14), the prophet proceeds to set forth the causes and the manner of the judgment which in the first three verses had been announced in general terms.

Let us first take the briefest possible glimpse at the main contents of this paragraph: " Israel, prophetically viewed as given over to judgment, is called צֹאן הַהֲרֵגָה (*tson ha-haregah*), " sheep of slaughter," or, " of slaughtering."

As a manifestation of God's mercy, however, an effort is to be made to save them. The prophet, representing the Lord as the True Shepherd of Israel, is commanded to feed them, and he, in obedience to the command, takes upon himself the office of the shepherd and endeavours to rescue them from the wicked shepherds who are leading them to certain destruction. The obstinacy of the majority of those whom he seeks to save, however, compels him to give up the office and leave the flock to their utter misery and ruin. Then (in order to make manifest the ingratitude, as well as the wickedness, of those on whom such care had in vain been bestowed) the shepherd asks for his wages, and they in mockery offer him thirty pieces of silver—the sum which, according to the law, was to be paid in compensation for a slave who had been killed (Ex. xxi. 22). This money the prophet, by God's command, throws down contemptuously in the Temple, in the presence of all the people, " to the potter," after which he breaks the last emblem of his relation to them as shepherd.

This is the briefest outline which we shall endeavour to fill in when we come to the exposition, but before doing this one or two further preliminary remarks are still necessary.

'Because it makes white the sins of Israel.' Rav. Zutra, the son of Tobiah, says: ' Why is the Temple called "forest"'' (Zech. xi. 2)? Answer: Because it is written, ' The house of the forest of Lebanon' (1 Kings vii. 2), etc."

(1) As just stated, the prophet must be viewed as acting in this chapter not in his own person, but, in a very special sense, as the representative of God. This is clear from such expressions as, " I cut off three shepherds in one month " (ver. 8), " that I might break my covenant which I have made with all the peoples " (ver. 10), etc. ; which neither Zechariah nor any other prophet did, or could do, but the Lord only.

Hengstenberg, Pusey, and others think that the prophet acts here directly as the type, or representative, of the Angel of Jehovah or the Messiah ; but to this most modern commentators object, on the ground that, while in the visions recorded in the first part of Zechariah the Angel of Jehovah is indeed spoken of as an actor, " no intimation whatever is given in this chapter that the Angel of Jehovah is to be regarded as the doer of the things which are here related, and we have no right to assume that the prophecy is a continuation of the visions in the earlier part of this book."

But it practically comes to much the same thing, whether we regard the prophet as representing in his actions as shepherd, Jehovah, or more directly the Messiah, for the coming of the Messiah is often spoken of in the Old Testament as the coming of Jehovah. In Ezek. xxxiv., for instance, Jehovah Himself is represented, in His capacity as the true Shepherd of Israel, as seeking, saving, strengthening, healing, and satisfying His people ; but as we read on in that chapter we become aware that it is not Jehovah directly who is going to do all this, but *mediately* through the Messiah. " *And I will set them up one shepherd over them, and He shall feed them, even My servant David ;* He shall feed them, *and He shall be their shepherd* "— namely, the true David, the Messiah, as the Jews themselves have always rightly interpreted this passage.

And so it is always : in all His relations and dealings with men, both *in mercy and in judgment*, it is God *in Christ* who acts. As a matter of fact, this prophecy (as is admitted by one who is not inclined to see many references to Christ in the Book of Zechariah) " is one of a peculiarly

---

Messianic character, and (as we shall see more clearly farther on) what Jehovah is said here to perform was done in very deed by the Messiah."

(2) The second preliminary question to be settled is the time to which this prophecy, and more especially the symbolical action described in vers. 7–14, is to be referred. Two or three Jewish commentators, who are influenced in their interpretations by their hostility to Christianity, and some of the "modern" rationalistic Christian theologians, to whom Christ and the New Testament are non-existent, or of no account in their interpretations of the Old Testament, refer it to some event, or events, which they imagine occurred in the time of the First Temple before the Babylonian Exile.[1]

A full and lengthy refutation of this view is, however, supplied by another Jewish commentator, namely, Abarbanel. One argument of his is, of itself, quite sufficient.

"To what purpose," he asks, "should God show the prophet past events, which he had seen with his own eyes and with the eyes of his father; and what necessity was there to make known to him the captivity of the tribes and the desolation of the first house, which had occurred but a short time before; and (above all) to do this in parables, which are only employed in reference to the future, to make events known before they happen? But with regard to the past, information is not conveyed in parables. It is not possible to suppose that God would communicate a plain matter of recent history in obscure symbols, and, therefore, the symbolical representation cannot refer to the past, and must predict what was to happen during the time of the Second Temple."[2]

[1] I may quote as an instance, Professor Driver, who says that this scripture "is to be interpreted in all probability, not as a prediction, but as a symbolical description of events which had happened recently when the prophet wrote."

[2] It is of interest to observe that as far as the "Jewish interpretation" is concerned, not only Abarbanel, but the Talmud (both the Jerusalem and the Babylonian), Joseph Ben Gorion (Breithaupt's edition, p. 889), Aben Ezra, Abraham "the Levite," Alshech, and even R. Isaac of Troki in his polemical work against Christianity—all agree with Christians in applying this prophecy to the time of the Second Temple.

But even among those who rightly apply this prophecy to the time of the Second Temple, there is still a difference of opinion. According to some, the whole of the dealings of God with Israel during the time of the Second Temple are alluded to. This is the view of most of the Jewish interpreters and of eminent Christian commentators. Thus, according to Calvin, " the Lord discharged the duties of a shepherd by means of all His faithful servants in the time of the Second Temple, but most perfectly of all by Christ "; and Koehler sees in this scripture " a representation of the mediatorial work in the plan of salvation, of which Daniel was the first representative, and which was afterwards exhibited on the one hand by Haggai and Zechariah, and on the other hand by Zerubbabel and his successors as the civil rulers of Israel, and by Joshua and those priests who resumed the duties of their office along with him." But the ground on which this view is chiefly based—namely, that because the prophecy in chaps. ix. and x. embraces the whole period of the Second Temple, from Alexander the Great to the coming of Christ, and even merging into the time of the end—therefore, this one in chap. xi. must be equally comprehensive, and start from the same historical point of time, is, to say the least, a very uncertain one.

For my own part, I believe that the more carefully we look into this solemn scripture, the more manifest it becomes that the state of things which it prophetically depicts answers exactly to the condition of the Jewish nation immediately preceding the final catastrophe at the destruction of the Second Temple, and the dissolution of the Jewish polity by the Romans, and does not correspond to their condition and experience during the whole, or even greater part, of their history after the partial restoration from Babylon.

For this, and other reasons which for lack of space I cannot enter here, I must confess myself on the side of those who view this 11th chapter as restricted to the *principal object* of the preceding great prophecy (chaps. ix.

and x.), namely, the prediction concerning the coming of the Messiah (ix. 9–10), which is in this 11th chapter presented from another point of view, in order that the meaning may be fully understood, and "not be so perverted by a one-sided and worldly interpretation as to become pernicious instead of salutary";[1] or, in other words, that this prophecy refers particularly to the office of shepherd which was to be filled by the Messiah, and to His blessed labours and experience in seeking to save the "lost sheep of the house of Israel."

Let us now examine the scripture itself. There is discussion among commentators whether the phrase צֹאן הַהֲרֵגָה, tson ha-haregah — "sheep of slaughter," describes the Jewish nation as a flock which is already being slaughtered, or as one which is marked out for slaughter at a future time. There is no doubt that the condition of the people was deplorable enough in the time of the prophet, for already in the 10th chapter he describes them as those who "go their way (or 'wander') like sheep," and "are 'afflicted' (or 'oppressed') because there is no shepherd."[2]

Already they were a prey to false shepherds, and subject to the abuse and oppression of their own unfaithful civil and religious rulers and foreign tyrants; but, as may be gathered from the introductory remarks, I regard it as a special prophetic designation of the people during the time to which this prophecy has particular reference when it became more terribly and literally true.

The 5th verse illustrates the truth of the designation in the 4th verse. They may, indeed, be described as sheep of slaughter, for "*their possessors* (literally, '*buyers*') *slay* (or '*strangle*') *them, and hold themselves not guilty; and they that sell them say, Blessed be Jehovah, for I am rich.*"

The buyers and sellers are those into whose hands the nation is delivered, and who do with them as they please, namely, the Gentile powers. They are represented as thinking themselves "not guilty" in all their cruel actions in relation to the Jewish people. This reminds us of

[1] Hengstenberg. [2] Chap. x. 2.

Jer. l. 6–7, which was most probably before the mind of Zechariah. "*My people hath been lost sheep : their shepherds have caused them to go astray : . . . all that found them have devoured them : and their adversaries say we offend not (are 'not guilty'* [1]), *because they have sinned against Jehovah, the habitation of justice, Jehovah, the hope of their fathers.*"

But, though it is true that Israel on account of their most terrible sins have been handed over by God as a righteous punishment into the hands of the Gentile world-powers, they are not held innocent for their cruel deeds towards them. This we see from the same 50th chapter of Jeremiah, where God says : "*Israel is a scattered sheep ; the lions (the Gentile world-powers who are likened to ferocious wild beasts) have driven him away : first, the king of Assyria hath devoured him ; and last this Nebuchadnezzar king of Babylon hath broken his bones. Therefore thus saith Jehovah of hosts, the God of Israel : Behold, I will punish the king of Babylon and his land, as I have punished the king of Assyria.*" [2]

And what God did to Assyria and Babylon, He did also to Medo-Persia, Greece, and Rome, and still will do to nations and individuals whom He uses as a scourge against His own people, for His word in another part of Jeremiah still holds true : "*Therefore all they that devour thee shall be devoured ; and all thine adversaries, every one of them, shall go into captivity ; and they that spoil thee shall be a spoil ; and all they that prey upon thee will I give for a prey.*" [3]

But to return more directly to our scripture. Not only will they be thus abused and "slain" by Gentile oppressors, but "*their own shepherds,*" by which we must understand their own civil and religiou. rulers, those who ought to have fed and defended them—"*pity them not*" [4]—thus proving themselves false shepherds, who only sought their own, and were the chief cause of the sheep becoming a prey.

---

[1] נֶאְשָׁם לֹא—the same verb as in Zech. xi. 5.

[2] Jer. l. 17, 18.   [3] Jer. xxx. 16.

[4] יֹאמַר לֹא יַחְמֹל—*yomar lo-yachmol*—the verbs "sayeth" and "hath no pity" are singular — an emphatic mode of expression, by which each individual is represented as doing or not doing the action of the verb.

There is a sad gradation in the wretchedness of the people thus given over to judgment, as described in vers. 5–6. First, the Gentile nations pity them not, but buy and sell and slay them as " sheep of slaughter." Secondly, their own shepherds, from whom something different might have been expected, have no compassion for them ; and thirdly, and most terrible of all, " *I will no more pity the inhabitants of the land, saith Jehovah,*" for long-continued obduracy exhausts even the patience of Jehovah ; and there comes a time in the history of nations and of individuals when the long-suffering God has to say " there is no more remedy " (or " healing "[1]), and His righteous anger has to manifest itself in judgment.

In the solemn words of the 6th verse we have a forecast of what would take place after the rejection of the Good Shepherd, and the care and protection of God over His people would be withdrawn. God's anger will show itself, not only in a negative manner (" I will no more pity "), but also in a positive way.

" *And, lo* " (or " behold "), this is God's way of calling attention to something great which He is going to do either with nations or individuals—" *I will deliver the men every one into the hands of his neighbour, and into the hand of his king : and they shall smite* (literally, ' *break down,*' i.e., *lay waste*) *the land*"—solemn and awful words which well describe in advance the confusion, captious strife, hatred, and mutual destruction, which followed soon after the rejection of our Lord Jesus, their true Messiah and Shepherd, the detailed accounts of which may be read in Josephus, and even in the Talmud.

A parallel passage is found in Jer. xix. 9, which was fulfilled in the siege of Jerusalem by the Chaldeans, and the destruction of the First Temple : " *And I will cause them to eat the flesh of their sons and the flesh of their daughters, and they shall eat every one the flesh of his friend in the siege and in the straitness, wherewith their enemies, and they that seek their lives, shall straiten them* "—where

[1] 2 Chron. xxxvi. 16.

also a twofold cause of their ruin is given, namely, strife among themselves, which is heightened by sufferings and oppression inflicted by the foe without. Contention within, and the enemy without, are not only mentioned in the passage just quoted from Jeremiah, but they are linked together by Zechariah himself in chap. viii. 10, as the two chief methods of punishment employed by God for the chastisement of His people. "*There was no peace to him that went out or came in because of the adversary, and I set all men every one against his neighbour*"—"which miserable state of things existed before the Babylonian Captivity and is represented in the 11th chapter as returning with still greater force on account of the base ingratitude and relapse into apostasy on the part of the people." [1]

The phrase, "*into the hand of his king*," must be understood as referring to the king of "his," *i.e.*, Judah's own choice. That it is of a foreign oppressor, and not of a native ruler, that the prophecy speaks, is evident, among other things, from the fact that the Jews had no king at the time of Zechariah, and that this prophet never (either in the first or second half of the book), even in his descriptions of the future, speaks of any king, with the exception of the Messiah.

When, on that fateful eve of the Passover, Pilate brought Jesus out before the Jews, and half in mockery said, "Behold your king," they cried, "Away with him, crucify him ! " and when he again appealed, " Shall I crucify your king ? " the chief priests, who constituted themselves the leaders of the people, answered : "We have no king but Cæsar ! " and, having thus deliberately made this terrible choice, they were "delivered " into Cæsar's hand ; and soon after the Roman armies, under Vespasian and Titus, laid waste the land and destroyed the people.   How terrible was the retribution.   "If we let this man thus alone," said the chief priests and Pharisees in council, "all men will believe on him, and the Romans will come and take away both our place and our nation."   So they decided to carry

---

[1] Hengstenberg.

out the wicked counsel of Caiaphas, who said: "It is expedient for you that one man die for the people, and that the whole nation perish not," and handed Him over to the Romans. But the very thing they feared, and on account of which they decided on committing the great national crime of betraying their Kinsman-Redeemer into the hands of the Gentiles, came upon them, for these very Romans did come, "and take away both their place and their nation."

But, terrible as is the punishment which came upon the Jewish nation in consequence of their rejection of the Good Shepherd, we must beware of wrong conclusions, and of perverting Scripture by false interpretation. Thus, Hengstenberg, Pusey, and other commentators—who are great literalists as far as the threatenings and curses are concerned in applying them to the Jewish people, but "spiritualise" and misapply all the *promises*—lay great stress on the last words of the 6th verse : " I will not deliver them," in proof that the captivity of the Jewish nation brought about by the Romans "shall be without remedy or end." Pusey, for instance, quotes with great approval the words of Jerome: " Hear, O Jew, who holdest out to thyself hopes most vain, and hearest not the Lord strongly asserting, '*I will not deliver them out of their hands,*' that thy captivity among the Romans shall have no end."

But this is a one-sided perversion of the truth. As far as the generation which is contemplated in this prophecy is concerned, there was "no remedy," or "deliverance," as was the case also with the generation of the time of the first Captivity and the destruction of the Temple by the Babylonians, of which similar expressions are used ; and as is the case in every generation with those who prove themselves obdurate, and persistently harden their hearts and refuse God's gracious call: " Turn ye, turn ye, from your evil ways : for why will ye die, O house of Israel."

But, as far as the purpose of God with the Jewish nation is concerned, it ever abides unchanged and unalterable, for the unchangeable God remains true and faithful,

though all men prove liars. This same prophet, who in
the 11th chapter predicts Israel's rejection of the Good
Shepherd, and their consequent rejection of God for a time,
graphically describes in the last three chapters, which deal
with the last events of this age, Israel's restoration and
conversion when the spirit of grace and of supplication shall
be poured upon them, and they shall bitterley lament and
repent of their great national sin, and look upon Him
whom they have pierced.

And this is in accord also with the clear statements of
the New Testament, which tells us that "all Israel shall be
saved, even as it is written : There shall come out of Zion
the Deliverer, and shall turn away ungodliness from Jacob ;
for this is My covenant unto them when I shall take away
their sins."

And even in the generation of which the terrible words
are written, " I will not deliver them out of their hands,"
there were "the poor of the flock " (vers. 7, 11) who did
"give heed " and " knew the word of Jehovah," who (as we
shall see) are none other than the remnant, according to
the election of grace, which, blessed be God! has never
been wanting even in the darkest period of Israel's history.

We proceed to what may be said to constitute the
heart of this remarkable prophecy, namely, the actual
"feeding," or shepherding, of the flock which, through their
own obstinacy, became "the flock of slaughter."

" So I fed the flock of slaughter, verily the poor of the
flock.   And I took unto me two staves : the one I called
Beauty, and the other I called Bands, and I fed the flock.
And I cut off the three shepherds in one month ; for my
soul was weary of them, and their soul also loathed me.
Then said I, I will not feed you : that that dieth, let it die ;
and that that is to be cut off, let it be cut off ; and let them
which are left eat every one the flesh of another.   And I
took my staff Beauty, and cut it asunder, that I might break
my covenant which I had made with all the peoples.   And it
was broken in that day ; and thus the poor of the flock
that gave heed unto me knew that it was the word of the

Lord. And I said unto them, If ye think good, give me my hire; and if not, forbear. So they weighed for my hire thirty pieces of silver. And the Lord said unto me, Cast it unto the potter, the goodly price that I was prised at of them. And I took the thirty pieces of silver, and cast them unto the potter, in the house of the Lord. Then I cut asunder mine other staff, even Bands, that I might break the brotherhood between Judah and Israel" (Zech. xi. 7–14).

We may pause for a moment to ask whether the symbolical transaction which is here described was an inward or outward one. Most of the Jewish commentators take the latter view. Thus Abarbanel, for instance, says: "God commanded the prophet to perform a real action, and in a waking state, which action was to be an intimation and a sign of that which was to happen in God's dealings with Israel," and adds: "By attending to the affairs of the prophets thou mayest know that God, blessed be He, sometimes commanded them to perform real actions, and in a waking state, and afterwards explained to them the reason of the command according to the sign that was in them.[1] . . . But sometimes the blessed God commanded the prophets to do things foreign to their character, and unnecessary for them to do; which things were also to be a sign and a type of coming events, and did not expound the meaning, because He knew that the thing itself could be understood" (as, for instance, Isa. viii. 1–2; Ezek. iv. 1–2, v. 1). But, as has been observed, the narrative in this chapter differs in some respects from the symbolical actions of the prophets and from Zechariah's own visions.

"The symbolical actions of the prophets are actions of their own: this involves acts which it would be impossible to represent, except as a sort of drama. Such are the very central points, the feeding of the flock, which yet are intelligent men who understand God's doings: the cutting off of the three shepherds; the asking for the price; the unworthy price offered; the casting it aside. It differs

[1] He quotes Isa. xx. 2, viii. 4; Jer. xiii. 1, etc., and Ezekiel as examples.

from Zechariah's own visions, in that they are for the most part exhibited to the eye, and Zechariah's own part is simply to inquire their meaning and to learn it, and to receive further revelation. In one case only (chap. iii. 5) he himself interposes in the action of the vision ; but this, too, as asking that it might be done, not as himself doing it. Here (in chap. xi.) he is himself the actor, yet as representing Another, Who alone could cut off shepherds, abandon the people to mutual destruction, annulling the covenant which He had made."[1] Maimonides, then, seems to say rightly : " This, ' I fed the flock of the slaughter,' to the end of the narrative, where he is said to have asked for his hire, to have received it, and to have cast it into the Temple, to the treasurer—all this Zechariah saw in prophetic vision. For the command which he received, and the act which he is said to have done, took place in prophetic vision or dream. This," he adds, "is beyond controversy, as all know who are able to distinguish the possible from the impossible."

Let us bear in mind also that, as has been well observed by an old writer, the actions of the prophets are not always to be understood as actions, but as *predictions*—as, for instance, when God commands Isaiah to " make the heart of the people fat and their ears heavy " ;[2] or when He says that He appointed Jeremiah over the nations, 'to root out, and to break down, and to destroy, and to overthrow, and to build, and to plant " ;[3] or when He commanded the same prophet to cause the nations to drink the cup whereby they should be bereft of their senses.[4] Neither Isaiah nor Jeremiah actually did this, but foretold in advance in this manner what would be. So it is here.

But to proceed to the exposition. And, first, I will deal with what I believe to be a parenthetical sentence in the 7th verse, which occurs again in the 11th verse, and which has greatly puzzled the commentators, and of which all sorts of explanations have been given : " So I fed," we

---

[1] Pusey.
[2] Isa. vi. 10.
[3] Jer. i. 10.
[4] Jer. xxv. 15-27.

read, "the sheep of slaughter"; after which there follow
the three Hebrew words, הַצֹּאן עֲנִיֵּי לָכֵן, *lachen aniyye hatson*,
which the Authorised Version has rendered, "Even you, O
poor of the flock"; and the Revised Version, "Verily, the
poor of the flock"; and the explanation usually given is
that "the poor of the flock" is practically only another
name for "the sheep of slaughter." But this is very
unsatisfactory, for, first, the primary and natural meaning of
the adverb לָכֵן, *lachen*, is not "even" or "verily," but
" *therefore* "; and secondly, the designation " *aniyye ha-am*,"
"the poor of the people," or as the word also means, "the
needy," "the weak," "the afflicted," is almost invariably
used in the Hebrew Bible of the pious or *godly* in the nation
who are persecuted and oppressed by the godless—of those
whom the wicked in his pride "hotly pursue," or persecute,
but who, knowing God to be their refuge, can look up to
Him and say: "But I am *poor* and needy, yet the Lord
thinketh upon me." [1]

Certainly in the 11th verse the "*aniyye hatson*," who
"observed" the prophet, and knew that it was the word of
Jehovah, must refer to the God-fearing portion of the nation.
In brief, I believe that the sentence should be rendered,
" *therefore* (on this account) the poor of the flock," [2] and
that in these three words in the Hebrew there is summed
up the result, or blessed fruit of the labours of the Good
Shepherd. Not altogether in vain, or fruitless, would His
self-sacrificing effort to save the lost sheep of the House of
Israel prove. The mass would indeed prove obstinate,

---

[1] Compare Ps. x. 2-9, xiv. 6, liii. 6, xxxv. 10, xxxvii. 14, xl. 17, lxx. 5,
lxxii. 4, lxxxvi. 1, cix. 16-22; Isa. x. 2, xiv. 32, xli. 17; and many other
places where עָנִי, *ani*, is used.

[2] The LXX has evidently made a great blunder over these sentences, for in
ver. 7 it has for לָכֵן עֲנִיֵּי הַצֹּאן—εἰς τὴν Χαναανῖτιν, "in the land of Chanaan" (or
Canaan), leaving out the word for "sheep" or "flock" altogether; and in ver.
11 it has got οἱ Χαναναῖοι—the Canaanites, or "merchants." And yet some
modern scholars adopt these evident misreadings as the basis of emendations of
their own of the Hebrew text—as, for instance, Sir George Adam Smith, who
has translated the sentence in ver. 7 "for the sheep merchants," and in ver. 11,
"the dealers of the sheep." But the Hebrew text in this place needs no
emendation or alteration when properly understood.

and by rejecting Him choose death rather than life, and thus experience the truth of the awful designation, *tson ha-haregah*, "sheep of slaughter"; but, as has been the case even in the very darkest periods of Israel's history, God would leave in the midst of them "an afflicted and poor people," who would trust in the Name of Jehovah,[1] the remnant according to the election of grace, in and through whom the purposes of God would be carried forward. The New Testament parallel and ultimate fulfilment is in John i. 11: "*He came unto His own, and they that were His received Him not. But as many as received Him, to them gave He the right* (or '*power*') *to become children of God, even to them that believe in His Name.*"

"The elect are the end of all God's dispensations," observes another writer. "He fed all; yet the fruit of His feeding, His toils, His death, the travail of His soul, was in those only who are saved. So also the apostle says: 'Therefore, I endure all things for the elects' sake, that they also may obtain the salvation which is in Christ Jesus with eternal glory.' He fed all; but the poor of the flock alone, those who were despised of men because they would not follow the pride of the high priests and scribes and Pharisees, believed on Him."

On entering his office as shepherd, the prophet "took two staves." The Eastern shepherd, to quote from Dr. Thomson's *The Land and the Book*, "invariably carries a staff or rod with him when he goes forth to feed his flock. It is often bent, or hooked, at one end, which gave rise to the shepherd's crook in the hand of the Christian bishop. With this staff he rules and guides the flock to their green pastures, and defends them from their enemies. With it, also, he corrects them when disobedient, and brings them back when wandering. This staff is associated as inseparably with the shepherd as the goad is with the ploughman."

That on certain occasions, at any rate, it was customary for the shepherd to have not only one but two staves—one

[1] Zeph. iii. 12.

for keeping off wild beasts and thieves, and the other for feeding the flock—is manifest from the reference so familiar to us in the 23rd Psalm: " *Thy rod and Thy staff, they comfort me.*"

The names of the staves, like everything else in this symbolical transaction, were significant. One he called נֹעַם, *noam*, which means " beauty," " pleasantness," " favour " —and had reference, as we see from the 10th verse, to the grace and loving-kindness of God in keeping off their enemies from destroying them ; and the other he called חֹבְלִים, *hobhlim*, " bands," or literally " binders," and symbolised, as we see from the 14th verse, that part of the shepherd's rule by which the sheep were kept united among themselves as one flock. " And so " (thus equipped), he says again at the end of the 7th verse, " I fed the flock."

There is, perhaps, not another scripture in the Old Testament which has been more variously interpreted than the first part of the 8th verse of this chapter : " *And I cut off the three shepherds in one month.*" Who are the three shepherds, and what are we to understand by the expression, " in one month " ?

The following are a few out of the many answers which have been given to these questions : (1) Von Hoffmann, Koehler, Keil, Dr. C. H. H. Wright, W. H. Lowe, and others understand by the three shepherds *Gentile rulers*, in whose power the Jews were, and who ought to have acted to them as " shepherds " ; but they differ as to who these rulers were, and also in their interpretation of the " one month." Thus, Von Hoffmann identifies the three shepherds with three empires, namely, the Babylonian, the Medo-Persian, and the Macedonian. According to him the " one month " signifies a prophetic period of thirty prophetic days, each of seven literal years' duration. This would be equivalent to 210 years. The three empires named actually lasted 215 years, reckoning from the Babylonian Captivity to the death of Alexander the Great ; but the slight discrepancy of five years is considered of little consequence in reckoning sabbatic periods.

The chief objection to this interpretation is that it cannot be shown that "a day" is ever used in the prophetic Scriptures to represent seven years. His reference to Dan. ix. 24, in support of his theory, does not apply, for there the "*seventy weeks*" (or "seventy sevens") are seventy weeks of years, *i.e.*, 490 years, and on that principle the "one month" could only signify thirty years. "Moreover," as Wright observes, "it is not in accordance with fact, or with Daniel's prophecy in chap. viii., to view the death of Alexander as the destruction of the Macedonian empire, which continued to exist, though no longer as a united empire, under the rule of the Diadochi, or successors of Alexander."

Koehler, Kliefoth, and Keil also identify the three shepherds with the Babylonian, Medo-Persian, and Macedonian empires; but, according to them, the only way in which the expression "in one month" can be symbolically interpreted is by dividing the month as a period of thirty days into three times ten days, according to the number of the shepherds, and taking each ten days as the time employed in the destruction of a shepherd. "Ten is the number of the completion or the perfection of any earthly act or occurrence. If, therefore, each shepherd were destroyed in ten days, and the destruction of the three was executed in a month, *i.e.*, within a space of three times ten days following one another, the fact is indicated, on the one hand, that the destruction of each of these shepherds followed directly upon that of the other; and, on the other hand, that this took place after the full time allotted for his rule had passed away." I agree with another writer that this explanation as to what is meant by the "one month" appears highly artificial.

Dr. Wright explains the "one month" on the year-day principle ("each day for a year," Ezek. iv. 6), and identifies the thirty years with the period "between B.C. 172, when Antiochus Epiphanes desecrated the Temple, and B.C. 141, when the three alien shepherds, Antiochus Epiphanes, Antiochus Eupator, and Demetrius I. were cut off, and the last trace of Syrian supremacy was removed by the expulsion of the Syrian garrison from its fortress in Jerusalem."

But this is in accord with his general interpretation of the chapter (as is the case also with all the others who seek to identify the shepherds with Gentile rulers or kingdoms); by which also the "shepherds" in the 5th verse, and the solemn words of judgment in the 6th verse, are made to apply, not to the Jews, but to their Gentile oppressors—a view which seems to me untenable; for first, there is no mention or reference to the Gentiles in the announcement of the devastating judgment in the first three verses of the chapter, which I regard as the prelude to the whole prophecy, but only to the borders of the promised land from the north to the south.

Secondly, the awful condition of things depicted in the 5th verse is just that which, according to vers. 9 and 11, is to happen to "the sheep of slaughter" after their rejection of the Good Shepherd; and thirdly, the very usage of the term "shepherds" precludes, it seems to me, the interpretation which makes it to mean Gentile tyrants, or oppressors—its almost exclusive application, when used in the Hebrew Bible in its figurative sense in relation to a flock of men, being to native Israelitish rulers or leaders, whether civil or religious,[1] most of whom, alas! proved themselves to be only false shepherds without any heart for the sheep.

(2) Maurer, Hitzig, Ewald, Bleek, Bunsen, S. Davidson, and other writers have fastened upon this passage as containing, according to them, "one of the clearest proofs" of the pre-exilic authorship of the second part of Zechariah, inasmuch as the "three shepherds" are supposed to refer to three kings of the northern or ten-tribed kingdom of Israel who were "cut off in one month" (which they take

---

[1] The only exception is Isa. xliv. 28, where God says of Cyrus, "He is My shepherd"; but there he is so called because he is raised up to play the rôle, not of an *oppressor* of Israel, but as performing God's pleasure, even saying to Jerusalem she shall be built, and to the Temple, "Thy foundations shall be laid."

in its literal significance), and, therefore, contend that this prophecy must have been written before the destruction of that kingdom by the Assyrians in 721 B.C., and not, as is generally accepted, before the restoration from Babylon.

The historical event, or events, to which our passage is made by these writers to refer, is 2 Kings xv. 8–14, where we read of the assassination of Zechariah, son of Jeroboam II., by Shallum, who very shortly was himself smitten by Menahem. But we need only look into this passage in 2 Kings to see the baselessness of this interpretation and of the theory based upon it. Shallum, who murdered Zechariah, himself reigned "a full month" before he was in turn murdered by Menahem, who was not killed at all, but reigned ten years, and was succeeded by his son Pekahiah. Maurer, Ewald, Bunsen, and S. Davidson, in support of this theory, have invented "a third unknown usurper," who succeeded Zechariah for a very brief period before Shallum actually reigned, or "possibly on the other side of the Jordan," and who also met with a violent end; but such inventions, of which history knows nothing, and for which there is no place in the historical narrative in the Scriptures, are not worthy to be refuted.[1]

(3) There remains one other explanation which, though not altogether free from difficulties, seems to me the correct one, namely, that the prophet is speaking, *not of three individuals*, but of three orders, or *classes*, of shepherds. But even among those holding this view there have been

---

[1] I may mention a few other interpretations, or rather guesses and conjectures, respecting the three shepherds. Abarbanel explains them to mean the three Maccabees—Judas, Jonathan, and Simon; Kimchi refers them to Jehoahaz, Jehoiakim, and Zedekiah; Jerome (following the Talmud), to Moses, Aaron, and Miriam; Grotius, to David, Adonijah, and Joab; Burger, to Eli and his two sons, or to Samuel and his two sons; and Kalmet explains them of the three Roman emperors—Galba, Otho, and Vitellius. Another theory contended for is that the three shepherds are John, Simon, and Eleazer, the three desperate leaders of the Jewish factions in the last struggle against Rome; but, as a matter of fact, John of Gischala and Simon Bar Giora were taken alive to Rome, and Simon was slain in Rome during the triumphal procession of Vespasian and Titus about three years after the destruction of the Temple; so that they certainly could not be the three shepherds who were to be "cut off in one month."

differences of opinion. Some, among them Lightfoot, thought the Pharisees, Sadducees, and Essenes are referred to; others have imagined that the civil, ecclesiastical, and military authorities are meant. But I agree with Hengstenberg, that if it may be regarded as certain that the three shepherds represent the *three classes of shepherds* existing in the theocracy—in other words, the leaders of the nation —then " Zechariah could not possibly have thought of any others than the *civil authorities* (*the rulers*), *the priests, and the prophets*," who are frequently spoken of in the earlier scriptures as the " shepherds," or leaders of the people, and to whose misguidance is attributed the ruin of the nation.[1]

" The only difficulty in connection with this view is to explain the fact that the prophetical order should be introduced as one of the three, seeing that this had been extinct for a long time before the period of fulfilment. We reply that, in accordance with the essential character of prophecy, the prophet represents the future by means of the analogous circumstances of his own time. Just as the order of the civil shepherds continued to exist though the kings had ceased to reign, so did the order of prophets continue, so far as everything essential was concerned, even after the suspension of the gift of prophecy. The vocation of the prophet was to make known to the people the word and will of God (Jer. xviii. 18). Before the completion of the canon this was done by means of revelations under the guidance of the Spirit of God, and the application of the results to the peculiar circumstances of the age. The place of the prophets was occupied by the scribes, on whom, according to the Book of Ecclesiasticus (chap. xxxix.), the Lord richly bestowed the spirit of understanding, who studied the wisdom of the ancients, investigated the prophets, delivered instruction and counsel, and who were noted for wise sayings. They stood in the same relation to the prophets of the Old Testament, as the enlightened teachers of the Christian Church to the prophets of the New. The three constituent elements of

[1] Comp. Jer. ii. 8-26, xviii. 18.

the Jewish Sanhedrim answer to the three shepherds mentioned here, namely, the leading priests, the scribes, the elders, ἀρχιερεῖς, γραμματεῖς, πρεσβύτεροι (Matt. xxvi. 3)."

It is interesting to note that among Christian interpreters this is the oldest view. Thus, Theodoret[1] says: " He speaks of the kings of the Jews, and prophets, and priests; for by the three orders they were shepherded"; and Jerome,[2] who, himself following the Talmud, interprets the three shepherds of Moses, Aaron, and Miriam, says: " I have read in some one's commentary that the shepherds cut off in the indignation of the Lord are to be understood of priests, and false prophets, and kings of the Jews, who, after the Passion of Christ, were all cut off in one time."

So also Cyril,[3] who says: " The three shepherds were, I deem, those who exercised the legal priesthood, and those appointed judges of the people, and the interpreters of Scripture, *i.e.*, lawyers "; who, as shown above in the quotation from Hengstenberg, really took, at the time of Christ, the place of the prophets.

As will have been already inferred, I do not understand the expression " in one month " in a literal sense, but as a period of time—long, when compared with that which might be figuratively expressed by " one day," as in chap. iii. 9; but brief, as contrasted with other periods of time.

In short, it might be said to embrace the period during which our Lord Jesus "sought by repeated efforts, but without avail, to deliver the lost sheep of the house of Israel from the spiritual tyranny of its blind and corrupt guides."

Anyhow, this is an historic fact, that it was consequent on the rejection of the Messiah, the Good Shepherd, that the Jewish polity was broken up, and that since then, and now for " many days," the children of Israel have been not only without a king and without a prince, but also without a prophet and without a priest. On the other hand, these three offices were, on the testimony of the prophets, to be

---

[1] Died in 420 A.D.   [2] 423-457 A.D.   [3] Died 444 A.D.

united in the person of the Messiah, and have always in the consciousness of the Church been associated with Christ. If Israel had received Him, they would have found *in Him* their Prophet, Priest, and King ; they might even, as Pusey suggests, " have been held under Him " (*i.e.*, by human representatives of Him); but having rejected Him, these three offices, which, originally appointed by God, were mediatorial in their character, and were held on earth by those who were meant to represent and foreshadow Him who is the " One Mediator between God and man "—were " cut off," that is, abolished, as an outward sign that through their rejection of Christ their relations with God were broken off.

The second half of the 9th verse describes the rupture between the Good Shepherd and the people as a whole, including those who ought to have acted as shepherds, but only misled and devoured the flock. It also, it seems to me, indicates the reason why " the three shepherds " were cut off.

Commentators generally view the cutting off of the three shepherds " as an act of God's loving-kindness toward the sheep of His pasture,"[1] and as part of the beneficent care of the Good Shepherd for the flock. So it might have been, if delivered from their false shepherds, the people as a whole had turned to Him Who was sent to them of God to seek and to save, and Who in His one person combined the offices of Prophet, Priest, and King. But as not only the leaders, both civil and religious, but the people in general, took up more and more an attitude of opposition and hostility toward Him, the " cutting off " of the three " shepherds," or the abolition of the three mediatorial offices, which is the outward sign of the suspension of God's covenant relationship with them, must certainly be regarded also as an act of judgment on the nation as a whole.

And, if it be asked, what other expression of the beneficent activity of the Good Shepherd on behalf of the

[1] Wright.

sheep of slaughter do we find in this prophecy, if the cutting off of the shepherds is not to be regarded as an effort on His part for the deliverance of the flock, my answer is, that a full, though compressed, summary of the beneficent character of the activities of the Good Shepherd is given in the 8th verse. There we see the Shepherd fully equipped with the two staves of Beauty (or " Favour "), and " Bands " (or " Binders "), feeding the flock. " So I fed the flock "; and in that blessed shepherding everything was included—protection and deliverance from without, and safety, guidance, and provision within. Oh! that my people had hearkened unto His voice, and that Israel had walked in His ways! Then would it, indeed, have been well with them. Not only would He soon have subdued their enemies and turned His hand in judgment against their adversaries, but their peace should have been as a river, and their righteousness as the waves of the sea.

But the frequent complaint of God of the attitude of His stiff-necked people in the time of the prophets, culminated in their spirit of opposition and hostility to Him, Who was the last and greatest of the prophets, and the very image of God. " My people hearkened not to My voice; Israel would none of Me. So I let them go (or ' sent them forth') after the stubbornness of their heart, that they might walk in their own counsels." [1]

This, in brief, is the meaning of vers. 8 and 9: " And my soul was wearied (lit., ' was shortened,' i.e., became impatient) [2] with them." Oh! how much stubborn disobedience on the part of the flock is presupposed in this complaint on the part of the shepherd, " And their soul also loathed (בָּחַל, bachal—a word expressive of intense disgust) me ": sad and solemn words which in their fulness were fulfilled in the intense loathing which the leaders of the Jewish nation manifested to Jesus of Nazareth.

The terrible consequence was, that even the long-

---

[1] Ps. lxxxi. 12–16 ; Isa. xlviii. 18.

[2] The expression קָצְרָה נֶפֶשׁ is the same as in Num. xxi. 4, where it is rendered in the A.V., " The soul of the people was much discouraged."

suffering of God as manifested in Christ was exhausted ; " *Then said I, I will not feed you : that which dieth, let it die ; and that which perisheth* (or ' *is cut off* '), *let it perish ; and those that remain, let each one eat the flesh of another* " —all which became terribly and literally true when, after the rejection of the Good Shepherd, the terrible calamities of war, famine, pestilence, intestine strife, and mutual destruction overtook the poor deluded people.

The first outward visible sign of the rupture between the Shepherd and the sheep was the breaking of one of the staves : " *And I took My staff ' Beauty '* (or ' *Favour* ') *and cut it asunder, that I might break My covenant which I had made with all the peoples.*"

This staff was called נֹעַם, *noam*—" Beauty," or " Pleasantness," or " Favour "; because, as already said above, it was the symbol of God's protection over them in keeping off the nations from attacking them from without.

The covenant which He says He will break is not the covenant which He made with the people. The word for people in the original is in the plural, and refers to the *Gentile* nations, and the covenant is that which God, so to say, made with the Gentile peoples on their behalf. When Israel was in God's favour and under His gracious protection, then He caused even their enemies to be at peace with them ; and when the Gentile nations gathered against them ready to devour, the Shepherd of Israel soon broke the arm of their strength and prevented them doing harm to His people. But when He ceased to be their defence, then they became a ready prey to the Gentile world-powers, which are well symbolised in the Bible by wild beasts— " The boar out of the wood doth waste it, and the wild beast of the field doth devour it."

Again, however, it is declared in the same word of prophecy that restored and converted Israel will be taken under the special protection of God, and a covenant will be made by Him on their behalf, not only with the nations, but with the beasts of the field. " *In that day will I make a covenant for them with the beasts of the field, and with the*

*fowls of heaven, and with the creeping things of the ground :
and I will break the bow and the sword and the battle out of
the land, and will make them to lie down safely. And I
will betroth thee unto Me for ever ; yea, I will betroth thee
unto Me in righteousness, and in judgment, and in loving-
kindness, and in mercies. I will even betroth thee unto Me
in faithfulness : and thou shalt know that I am the Lord."* [1]

We proceed to the 11th verse : " *And it was broken*
(namely, ' the covenant ') *in that day ; and thus the poor of
the flock that watched Me* (or ' gave heed unto Me ') *knew
that it was the word of Jehovah.*"

The manifest proof that the covenant which the
Shepherd of Israel had made with the nations on Israel's
behalf was broken, served as a demonstration to the poor
of the flock that what had been foretold was indeed the
Word of God.

The point of time in the expression " in that day " is
prophetic from the prophet's point of view, and refers to the
time and events following the breaking off of the relations
between the True Shepherd, whom the prophet represented,
and the flock. It is true that he speaks of the breaking of
the covenant with the nations on Israel's behalf as past,
because *in the vision* which passed before his mind the
things described had actually occurred. " If the prophecy,"
remarks Hengstenberg, " had been couched in literal terms,
instead of being clothed in symbol, it would have run thus :
When, therefore, My covenant, or treaty, with the nations
is brought to an end, those who fear Me will discern in the
fulfilment the divine character of this sentence of Mine upon
Israel."

By the הַצֹּאן עֲנִיֵּי, *aniyye hatson*—" the poor of the
flock "—we can understand (as already explained) nothing
else than the believing remnant who were saved out of the
" flock of slaughter." They are described as " *Hashshomerim
othi*," rendered " that waited upon Me," in the Authorised
Version ; and, " they that gave heed unto Me," in the
Revised Version. Literally, it is those that " *watched* with

---

[1] Hos. ii. 18–20.

Me," or, "those that observed Me "—that is, "kept their eyes constantly fixed on Me, ready to act according to My direction and will "—a beautiful designation not only of the believing remnant of Israel, but of those from all nations who have learned in truth that what was spoken by prophets and apostles, and Christ Himself, was indeed the Word of the living God, and whose eyes are fixed upon Him with ready obedience to do His will.

We come now to vers. 12 and 13, which form perhaps the most difficult passage in the whole prophecy:

"*And I said unto them, If ye think good, give me my hire; and if not, forbear. So they weighed for my hire thirty pieces of silver.*

"*And the Lord said unto me, Cast it unto the potter, the goodly price that I was prised at of them. And I took the thirty pieces of silver, and cast them unto the potter, in the house of the Lord.*"

As an indication that his service as shepherd was coming to an end, he asks his wages. I need not again remind the reader that we have to do here with symbols and figures, and that the symbolical transaction in the vision in which the prophet was himself the chief actor was designed to set forth great spiritual truths.

That the prophet only represented Jehovah, the *true Shepherd of Israel*, who in fulness of time was especially to manifest Himself in this character in His only-begotten Son, the Messiah, comes out very clearly in these verses, for the contemptible wages which they did offer, Jehovah says (in ver. 13), ironically, is "the goodly price *that I was prised at of them.*"

The wages (שָׂכָר, *sakhar*, "hire," or "reward"), which He actually sought from them for all His Shepherd care, was, as the commentators rightly understand, the spiritual fruit of His labours—repentance, faith, true heart piety, humble obedience and grateful love. This is brought out clearly in the Lord's parable of the Vineyard, which is Israel, to whom He first sent His servants, and then His own Son, "that He might receive the fruits of it."

And although He has every right to *demand* this "hire," He leaves it to His professed people, upon whom such bounteous care and attention has been lavished by Him, to make a free return to Him of their love and gratitude in order that the actual condition of their hearts towards Him may be thus tested. "Give me," He says, "my 'hire' or 'reward,' for all that I have been and done for you, *if you think well* (lit., '*if it seem good in your eyes*'), *and if not, forbear.*" For, as has been well expressed by another writer, "God does not force our free will or constrain our service. He places life and death before us, and bids us choose life. By His grace alone we can choose Him; but we can refuse His grace and Himself."

That which they did offer the prophet in return for His services is meant to express the black ingratitude of their hearts for the shepherd care of Jehovah. Instead of "wages," as Keil well expresses it, they offer Him an insult—"*so they weighed for My hire thirty pieces of silver*," which was exactly the amount which, according to the law, was to be paid in compensation for a slave gored to death by an ox.[1] "*And Jehovah said unto me, Cast it*" (*hishlikh* —"fling it" with contempt as a thing unclean[2]) "*unto the potter, the goodly price* (or, 'the magnificence of the price') *that I was prised at of them : so I took the thirty pieces of silver, and cast them, in the house of Jehovah, unto the potter.*

There are two or three important points in this passage which need explanation :

(1) What is meant by casting to the potter? Many different conjectures have been advanced in answer to this question. The most generally accepted explanation by evangelical writers is that given by Hengstenberg, namely, that it is equivalent to casting a thing into an unclean place. This explanation rests on the supposition that the

---

[1] Ex. xxi. 32.

[2] The verb *hishlikh* is used for casting torn flesh to the dogs, Ex. xxii. 31 ; of a corpse which was cast unburied, Isa. xiv. 19 ; and in many other such connections ; and of idols "cast" to the moles and bats, Isa. ii. 20.

potter who worked for the Temple had his workshop in the
valley of Ben Hinnom, "which having been formerly the
scene of the abominable worship of Moloch, was regarded
with abhorrence as an unclean place after its defilement by
Josiah, and served as the slaughter-house for the city.[1]
But, as Keil observes with truth, "It by no means follows
from Jer. xviii. 2 and xix. 2 (on which Hengstenberg bases
his supposition), that this potter dwelt in the valley of Ben
Hinnom."

On the contrary, the passages in Jeremiah which are
referred to would rather lead us to the opposite conclusion,
for when we read that God said to the prophet, "*Go, and buy
a potter's earthen bottle* (or '*pitcher*'), *and take of the elders
of the people, and go forth unto the valley of Hinnom, which
is by the entry of the gate Harsith*" (or "*pottery gate*"),[2] it
seems pretty clear that the pottery itself, where the pitcher
was to be bought, stood *inside* the city gate, since he had
to "go forth" from it toward the valley. But even if the
potter had had his workshop in the valley of Hinnom,
which was regarded as unclean, he would not necessarily
have become unclean himself in consequence; "And if he
had been looked upon as unclean, he could not possibly
have worked for the Temple, or supplied the cooking
utensils for use in the service of God—namely, for boiling
the holy sacrificial flesh."

Without stopping to analyse here other unsatisfactory
explanations, I would briefly state that the reason why the
thirty pieces of silver which Jehovah ironically calls the
"magnificence of the price" at which He was valued by
them, were to be flung to the potter, was most probably
because the potter was one of the lowest of the labouring
classes, whose labour was estimated as of comparatively
trifling value, and "whose productions, when marred by
any trifling accident, could be easily replaced at an insignificant expenditure." The phrase, "Throw to the
potter," may perhaps have been "a proverbial expression
for contemptuous treatment"; but this also is only a con-

---

[1] 2 Kings xxiii. 10.   [2] Jer. xix. 1, 2.

jecture. That it is meant to express the *valuelessness* of a thing is pretty certain.

(2) In the command that the prophet should cast the money to the potter, there is nothing said about his going to the Temple, but in the performance we read, " And I took the thirty pieces of silver and cast them, *in the house of Jehovah, to the potter.*"

Hengstenberg understands this to mean that the money was thrown there that it might be taken thence to the potter; but I agree with another Bible student that, " as the words read they can only be understood as signifying that the potter was in the Temple when the money was thrown to him; that he had either some work to do there, or that he had come to bring some earthenware for the Temple kitchen." [1]   And the reason why the prophet went to the house of Jehovah was not merely to show that it was as the servant of the Lord and by His command that he was acting, but because " the Temple was the place where the people of the covenant were wont to assemble to present themselves before the Lord.   In that holy place the awful repudiation on the part of the nation of Him, who was the Shepherd of Israel, was to be *publicly* made known.   The base transaction (however done in a corner) was to be proclaimed upon the housetops.   In the place where the solemn covenant between Jehovah and His people had so often been ratified by sacrifices, the fearful separation between the people of Israel and Himself was to be declared.   What was done in the Temple was done in the presence of both parties to the covenant : in the presence of Jehovah, in whose honour the Temple had been erected, and in the presence of the nation, who, by its erection of that Temple, had accepted Jehovah as their Lord and God. In the presence of both parties the rejection of the Lord as the Shepherd of Israel was to be announced, and the dissolution of the covenant made by Jehovah to be publicly proclaimed by the act of His representative." [2]

[1] In chap. xiv. 20 there is a mention of earthenware " pots " as being used in the Temple.   [2] Dr. C. H. H. Wright.

We have now reached the place where we must refer more fully to the fulfilment of this prophecy in our Lord Jesus. As regards the solemn prediction of the chapter as a whole (when viewed in the light of other prophecies in the Old Testament), its chief points have been thus summarised :

(1) That before the destruction of Jerusalem, Jehovah, in the person of the Messiah, would appear as the Shepherd of Israel.

(2) That only "the poor of the flock" would attend to His word ; but the rest, both leaders and people, would reject and abhor Him.

(3) That the Good Shepherd should be valued at the price of a common slave.

(4) That the people would in consequence be given over to be the prey of the Gentile powers from without, and to civil feuds within. Now even the most superficial acquaintance with the Gospel narrative, and of the subsequent history of the Jewish people, must lead one to see how strikingly all this has been fulfilled in Jesus of Nazareth, and in the events which took place in consequence of His rejection by His own nation.

If there had been no allusion at all in the New Testament to this prophecy, we should still, from the mere Gospel narrative, be led to see its true and full fulfilment in Christ. But the New Testament does cite vers. 12 and 13 as a direct prophecy of our Lord Jesus. After describing in chap. xxvi. the betrayal of Jesus by Judas, to whom the chief priests weighed thirty pieces of silver, and His condemnation to death by Pontius Pilate, at the instigation of the high priests and elders of the Jews, the evangelist Matthew proceeds :

" Then Judas, which betrayed Him, when he saw that He was condemned, repented himself, and brought back the thirty pieces of silver to the chief priests and elders, saying, I have sinned in that I betrayed innocent blood. But they said, What is that to us ? see thou to it. And he cast down the pieces of silver into the sanctuary, and

departed ; and he went away and hanged himself. And
the chief priests took the pieces of silver, and said, It is not
lawful to put them into the treasury, since it is the price of
blood. And they took counsel, and bought with them the
potter's field, to bury strangers in. Wherefore that field
was called, The field of blood, unto this day. Then was
fulfilled that which was spoken by Jeremiah the prophet,
saying, And they took the thirty pieces of silver, the price
of Him that was priced, whom certain of the children of
Israel did price ; and they gave them for the potter's field,
as the Lord appointed me." [1]

It has been objected by Jews and others that there are
certain discrepancies between the words of the prophecy
and its fulfilment as recorded by Matthew. One of the
alleged discrepancies is contained in the fact that " in the
prophecy the thirty pieces of silver were weighed as wages
for the shepherd," whereas in the Gospel narrative they are
said to have been paid to Judas for the betrayal of Jesus.

" But, in truth, as soon as we trace back the form of the
prophecy to its idea, the difference is resolved into harmony.
The payment of the wages to the shepherd in the prophetical announcement is simply the symbolical form in
which the nation manifests its ingratitude for the love and
fidelity shown towards it by the shepherd, and the sign that
it will no longer have him as its shepherd, and therefore a
sign of the blackest ingratitude and of hard-heartedness in
return for the love displayed by the shepherd. The same
ingratitude and the same hardness of heart are manifested
in the resolution of the representatives of the Jewish nation,
the high priests and elders, to put Jesus, their Saviour, to
death, and to take Him prisoner by bribing the betrayer.
The payment of thirty silverlings to the betrayer was, in
fact, the wages with which the Jewish nation repaid Jesus
for what He had done for the salvation of Israel ; and the
contemptible sum which they paid to the betrayer was an
expression of the deep contempt which they felt for Jesus.

" There is no great importance in this difference, that

[1] Matt. xxvii. 3-10.

here the prophet throws the money into the house of
Jehovah to the potter; whereas, according to Matthew's
account, Judas threw the silverlings into the Temple, and
the high priests would not put the money into the Divine
treasury, because it was blood-money, but applied it to the
purchase of a potter's field, which received the name of a
field of blood. For by this very fact not only was the
prophecy almost literally fulfilled; but, so far as the sense
is concerned, it was so exactly fulfilled that every one could
see that the same God who had spoken through the prophet had, by the secret operation of His omnipotent power,
which extends even to the ungodly, so arranged the matter
that Judas threw the money into the Temple, to bring it
before the face of God as blood-money, and to call down
the vengeance of God upon the nation; and that the high
priest, by purchasing the potter's field for this money,
which received the name of 'field of blood' in consequence
'unto this day,' perpetuated the memorial of the sin committed against their Messiah. Matthew indicates this in
the words 'as the Lord commanded me,' which correspond
to 'and Jehovah said unto me,' in ver. 13 of our prophecy; on which H. Aug. W. Meyer has correctly observed,
'That the words, "as the Lord commanded me," express the
fact that the application of the wages of treachery to the
purchase of the potter's field took place *in accordance with
the purpose of God*, whose command the prophet had
received. As God had directed the prophet how to proceed
with the thirty silverlings, so was it with the antitypical fulfilment of the prophecy by the high priests, and thus was
the purpose of the Divine will accomplished.'"[1]

There remains, however, one real difficulty in the
citation of this prophecy by Matthew, namely, in the fact
that Matthew quotes the words of Zechariah as *that which
was spoken by Jeremiah the prophet.*

It was the attempt to justify the inerrancy of this
quotation in Matthew, which, as I have shown in my
"Introduction" to the second part of Zechariah, led the

[1] Keil.

earliest English critics, who were believing men, to the conclusion that these chapters in Zechariah were not attributed
by the Jews to their right author, who, in truth, was not
Zechariah, but Jeremiah.   But, as I have tried to show,
there is no basis in fact for this theory.   A more elaborate
attempt to justify the occurrence of Jeremiah's name in this
passage in Matthew was first made by Grotius, and afterwards developed by Hengstenberg.   Stated in the briefest
form, the reason for the introduction of Jeremiah's name in
the place of that of Zechariah's is, according to these
writers' explanation, " because, as far as the principal
features are concerned, Zechariah's prophecy in chap. xi. is
simply a renewal and repetition of the prophecy in Jer.
xix. (or, according to others, of chaps. xviii. and xix.), and
Zechariah announced a second fulfilment of that prophecy."   Or, to quote for the sake of elucidation a longer
summary :
    St. Matthew intentionally ascribed the words of
Zechariah to Jeremiah, because he wished to impress upon
his readers the fact that Zechariah's prediction was a
reiteration of two fearful prophecies of Jeremiah (Jer. xviii.,
xix.), and should, like them, be accomplished in the
rejection and destruction of the Jewish people.   He wished
to remind them that " the field of blood," purchased with
the money that testified the fulness of their guilt, was a
part of that valley of the son of Hinnom which their fathers
had made a " field of blood " before them, and where
Jeremiah had twice by the symbol of a potter's vessel,
announced their coming destruction.   The words of the
prophet, " Cast it to the potter," were in themselves
sufficient to direct the attention of readers acquainted with
the prophecies to those two chapters of Jeremiah ; but the
manner in which St. Matthew introduces his quotation
makes the allusion still more plain.   He first relates the
purchase of the potter's field, thereby pointing out the
locality of Jeremiah's prophecy ; then he mentions the fact
that it was called " the field of blood," thereby referring to
a very similar expression in that prophet, " Behold the days

come, saith the Lord, that this place shall no more be called Tophet, nor the valley of the son of Hinnom, but the valley of slaughter " (Jer. xix. 6); and then cites the words of Zechariah, as spoken by Jeremiah, in order to make all mistake impossible. St. Matthew had, therefore, a direct purpose in introducing the name of Jeremiah; it was to warn the Jews against the coming judgments. They fondly hoped that, as the chosen people of God, they were safe. St. Matthew points them to the potter's field, and thus reminds them of the calamities which had already come upon them for past sins, less heinous than that of which the potter's field now testifies. [1]

I have entered somewhat fully into this explanation because it has commended itself to many devout and scholarly Bible students ; but, at the same time, I must confess that I myself do not feel at all positive of the connection between our passage in Zechariah and the particular prophecy in Jeremiah to which reference has been made. The whole rests upon the presupposition (1) that the potter, of whom Jeremiah purchased the pot, had his workshop in the valley of Hinnom, which was regarded with abhorrence as an unclean place; (2) that Zechariah threw the thirty pieces of silver at the spot in that valley where the potter's workshop was, with evident and intentional allusion to Jeremiah's prophecy which the people are assumed to have had in their minds. But, as shown above, it is not at all proven that the potter in Jeremiah had his workshop in the

---

[1] Dr. Alexander McCaul. This seems to be also the view of Dr. Alfred Edersheim. Speaking on "the potter's field," in the passage in Matthew, he says : "The very spot on which Jeremiah had been Divinely directed to prophesy against Jerusalem and against Israel, how was it now all fulfilled in the light of the completed sin and apostasy of the people, as prophetically described by Zechariah ! This Tophet of Jeremiah, now that they had valued and sold at thirty shekels Israel's Messiah-Shepherd—truly a Tophet—and become a field of blood ! Surely, not an accidental coincidence this, that it should be the place of Jeremy's announcement of judgment : not accidental, but veritably a fulfilment of his prophecy ! And so St. Matthew, targuming this prophecy in form as in its spirit, and in true Jewish manner stringing to it the prophetic description furnished by Zechariah, sets the event before us as the fulfilment of Jeremy's prophecy."—Edersheim, *Life and Times of Jesus the Messiah*, vol. ii. p. 576.

valley of Hinnom,[1] and, as far as the words in Zechariah
are concerned, the obvious sense of the words is that the
money was thrown to the potter " in the house of Jehovah "
or Temple.

Failing any other satisfactory explanation, we shall
have to assume that the name of Jeremiah has crept into
the passage in Matthew by error in one of the following
ways : By a simple slip of memory, according to Augustine,
Luther, Beza, Koehler, Keil, and almost all writers of the
modern school ; or secondly, and to my mind much more
probable, as a very old copyist's error more ancient than
the date of any of the MSS which have come down to us. [2]

The insult to the Shepherd of their offering Him for
His hire nothing more than the price of a dead slave is fol-
lowed by the completion of the severance of the relations
which existed between the Shepherd and flock, and the
final giving over of the sheep to their own evil devices :
" *And I cut asunder Mine other* (or ' *second* ') *staff, even
Bands* (or ' *Binders* '), *to destroy the brotherhood between
Judah and between Israel.*"

The retention by the Shepherd of this second staff for
some time after the first had already been broken, is
probably meant to indicate His reluctance to give up the
flock which had been so dear to Him, and His waiting to
the very end to be gracious to them if they had but turned
from their evil ways.   His very request for His " wages,"
or " hire," after the first staff was broken, was really, if they

---

[1] It is clear, however, from Matt. xxvii. etc., that in our Lord's time there
was a spot in that valley which was known as "the potter's field," probably
because of the accumulation of potsherds and débris from potteries, or, as some
suppose, because it furnished a sort of clay suitable for potters' ware.

[2] In connection with this two suggestions have been made, either of which is
quite probable.   (*a*) That in the original MS the name Ζαχαρίου (Zechariah)
stood in abbreviated form as Ζρίου, which a very early copyist mistook for 'Ιρίου
(the abbreviation for 'Ιερεμαίου—Jeremiah), and thus the error was afterwards
perpetuated ; (*b*) that in the original text of the evangelist there was no name at
all, but simply "as was spoken by the prophet"—διὰ τοῦ προφήτου—a formula
which Matthew uses again and again (see i. 22, ii. 5–15, xiii. 35, etc.) ; and that
the early copyist made a double error of inserting a name which was not in the
original, and that a wrong one.

had only properly understood it, a call to repentance; but instead of "fruit" as the result of His care and blessed labours, they brought Him forth the "wild grapes" of contempt and black ingratitude. And thus reluctantly He had to give over "the dearly beloved of His soul," not only into the hands of their enemies without, which was symbolised by the breaking of the first staff called "*Noam*," but the still more terrible calamity of civil strife and destructive feuds among themselves, which is symbolised by the breaking of the staff called *Ḥobhlim* ("Bands" or "Binders").

The אַחֲוָה, *achavah*, "brotherhood," which was to be destroyed "between Judah and between Israel," is not to be understood in the sense "that the unity of the nation would be broken up again in a manner similar to that in the days of Rehoboam, and that two hostile nations would be formed out of one people," although the disruption of national unity which took in the days of Jeroboam may be referred to as *an illustration* of that which would occur again in a more serious form. "The schism of Jeroboam had a weakening and disintegrating effect on the nation of the twelve tribes, and the dissolution of the brotherhood here spoken of was to result in still greater evil and ruin; for Israel, deprived of the Good Shepherd, was to fall into the power of the 'foolish,' or 'evil,' shepherd, who is depicted at the close of the prophecy."

The preposition בֵּין, *bein*, which is twice repeated, has the meaning not only of "*between*," but also of "*among*,"[1] and the formula, House of Judah and House of Israel, or simply, "Judah and Israel," is, as we have had again and again to notice, this prophet's inclusive designation of the whole ideally (and to a large extent already actually) reunited one people. I think, therefore, that we may rightly render the sentence "to destroy the brotherhood *among* Judah and among Israel"—that is to say, among the entire nation. The consequence of it would be the fulfilment of the threat in the 9th verse: "Let them which are left eat every one the

[1] See, *e.g.*, Isa. xliv. 4.

flesh of another"—solemn and awful words, which, as already shown above, had their first literal fulfilment in the party feuds and mutually destructive strife, and in the terrible "dissolution of every bond of brotherhood and of our common nature, which made the siege of Jerusalem by the Romans a proverb for horror, and precipitated its destruction."

There remains yet one act in this prophetic drama which sets forth the terrible fact that as a consequence of their rejection of the Good Shepherd they would be given over to the domination of one who would be the very opposite of Him Who came to seek and to save that which was lost.

"*And Jehovah said unto me, Take unto thee yet again the instruments of a foolish shepherd.*"

The word עוֹד, *od* ("yet again") connects this action with the previous one (vers. 4–8), for it implies that the prophet had already acted in the capacity, and had had in his hands the emblems of the shepherd's office once before. The adjective אֱוִלִי—*evili* (the sound of which is very much like the English word *evil*)—expresses more than the English rendering "foolish" given in this passage. It may almost be rendered "wicked."[1] "Folly and sin were almost identical terms in the eyes of the sacred writers," and the word is frequently used as the synonym for *ungodliness*.[2]

What the instruments of the foolish shepherd were, and in what respects they differed from those of the Good Shepherd, are matters for speculation, since we are not told. Hengstenberg supposes that the "instruments of the foolish shepherd consisted of a strong stick mounted with iron, with which the sheep were hurt and wounded, whereas the Good Shepherd was wont to keep the sheep in order with a thin staff and gentle strokes"; but this is only conjecture.

[1] See Job v. 3, where the same word is used.
[2] See Ps. xiv. 1 ; Prov. i. 7, etc.

The interpretation of this symbolical act is given by God Himself: "*For I will raise up a shepherd in the land, which shall not visit* (or '*observe,*' or '*care for*') *that which is cut off* (or '*perishing*'), *neither shall he seek those that be scattered,*[1] *nor heal that which is broken; neither shall he feed that which is sound* (lit., '*standeth,*' i.e., *the strong*), *but he shall eat the flesh of the fat, and shall tear their hoofs in pieces.*"

The heartlessness and cruelty of this evil shepherd is strikingly described—first in a negative, and then in a positive, manner. Not only will he be utterly indifferent alike to the needs of those who are ready to perish as to those who are still sound, but he will positively devour the flock. He will even "tear their hoofs in pieces," not "by driving them along rough and stony roads," as Ewald and others explain, but "so that when he consumes the sheep he even splits or tears in pieces the claws to seize upon and swallow the last morsel of flesh or fat."[2]

And the most solemn fact in this forecast is that God says, "*I* will raise up" such a shepherd in the land. Yes, He will raise him up in the same sense as He raised up the Assyrians, the Babylonians, and the Romans, *i.e.,* as His scourge upon a godless generation.

And the readiness of the "sheep of slaughter" to follow such a shepherd will be but part of the punishment for their rejection of the Good Shepherd.

But who is meant by this foolish or wicked shepherd?

Jewish commentators interpret it of Herod;[3] some Christian interpreters, like Hengstenberg, apply it to "all the evil native Jewish rulers collectively," who, subsequent

[1] The word is הַנַּעַר, *hanaar,* and means a youth or young man (rendered in the A.V. "the young one"), but it is never used of the young of animals.

Moreover, the mention of the young of the flock would not be suitable here, since there would be no need to seek them, "for lambs which feed beside their mothers do not generally go astray."

The R.V. and modern scholars generally have adopted the explanation of Gesenius, that *na'ar* is an abstract substantive meaning "scattering," and used here for the concrete "that which is scattered."

[2] Keil.

[3] So, *e.g.,* R. Abraham of Toledo, quoted by Kimchi.

to the rejection of Christ, oppressed and devoured the flock, and ultimately brought about their own ruin ; others again identify him with the imperial Roman power.   Thus, in the words of one of the advocates of this view, " the Jews rejected Christ, the King of Israel, and accepted the Emperor of Rome.   In the madness of their rage against Jesus of Nazareth, they cried out : ' We have no king but Cæsar.'   They obtained their choice, and found it bitterness in the latter end."   " The description " (in ver. 16), the same writer proceeds, " is given in language suitable to the character of an evil shepherd under which the Roman Empire is described.   It is strikingly similar in meaning to that given of the fourth, or Roman word-empire in the Book of Daniel, as a wild beast more dreadful, terrible, and strong than those beasts that were before it, furnished with great iron teeth and brazen claws, devouring, breaking in pieces, and stamping even the residue of its prey under its feet (Dan. vii. 7, 19, 23).[1]

I have set forth this view at some length, because I believe that a reference to Rome as the more immediate scourge of God in the punishment of Israel after their rejection of Christ is probably included in this prophecy, and this is in accordance with the explanation I have given of the words in the 6th verse, " I will deliver the men every one . . . into the hand of his king." [2]   But whatever partial reference to Imperial Rome there may be in this scripture, and however many evil and foolish shepherds there have already arisen since the words were uttered who have devoured the Jewish flock, the full and final fulfilment of this solemn prophecy will take place in *the final phase* of the development of the fourth great world-power (*i.e.*, the Roman), when amid the ten horns, or kingdoms, there shall come up " a little horn " who shall be master of them all, and in whom all the beast-like qualities of apostate anti-Christian world-power shall be concentrated and reach their climax.

---

[1] C. H. H. Wright.
[2] See above the remarks on ver. 6.

For just as the Good Shepherd, whose part the prophet acted in the first part of the chapter, is in the highest and truest sense none other than the Messiah, so the "foolish," or wicked, shepherd is in the last resort none other than the one who is in every sense his opposite—the personal Antichrist, under whose brief reign all Israel's previous sorrows and sufferings shall reach their climax in the final great tribulation; even though it may be granted that, as in the case of the Christ, so of the Antichrist, there have been, so to say, shadowy precursors in whom a certain partial historical fulfilment of the prophecy may be discernible.

And he will indeed be the "foolish" shepherd; for as the Messiah is sometimes spoken of as Wisdom personified, so the Antichrist, in spite of his being wise in all the wisdom which is from beneath, will be the very embodiment of folly; for (to quote from an old writer) "since the extremest folly consists in the extremest wickedness, he will be the most foolish who reacheth the highest impiety, and this he will do by arrogating to himself divinity, and claiming divine honours."

But the career of this evil shepherd shall be short, and his end will be sudden destruction—" *Woe to the idol* (or '*worthless*') *shepherd*"—the prophecy ends, or, as some would render, the shepherd of "*nothingness*," or "*uselessness*."[1]   This is God's estimate and description of him, even while he exalts himself unto heaven and seeks to be worshipped as God—" *that leaveth* (or '*forsaketh*') *the flock*"—and thus proves himself a false shepherd and hireling,[2] " *the sword shall be upon his arm and his right eye.*"

The arm is the emblem of might and the eye of intelligence—the two things in which the one who will sum up in himself anti-Christian world-power will trust, and in which he will boast himself.   Very well, he shall be smitten

---

[1] The word אֱלִיל, *elil*, is frequently used as an adjective to describe idols as vain and useless (see Lev. xix. 4, xxvi. 1; Ps. xcvi. 5, and other places). In the prophets it is often used also as a name for idols. The probable underlying etymological idea is that of vanity or nothingness.

[2] John x. 12, 13.

27

in these very parts—" *his arm* (the emblem of strength) *shall be utterly withered up, and his right eye* (the symbol and instrument of intelligence) *shall be utterly darkened.*" And this shall be the end of him who shall be slain with the breath of Messiah's mouth, and be destroyed by the brightness of His appearing.

Chapter 17

ISRAEL'S FINAL CONFLICT AND
GREAT DELIVERANCE
Zechariah 12

The burden of the word of Jehovah concerning Israel. Thus saith Jehovah, who stretcheth forth the heavens, and layeth the foundation of the earth, and formeth the spirit of man within him : Behold, I will make Jerusalem a cup of reeling unto all the peoples round about, and upon Judah also shall it be in the siege against Jerusalem. And it shall come to pass in that day, that I will make Jerusalem a burdensome stone for all the peoples ; all that burden themselves with it shall be sore wounded ; and all the nations of the earth shall be gathered against it. In that day, saith Jehovah, I will smite every horse with terror, and his rider with madness : and I will open Mine eyes upon the house of Judah, and will smite every horse of the peoples with blindness. And the chieftains of Judah shall say in their heart, The inhabitants of Jerusalem are my strength in Jehovah of hosts their God. In that day will I make the chieftains of Judah like a pan of fire among wood, and like a flaming torch among sheaves ; and they shall devour all the peoples round about, on the right hand and on the left : and they of Jerusalem shall yet again dwell in their own place, even in Jerusalem. Jehovah also shall save the tents of Judah first, that the glory of the house of David and the glory of the inhabitants of Jerusalem be not magnified above Judah. In that day shall Jehovah defend the inhabitants of Jerusalem ; and he that is feeble among them at that day shall be as David ; and the house of David shall be as God, as the Angel of Jehovah before them. And it shall come to pass in that day, that I will seek to destroy all the nations that come against Jerusalem. And I will pour upon the house of David, and upon the inhabitants of Jerusalem, the spirit of grace and of supplication ; and they shall look upon Me whom they have pierced : and they shall mourn for Him, as one mourneth for his only son, and shall be in bitterness for Him, as one that is in bitterness for his first-born. In that day shall there be a great mourning in Jerusalem, as the mourning of Hadadrimmon in the valley of Megiddon. And the land shall mourn, every family apart ; the family of the house of David apart, and their wives apart ; the family of the house of Nathan apart, and their wives apart ; the family of the house of Levi apart, and their wives apart ; the family of the Shimeites apart, and their wives apart ; all the families that remain, every family apart, and their wives apart.

Chapter 17

IN commencing my notes on the last section of Zechariah (chaps. xii.–xiv.), I take the liberty of repeating a brief paragraph from my introductory remarks to the 9th chapter to which I would again draw the attention of the reader.

The overthrow of world-power, and the establishment of Messiah's Kingdom, may be given as the epitome of the last six chapters of Zechariah. The two oracles which make up the whole of the second half of the book (chaps. ix.–xi. and xii.–xiv.) show by their headings, as well as by their contents, and even by their formal arrangement, that they are corresponding portions of a greater whole. Both sections treat of war between the heathen world and Israel, though in different ways.

In the first (chaps. ix.–xi.), the judgment *through which Gentile world-power over Israel is finally destroyed*, and Israel is endowed with strength to *overcome all their enemies*, forms the fundamental thought and centre of gravity of the prophetic description. In the second (chaps. xii.–xiv.), the judgment *through which Israel itself is sifted and purged* in the final great conflict with the nations, and transformed into the holy nation of Jehovah, forms the leading topic.

The foreground, or more immediate future of the first main section of the second half of the book (chaps. ix.–xi.), were, as shown in my notes on those chapters, the victories of Alexander the Great, the overthrow of the Persian Empire, the advent of the Messiah, and His rejection by Israel—though even there, as we had occasion to observe more particularly in connection with chap. ix. 9, 10, and chap. x. 4–12, the foreground of the more immediate or

421

proximate future, and the events which were to precede
and accompany the First Advent, merge into the great and
solemn events of the Second Advent, and the time of the
end.

The second or last section, on the other hand (chaps.
xii.–xiv.), seems to me to carry our thoughts altogether
to the more distant future, and is eschatological and
apocalyptic in its character, for it is impossible to apply
the solemn predictions in these chapters to events at the
time of the destruction of Jerusalem by Nebuchadnezzar,
which is the favourite theory of those who assign a pre-
exilic origin for the second half of Zechariah, and who
degrade this great prophecy to the level of a mere
" political divination of the affairs of the kingdom of Judah
in which ardent hopes were expressed by the unknown
prophet—hopes destined, however, to be sadly disappointed
—respecting the final result of the struggle of the Jewish
kingdom with the Babylonian power." [1]

Neither can we, without doing great violence to the
prophecy, interpret it of the taking of Jerusalem by
Antiochus Epiphanes, as some do, nor to the destruction
of the city and Temple by the Romans ; for (to quote from
words of my own) in none of those calamitous events in
the past history of Israel did God in the person of the
Messiah visibly appear on the Mount of Olives with His
angelic hosts as the Deliverer of His people and the
destroyer of many nations which were gathered against
them ; nor was the spirit of grace and supplication ever yet
poured out upon the Jewish nation, so that they might look
upon and recognise " Him whom they have pierced " ; nor
has the Lord, from any of those past events onward, become " King over the whole earth " (chap. xiv. 9) ; not to
mention many other great and solemn events which are
predicted in these chapters which cannot be allegorised or
explained away. We must reject, therefore, the view of
some of the " orthodox " commentators that this last
section traverses the ground already trodden in the previous

[1] Thus, for instance, Ewald in *Die Propheten des alten Bundes*.

chapters, and " refers to the events which took place in the period between the time of the prophet and the day of the Messiah."

The הַהוּא יוֹם, *yom ha'hu*, the "that day" which is mentioned no less than fourteen times in these last three chapters, is indeed "the day of the Messiah," but it is the day not of His first advent in humiliation, but of His manifestation in glory. It is, therefore, pre-eminently called יוֹם לַיהוָה, *yom la-Yehovah*—a day for Jehovah—the day set apart and appointed by Him not only for the display of His majesty and vindication of the holiness and righteousness of His character and ways, but it is "the day" of the manifestation of His Divine might and glory in the destruction of Israel's enemies, and the salvation of His own people.

The main theme of the first nine verses of chap. xii. is Israel's sudden deliverance by the interposition of God and the destruction of the armies of the confederated anti-Christian world-powers in the final siege of Jerusalem. But inasmuch as this siege, or " straitness," and the solemn events of "that day" synchronise with "the time of Jacob's trouble," and covers the period of unparalleled sufferings and "tribulation" by means of which the Jewish nation *is itself first purged as in a fiery furnace*, the prophecy properly begins with the words מַשָּׂא דְבַר יְהוָה עַל יִשְׂרָאֵל, *massa debhar Yehovah al Israel*—" the burden of the word of Jehovah upon (or ' over ') Israel"; the word *massa*, as we have seen, when dealing with the 1st verse of chap. ix., being as a heading confined entirely to prophecies which contain threatenings and announce judgments.

But though it will be a time of unspeakable anguish for Israel, the climax of all their sufferings and tribulations through all the centuries since the commencement of "the times of the Gentiles," they "shall be saved out of it." Yea, in their greatest extremity, and in the time of their most dire need, God Himself in the person of their Messiah shall interpose on their behalf, and He will be "jealous for His land, and have pity on His people," or, in the words of

the inspired prophetic song which Moses was commanded
to teach the children of Israel, so that it " should not be
forgotten out of the mouth of their seed," and which sets
forth in advance all the vicissitudes of their history to the
very end—

> " *Jehovah shall judge His people,*
> *And repent Himself for His servants :*
> *When He sees that their strength is gone,*
> *And that there is none remaining, shut up or left at*
> *large.*"

Then He will " lift up His hand to heaven " and swear,
saying :

> " *As I live for ever.*
> *If I whet my glittering sword, and Mine hand take*
> *hold on judgment ;*
> *I will render vengeance to Mine adversaries,*
> *And will recompense them that hate Me.*
> *I will make Mine arrows drunk with blood,*
> *And My sword shall devour much flesh.*" [1]

For the enemies of His people will then be accounted as
His enemies, which in reality they are.

But to return to our chapter.

To remove all possibility of doubt of the fulfilment of
the great and wonderful things which the prophet is about
to announce from the mouth of Jehovah, we are reminded
of the almighty-creative and sustaining power of the everlasting God. This surely is a sufficient basis for our faith
in His word, however great the human improbabilities and
natural impossibilities of their ever being literally fulfilled,
may appear to us.

" *Thus saith* (or ' the saying ' of) *Jehovah, which stretcheth
forth the heavens, and layeth the foundation of the earth, and
formeth the spirit of man within him.*"

A similar declaration of God's almighty-creative and

---

[1] Deut. xxxii. 36–42.

sustaining power is made in Isa. xlii. 5, and with the same
purpose, namely, to remove all doubt as to the realisation
of the great and mighty things which the prophet there
predicts : *"Thus saith God, Jehovah, He that createth the
heavens and stretcheth them forth ; He that spread abroad
the earth, and that which cometh out of it*; He that giveth
breath (נְשָׁמָה, *neshamah*—soul) unto the people upon it ;
and spirit (רוּחַ, *ruach*) to them that walk therein."

The participial verbs in our passage in Zech. xii.—
נֹטֶה, יֹסֵד, יֹצֵר—*noteh, yosed, yotzer*—" stretcheth," " layeth "
(literally, *foundeth*), and *"formeth"*—are intended to
remind us of God's omnipotence and the *continuous* active
display of His power and wisdom in the universe which
He has created.

Jehovah is altogether a different being from the god of
the deist. He not only once for all " in the beginning "
created the heavens and the earth, and appointed certain
" laws " to regulate their motions, without troubling Himself
further about them, or about man, who is admittedly the
goal and climax of His creative work on earth. No.
" My Father worketh hitherto," said our Lord Jesus, " and
I work ";[1] and this is equally true in the sphere of creation,
providence, and redemption. According to the Biblical
view, as a Bible scholar well observes, " God stretches out
the heavens every day afresh, and every day He lays the
foundation of the earth, which, if His power did not uphold
it, would move from its orbit and fall into ruin."[2] In like
manner, when it is said that " He formeth the spirit of man
within him," it does not refer merely " to the creation of
the spirits or souls of men once for all, but denotes the
continuous creative formation and guidance of the human
spirit by the Spirit of God."[3]

Now let us hear what Jehovah, the Author of all being
and all life, the Creator of heaven and earth, proceeds to
say, and be assured, without any shadow of doubt, that
what He hath spoken He will in His appointed time bring
to pass : *" Behold, I* (which is very emphatic) *will make*

----

[1] John v. 17.   [2] Hengstenberg.   [3] Keil.

Jerusalem a goblet (or 'basin') *of reeling* (or 'giddiness') *unto all the peoples round about.*"

The cup of reeling, or giddiness, is frequently used in Scripture as a symbol of the judgment of God which brings man into a condition of helplessness and misery like unto that of the staggering, intoxicated man who is unable to stand, or walk. "*For in the hand of Jehovah,*" we read in the Psalms, "*is a cup, and the wine is red* (or '*foameth*'); *it is full of mixture, and He poureth out of the same; surely the dregs thereof, the wicked of the earth shall wring them out, and drink them.*"[1]

In Isa. li. 21–23 the figure is used of the judgments which Israel itself first experiences: "*Therefore hear now this, thou afflicted, and drunken, but not with wine: thus saith thy Lord the Lord, and thy God that pleadeth the cause of His people, Behold, I have taken out of thine hand the cup of staggering* (or '*reeling*'), *even the bowl of the cup of My fury; thou shalt no more drink it again: and I will put it into the hand of them that afflict thee; which have said to thy soul, Bow down, that we may go over: and thou hast laid thy back as the ground, and as the street to them that go over.*"

In those passages, however, it is the כּוֹס, *kos* (cup), that is spoken of, but here in Zech. xii. it is the סַף, *saph*,[2] the *bowl*, or "*basin* of reeling*"; the thought expressed in this instance is that of a vessel large enough for all nations to drink out of it, "either together, or one after another in succession." And they shall all drink of this intoxicating cup of God's judgment and stagger and fall, not to rise again.

The structure of the second half of the verse presents some difficulty, and has been variously rendered and interpreted by commentators. Literally, the clause in Hebrew reads, "*And also upon Judah shall be in the siege against Jerusalem.*"

The question is, What subject must be supplied to the

---

[1] Ps. lxxv. 8.

[2] סַף, *saph*, has also the signification of *threshold*, and the LXX, Vulgate, Calvin, etc., have translated it in that sense; but the rendering *basin* is the only suitable one here. It is used of the vessel containing the blood of the Paschal Lamb; also in 2 Sam. xvii. 28 and 1 Kings vii. 50, etc.

verb "shall be"? Ewald and others have rendered it thus : "*And also upon Judah shall it be (incumbent to be occupied) in the siege against Jerusalem.*" Similarly, already the Targum, Kimchi, Jerome, and many of the modern commentators have explained the passage as " containing a prediction that the people of Judah should be arrayed among the hostile forces marshalled against Jerusalem, that they should be forced to assume such a position by reason of the enemies round about, but that after a certain time the people should be able to break away from the ranks of the hostile army, and would ultimately assist the beleagured citizens of Jerusalem."

I cannot enter on a minute examination of the critical grounds on which this view has been advocated, but I believe the explanation to be an erroneous one. It is asserted that it is to be inferred from the context that Judah is regarded as in the camp of the enemy,[1] but I agree with Keil, who truly observes that in what follows—

" There is no indication whatever of Judah's having made common cause with the enemy against Jerusalem ; on the contrary, Judah and Jerusalem stand together in opposition to the nations, and the princes of Judah have strength in the inhabitants of Jerusalem (ver. 5), and destroy the enemy to save Jerusalem (ver. 6). Moreover, it is only by a false interpretation that any one can find a conflict between Judah and Jerusalem indicated in chap. xiv. 14. And throughout it is incorrect to designate the attitude of Judah towards Jerusalem in these verses as ' opposition,' a notion upon which Ebrard (*Offenb. Joh.*) and Kliefoth have founded the marvellous view, that by

---

[1] The following is from Kimchi's commentary : " The sense of the whole passage is, that when Gog and Magog come against Jerusalem after the redemption, they will go up by the land of Judah, for the desire of their faces will be to come against Jerusalem first ; and they will not be anxious first to subdue the whole land of Israel, for they will think, when we have subdued Jerusalem, the whole land will fall before us. But they will go up to Jerusalem by the way of the land of Judah, which is their natural route, and they will take with them the children of Judah against their will to go with them to besiege Jerusalem ; and so Jonathan has interpreted."

Jerusalem with its inhabitants and the house of David we are to understand the unbelieving portion of Israel ; and by Judah with its princes, Christendom, or the true people of God, formed of believing Israelites and increased by believing Gentiles. Judah is not opposed to Jerusalem, but simply distinguished from it, just as the Jewish kingdom or people is frequently designated by the prophets as Jerusalem and Judah. The גַם, *gam*, which does not separate, but adds, is of itself inapplicable to the idea of opposition. Consequently, we should expect the words ' also upon Judah ' to express the thought that Judah will be visited with the same fate as Jerusalem— as Luther, Calvin, and many others follow the Peshito in supposing that they do."

The best rendering of the clause in my view is that suggested by a Hebrew student,[1] namely : " *And also on Judah shall be* (or, *fall, this reeling*) *in* (or ' *during*') *the siege* (*which is to take place*) *against Jerusalem* "—the sense being that already expressed by Keil, that Judah, which stands here for all the rest of the people of the land, shall experience the same ordeal of suffering in that siege as the inhabitants of Jerusalem, ere the Lord finally interferes on their behalf as the destroyer of their enemies.

The prediction of judgment against the nations who will be gathered against Jerusalem " in that day," is strengthened in the 3rd verse by the use of another figure : " *And it shall come to pass in that day, that I will make Jerusalem a burdensome stone* (lit., *a stone for lifting*) *for all the peoples ; all that burden themselves with it* (lit., *all that lift it*) *shall be sore wounded* (or ' *lacerated*,' or ' *tear rents for themselves*') ; *and all the nations of the earth shall be gathered together against it*." [2]

[1] W. H. Lowe, M.A., in his *Hebrew Student's Commentary*. Pusey thinks that the " Burden of the Word of the Lord " is the subject to be supplied, *i.e.*, the burden which was to be, or should be, upon Judah, *i.e.*, upon all great and small ; but that phrase is too remote from the verb to admit of its being regarded as the " natural subject."

[2] The figure of the " burdensome stone " is, according to Jerome (died 420) and others, based on a custom which prevailed in Palestine. That " old

It has been pointed out that there is a gradation in the thought, both in the figure of the " burdensome stone," which cuts and wounds those who try to lift it, whilst the " reeling cup " in the 2nd verse only makes powerless; and also in the description given of the hosts gathered for the attack. In the 2nd verse the nations round about Jerusalem are spoken of, but in the 3rd verse it is " all peoples " and " all nations of the earth."

The magnitude of the danger and of the sufferings of Jerusalem are brought before our minds in the last clause of the 3rd verse, and are to be inferred from the fact that " *all nations of the earth,*" represented, no doubt, by the flower of their armies, " will be gathered against it."

" The gathering of these hosts is not unfrequently referred to in the Scripture, and always in language calculated to impress the mind with the peculiar magnitude of the power to be displayed in this last great effort of man under Satan. In the Revelation, for example (chap. xvi. 14), it is said that ' spirits of devils,' working miracles, shall go forth to gather the kings of the whole world to the battle of that great day of God Almighty."[1] Joel also speaks of the same mighty confederation : " Proclaim ye this among the Gentiles, prepare war, wake up the mighty

usage," he says, "is kept up to this day throughout Judea, that in villages, towns, and forts round stones are placed, of very great weight, on which young men are wont to practise themselves ; and, according to their varying strength, lift them—some to the knees, others to the navel, others to the shoulders and head ; others lift the weight above the head, with their two hands raised up, showing the greatness of their strength. In the Acropolis at Athens I saw a brass globe, of very great weight, which I, with my little weak body could scarcely move. When I asked its object, I was told by the inhabitants that the strength of wrestlers was proved by that mass, and that no one went to a match until it was ascertained, by the lifting of that weight, who ought to be set against whom."

But, as it has been observed, the stone of which the prophet speaks here was not such a round stone, but one with sharp edges by which those who sought to raise it were lacerated. Keil may be more correct in considering that the figure is taken from operations connected with building. Another has suggested that the reference is to " one of the large stones half buried in the earth, which it is the effort of the husbandman to tear from its bed and carry out of his field before he ploughs it."

[1] B. W. Newton.

men, let all the men of war draw near, let them come up;
beat your ploughshares into swords and your pruning-hooks
into spears; let the weak say, I am strong. Assemble
yourselves, and come, all ye Gentiles, and gather yourselves
together round about" (Joel iii. 9–12).

But the extremity of Israel's need, as already stated,
will be God's opportunity for the display of His power in
the destruction of their enemies, and His grace in their
deliverance, It is to "that day" that the prophetic words
in Ps. cxviii. refer:

> *" Out of my distress* [1] *I called upon Jehovah :*
> *Jehovah answered me and set me in a large place.*
> *Jehovah is on my side ; I will not fear :*
> *What can man do unto me ?*
>
> .   .   .   .
>
> *All nations compassed me about :*
> *In the Name of the Lord I will cut them off.*
> *They compassed me about ; yea, they compassed me about :*
> *In the Name of the Lord I will cut them off.*
> *They compassed me about like bees ; they are quenched*
> *   as the fire of thorns :*
> *In the Name of the Lord I will cut them off."*

The *manner* of God's interposition on Israel's behalf is
described in the verses which follow: *" In that day, saith
Jehovah, will I smite every horse with astonishment* (lit., *with
' bewilderment ' or ' stupefaction '), and his rider with madness :
and upon the house of Judah will I open Mine eyes, and every
horse of the peoples* (i.e., *of their attacking cavalry) will I
smite with blindness."*

It is interesting to note that the three nouns *timmahon*,
"astonishment" or "bewilderment"; *shigga'on*, "mad-
ness"; and *'ivvaron*, "blindness," which here describe
God's judgment on the confederated armies of the anti-
Christian world-powers which will be gathered against
Jerusalem, are used elsewhere only of the judgment which

---

[1] מִן הַמֵּצַר. The word also means "straitness," "siege," and is the same as is
used in Zech. xii. 2 of the "siege."

was to come upon Israel in case of their apostasy. In the 2nd verse the prophet uses the symbol of the cup, or goblet, of reeling, which, as we have seen, had also been used in the first instance of Israel. Among the other plagues which Israel has had long to drink out of that "cup" are those enumerated in Deut. xxviii. 28: "*Jehovah shall smite thee with madness, and with blindness, and with astonishment, or bewilderment.*" But when Zion's warfare shall be accomplished and her iniquity pardoned, and God's time to favour Zion comes, He says: "*I will take out of thine hand the cup of reeling, even the bowl of the cup of My fury: thou shalt no more drink again, and I will put it into the hand of them that afflict thee,*" and they shall drink to the dregs these very plagues.

The effect of the enemies of Israel being smitten with these three plagues has been thus described: "The terrified horses of the cavalry of the assembled hosts (being thus suddenly smitten with bewilderment, or terror, are represented as unable any longer to be guided by bit and bridle. The riders in their madness are described as unable to manage their steeds, while the steeds themselves are portrayed as struck with blindness (or 'blind staggers'), and therefore unable to escape from the dangers around them. And while the enemies of God's people will find themselves in such straits at the very moment when they imagined that they had gained the victory, and while, instead of chasing the vanquished Jews in headlong flight, they themselves are described as rushing upon destruction, Jehovah will '*open His eyes upon the house of Judah,*' which stands here for the whole covenant nation."

And that look of Jehovah, through the eyes of their Messiah Jesus, upon His long unbelieving and rebellious people—a look of love and pity, not unmixed with tender reproach—will have something of the same effect on stubborn Israel as the look of the Lord Jesus on Peter from the hall of Caiaphas the high priest,[1] when that apostle had thrice denied Him. It will at last soften and

[1] Luke xxii. 61, 62.

melt their hard heart to true repentance, and cause them to "weep bitterly." But this is set forth fully in the last part of this chapter, and for the present we must return to the prophet's description of their outward deliverance and the destruction of their enemies.

While terror and confusion seize the ranks of the assembled hosts as the result of the plagues with which they shall be smitten, unity, confidence, and assurance of victory take possession of the "heart" of the reduced, and till then demoralised, remnant of Judah, from the moment that they become conscious that the eye of Jehovah is upon them for good, and that the "Captain of the Lord's host" Himself is with them : "*And the governors* (or '*princes*' [1]) *of Judah shall say in their hearts, The inhabitants of Jerusalem are my strength* (or, '*a strength to me*') *in Jehovah of hosts their God.*"

"The princes of Judah," as Keil truly observes, "recognise in the inhabitants of Jerusalem their strength or might—not in the sense that Judah, being crowded together before Jerusalem, expects help against the foe from the strength of the city and the assistance of its inhabitants, as Hoffmann and Koehler maintain, for 'their whole account of the inhabitants of the land being shut up in the city' (or crowded together before the walls of Jerusalem, and covered by them) is a pure invention, and has no foundation in the text—but in this sense, that the inhabitants of Jerusalem are strong through Jehovah their God, *i.e.*, through the fact that Jehovah has chosen Jerusalem, and by virtue of this election will save the city of His sanctuary" (comp. x. 12 with iii. 2, i. 17, ii. 16).

It is the fact that *Jehovah hath chosen Jerusalem*, and has returned to her with mercies,[2] which makes the princes of Judah confident in her invincibility. "God is in the midst of her," sings the Psalmist, looking on to the solemn

---

[1] אַלֻּפֵי, *alluphei.* See the footnote on the meaning of "*alluph*" in chap. ix. 7. The root-idea is expressed in the LXX, which renders "captain of thousands."

[2] Chap. i. 16.

events of "that day" in the spirit of prophecy—"she shall
not be moved; God shall help her" (lit., "*at the dawn of
the morning*,"[1] *i.e.*, after the long night of sorrow and
weeping.

A slight alteration in the original text of this verse
has been suggested already in the Targum, which would
read: "The princes of Judah shall say in their heart, The
strength of the inhabitants of Judah is in Jehovah their
God." But the "correction" is not needed, for this is not
the only instance, even in Zechariah, where a collective
body is represented as speaking in the singular as one man.
Thus, the inhabitants of Bethel speak to the prophet
through the deputation which they sent to him (chap. vii.
1–5), saying, "Should I weep, etc.?" The singular pronoun, לִי, *li* ("my," or, "to me") is meant to express the
fact that *each individual* says, "*in their heart*" (which is
also in the singular), because all are *as one* in this confidence that there is strength for them in Jehovah their
God, whose power is now displayed on behalf of Jerusalem.
"*And in that day*," the prophecy proceeds, "*will I make the
princes of Judah as a pan* (or '*basin*') *of fire among wood,
and like a torch of fire among sheaves, and they shall devour
all the people round about on the right hand and on the left,
and Jerusalem shall yet again dwell in her own place in
Jerusalem*" (*tachteah*, lit., "*under her place*," i.e., "*in her
place*")—the name "Jerusalem" in this last clause standing
in the first instance for the people personified as a woman,
and in the second for the city as such.

That this great deliverance will be all of grace and by
the power of God is brought out in the verses which
follow: "*And Jehovah shall save the tents of Judah first,
that the glory of the house of David, and the glory of the
inhabitants of Jerusalem, be not magnified against Judah.*"

The reason that "Judah" (which stands here for the
people of the land generally in contrast to those who are
within the city of Jerusalem) are saved "first," is not, as is
mistakenly supposed by some, because Judah, having,

though unwillingly, joined the foe in the siege, " will be found in a place more rebellious and more evil than that of Jerusalem," but because of their weak and defenceless condition (as indicated by the fact that they dwell in "tents ") as contrasted with those within the city walls. Or, in the words of another, " The defenceless land will be delivered sooner than the well-defended capital, that the latter may not lift itself up above the former, but that both may humbly acknowledge (as Jerome expresses it) that the victory is the Lord's," and that both alike may magnify the grace of God in their deliverance. " The glory (or 'splendour,' תִּפְאֶרֶת, *tiphereth*) of the house of David " consists in the fact that it is the God-appointed *royal line* in Israel, which was continued in Zerubbabel, the prince who was Zechariah's contemporary, and culminated in our Lord Jesus, the true Son and Heir of David ; and " the glory " or " splendour " of the inhabitants of Jerusalem may be regarded as consisting in the fact that they may consider themselves as especially privileged and exalted above the rest of the people of the land as dwellers in the city which God has especially chosen as the seat of His earthly throne.

But the deliverance of the defenceless people of the land will be only the " first " act of God's interposition on behalf of Israel in that day.

The heart of the great conflict will be in and around the walls of Jerusalem, for on it all the fury of the enemy's attack will be directed. But " *in that day shall Jehovah defend* (lit., ' *shield*') *the inhabitants of Jerusalem, and he that is feeble among them shall be as David ; and the house of David shall be as God, as the Angel of Jehovah before them*." Not its walls or bulwarks will constitute the " defence " of the remnant of the people which shall be left in Jerusalem in that solemn day. From chaps. xiii. 8, 9 and xiv. 1–6, which, as we shall see, refer to the same invasion of the land and siege of Jerusalem by the Gentile hosts, we learn that the city, or a great part of it, will actually be " taken " and spoiled, and half of the city (that is, of the population) " go forth into captivity," and that then, when the enemy lifts his hand for the last blow in order utterly to destroy them, " that the name of Israel may be no more in remembrance "—the visible appearance of Jehovah in the person of their Messiah Jesus takes place. The uplifted arm of the adversary becomes suddenly withered; and because Jehovah intervenes as the shield of the remnant that remains, therefore " the residue of the people shall not be cut off from the city " (xiv. 2). " *For thus saith the Lord unto me, Like as when the lion growleth, and the young lion over his prey, if a multitude of shepherds be called forth against him, he will not be dismayed at their voice, nor abase himself for the noise of them : so shall the Lord of hosts come down to fight upon Mount Zion, and upon the hill thereof. As birds flying, so will the Lord of hosts protect Jerusalem ; He will protect and deliver it ; He will pass over and preserve it.*" [1]

And not only shall Jehovah Himself " go forth and fight against those nations," but when once the weak and broken remnant of the people recognise their Divine Saviour, and hear the shout of the King in their midst, they are suddenly girt with superhuman strength. The feeblest of them, *hannikhshal* (lit., " he that stumbleth," *i.e.*, the one so weak that he could not even stand, much less fight), shall in that day be as David—the greatest of Israel's national heroes, and " to the Jew, therefore,· the highest type of strength and glory on earth "—and the house of David shall be as *Elohim* (*i.e.*, " God " in His might and majesty), and as the Divine " Angel of Jehovah," who of old went " before them " in the desert and through the Red Sea smiting down their enemies, and therefore, " the highest type of strength and glory in heaven."

No wonder, therefore, that through *Him* they " will push down their adversaries," and " *through His Name* tread them under that had risen up against them " ; [2] and, if I may venture a brief digression, I would say that there is a message in this scripture for you too, dear Christian reader. It is this, that however weak in yourself and ready

[1] Isa. xxxi. 4, 5 (R.V.).   [2] Ps. xliv. 4, 5.

to " stumble," you may be strong in the Lord and in the
power of His might, and that " more " and " greater " is He
that is for us, and with us, than all that can be against us.
" *Through God*," exclaims the Psalmist, " we shall do
valiantly " (or, as it might be rendered, " *in God* we shall
form an host"—however weak and few and insignificant in
ourselves), for He it is that shall tread down our adversaries.[1]

But to return to our chapter. While Jehovah endows
the inhabitants of Jerusalem with supernatural strength so
that they perform exploits, He will " *seek to destroy all
nations that come against Jerusalem* " (*i.e.*, in martial array
to attack, as the phrase in the original implies). The
expression " seek to do " is always used in the Bible " of
seeking to do what it *is a person's set purpose to do if he
can*." Man may seek to do a thing and fail, but " woe
indeed to those whom Almighty God shall seek to
destroy " ; for that on which His heart is once set He will
assuredly accomplish, whether it will be in blessing on His
people or in vengeance on His enemies.

The Great Spiritual Crisis in Israel's History

The first nine verses of the 12th chapter of Zechariah
describe prophetically, as we have seen, Israel's great
national deliverance and the destruction of the armies of
the confederated anti-Christian world-powers which shall be
gathered in the final siege of Jerusalem. That will, indeed,
be a great and wonderful day in their history, " an hour of
triumph such as they have never known before, greater than
when they quitted Egypt ; greater than when they triumphed
over Pharaoh and his host at the Red Sea ; greater than
when they entered the Promised Land, and the walls of
Jericho fell down before them."

But yet there is something greater, more solemn and
more blessed, than mere outward deliverance and triumph
over their enemies that Israel is to experience on " that day,"
and that is God's final conquest *over them*. Ah! yes, Israel

[1] Ps. lx. 12.

shall then learn the truth of the saying, that "our only true triumphs are God's triumphs *over us*, that *His defeats of us* are our only true victories"; [1] and will learn with the great apostle —whose history and experiences are in many ways a foreshadowing of the history and experience of his nation—to say, " Thanks be unto God, who always leadeth us in triumph in Christ " [2]—that is, as former enemies who have been vanquished, and whom He is now leading about as manifest trophies of His all-subduing grace and power.

" On former occasions, when Jeshurun had been made to ride on the high places of the earth, he had waxed fat and kicked ; then he forsook God which made him, and lightly esteemed the Rock of his salvation. But it will never be so again. He who comes to conquer their foes comes also to subdue their hearts." Hence, great as their triumph will be, great as will have been their individual might in the last stage of their conflict with the surrounding hosts (so that "he that is feeble among them will be as David "), yet, when they return from their victory, this their glorious day of triumph will end in self-abasement and tears.[3] How this wonderful change will be brought about, how the stubborn heart of unbelieving and gainsaying Israel will at last be broken, we are told in the 10th verse: " *And I will pour upon the house of David and upon the inhabitants of Jerusalem the spirit of grace and supplication ; and they shall look upon Me whom they have pierced : and they shall mourn for Him, as one mourneth for his only son, and shall be in bitterness for Him, as one that is in bitterness for his first-born.*"

" I think," said a great master in Israel, "there is nothing in the whole range of scripture more touching than the promise contained in these simple, unadorned words. As they touch the heart they fix themselves on our memory. Who can ever forget them ? ' They shall look unto (or " upon ") Me whom they have pierced.' " [4]

And yet there is not another scripture in the Old

---

[1] Dean Alford.   [2] 2 Cor. ii. 14 (R.V.).
[3] B. W. Newton.   [4] Adolph Saphir.

Testament around which more controversy has raged than around "these simple, unadorned," and, to the Christian, most precious words. Jewish commentators and some rationalistic Christian writers who seem not less biased in their anti-Christological methods in interpreting the Old Testament,[1] have tried their utmost to divert this scripture from Him whose rejection and suffering unto death, and yet future recognition and penitent reception on the part of " His own " nation, it foretells.

The modern Jewish translation of the passage as given, for instance, in the " Appendix of the Revised Version," issued by the Jewish Community in England for the use of Jews, in 1896, is as follows : " And they (*i.e.*, the house of David and the inhabitants of Jerusalem) shall look up to Me because of Him whom they (*i.e.*, the nations which come against Jerusalem) have pierced." This translation, first suggested by Rashi, adopted by Kimchi in his commentary on Zechariah, was fully elaborated by Rabbi Isaak of Troki [2] in his polemical work against Christianity, *Chizzuk Emunah* (" Strengthening of the Faith "), who thus explains :

" If it should happen that any of the Israelites should be pierced, namely, in that war, even though it should be one of the most inconsiderable, they shall wonder greatly how this could happen, and will think that this is the

[1] Thus, for instance, Ewald, one of the fathers of the " Higher Criticism," and who has a very large following among Christian commentators and theological writers in this country, considers the mourning pictured by the prophet in the scripture " as a mourning ·over the Jews fallen in the defence of their city," as martyrs for their country and faith ; those slain in the battlefield he considers to be " those pierced by the heathen." Canon Driver, in his *Introduction to the Literature of the Old Testament*, makes this passage to refer to some " deed of blood " in which the house of David, together with the people, became implicated some time *before these chapters were written*, which, according to him (and in opposition to Ewald and his school, who assign a pre-exilic origin to the second half of Zechariah) was some time between 518 and 300 B.C., of which deed of blood, as pointed out in my " Introduction to the second half of Zechariah," which could occasion such deep and universal mourning, *history knows nothing*.

[2] Isaac Ben Abraham of Troki, a Karaite Rabbi—born in 1533, died in 1594. His book is still the chief arsenal whence many arguments of modern Jews in their polemics against Christianity are drawn.

beginning of a fall and defeat before their enemies, as Joshua did. When the men of Ai smote thirty-six of Israel, he said : ' Alas ! O Lord God, why didst Thou cause this people to pass the Jordan ? ' And again : ' What shall I say when Israel turn their backs before their enemies ? ' (Josh. vii.). So will it be at that time if they should see any of them pierced, they will be astonished, and look on Me on account of Him whom they pierced."

This translation, however, to which English-speaking Jews have, as we have seen, officially committed themselves, only shows the length which modern Judaism will go in misinterpreting the plainest scriptures so as to evade the Christian argument drawn from them in support of the claims of Jesus of Nazareth.[1]

It is a rendering which is contrary to grammar and to the natural sense, for, first, the word אֶת אֲשֶׁר (*eth asher*) cannot possibly mean " because of Him whom," but simply " whom," emphatically and definitely expressed. And, secondly, the modern Jewish rendering or paraphrase implies that the subject of the second verb of the first verse, דָּקָרוּ, *daqaru*—" pierced," is a different one from that of the first verb, וְהִבִּיטוּ, *v'hibitu*—" *shall look*," in the same short sentence. But it is altogether unnatural to suppose that two

---

[1] An instance of departure not only from the plain sense and grammar, but from the more ancient Jewish traditional interpretations of Messianic passages for controversial reasons, is found in Rashi (Rabbi Solomon Bar Isaac), the most popular commentator on the Bible and Talmud—born at Troys in 1040, died in 1105. In his commentary on this passage in the Bible he says : " They shall look back to mourn because the Gentiles had pierced some amongst them, and killed some of them."

But in his commentary on the Talmud he says : " The words, ' the land shall mourn,' are found in the prophecy of Zechariah, and he prophesies of the future that they shall mourn on account of Messiah, the son of Joseph, who shall be slain in the war of Gog and Magog " (Sukkah, fol. 52, col. 1). That this manifest contradiction is not accidental, but intentional, appears from the fact that this writer has dealt similarly by other controverted passages ; for instance, Isa. liii., which, in his commentary on the Bible, he expounds of the Jewish people ; but in his commentary on the Talmud he explains of Messiah. Indeed, his determination to get rid of any explanation that could favour Christianity is plainly avowed in his commentary on Ps. xxi., where he says : " Our Rabbis have expounded it of the King Messiah, but it is better to expound it further of David himself, in order to answer heretics."

parties were in the prophet's mind, and that "they" who "shall look" are the Jews, and "they" who "have pierced" are the Gentile nations.

Another "Jewish" rendering of the passage, equally unfair and even less tenable, but contradictory of the above, is that found in the bulky "Jewish Family Bible," which has also a kind of "official" air about it, inasmuch as it was "printed with the sanction of (the late) Rev. Dr. Adler, the chief Rabbi."[1] The critical passage in question is translated thus: "But I will pour upon the house of David, and upon the inhabitants of Jerusalem, the spirit of grace and of supplication, and they *whom the nations are piercing* shall look upon Me, and shall mourn over it," etc. But a translation which does not scruple to interpolate words and expressions is not worth noticing, except to point out that it can claim, at best, to be only a polemical *Targum*, or commentary, the chief aim of which is the elimination of all references to a suffering, atoning Messiah from the pages of the Old Testament. It is not necessary to point out to any one who can read the original that the words, "whom the nations were piercing," are not found in the Hebrew text, and are an unjustifiable gloss of the "reviser."

But there is a more ancient Jewish interpretation of this prophecy than those to which I referred, which were invented by Jews for controversial reasons; it is that, namely, which applies the passage to Messiah ben Joseph. Thus Aben Ezra,[2] who wrote after Rashi, says: "All the heathen shall look to me to see what I shall do to those who pierced Messiah, the son of Joseph"; and Abarbanel,[3] after noticing the interpretation of Rashi and Kimchi, says:

---

[1] It claims to be the Authorised or "Anglican" version, revised by Dr. M. Friedländer, Principal of the Jews' College, published in 1881. Its honesty as a translation, or "revision," may be judged from its rendering of this and other Messianic passages.

[2] Aben Ezra—Rabbi Abraham ben Ezra—one of the greatest of Jewish commentators and grammarians: born, 1088; died, 1176.

[3] Abarbanel (or Abravanel), Rabbi Dan Isaac ben Jehudah, the celebrated Jewish statesman and philosopher, theologian and commentator: born, 1437; died, 1508.

" It is more correct to interpret the passage of Messiah, the son of Joseph, as our Rabbis, of blessed memory, have interpreted it in the treatise Sukkah,[1] for he shall be a mighty man of valour of the tribe of Joseph, and shall at first be captain of the Lord's host in that war (namely, against Gog and Magog), but in that war shall die."

This interpretation is of interest and importance to the Christian student, in so far as it shows that the disciples of Christ, when the New Testament was written, were not alone in interpreting this scripture of the Messiah. The Jewish Rabbis explained it in the same way, only they applied it to Messiah ben Joseph, who does not exist in Scripture, and is an invention of their own brains.

Let me, while dwelling on the Jewish interpretation of this passage, reproduce a striking passage from Alshech,[2]

[1] The passage will be found in Bab. Talmud, Sukk. 52a.

[2] Moses Alshech flourished in Safed, Palestine, in the second half of the sixteenth century. The doctrine or theory of two Messiahs—a Messiah ben Joseph, who should suffer and die, and the Messiah ben David, who shall reign in power and glory—can be traced back to the third or fourth century A.D., and very probably originated in the perplexity of the Talmudists at the apparently irreconcilable pictures of a suffering, and yet a glorious Messiah, which they found in the prophecies. Instead of finding the solution in two advents of the one person, they explained the different scriptures as referring to *two different persons.*

" But whom did the Rabbis mean by the epithet Messiah ben Joseph ? " writes a learned Hebrew Christian brother. We do not hesitate to answer : " None other person than Jesus, whom, after their great disappointment in the revolution of Bar-Cochba, they tacitly acknowledged as the suffering Messiah, and denominated Him by the name that He was commonly called in Galilee, in order perhaps to screen themselves against the hatred and persecution of their own followers, or of their Roman masters. This idea has been hinted at by the Rev. M. Wolkenberg in his translation of *The Pentateuch according to the Talmud*, p. 156, and broadly asserted by Dr. Biesenthal in his Hebrew commentary on St. Luke (chap. xxiii. 48). This accounts for the remarkable fact that on the Feast of Trumpets, before the blowing of the ram's horn, God's mercy is besought through ' Jesus, the Prince of the Presence of God, the Metatron,' or the One who shares the throne of God. At this same service, verses, mostly from Ps. cxix., are repeated, whose first letters form the name of ' Christon,' but so ingeniously chosen, that they should at the same time read קרע שטן, ' the Bruiser of Satan.' This name also is written on amulets and in Jewish houses when a child is born, as well as the name of the angel, מצמצ׳ה, which is mentioned in the said service, with alteration of only one accountable

which, barring the mention of Messiah ben Joseph, might almost be accepted as a statement of the Christian view of this scripture.

" I will do yet a third thing, and that is, that 'they shall look unto Me,' for they shall lift up their eyes unto Me in perfect repentance, when they see Him whom they pierced, that is, Messiah, the Son of Joseph ; for our Rabbis, of blessed memory, have said that He will take upon Himself all the guilt of Israel, and shall then be slain in the war to make an atonement in such manner that it shall be accounted as if Israel had pierced Him, for on account of their sin He has died ; and, therefore, in order that it may be reckoned to them as a perfect atonement, they will repent and look to the blessed One, saying that there is none beside Him to forgive those that mourn on account of Him who died for their sin : this is the meaning of ' They shall look upon Me.' "

There is another critical point on which I must very briefly touch before proceeding with the exposition. The reading of the Massoretic text, וְהִבִּיטוּ אֵלַי, *v'hibitu elai* (" they shall look *unto Me* "), has been much disputed by Jews and modern writers, but it is supported by all the ancient versions and extant MSS with very few exceptions, and is the reading which is accepted in all the Rabbinic quotations made above. In a few MSS, how-ever, the marginal correction—אֵלָיו, *alav*—" unto Him," instead of אֵלַי, *elai*—" unto Me," was made by Jewish hands ; and in several instances this " Keri," or marginal reading, has, as is sometimes apt to be the case, crept into the text itself.

letter, and which stands for the King our Righteousness, ' the King our Righteousness, Jesus the Messiah.' To this Metatron is again applied in the Talmud (*Sanhed.* p. 256), the passage Ex. xxiii. 20, and it is added that ' His name is the name of His Master.' And in the liturgy of the Feast of Tabernacles reference is made to the glorious and dread Metatron, who was transformed from flesh to fire.

" Who cannot see in these mysterious hints a purposely covered belief in the Messiahship of Jesus, and that in a most orthodox manner ? " (From *Rays of Messiah's Glory*.)

But we need not impute any dishonest intention to the Jews in this matter, as some have done,[1] and of a desire to corrupt the text; for, as a matter of fact, however much they obscured and perverted the true sense of Scripture, through their *misinterpretations*, and in their paraphrases and commentaries, they always most jealously guarded the *original letter* and text of Scripture from alteration or corruption.

The marginal reading in the few MSS which is also accepted in the Talmud, is, however, not recognised as a *Keri*, or proper reading, in the Massoretic text. It originated in the very natural difficulty, from the Jewish point of view, of conceiving how God, who is undoubtedly the speaker in the first part of the verse, since He promises to pour out the spirit of grace and supplication, can be "pierced." It requires the light which is thrown on Messianic prophecy by the New Testament; and a knowledge of Him in whom dwelt the fulness of the Godhead bodily, and who could say, "I and the Father are 'One,'" for men to grasp this mystery.[2]

But we are told by Jewish and rationalistic writers that we must not "read the New Testament into these Old Testament prophecies, "but rather ask ourselves what meaning the people in the prophet's own time would attach to them. To this we reply. First: Though it is true, generally speaking, that the prophets spoke first and primarily to those in their own time, there is, never-

---

[1] As, for instance, Martini.

[2] It need not, it seems to me, be supposed that the Apostle John, in John xix. 37, quoted from a manuscript which read, "They shall look *on Him*." It is rather his adaptation and *application* of the prophecy in the light of fulfilment (as far as the piercing is concerned) to our Lord Jesus. He knew well that in its connection, in Zech. xii., it is spoken of God; but this passage, like many other prophecies and promises which in the Old Testament centre in Jehovah, find their fulfilment and realisation in history in the person of the Messiah, whom this beloved apostle depicts to us as "the Word made flesh," and in whose face he beheld the glory of the only-begotten of the Father. Hence, as he now gazes upon Him on the Cross, and beholds the Roman soldier plunging his spear into His side, he says, "Here, truly, is the One to whom this Scripture applies—they shall look *on Him* whom they have pierced."

theless, a predictive element in Holy Scripture, and that many of the prophetic utterances concerning " the sufferings of Christ and the glory that should follow " were not only not fully comprehensible to the people to whom they spoke, but to the prophets themselves,[1] and could only be fully understood after, and in the light of, their fulfilment.

Secondly: Even the Jews in the prophet's own time, if they pondered on the prophet's word, must have understood, at any rate this much, that the prediction refers to " a national mourning over some one who stood in an intimate connection with Jehovah, and whose rejection and death was to be bitterly bewailed by the people of Israel. Such would have been the meaning conveyed by the passage to the Jews of the time of Zechariah. Assuming that the prophecy proceeded from the same author as that of the previous chapter—and there are not sufficient grounds on which to deny it— the rejection of the representative of Jehovah (namely, the Good Shepherd, whose rejection is there spoken of as followed by a terrible punishment), and the national mourning described as taking place for one who should be, in some mysterious manner, ' pierced ' by the nation when acting in the capacity of the representative of Jehovah, must both have been considered by the hearers of the prophet to refer to one and the same event."

But now, to be done with criticism and controversy, let us look into the heart of this great prophetic promise.

We will take the words in the order in which they stand in the Hebrew. " *And I will pour* "—וְשָׁפַכְתִּי, *v'sha-phachti*—the word expresses the *fulness* and abundance of the gift of the Spirit which shall then be bestowed upon the people. The promise points back to Joel ii. 28, 29 : " *And it shall come to pass afterward that I will pour out My spirit upon all flesh,*" etc.; or, as we read in Isaiah : " *I will pour My spirit upon thy seed, and My blessing upon thine offspring*"—in the same abundance and with the

---

[1] 2 Pet. i. 10–12.

same blessed quickening and fertilising effects as " waters "
and " streams " are poured " upon the dry and thirsty
ground." [1]

" *Upon the house of David and upon the inhabitants of
Jerusalem.*" Jerusalem and its inhabitants are mentioned
alone in the text, "not as though the blessing of the
gracious outpouring of the spirit was to be confined to
them, but because Jerusalem is used as a designation for
the whole people, in accord with the custom of regarding
the capital as the representative of the whole nation ";[2] for
it is clear enough from the whole context that, if the great
penitential sorrow which is to be the fruit of this outpouring commences in Jerusalem as the centre, and with
" the house of David," which stands for the highest among
the people, it extends to " the whole land " (ver. 12), and
to all " the families of the people."

" *The spirit of grace and of supplication* "—רוּחַ חֵן וְתַחֲנוּנִים,
ruach hen v'thachnunim—is the Holy Spirit of God who
conveys grace and brings our hearts into a condition of
grace. Just as " *The spirit of wisdom and understanding* "
is the spirit infusing wisdom and understanding, and " *the
spirit of counsel and might* " is that same spirit imparting
the gift of *counsel* to see what is to be done, and of *might*
to do it, and " *the spirit of knowledge, and of the fear of
the Lord,*" is that same spirit infusing intimate acquaintance
with God with awe at His infinite majesty ; so " the spirit
of grace " is that same spirit infusing grace and bringing
into a state of favour with God, and a " *spirit of supplication* " is that spirit calling out of the inmost soul the cry
for a yet larger measure of the grace already given.[3] But
the simplest way to understand the two kindred terms,
hen and *thachnunim*—" grace and supplication "—is to view
them in the light of cause and effect, for grace is that
which God bestows and the Holy Spirit conveys, and
" supplication " is the *fruit* of that *condition of heart*, or
soul, which that same spirit creates within us.

[1] Isa. xliv. 3 ; see also Ezek. xxxix. 29, xxxvi. 26, 27.
[2] Keil.   [3] Pusey.

The blessed effect of the outpouring of the spirit of
grace and supplication on the house of David and the
inhabitants of Jerusalem " in that day " will be that " *they
shall look upon Me whom they have pierced, and mourn.*"

(*a*) They shall look (וְהִבִּטוּ, *v'hibitu*) with no ordinary
or mere passing look, but " with trustful hope and longing," as one has paraphrased it. Among the other meanings which this particular verb has is that of " to regard,"
" to consider," " to contemplate," " to look upon with
pleasure." It is used, for instance, in that remarkable
story of the brazen serpent in Num. xxi. 9, which, as
it seems to me, was in the mind of Zechariah when he
uttered this prophecy : " *And Moses made a serpent of brass,
and set it on a pole* (or ' *the standard* '), *and it came to pass
that if a serpent had bitten any man, when he beheld it* (or
looked unto—וְהִבִּיט, *v'hibit*), *the serpent of brass, he lived.*"
With this same eager look of faith and hope shall Israel
in that day behold and contemplate Him, who is the great
antitype of the brazen serpent, and who was " lifted up "
for us on the Cross, that whosoever believeth on Him
should not perish but have everlasting life. It is this
word also which is used in Num. xii. 8, as describing the
beatific view of the very " form " or " similitude " of God,
which it was the distinction and privilege of Moses above
the other prophets to " behold." Thus also, not " in a
vision " or " in a dream," but face to face, and with no
longer any veil to hide His glory, shall Israel in that day
" look upon " Him who came once in humiliation to suffer
and die, but who shall be manifested now in the glory of
His Father and with His holy angels.[1]

(*b*) " Unto Me," or " Upon Me (אֵלַי, *elai*).

This sets forth the character and majesty of Him
whom they shall behold as their great Deliverer, for the
One who speaks throughout the chapter, as already

---

[1] See also, for instance, Ps. xxxiv. 5 : "They *looked* unto Him and were
lightened"; and Isa. li. 1, 2 : "Look unto the Rock whence ye were hewn";
"Look unto Abraham," etc. ; where the same word is used to express the
"look," not only of faith, but of contemplation.

observed, is none other than Jehovah, "which stretcheth forth the heavens, and layeth the foundation of the earth, and formeth the spirit of man within him" (ver. 1); and who in this 10th verse says: "*I will pour* out the spirit of grace and of supplications." This, as already observed above, is a great mystery comprehensible only to faith based on the Biblical revelation of the twofold nature of the Messiah; but when perceived it is very precious and beautiful.

"They shall look *upon Me.*"

The Jewish nation has hitherto regarded faith in our Lord Jesus as irreconcilable with faith in God, and have conceived of Him *as being in opposition* to God.

This was the chief ground of the blind hostility to Christ on the part of the scribes and Pharisees during His earthly ministry, and has continued to this day, not knowing that their hatred of Christ was in its essence nothing else than hatred of God, and their opposition to Him nothing else than a fighting against God. But, as Saul of Tarsus (whose experience and history are in many ways a foreshadowment of the history of his people in relation to Christ) was startled and surprised to learn from that voice on his way to Damascus, "*I am Jesus whom thou persecutest,*" that those hated Nazarenes whom he was persecuting, even unto death, were one with Him who was now revealed to him as the risen and living Son of God, and that he who was touching them was touching "the apple of His eye"; so shall the Jewish nation in the day when the spirit of grace and of supplication is poured upon them, and "the eyes of the blind are opened" to behold the divine glory of their Messiah, be startled and surprised to discover that their having persecuted and "pierced" Him was equivalent to their having persecuted and pierced God, because of His being one with God, in a higher and deeper sense even than believers are with Christ.

But just as the words, "they shall *look unto Me,*" set forth the essential oneness of the pierced One with Jehovah, so does the sudden transition in the same verse from the first person to the third, and the words, " they shall mourn *for Him*," teach us that, as to His person, He is yet *distinct* from God. The same mystery and apparent paradox meet us in many other Old Testament scriptures which speak of the Messiah as " Jehovah " the " mighty God," and yet as one sent by, and coming in the name of God, and is—a mystery which (as already stated above) is solved to all whose eyes have been opened to the Biblical doctrine of the *Tri-unity* of the blessed Godhead, and to the twofold nature of the promised Redeemer, who is perfect God and perfect Man—the Son of David and the Son of the Highest.

(*c*) " Whom they have pierced."

The verb דָּקַר, *daqar*, means " to pierce," or " thrust through with a spear or lance,"[1] and points to " the climax of our Saviour's mortal sufferings " when, as the Gospel narrative bears witness, " one of the soldiers with a spear pierced His side, and straightway there came out blood and water."[2]

It was a Roman soldier who did the actual deed; Roman soldiers also were they who pierced His blessed brow with the crown of thorns, and His hands and feet with those cruel nails; but the guilt and *responsibility* for

[1] See Num. xxv. 7, 8, where the same verb is used in connection with רֹמַח, "spear " or lance; the same verb is used also in Zech. xiii. 3.

[2] It has been urged that stress must not be laid on the literal fulfilment of this item in the prophecy as recorded in the Gospel narrative, since the prophet uses language in chap. xiii. 7 " which if its literal signification be insisted on, would imply death by the sword "; but this is a misapprehension. חֶרֶב, "sword," is used frequently, in *a general way*, as the instrument of death by violence, without in many cases defining that it would be brought about by being literally slain with the sword. In Ps. xxii. 20, *e.g.*, we read : " Deliver my soul from the sword (*i.e.*, from death), my darling (my only one) from the power of the dog "; yet in the immediate connection we read : " They pierced My hands and My feet." We take it then that in chap. xiii. 9 we have a prophecy of Messiah's sufferings unto death in a general way, by the use of a figure well understood as having this signification, but that chap. xii. 10 refers to the definite act in process of the infliction of the sufferings unto death on our Lord, on the literal fulfilment of which the Apostle John lays such emphasis (John xix. 34–37).

these actions will be brought home to the heart and conscience of the Jewish nation in that day, and they will then
acknowledge that both directly, by delivering Him into
the hands of the Gentiles, and indirectly, on account of
their sins, it was *they* who pierced Him.

(*d*) "*And they shall mourn for* (or '*over*') *Him*"—
vesaphedhu alav—not only with the ordinary " mourning,"
as those who mourn for the dead (in which sense the verb
סָפַד, *saphad*, is generally used), but with a *deep and intense*
mourning, namely, " as one that mourneth for his only son "
(or, literally, "*with the mourning for an only one*"), and
"they shall be in bitterness for Him as one that is in
bitterness for his first-born." Mourning for an " only son "
was proverbial as descriptive of the magnitude of the grief,
as we read in Jer. vi. 26 : "*O daughter of my people, gird
thee with sackcloth, and wallow thyself in ashes : make thee
mourning as for an only son, most bitter lamentation.*" And
again in Amos viii. 10 : "*I will make it as the mourning
for an only son.*"

But not only on account of their proverbial use to express the intensity and bitterness of the sorrow and grief,
are these names " the only one " and " first-born " introduced
here in connection with Israel's mourning over the Messiah
whom they had pierced, they are peculiarly appropriate
designations of Him who is " the First-born of every creature," and of whom the apostle exclaims : " We beheld His
glory, the glory as of *the only-begotten of the Father full of
grace and truth.*" And He is not only the " first " and
" only-begotten " as the Son of God, in relation to the
Father, but as the Son of Man, and more particularly in
relation to the Jewish nation. He was *their child of promise*
upon whom the hopes and expectations of the nation had
been centred through the centuries. He is the " only One "
whom this nationally barren woman, who was betrothed
unto Jehovah, had brought forth, as it were, miraculously,
by the power of God. And it was ordained that He should
be " the First-born among many brethren," first and foremost to them who, according to the flesh, are " His own,"

as well as in relation to men generally—and *Him* they have with wicked hands " pierced " and slain ! No wonder that " in that day," when the spirit of grace and supplication is poured upon them, and their eyes are open to behold Him, and to recognise the fearful national crime which they committed, to their own sorrow and hurt, they shall mourn over Him " with the mourning for an only one," and shall be in bitterness for Him as he is in bitterness " who mourneth for his first-born."

It is in that day of their deep sorrow and contrition that they shall, amid their broken-hearted sobs, utter that great national confession and lament contained in that wonderful chapter in Isaiah :

" He was despised, and rejected of men ; a Man of Sorrows, and acquainted with grief ; and as one from whom men hide their face He was despised ; and we esteemed Him not.   Surely He hath borne our griefs, and carried our sorrows ; yet we did esteem Him stricken, smitten of God, and afflicted.   But He was wounded for our transgressions ; He was bruised for our iniquities ; the chastisement of our peace was upon Him ; and with His stripes we are healed. All we like sheep have gone astray ; we have turned every one to his own way, and the Lord hath laid on Him the iniquity of us all."

(*e*) And not only will the mourning be great and intense, it will also be *universal* and yet *individual* : " *In that day shall there be a great mourning in Jerusalem, as the mourning of Hadadrimmon in the valley of Megiddon. And the land shall mourn, every family apart ; the family of the house of David apart, and their wives apart ; the family of the house of Nathan apart, and their wives apart ; the family of the house of Levi apart, and their wives apart ; the family of the Shimeites apart, and their wives apart : all the families that remain, every family apart, and their wives apart.*"

One or two points in these verses need explanation :

(1) Israel's great penitential mourning over their Messiah is likened by the prophet for magnitude to

"the mourning of Hadadrimmon [1] in the valley of Megiddon."

The reference can be nothing else than to the national mourning over the pious young king Josiah, who was slain by Pharaoh Necho " in the valley of Megiddon," as recorded in 2 Kings xxiii. 29, 30, and more fully in 2 Chron. xxxv. 20–27. His death was the greatest sorrow which had till then befallen Judah, inasmuch as he was "the last hope of the declining Jewish kingdom, and in his death the last gleam of the sunset of Judah faded into night." In that great mourning for Josiah the prophet Jeremiah took part, and wrote dirges for it (2 Chron. xxxv. 25), and the national lamentations over him continued and became "an ordinance" in Israel, which survived the seventy years'

---

[1] "Hadadrimmon" was, according to Jerome, a city near Jezreel ("in the valley of Megiddo"), which in his day was called Maximianopolis, and has been identified by others with the site of the modern village of *Rammaneh*, or *Rūmani*, in the same "valley," or "plain"; but the identification is doubtful.

Hitzig, who first held that the reference might be to some mourning for Ahaziah, king of Judah, who was wounded by Jehu when the latter rebelled against Joram, and who fled to Megiddo, and died there (2 Kings ix. 27), afterwards, in his commentary, propounded the still more absurd view, which, however, has been adopted by some modern writers, *i.e.*, that the mourning of Hadadrimmon refers to the mourning for the god Adonis, who, according to mythology, was slain by a boar, and whose orgies probably had their origin in Phœnicia.

A plausible ground for the conjecture that Hadadrimmon, instead of being a place-name, might rather be the name of the object of mourning—that is, the god Adonis—is advanced by these critics, namely, that according to 2 Chron. xxxv., Josiah, though mortally wounded in Megiddo, was brought to Jerusalem, where he died, and that the great mourning for him took place there.

But to this it has been properly replied that "the mourning may be considered as having commenced at Hadadrimmon, where the good king received his deadly wound, even though the great national mourning took place in Jerusalem, whither his body was brought from the fatal field."

Moreover, as it has been suggested, "the mourning of Hadadrimmon" may be explained as "the mourning over Hadadrimmon," *i.e.*, over the national calamity which took place there.

Other suggestions—such as that of Pressel, who considers that the mourning refers to the wailing of the mother of Sisera over her son, the great chieftain of the Canaanites, who was slain by Jael not far from Megiddo—are not worth examining. It is quite wonderful to what absurd theories and conjectures some scholars will resort when the simple and obvious sense of these prophecies is passed over.

captivity and continued " to this day," when the chronicles were closed.   It was worthy, therefore, to be referred to by the prophet, and to be compared with the still greater and more bitter mourning of repentant Israel in the future.

(2) In the universal, yet individual, mourning which, commencing in Jerusalem, will spread throughout the whole land, four " families " are especially singled out as being conspicuous.   Of these four, two are well known, namely, " the family of the house of David " and " the family of the house of Levi."   But who are meant by " the family of the house of Nathan " and " the family of Shimei " (or of " the Shimeites ") ?

It would require a treatise to analyse the various conjectures and explanations which have been advanced on this point by Jewish and Christian commentators.

Let me in the briefest possible manner give here what seems to me the most satisfactory explanation.   And first, we may say with certainty that " the family of the house of Nathan " does not refer to the posterity of Nathan the prophet, as representing the prophetic order, as the Rabbis and some Christian writers have supposed, but to the family of Nathan, the son of David and brother of Solomon (2 Sam. v. 14), whose name figures also in the genealogy of our Lord in Luke iii. 31.   Likewise, " the family of the Shimeite " does not refer to the tribe of Simeon, which, according to rabbinic fiction, furnished the teachers of the nation ;[1] for in that case, apart from other considerations, the name would be differently written in the Hebrew,[2] but refers to Shimei, the son of Gershon and grandson of Levi (Num. iii. 18).   We have thus two families of the royal and two of the priestly line, and of these one stands for the

---

[1] Jerome sums up the Jewish view, which he seems to have adopted, thus : "In David the regal tribe is included, *i.e.*, Judah.   In Nathan the prophetic order is described.   Levi refers to the priests from whom the priesthood sprang.   In Simeon the teachers of Israel are included, as companies of masters sprang from that tribe.   He says nothing about the other tribes, as they had.no special privilege or dignity."   But, as stated above, these conjectures rest on no historic basis of fact.

[2] שִׁמְעֹנִי, Simonite—instead of as it is in the text—שִׁמְעִי.

chief (David for the royal, and Levi for the *priestly*), and
the other (Nathan for the royal, and Shimei for the priestly),
for the *subordinate* families of their lines—*as including and
representing the whole* — to indicate, as Hengstenberg
suggests, that the mourning spoken of would pervade every
family (of these lines) from the highest to the lowest.

But though these, as the two aristocratic and privileged
lines, the rulers and priests, who, alas! in times past often
set an *evil* example to the whole nation, will now be foremost in their self-contrition and mourning over the great
national sin, their example for *good* will now also be
followed by all the rest of the people. This is expressed
in the last verse of the chapter, which tells us that " *all the
families that remain shall mourn, every family apart, and
their wives apart.*"

In the last sentence of the chapter, not only the magnitude and universality, but the depth and intensity, as well
as the *individual character* of this unprecedented mourning,
is once again described. It is strikingly pictured as a
mourning which shall not only be manifested in public, but
be participated in by each family apart. And not only are
families spoken of as mourning apart from families, but
individuals, compelled by the deep sorrow which shall
overwhelm them, shall weep apart by themselves.

This depicts a sorrow greater than any previous sorrow.
Even husbands shall mourn apart from their wives, and
wives apart from their husbands, because each individual
man or woman will be overwhelmed with his or her own
individual share in the guilt of having slain their Messiah.

It will thus be both a national and individual mourning
at the same time, and no mere *ceremonial* lamentation, but
a genuine sorrow of heart. " Each individual shall experience the grief so keenly as to desire to hide himself from
the eyes of others "[1]—even from those nearest to them.

The only one who will be able effectually to comfort
them in this great mourning will be the Lord Himself, *He
over whom they shall mourn.* And He shall comfort them

[1] Wright.

in that day as "him whom his mother comforteth," and they "shall be comforted in Jerusalem."

When once this great but godly sorrow shall have accomplished its blessed end in working a repentance never to be repented of, He shall pour His consolations into their broken hearts, and give unto them the "oil of joy for mourning, the garment of praise for the spirit of heaviness." Like Joseph to his brethren (in whom the history of Christ and Israel is depicted), He will say unto them: "As for you, ye thought evil against me, but God meant it unto good, to bring to pass, as it is this day, to save much people alive: now, therefore, be not grieved nor angry with yourselves." [1]

We are done with the exposition of this great Messianic prediction. The ultimate literal fulfilment of it lies yet in the future, in the day for which we watch and pray, when our Lord Jesus shall, according to His promise, appear in His glory, and the Jewish nation shall literally look upon Him whom they have pierced, and be, as it were, "born in a day." But there is a *forestalment*, so to say, in the fulfilment of this prophecy in the case of the individual even now. "And thus," to quote the words of an honoured Hebrew Christian brother and true master of Israel, "every Jew who, by the grace of God since the Day of Pentecost, has been brought to Christ, fulfils this prediction; he looks unto Him whom he has pierced. It is the look of repentance; for only a sight of the crucified Jesus shows us our sin and grief. It is the look of supplication and faith; for He only can bless and save, and He saves all who believe. It is the look of peace and adoration; for His love is infinite, unchanging, and omnipotent. It is the look which never ceases and never ends; for now the veil is taken away, and we with open face, beholding the glory of the Lord, are changed into the same image from glory to glory." [2]

And as it is with the individual Jew, so it is with the individual Gentile. Yes, thanks be to God, as we all,

---

[1] Gen. xlv. 5, l. 20.　　　　[2] Adolph Saphir.

whether Jew or Gentile, had our share in the guilt of Christ's crucifixion because of our common *sin*, so also may all have their share in the *salvation* which comes through a penitent look of faith on Him whom we have pierced.

The Cross has been from the beginning, and must continue to be, the centre of all true Christian devotion, "the security against passion, the impulse to self-denial, the parent of zeal for souls, the incentive to love. This has struck the rock, that it gushed forth in tears of penitence; this, the strength and vigour of hatred of sin—to look to Him whom our sins have pierced."

Let us all then look to Him for our salvation, and have our gaze fixed upon Him for our sanctification, and so have no occasion to dread that awful day when "*He cometh with clouds ; and every eye shall see Him, and they which pierced Him : and all the kindreds of the earth shall wail because of Him. Even so, Amen*" (Rev. i. 7).

Chapter 18

THE OPENED FOUNTAIN AND ITS CLEANSING POWER

Zechariah 13:1-6

In that day there shall be a fountain opened to the house of David and to the inhabitants of Jerusalem, for sin and for uncleanness. And it shall come to pass in that day, saith Jehovah of hosts, that I will cut off the names of the idols out of the land, and they shall no more be remembered : and also I will cause the prophets and the unclean spirit to pass out of the land. And it shall come to pass that when any shall yet prophesy, then his father and his mother that begat him shall say unto him, Thou shalt not live ; for thou speakest lies in the name of Jehovah : and his father and his mother that begat him shall thrust him through when he prophesieth. And it shall come to pass in that day, that the prophets shall be ashamed every one of his vision, when he prophesieth ; neither shall they wear a hairy mantle to deceive : but he shall say, I am no prophet, I am a tiller of the ground ; for I have been a bondman from my youth. And one shall say unto him, What are these wounds between thine arms ? Then shall he answer, Those with which I was wounded in the house of my friends.

Chapter 18

THE first six verses of the 13th chapter stand in closest connection with the great prophecy in the 12th chapter.

There the prophet depicts in the last verses the great national repentance and sorrow of Israel over Him "whom they have pierced," as the result of the pouring out upon them of the spirit of grace and supplication. Here we see how that same blessed Spirit, who shall have wrought in them this godly penitential sorrow on account of their great national sin, shall also bring them into the experience of forgiveness, and open their eyes to the provision God has made for their justification and cleansing.

"In *that day*"—the goal of prophetic vision in relation to the nation, the great "day" of Israel's national atonement—when "the iniquity of that land shall be removed in one day,"[1] and when a whole nation shall, as it were, "be born at once,"[2] "*shall a fountain be opened to the house of David and to the inhabitants of Jerusalem for sin and for uncleanness.*"

The word employed here for "fountain" is מָקוֹר, *maqor*, which, according to its etymological meaning, describes a place "dug" out,[3] and perhaps originally standing for "well," or artificially made "cistern," came to mean spring or fountain. It is the substantive used in Ps. xxxvi. 9: "*For with Thee is the fountain of life*"; and in Jer. ii. 13 and xvii. 13 it is used as the figure of Jehovah Himself, "*the Fountain of living waters.*"

Here in Zech. xiii., however, it is not primarily as the

---

[1] Zech. iii. 9.   [2] Isa. lxvi. 8.
[3] From the verb קוּר, *qur*, "to bore," "dig," or "scoop out."

source of life and refreshment, but as the means of *puri-fication* from sin and moral uncleanness, that the figure of the fountain is introduced.

The background of the figurative language in this prophetic scripture are the Divine appointments in the Levitical ritual. The primary allusion may be to the water used for the purification of the Levites on their con-secration, which is called מֵי חַטָּאת, *mei ḥattath*, literally, "sin water" or "water of expiation."[1]

It is this Levitical ordinance which was very probably also in the mind of the priestly prophet Ezekiel in his great prophecy concerning Israel's future in chap. xxxvi.: "*And I will sprinkle clean water upon you, and ye shall be clean: from all your filthiness and from all your idols will I cleanse you.*"

In our passage in Zechariah, however, the figure is a much stronger one. Instead of water being *sprinkled* upon the defiled, a *fountain* of cleansing water is opened, in which the guilty may wash and be clean. But the words *le-ḥattath u-leniddah*—"for sin and for uncleanness"—seem almost an echo of Num. xix. 9, where these two words are used. The ashes of the red heifer, we read, shall be laid up in a clean place without the camp, "*lemai niddah, ḥattath hi*,*" literally, "for water of purification, a means of removing sin it is."

The Revised Version renders the words "a water of separation; it is a sin offering." The fact is that *ḥattath* means "sin," and also "offering for sin," or "means of removing sin." The same is true of the word *niddah*, translated "uncleanness" in Zech. xiii. 1, 2, and "separa-tion" in the Authorised and Revised Versions in Num. xix. 9, which means primarily that kind of ceremonial uncleanness which requires "separation,"[2] but denotes also the *means of the removal* of this particular uncleanness.

But, to repeat, it is not for the purification from bodily, or ceremonial uncleanness, that the fountain shall then be opened to the house of David and to the inhabitants of

---

[1] Num. viii. 7.   [2] Lev. xii. 2, xv. 19–24.

Jerusalem—which in this passage also, as in chap. xii. 10, represents the whole nation—but for purification from the guilt and the moral defilement of *sin*, of which bodily uncleanness is often used in the Bible as a figure. Thus, for instance, in Ps. li. 7 David prays : " Purge me (literally, if one may invent an expression, '*unsin me*,' or ' rid me of my sin ') with hyssop "—which is a distinct allusion to the cleansing of the leper from his bodily plague,[1] in connection with which a Jewish commentator rightly observes : " What has befallen the soul is like unto the plague of leprosy in the body."[2] To pass from the figure to the reality, from the shadow to the substance, the " fountain " which shall then be opened to the house of David and the inhabitants of Jerusalem for the national and individual cleansing from guilt and sin, is nothing else than the blood of their Messiah whom they have pierced. Hence, those are not far wrong who trace a connection between מָקוֹר, *maqor* (" fountain ") in chap. xiii. 1 and דָּקַר, *daqar* (" pierced ") in chap. xii. 10, and say that the opening of the fountain took place when the Roman soldier with his spear pierced our Saviour's side, and " there came out of it blood and water "—though the basis for the connection is not in philology (the root of the two words not being the same though of cognate significance), but in *fact*.

Yes, Israel " in that day " shall experience the wonderful and everlasting efficacy of the blood of Jesus their Messiah, God's Son, which cleanseth from all sin. In quite another and *blessed* sense shall that fearful prayer once uttered in ignorance, " His blood be on us and our children," which has haunted the Jewish conscience through all the centuries since, and has, like the blood of Abel, brought down the curse of Cain on the whole nation, be fulfilled " in that day." It shall be upon them for life and not for death, for cleansing and not for defilement.

They shall experience then the truth of the inspired words in Heb. ix. 13, that " *if the blood of bulls and of goats, and the ashes of an heifer sprinkling the unclean,*

---

[1] See Lev. xiv. 1-9.　　　　[2] Eben Ezra.

sanctifieth to the purifying of the flesh, how much more shall the blood of Christ, who through the eternal Spirit offered Himself without spot to God, purge our[1] conscience from dead works to serve the living God."

But, it may be objected, if it is the blood of Christ which constitutes the cleansing stream which shall wash away Israel's " sins and uncleanness," then the fountain was " opened " nineteen centuries ago on Calvary; whereas this is a prophecy of the national purification of Israel which is to take place " in that day " which is yet future.

For answer, I repeat what I stated in my notes on chap. iii. 9 : " I will remove the iniquity of that land in one day "—namely, that what is here predicted will assuredly be fulfilled only on the ground and as a blessed consequence of " the day of Golgotha," when Christ, through the eternal Spirit, offered Himself without spot unto God ; but *actually* and experimentally the great " day " of Israel's national repentance and of cleansing will take place when the spirit of grace and of supplications shall be poured out upon them, and they shall look upon Him whom they have pierced. The cleansing fountain for sin and for uncleanness was opened once and for all when " the Lamb of God " was slain and His precious blood shed ; but to the sinner actually and *experimentally* the Day of Calvary is the day his eyes are opened to the true meaning to *himself* of the great redeeming work there accomplished, and when the Spirit of God *applies* Jesus' blood and righteousness and high-priestly intercession to his own need. Thus " in that day " it will be with Israel nationally. The fountain will be opened *then* " to *the house* of David and the inhabitants of Jerusalem," because " *then the eyes of the blind shall be opened* "[2] for the first time to *behold* the Lamb of God, and to perceive the atoning value and efficacy of the offering which He once made for the sins of many.

Blessed be God ! the fountain once opened shall never

---

[1] Many ancient authorities read " our," and not " your," as in the Authorised and Revised Versions."

[2] Isa. xxxv. 5.

be closed, for the force of the Hebrew words [1] which are used, is not only "shall be opened," but "shall remain open "—ever free and accessible to all, and everlastingly efficacious for " sin and for uncleanness."

From the inward cleansing of the people from the guilt and moral defilement of sin, the prophet passes in vers. 2–6 to the cleansing of the land and the purification of the *environment* in which the forgiven and sanctified people shall then live and move.　Nothing that defileth shall be permitted in the restored Jewish state in the day when " Jehovah shall inherit Judah, His portion *in the holy land*, and shall choose Jerusalem again."

The two chief sources of moral pollution and the great besetting sin of Israel in the land were idolatry and false prophecy.　These shall be utterly purged out of their midst. *" And it shall come to pass in that day, saith Jehovah of hosts, that I will cut off the names of the idols out of the land, and they shall no more be remembered : and I will also cause the prophets and the unclean spirit to pass out of the land."*　Not only shall the idols—the objects of idolatrous worship— themselves be " cut off," but their very names and *remembrance* shall perish in the land ; and not only shall false prophets disappear, but the unclean spirit—the *author* and *inspirer of false prophecy* as well as the instigator of idolatry —shall be cast out from the midst of the people, whose ears shall then be circumcised to hearken only to words of truth and purity, and whose heart's love and worship shall be centred in Jehovah alone.

The evil spirit is particularly designated as the *ruach hattumah* ("the spirit of uncleanness "), in contrast to " the spirit of grace and of supplications " in chap. xii. 10, who is pre-eminently the *Ruach Ha-qodesh*—the " *Holy* Spirit "— because He is the representative and revealer of the blessed Godhead, whose chief attribute is that of holiness, and who dwells in the midst of His people to sanctify them and to make them holy, because Jehovah their God is holy.

Some have argued from the mention of idols and false

---

[1] יִהְיֶה נִפְתָּח, *Yeeyhe niphtach.*

prophecy in this passage that these last chapters of
Zechariah must have been written in the pre-exilic period
when these two great national sins were still prevalent in
the land.   But there is no real foundation, in fact, for this
any more than for the other " proofs " of a pre-exilic
authorship of these chapters, as I have already shown else-
where.¹   In reference to this particular point, though it be
true that idolatry, and false prophecy, which was usually
associated with it, did not exist any more in their gross
form among the Jewish people after the Babylonian captivity, such passages as Neh. vi. 10; Ezra. ix. 1 ; Neh.
xiii. 23, 24, etc., which speak of the lying prophets which
existed at that time, and of marriages contracted, even by
priests, with Canaanitish and other heathen women, whose
children could not even speak the Jewish language—show
very clearly, as Keil and others point out, that " the danger
of falling back into idolatry was not a remote one."

The range of the prophetic vision, however, in the six
last chapters of Zechariah does not terminate with the mere
immediate future, but finds its goal in the time of the end,
when the great sins of idolatry and false prophecy shall
reach their climax in the worship of the beast and his
image, and in the " unclean spirits " ² which shall go forth
upon the earth to deceive the anti-Christian nations.

The four verses which follow are an amplification of the
announcement in ver. 2 that idolatry and false prophecy
would be utterly exterminated from the land " in that
day."   They set forth in realistic—we might almost say
dramatic — form the great change which will then come
over the Jewish nation, and their zeal against those sins
which formerly were the chief causes of their national
ruin.

The 3rd verse introduces an hypothetical case: "*And
it shall come to pass that, when any shall yet prophesy, then
his father and his mother that begat him shall say unto him,
Thou shalt not live : for thou speakest lies in the Name of*

¹ See the introduction to the second part of this book.
² 2 Thess. ii. 4 ; Rev. xiii. 1–6 ; xvi. 13, 14.

the Lord : and his father and his mother that begat him shall thrust him through when he prophesieth."

The allusion is to Deut. xiii. 6–10, where we read : "*If thy brother, the son of thy mother, or thy son, or thy daughter, or the wife of thy bosom, or thy friend, which is as thine own soul, entice thee secretly, saying, Let us go and serve other gods, . . . thine eye shall not pity him ; neither shalt thou spare, neither shalt thou conceal him, but thou shalt surely kill him : thine hand shall be first upon him to put him to death.*"

The same injunction holds true in relation to the false prophet who either speaks "presumptuously" or falsely in the Name of Jehovah, or in the name of other gods. "*That same prophet shall die.*" [1]

Now the prophet, to illustrate the zeal for Jehovah and His truth which shall then characterise converted and regenerated Israel, supposes such a case. Even if it should be their own son who should presumptuously "prophesy," either to entice them from their allegiance to Jehovah or to spread error in His Name, his own parents will not spare or pity him ; but his father and his mother that begat him shall thrust him through (*ud'qaruhu*—the verb is the same as in chap. .xii. 10 for "pierced") when he prophesieth (בְּהִנָּבְאוֹ, *b'hinnabho*), which may mean either *when he is in the act of prophesying*, or, "*because of his prophesying.*" Zeal for Jehovah and His law will be so strong as to overmaster even parental affection ; the people themselves would stop short at nothing in order utterly to exterminate the evil should it be possible once again to assert itself.

And not only will false prophets no longer be tolerated in their midst, the pretended prophets themselves will be ashamed of their calling. "*And it shall come to pass in that day that the prophets shall be ashamed every one of his vision when he prophesieth ; neither shall they wear a hairy mantle to deceive.*" "In former days the false prophets had been bold enough to assert their claims even in the very face of the true prophets raised up by Jehovah. Now, popular feeling will run so strongly in an opposite direction that

[1] Deut. xviii. 20.

persons will be ashamed of making any pretence to supernatural visions, and confounded when charged with having
made such assumptions. Instead of being anxious to be
considered as prophets, they will rather seek in every way
to avoid the reputation of such a dangerous and unpopular
profession."[1]

The "hairy mantle" was the distinguishing garb of
some of the great prophets. Some (as Koehler) suppose it
to have been made of untanned skins; others think it was
a garment formed of camel's hair, such as that worn by
John the Baptist. Thus, Elijah was recognised by Ahaziah
when described by his messengers as "a hairy man, and
girt with a girdle of leather about his loins."[2]   The "rough
garment" was not only the outward sign of "the strict
course of life and abstinence from worldly pleasures"—
"the frugality alike in food and attire," which marked the
true prophets of Jehovah—but, also (on certain great
occasions, at any rate), it was the symbol of grief and
mourning for the sins of the nation, and the consequent
judgments which they were commissioned to announce.

In the case of the false prophets it was a cloak of
hypocrisy, and was assumed "in order to lie," or "deceive";
for, though outwardly they may be clothed like "sheep," or
even like the true prophets of God, inwardly they are
"ravening wolves."

The prophet having shown the opposition which would
be exhibited by the Jewish nation to the false prophets,
who in the past were the chief cause of their national un-
doing—first, by the hypothetical instance of a son who
should venture to prophecy falsely being slain by his own
parents; and secondly, by the general statement that the
pretended prophets would themselves be ashamed of their
evil profession and seek in every way to avert suspicion
that they ever had to do with such evil practices, with a
view to deceive the people—proceeds in the next two verses
still more fully to illustrate the condition of the time.

In a few but graphic touches he pictures a dramatic

---

[1] Dr. Wright.   [2] 2 Kings i. 8.

incident. One who is suspected of being a false prophet is suddenly challenged by a zealous Israelite. He, however, vehemently answers, "*I am no prophet*"; far from ever having professed to be an inspired teacher of the people, "*I am a tiller of the ground* (*i.e.*, belonging to the humblest class of the people), *and I have been made a bondsman* [1] (or, '*a man has bought me*') *from my youth.*"

A certain similarity has been pointed out between the words of this false prophet and those of Amos, when in answer to Amaziah, the priest of the idolatrous worship of Bethel, who warned him to flee to Judah and prophesy there, but to cease prophesying in Bethel, because it was the chief sanctuary and a royal residence of the kings of Israel, the prophet said: "*I was* (or '*am*') *no prophet, neither was I a prophet's son, but I was a herdman, and a dresser of sycomore trees.*"

But the purport of the two passages is very different. Here, in our passage in Zechariah, the false prophet, when accused with exercising the functions of a prophet, utterly denies the charge; but Amos, though he disclaims having been a prophet by profession and training, is nevertheless conscious of a direct call from God, and boldly asserts his Divine mission in the words which immediately follow: "*Jehovah took me from following the flock, and Jehovah said unto me, Go, prophesy unto My people Israel.*" [2] Far, therefore, from being intimidated by the threats of Amaziah, or his royal master Jeroboam II., he proceeds: "*Now therefore hear thou the word of Jehovah.*"

---

[1] הִקְנָנִי—*hiqnnani.* The verb קָנָה in the Kal means to "originate," "acquire," "possess"; but since it occurs nowhere else in the Hebrew Bible in the Hiphil there is great difficulty in determining its exact force in this sentence. Some take it as a stronger Kal, "to purchase," others "to sell." Some taking it as a denominative from מִקְנָה, *miqneh,* "possession," deduce the same meaning, *i.e.*, "to buy."

Rashi and Kimchi derive *hiqnnani* from "*miqneh*" in the sense of a *flock,* and translate "made me a shepherd, or set me to keep his flock."

But in the words of W. H. Lowe: "Whatever be the exact meaning of the word it is clear that the person accused here of assuming prophetic powers disavows all such assumption, and claims to be looked on as a simple rustic."

[2] Amos vii. 10-14.

But to return to the dramatic incident in our passage in Zechariah. Not easily put off by the vehement protestations of the false prophet that he is not at all likely to have performed the functions of a prophet, seeing he is only a simple peasant—in fact, a slave from his youth—his interrogator proceeds: " *What are these wounds between thine hands ? And he shall say* (They are) *those with which I was wounded in the house of my friends.*"

The two clauses in this 6th verse are to be understood as " speech and reply, or question and answer." It was very probably these *makkoth* — " wounds " — which the zealous challenger of the false prophet had observed which first aroused his suspicion. He evidently regards them as self-inflicted on his person in order to arouse his prophetic frenzy, or in connection with idolatrous rites. " It must not be forgotten," to quote the words of another, " that such rites were sometimes observed even where Jehovah was acknowledged to be the highest object of adoration. In the idolatrous court of Ahab there were hundreds of false prophets who were wont to prophesy in the Name of Jehovah,[1] and yet at the same court priests and prophets of Baal cut themselves with knives and lancets until blood gushed out upon them,[2] in order to procure answers from their god." That such practices were common among Israelites in the days of apostasy is plain from the passage referred to, as well as from the prohibition of similar doings in Deut. xiv. 1, in cases of mourning for the dead, which were employed in later times by the Israelites.[3]

The expression " between thy hands " is an idiom which may mean on the palms of the hands, or on the arms, or on the chest between the hands ; but the explanation of Rashi that it means " between thy shoulders," where persons are wont to be scourged, is a very unlikely one. There is difference of opinion among commentators as to the meaning of the answer of the false prophet in the second half of the verse. It greatly depends on the mean-

---

[1] 1 Kings xxii. 5, 6, 7, 11, 12.   [2] 1 Kings xviii. 28.
[3] Jer. xvi. 6, xli. 5.

ing we attach to the word מְאַהֲבָי—rendered " of my friends,"
in the Authorised Version, but which might more properly
be translated " my lover." Now Hengstenberg and others
understood the " lovers " to signify *idols*, and regard the
answer as a humble confession on the part of the false prophet
who is thus detected, either that his wounds were received
during some idolatrous rites, or, though self-inflicted, he was
only the instrument—the real authors of the wounds beings
his " lovers," namely, the idols whom he worshipped. But
I agree with Koehler, Keil, Dr. Wright, and others, that,
though it be true that the special conjugation of this verb
(*piel*) is used in other cases of dishonourable love, and
might therefore be figuratively used of idolatry and idols,
" there is nothing in the form of the verb to render that
meaning *necessary*. *Intensity* of love is all that is expressed
in the word ; and the expression might, as far as the form
is concerned, be used with reference to parents or any
friends, whether good or bad."

It is very probable, therefore, that far from being a
humble confession of his guilt, " this answer is also nothing
but an evasion, and that he simply pretends that the marks
were scars left by the chastisements which he received when
a boy in the house of either loving parents, or some other
loving relations or friends." [1]

This seems to me more in accord with the context, and
illustrates the general statement that the false prophets
would in that day themselves be ashamed of their former
evil profession, and when detected would stop short of no
falsehood in order to avert or dispel suspicion.

[1] Keil. Kimchi explains as follows : " He shall say these wounds are not on
account of prophecy, but my friends wounded and chastised me because I was
abandoned, and was not industrious in cultivating the land in my youth ; and
they beat me that I should cease from the profligacy of young men, and should
set to my work. And the reason of the wounds being in the hands is, that they
used to bind his hands and feet that he should not go out."

Chapter 19

THE SMITTEN SHEPHERD AND
THE SCATTERED SHEEP

Zechariah 13:7-9

Awake, O sword, against My Shepherd, and against the man that is My Fellow, saith Jehovah of hosts : smite the Shepherd, and the sheep shall be scattered ; and I will turn My hand upon the little ones.   And it shall come to pass, that in all the land, saith Jehovah, two parts therein shall be cut off and die ; but the third shall be left therein.   And I will bring the third part into the fire, and will refine them as silver is refined, and will try them as gold is tried : they shall call on My Name, and I will hear them : I will say, It is My people ; and they shall say, Jehovah is my God.

Chapter 19

INTRODUCTORY

WITH the 7th verse begins a new section in this last great prophecy (chaps. xii.–xiv.), which has for its main theme *the judgment by means of which Israel will be finally purged and transformed into the holy people of Jehovah.* It is in the first instance an expansion and enlargement of what has gone before. But, whereas the preceding section (xii. 1–xiii. 6) announces how the Lord will protect Israel and Jerusalem against the pressure of the world-powers, how He will smite their enemies, and not only endow His people with miraculous power which ensures their victory, but also by pouring out His spirit of grace and of supplications upon them, lead them to a knowledge of the guilt they have incurred by putting the Messiah to death, and to repentance and renovation of life ; the second half (xiii. 7–xiv. 21) depicts the judgment which will fall on Jerusalem itself, by means of which the ungodly shall be cut off, and the righteous remnant and the land itself be purified and made fit to be the centre of God's kingdom on the earth.

This second half is divided again into two parts, the former of which (chap. xiii. 7–9) gives a summary of the contents, whilst the latter (chap. xiv.) expands it into fuller detail.[1]

THE EXPOSITION

From the false prophet " wounded in the house of his friends," or " lovers," upon whom his attention had been fixed in the verses immediately preceding, the Spirit of God abruptly turns the prophetic gaze of Zechariah on to

[1] Condensed from the valuable remarks of Keil.

another and altogether different figure, who is now made to pass before his vision, and whose experience, if not foreshadowed, is at least *suggested* by the treatment which had been meted out to the false prophet. He was the true prophet, and much more than a prophet, but He also was "wounded," yea, "smitten" even unto death, in the house of His friends (*i.e.*, "His own" nation), who in their blind and ungodly zeal even thought that they rendered God a service in slaying the Prince of Life; because, having become alienated in their hearts from God, they did not recognise Him Who is the very "image of the invisible God," and charged Him with blasphemy, because He claimed to speak to them in the Name of God, as one who is "equal with God."

But this great national crime, which has occasioned them unparalleled sorrow and suffering, was nevertheless overruled of God to the greatest good for the world as a whole, and is the very ground of Israel's future national redemption. The slaying of the Messiah, therefore, which, in chap. xii. 10–14, is viewed as being the act of the Jewish nation, of which they shall yet repent with such deep and godly sorrow, is in the passage now before us described as an act of God. "*Awake, O sword, against My Shepherd, and against the man that is My Fellow.*" This aspect of Messiah's sufferings and death, namely, that they were inflicted upon Him by God in order to make His soul "an offering for sin," is set forth more fully in Isa. liii., where we read that "*it pleased Jehovah to bruise Him; He hath put Him to grief,*" etc. It was indeed by the hand of man that "He was led as a lamb to the slaughter"; but, "human malice acting freely" could do no more than what "His hand and His counsel had fore-ordained to come to pass." [1] Yes, "the envy and hatred of Satan, the blind fury of the chief priests, the contempt of Herod, the guilty cowardice of Pilate, freely accomplished that death which God had before decreed for the salvation of the world." [2]

---

[1] Acts iv. 28. [2] Pusey.

But let us look more carefully at this remarkable passage: "O sword, awake!" (*ḥerebh uri*)—the sword being addressed as a person, and called upon to rouse itself, as it were, from sleep in order to execute Divine justice.[1]

But upon whom shall it fall? Not, in this instance, upon the wicked and the ungodly, but, mystery of mysteries! upon Him who is not only absolutely innocent and holy, but who stands in the nearest and closest relationship to Jehovah. This would be the most inexplicable thing in God's moral government of the universe were it not for the wonderful counsel of God in the salvation of man revealed in the Scriptures, according to which the Messiah willingly becomes the Lamb of God in order to save a lost world, and is " wounded (lit., ' pierced through ') for our transgressions, bruised (or ' crushed ') for our iniquities," and " pours out His soul unto death," in order that sinners might not only be saved from the penalty of their sin, but obtain eternal life.

" *Against My Shepherd*"—Jehovah Himself is "the Shepherd of Israel," but He fulfils all that is implied in this relationship and office *mediately*, in and through the Messiah. This is fully set forth in Ezek. xxxiv., where, after announcing that He will *Himself* " seek " and " save," " heal " and " strengthen," " feed " and " satisfy," His now scattered flock, He says : " *I will set up one shepherd over them, and He shall feed them, even my servant David*" (*whom the Jewish commentators themselves identify with the Messiah, " David's greater Son "*). " *He shall feed them, and He shall be their Shepherd.*" God, therefore, calls Him " *My* Shepherd," for He is not only specially called and appointed by Him to this office, but because He is in the fullest sense His Representative, in and through whom the shepherd relationship between God and His people is realised.

---

[1] Compare for a similar personification of the sword of Jehovah Jer. xlvii. 6, 7. As already explained in a note on chap. xii. 10, the sword is used in a general way as an emblem of death, or as a weapon used for killing, and is not intended to describe the manner of Messiah's death.

The unique and peculiar relationship between this
" Shepherd " and Jehovah is fully brought out in the words
which follow : עַל גֶּבֶר עֲמִיתִי (*'al gebher 'amithi*)—" the man
that is my Fellow." The word עָמִית (*'amith*) is found elsewhere in the Hebrew Bible only in Leviticus.   It seems
to be a substantive, and denotes " fellowship," " neighbour-
ship," in the abstract.   But the only other place in the
Hebrew Bible where this word is found, namely, in Leviticus, it is used only as the synonym of אָח (" brother "), in
the concrete sense of the nearest one.[1]   The two words
gebher (" man ") and " *'amithi* " (" my Fellow ") must therefore be regarded as apposites, and have been properly so
rendered in the English Bible.

Some rationalistic writers have sought to identify the
smitten Shepherd in this passage with " the foolish
shepherd " in chap. xi. 15–17, who is permitted to destroy
the flock in punishment for their rejection of the Good
Shepherd, and who is himself in the end smitten with a
sword on his right arm and his right eye.[2]   If the expression,
" My Shepherd," stood alone, there might be some
slight plausibility for this view, for the " foolish," or evil
shepherd is, in a sense, also raised up of God as a scourge
on the " sheep of slaughter " after their rejection of the Good
Shepherd ; but the further description of the Shepherd in
this passage as *gebher 'amithi*—" the man who is my
Fellow," or " my nearest one "—implies much more than
mere *appointment* to this office by Jehovah.   More also
than mere "unity or community of vocation," or that he is
so styled because he had to feed the flock *like* Jehovah,
and as His representative.

" No owner of a flock, or lord of a flock, would call a
hired or purchased shepherd his *'amith*.   And so God
would not apply this epithet to any godly or ungodly man
whom He might have appointed shepherd over a nation.

---

[1] Comp. Lev. xxv. 15.   It occurs altogether eleven times in Leviticus.   Pusey
observes : " It stands alone in the dialects, having probably been formed by
Moses to express more than " neighbour "—" our common nature," as we speak.

[2] See the exposition of that passage, page 414 ff.

The idea of nearest one (or fellow) involves not only similarity in vocation, but community of physical or spiritual descent, according to which he whom God calls His neighbour cannot be a mere man, but can only be one who participates in the Divine nature, or is essentially Divine. The Shepherd of Jehovah, whom the sword is to smite, is therefore no other than the Messiah, who is also identified with Jehovah in chap. xii. 10; or the Good Shepherd, who says of Himself, ' I and My Father are one ' (John x. 30)."

No, the Shepherd of this passage is the *Good* Shepherd, who, in chap. xi. 4–14, is mysteriously identified with Jehovah, the same over whom the nation will mourn with a deep universal mourning in the day when the spirit of grace and of supplication is poured upon them, and their eyes are opened to perceive that in piercing Him they pierced Jehovah.[1]

The Jews accused our Lord Jesus of blasphemy, because He claimed not only to have come from God, but that He was "equal with God"; or because when speaking of Himself as "the Good Shepherd" who layeth down His life for the sheep, He said (with probable allusion to this very passage in Zechariah): "*I and My Father are one.*"

It was indeed a mystery passing mere human comprehension how this could be true of a *man* who stood in their midst. But this mystery faces us, not only in the pages of the New Testament, but in the inspired Scriptures of the prophets. There, too, the promised Redeemer is depicted as a *babe* born in Bethlehem, " whose goings forth are from everlasting,"[2] "a child born" in the midst of the Jewish nation, whose name is "Wonderful, Counsellor, Mighty God, Father of Eternity, Prince of Peace,"[3] a son of David, yet Jehovah Tzidkenu,[4] a "man," and yet Jehovah's "Fellow," or equal. This mystery, like others in the pages of the Old and New Testaments, can be solved only by faith in things which are revealed, to the knowledge of

---

[1] Chap. xii. 10.
[2] Mic. v. 2.
[3] Isa. ix. 6.
[4] Jer. xxiii. 6.

which man can never attain by a mere process of reasoning.

But when thus laid hold of with a pure heart and in childlike simplicity, we are brought also *to understand* that the doctrine of the twofold nature of the Messiah—the fact that He is Man according to His human nature and, according to His Divine nature " God blessed for ever," is a necessary part in the Divine philosophy of Redemption unfolded in the Scriptures, for it is only a Divine Saviour who could redeem man from sin and death; only one in whose person the human and the Divine meet who can be the true Mediator between God and man, in and through whom the broken fellowship between heaven and earth, between the Holy God and fallen man, can be fully restored. Only as man, and one who in all points was tempted even as we are, could He become the compassionate High Priest touched with the feeling of our infirmities, and able with a perfect human sympathy to enter into all our griefs and sorrows; but only as the Holy One, who Himself was pure from sin—the everlasting Son of the Father in whom dwelt " the fulness of the Godhead bodily," could He effectually succour and deliver us, and *lift us out* of our own innate wretchedness and sin.

Therefore, this doctrine of the twofold nature of the Messiah, which to the unbelieving is such an occasion of stumbling, is to the child of God a source of unspeakable comfort, and an occasion for unceasing praise.

But this is somewhat of a digression. To return to the passage immediately before us, it is interesting to observe that Jewish commentators themselves have admitted that the word " *'amithi* " (" my Fellow ") implies equality with God; " only since they own not Him who was God and Man they must interpret it of a *false claim* on the part of man," overlooking that it is *God Himself* who thus speaks of the shepherd of his text.[1]

---

[1] Aben Ezra (1088–1177) interprets it of the Gentile kings, who in their arrogance are styled Divine, and thus called themselves " God's fellows." Kimchi adopts the same interpretation, adding, "thinks himself my Fellow." Rabbi

The immediate consequence of the smiting of the Shepherd is that "*the sheep shall be scattered*," or, as the Hebrew verb more accurately expresses it, "*that the sheep may be scattered.*" For, although the slaying of the Messiah is (as stated above) overruled of God to the eventual gathering and blessing, not only of the Jewish nation, but of those many millions of "other sheep" from among the Gentiles, who are, as the result of Messiah's death, brought into the one fold—yet the fact of the removal by a violent death, as the direct consequence of national sin and rebellion against God, of Him who was appointed to be their Shepherd, could not but bring calamity on the flock. And this—the consequent disaster which it would bring on the people—is the primary thought associated with the slaying of the Messiah in this particular passage. It announces the fact that Jehovah will scatter the flock by smiting the shepherd: "That is to say, He will give it up to the misery and destruction to which a flock without a shepherd is exposed."

The flock which is to be thus "scattered" is neither the human race nor the Christian Church, as some commentators would have us think, but the Jewish nation, or those which the Good Shepherd was appointed to feed, according to chap. xi. 1–14, but who, because of their wilful obduracy, are designated "*sheep of slaughter.*"

It was primarily fulfilled when, after the crucifixion of our Lord, "the people of the prince that shall come"[1]— that is, the Romans—destroyed the city and the sanctuary,

---

Izaak of Troki, in the *Chizzuk Emunah*, interprets the whole of the King of Ishmael, "called also the King of Turkey," who in his pride and greatness of his heart "accounts himself like God." This is a modification and enlargement of the interpretation given by Abrabanel, who explains the words "My Shepherd" of Mohammed, and the words "the man my Fellow" of our Lord Jesus, in a bitter controversial spirit, thus: The words, "the Man my Fellow," are spoken of Jesus the Nazarene, for, according to the sentiment of the children of Edom (*i.e.*, the Christians) and their faith, He was the Son of God, and of the same substance, and therefore He is called, according to their words, "the Man my Fellow,"—overlooking the fact pointed out above that it is not man but Jehovah *Himself* who calls Him "My Shepherd" and "My Fellow."

[1] Dan. ix. 26.

and brought about the new and more universal phase of the dispersal of the Jewish people among all the nations of the earth, *which is continued to this day.*

But while this terrible judgment would fall on the nation, a little remnant would remain the object of His compassion and care. This is expressed in the words וַהֲשִׁבֹתִי יָדִי עַל הַצֹּעֲרִים (*vehashibhothi yadi al hatsoarim*)—" I will turn My hand upon (or ' back upon ') the little (or ' small ' ones)."

The idiomatic phrase, " to turn (or ' bring back ') the hand over a person," is usually used in connection with the infliction of judgment; as, for instance, in Amos i. 8, " I will turn My hand over (or ' against ' Ekron "); or Ps. lxxxi. 14 : " I should soon have subdued their enemies, and turned My hand over (' against ') their adversaries." But I agree with Keil, Hitzig, Dr. Wright, and others, that the phrase is used here in a good sense, namely, that God will turn His hand upon " the little ones," for salvation, though that salvation may be brought about by means of chastisement. It occurs in this sense in Isa. i. 25, " in relation to the grace which the Lord will manifest towards Jerusalem by purifying it from its dross "; and it is used here in Zech. xiii., also in that same sense as vers. 8 and 9 clearly show, according to which the judgment which is to come upon Israel in consequence of the Shepherd being smitten, will only be the cause of ruin to the greater portion of the nation, whereas it will bring salvation to the remnant.

The particular form of the word translated " little ones " (*tsoarim*) does not occur elsewhere in the Hebrew Bible. Its true signification is, " those *who appear as little*," " those who make themselves small, or," *the patient*, the humble ones.[1]

They are to be identified with " the poor of the flock " of chap. xi. 7, namely, the poor and righteous in the nation who suffer oppression from the godless majority.

---

[1] צֹעֲרִים is not equivalent to the adjective צְעִירִים. It is the active participial form of the verb צָעַר, and is found only in this passage.

The prophetic message, then, in the whole of the 7th verse is briefly this: The Shepherd would be smitten on account of the sin of the people, who would in consequence be scattered, but Jehovah would remember in mercy a little remnant of the flock, namely, the poor in spirit, the humble ones who are little in their own eyes, and who give heed to the word of the Lord.[1]

The prophecy finds its fulfilment in Christ: "The Shepherd was slain"; as another writer truly observes: "When Jesus of Nazareth was crucified—an act ascribed in the New Testament no less to the determinate counsel and foreknowledge of God, on the one hand, than to the malice of men on the other." And there, in the same inspired narrative which tells of the smiting of the Shepherd, we read also of another fulfilment of the scattering of the flock, which is, so to say, additional to the primary meaning of the prophecy, but is not altogether unconnected with the scattering of Israel and the saving of the remnant.

On the night of His betrayal, after He had partaken for the last time of the Paschal Supper, and transformed it to be henceforth the memorial supper of His death "till He come," our Lord Jesus said to His disciples: *"All ye shall be offended in Me this night, for it is written, I will smite the shepherd, and the sheep of the flock shall be scattered abroad. But, after I am raised up, I will go before you into Galilee."* [2]

The reference is to this passage in Zechariah, though the quotation is a free one, and does not in every detail correspond with the words in the Hebrew. The meaning of the passage is, however, preserved intact. Where the words are slightly modified, it is (as is usually the case with free quotations from the Old Testament in the pages of the New) designedly so, with a view to throw a new, or additional, meaning on Old Testament prophecy in the light of the fuller unfolding of God's purpose brought about by the actual advent of the Messiah. Thus, the address to the sword to awake and smite, resolves itself in the quota-

---

[1] Chap. xi. 11.   [2] Matt. xxvi. 31, 32; Mark xiv. 27 (R.V.).

tion into its actual meaning, "*I will smite.*" The offend-
ing of the disciples took place when Jesus was taken
prisoner, and they all fled. This flight was a prelude to
the dispersion of the flock at the death of the Shepherd.
The closing words of our Lord, "I will go before you into
Galilee," is, I think, rightly taken by Keil and others as a
practical exposition of the words of the prophet, "*I will
turn My hand upon the little* (or '*humble*') *ones,*" inasmuch as
it was a promise of their re-gathering to Him and of His
care for them after His resurrection.

But, to repeat, this special fulfilment did not exhaust
the meaning of the prophecy as some erroneously think.
"The correct view," to quote again from an English writer,
"appears to be that the desertion of Christ in the hour of
trial by His most faithful followers, whereby they were
scattered every man to his own, and left the Saviour alone [1]
—a desertion which added so much to the bitterness of
that 'hour of darkness'—was indeed of importance in itself,
but still more so as prefiguring the rejection of Christ by
the Jewish nation, and the terrible scattering of the flock of
Israel." [2]

That the primary reference of the words, "the flock
shall be scattered," etc., is to the Jewish nation, is placed
beyond a doubt by the verses which follow, for the 8th
verse sets forth the misery which the dispersion of the flock
brings upon Israel, and the 9th verse shows how the words,
"I will turn My hand upon (or, 'back upon') the little
ones," would be realised in the final deliverance and salvation of the remnant: "*And it shall come to pass that in all
the land, saith Jehovah, two parts therein shall be cut off, shall
die, and the third part shall remain therein. And I will
bring the third part through* (lit., '*into*') *the fire, and refine*
(or '*melt*') *them as silver is refined.*"

The idiomatic expression פִּי שְׁנַיִם (*pi sh'nayim*) is found
in Deut. xxi. 17 and 2 Kings ii. 9, and is primarily used
of the "double portion" inherited by the first-born; but
here, in Zechariah, it means *two-thirds*, as is shown by the

[1] John xvi. 32.   [2] C. H. H. Wright.

use of the word *ha-shelishith* (" the third part ") in the second half of the verse.

A parallel to this scripture is found in Ezek. v. 12, where the nation is also divided into three parts: " *A third part of thee (shelishith) shall die with the pestilence,* . . . *and a third part shall fall by the sword,* . . . *and a third part I will scatter unto all the winds.*"

" The whole of the Jewish nation," observes Hengstenberg, " is introduced here as an inheritance left by the Shepherd who has been put to death, which inheritance is divided into three parts: death claiming the privilege of the first-born, and so receiving *two* portions, and life one—a division similar to that which David made in the case of the Moabites."[1] The literalness of this division must not, however, be pressed. Isaiah, for instance,[2] speaks of only a *tenth* part as escaping from the great purging judgment. Both expressions, as Dr. Wright properly observes, are to be regarded as emblematic for a comparatively small number, and not as describing the exact proportion of the remnant that should escape.

The emphatic word, בָּהּ (" therein "), or literally, " in it," which is twice repeated, refers to the land and not to the flock, as some interpreters explain: " *In all the land* . . . *two-thirds in it shall be cut off, shall die.*" It seems to me, therefore, that, though the fulfilment may not be entirely *limited* to it, yet, that the reference is chiefly to the judgments which would come on the people *in the land,* namely, immediately after the " smiting of the Shepherd," while they were yet recognised as a nation in Palestine, though no longer in a nationally independent condition ; and again after the restoration of a representative remnant in unbelief at the end of the long parenthetical period, when God's national dealings with them shall be resumed, and His long controversy with them as a nation on account of their great sin finally settled *on the same soil* where it originated.

And with what terrible literalness has this Divine fore-

---

[1] 2 Sam. viii. 2. [2] Isa. vi. 13.

cast been verified! During the futile, but heroic, struggle
with the great Roman power, which commenced so soon
after the crucifixion of the Messiah, and lasted seven years,
about one million and a half Jews perished in the land by
the sword and by famine and pestilence. Great numbers
of Jews were crucified by the Romans outside the walls of
Jerusalem, while many thousands were taken in ships to
Egypt and sold as slaves. Then, not to speak of the great
numbers of Jews who were during the same time done to
death in different parts of the Roman Empire, only some
sixty years after the destruction of Jerusalem by Titus, a
calamity of almost equal magnitude overtook the Jewish
people "throughout all the land," consequent on their
renewed rising under the false Messiah, Bar Cochba.[1]

Then, after the "two-thirds" in the land were "cut off,"
the remainder of "the sheep of the flock" were "scattered";
for a new stage—the *universal* phase in the dispersion of
the Jewish nation took place consequent on the culmination
of Israel's apostasy in the rejection of their Messiah.

Throughout all these centuries the Jews have suffered
as no other nation on earth. At the beginning of the
sixteenth century, according to reliable computations, there
were only about one million Jews left in the whole world
after the centuries of oppression and unparalleled sufferings
which they had had to endure, especially throughout the
dark Middle Ages.

And there is yet a *climax* to all their sufferings to be
reached in the "Day" of Jacob's final great "trouble,"[2]
when they are once again "in the land" and God's "fire"
is kindled in Zion, and His "furnace" set up in Jerusalem[3]

---

[1] Five hundred and eighty thousand Jews are said, by Jewish historians, to
have perished by the sword in the siege at the fall of Bithar, besides those who
perished by famine and sickness. "Judea was almost wholly a wilderness."
Fifty castles and two hundred and eighty-five villages were entirely destroyed.
At the yearly market, by Abraham's Oak, at Hebron, Jewish slaves were sold
at a nominal price; a Jew was worth no more than a horse. See the summary
of Jewish History since the Dispersion, in *The Shepherd of Israel and His
Scattered Flock.*

[2] Jer. xxx. 7.   [3] Isa. xxxi. 9.

for the final purging of the nation. And yet in this very prophecy we see mercy blended with judgment.

Two-thirds may be " cut off " and die, but the nation can never be *utterly* destroyed. There is always " a third," or " a tenth," which forms the indestructible " holy seed," [1] which God takes care to preserve as the nucleus of the great and blessed nation through whom His holy will and His wonderful purposes in relation to this earth shall yet be realised. " I will make a full end," He says, " of all nations whither I have scattered thee, but I will not make a full end of thee."

Hence, no fires of tribulation, however hot, have been able utterly to consume them ; and no waters of affliction, however deep, to drown them.

And the end of the Lord in all the chastisements and judgments with which He has to visit His people on account of their great and manifold sins, is not their destruction, but that they may, by these very judgments, as well as by the abundant mercy which He will reveal to them " in that day," be brought as a nation *fully, and for ever*, to know Him, in all the Divine perfections of His glorious character, so as to be able to fulfil their fore-ordained mission to show forth His praise, and to proclaim His glory among the nations.

Hence the " refining " and the " trying," or " testing," of even " the *third* part," or little remnant, as set forth in the 9th verse. This, I believe, refers more particularly to the remnant in the land at the time of the very end, immediately before their final glorious deliverance. Then, particularly, He will " refine them as silver is refined, and will try them as gold is tried," for in the words of Malachi, " He will be like a refiner's fire, and like fullers' sope." He shall sit as a refiner and purifier of silver, " and shall purge and purify them that they may offer unto Jehovah offerings in righteousness." [2]

But from the midst of this fiery furnace of tribulation " *they shall call on My Name and I will hear them : I will*

[1] Isa. vi. 13. [2] Mal. iii. 2-4. See also Ps. lxvi. 10-12.

*say, Ammi-hu.   It is My people ; and they shall say, Yehovah
Elohoi, Jehovah is my God.*[1]

Blessed and most glorious consummation! The covenant relationship between God and His people, so long
interrupted though never broken, is restored again; she
that was, during the time of her wanderings from her God,
Lo-ammi—" not My people," is " *Ammi* "[2]—" My people "
again; the national vow of Israel by which they avouched
Jehovah to be their God, to walk in His ways, and ever to
hearken to His voice, is now renewed, never to be broken
again.[3] Well might the prophets—contemplating the day
when restored and converted Israel shall once again be, as
it were, pressed to God's own heart, and in view of *the
glorious issues* which shall result to the whole world from
this restoration of covenant relations between God and
" His own " people—call upon the whole creation to join in
a grand chorus of praise.

> " *Sing, O heavens ; and be joyful, O earth :
> And break forth into singing, O mountains :
> For Jehovah hath comforted His people,
> And will have compassion upon His afflicted.*" [4]

[1] See Jer. xxxii. 38-42 ; Ezek. xxxvii. 23-28, and other places in the former
prophets, of which this is an inspired echo and reiteration.
[2] Hos. i. 9-11.   [3] Deut. xxvi. 17-19.   [4] Isa. xlix. 13.

Chapter 20

THE GLORIOUS CONSUMMATION
MESSIAH'S VISIBLE APPEARING AS THE DELIVERER OF ISRAEL AND THE ESTABLISHMENT OF GOD'S KINGDOM ON EARTH

Zechariah 14

Behold, a day of Jehovah cometh, when thy spoil shall be divided in the midst of thee. For I will gather all nations against Jerusalem to battle ; and the city shall be taken, and the houses rifled, and the women ravished : and half of the city shall go forth into captivity, and the residue of the people shall not be cut off from the city. Then shall Jehovah go forth, and fight against those nations, as when He fought in the day of battle. And His feet shall stand in that day upon the mount of Olives, which is before Jerusalem on the east, and the mount of Olives shall be cleft in the midst thereof toward the east and toward the west, and there shall be a very great valley ; and half of the mountain shall remove toward the north, and half of it toward the south. And ye shall flee by the valley of My mountains ; for the valley of the mountains shall reach unto Azel : yea, ye shall flee, like as ye fled from before the earthquake in the days of Uzziah king of Judah : and Jehovah my God shall come, and all the holy ones with Thee. And it shall come to pass in that day, that there shall not be light : the bright ones shall withdraw themselves : but it shall be one day which is known unto Jehovah ; not day, and not night : but it shall come to pass, that at evening time there shall be light. And it shall come to pass in that day, that living waters shall go out from Jerusalem ; half of them toward the eastern sea, and half of them toward the western sea : in summer and in winter shall it be. And Jehovah shall be King over all the earth : in that day shall Jehovah be one, and His name one. All the land shall be made like the Arabah, from Geba to Rimmon south of Jerusalem ; and she shall be lifted up, and shall dwell in her place, from Benjamin's gate unto the place of the first gate, unto the corner gate, and from the tower of Hananel unto the king's winepresses. And men shall dwell therein, and there shall be no more curse ; but Jerusalem shall dwell safely. And this shall be the plague wherewith Jehovah will smite all the peoples that have warred against Jerusalem : their flesh shall consume away while they stand upon their feet, and their eyes shall consume away in their sockets, and their tongue shall consume away in their mouth. And it shall come to pass in that day, that a great tumult from Jehovah shall be among them'; and they shall lay hold every one on the hand of his neighbour, and his hand shall rise up against the hand of his neighbour. And Judah also shall fight at Jerusalem ; and the wealth of all the nations round about shall be gathered together, gold, and silver, and apparel in great abundance. And so shall be the plague of the horse, of the mule, of the camel, and of the ass, and of all the beasts that shall be in those camps, as that plague. And it shall come to pass, that every one that is left of all the nations that came against Jerusalem shall go up from year to year to worship the King, Jehovah of hosts, and to keep the feast of tabernacles. And it shall be, that whoso of all the families of the earth goeth not up unto Jerusalem to worship the King, Jehovah of hosts, upon them there shall be no rain. And if the family of Egypt go not up, and come not, neither shall it be upon them ; there shall be the plague wherewith Jehovah will smite the nations that go not up to keep the feast of tabernacles. This shall be the punishment of Egypt, and the punishment of all the nations that go not up to keep the feast of tabernacles. In that day shall there be upon the bells of the horses, Holy unto Jehovah ; and the pots in Jehovah's house shall be like the bowls before the altar. Yea, every pot in Jerusalem and in Judah shall be holy unto Jehovah of hosts : and all they that sacrifice shall come and take of them, and boil therein : and in that day there shall be no more a Canaanite in the house of Jehovah of hosts.

Chapter 20

INTRODUCTORY

PERHAPS in connection with no other scripture do the contradictions and absurdities of the allegorising commentators appear so clearly as in their interpretations of this 14th chapter of Zechariah. Thus, according to Hengstenberg, Keil, and others of the older German expositors, who are followed by such English scholars as Pusey and C. H. H. Wright, to whose works I have so often referred in this exposition, "Israel," in this last section of Zechariah, "denotes the people of God in contradistinction to the peoples of the world; the inhabitants of Jerusalem with the house of David, and Judah with its princes, as the representatives of Israel, are typical epithets applied to the representatives and members of the new-covenant people, namely, the Christian Church; and Jerusalem and Judah, as the inheritance of Israel, are types of the seats and territories of Christendom." [1]

And yet, when it is a question of judgment, as, for instance, the statement that "two thirds shall be cut off and die in the land," then, of course, they are agreed that those "cut off" are literal Jews, and "the land" Palestine.

Or again, when it is a prediction *which has already been fulfilled*, such as the piercing of the Messiah in chap. xii. 10, or the smiting of the shepherd and the scattering of the flock in chap. xiii. 7, then it is to be understood literally; but when the prophet speaks of things of which no fulfilment can yet be found in history, then the words, however definite and particular, must be spiritualised, and "Jerusalem" is no longer the capital of the Promised Land, but

[1] Keil.

"the Church," and "Israel" no longer the literal descendants of Abraham, Isaac, and Jacob, but "the people of God," by which, as is seen in the quotation given above, is meant "Christendom."

But that is not really a spiritual way of interpreting Scripture, which robs it of its simple and obvious sense.

Kliefoth, Keil, etc., speak of the views expressed by Koehler and Hoffmann in their works on Zechariah, that this chapter refers to a yet future siege of Jerusalem after the return of the Jews in a condition of unbelief, and of their deliverance by the appearing of Christ, as "Jewish Chiliasm," but Jewish Chiliasm was not *all* wrong. *There is* a Messianic Kingdom—a literal reign of peace and righteousness on the earth, with Israel as its centre; but where Jewish Chiliasm erred was that it overlooked, or explained away, the sufferings of the Messiah which precede the glory. The question is if these allegorising commentators are not as much in the dark in relation to the Second Coming and the glory that should follow, as the Jews were in relation to His First Advent and His atoning suffering and death.

In the words of a true master in Israel: "The literal fulfilment of many prophecies has already taken place. It belongs to history. But the Christian has no more difficulty in believing the future fulfilment of prophecy than in crediting the record of history. He believes because God has spoken, because it is written. To believe that the Jews are scattered among all nations, that Jerusalem was destroyed by the Romans, that of the Temple not one stone was left upon another, requires no spiritual faith—it requires only common information. But to believe that Israel will be restored, Jerusalem rebuilt, and that all nations shall come up against the beloved city and besiege it, and that the Lord Jehovah shall appear and stand on the Mount of Olives, requires faith, for it is as yet only written in the Bible. But what difference does it make to the child of God whether the prophecy is fulfilled or not? Can he for a moment doubt it?

" And when we remember how literally prophecy has been fulfilled, we cannot but expect as literal a fulfilment in the future.

" How natural it would have been for those who lived before the First Advent, to think that only the spiritual features of the Messiah's Coming and Kingdom could be the object of inspired prophecy, and that the outward and minute circumstances predicted were either allegorical and figurative, or only the drapery and embellishment of important and essential truths. And yet the fulfilment was minute even in subordinate detail." [1] For our own part, it is unnecessary to say, after what we have already written on chaps. xii. and xiii., that we have here a great and solemn prophecy which will yet be literally fulfilled in the future. And when it is objected by some of the modern writers that the literal fulfilment is " impossible," because it would involve not only national upheavals, but physical convulsions of nature, our answer is that *this is just what the prophet declares as most certainly to take place ;* and, as if to anticipate the objection on the ground of its being naturally " impossible," or, according to human judgment, " improbable," he reminds us at the very outset of this section of his prophecy that it is *the word of Jehovah*, " *Who stretcheth forth the heavens, and layeth the foundation of the earth, and formeth the spirit of man within him*," [2] *with whom nothing is impossible.*

THE EXPOSITION [3]

The first verses of this fourteenth chapter, which are an expansion and amplification of the last three verses of the preceding chapter, lead us back, I believe, to the point of time with which the *twelfth* chapter opens, and tells us

---

[1] Adolph Saphir.   [2] Chap. xii. i.

[3] The exposition of the first seven verses of this chapter—now slightly altered —was originally written out and read as "a paper" at a meeting of the " Prophecy Investigation Society," which also printed it for private circulation among the members. This will account for its being slightly different in form and style from my exposition generally.

of the judgment which is first allowed of God to be inflicted on Jerusalem in the final great siege by means of the marshalled Gentile armies, whose subsequent sudden destruction these chapters prophetically set forth with all the vividness of an historic event depicted by an eye-witness.

Nor need we be surprised to find in this chapter a partial reiteration of events which had already been announced by the prophet in chaps. xii. and xiii.; for, to quote a few sentences from a writer with whose interpretation of the last chapters of Zechariah I am utterly at variance, " the prophets frequently speak generally of the final results of an event, and afterwards proceed to give further details. Any attempt to regard all the statements of the prophets as necessarily succeeding one another in chronological order, would reduce many of these prophecies to a mass of confusion." This observation is true.

But it is necessary briefly to summarise the probable events which lead up to the supreme crisis into the midst of which we are introduced in this last chapter of Zechariah.

First of all we have to suppose a restoration of the Jews in a condition of unbelief—not a complete restoration of the whole nation, which will not take place till after their conversion, but of a representative and influential remnant.

It seems from Scripture that in relation to Israel and the land there will be a restoration, before the Second Advent of our Lord, of very much the same state of things as existed at the time of His First Advent, when the threads of God's dealing with them nationally were finally dropped, not to be taken up again " until the times of the Gentiles shall be fulfilled."

There was at that time a number of Jews in Palestine representative of the nation ; but compared with the number of their brethren, who were already a diaspora among the nations, they were a mere minority, and not in a politically independent condition.

So it will be again. There will be at first, as compared with the whole nation, only a representative minority in Palestine, and a Jewish state will be probably formed, either under the suzerainty of one of the Great Powers, or under international protection.

The nucleus of this politically independent Jewish state is already to be seen in the 120,000 Jews who have wandered back from all regions of the earth to the land of their fathers.

Already Jerusalem before the war was almost a Jewish city, while the thirty and more Jewish colonies which dotted the land were described by a prominent English Jew as " so many milestones marking the advance which Israel is making towards national rehabilitation." And in no other country in the world do the Jews, to the same extent, represent the nation. In Jerusalem and in the other Jewish settlements in Palestine I have personally, in the course of my seven different visits to the land since 1890, met Jews from all parts—from the east and the west; from India and the burning plains of Southern Arabia, and from the extreme north of Siberia and the Caucasus; and have heard them speaking in nearly all languages under heaven.

Around this nucleus a large number more from all parts of the world will in all probability soon be gathered; but we shall only be able to speak of a restoration of the Jews as an accomplished fact when Palestine becomes by international consent (to quote from the Zionist programme) the " openly recognised and legally assured home " of the Jews, *i.e.*, when the Jews are once more acknowledged as a nation with a land of their own to which they might go.[1]

But what follows? After a brief interval of prosperity there comes a night of anguish. What occasions the darkest hour in the night of Israel's sad history since their rejection of Christ is the gathering of the nations and the siege predicted in this chapter.

---

[1] How rapidly things have developed on the lines here forecast since the above was originally written four or five years ago.

The " Declaration " of the British Government recognises the Jews as once more a nation, and promises to facilitate their re-establishment in Palestine ; while Jerusalem has been captured by the victorious British Army !

If we interpret Scripture rightly, they shall have entered into covenant and sworn allegiance to a false Messiah, thus culminating their national apostasy, and fulfilling the word of Christ, "If another shall come in his own name, him ye shall receive."

But the covenant of iniquity based upon apostasy will not stand. Infuriated, probably by the faithfulness to the covenant God of their fathers on the part of the godly remnant who shall then be found in the land, the Antichrist forms the purpose of utterly and finally exterminating this people, who can never cease, even in apostasy and unbelief, to be witnesses for the living God and His truth. The armies of the confederated nations, the very flower of their strength, are marshalled together in Palestine, their watchword being, "Come, let us cut them off from being a nation, that the name of Israel may be no more in remembrance."

The dreadfulness of these hosts I have already dwelt on in my notes on the 12th chapter. They march in triumph through the land, easily treading down all opposition. And now the enemy in overwhelming force and irresistible fury attacks Jerusalem, which is soon at his mercy. The city is taken, and the "spoil" or booty leisurely "divided in the midst" of her, without any fear on the part of the enemy of interruption or molestation. There ensue scenes of cruel brutality, and lust, and horrors, which usually accompany the sack of cities by enraged enemies, only intensified in this particular case by the accumulated hatred of these confederated hosts against this land and people. Half of the remaining population in the city is dragged forth into captivity, and there is but a small and wretched remnant left, which probably, in the intention of the enemy, are also devoted to destruction.

Well might another prophet exclaim, "*Alas! for that day is great, so that none is like it; it is even the time of Jacob's trouble.*"

But though it is a day which begins with calamity and judgment to Israel, it is not going to end in triumph to

Israel's enemies.   It is pre-eminently the יוֹם לַיהֹוָה (*yom la-Yehovah*)—"a day for Jehovah"—the day set apart and appointed by Him, not only for the display of His majesty and the vindication of the righteousness of His character and ways, but it is the day of the manifestation of His Divine might and glory in the destruction of Israel's enemies, and the salvation of His own people.   "*Then shall Jehovah go forth, and fight against these nations, as when He fought in the day of battle*"; or, "as in a day of His fighting in a day of conflict"—as the words in the original may more properly be rendered.

There are many instances recorded in the Old Testament when Jehovah manifestly fought for His people.   In Josh. x. 14, for instance, we find words which seem echoed in this prophecy.   "*And there was no day like that before it or after it,*" we read there, "*for Jehovah fought for Israel.*"   But I think we must agree with the Jewish Targum and those commentators who regard the reference as being particularly to the conflict between Jehovah and the Egyptians at the Red Sea ; for, "of all the wars in which human insolence could claim no part of the glory," to quote the words of a well-known writer, "none was more wondrous than that in which Pharaoh and his army were sunk in the deep."   It was after that great act of judgment on Israel's enemies on the part of God that Israel sang, "*Jehovah is a man of war ; Jehovah is His Name*" (Ex. xv. 3).   The reference is more likely to be to this outstanding event in the past history of the Jewish people, since we know that the prophetic Scriptures generally regard the deliverance from Egypt as typical, not only of the greater spiritual redemption accomplished by Christ, but of the future greater national deliverance of Israel ; and the overthrow of Pharaoh and his hosts as a foreshadowment of the final overthrow of the enemies of God and of His people at the time of the end.

And it will be no other than Jehovah-Jesus, the El Gibbor, "God the Mighty Man," who will thus suddenly appear as Israel's deliverer in the hour of their sorest need :

" *And His feet,*" we read, " *shall stand in that day upon the Mount of Olives, which is before Jerusalem on the east.*"

The mountain which is so clearly defined and located in this prophecy is already associated with many events and crises in Israel's history. We especially remember that before the final overthrow of the Davidic throne and the commencement of the Times of the Gentiles, it was from this mountain, which is before Jerusalem on the east, that the prophet Ezekiel saw the glory of Jehovah finally taking its departure.

It was from this mountain also that He, who was not only the symbol, but the living personal revelation of the glory of Jehovah, finally took His departure from the land, after He had already been rejected by the nation. He led His handful of disciples out as far as Bethany (on the Mount of Olives), and He lifted up His hands and blessed them. "And it came to pass while He blessed them, He was parted from them, and carried up into heaven " ;[1] since when a still darker era in the long Ichabod period of Israel's history commenced.

But from the same direction whence he saw the departure of the Glory of Jehovah, the prophet Ezekiel saw also its return. " *Afterwards,*" we read, " *He brought me to the gate that looketh toward the east, and behold, the Glory of the God of Israel came from the way of the east, and His voice was like the noise of many waters, and the earth shined with His glory.*" And what is this but a prophecy in symbolic language of the same event which the heavenly messengers announced to the men of Galilee, that " *this same Jesus, which is taken up from you into heaven, shall so come in like manner as ye have seen Him go up into heaven.*" And not only " in like manner "—that is, bodily, visibly—but He shall come *to the same place* whence He finally departed.

We love to think that this same mountain on which He once shed tears of sorrow over Jerusalem, the slope of which witnessed His agony and bloody sweat, shall be the

---

[1] Luke xxiv. 50, 51.

first also to witness His manifestation in glory; and that
His blessed feet, which in the days of His flesh walked
wearily over this mountain on the way to Bethany shall,
" in that day," be planted here *in triumph and majesty.*

In response to the actual presence of the Divine
majesty of the Son of God on this earth, the Mount of
Olives, on which He shall descend, shall be cleft in two
from east to west; half of it moving to the north and half
to the south, forming " a very great valley."

Into this valley the remnant still remaining in Jerusalem will flee,[1] " like as ye fled from before *the earthquake
in the days of Uzziah king of Judah,*" of which earthquake
there is no other mention in Scripture except in Amos i. 1.
But it must have been very terrible indeed, since the
memory of it survived for more than two centuries, and
could still be referred to by the prophet as an occurrence
fresh in the minds of the people. " Ye shall flee," as the
Hebrew Text reads, " into MY mountains " — the lofty
precipitous sides of this newly-formed chasm, or valley, being
called *His* mountains, because they were formed by an act of
His power. This may, in a sense, be regarded as a
parallel to the passage through the Red Sea after it was
divided by the power of God, and " the waters were a wall
unto them on their right hand and on their left " (Ex. xiv.
22).

The occasion of this flight will not only be fear of the
destroying enemy, and the terror inspired by the earthquake, but they shall flee most of all " for fear of Jehovah,
and the glory of His majesty," when thus suddenly and
unexpectedly " *the Lord my God shall come,*" in the person
of their long-rejected Messiah, " *and all the holy ones with
Thee* "—by which are meant, not only the myriads of His
holy angels, but His saints, who are also called קְדשִׁים,
qedoshim (" holy ones "), and who shall have been caught up
to meet the Lord in the air.

---

[1] The Massoretic reading, וְנַסְתֶּם, *venastem*, " Ye shall flee," is doubtless the
correct one, and not וְנִסְתַּם, *venistam*, " shall be stopped up," which is found in
several MSS, and adopted in the Targum, the Septuagint, and other versions.

It is at this point, I believe, that the solemn events announced from the 4th verse of chap. xii. to the 2nd verse of chap. xiii. will transpire.

The first proof of the Lord's interposition on behalf of His people and land, will be His act of judgment on the besieging hosts. The pride of the glory of the marshalled armies will probably be in the mounted squadrons, which will no doubt include the finest horsemen of Europe and Arabia, and against them the Captain of the Lord's host shall first direct His hand : " *In that day I will smite every horse with astonishment, and his rider with madness.*" [1]

Then the extended ranks of infantry shall be visited with the plague described in chap. xiv. 12, and a great tumult from the Lord shall ensue among the confederated hosts, as happened in the past, when Jehovah fought for Israel ; so that each man's hand shall be against his neighbour.

And not only by the direct act of God shall the enemy be destroyed, but, as already shown in my Notes on chap. xii., with the shout of a king in their midst, and conscious that Almighty power is now on their side, the remnant of Judah, too, will do valiantly, and tread down their enemies under their feet: " *He that is feeble among them at that day shall be as David, and the house of David shall be as God, as the Angel of the Lord before them.*"

But suddenly the noise of war and the shout of triumph is turned into wailing and lamentation as the spirit of grace and supplication takes possession of the heart of the remnant of Israel, and the eyes of the blind are opened, and they behold in the King of Glory, at whose presence the earth trembles and the mountains are cleft, and who has so marvellously delivered them in the hour of their greatest need, none other than the one whom they have pierced, and whom for so many centuries they have rejected and despised. This look of recognition, as we have seen in chap. xii., will break Israel's heart, and " they shall mourn for Him as one mourneth for his only son, and

[1] Chap. xii. 4.

shall be in bitterness for Him as one that is in bitterness for his firstborn."

And not only will the sorrow and mourning spread from Jerusalem to the whole land, but also to the whole earth; for, though Jerusalem and Palestine will be the centre of these awful and solemn events, the whole world will be more or less involved in them.

When the final judgments of God are abroad in the earth, and when the anti-Christian rage and persecution will be everywhere directed not only against the confessors of Christ, but against those in Israel who are faithful to the God of their fathers, there will be weeping, and mourning, and heart-searching among the scattered tribes of Israel in all the lands of their dispersion.

And when at last, in the hour of their deepest need, their long-rejected, crucified Messiah appears for their deliverance—when His blessed feet shall stand in that day upon the Mount of Olives—they will almost simultaneously be made aware of it; for, though they may not all at once behold Him with their eyes, the whole world, and nature generally, will be conscious of, and respond to, the visible appearing and presence of the Son of God.

And the spared remnant of the dispersed of Israel will, like their brethren in Jerusalem, hail Him—though at first it may be from a distance—whom they crucified, and turn to Him in true repentance.

But to proceed to the 6th verse.

In keeping with the awful solemn events shall be the outward natural phenomena and physical characteristics of that fateful day. It shall be a day of preternatural gloom. " *There shall be no light*, the " precious ones " (*i.e.*, the stars, " the splendid heavenly bodies ") will contract themselves (or " *wane* "), which I believe to be the true meaning of the two last, somewhat difficult Hebrew words of the 6th verse, which have been variously rendered and interpreted by commentators.[1] This is in harmony with the plain declara-

---

[1] The words in the Hebrew text are יְקָרוֹת יְקִפָּאוֹן, *yeqaroth yeqipa'un* : קָר, *yaqor* (" precious," " rare," " splendid ") is applied *to the moon* in Job xxxi. 26,

tions of other prophetic announcements concerning that day ; as, for instance, " *The sun and the moon shall be darkened, and the stars shall withdraw their shining*," [1] or, in the words of Isaiah : " *The moon shall be confounded and the sun ashamed when the Lord of Hosts shall reign in Mount Zion and in Jerusalem, and before His ancients gloriously*" ; [2] and again : " *The stars of heaven, and the constellations thereof, shall not give their light : the sun shall be darkened in his going forth, and the moon shall not cause her light to shine.*" [3]

" *But in those days after that tribulation the sun shall be darkened and the moon shall not give her light, and the stars shall be falling from heaven, and the powers that are in the heaven shall be shaken.*" [4]

And it shall be *yom echad*, " one day," we read in our prophecy—" one " primarily in the sense of its being unique

which is described as " *sailing resplendent*," and it seems most probable that the plural *yeqaroth* is used here of " the resplendent heavenly bodies," *i.e.*, the stars. The verb קָפָא, *qapha* (" thicken," " condense," " congeal ") is found in Ex. xv. 8, and describes the depths as becoming *congealed*, or *consolidated*, in the midst of the seas. But the difference of the gender in the combination of the feminine substantive *yeqaroth* with the masculine verb *yeqipa'un*, the irregularity of construction, and the rarity with which these words are met with in the Hebrew Bible, have occasioned many conjectural readings and explanations. The "*keri*" (marginal alternative reading in the Massoretic text) has יְקָרוֹת וְקִפָּאוֹן, *yeqaroth v'qipa'un*—the meaning of which is also not quite clear, but may be rendered " intense brightness, and waning." But it is pretty generally agreed by all scholars that the *kethib* (the Hebrew text) and not the *keri*, or margin, has the true reading. The " Jewish " explanation is embodied in Kimchi's comment, which is as follows : " In that day in which he says that this miracle shall occur, there shall also be this circumstance, that the light shall neither be *yeqaroth* (" precious ") nor *yeqipa'un* (" thickness "). The meaning is figurative, that the light of that day shall not be bright, which is the meaning of "precious lights," or "the moon walking in brightness" (Job xxxi. 26), nor light of thickness, *i.e.*, dense and thick, which is like darkness. The sense is, the day shall not be entirely light nor entirely dark, *i.e.*, it shall not pass entirely in tranquillity nor in affliction, for they two shall be in it ; and so he says afterwards, not day nor night. Jonathan has interpreted, " There shall be nothing that day but privation and coagulation."

The LXX reads καὶ ψύχη καὶ πάγος, " and cold and frost."

The translation which I have given in the text seems to me the most satisfactory.

[1] Joel iii. 15. [2] Isa. xxiv. 23.
[3] Isa. xiii. 10. [4] Mark xiii. 24, 25.

and different to all other days in the world's history, "so that none is like it," as Jeremiah expresses it, "*and it shall be known to Jehovah*," which phrase certainly reminds us of the words of our Lord : "Of that day and hour knoweth no man, not even the angels which are in heaven, neither the Son, but the Father"[1]—"*Not day nor night*"—"like mysterious light when day and night are contending together." It shall not be day, for the natural sources of light will be withdrawn ; but it cannot be like the darkness of night, for there will be the transplendent light of the glory of the Lord, and the myriads of His holy angels, and of the glorified saints reflected on the earth.

"*And it shall come to pass that at evening time*"—when in the order of nature everything should sink into darkness—"*there shall be light*" ; out of the contest between light and darkness on that eventful day light shall emerge victorious —"the light of salvation breaking its way through the night of judgment," as Von Orelli observes ; and out of the apparent chaos beauty and order.

As far as its *primary* literal significance is concerned, the statement that "at evening time there shall be light," may perhaps be explained by the words of Isaiah : "The light of the moon shall be as the light of the sun, and the light of the sun shall be sevenfold, as the light of seven days, in the day that Jehovah bindeth up the hurt of His people and healeth the stroke of their wound."[2]

But this literal physical phenomenon will answer also to the spiritual condition of the spared remnant. "At evening time" of that great and most solemn day—the great Atonement Day for the nation—when the long dark period of their national history shall end in bitter sorrow and universal mourning, not on account of their suffering, but for their sin ; when the glorious Sun of Righteousness shall at last rise upon them with healing in His wings, "*there shall be light*"—the light and the joy of forgiveness and eternal reconciliation ; the light of the glory of God in the face of Jesus Christ which shall shine upon them.

[1] Mark xiii. 32.   [2] Isa. xxx. 26,

"We can in part conceive the feelings with which the
spared remnant of Israel will behold the light of that
evening—the evening which is to introduce the new order
of God. They have been described in the 12th chapter as
subdued, contrite, and mourning. And no marvel: carried
as they will have been by a power that they knew not,
through such a day of terror, strengthened for the Lord in
it, and left at last in a scene of tranquil blessing received
from the hands of One whom they had despised, but to
whom they have now learned to say ' My Lord, and my
God '; it would be strange indeed if they should not, numbering such mercies, be bowed in contrition of spirit. And
when they shall at last be comforted, and the Spirit be
poured out upon them from on high, when the knowledge of
their own past history and of the Church's history will all
be opened to them in the light of God, then, like so many
Pauls, monuments of Sovereign grace, they shall go forth
to the dark places of the earth, rich in experience and in
the knowledge of God, and from them shall flow rivers of
living waters." [1]

The blessed issues of the great and solemn events of
"that day," as set forth in the first seven verses, are
described in the verses that follow :—

I. By means of the great earthquake spoken of in
vers. 4 and 5, and other convulsions of nature which are
immediately to precede and to accompany the visible
appearing of the Messiah, when His feet shall stand in that
day upon the Mount of Olives—great physical changes will
take place in Palestine and the whole land, but particularly
the position of Jerusalem will be greatly altered and transformed.[2] " *And it shall come to pass in that day that living
waters shall go out from Jerusalem, half of them toward the
eastern sea, and half of them toward the western sea ; in
summer and in winter shall it be.*"

The " eastern " (*haqqadmoni*, which has sometimes also
the meaning of " ancient ") is the Dead Sea, which shall
then be healed by the streams of fresh, or " living,"

---

[1] B. W. Newton.   [2] Isa. xxx. 25, 26.

water which will flow through it; and the western *ha-acharon* (literally, the "last" "or hindermost") is the Mediterranean. And these waters will never run dry, as the streams in the south[1] are apt to do now: "summer drought shall not lessen them, nor winter cold bind them," but they shall ceaselessly flow "in summer and in winter." To these perennial waters flowing from the "river of God,"[2] primarily so called, because it is formed, as it were, by a direct act of His power, there are many references in the prophetic Scriptures.

Thus Joel, speaking of the time when Jehovah shall manifestly dwell in Zion, and "Jerusalem shall be holy," into which nothing that defileth shall enter, says, "*And a fountain shall come forth from the house of Jehovah and shall water the valley of Shittim*";[3] and in Ps. xlvi., which is a great prophecy of the same solemn events which are described in these last chapters of Zechariah, the inspired Psalmist beholds in vision "*a river the streams whereof make glad the city of God*,"[4] namely, restored and renewed Jerusalem, the vestibule, as it were, during the millennial period of the Jerusalem which is above—which shall emerge from the catastrophe described in the first verses, when the earth shall "be removed," or "changed," and the "mountains shaken into the heart of the seas, and the waters roar and be troubled."

The allusion in all these scriptures, which speak of the river of living waters dividing themselves into streams flowing in different directions, is probably to Gen. ii. 10. There we read: "*And a river went out of Eden to water the garden; and from thence it was parted and became four*

---

[1] Ps. cxxvi. 4. [2] Ps. lxv. 9.

[3] Joel iii. 18. Some modern writers understand this as referring to a valley somewhere in the neighbourhood of Jerusalem ("a valley in connection with the Kidron Valley"—Von Orelli), but I am inclined to think that the reference is to the Shittim of Num. xxv. 1, the last encampment of the Israelites on the steppes of Moab before their entrance into Canaan—the barren valley of the Jordan above the Dead Sea. Shittim means acacias, which grow only in arid regions, and the words of the prophecy imply that even the arid desert shall be fertilised by the waters issuing from this fountain.

[4] Ps. xlvi. 4.

heads," or *streams.* Now, since for beauty and fertility, and as the earthly centre of God's dwelling and worship, Jerusalem and Palestine will, in the millennial period, answer, as it were, to the garden of Eden—there is again the River, the streams whereof make glad the city of God, and flowing thence fertilise other parts of the earth.

Now, to repeat, we believe, in a literal fulfilment of this prophecy in Zechariah, and when we are told by a scholarly English writer that a literal fulfilment is out of the question because " the physical nature of the whole land would have to be changed to permit literal rivers to flow forth from Jerusalem,"[1] our answer is, " Certainly ; *this is just what the prophecy says will be the case."* The physical nature of the whole land will be changed through the convulsions of nature, which are described here and in other scriptures, and which will be brought about by the Almighty power of God, with whom nothing is impossible. But while this literal fulfilment cannot be emphasised too strongly in order to a true understanding of these prophecies, it is important also to note that the literal, material river will be at the same time the visible symbol of the mighty river of God's grace and salvation, which, during the millennial period dividing itself into full streams of Messianic blessings, will start from Jerusalem as its source and centre, and carry life and salvation to all nations.

" We read in many parts of the Scripture that the land of Israel will in that day teem with evidences of the miraculous power of God in dispensing blessings. On the sides of Zion, for example, the wolf and the lamb, the leopard and the kid, shall be seen together, and a little child shall lead them. Nothing shall hurt or destroy throughout God's holy mountain. These will be sights

---

[1] Dr. C. H. H. Wright, *Zechariah and his Prophecies.* His long chapter of nearly one hundred pages on " The Eschatology of Zechariah, or the Last Things as seen in the Light of the Old Dispensation," is an illustration and specimen of the phantomising method of interpreting Old Testament prophecy, to which I referred in the introductory remarks to this chapter. But though very dogmatic in his style, Dr. Wright succeeds, not in explaining, but in explaining away, these great prophecies.

that no one will deny to be in themselves blessed. But they are symbols also, living symbols, speaking of higher blessings; for they indicate the peace and harmony and love that shall pervade all hearts and all peoples whom the power of Zion shall effectually reach. And if God has appointed that the spiritual influence of which I have spoken above should go forth from His forgiven and privileged nation in Jerusalem, we might expect to find some outward symbol of this, its relation. And, accordingly, a symbol is given in the perennial flow of those streams which, going forth from the sanctuary in Jerusalem, shall heal waters, which, like the Dead Sea, have been accursed, and spread life and refreshment in the midst of desolation." [1]

As the symbol of the greater spiritual reality, let us pause and contemplate for a moment this " river of God." Its source is God Himself. " *There,*" exclaims the prophet Isaiah—that is, in renewed and glorified Jerusalem—" *The glorious Jehovah* " (or, " *Jehovah in His Majesty*") " *will be unto us a place of broad rivers and streams.*" [2] Or, in the language of the beloved John in the Apocalypse, " *He showed me a river of water of life bright as crystal proceeding out of the throne of God and of the Lamb.*" [3] Yes, " and *of the Lamb,*" for though God is the Source, the Eternal Fountain of this pure Water of Life, the Lamb slain is the channel through which it flows.

Another glorious fact emphasised in the Scriptures in connection with these living waters is their fulness—indicative of the abundance of God's grace and salvation, which shall go forth during the period of Messiah's reign, from Jerusalem as its centre, into all parts of the world. The " River of God," we read, " *is full of water,*" [4] and Ezekiel beholds it in vision " *as a river which he could not pass through, for the waters were risen, waters to swim in, a river that could not be passed through.*" [5]

And as they are abundant in quantity, so also is the

[1] B. W. Newton.   [2] Isa. xxxiii. 21.   [3] Rev. xxii. 1,
[4] Ps. lxv. 9.   [5] Ezek. xlvii. 1–12.

healing, life-giving efficacy of the living waters wonderful.
The very desert shall be transformed by them, and the
stagnant waters of the Dead Sea healed. *" Everything,"*
says Ezekiel, *" and every living creature which swarmeth in
every place whither the river shall come, shall live ; . . . and
by the river upon the bank thereof on this side, and on that
side, shall grow every tree for meat, whose leaf shall not
wither, neither shall the fruit thereof fail ; it shall bring forth
new fruit every month, because the waters thereof issue out of
the sanctuary ; and the fruit shall be for meat, and the leaf
thereof for healing."* Yes, *" for the healing of the nations,"* [1]
as the beloved Apostle adds in the last chapter of the
Apocalypse, where Ezekiel's imagery of the earthly but
glorified Jerusalem during the millennial period is transferred also to the heavenly Jerusalem.

A foretaste of the great spiritual realities, which in the
age to come will be symbolised also by literal and visible
objects, we have indeed in the present dispensation, for
those are not wholly wrong who point to the Gospel of our
Lord Jesus Christ as embodying the very qualities ascribed
to these " living waters," and many there be who can testify
from experience to its life-giving, healing, sanctifying
power, and to the great and glorious transformations which
it has effected in the world since Christ's first Advent.
But, whereas its course now and all through the present
period is an intermittent, chequered one, and its quickening
power has been experienced only by individuals, by-and-by,
when Israel as a nation is first quickened and transformed
by it, and the national Saul of Tarsus is turned into a
nation of Pauls, with the same burning love and self-
consuming zeal for their Redeemer-King, which characterised
the great Apostle to the Gentiles — the blessings of
Messiah's Gospel, and the beneficent effects of His reign—
will flow from Jerusalem *as mighty rivers and streams* into
all parts of the world, so that it will not be long before
" the earth shall be filled with the knowledge of the glory
of Jehovah as the waters cover the sea." [2]

¹ Rev, xxii. 2.   ² Hab. ii, 14.

II. Another glorious issue of the solemn events described in the first seven verses of our chapter will be the establishment of Messiah's righteous and beneficent rule on earth, and the fulfilment of the prayer which has ascended from the yearning hearts of the faithful in all ages : " Thy Kingdom come." This is announced in the 9th verse : " *And Jehovah shall be King over all the earth : in that day shall Jehovah be one and His Name one.*" In this great and comprehensive prophecy we note especially two or three points : (*a*) " *Jehovah* shall be King "—but according to the united and harmonious testimony of the prophetic Scriptures it will be Jehovah in the person of the Messiah, Jehovah-Jesus, Immanuel—He whose feet shall in that day stand on the Mount of Olives which is before Jerusalem on the east—who will thus set up His Kingdom and rule on this earth. And He will be King, not only in virtue of His being the Son of God, in whose coming and reign the long-promised rule of God Himself on this earth shall at last be realised in the fullest possible measure, but by reason of His being the Son of Man—the second Adam —the appointed Lord of creation, in whom the original purpose of God in the creation of man and of the world shall be fulfilled, and as the Son of David, in whom all the promises of the Messianic Kingdom are centred, before whose birth it was announced by the angel from heaven, " *He shall be great, and shall be called the Son of the Highest ; and the Lord God shall give unto Him the throne of His father David. And He shall reign over the House of Jacob for ever ; and of His Kingdom there shall be no end.*"

All that is implied in the blessed announcement that Jehovah Himself shall at last be King over this earth, and in the person of His own Son, who is at the same time the man after His own heart, visibly rule among the nations, we cannot yet fully conceive. " Our ideas of kingship," to quote the words of a master in Israel, " are limited, and do not come up to the Divine conception." [1] Man has had experience of rule, or kingship on earth. but " the true or

[1] Adolph Saphir.

real king among men has not appeared yet." The nearest approach to His rule was David's; but what are the last words of the son of Jesse, the man who was raised up on high, the anointed of the God of Israel and the sweet Psalmist of Israel? His last testimony was that the Spirit of the Lord had spoken by him, and that he had heard the Rock of Israel, and that the sum and substance of these Divine revelations was the coming of the perfect King: "*One that ruleth over men righteously, that ruleth in the fear of God, He shall be as the light of the morning when the sun riseth, a morning without clouds, when the tender grass springeth out of the earth through clear shining after rain.*"[1]

For this ideal King, for this glorious "Sun" to usher in "the morning without clouds" on this groaning earth, the nations have long waited; but He shall come, and the world will experience the blessedness of His righteous and beneficent sway.

(*b*) The extent of His rule—"*over all the earth.*" As explained more than once in the course of these notes, אֶרֶץ, *eretz*, translated "earth," means both "land" and "earth"; and the primary reference in this prophecy is doubtless to "the holy land,"[2] as the enlarged and purified Land of Promise shall then be called. The word is used in this more restricted sense in the very next verse of our chapter, where it is rightly translated "land." But while the holy hill of Zion shall be the *seat* of His throne, and Palestine, with restored and converted Israel, the centre of His blessed rule, "He shall have dominion also from sea to sea, and from the river unto the ends of the earth"; yea, all kings shall fall down before Him, all nations shall serve Him,[3] for all the kingdoms of this world shall then become the Kingdom of our Lord and of His Christ, and He shall reign for ever and ever.

That the prophet's vision of the theocratic kingdom ranged beyond even the enlarged boundaries of the "land," and extended to the whole "*earth*," is seen also from the 16th verse, where he speaks of *all the nations* coming up

[1] 2 Sam. xxxiii. 1-4 (R.V.).   [2] Chap. ii. 12.   [3] Ps. lxxii. 8-11.

to Jerusalem "to worship the King-Jehovah of Hosts," whose sole rule they will then acknowledge. Yes, Messiah's kingship is to extend over *the earth.* God's will, according to the petition which He teaches His disciples, is to be done *on earth* as it is in heaven.

"It is on earth, where God has been denied and forgotten; where His honour has been disregarded and His commandments have been transgressed; where nations and kingdoms, instead of seeking His glory and showing forth His praise—have not bowed to His authority and reverenced His law; it is on earth that the Lord shall reign; injustice, cruelty and war shall be banished; and instead of idolatry, selfishness and sin, the fear and love and beauty of God will be manifest. Christ and the glorified saints shall reign over Israel and the nations. The appearings of the risen Lord to His disciples during the forty days seem to be a prophetic parallel of the relation of the transfigured Church to the earth. Jerusalem is the centre of the world; the land of Israel is restored to wonderful fertility and blessedness. We may not be able clearly to conceive the fulfilment of the predictions concerning this earth during the Christocracy, but our danger does not lie in believing too implicitly or too literally what is written."[1] And this kingship *over the "earth"* is due to our Lord Jesus as an answer to His humiliation. "It is not sufficient that He is glorified in heaven—it is a perfect delight to His own that He is to be glorified and adored in the very scene of His rejection and shame. God will see to this. Here, where His royal claims were scorned, every knee shall bow to Him; here, where He was reviled and insulted, every tongue shall own that "He is Lord to the glory of God the Father. His Name shall be excellent *in all the earth."*

III. "*In that day,*" the prophet adds, "*shall Jehovah be One*"—that is, recognised and *acknowledged* as such, and be known and called the "God of the whole earth,"[2] the only

---

[1] Adolph Saphir, *Lectures on the Lord's Prayer.*
[2] Isa. liv. 5.

and blessed Potentate;[1] for the false gods of the nations, to whom even Israel was tempted in former days of apostasy to render worship, shall be "cut off," and all idols utterly abolished.

"*And His Name*"—which embodies His revealed character as the God of Redemption, the faithful covenant-keeping God of Abraham, Isaac, and Jacob, now fully made known to us by our Lord Jesus Christ, who is Himself the fullest revelation of the Name, shall be "*One*"—to the exclusion of all others—as the only object of reverence, praise, and worship, "*so that he who blesseth himself in the earth shall bless himself in the God of truth; and he that sweareth in the earth shall swear by the God of truth*;[2] and the nations, even from "the ends of the earth," confess that the gods which they had formerly worshipped were "no gods," and the idolatries which they had inherited from their fathers were "nought but lies, even vanity, and things wherein there is no profit."[3]

IV. As "the city of the great King" (Ps. xlviii. 2), whose dominion extends to earth's utmost bounds, and as the centre whence God's light and truth shall go forth among all the nations, Jerusalem is also to be physically exalted above the hills by which she has hitherto been surrounded and overshadowed. This is the announcement in the 10th verse: "*All the land shall be turned*" (or "*changed*," so that it shall become "*as*," or) "*like the Arabah.*" Then the district to be thus transformed is more closely

---

[1] 1 Tim. vi. 15.   [2] Isa. lxv. 16.

[3] Jer. xvi. 19–20 (R.V.). Von Orelli thinks that by the unity of the name Jehovah "is to be understood primarily *unity of designation*, which is important as the plurality of designations of the one God has led in various ways to plural conceptions of the Godhead," and refers to Hos. ii. 16. Lange, by simply referring his readers for an explanation of this clause to Hitzig, seemingly adopts it as his own—namely, "that in consequence of the display of Jehovah's glory, the heathen who had hitherto worshipped God under other names, such as Moloch, Baal, etc., should from henceforth honour and adore Him as 'Jehovah,' under which Name He had made Himself known to the people of Israel." But, as another has observed, "The idea that the heathen under the various names of their gods really meant to worship Jehovah, appears to be an attempt to engraft modern ideas (which, I venture to add, have no basis in fact) upon those of the Old Testament prophets."

defined, namely, "*from Geba to Rimmon, south of Jerusalem.*"
Geba, probably the same as Gibeah of Saul, was in the
tribe of Benjamin,[1] and is mentioned in 2 Kings xxiii.
8 as one of the northern border towns of the land of Judah.
Rimmon was on the southern border of Palestine, and is
identified by some scholars with the modern Umm-er-
Rummamin, north of Beersheba. The words "south of
Jerusalem" are added, to distinguish this latter place from
the town Rimmon in Galilee[2] (identified with Rummaneh),
and from the rock Rimmon in the hill range of Benjamin.[3]

All this district from Geba to Rimmon is to be changed
and become "as the Arabah" (כָּעֲרָבָה). This word, translated "plain" in the A.V., is the proper name of the Jordan
valley—"that remarkable depression which runs from the
slopes of Hermon to the Red Sea, known as the deepest
depression in the surface of the globe"; the sea of Galilee
situated within it being 652 feet below the level of the
Mediterranean, while the Dead Sea, which is also included
in its course, is 1316 feet below that level, or the level of
the Red Sea. Parts of this valley were distinguished for
their luxurious vegetation, but the reference here is not to
its fertility nor to its deep depression, which probably will
itself undergo modification in that day of great physical as
well as moral upheavals, but to the fact of its being a plain.

The whole hill-country specified shall be levelled or
become a plain, "*and she*" (i.e., *Jerusalem*) "*shall be lifted
up*" (or "*exalted*") "*and shall dwell*" (or "*become settled*")
"*in her place,*" literally, "upon that which was under her,"
upon her own *tel*, or mound, as Jeremiah expresses it.[4]

In this brief statement about the towering position of
Jerusalem in that day the prophet Zechariah gives us also,
as is his wont, a terse summary of the longer predictions
of the former prophets; for already Isaiah and Micah, as
well as Ezekiel, announced that "*it shall come to pass in the
latter days that the mountain of Jehovah's house shall be*

---

[1] Josh. xviii. 24.   [2] Josh. xix. 13.
[3] Judg. xx. 45-47.
[4] עַל תִּלָּהּ, Jer. xxx. 18. Translated in the A.V., "Upon its own heap."

established on the top of the mountains, and shall be exalted above the hills." [1]

And here again, as in the case of the "living waters" in the 8th verse, the literal fact will at the same time be emblematic of a great spiritual truth. Zion in the millennial age will be the city of truth, "*the habitation of righteousness and mountain of holiness,*" and therefore will be raised *conspicuously aloft* in the view of all the nations ; it will be the source whence the living waters of God's grace and salvation are to issue in all directions, and therefore every obstacle which might hinder their flow shall be "changed" and turned into a plain. It will be the centre of God's governmental rule of the world, and the place to which "all nations shall flow" for instruction and guidance, and therefore it must be lifted high, and approach to it rendered easy.

In the words of the beautiful paraphrase of the prophetic announcement by Isaiah and Micah :

> Behold ! the mountain of the Lord
> In latter days shall rise
> On mountain-tops above the hills,
> And draw the wond'ring eyes.
>
> To this the joyful nations round,
> All tribes and tongues, shall flow ;
> "Up to the hill of God," they'll say,
> "And to His house we'll go ! "
>
> The beam that shines from Zion's hill
> Shall lighten ev'ry land ;
> The King who reigns in Salem's towers
> Shall all the world command.
>
> Among the nations He shall judge—
> His judgments truth shall guide ;
> His sceptre shall protect the just
> And quell the sinner's pride.

The second half of the 10th verse describes the bounds of the restored and enlarged city, which shall thus be "lifted up" and settled down to dwell safely "in her own place."

"*From Benjamin's gate unto the place of the first* (or

[1] Isa. ii. 2.

'*former*') *gate, unto the corner gate, and from the tower of Hananel unto the king's winepresses.*"

I shall not trouble my readers with topographical details, all the more as by general confession the gates and towers here named cannot with any certainty be identified. Suffice it here to say that " Benjamin's gate," which is very probably the same as " the gate of Ephraim," mentioned in 2 Kings xiv. 13, was in the north wall of the city through which the road to Benjamin, and thence to Ephraim, ran.

The first (or " former ") " gate," which no longer existed in Zechariah's time, since only the place where it once stood is referred to, is supposed to have been at the north-eastern corner, and the " corner gate " (which is also mentioned in 2 Kings xiv. 13 as well as in Jer. xxxi. 38) at the north-western corner.

If these suppositions be correct, this line would describe the whole breadth of the city from east to west, while the tower of Hananel,[1] which stood at the north or *north-east* corner, and " the king's winepresses," which all are agreed were in the king's gardens south of the city, would indicate the northern and southern boundaries. But the chief importance of these local and topographical details in this great prophecy is the proof which they afford that it must be literally understood, and that it is of Jerusalem and Palestine that the prophet primarily speaks, or what can the allegorising commentators make of these physical landmarks and boundaries, such as " the gate of Benjamin " and " the corner gate " ? And in what part of the heavenly Jerusalem can " the tower of Hananel " and " the king's winepresses " be located ?

V. The 11th verse gives us in three brief sentences a glimpse of the blessed condition of the inhabitants of Jerusalem, which shall be thus renewed and established.

(*a*) " *And they shall dwell in her,*" that is, *permanently* and *at peace,* " nevermore to go forth from it either in captivity or in flight." [2] In the words of one of the former prophets,

---

[1] See Jer. xxxi. 38 ; Neh. iii. 1, xii. 39.　　　　[2] Koehler.

Jacob then "shall be quiet and at ease, and none shall make him afraid." [1]

(b) "And there shall be no more curse" (or "ban," or "sentence of destruction," as the word may be rendered), because the causes which previously provoked the Holy One to inflict desolating and destructive judgments upon the land and people shall be no more. [2] Another glorious and blessed contrast with the past, when on account of manifold and continuous transgressions He had to "profane the princes of the sanctuary, and give Jacob over to the curse (הֵרֶם, herem) and Israel to reproaches" (or "reviling"). [3]

(c) "And Jerusalem shall dwell (or 'shall be inhabited') safely, or literally, in conscious security" (לָבֶטַח, labhetach) or "in confidence"; for, though it shall be surrounded neither by walls, nor fortifications, it shall have nothing to fear. "For I, saith Jehovah, will be unto her a wall of fire round about, and the glory in the midst of her," [4] and "salvation" will Jehovah appoint for walls and bulwarks. [5] This outline picture of the blessed condition of restored and purified Jerusalem, which in the millennial period will be, so to say, the earthly vestibule and the reflection of the glory

[1] Jer. xxx. 10.

[2] The word הֵרֶם, herem (which is a masculine noun), describes primarily something devoted—usually for utter destruction, but occasionally also for sacred uses. Thus, for instance, the cities and inhabitants of Canaan were devoted by God to utter destruction, and of Jericho particularly we read: "And the city shall be חֵרֶם, herem (devoted)—even it and all that is therein to Jehovah" (Josh. vi. 17). Achan, by taking מִן הַחֵרֶם, min hacherem, "of the devoted thing," made the whole camp of Israel חֵרֶם, "accursed," or devoted to destructive judgment, until it was purged by the discovery and stoning of the transgressor, who became himself herem, like the "devoted" thing which he had stolen (Josh. vi. 18, vii. 11-13). If an individual or a whole city in Israel forsook Jehovah and turned to serve other gods, they became herem, devoted to utter destruction (Deut. vii. 25, 26, xiii. 12-17). In Lev. xxvii. 29, where we read, "All devoted (herem), that shall be devoted from among men, shall not be ransomed, he shall surely be put to death," it is such cases which are contemplated, i.e., those devoted by God "from among men" for utter destruction, either on account of apostasy or because of some special crime. Thus Benhadad is called אִישׁ חֶרְמִי, "a man under my herem, or ban," "one whom I have devoted to utter destruction" (1 Kings xx. 42). So likewise were the Amalekites, etc. The Septuagint properly renders הֵרֶם in Zech. xiv. 11, by anathema.

[3] Isa. xliii. 28.   [4] Zech. ii. 4, 5.   [5] Isa. xxvi. 1.

of the new or heavenly Jerusalem, which shall come down from God out of heaven, is filled in by the inspired utterances of the "former" prophets (on which the prophecies of Zechariah are more or less based), but particularly in the last chapters of Isaiah: "*For behold, I create new heavens and a new earth : and the former things shall not be remembered, nor come into mind. But be ye glad and rejoice for ever in that which I create : for behold, I create Jerusalem a rejoicing, and her people a joy. And I will rejoice in Jerusalem, and joy in My people : and the voice of weeping shall be no more heard in her, nor the voice of crying. There shall be no more thence an infant of days, nor an old man that hath not filled his days : for the child shall die an hundred years old, and the sinner being an hundred years old shall be accursed. . . . They shall not labour in vain, nor bring forth for calamity : for they are the seed of the blessed of the Lord, and their offspring with them. And it shall come to pass that, before they call, I will answer, and while they are yet speaking I will hear. The wolf and the lamb shall feed together, and the lion shall eat straw like the ox : and dust shall be the serpent's meat. They shall not hurt nor destroy in all My holy mountain, saith the Lord.*" [1]

[1] Isa. lxv. 17–20, 23–25. Some have professed to find a contradiction between the words of Zechariah, "There shall be no curse," and this statement of Isaiah that "the sinner being an hundred years old shall be accursed." But first the passage in Isaiah instances what are probably two *hypothetical* cases illustrative of the general longevity and the very *rare* occurrence of sin in renewed Jerusalem. He that should happen to die "a hundred years old" will be regarded but as a mere "child," compared with the average length of days to which man shall then attain ; and "the sinner" who is visited with God's curse and overwhelmed with the punishment, will not be swept away before the hundredth year of his life. Secondly, the words in the original are not the same. There will be rare, or isolated, instances of sin in the Millennium, and God's curse, קְלָלָה, *qelalah* (Isa. lxv. 20—literally, "a reviling" "a thing lightly esteemed"), will descend on *individuals* ; but there shall be no more חֵרֶם, *ḥerem* (Zech. xiv. 11), *i.e.*, a ban, or a devoting to utter destruction of *the city and people*, which shall then in the aggregate be cleansed and holy. Isa. xxv. 8 carries us on to the glorious *consummation*. Before millennial dawn finally merges into the Eternal Day, every vestige of sin and death shall be swept away. "He will swallow up death for ever, and the Lord God will wipe away tears from off all faces, and the reproach of His people shall He take away from off all the earth : for Jehovah hath spoken it."

The glorious picture of salvation in vers. 8–12 has its obverse side, namely, the judgments which will be inflicted on the enemies of God and His people. Chronologically, vers. 12–15 follow ver. 3, for the terrible punishment of the confederated anti-Christian hosts which they describe (and which are an amplification and supplement to the prophetic announcement of the destruction of these same Gentile hosts in chap. xii. 4–10) are the immediate consequence of the manifest interposition of Jehovah in the person of the Messiah as the Deliverer of His people, when He shall " go forth and fight against those nations as when He fought in the day of battle "; but the detailed description of the judgments on Israel's enemies is passed over by the prophet for a time in order that the wonderful deliverance of God's people and the glorious transformation of Jerusalem and the " Holy Land " might be first fully described.

Three weapons will be used by God for the destruction of the enemies of His Kingdom : (1) The fearful plague described in verse 12; (2) mutual destruction in consequence of a great panic of terror " from Jehovah "; and (3) the superhuman strength of the saved remnant of Judah, who shall suddenly become like " a pan of fire " among wood, and like " a flaming torch among sheaves "[1] and shall devour their enemies round about, on their right hand and on their left. Of these three simultaneous judgments, the first two are spoken of as being inflicted by God's own hand, for *maggepha*, rendered " plague " (which is used in the Hebrew for " *infliction*," " slaughter," " plague," " pestilence "), always denotes a plague or judgment sent direct by God.[2]

The description of the " plague " is terribly realistic. Literally, " *He (Jehovah) makes his flesh to rot* (or *consume away*), *while he standeth on his feet* " (וְהוּא עֹמֵד עַל רַגְלָיו, *vehu omed al raglav*), which is perhaps intended to express the suddenness with which God's stroke will alight upon him : " *And his eye (singular) shall consume away in their sockets*

---

[1] Chap. xii. 6.   [2] See Ex. ix. 14 ; Num. xiv. 39 ; 1 Sam. vi. 4.

(plural); and his tongue (singular) shall consume away in their mouth (plural)." The thought which the prophet probably intends to express, by the use of the singular suffix, is that this terrible catastrophe shall overtake each one and the whole company. "It is," as another has expressed it, "the act of God in His individual justice to each one of all those multitudes gathered against Him." One by one *their eyes*, of which they said, "Let our eye look (or ' gaze ') upon Zion "[1] (*i.e.*, with joy at her desolation), shall consume away in their sockets, and their tongue, with which (like Rabshakeh and the Assyrians in a former siege of Jerusalem [2]) they blasphemed God, shall consume away in their mouth—a truly terrible judgment, intended as a warning to men that it is a fearful thing to be arrayed against Jehovah and His Anointed, or against the people and the city with which He and His cause shall in that day be identified.

The מְהוּמַת יְהוָֹה, *m'humath Yehovah*—literally, a "tumult of Jehovah," with which the gathered hosts shall also be seized in that day, is the supernatural panic and "confusion" which Jehovah sends among His enemies, with a view to their utter discomfiture and self-destruction. It is the same as the "astonishment" and "madness" with which the horses and the riders of these same hosts are spoken of as smitten in chap. xii. 4, and as a consequence "they shall lay hold" (הֶחֱזִיקוּ, *hech'ziqu*, a verb which is used generally but not exclusively of "laying hold," or "seizing violently" with evil intent) "every one on the hand of his neighbour." Each in that tumultuous, panic-stricken throng shall seize the other's hand, "mastering him powerfully," with a view to his destruction—"and his hand (*i.e.*, each man's hand) shall be lifted up against the hand of his neighbour," with a view to deliver a deadly blow.

Such "confusions" or tumult the Lord had sent before in the midst of Israel's enemies. Thus the hosts of Midian were discomfited before Gideon and his little band,

---

[1] Mic. iv. 11.
[2] Isa. xxxvi. 18–22, xxxvii. 4.

and the multitude of Philistines at Michmash "melted away" before Jonathan and his armour-bearer.[1]

But *the* historical instance of the self-destruction of the enemies of God's people by means of such a "confusion" or panic sent by the Lord, to which the prophet seems specially to allude as an illustration of what will overtake the confederated anti-Christian hosts in the future, is that recorded in 2 Chron. xx., when, in answer to the prayer of Jehoshaphet, the hosts of Ammon, Moab, and Mount Seir, which were gathered against Judah, suddenly fell on one another. "*And when they began to sing and to praise, the Lord set liers in wait against the children of Ammon, Moab, and Mount Seir, which were come against Judah ; and they were smitten. For the children of Ammon and Moab stood up against the inhabitants of Mount Seir, utterly to slay and destroy them : and when they had made an end of the inhabitants of Seir, every one helped to destroy another.*"

The first clause of the 14th verse has been rendered by some, "*And Judah also shall fight against Jerusalem,*" but there is no justification for it in grammar, and it is altogether contrary to the context :[2] literally, "*And Judah also*"—which stands here for the whole remnant of the people—"*shall fight at* (or '*in*') *Jerusalem.*" It indicates the third weapon which (in addition to the "plague" and the "tumult") will be used by God for the destruction of

---

[1] Judg. vii. 22 ; I Sam. xiii. 16-20.

[2] The Targum has the mistranslation "against," and so also the Vulgate ; but the Septuagint and the Syriac render properly "at" or "in." Luther, Calvin, Ewald, etc., follow the Vulgate ; but Koehler, Hengstenberg, Keil, Von Orelli, Pusey, Dr. Wright, and almost all competent modern Hebrew scholars, translate "in" or "at Jerusalem." After the verb נִלְחַם (fight) the preposition ב (be) is often used in a *local* sense, especially when used in relation to places. The very same idiom as in this passage in Zech. xiv. 14 (בּ תִּלָּחֵם) is found in Judg. v. 19, where it certainly means "fought in Taanach," and Ex. v. 8. Then came Amaleh and fought with Israel, בִּרְפִידִם—"in" or "at" (certainly not "against") Rephidim, and so in other places. The English Revised Version is very inconsistent ; for whereas it renders "against" in Zech. xiv. 14, it has translated the same proposition "at" or "in" in the other passages just quoted, and in other places. It is properly rendered "at Jerusalem" in the "American Standard Edition."

the confederated hosts, which had all but succeeded in utterly exterminating the remnant of His people.

While their foes are consumed by the "plague" and engaged in fighting with one another in consequence of the "confusion" or tumult sent among them by the Lord, the remnant of Judah, "also" conscious now that the Captain of the Lord's host is with them, and that Almighty power is now on their side, are suddenly stirred up to do valiantly and have a share in utterly destroying them.

One consequence of the utter discomfiture of these hosts around Jerusalem is that "*the wealth of all the nations round about shall be gathered together, gold and silver and apparel in great abundance*"; where again we have an allusion by the prophet to historical incidents in the past history of the nation as foreshadowments of the future.

Thus, in 2 Chron. xx., to which reference has already been made, after the overthrow of the hosts of Ammon and Moab and the inhabitants of Mount Seir, we read that Jehoshaphat and his people gathered into Jerusalem "*spoil in abundance, both riches and garments and precious jewels*"; and thus also, when the hosts of Syrians, who were besieging Samaria, were suddenly seized with panic, fled because the Lord had made them "hear a noise of chariots and horses and of a great host"—they left behind abundance of silver and gold and raiment.[1]

And inasmuch as these hosts, by their enmity against God and His people, have brought themselves under His ban for utter destruction, the animals which they have brought with them for this campaign against the holy land and city, will also be overtaken with the same fate as their masters.

"*And so shall be the plague of the horse, of the mule, and of the camel, and of the ass, and of all the beasts that shall be in those camps as their masters.*"

This, as Hengstenberg points out, is in accord with the Mosaic law in reference to the *cherem*, or "ban." When a whole city had committed the crime of idolatry, not only

[1] 2 Kings vii. 2–8.

the inhabitants, but the animals also, were put to death ; in which case the same law affecting the relation between the irrational and rational portions of the creation was repeated on a small scale as that which caused the animal creation to be " subject to vanity," not willingly, " on account of the sin of man." An instance of this we have in the case of Achan, whose oxen, asses, and sheep were stoned and burned, along with himself and his children.[1]

Blessed be God, " creation," which has become involved in the sin and consequent suffering and death of man, is to participate also in the benefits of the great redemption which has been accomplished by our Lord Jesus Christ, and shall yet be delivered from the bondage of corruption into the glorious liberty of the children of God.[2]

But there is a beneficent end in the very judgments of God, for through them the nations will at last learn righteousness, and the fruit will be " universal homage to the Universal Ruler," [3] Jehovah of Hosts, and in the person of the Messiah, under whose sway all nations shall then be blessed. "*And it shall come to pass that every one that is left of all the nations that come up against Jerusalem shall go up from year to year to worship the King, Jehovah of Hosts, and to keep the Feast of Tabernacles.*"

First, it should be observed that when it is said that all nations and families of the earth shall come up to Jerusalem from year to year to worship Jehovah, and in acknowledgment of Israel's national supremacy in the millennial earth, it is not meant that every individual in each nation shall come up, but that the nations shall come up *representatively.* " The actions of nations and all corporate bodies is always spoken of in Scripture with reference to those who are officially appointed to express or carry out their will. Thus in the great gathering against Jerusalem the nations concerned therein are represented by their armies. Every individual in each nation will not be present, yet each nation is said to be there." [4]

[1] Josh. vii. 24, 25.   [2] Rom. viii. 20-22.
[3] Von Orelli.   [4] B. W. Newton.

The commentators differ as to *why* the Feast of Tabernacles is singled out as the one which all the nations are represented in this prophecy as coming up to Jerusalem to celebrate; and very few see the deep typical and spiritual truth set forth by this "*Hag-Yehovah*"—the "Feast of Jehovah,"[1] as it is emphatically called in Lev. xxiii., which has been properly styled "The Sacred Calendar of the History of Redemption," because it sets forth, by a series of striking types, not only the great facts, but the *very order* in which the various stages of God's great redemption scheme for the world were to unfold themselves in the course of time. Briefly, it may be said that the nations are represented as coming up to Jerusalem to keep the Feast of Tabernacles because the spiritual truths set forth by this particular type shall then be realised—for Jerusalem shall then be the metropolis of God's Kingdom on earth, and the joy and blessedness foreshadowed by that feast will then not only be the portion of saved Israel, but shall also pervade all nations of the earth.

But to understand this more clearly we must examine a little more fully the historical and prophetic character of this feast. Primarily[2] Tabernacles was, above all the other

---

[1] Lev. xxiii. 39. Dr. Wright and others have built an argument against the literal interpretation of this prophecy on Isa. lxvi. 23, which, according to them, represents the Gentile nations as going up to Jerusalem to worship, not only once a year, but at all the festivals, and even on the new moons and Sabbaths. But the words of Isaiah are these: "*And it shall come to pass that from one new moon to another, and from one Sabbath to another, shall all flesh come to worship before Me, saith Jehovah.*" He says nothing about their going up *to Jerusalem* to keep these weekly and monthly festivals. Even Israel in the land did not go up to Jerusalem to celebrate their Sabbaths and their new moons, but worshipped God *wherever they were*. And so "all flesh" in that renewed earth, in which shall dwell righteousness, shall come together (in their own lands) to worship Jehovah on these frequent regular occasions. Zechariah, however, speaks distinctly of their going *up to Jerusalem* at the annual Feast of Tabernacles—not at all an impossible thing. An argument has been based on the opinion that the more distant nations could not obey this command because of the time required for the journey, but we do not yet know what the facilities of travel will be in the Millennium.

[2] This section on the Feast of Tabernacles is quoted here from the 1st chapter of *Types, Psalms, and Prophecies*, entitled "The Sacred Calendar of the History of Redemption."

feasts, " the harvest festival of joy and thanksgiving, in celebration not only of the full ingathering of the ' labours of the field,' but also of the fruit and of the vintage, and is therefore pre-eminently styled ' the Feast of Ingatherings ' " (Ex. xxiii. 16; xxxiv. 22; Deut. xvi. 13).

It had, moreover, a clear retrospective or commemorative significance, as is plainly stated in the command that they should dwell in booths : " *And ye shall take you on the first day the fruit of the goodly trees, branches of palm trees, and boughs of thick trees, and willows of the brook, and ye shall rejoice before Jehovah your God seven days ; . . . ye shall dwell in booths seven days, . . . that your generations may know that I made the children of Israel to dwell in booths when I brought them out of the land of Egypt : I am Jehovah your God*" (vers. 40–43)—an ordinance well calculated indeed to keep alive in their mind the grateful remembrance of the God of Israel, who sustained them miraculously in the wilderness, and led them by the hand of Moses, Aaron, and Joshua, safely into the promised land.

The Rabbis in later times regarded the *Sukkah* (tabernacle), in which they dwelt during the feast, as more especially symbolical of the cloud of glory which hovered over the Tabernacle, and which led and shielded Israel by day and illumined them by night in their forty years' wilderness wanderings ; but even the Mishna and the Talmud single out this feast from all the others as being of an *anticipative* or prophetic character, while Christian scholars and Bible students are in agreement that there is nothing in this dispensation to answer to the Feast of Tabernacles. No, its fulfilment is yet in the future, when, after Israel's national Day of Atonement shall have come to pass, and the nation which was destined of God from the beginning to be the channel of blessing to the world shall have been reconciled and cleansed, and equipped by the power of God to go forth on its mission of spreading the knowledge of their Messiah over the whole earth, the great " Feast of Ingathering " shall take place, and " all peoples " shall sit down to the " feast of fat things, yea, a feast of wines on the lees, of fat things full of marrow," which Jehovah of hosts has prepared for them on Mount Zion.[1]

Though not part of the original Mosaic appointment, the ceremonial service of this feast, which was in practice in the Temple, was also designed to point and emphasise its symbolic and prophetic significance. I will mention only two or three features of that ritual.

1. *Simchat-bet-ha-Sho'ebhah* — literally, "Joy of the House of Drawing (the water); or, the Ceremonial of Water Libation."

Every morning of the feast, a joyous procession, accompanied by music and headed by a priest bearing a golden pitcher, measuring just a little over two pints, made its way from the Temple courts to the Pool of Siloam. At the same time another procession went to the place in the Kedron valley called Moza, or Colonia, whence they brought willow branches, which they bound on either side of the altar of burnt-offering, " bending them over towards it so as to form a kind of leafy canopy."

Then the ordinary sacrifice proceeded, "the priest who had gone to Siloam so timing it that he returned just as his brethren carried up the pieces of the sacrifice to lay them on the altar. As he entered by the 'Water Gate,' which obtained its name from this ceremony, he was received by a threefold blast from the priests' trumpets." Amid great demonstrations of excitement and joy this water was poured into a silver basin, or tube, on the altar, simultaneously with the prescribed libation of wine, which was poured into another tube.

On the seventh day, called the " Hoshanna rabba," the

---

[1] Isa. xxv. "That these are not ideal comparisons, but the very design of the Feast of Tabernacles, appears not only from the language of the prophets and the peculiar services of the feast, but also from its position in the Calendar, and even from the names by which it is designated in Scripture. Thus in its reference to the harvest it is called 'Feast of Ingathering'; in that to the history of Israel in the past, the 'Feast of Tabernacles'; while its symbolic bearing on the future is brought out in its designation as emphatically '*the* feast' and 'the Feast of Jehovah.' "—Edersheim.

great Hosanna, the joy and excitement of the people reached their climax. The joyous crowds of worshippers on that day, seen from one of the flat roofs of Jerusalem overlooking the Temple area, would resemble a forest in motion, for all carried palm branches in their hands which were more than a man's height in length. Great silence would fall on the assembled throng as the choir of Levites commenced to sing the Hallel (the specially prescribed " Praise " for the great festivals, consisting of Pss. cxiii.– cxviii.), to each line of which the people had to respond with " Hallelujah." Soon the whole crowd fell into order, and, led by the priests, marched in procession round the altar. Seven times they encompassed it. As the singers reached vers. 25 to 29 of Ps. cxviii., and joined in the words, " *Ana Adonai Hoshio-na !* " (" Hosanna, make Thy salvation now manifest, O Lord ! "), " *Ana Adonai Hatslicha-na !* " (" O Lord, send now prosperity ! "), the people waved their palm branches and accompanied the song with loud exclamations of joy. And as they reached the words, " *Blessed is He that cometh in the Name of Jehovah*," the godly and spiritual among them would in their hearts greet the coming Messiah and King, to whom they well knew these words applied.

The joy accompanying this ceremonial was so great that it became a proverb. " He that hath not seen *Simchat-bet-ha-Sho'ebhah*, the joy of the drawing (and the pouring) of the water, hath not seen joy in this life." Now, though the Rabbis attached a symbolic significance to the ceremonial in connection with the dispensation of the rain, the amount of which for the year they imagined was determined by God at this feast ; and perhaps also a commemorative sense, as reminding them of the wonders God wrought in the wilderness in giving them water out of a rock, the main reference according to themselves, as already said, was to the future blessings to be bestowed on them in Messiah's time, and especially pointed to the pouring out of the Spirit ; as is to be inferred from the singing by the multitude of Isa. xii. 3, and from the distinct statement in the Talmud (Jer., Sukkah v., also Tosefta Sukkah iv.). " Why is it called *Bet-ha-Sho'ebhah* ? (the joy of drawing or pouring). Because of the pouring of the Holy Spirit, according to what is said : ' *With joy shall ye draw water out of the wells of salvation.*' " Now, in a limited though very blessed degree, this has already been fulfilled, for it was in reference to this ceremonial of the pouring of water that our Lord Jesus " on the last day— the great day of the feast "—stood and cried, saying, " *If any man thirst, let him come unto Me and drink. He that believeth on Me, as the Scripture hath said, out of His belly shall flow rivers of living water : and this He spake of the Spirit which they that believed were about to receive*"; in accordance with which, when once Jesus was glorified, on being raised from the dead and taken up to the right hand of God, the Spirit came down from heaven like a rushing mighty wind, and the Church of this dispensation was formed, every living member of which knows experimentally of the indwelling of this blessed heavenly Paraclete.

In its fulness, however, such a prophecy as Isa. xii. and the wonderful prediction of Joel—" *And it shall come to pass afterward that I will pour out My Spirit upon all flesh*"—will only be realised subsequent to Israel's great national Day of Atonement. Then " the ransomed of Jehovah shall return and come to Zion with songs and everlasting joy upon their heads ; they shall obtain joy and gladness, and sorrow and sighing shall flee away " (Isa. xxxv. 10). Then shall Israel *nationally* experience the truth of Christ's word, " But the water that I shall give him shall be in him a well of water springing up into eternal life "; and then also " shall living waters go out from Jerusalem " for the quickening and refreshing of the whole world (Zech. xiv. 6).

2. Another feature in the Temple service of the Feast of Tabernacles also deserves mention, because of its rich symbolic import.

At the conclusion of the first day of the feast the worshippers congregated in the Court of the Women, where a great illumination took place. Four huge golden lamps or candelabras were there, each with four golden bowls, against which rested four ladders. Four youths of priestly descent ascended these with large pitchers of oil from which they filled each bowl. The old worn breeches and girdles of the priests served for wicks for these lamps. So great and brilliant was the light that, according to a saying, "There was not a court in Jerusalem that was not lit up by it." Around these great golden burning lamps a sacred dance took place, in which even the *hassidim* (saints) and "the men of deed," or prominent leaders of the people, with flaming torches in their hands, danced before the people and sang before them hymns and songs of praise. " The Levites also, with harps, and lutes, and cymbals, and trumpets, and with instruments of music without number, stood upon the fifteen steps which led down from the Court of Israel to that of the Women, according to the number of the fifteen ' Songs of Degrees' in the Book of Psalms."

This illumination, too, was regarded as of the same twofold symbolic significance as the pouring of the water. It reminded them of the past when God led them in the wilderness with the cloud of glory and the pillar of fire— of the Shekinah glory which dwelt in the first Temple, but was, alas! already absent in the second; but it also, and chiefly, was meant to remind them of the Messianic promises in the future when the light of Jehovah should arise upon their land and people.

Now this, too, has, in a partial degree, been already fulfilled, for He who cried, "If any man thirst let him come unto Me and drink," at this same feast, and in reference to this illumination, again spake unto them, saying, "I am the Light of the world; he that followeth Me shall not walk in darkness, but shall have the Light of Life "; and since then hundreds of millions who have heard His voice, and have followed in His steps, have had their hearts and souls, their present and their future eternity illumined by His Gospel. But while this is so, Israel, *as a nation*, still walks in darkness, and the other peoples of the earth are still covered by the shadow of death—until the Sun of Righteousness shall arise with healing in His wings, and the word shall go forth: "Arise, shine, for thy light is come, and the glory of Jehovah is risen upon thee." Then "*nations*," as nations, "*shall come to thy light*; and kings to the brightness of thy glory" (Isa. lx. 1–3); and the promise confirmed by the oath of Him who cannot lie shall be fulfilled: "As truly as I live, all the earth shall be filled with the glory of Jehovah" (Num. xiv. 21).

The Feast of Tabernacles was the only one that had an octave, "the last and great day of the feast," the *Azereth* —"conclusion," or "*crowning feast* of all the feasts of the year," as Philo, the Alexandrian, called it; on which Israel dwelt no longer in booths to remind them of the wilderness but returned to their homes to rejoice there, and to begin, so to say, a cycle beyond the one of seven which they had just completed.

Now the eighth day in Scripture is the *Resurrection Day*, and points, I believe, to the Eternal Day, after the cycle of time in which the history of the earth, as set forth in the Sacred Calendar of the History of Redemption, shall have been finished, when the *consummation* of earthly rest shall synchronise with the *commencement* of heavenly glory —"when a great voice out of the throne shall go forth, saying: *Behold, the tabernacle of God is with men, and He shall dwell with them, and they shall be His people. And God Himself shall be with them and be their God. And God shall wipe away every tear from their eyes, and there shall be no more death, neither sorrow, nor crying, neither shall there be any more pain: for the former things have passed away*" (Rev. xxi. 1–8).

"Then," to conclude with the words of an old divine, "the mystery of the water which was poured upon the sacrifices shall be fulfilled, when He who is the Alpha and the Omega shall proclaim, *It is done.* '*I will give to him that is athirst of the water of life freely.*' Then He who, at the Feast of Tabernacles, invited sinners to come to Him and drink, shall lead His redeemed people *by living fountains of water, and make them drink of the river of His pleasures.* Then, too, the symbol of the palm branches shall be accomplished in the final victory of the redeemed over Death and Hades; and they shall realise the blessed fulfilment of the promise, '*He that overcometh shall inherit all things; and I will be his God, and he shall be My Son.*'

"Then, too, shall be *the great Hosanna*, when that great multitude, which no man could number, out of all nations, and kindreds, and people, and tongues, shall stand before the throne of God, and *before the Lamb*, clothed with white robes, *and palms in their hands*, and shall ' cry with a loud voice, saying: Salvation to our God which sitteth upon the throne, and unto the Lamb ' (Rev. vii. 9, 10)."

During that blessed millennial period the knowledge of the glory of Jehovah shall indeed cover the earth, and all nations shall walk in His light. Sin and iniquity will no longer be allowed to lift up their head, and apostasy and rebellion will be visited with instant punishment whenever they manifest themselves. Yet we know from prophetic Scripture that the hearts of multitudes among the Gentile nations will not be fully subdued to God and His truth, even in the Millennium, and that many of them will render only a feigned submission to the Divine King, whose throne shall be on Mount Sion. There follows therefore the warning to the nations against disobedience to His command to come up to Jerusalem to render homage to the King, Jehovah of hosts. "*And it shall be that whoso of the families of the earth goeth not up unto Jerusalem to worship the King, Jehovah of Hosts, upon them there shall be no rain*," which commentators take to mean the " early rain," which generally falls in Palestine about the end of October and the beginning of November soon after Tabernacles, but גֶּשֶׁם (*geshem*—the word here used) usually stands simply for heavy, torrential rain, יוֹרֶה (*yoreh*), being the special word for the " early rain." Besides, this is a threat uttered, not against Israel and Palestine, but the Gentile nations, whose seasons and climates may be altogether different.

The word is to be taken first of all in its literal sense.

The withholding of rain was one of the ways by which God was wont to punish the apostasy of His own people in the days of the theocracy,[1] and He now threatens to inflict it on the Gentile nations in case of disobedience. At the same time, there is also here a blending of the literal and the spiritual, and the punishment threatened includes also the withholding from the disobedient nations, or "families," of the showers of God's grace and blessing, of which the literal rain is often used in Scripture as an emblem.

For this punishment, in case of disobedience, there will be no exception and escape. This is the thought expressed in the two following verses : " *And if the family of Egypt go not up, and come not, then also not upon them ; there shall be the plague wherewith Jehovah will plague the nations that go not up to keep the Feast of Tabernacles.*"

This is the literal rendering of the words as they stand in the Hebrew text, but the actual meaning is not absolutely certain.[2]

Egypt is especially named according to Von Orelli, Koehler, and others, because of its peculiar conditions and climate—for however it ultimately depended on the equatorial rains, which overfilled the lakes which supply the Nile, it did not need that fine arrangement of the rains of autumn and spring which were essential to the fruitfulness of Palestine. Hence it may perhaps encourage itself in the thought that the threatened infliction in case of disobedience would be no punishment to them. The prophet therefore

---

[1] Comp. 1 Kings xvii., xviii.

[2] Most commentators supply the words יִהְיֶה הַגֶּשֶׁם, *yihyeh haggashem*, " and not upon (or ' neither upon them ') shall be the rain." It is possible, however, that the adverb, לֹא (" not ") before the word עֲלֵיהֶם, "upon them," has crept in by mistake from the previous line, and that the Septuagint is in this case likely to be correct. By omitting one of the negatives, it reads simply, "And if the tribe of Egypt does not go up nor come, the plague will be upon them with which Jehovah will smite all the nations." Lange, following Hitzig and Bunsen, renders the passage interrogatively : "And if the family of Egypt will not go up and will not come, then will the plague not fall upon them with which Jehovah shall smite the nation which will not go up in order to keep the Feast of Tabernacles ?" to which question the 19th verse is, according to this rendering, supposed to be the answer. But this translation is rejected by most scholars on grammatical grounds.

emphasises the fact that, notwithstanding Egypt's apparent independence of rain, it would suffer the consequences that follow the withholding of rain, as much as the other nations that are dependent on it. It may be also, as Pusey suggests, that the words are left undefined "with a purposed abruptness" (the word rain not being mentioned in the Hebrew in the 18th ·erse), " *there shall not be upon them*," namely, "whatever they need." [1]

The thought that Egypt if disobedient will be overtaken in the same judgment is solemnly repeated in the 19th verse : " *This shall be the punishment of Egypt and the punishment of all the nations that go not up to keep the Feast of Tabernacles.*" The word used here for punishment is חַטָּאת, *ḥattath*, which primarily means " sin "; but it signifies also sin *in its effects*, as bringing *punishment* in its train. The word stands also sometimes for " sin-offering," which reminds us of the intimate relation that exists in God's moral government of the world between sin and its punishment, and helps us to understand such a statement as that Christ, who knew no sin, was *made sin* for us— namely, a *sin-offering*, enduring and bearing the consequence of sin on our behalf.

In the last two verses we reach the glorious goal and climax of vision and prophecy. God's original purpose in the calling and election of Israel—" Ye shall be unto Me a Kingdom of priests, an holy nation "—shall at last be realised ; the aim and purpose of the whole law,—namely, that His people might learn the meaning of holiness and become holy because Jehovah their God is holy ; but to which, so long as they were in bondage to the law, they could not attain, shall at last be fulfilled when they are brought into a condition of grace, and when God shall put His law *into their inward parts* and write it on their hearts

---

[1] Kiel, Bredenkamp, and others contend, however, that the prophet mentions Egypt especially, not because of the fact in natural history that this land owes its fertility not to rain, but to the overflowing of the Nile—but as the nation which showed the greatest hostility to Jehovah and His people in the olden time, and for the purpose of showing that this nation was also to attain a full participation in the blessings of salvation bestowed upon Israel (comp. Isa. xix. 19-25).

Then the world shall witness for the first time the glorious spectacle of a whole nation, and every individual member of it, wholly consecrated to Jehovah, and an earthly capital which shall truly answer to its name, "The Holy City," because it shall in many ways be the earthly counterpart and reflection of the glory of the New Jerusalem, which will come down out of heaven from God.

And not only shall קֹדֶשׁ לַיהוָֹה, *Qodesh la-Yehovah*— "Holiness (or 'holy') unto the Lord" be written on their persons, and on all the outward and inward life of the whole community, but on everything they possess. "*In that day shall there be (engraven) on the bells of the horses, Holy unto Jehovah: and the pots in Jehovah's House*"— which were used for the boiling of the sacrificial flesh, of which the common people, as well as the priests, could eat, and were therefore regarded as less holy—"*shall be like the bowls before the altar*"—in which the blood of the sacrifices was received, and out of which it was sprinkled, or poured, upon the altar, and therefore regarded as most holy. In the words of a deep student of Scripture, "The whole external character of life—that which is exhibited in the streets of a city (represented by the tinkling sound of the bells of the passing horses) shall bear in all its parts, throughout all its detail, the impress of holiness unto the Lord. Religious life and fellowship shall be holy also; for the pots in the Lord's House, vessels which of old the priests had so often defiled, shall be like the bowls of the altar. Private and domestic life shall be hallowed too; for '*every pot in Jerusalem and in Judah (that is, throughout the holy land) shall be holy unto Jehovah of Hosts: and all they that sacrifice shall come and take of them and seethe (or boil) in them.*' For everything alike shall be holy, and all such distinctions as 'profane,' 'holy,' and 'most holy,' shall completely cease 'in that day.'"

"The distinction between holy and profane can only cease, however," to quote yet another writer, "when the sin and moral defilement *which first evoked this distinction*, and made it necessary that the things intended for the service of God should be set apart and receive a special consecration, have been entirely removed and wiped away. To remove this distinction, to prepare the way for the cleansing away of sin, and to sanctify once more that which sin had desecrated, was the object of the sacred institutions appointed by God. To this end Israel was separated from the nations of the earth; and in order to train it up as a holy nation, and to secure the object described, a law was given to it, in which the distinction between holy and profane ran through all the relations of life. And this goal will be eventually reached by the people of God, and sin with all its consequences be cleansed away by the judgment. In the perfected Kingdom of God there will be no more sinners, but only such as are righteous and holy." [1]

Finally, " *there shall be no more a Canaanite in the House of Jehovah of Hosts in that day.*" The Hebrew word כְּנַעֲנִי, *Khena'ani*, means also " trader," or " merchant," because in early times the Canaanites, especially the Phœnicians, were known in the world as traders. Some therefore prefer to render the clause, " There shall no more be a trafficker in the House of the Lord," which is also the rendering of the Jewish Targum. But whether we take the term Canaanite to stand for the unclean and the godless, or understand it as meaning merchant or trafficker, the sense is practically the same. Nothing that defileth, or that maketh an abomination or a lie, or that could disturb the peace or mar the holiness, shall in anywise be permitted to enter that House, which " in that day " shall be the House of Prayer for all nations.

" For this shall be the law of the House: upon the top of the mountain the whole limit thereof round about shall be most holy. Behold, this is the law of the House." [2]

[1] Keil.   [2] Ezek. xliii. 12.

GENERAL INDEX

Abarbanel, commentary of, 109; on "And I cut off three shepherds in one month," 380, 381; on the "breaking of the staves," 389; the four horns, 46.

Abarbanel (Abrabanel), repentance and recognition of the Messiah by Israel, 440.

Aben Ezra, 191; on twofold nature of the Messiah, 478.

Abraham ben Ezra, Rabbi, repentance and recognition of the Messiah by Israel, 440.

Abraham, God's covenant with, antitypical ratification of, 318.

Abraham, Isaac ben, Rabbi, of Troki, *Chizzuk Emunah*, 438; on repentance and future recognition of the Messiah by Israel, 438.

Abraham, Rabbi, of Toledo, "foolish" (wicked) shepherd, 415.

Actions of the Prophets to be understood as predictions, 390.

Alexander the Great, victories of, prophesied, 286.

Alford (Dean), on passage in Epistle of Jude referring to "The Body of Moses," 124; what Israel will learn on "that day," 436, 437.

Alshech, Moses, sixteenth century, on repentance and recognition of Messiah (Messiah ben Joseph) by Israel, 441.

Angel attendants, referred to as "these that stand by," 105.

Angelic riders, the, 23, 24; symbolism of, 27, 28; their report concerning the Gentile world, 32.

Angel of Jehovah, the, His character, 23; answer of, to accusations of Satan, 94; answer to intercession of, 35; appearance in Temple of, 88; as advocate, 33, 34, 35, 88, 91, 95; as judge, 89; identity of interpreting Angel with the; arguments for and against, 28-31; identity of "the man" in first vision with the; arguments for and against, 23, 24, 59; the identity of the Angel of Jehovah with the "Angel of His Face," 87.

Angels, chariots and winds in eighth vision identified with, 175; ministering, 31, 32, 91.

Apocrypha, the, "The Ascension," or "Assumption of Moses," 123.

Apostasy of the people of Israel, judgment as punishment for, causes and manner of, 379; judgment consequent on, predicted, 376, 377.

Atonement, Day of, the, redeeming work of Christ prefigured by, 119, 121, 140.

Augustine, 327.

Autocratic ruler, or "Exactor," the, emblematic of the Messiah at His second coming, 355-357.

Babylon, command to flee out of, 69, 70; prophecies concerning, 167, 168.

Babylonia, recuperative power of, 169, 170.

Bagdad railway, importance of, 169, 170.

"Battle Bow," the, emblematic of the Messiah, 354, 355.

Baumgarten, *Die Nachtgescichte Sacharias*, 124; on mountains of brass, 174; the stone laid before Joshua,

"Horns" and the "carpenters," the, 45–54.

Horns, the four, symbolism of, 45, 46.

Horses, colours, divergence of opinion concerning, 176, 177, 178, 180, 181 ; in first vision, significance of their colours, 23, 27, 28 ; significance of number of chariots and colour of, in eighth vision, 175–181 ; symbolic mission of, in eighth vision, 179, 180.

Isaak ben Abraham (Rabbi) of Troki, *Chizzuk Emunah*, 307.

Isaiah, chief message of, 12.

Israel, affliction and scattering of, by Gentile world-powers, 45–48, 57, 127, 128, 231 ; analogy between Church of Christ and, 322, 323 ; apostasy of, 484, 494 ; as a type of man, 11, 12 ; calling and election of, 530 ; compared with "lost sheep" and "scattered sheep," 383, 384 ; continued and marvellous preservation of, 48–51 ; deliverance of, predicted, 388 ; desolation of land, accompanied by destructive judgment of the people predicted, 376, 377 ; dispersion of Judah and, definite prophecies concerning, 47 ; Egypt earliest home of, 49 ; enemies of, consequences to Jerusalem of their destruction, 516–518 ; enemies of, predicted punishment of kings of Assyria and Babylon, 384 ; enemies of, smitten with plagues, 431–432 ; weapons for their destruction, 516–520 ; final national deliverance of, 299 ; gathering together of the houses of Judah and Joseph at the second coming of the Messiah, 362–368 ; Gentile world contrasted with that of, 32, 33 ; God's interposition on behalf of, on "that day" ; history of, lesson taught by, 235–237 ; *Ichabod* period of, 232, 233 ; increase of nation, prediction as to, 364, 365–370 ; jealousy of ancient nations with regard to, 49, 50 ; Judah and, union

of, 245, 246 ; living and prevailing power of, 50, 51 ; predictions concerning, by early prophets, 360 ; prophetic promises as to restoration of, 232–240, 249 ; refusal of, to hear and receive law of Moses, 221, 222 ; religious and ecclesiastical position of, as typified by the golden candlestick, 131, 132 ; restoration of, Divine promises as to, 230, 231; its effect on history of world, 245, 246, 249, 250–255 ; blessed and prosperous condition of, foretold, 337 ; promise of God's covenant with, 401–402 ; wanderings to cease in restored relationship of Jehovah with Israel at second coming of the Messiah, 359 ; without king, prince, prophet, or priest since their rejection of the Messiah, 398 ; wretchedness of the people under Gentile rule, 385.

Israelites. See under *Jews, Jewish.*

Israel's Prince of Peace, His Kingdom's foundation, 314, 315 ; His mission in the world, 302–322.

Jaddua, high priest, Jerusalem, dream of, 300–301.

Jehovah, glory of, its departure from Israel, 232, 233.

Jehovah, repetition of name, reason for, 11, 230.

Jeremiah, prophecy of, concerning moral purification and deliverance of Israel, 86.

Jerome, 230 ; on "And I cut off three shepherds in one month," 396, 398 ; on Jerusalem as the "burdensome stone," 428 ; on symbolism of measure in seventh vision, 156, 160.

Jerusalem, blessed condition of inhabitants on and after "that day," 513–515 ; chosen by Jehovah as city of His sanctuary, 432 ; divine protection promised for, 62, 434–436 ; earthly kingdom of, reasons for supposition that reference in third vision is to a literal, 62, 63, 64, 65, 240, 241 ; fountain of living water to flow

276 ; *The Book of the Twelve Prophets,* 268, 270.

Sorrow and mourning of Israel, their rejection of the Messiah causing spread to whole world of, 498–499.

Stade, Bernard, on authorship of final chapters of Zechariah, 270, 276.

Stähelin, *Einleitung in die Kanonische Bücher des Alten Testaments,* 271.

St. Gregory, quoted by Pusey, 116.

Svedberg, Jasper, on mountains of brass, 174.

Tabernacle, the, candlestick in. See *Candlestick.*

Tabernacles, feast of, celebration of, at Jerusalem by those left from the enemies of Israel, 520 ; ceremonial service, features of, and symbolic significance attached to, 521–527 ; Egypt especially threatened if absent from, 529 ; historical and prophetic character of, 521–522.

Tables of the Law, duty of man to God and his neighbour contained in third and eighth commandment of, 146 ; resemblance between Flying Roll and, 145.

Talent, significance of, as cover to ephah, 159.

Talmud, the, 16, 78, 117, 123, 148 ; legends in, 123 ; quotation from, 122 ; tradition from, concerning foundation-stone of Second Temple, 115, 117.

Targum of Jonathan, the, 191 ; titles of the Messiah as interpreted by, 109.

Targum, the Jewish, 95, 138 ; on colours of horses in eighth vision, 177 ; view of, with regard to promise made to Joshua, 105.

Temple, the, building of, 40, 88, 95, 209 ; building of second, 191, 192 ; completion of, 40 ; courts of, as described by Josephus, 188, 189 ; foundation-laying of, 242 ; foundation of second, probable allusion to, 115, 117 ; rebuilding of, 9, 21 ; as a visible proof and symbol, 137 ;

commenced, 243 ; hindrances with regard to, 138, 242 ; sacred letters " graven " on foundation-stone of, 116, 117 ; symbolic meaning of, 195–198.

Ten, the number, different use of, in Scripture, 253, 254.

Teraphim, the, 280 ; modern Christian, 343 ; nature of, 341 ; passages of Scripture in which referred to, 341, 342.

Tertullian, quotation from, 252.

" That day," blessed issues of the great and solemn events of, foretold, 502–532 ; day of the manifestation of the Messiah in His glory, 423 ; light at evening time after dark and gloomy day foretold, 501 ; natural phenomena and physical characteristics foretold, 499–501 ; on which the names of idols, prophets, and unclean spirits will be put out of the land of Israel, 463–464 ; prophecies shall be discredited and prophets " thrust out " of the land of Israel, 465 ; prophets will then become ashamed of telling their visions, 465 ; reference to, in Ps. cxviii., 430 ; the great day of Israel's national atonement, 119–122, 459–463.

Theodoret (423–457 A.D.), on " And I cut off three shepherds in one month," 398.

" Third part," remnant of Israel, " refining "—" trying "—" testing " of, 485.

Thomson (Dr.), *The Land and the Book,* 392.

Trypho, quotation from, 252.

Tyre, conquest of, by Alexander the Great, 293–294 ; siege of, by Nebuchadnezzar, 292 ; wisdom of, how shown, 291.

Unity of God the Father and God the Son, Jews unable to grasp idea, 443.

Vatke, on authorship of final chapters of Zechariah, 270, 276.

SCRIPTURE INDEX

Old Testament

ISRAEL

IN THE PLAN OF GOD

DAVID BARON

was raised in a devout Jewish family and
rew in rabbinical school. After completing
he Scriptures, he converted to Christianity
nself to a twofold ministry: explaining
Christianity to the Jews and explaining Jews to Christianity.
These two objectives form the basis for his classic work *Israel
in the Plan of God.*

Israel's past and future, from her national election by God
to the final judgment of her enemies, is covered in this
balanced, biblical study.

ISBN 0-8254-2089-X • 320 pages